THE ROUGH GUIDE TO
BATH, BRISTOL & SOMERSET

ROUGH
GUIDES

Written and rese...
Robert Andre...

D1331383

90710 000 447 042

Contents

GLASTONBURY TOR

Introduction to

Bath, Bristol and Somerset

Somerset: the very name – seemingly derived from the Anglo-Saxon for "people dwelling in a summer pasture" – evokes a picture of bucolic bliss, a soft undulating landscape grazed by sheep and populated by straw-chewing yokels speaking in a quaint "zummerzet" drawl. Early railway posters traded on the cliché, portraying thatched cottages, tottering hayricks and castellated church towers. And while the modern reality is much more complex and nuanced, parts of the caricature are still identifiable today, where rounding a bend will bring you face to face with a heart-stoppingly lovely picture of quiet lanes meandering through hushed valleys, landscapes essentially unchanged for centuries, and yes, even a castellated church tower or two in the distance.

Somerset stands out among English counties for its breadth and diversity. The distance from the Wiltshire border in the east to the Devon border in the west stretches some seventy miles, within which every kind of landscape features, from limestone gorges to marshy flatlands, and from lush meadows to windswept moorland. There are forty miles of coastline, ranging from busy and brash holiday resorts to bleakly beautiful wetland reserves. Populous towns and cities give way to one-horse villages, and the historical traces take in stone circles, ruined castles and Renaissance palaces.

Where to go

The Romans knew a good thing when they saw it, and in **Bath**, in the northeast corner of the county, they hit gold. Possessing Britain's only natural hot springs, the town quickly developed as a home from home for the baths-loving Romans, and it was the presence of these thermal waters that came to define Bath throughout its subsequent history. Visitors from far and wide came to wallow in the healing waters, with the town reaching its greatest glory in the eighteenth century, when fashion and great architecture came together to create the apotheosis of the Georgian urban centre. Today, Bath has plenty to offer: some of the finest museums outside London, inviting shops and a vibrant cultural life that belies its size – all contained within a compact area that makes for easy strolling, often through traffic-free lanes.

Within easy distance of Bath is a cluster of towns and villages on the Somerset-Wiltshire border that make alluring day-trips: **Bradford-on-Avon**, with its medieval bridge and terraces of ex-weavers' cottages; **Lacock**, whose abbey-turned-stately home incorporates a museum of photography; and **Corsham**, with its prized collection of Old Masters at Corsham Court.

West of Bath, **Bristol**, while not technically part of Somerset, is the dominant urban centre in the region. The city shares some of Bath's most characteristic features, such as an impressive array of Georgian architecture and the River Avon winding through. Here, though, the tidal Avon was harnessed, and the city's skyline owes much to the riches that were funnelled through its harbour, fuelled by the transatlantic trade of tobacco, sugar and slaves. With its fierce creative energy and urban bustle, Bristol takes in more extremes, and has more of a contemporary, cosmopolitan view of life than Bath. Its verve and panache are expressed in everything from genre-defying music and

eye-catching street art to cutting-edge design and technology, as well as a dynamic range of bars, restaurants and clubs. The M Shed museum celebrates Bristol's rich history and cultural diversity, which you can explore further in the city's galleries and collections, its venerable churches and miscellaneous markets.

South of the Bath-Bristol axis, the countryside soon takes over, and some of Somerset's most appealing small towns are nestled among its rolling hills and sweeping marshland. **Wells** has one of the earliest and finest English Gothic cathedrals, and lies within easy reach of the **Mendip Hills**. Cutting through the county, they're not particularly high, but they are quite a bit wilder than you'd expect, and surprisingly

WHERE THE WILD THINGS ARE

Somerset isn't all rolling green fields and rich fertile pasture. From gorse-covered moors to towering sea cliffs, dry valleys to reed-swathed marshland, its varied landscapes cover a wide spectrum of habitats that are home to all creatures great and small. In the **Quantock Hills**, Somerset has the country's first Area of Outstanding Natural Beauty (AONB), a compact outcrop of upland heath and wooded combes harbouring nightjars and red deer. The Quantocks share similar flora and fauna with nearby **Exmoor**, the region's only national park and the other destination for deer spotters. The more pronounced hills of the **Mendips**, another AONB to the northeast, are riddled with caves and cut through by two dramatic gorges, most famously at Cheddar, and are a great place to see badgers, bats and peregrine falcons. Lying between the two ranges, the mesmerizing wetlands of the **Somerset Levels** provide hands-down the best birdwatching in the South West, particularly among the reedbeds and former peat bogs of the Avalon Marshes; a number of the waders and migrants that call in here can also be seen in the estuaries, sand dunes and cliffs that make up Somerset's **coast**.

TOP 5 NATURE RESERVES

Exmoor Strikingly scenic national park abutting the Bristol Channel, blanketed in heather and gorse and home to herds of majestic red deer. See page 246

Shapwick Heath This vast reserve – the largest in the Somerset Levels – is rich in birdlife and makes a great place to watch otters swimming among the reeds. See page 170

Ubley Warren Former mining landscape, now buzzing with a variety of butterflies and birds. See page 150

West Sedgemoor Migrant waders out on the wet meadows and a huge heronry in the Swell Wood section. See page 177

Westhay Moor Brilliant birdwatching, and a reliable spot to catch the winter starling migration. See page 172

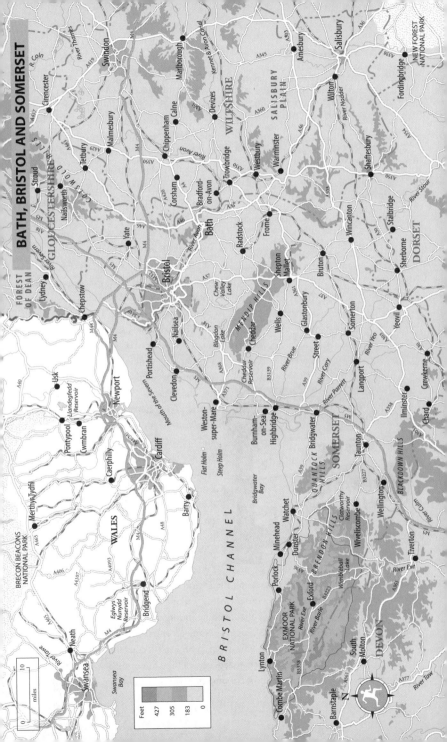

BATH, BRISTOL AND SOMERSET

WHAT'S IN A NAME?

Perhaps more than any other county in England, Somerset is blessed with some truly spectacular **place names**. Where else would you find such intriguing-sounding villages as Nempnett Thrubwell, Furzy Knaps, Charlton Mackrell and Haselbury Plucknett? Many of these can be traced back to their **Celtic origins** – *crug*, the old Celtic word for "hill", for example, is buried away in names like Crewkerne and Cricket St Thomas. Others are derived from **Anglo-Saxon words**, such as Huish Episcopi, the prefix of which stems from *hus*, or "house", the suffix recalling the time when the Bishop of Bath and Wells played landlord to much of the county.

You'll see Currys (from *cwr*, meaning "border" or "edge"), Camels (a combination of *cant* and *mel*, which literally translates as "bare district") and Chews (a stream or river), but nothing crops up quite as much as Combe. From Monkton Combe to the extravagantly named Nyland cum Batcombe, it indicates a hollow or valley and is most often linked to the Celtic word *cwm*, though it also appears in Saxon, Norse and Irish languages.

dramatic in parts, most jaw-droppingly so at **Cheddar Gorge**.

A short distance down the road, **Glastonbury** is distinguished for the ruins of its once-mighty abbey, but resonates among the New Age crowd for its tangled knot of Arthurian links and other mystical associations. Even the most cynical of sceptics would find it hard to deny that there's a certain aura about the town, not least in the peculiar promontory that is **Glastonbury Tor**. From the Tor, you can survey the **Somerset Levels** stretching out to the west – a captivating latticework of rhynes and ditches that's excellent terrain for walkers, cyclists and birders.

Continuing south, you'll find a mix of modern and ancient sights around the unassuming towns of **Yeovil** and **Chard**, ranging from **Cadbury Castle** (another place recalling the mythology of King Arthur) and the Renaissance mansion of **Montacute House** to collections of cars and aeroplanes – though the pretty little hamstone hamlets and orchards heavy with cider apples are just as much of a draw. To the west lies **Taunton**, home to the **Museum of Somerset**, a must-see for visitors to the region, and **Bridgwater**, with its Civil War memories. Either place would make a good departure point for forays into the **Quantock Hills**, perfect country for gentle hikes and home to some of Somerset's most exquisite churches.

In the far west of the region, straddling the Devon border, the wide open spaces of **Exmoor** beckon, traversed by a good network of walking routes. The moor reaches all the way to the coast, with high cliffs affording unforgettable vistas, and a string of picturesque villages providing shelter and refreshment. If it's seaside fun you're after, however, you'd do better to let your hair down in Somerset's coastal resorts, the biggest of which, **Weston-super-Mare** and **Minehead**, offer all the fun of the fair, though the smaller centres of **Clevedon** and **Burnham-on-Sea** have a more low-key, old-fashioned charm of their own.

SOMERSET SPECIALITIES

The pastoral landscape that constitutes much of Somerset provides a wealth of high-quality **produce**, the majority of it making the short journey from field to local farm shop, market stall or restaurant menu. The region is well known for its tangy cheeses and punchy ciders – all of which would make a gourmand giddy – but it's also worth sampling a few less familiar dishes. Here are five to try…

Bath chap Pigs' cheeks (and sometimes jawbones), salted, smoked and covered in breadcrumbs, served cold.

Chew Valley trout Brown trout, freshly hooked out of Chew Valley Lake, is a regional speciality, at its best when the cook lets the fish do the talking.

Eels Svelte and silky in texture, and delicious when smoked over beech and apple wood, as they are at Brown & Forrest in the Somerset Levels (see page 178).

Mendip wallfish Fairly hard to find nowadays, but well worth trying if you do: large garden snails, purged and then cooked in butter, herbs and cider.

Salt-marsh lamb Tender meat that owes its sweet, unusually aromatic taste to the variety of herbs and wild grasses that the lambs feed on in the low-tide marshes of the Severn Estuary.

At the other end of the region, East Somerset has an almost industrial feel around **Radstock** – once a booming coal-mining centre – but reverts to a more rural theme in places nearby, such as **Iford Manor**, where a gorgeous Italian Renaissance garden has been created, or along the **Colliers Way** cycle and walking route. The distant past can be explored in the remote **Stoney Littleton Long Barrow**, while two ruined fortresses – **Farleigh Hungerford Castle** and **Nunney Castle** – recall a time of medieval strife. Close to Nunney, the vibrant shops and thriving cultural scene in **Frome** have placed this small town firmly on the map in recent years, while two nearby country piles across the Wiltshire border, **Longleat** and **Stourhead**, present a hoard of magnificent treasures – paintings, furniture and assorted gewgaws of every description. Longleat also boasts a panoply of family amusements and a safari park, while Stourhead has some of England's finest landscaped grounds.

Venturing further into Wiltshire, you can make easy excursions to **Salisbury**, one of England's greatest cathedral cities, and to one of the country's most iconic prehistoric sites, **Stonehenge**; much more than the famous stone circle, the site encompasses a range of archeological splendours that demand prolonged exploration.

When to go

If you're aiming to hit the beaches in and around Somerset's coastal resorts, you'll want to catch the hottest months between June and September, but if it's peace you're after, avoid the hectic **school summer holidays** (late July to early Sept), when accommodation can be hard to find and tough on the wallet. Otherwise, the region doesn't have much in the way of a seasonal pattern – any time of the year is a good time to visit. **Weekends and bank holidays**, however, can be busy in Bristol, Bath, and, to a lesser extent, Wells, where early booking of accommodation is recommended and (in Bath particularly) there will often be a minimum-stay requirement of a couple of nights. If you're intent on pursuing **outdoor activities**, the increased likelihood of cold and rainy days in **winter** can make a trip at this time of year risky, especially on Exmoor, which attracts more rain than the rest of the region, not to mention fog and wind.

Author picks

Our authors have spent years living, working and travelling in Bath, Bristol and Somerset, delighting in the region's hidden gems as much as its heavyweight sights. Here are a few of their unsung heroes...

Hidden in the City Tucked away down Bristol's Broad Street, the striking facade of the former Everard's Printing Works is one of the most startling in the city, even when you know it's there. See page 91

Cider Inside Pulling in at Land's End Farm on the edge of the Wedmore plateau and sampling a generous taster of Roger Wilkins' farmhouse cider makes you feel like you've truly arrived in Somerset. See page 173

Art and Soul A former farmhouse makes an inspired setting for Hauser & Wirth's contemporary art gallery, as does the refreshingly unlikely location of rural South Somerset. See page 186

Making a Comeback Cranes have returned to the Somerset Levels (see page 175), otters are out in force and the rare bittern is breeding again in Ham Wall National Nature Reserve (see page 171), showing that conservation can work, given half a chance.

Holier Than Thou Once you get the church bee in your bonnet, it quickly becomes an obsession. Somerset's churches are especially renowned for their pinnacled towers and amazing oak bench-ends, for example at Crowcombe (see page 220) and Bishops Lydeard (see page 219) in the Quantocks.

Arts and Crafts Marvels abound at Tyntesfield, a flamboyant mansion outside Bristol that's being painstakingly returned to its glory days of Gothic grandeur. See page 230

Our author recommendations don't end here. We've flagged up our favourite places – a perfectly sited hotel, an atmospheric café, a special restaurant – throughout the Guide, highlighted with the ★ symbol.

EVERARD'S PRINTING WORKS, BRISTOL

A CRANE ON THE SOMERSET LEVELS

20

things not to miss

It's not possible to see everything that Somerset has to offer in one trip – and we don't suggest you try. What follows, in no particular order, is a selective taste of the region's highlights, from ancient ruins and outstanding national parks to fascinating wildlife encounters and unforgettable city sights. All highlights have a page reference to take you straight into the Guide, where you can find out more. Coloured numbers refer to chapters in the Guide.

1

1 CIDER
See page 29
Tasting traditional farmhouse cider straight from the barrel, and fresh from the surrounding orchards, is a quintessential Somerset experience.

2 THERMAE BATH SPA
See page 48
Take the waters at this cutting-edge facility in the UK's original spa town.

3 GLASTONBURY FESTIVAL
See page 168
The legendary musical mud bath in fields near Glastonbury has become a modern-day rite of passage.

4 BRISTOL INTERNATIONAL BALLOON FIESTA
See page 129
Night glows, novelty inflatables and the uplifting sight of a hundred hot-air balloons taking flight over the city.

5 ROYAL CRESCENT
See page 54
John Wood the Younger helped shape many of Bath's most beautiful buildings, but nothing matches the splendour of this famous arc of houses.

6 FLEET AIR ARM MUSEUM
See page 193
A buzzing airbase makes the perfect setting for this brilliantly interactive museum, home to dozens of fighter planes, bombers and military helicopters.

7 FARMERS' MARKETS
See page 28
The smorgasbord of local cheeses, freshly pressed apple juices, farmhouse bread and home-made chutneys is a regular feature at dozens of towns across the county.

8 ROMAN BATHS
See page 46
The baths that gave Bath its name: an evocative ensemble of hot springs and pools, cloaked in swirling clouds of steam.

9 WELLS CATHEDRAL
See page 137
Watch sunlight play on the magnificent west front then return for Evensong, when one of the best choirs in the world brings this beautiful building to life.

10 SS GREAT BRITAIN
See page 100
Superb museum charting the history of the one-time largest ship in the world, now back in the dock where it all began.

11 WALKING

See page 30

Taking to the hills –or to the Levels or the coast – is one of the joys of Somerset, whether it's a one-hour walk or a multi-day cross-county ramble.

12 GLASTONBURY ABBEY

See page 159

King Arthur, St Patrick and Christ himself have all reputedly visited this dramatic site in the heart of Glastonbury.

13 STREET ART IN BRISTOL

See pages 92 and 113

Banksy is just the most famous of a gifted group of graffiti artists who have together created the most exciting street-art scene in the country.

14 CLIFTON SUSPENSION BRIDGE

See page 109

Brunel's phenomenal bridge provides jaw-dropping views along the Avon and over Bristol's Floating Harbour.

15 STOURHEAD

See page 288

Immaculately landscaped grounds, dotted with a lavish collection of monuments set around a tranquil lake.

11

12

13

14

15

16

17

18

19

20

Itineraries

The following itineraries will take you right across the region, from the urbane delights of Bath and Bristol to longer stays in the countryside beyond. Dipping into Somerset's varied landscapes and exploring its rich tradition of folklore, they take in major destinations such as Glastonbury and Exmoor, as well as lesser-known gems like the island of Steep Holm.

A WEEKEND IN BATH

FRIDAY

Pulteney Bridge Take an introductory amble along the river and over Robert Adam's graceful bridge. See page 50

Dinner Sample some coffee-infused cauliflower at *Acorn* vegetarian restaurant. See page 65

SATURDAY

Roman Baths You'll need a whole morning for the informative showpiece that gives Bath its name. See page 46

Bath Abbey It's a short stroll across bustling Abbey Churchyard to the towering abbey and its superb vaulted ceiling. See page 45

Shopping Wander the Upper Town's warren of lanes, crammed with antique shops. See page 69

Dinner Treat yourself to a refined meal at the Michelin-star *Olive Tree*. See page 67

SUNDAY

Thermae Bath Spa Relax at this state-of-the-art spa, complete with indoor bath, steam rooms and a rooftop pool. See page 48

The Circus and the Royal Crescent Admire John Wood the Elder's architectural masterpiece, before taking in his son's majestic crescent, just a few steps away. See page 54

A WEEKEND IN BRISTOL

FRIDAY

M Shed Start with a thought-provoking rundown of Bristol and the people that make it tick. See page 100

Dinner Tuck into exquisite British dishes in the confines of a shipping container at bijou *Box-E*. See page 119

SATURDAY

St Nicholas Market Browse the eclectic stalls in the Exchange before grabbing brunch in the Glass Arcade. See page 91

Park Street and Clifton Have a nose round Bristol Cathedral (see page 104) on your way up to Clifton (see page 108), where you can join a tour of the dramatic Suspension Bridge.

Dinner More meat than you can eat at *The Cowshed* (see page 120) or trendy poolside dining at *Lido* (see page 120).

Create your own itinerary with Rough Guides. Whether you're after adventure or a family-friendly holiday, we have a trip for you, with all the activities you enjoy doing and the sights you want to see. All our trips are devised by local experts who get the most out of the destination. Visit **www.roughguides.com/trips** to chat with one of our travel agents.

Afters Follow a cocktail at easy-going *Kinakjou* (see page 123) with one or two more at hidden speakeasy *Hyde & Co* (see page 123).

SUNDAY

SS Great Britain Take a ferry to the Great Western Dockyard to explore Brunel's beautifully restored iron ship. See page 100

THE GREAT OUTDOORS

Allow a week to tick off all these walking, climbing and caving excursions, including a day to recover in a spa afterwards.

❶ Ballooning in Bristol Pick a still, sunny morning and float up, up and away, past the Suspension Bridge, over Bristol Harbour and across the city beyond. See page 128

❷ Bath Skyline Walk The six-mile circuit above Bath cuts through meadows and woodland and affords fantastic views over its mellow terraced crescents. See page 59

❸ Cheddar Gorge The country's biggest gorge is the region's best activity centre, whether climbing, abseiling, caving or walking – or all of the above. See page 146

❹ Steep Holm Take a boat trip out into the Bristol Channel to this island nature reserve with its population of Muntjac deer. See page 234

❺ Westhay Moor National Nature Reserve Whether out on the trails or at a poolside hide, you'll spot plenty of birdlife at this tranquil reserve in the heart of the Avalon Marshes. See page 172

❻ Exmoor Expansive national park that sprawls across the border into Devon: join a red-deer safari, hit the bridleways on the back of a horse or set off on a windswept walk along Britain's tallest sea cliffs. See page 246

MYTHS AND LEGENDS

There should be enough intrigue here to keep you busy for a week or so, more if you want to tackle all of Glastonbury's legends.

❶ Stanton Drew The third-largest stone circle in the country is actually a ring of petrified locals, punished for celebrating on the Sabbath – or so they say. See page 130

❷ Jack and Jill Hill Take care climbing to the hilltop well in the village of Kilmersdon – people have been known to break their crown up here. See page 286

❸ Wookey Hole Cast into stone, the figure of the Wookey Hole Witch awaits visitors who venture underground at this network of atmospheric caverns. See page 145

❹ Glastonbury Take your pick, from Joseph of Arimathea to King Arthur, by way of holy thorns, fairy kings and the final resting place of the Cup of Christ. See page 156

❺ Burrow Mump Allegedly part of the fort that once sheltered Alfred from the Danes, the "mump" overlooks the marshland where the king charred his cakes. See page 175

❻ Cadbury Castle Soak up the spectacular views from this Iron Age hillfort, reputedly the sixth-century site of King Arthur's fabled Camelot. See page 187

❼ Stonehenge The enigmatic circle of sarsens is one of those rare places that can still send a shiver down your spine. See page 302

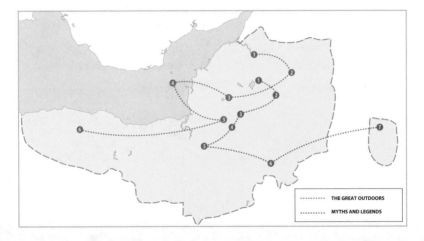

·········· THE GREAT OUTDOORS

·········· MYTHS AND LEGENDS

WEST SOMERSET RAILWAY

Basics

Getting there

Somerset's main centres – Bristol, Bath and Taunton – are well integrated into the UK's transport infrastructure, easily accessible by air, road and rail. Domestic and foreign flights use Bristol Airport, eight miles south of the city, while Exeter International Airport and Southampton Airport are also useful arrival points from elsewhere in the UK or from abroad – Exeter only an hour or so from Somerset's western reaches, Southampton with good links to Salisbury.

Bristol, Bath, Taunton and some other towns (such as Bradford-on-Avon, Bridgwater, Yeovil and Salisbury) are on the main rail network, while National Express and a few other private companies run bus services connecting these to all the UK's major cities. Drivers can access the region along the M4 motorway between London and Wales (passing close to Bristol and Bath) and the M5 between Birmingham and Exeter (good for Bristol, Glastonbury, the Quantock and Mendip hills and the coast).

Flights

Bristol International Airport (Ⓦbristolairport. co.uk) is the West Country's busiest airport, with regular **flights** from Newcastle, Edinburgh, Glasgow, Aberdeen, Inverness, Isle of Man, the Channel Islands and Belfast in the UK, and from Rome, Milan, Madrid, Barcelona, Malaga, Prague, Dublin, Cork, Shannon, Amsterdam, Copenhagen, Paris, Toulouse, Nice, Berlin, Cologne and Brussels among other cities in Europe. Located on the south coast, **Southampton Airport** (Ⓦsouthamptonair-port.com) has regular flights from Leeds-Bradford, Edinburgh, Glasgow, Belfast, the Channel Islands, Manchester and Newcastle in the UK, and from such European centres as Dublin, Amsterdam, Paris, Bordeaux, Limoges, Rennes, Geneva, Düsseldorf and Verona. In Devon, **Exeter International Airport** (Ⓦexeter-airport.co.uk) has flight connections to London, Edinburgh, Belfast, Manchester, Newcastle and the Channel Islands in the UK, and international connections to Paris, Bergerac, Geneva, Dublin, Amsterdam, Naples, Malaga, Alicante and Faro. There are also seasonal flights to and from a range of other European towns and cities from these airports. Operators include budget airlines and smaller companies such as easyJet and flybe, with single fares as low as £50, dependent on season and demand.

There are frequent **bus connections** from Bristol Airport to Bristol (see page 114) and Bath (see page 62), and hourly services to Weston-super-Mare and Taunton. If you're arriving at London's Heathrow Airport, you'll find direct connections to Bristol and Bath on National Express buses.

By train

GWR (Ⓦgwr.com) is the main **train** company serving the region, with twice-hourly services to Bath (1hr 30min) and Bristol (1hr 45min) from London. There are also frequent services to Bristol from Cardiff, Birmingham and Exeter, and direct services from London Paddington and Reading to Westbury, Castle Cary and Taunton. South Western Railway (Ⓦsouth-westernrailway.com) operate from London Waterloo to Salisbury (twice hourly; 1hr 25min), with some trains continuing to Westbury and Yeovil. There are regular connections between Salisbury, Bath and Bristol, stopping at Westbury and Bradford-on-Avon en route. For other stations on the rail network (Weston-super-Mare, Highbridge & Burnham, Avoncliff, Frome and Bruton) you'll usually need to change at Bristol or Westbury.

Train **tickets** in the UK are notoriously expensive, but you can often find cheaper fares by booking early. As a rule, the earlier you buy them, the cheaper they will be, but the more subject to restrictions; the most expensive ones are those sold on the day of travel and those with more flexibility. Railcards and concessionary fares are available (see page 24).

By bus

National Express (Ⓦnationalexpress.com), covering most of the UK's long-distance **bus** routes, has direct services from London's Victoria Coach Station to Bath (3hr) and Bristol (2hr 40min), as well as Frome, Weston-super-Mare, Clevedon, Burnham-on-Sea, Salisbury, Bridgwater, Taunton and Wellington. Bristol also has direct links with Birmingham, Swansea, Cardiff, Manchester and Southampton, while Salisbury has connections from Southampton and Portsmouth. The budget bus service Megabus (Ⓦmegabus.com) runs coaches to Bristol from London, Birmingham, Exeter, Plymouth, Cardiff, Manchester and Leeds. Berry's Coaches (Ⓦberryscoaches.co.uk) operates a service two or three times daily from London's Hammersmith Bus Station to Glastonbury, Shepton Mallet, Frome, Warminster, Yeovil, Wincanton, Bridgwater, Taunton and Wellington. As with trains, National Express and Megabus **tickets** bought on the day cost more.

Getting around

Getting from A to B is one of the pleasures of Somerset. Inevitably, however, the way isn't always smooth. Drivers will face motorway snarl-ups and slow-moving traffic on minor roads, while negotiating Bath and Bristol by car can be a nightmare. Users of public transport will find high fares and limited networks, and even walkers and cyclists will occasionally despair at the ubiquity of motor traffic. Nonetheless, public transport will get you to the vast majority of places mentioned in the Guide. For all public transport routes and timetables, contact Traveline (see box). Travelwest (see box) provides nearly-live updates on schedules in Bristol, Bath and North Somerset.

By train

The main operators for train travel in the region are South Western Railway and GWR. Trains provide the easiest means of moving between Bath and Bristol (taking less than 15min), and are useful for reaching some points further afield – the snag is that there aren't that many places in the area that you can reach by train. Heading southwest from Bristol, you can get to Weston-super-Mare, Highbridge & Burnham (for Burnham-on-Sea), Bridgwater, Taunton and Tiverton (for Exmoor); from Bath there are trains to Avoncliff, Bradford-on-Avon, Westbury and Salisbury, and from Westbury you can board a train to Frome, Bruton, Castle Cary and Yeovil. And that's about it. Of the two heritage train routes in the region – both seasonal – the **West Somerset Railway** (see page 222) is moderately useful for exploring the western flank of the Quantock Hills and the coast to Minehead, though the stations are often quite far from the villages and the best walking country. Elsewhere, train stations are fairly well placed for town centres, and the services that exist are usually punctual.

Cyclists should be aware that they won't always find space for bikes on trains, though places can be booked at least 24 hours before travel. For all reservations and information on services, contact **National Rail Enquiries** (see box).

Tickets can be bought at the station or online, or onboard if a station is unstaffed; otherwise, ticketless travel can result in having to pay the maximum fare for the journey. On all rail journeys, under-5s travel free and children aged 5–15 normally qualify for a fifty percent discount of the full fare. If you're travelling exclusively in Somerset and for a limited period, it probably won't be worth investing in one of the various **railcards** available, which give a year's discounted travel over the national train network to families, travellers with disabilities, those aged 16–25 or 26–30, and those aged 60 or over (the National Rail website has full details of these). More useful for limited periods is the **Freedom Travelpass**, valid for travel on all trains and most buses in Bristol, Bath and North Somerset, and available from bus drivers, train conductors and stations. A one-day Freedom Travelpass costs £6 for travel in Bristol; £11.50 for Bristol and Bath or Bristol and Clevedon; £13.50 for Bristol, Bath and Clevedon or Bristol, Clevedon and Weston-super-Mare, and £18 for Bristol, Bath, Clevedon and Weston-super-Mare; a one-week Freedom Travelpass costs £27 for Bristol; £50 for Bristol and Bath or Bristol and Clevedon; £59 for Bristol, Bath and Clevedon or Bristol, Clevedon and Weston-super-Mare, and £76 for Bristol, Bath, Clevedon and Weston-super-Mare. Monthly passes are also available.

By bus

Somerset's **bus** network is far more comprehensive than that of the trains, though even buses don't reach some of the remoter corners of the county, particularly on Exmoor. The main operator in the region is First, operating in much of the region as Buses of

PUBLIC TRANSPORT CONTACTS

Berry Coaches ☎01823 331356, ⊛berrycoaches.co.uk
Dartline ☎01392 872900, ⊛dartline-coaches.co.uk
Filers ☎01271 863819, ⊛filers.co.uk
First ☎0345 646 0707, ⊛firstgroup.com
GWR ☎0345 700 0125, ⊛gwr.com
National Express ☎08717 818181, ⊛nationalexpress.com
National Rail Enquiries ☎03457 484950, ⊛nationalrail.co.uk

Quantock Heritage ☎01984 624906, ⊛quantockheritage.com
Ridlers ☎01398 323398, ⊛ridlers.co.uk
South West Coaches ☎01935 475872, ⊛southwestcoaches.co.uk
South Western Railway ☎0345 600 0650, ⊛southwesternrailway.com
Stagecoach ☎01452 418630 or 01392 427711, ⊛stagecoachbus.com
Traveline ☎0871 200 2233, ⊛travelinesw.com
Travelwest ⊛travelwest.info

Somerset though Stagecoach, Filers, Dartline, Ridlers and Quantock Heritage also operate some services. Summaries of schedules and routes are given in every chapter of the Guide; bear in mind that these normally only refer to direct services, and many more places than those listed are reachable by bus with a change or two. Services on Sundays drop sharply, and winter also sees a reduction of routes and frequencies.

Tickets are purchased on boarding the bus. Return tickets are normally cheaper than two singles. Children under 5 travel free and those aged 5–15 get a discount of around a third depending on the route. Apart from journeys made during peak times (Mon–Fri before 9am), free travel is available for those aged 60 and over and for travellers with disabilities on presentation of a concessionary pass, available from the local authority where you reside.

Dedicated bus travellers can benefit from **travel passes**. First offers a West of England pass, valid for travel on all First bus routes around Bristol, Bath, Clevedon, Weston-super-Mare and the western fringes of Wiltshire (£7 for one day, £26 for a week, with separate prices for children, students, seniors and families, and small discounts when bought before boarding). West of England Plus also takes in Buses of Somerset in the rest of Somerset, but is only available for one day's travel (£12 or £24 for a group of five). Buses of Somerset also offers a Travel Anywhere ticket (£13 or £26 for a family for one day, £28 or £56 for a family for one week). Alternatively, AvonRider allows travel on services operated by any bus company in the Bristol, Bath and North Somerset area (£7 for one day, £32.50 for a week). Stagecoach, with a much more limited network in the region, offers a South West Explorer ticket (£8.30) covering the whole Stagecoach South West network including Taunton, Wellington, Chard and Yeovil over one day, and a Megarider valid for one week that covers the same area (£30). There's also the Freedom Travelpass (see page 24), which applies to train travel too.

By car

Touring Somerset **by car** may free you of the limitations of the public transport network but it does have its downsides. Most of the county's roads were originally designed for horses and carts, and the M5 motorway, while providing an easy way to cover the distance between Bristol and West Somerset, can get horrifically jammed, especially during school holidays and on bank holiday weekends. Somerset's "A" roads – mostly single-carriageway – are subject to long hold-ups too, as a result of roadworks, farm traffic and slow-moving caravans. Drivers should keep alert for constantly changing speed limits (speed cameras are fairly ubiquitous, particularly around Bristol and Bath) and, on Exmoor above all, should be aware of sheep and ponies wandering onto the roads (including at night) – game birds can also be a hazard.

A car can prove an encumbrance when visiting towns and villages. The only way to get acquainted with many of the places covered in this Guide is on foot, and the first thing drivers should do on arrival is to find somewhere to stow the car. Consequently, **parking** can be a constant preoccupation, and you'll save a lot of time by either heading straight for a central car park, or, where it exists, by seeking out a **Park & Ride** (Ⓦ parkandride.net), where free car parks on the periphery of towns are connected to the centre by frequent buses. Bristol, Bath, Salisbury and Taunton all have Park & Ride schemes. For other car parks, keep a bundle of change handy; Bristol and Bath are more expensive, but elsewhere you'll pay around £1 for an hour; parking at meters will be more expensive and time restricted.

If you want to **rent a car**, all the main rental companies have branches in Somerset, mostly in Bristol and Bath. You'll normally pay from around £20 for a day, £30 for a weekend, and £60 for a week; check out Ⓦ carrentals.co.uk for the best deals.

Consult local radio stations and websites such as Ⓦ trafficengland.com for live traffic updates. In the event of an **emergency breakdown**, contact the RAC (Ⓣ 0330 159 8757 or 0330 159 8743, Ⓦ rac.co.uk), the AA (Ⓣ 0800 887766, Ⓦ theaa.com) or Green Flag (Ⓣ 0800 400600, Ⓦ greenflag.com) for roadside assistance – though this will be expensive unless you're already a member. They also provide **route-planning** information and notice of traffic conditions.

Accommodation

Somerset has every kind of accommodation, with options to suit all tastes and budgets. The choice is of course widest in Bath and Bristol, and the seaside resorts of Weston-super-Mare and Minehead also have a good selection, while village inns, farmhouse B&Bs and campsites add to the stock outside the towns.

However, even this wide choice can narrow down drastically at certain times. Accommodation in Bath is scarce at weekends and during festivals, seaside resorts get booked up early over the summer, and vacancies are at a premium in and around places like Glastonbury during the Glastonbury Festival, and Shepton Mallet while the Royal Bath & West Show is on. Moreover, some places impose conditions, such as a minimum stay of two nights in Bath at weekends and up to a week in the seaside resorts in summer. For greater availability and lower rates, it's always worth considering other options close by: Bradford-on-Avon instead of Bath, for example, or Dunster rather than Minehead. Most tourist offices keep abreast of local vacancies and provide a free booking service.

Hotels, inns and B&Bs

Hotels in Somerset range from luxurious country-house retreats to seedy seaside dives with peeling wallpaper. At the top end, with rates starting from around £150 per room per night, you can expect every comfort, with a decent restaurant, good leisure facilities and spacious rooms, perhaps overlooking acres of grounds. Many have the air of exclusive clubs, with deliberately old-fashioned style and trappings; others might come into the "boutique hotel" category, with dark colours, sleek bathrooms and a blend of traditional and contemporary design. At the lower end of the scale, starting from around £80 a night, hotels are pretty indistinguishable from B&Bs (the legal distinction is largely technical) – a few rooms, perhaps with parking spaces and a part-time reception desk. That's not to say the cheaper places are necessarily tawdry; many smaller hotels offer heaps of character as well as the most attentive service.

Increasingly, **room rates** are determined according to demand, with prices generally higher at weekends and other peak periods. In any case, it's always worth looking online for cheaper deals than the official tariffs, and various sites such as ⓦ lastminute.com will often throw up top-notch hotels at rock-bottom prices.

Somerset has a rich selection of **inns**, or pubs with rooms, which at their best are traditional old coaching inns, thatched and rickety, and often found in the most out-of-the-way places. They're not all wonderful, but the best ones are worth seeking out for a bit of authentic period atmosphere and a decent pint to boot. Choose your room carefully, though – you may not want to stay directly above the bar.

"**Restaurants with rooms**" represent the top end of this category, where a quality restaurant, usually in a rural area, offers two or three well-appointed guest rooms in a traditional setting. These places will often appeal to foodies unwilling to move very far from the table after a gastronomic blow-out, but they're usually smart and well maintained, making them a good option for anyone.

B&Bs, starting from around £60 per double room per night, are ubiquitous throughout Somerset and come in every shape and hue. The majority are just two or three simple rooms in a modestly sized house with minimal facilities, though most places now offer either en-suite or separate but private bathrooms. Grander ones, or "boutique B&Bs", may have a lot more style, more space and generous gardens, sometimes with a swimming pool or spa facilities as an added draw. Most B&Bs have free wi-fi connections, but note that many don't accept credit cards (we've mentioned where this is the case).

Hostels

Somerset has seven **hostels** belonging to the Youth Hostels Association (YHA, ⓦ yha.org.uk), in Bath, Bristol, Street, Exford, Cheddar and Minehead, while the area of Wiltshire covered by the Guide has one, in Cholderton, near Stonehenge. Modernized and less institutionalized than they once were, YHA hostels – affiliated to the global Hostelling International network and open to non-members with a surcharge of up to £3 – often have a choice of rooms catering to individuals, couples and families, as well as cooking facilities and canteens. Prices fluctuate according to demand, but might be £20–30 per person in high summer. Book early, as these places often fill up with groups.

As well as these, the region has a handful of independent or **backpacker hostels** in the region (most in Bath and Bristol), usually cheaper than YHA hostels, and with fewer restrictions, but often scruffier too. However, all have catering facilities and wi-fi connections, and are ideal for meeting up with other travellers.

ACCOMMODATION PRICES

For all accommodation reviewed in the Guide, we provide approximate prices **in high but not peak season** (July and Sept rather than Aug), referring to the lowest price for one night's stay in a **double or twin room** in a hotel or B&B, the price of a bed in a **dorm accommodation** in a hostel (and of a double room if available), and of a **pitch** in a campsite (sites sometimes charge per person, instead of, or in addition to, the pitch price). Prices in hotels and B&Bs may be lower between Sunday and Thursday and for stays of more than a couple of days; it's often worth looking online for the best deals.

SOMERSET'S QUIRKIEST ACCOMMODATION

Gypsy Caravan Breaks, Pitney Discover your inner gypsy in this cosy caravan parked in an apple orchard. See page 178.

Greenham Hall, Wellington Wake up to baronial splendour in this castellated Victorian pile set in beautiful grounds. See page 215.

Kildare Lodge, Minehead An eccentric, Lutyens-influenced version of Tudor architecture. See page 242.

Pack o' Cards Inn, Combe Martin As the name says, the building is modelled on a pack of cards. See page 271.

Yarlington Yurt, near Wincanton Glamping with a twist – a yurt furnished in eighteenth-century French style. See page 188.

Most hostels have single-sex dorms of 4 to 8 beds, and many also have en-suite doubles and family rooms; listings in the Guide show prices for individual beds and, where they exist, double rooms.

Campsites

Camping makes a great alternative to fully serviced accommodation, whether under canvas or in a motorhome or caravan. Somerset has a range of campsites, ranging from farmers' fields with basic washing facilities to mega-sites equipped for family holidays in or near the seaside resorts. Larger sites have shops, restaurants and evening entertainment, and even smaller places may have laundries, shops, swimming pools, playgrounds and other children's amusements. Areas holding tents are usually separated from parts reserved for motor-homes or caravans, and many of the larger sites offer static caravans to rent on a weekly basis. Most campsites close in the winter months, though dates tend to be flexible, varying according to the weather and demand. **Prices** for tent pitches start at around £5 per person per night in low season rising to around £15 in summer, depending on the facilities. Luxury camping – or "glamping" – in Mongolian-style yurts or other furnished and well-equipped large tents – will cost considerably more, of course. You'll find descriptions and reviews of most sites at ⓦ ukcampsite.co.uk, ⓦ campsites.co.uk and ⓦ coolcamping.com.

On Exmoor there are also one or two **camping barns**, amounting to little more than barns or large rooms with sleeping platforms and basic cooking and washing facilities. Prices are in the region of £8–15 a night. Unlike on Dartmoor, wild camping on Exmoor is illegal.

Rented accommodation

Rented accommodation in self-catering cottages or apartments can prove a more satisfying and economical option. Some places, such as those managed by the Landmark Trust and the National Trust, are in historic buildings with plenty of character. Most rentals are only available by the week (usually Friday to Friday or Saturday to Saturday), and the best ones are often booked up months in advance, especially on the coast, but it's always worth checking for cancellations, and shorter stays are often available in low season. Prices begin from around £350 for a week's stay in a one-bedroom property in high season. Local tourist offices can supply lists of properties.

HOLIDAY PROPERTY AGENCIES

Classic Cottages ☎ 01326 555555, ⓦ classic.co.uk. Rural properties in the West Country, with a small selection in Somerset.

Helpful Holidays ☎ 01647 433593, ⓦ helpfulholidays.com. A range of cottage rentals throughout the West Country, including several on Exmoor.

Hoseasons ☎ 0345 498 6060, ⓦ hoseasons.co.uk. Nationwide company whose Somerset properties include cottages, cabins with hot tubs and caravans, some in Glastonbury, in the Quantocks and on Exmoor.

Landmark Trust ☎ 01628 825925, ⓦ landmarktrust.org.uk. Stay in historic properties sleeping up to eight people, including Bath's Beckford's Tower, a priory near Weston-super-Mare and the attic rooms of a regimental museum in Salisbury's Cathedral Close.

National Trust Holiday Cottages ☎ 0344 335 1287, ⓦ nationaltrust.org.uk/holidays. Lodgings in 21 National Trust properties in Somerset and Wiltshire, including on the Tyntesfield, Montacute, Tintinhull, Lytes Cary, Fyne Court and Stourhead estates and in the Trust-owned villages of Lacock and Selworthy.

Rural Retreats ☎ 01386 897121, ⓦ ruralretreats.co.uk. Upmarket accommodation in restored historic buildings, including a Georgian apartment on Bath's Royal Crescent and a former toll house in Nether Stowey.

Food and drink

In recent decades, Somerset – and particularly Bristol – has embraced the Slow Food Movement, with seemingly even the simplest café now sourcing its products locally, and using seasonal (and often organic) ingredients where possible.

Cutting-edge cocktail bars are generally limited to Bristol and, to a lesser extent, Bath, though traditional pubs are still going strong, in many cases with a slight tweak of philosophy that sees them now combining real ales and refined food.

You'll be spoilt for choice in the big cities, with their huge range of independent cafés and innovative restaurants catering for every taste and budget. It's here (and in Castle Combe and the Chew Valley) that you'll find the region's **Michelin-star** restaurants – including *Casamia* (see page 119), *Restaurant Hywel Jones by Lucknam Park* (see page 67), *Bybrook* (see page 81), *Olive Tree* (see page 67) and *The Pony and Trap* (see page 131) – and the best **vegetarian** restaurants, such as *Flow* (see page 121) and *Acorn Vegetarian Kitchen* (see page 65).

There are some great **community cafés** elsewhere in the county, with teashops in notable abundance in Exmoor, though the traditional restaurant has faded of late, and in many smaller towns and villages you'll generally find the best chefs running the kitchens of **gastropubs**. The menus at many of these are often built around "Modern British" cuisine, which at its best memorably marries local, seasonal produce with ingredients and techniques from the Mediterranean and Southeast Asia.

No matter where you eat, though, the unifying factor throughout is Somerset itself, whose rich pastures provide a bounty of **meat** (particularly Mendip lamb and Exmoor horned sheep) and **dairy products** (good-quality Somerset brie and goat's cheese in addition to Exmoor blue and its world-famous Cheddar). There's also fruit from its plentiful **orchards**, while sharing a border with Devon means freshly caught **seafood** (scallops, mussels, hake and the like) is a given on most menus.

Markets and farm shops

Somerset's rich agricultural heritage is celebrated at numerous weekly or monthly **farmers' markets** and other showcase events: the Levels' Best market at Montacute House near Yeovil (see page 191), Bristol's Street Food Market (see page 92) and Bath's Guildhall Market (see page 72), which is becoming increasingly popular with foodies.

On a smaller scale, you can stock up on self-catering supplies or pick up a tasty souvenir or two at the resourceful little **farm shops** that dot the region, where the ciders are local, the chutneys home-made and the eggs still warm; we've highlighted some of the best ones in the Guide.

FOOD FESTIVALS

Love Food Festival Throughout the year; ⓦ lovefoodfestival.com. Annual festivals at Bristol's Paintworks and St Nicholas Market, championing local produce and producers.

Eat Festivals Throughout the year; ⓦ westonsuperfoodfestival.co.uk. Over a dozen regional festivals highlighting the best of local produce.

Feast Aug; ⓦ feasttaunton.co.uk. Three days of events showcasing the cooking of Somerset's best chefs, either at pop-up stalls or at sit-down dinners.

Drink

Somerset has a wealth of public houses, with a wide variety of contemporary **bars** and ancient coaching **inns** in Bath and Bristol, and some gloriously **traditional pubs** and **cider houses** in the countryside beyond: cosy, oak-beamed taverns with open fires that offer a fine range of naturally conditioned real ales and local ciders, usually served from a barrel.

As well as the region's famous farmhouse **ciders**, there are also plenty of very good **apple juices** available, with some cider-producers making up to twenty varieties.

FARMERS' MARKETS

Axbridge	First Sat 9am–1pm	**Martock**	Second Sat 10am–1pm
Bath	Every Sat 9am–1.30pm		
Bradford-on-Avon	Third Thurs 9am–1pm	**Midsomer Norton**	First Sat 9am–1pm
	Last Sun 10.30am–2pm	**Minehead**	Every Fri 8.30am–2pm
Bridgwater	Every Fri 9am–2pm	**Taunton**	Every Thurs 8am–3pm
Bristol	Every Wed 9.30am–2.30pm	**Watchet**	Every Wed 9.30am–4pm
Burnham-on-Sea	Last Fri 9am–1pm	**Wellington**	First & third Sat 9am–1pm
Crewkerne	Third Sat 9am–1pm		
Frome	Second Sat 9am–1pm	**Wells**	Every Wed & Sat 9am–4pm
Glastonbury	Last Sat 9am–2pm		
Lynton	First Sat 10am–12.30pm	**Weston-super-Mare**	Second Sat 9am–1pm

DRINK UP YE CIDER

I am a cider drinker / I drinks it all of the day
I am a cider drinker / It soothes all me troubles away
Ooh arrh, ooh arrh ay / Ooh arrh, ooh arrh ay

"I am a Cider Drinker", The Wurzels

Nothing is quite as synonymous with Somerset as **cider**, a drink ingrained in the regional identity and one that – in some parts of the country, at least – still carries clichéd connotations of a sozzled yokel dozing in a hayfield with an empty flagon hanging from his hand. While the image is encouraged to some extent by so-called Scrumpy & Western groups like The Wurzels, the market has moved on, and cider has enjoyed something of a renaissance among younger drinkers throughout the UK in recent years.

Traditional farmhouse cider is made with a variety of **cider apples** (usually a mix of bittersweets and bittersharps) and nothing more. The apples are harvested in the autumn, a process also known as a "scrump" from the nineteenth-century practice of stealing apples from a neighbouring orchard – and from where scrumpy cider derives its name. The apples are pulped, mixed with straw and racked into layers (or "cheeses") to be pressed and then naturally fermented in oak barrels for between eight months and two years. The fermented juice is blended – the key to achieving a well-balanced cider in terms of sweetness and acidity – filtered, and sweetened if necessary (all cider apples press out dry).

Farmhouse cider is **dry, medium or sweet** (medium is usually a blend of the other two) and, more often than not, still rather than sparkling. What constitutes scrumpy varies between producers and can signify a rough, sharp and often potent cider, or simply draught (unpasteurized) cider served straight from the barrel; either way, it's always cloudy. In recent years, several producers have started creating single-variety ciders using just one of Somerset's 85 different types of cider apple, such as Yarlington Mill, Stoke Red, Dabinett or, perhaps most famously, Kingston Black. Burrow Hill (see page 196) also make a bottle-fermented sparkling cider, which is developed in the same way as champagne, as well as a highly regarded cider brandy.

You can learn more about the cider-making process at **cider farms** such as Sheppy's near Taunton (see page 211) and Perry's in Dowlish Wake near Ilminster (see page 198).

Cider and perry

Herefordshire folk may argue to the contrary, but if the apples haven't been freshly picked from a dew-kissed Somerset orchard, then it isn't really **cider**. It's widely recognized that England has three vintage areas for growing cider apples – and all of them are in Somerset. Consequently, the region is home to large-scale, supermarket-savvy producers like Gaymers (makers of Blackthorn) and Brothers, though the gap between their offerings and a pint of traditional Somerset farmhouse cider is so big that they're virtually a different drink.

There are around forty cider producers in Somerset, and most pubs will have at least one variety of **Thatchers** (see page 152) on tap; some will have half a dozen or so barrels out the back – specialist cider houses considerably more – with a good percentage coming from local producers such as **Wilkins** (see page 173) and **Hecks** (see page 165).

Most cider producers will also make a **perry** (pear cider), a slightly sweeter drink produced using pretty much the same method; it's been growing in popularity in recent years but is still difficult to find in pubs.

Beer

Traditionally overshadowed by their fruity cousins, Somerset's good local **beers** stand up well in comparison to any of the brews produced in more renowned centres. The vast majority are **real ales**, many of them CAMRA award-winners; CAMRA, the Campaign for Real Ale (Ⓦ camra.org.uk), also recognizes pubs that contribute to the survival of this brewing craft, of which the county has many.

The biggest local breweries, **Bath Ales** and **Butcombe Bitter**, own their own pubs – *The Salamander* in Bath (see page 68) is a great place to sample the former, *The Lamb* in Axbridge (see page 152) the latter – though an independent "freehouse" is best if you want to try a range of local beers. Breweries to look out for include: **Cheddar Ales**, with their zippy Potholer golden ale; **Moor Beer** (from Pitney on the Somerset Levels), who do a particularly good chocolatey porter; **Cotleigh** (from Wiveliscombe, on the edge of Exmoor National Park), notable for their Honey Buzzard; and **Exmoor Ales** (another Wiveliscombe brewer), creators of the first golden ale in the country, Exmoor Gold. The craft-beer revolution sweeping the UK has particularly taken hold in Bristol, where a growing list of experimental small breweries includes **Wild Beer Co** (whose Sourdough uses sixty-year-old yeast), **Arbor Ales** (whose Boomtown Brown uses Columbus hops and malted rye), and **Wiper and True** (who make an amber ale with vanilla, cinnamon and brandy-soaked currants).

Regional brewers making lagers and stouts are harder to come by, though Bristol has a couple of recommended outfits: **Zerodegrees** microbrewery, who produce both their own pilsner and black lager – as well as a German-style wheat beer – on site (see page 123); and **Bristol Beer Factory**, who stock Hefe (also a wheat beer) and Milk Stout at their floating pub, the *Grain Barge* (see page 123).

Sports and outdoor activities

Football and rugby are popular in Somerset – the former more so in the cities, the latter in the countryside – though perhaps cricket is the quintessential Somerset pastime. The county's rolling hills, dramatic coastline and network of trails make it classic walking and horseriding territory, while some of the best fishing in the country is to be had in its lakes, ponds, rivers and streams.

Spectator sports

Somerset sports fans have enjoyed a mixed time of it in recent years, with the fortunes of the local rugby and cricket teams ebbing and flowing, while Bristol City, the region's main football team, have flirted with promotion to the Premiership but never quite yet made the leap.

Football

Football is the main sporting passion in Somerset's towns, particularly in Bristol, though as in the rest of the South West, the Premier League has yet to be graced by a team from this neck of the woods. Bristol City (see page 128) were just one game shy of reaching the Promised Land in 2008, and currently try to repeat the feat each year in the Championship (despite the name, football's second tier). Other teams are Bristol Rovers, established in 1883 and the oldest club in the region (see page 128), in League One; Yeovil Town, who currently play in the National League (the fifth tier); and Bath City, a semi-professional team who play in the National League South (the sixth tier).

Rugby

Bath's sporting strength lies in **rugby**, and its rugby union team – known as Bath Rugby since the game turned professional in 1996 – play in the Aviva Premiership (see page 72). The club were the dominant force in English rugby during the mid-1980s and 1990s, winning seventeen trophies during that time, including the Heineken Cup in 1998. Their star has faded somewhat in the professional era, with the European Challenge Cup win of 2008 their only silverware since. Bristol – nicknamed the Bristol Bears (see page 128) – have long toiled in the shadow of their more illustrious neighbours but now play alongside them in the Premiership.

Cricket

The soundtrack of Somerset sport is the thwack of willow on leather, and **cricket** is the most popular game out in the countryside – there are over 75 cricket grounds in the county, with a dozen in Taunton alone. Cricket was first played here over 260 years ago, although it wasn't until 1875 that Somerset County Cricket Club was formed, when the "Gentlemen of Somerset" beat their opponents from Devon; the County Ground in Taunton (see page 209) has seen plenty of high and low points since, though. Ironically, Gloucestershire County Cricket Club play most of their home games in Bristol (see page 128).

Walking

Somerset's lush pastures and rolling hills make for glorious walking country – the Mendips, Quantocks and Blackdown Hills provide some particularly memorable hikes, while Exmoor National Park has the region's finest coastal walks, as well as plenty of scope for hikes along winding river valleys and windswept moors inland. There are countless rambles around the county's lakes and reservoirs, and gentle loops leading out from most county villages (check with local tourist offices or see ⓦ visitsomerset.co.uk).

Waymarked **long-distance walks** are often the best way of exploring a region (even just to sample a few miles of them, as they're generally routed to take in the best of the local scenery), and Somerset is no exception. The **River Avon Trail** (23 miles; ⓦ riveravontrail.org.uk), which heads upstream from Pill through the Avon Gorge to Pulteney Bridge, is a great introduction to Bristol and Bath; the thirty-mile **West Mendip Way** (see page 144) joins together the highlights of the Mendips; while the Somerset Levels and South Somerset are at their finest along the fifty-mile **River Parrett Trail** (see page 199). The best of the rest of the county is revealed on the **Leland Trail**

TOP 5 WALKS

Bath Skyline Walk Six-mile circuit around the hills surrounding Bath; meandering through woodlands and across peaceful meadows, it takes in a variety of sites, including an Iron Age fort and the eighteenth-century folly of Sham Castle. See page 59.

Charterhouse Numerous trails in a striking landscape, across lovely little nature reserves, past World War II bunkers and around the remnants of Roman and Victorian lead workings. See page 149.

Cheddar Gorge Walk Three-mile loop round Cheddar Gorge's precipitous cliffs, with great views over the towering rock faces and opportunities to strike off on longer hikes over the Mendips. See page 146.

Lynmouth to Watersmeet Two-mile riverside ramble, tracing the East Lyn inland to picturesque Watersmeet, where the river "meets" Hoar Oak Water. See page 264.

Wills Neck Follow the easy path from Dead Woman's Ditch to the equally oddly named Wills Neck, the highest point on the Quantocks. See page 221.

(28 miles), a rolling route from the Alfred Tower east of Bruton to Stoke-sub-Hamdon; the 36-mile **Quantock Greenway** (see page 221), which links the prettiest villages in that range; and Exmoor's northern end of the **Two Moors Way** (see page 265), which crosses Devon from Dartmoor.

The Exmoor section of England's longest National Trail, the **South West Coast Path** (see page 242) is particularly useful as a basis for short circular walks; it kicks off at Minehead, finishing some 630 miles (and around 55 days) later in Poole Harbour in Dorset, but just a few miles along it can be supremely rewarding. A couple of other long-distance cross-country routes run through the region: the **Monarch's Way** (615 miles; ⓦmonarchsway.50megs.com), which follows Charles II's escape route from the Battle of Worcester down to Shoreham in Sussex, spends more time in Somerset than any other county; while the **Macmillan Way** (290 miles; ⓦmacmillanway.org), from Boston in Lincolnshire to Abbotsbury in Dorset, cuts down past Bath and Bradford-on-Avon to Castle Cary, where Douglas Macmillan, the charity's founder, was born; a branch path from here, the **Macmillan Way West** (102 miles), heads across the Somerset Levels, the Quantocks and Exmoor to Barnstaple on the North Devon coast.

Trail maps for all walks are available online, and it's worth getting the appropriate Ordnance Survey map if you plan to go walking (see page 36).

Cycling

Hilly Somerset might not be the first place that springs to mind when it comes to getting about by bike, but the county has an impressive range of shared-use walking and cycling routes, some of them along old rail lines and canal towpaths, that make legwork comparatively painless. The obvious examples are the **Bristol and Bath Railway Path**, the **Kennet and Avon Canal**, connecting Bath and Bradford-on-Avon, and the **Bridgwater and Taunton Canal**.

Bike rental shops are available in Bath (see page 63), Bristol (see page 116), Glastonbury (see page 165), Taunton (see page 211), Minehead (see page 242) and Porlock (see page 256). Rates are around £15–25 per day.

The best areas for **mountain-biking** are the Quantocks, which has lots of twisting single-track trails that run down through its steeply wooded combes; Exmoor, particularly the descent from Dunkery Beacon and through Horner Wood; and the Mendips, which has some good trails around Black Down (see ⓦridemendips.org for route guides).

Bristol is the home of Sustrans, the **National Cycle Network** (ⓦsustrans.org.uk), whose first route – now part of Route 4 – was the Bristol and Bath Railway Path (see page 116). Bristol was also named the UK's first Cycling City in 2008, and is consequently pretty geared up for cyclists, with plenty of cycle lanes and green spaces.

Of the six other Sustrans routes that run through Somerset, **The West Country Way** (ⓦwestcountryway.co.uk), a regional section of Route 3, gives the best overview of the area: leaving Devon, it traverses Exmoor and follows canal towpaths to Bridgwater, before heading across the Somerset Levels – a great place for undemanding recreational cycling thanks to its pancake-flat terrain – and up to Bristol via Glastonbury, Wells, the Mendips and the Chew Valley. Route 410, also known as the **Avon Cycleway**, is an 85-mile circular route along country lanes around Bristol that takes in Clevedon and the Chew Valley, running near the stone circle at Stanton Drew. **Route 33** runs for 33 miles from Chard to Ilminster and Bridgwater, taking in Barrington (for Barrington Court), South Petherton, Langport (Muchelney Abbey) and

Burrowbridge (Burrow Mump) along the way, and tracing the River Parrett for some of its journey; part of this route is combined with routes 26 and 30 to form the waymarked eighty-mile **South Somerset Cycle Route**, looping between Yeovil, Castle Cary, Somerton, South Petherton, Ilminster and Montacute. **The Colliers Way**, a regional section of Route 24, runs from Frome to Radstock and the Dundas Aqueduct (see page 277); **The Strawberry Line** (Ⓦthestraw-berryline.org.uk), part of Route 26, connects Yatton with Cheddar but may be extended to Clevedon and Shepton Mallet (see page 151); while what's rather dramatically titled **The Ride to the North Somerset Coast** follows the Avon Gorge out of Bristol to the open-air lido at Portishead, along routes 33 and 41.

You can download leaflets and **route maps** for all of these from the Sustrans website, who also produce a more detailed series of waterproof maps (1:100,000). See Ⓦsomersetcycling.com for a list of bike shops in the area and other recommended routes.

Fishing

The best fishing in all of Somerset is on the **Chew Valley lakes** (see page 130), where Blagdon makes a superlative **fly-fishing** destination for trout, and Chew Valley itself serves up some monster pike. The county's numerous waterways provide some great **coarse fishing**, particularly on the **Somerset Levels**, where bream, tench and carp can be found in King Sedgemoor Drain, the Huntspill River and Combwich Ponds (see Ⓦbridgwaterangling.co.uk), and 30lb pike stalk the waters of the River Brue and River Tone. **Exmoor** is the place to head for wild salmon and trout fishing, notably the River Barle and River Exe. See Ⓦgo-fish.co.uk/somerset.htm for the details of over sixty fisheries, ponds, rivers, lakes, reservoirs and drains on which to cast a line. **Sea fishing** in the Bristol Channel can yield flounder, bass, wrasse and conger; try the seafront at **Weston-super-Mare** or **Burnham-on-Sea** or charter a boat for the day with a company like Seafire, in **Watchet** (Ⓣ01984 634507, Ⓦseafirefishing.co.uk).

Horseriding

Exmoor is a fantastic place for **horseriding**, with heather-clad moors stretching as far as the eye can see – though, as with walking, the Mendips and Quantocks are also crisscrossed with a number of bridleways worth following. There are nearly thirty riding schools across the county (see Ⓦepony.co.uk), while several companies offer riding holidays here, mostly in the national park. Some guesthouses (mostly those on

farms) can provide stables for anyone bringing their own horses on holiday with them.

Rock-climbing and caving

Somerset's best area for both **rock-climbing** and **caving** is the Mendip Hills, where the limestone walls of Cheddar Gorge and Burrington Combe are etched with a variety of challenging routes, as well as shorter ascents suitable for beginners (see page 146), and numerous sinkholes and cave systems provide plenty of opportunities for potholers (see page 145). Climbers can also tackle the deep quarry at Ham Hill in South Somerset, though it is forbidden to insert climbing gear into the rock face here.

SPECIALIST OPERATORS

Bath & West Country Walks Ⓣ 01761 233807, Ⓦ bathwestwalks.com. Guided and self-guided walking holidays around Bath, the Mendips and Exmoor, plus a Historic Somerset trip that includes Wells and Glastonbury.

Contours Ⓣ 01629 821900, Ⓦ contours.co.uk. Walking holidays and self-guided hikes, including the Mendip Way, the Coleridge Way and the Tarka Trail, which dips into Exmoor from Devon.

Footpath Holidays Ⓣ 01985 840049, Ⓦ footpath-holidays.com. Good selection of guided, self-guided and tailor-made itineraries, including Exmoor.

Let's Go Walking Ⓣ 0207 1931252, Ⓦ letsgowalking.com. UK walking specialists, organizing self-guided holidays on the South West Coast Path, Coleridge Way, Macmillan Way West, River Parrett Trail and Leland Trail.

Exmoor Riding Ⓣ 01643 862816, Ⓦ exmoor-ridingholiday. co.uk. Short rides, full days and three-day riding holidays, with a focus on barefoot riding, around the Vale of Porlock and along the Exmoor coast.

Festivals and events

As the cultural capitals of the South West, Bath and Bristol have an active calendar packed with festivals, events and seasonal celebrations, a love of a good party that spreads into the Somerset countryside in the form of music festivals, agricultural shows and village fetes. The following is a varied selection of the best of these, from ancient livestock fairs to fledgling music festivals; for details on local listings, either contact the relevant tourist office or see Ⓦvisitbath.co.uk, Ⓦvisitbristol.co.uk or Ⓦvisitsomerset.co.uk.

JANUARY TO MARCH

Wassail Jan 17 (region-wide). Cider-soaked ceremony dedicated to the health of apple trees and their forthcoming crop, dating back to Saxon times – the word comes from the Saxon weshal, "good health" – and held on the old (Julian calendar) Twelfth Night. You can join in the tradition at the Somerset Rural Life Museum in Glastonbury (see page 162) and Montacute House (see page 191), among other places.

Bath Literature Festival Late Feb to early March; Ⓦ bathfestivals.org.uk. Ten-day topical lit-fest that regularly attracts Nobel and Booker Prize winners, poet laureates and political heavyweights to historic venues across the city.

APRIL, MAY AND JUNE

Weston Sand Sculpture Festival April to Sept; Ⓦ westonsandsculpture.co.uk. Brilliant themed competition that will make your bucket-castle efforts look truly inept in comparison. Past creations include King Kong, Harry Potter and the Sagrada Família. See page 232.

Mayfest May (Bristol); Ⓦ mayfestbristol.co.uk. Wacky biennial festival of contemporary theatre that lasts a month and still manages to turn up something new every day, be it physical theatre, magic or storytelling.

Love Saves the Day Mid-May (Bristol); Ⓦ lovesavestheday.org. Proper inner-city weekend music festival from the people behind See No Evil (see page 92), taking in techno, grime and drum'n'bass.

The Bath Festival Mid- to late May; Ⓦ bathfestivals.org.uk. A cultural blockbuster of an event, combining classical, contemporary jazz, world and folk music with big-name authors, critics and Nobel Prize-winning scientists.

Dot To Dot Late May (Bristol); Ⓦ dottodotfestival.co.uk. Multi-venue music fest with a well-earned reputation for staging up-and-coming bands and soon-to-be big names.

Bath Fringe Festival Late May to early June; Ⓦ bathfringe.co.uk. Seventeen days of genre-defying performances across the city – in big venues, small cafés and on the streets in between.

Royal Bath & West Show Late May/early June (Shepton Mallet); Ⓦ bathandwest.com. Weighty agricultural show with loads of livestock, numerous displays, and the biggest cheese and cider competitions in the country.

Summer solstice June 21 (Stonehenge); Ⓦ english-heritage.org.uk. A mixed bag of druids, pagans, hippies and general partygoers gather to watch the sun rise over the Heel Stone on the longest day of the year. See page 306.

Glastonbury Festival Late June; Ⓦ glastonburyfestivals.co.uk. The music festival against which all other music festivals are measured, attracting the biggest names in the industry – and around 200,000 people to watch them. See page 168.

JULY AND AUGUST

Bristol Pride Early July; Ⓦ bristolpride.co.uk. Two-week-long celebration of Bristol's thriving LGBTQ community, culminating in a parade through the city centre and a festival on The Downs.

Frome Festival Early July; Ⓦ fromefestival.co.uk. This artsy East Somerset town ups the ante for ten days of open studios, exhibitions, cabaret, theatre and impromptu street performances.

St Pauls Carnival Early July (Bristol); Ⓦ stpaulscarnival.co.uk. A day-long parade of over-the-top costumes and elaborate floats forms the focus of this raucous celebration of Bristol's West Indian heritage. See page 129.

Priddy Folk Festival Mid-July; Ⓦ priddyfolk.org. Billing itself as the "friendliest folk festival in England", this well-respected event is focused around Priddy's pretty village green.

RNAS Yeovilton Air Day Mid-July; Ⓦ royalnavy.mod.uk/yeovilton-airday. Huge air show at one of the largest airfields in Europe, with aerobatic displays, flybys from historic aircraft, flight simulators and various military demonstrations. y

Bristol Harbour Festival Mid-July; Ⓦ bristolharbourfestival.co.uk. Water-based Harbourside event, the biggest in the city's calendar, with music, a circus and plenty of bobbing boats. See page 129.

Farmfest Late July; Ⓦ farmfestival.co.uk. Great-value rural music festival that prides itself on its alternatively low-key approach – cult bands and international DJs mix with hog roasts and hat competitions.

Taunton Flower Show Early Aug; Ⓦ tauntonfs.co.uk. Vivary Park makes a suitably bucolic setting for Britain's longest-running flower show, with designer gardens, arena events and more.

Bristol International Balloon Fiesta Early Aug; Ⓦ bristolballoonfiesta.co.uk. Atmospheric "night glows" and a battalion of odd-shaped balloons trying to take to the sky at once make for one of the city's most unusual festivals. See page 129.

RNLI Harbour Fest Minehead Mid-Aug; Ⓦ mineheadraftrace.co.uk. Weekend event at pretty Minehead Harbour including the RNLI Raft Race, a five-mile race from Minehead Bay.

Bath Folk Festival Mid-Aug; Ⓦ bathfolkfestival.org. A medley of concerts, ad-hoc amateur gigs and informal sessions taking place at venues across the city.

Ladies Day Mid-Aug (Bath); Ⓦ bath-racecourse.co.uk. Posh frocks and fancy hats at Bath racecourse's seminal event, with live music, fireworks and a bit of horseracing thrown in for good measure.

A CARNIVAL ATMOSPHERE

Somerset is rightly famous for its annual illuminated **carnivals**, a lightbulb-laden roadshow of spectacular floats and "squibbing" displays that date back to 1605, when the people of a predominantly Protestant Somerset took to the streets on torch-lit hay carts to celebrate the failure of the Gunpowder Plot. Between September and November each year (see Ⓦ cispp.org.uk for exact dates), fifteen towns put on their own one-night-only parade – **Bridgwater Carnival** (see page 217) is the one to catch, the biggest of its kind in the world, and renowned for its 100ft-long monster floats.

SEPTEMBER AND OCTOBER

Heritage Open Days Mid-Sept (region-wide); ⓦ heritageopendays.org.uk. An opportunity to spend the week nosing round historic buildings not normally open to the public.

Jane Austen Festival Mid-Sept (Bath); ⓦ janeaustenfestivalbath.co.uk. Celebrate the work of one of England's favourite authors at a variety of Austen-focused events, including a costumed parade through the city.

Somerset Art Weeks Late Sept/Early Oct (region-wide); ⓦ somersetartworks.org.uk. The best place to catch local art and artists, with more than a hundred venues hosting various events and exhibitions of the visual arts.

new music wells Mid-Oct (Wells); ⓦ wellscathedral.org.uk. Spread over five or six days and a great chance to hear choral music and organ recitals in beautiful Wells Cathedral (see page 139).

Halloween Oct 31 (region-wide). Take trick-or-treating to the next level at Wookey Hole caves (see page 145) or a late-night ghost tour around Dunster Castle (see page 258), where even the gift shop is supposedly haunted.

NOVEMBER AND DECEMBER

Bath Film Festival Mid-Nov; ⓦ bathfilmfestival.org.uk. The region's premier film fest, screening new documentaries and short films at various venues across the city.

Bath Mozart Fest Mid-Nov; ⓦ bathmozartfest.org.uk. Nine days of Mozart and Mozart-influenced music in historic venues that do justice to his work, and that of his contemporaries.

Bath Christmas Market Late Nov to mid-Dec; ⓦ bathchristmasmarket.co.uk. Wooden chalets fill Abbey Churchyard and surrounding streets for this popular annual market.

Travellers with disabilities

Somerset, and particularly Bath and Bristol, caters well for travellers with disabilities. All new public buildings – including museums and galleries – must provide wheelchair access, train stations are generally fully accessible and many buses have easy-access boarding ramps.

There are Shopmobility (ⓦ nfsuk.org) or similar schemes in **Bristol** (Cabot Circus and The Mall at Cribbs Causeway) and **Bath** (and in Taunton and Yeovil), which lend or rent out wheelchairs and/or powered scooters. Both cities have open-top bus tours with disabled access, though you'll need to contact Bristol's in advance for the schedule of its low-floor, step-free vehicle (see page 115). Dropped kerbs and signalled crossings are the rule, while the cities' big attractions also score highly on accessibility: Thermae Bath Spa, for example, has assistance chairs

that give access to the baths, while the SS *Great Britain* has won awards for its accessibility.

Getting around some of **Somerset**'s smaller villages (many of which don't even have pavements) can be more problematic, however, as can negotiating the county's historic buildings. That said, properties belonging to both the National Trust (Access Guide available at ⓦ nationaltrust.org.uk/features/access-for-everyone) and English Heritage generally have decent accessibility. Other more accessible attractions out in the country include **Haynes International Motor Museum** in South Somerset, whose owner has installed ramps throughout, and **Ham Hill** near Yeovil, where you can whizz round a designated route for free on an off-road scooter (available Mon–Fri 8am–4pm; call ☎ 01935 823617 at least 48hr in advance). Braille guides are available at several of the region's country homes, including **Lytes Cary Manor** and **Montacute House**.

Unfortunately, much of the finest **walking** (the Mendips and the Quantocks, for example) is up in the hills and across challenging terrain. The **nature reserves** in the Avalon Marshes, though, are particularly geared towards travellers with disabilities, with Shapwick Heath, Ham Wall and Catcott Lows all featuring accessible trails and boardwalks, some running to hides and viewing screens; furthermore, *Double-Gate Farm* (see page 173), six miles from both Shapwick Heath and Ham Wall, is a former AA Accessible Hotel of the Year.

RESOURCES

As well as the online resources listed below, *The Rough Guide to Accessible Britain* has detailed accounts of major attractions in the area – reviewed by writers with disabilities – with more places given the once-over by fellow travellers at ⓦ accessibleguide.co.uk.

Accessible South West ⓦ accessiblesouthwest.co.uk. Searchable directory of accommodation and restaurants, plus fairly detailed listings outlining the accessibility of local attractions.

Disability Rights UK ⓦ disabilityrightsuk.org. Campaigning organization with links and advice.

Tourism for All ⓦ tourismforall.org.uk. Excellent resource, with advice, listings and useful information.

Travel essentials

Costs

Although Bath and Bristol rank among the most expensive English cities outside London, Somerset is generally not much costlier than anywhere else in southwest England. What you spend depends entirely on your **budget**: buying your own food, staying in campsites or hostels, and walking or cycling everywhere might allow you to get by on as little as £30 per person per day, plus whatever you spend on sightseeing, while a couple staying in a B&B or modest hotel and eating out once a day can easily double this expenditure – after that, the sky's the limit. Your biggest expense will always be **accommodation**, which usually costs £60–120 per night for a double or twin room (singles cost around 75 percent of the full price of a double).

Admission prices for attractions given in the Guide are the full adult charges. The majority of fee-charging attractions have reductions for senior citizens, the unemployed, full-time students, under-26s and under-18s, with under-5s being admitted free almost everywhere; teachers, too, are sometimes given discounts. Anyone qualifying for reduced rates for attractions or travel should carry documentary proof.

Many of Somerset's **historic sites** – from long barrows to castles, abbeys and great houses – come under the aegis of the private **National Trust** (Ⓦnationaltrust.org.uk) or the state-run **English Heritage** (Ⓦenglish-heritage.org.uk), whose properties are denoted in the Guide with "NT" or "EH" respectively. Both bodies charge an entry fee for the majority of their historic properties, and these can be quite high, especially for the grander National Trust estates – though the expense can be partly offset at most NT properties by reductions for anyone arriving on foot, by bike or by public transport. If you think you'll be visiting more than half a dozen places owned by the National Trust or more than a dozen owned by English Heritage, it's worth taking out annual membership (£60–75), which allows free entry to the organizations' respective properties.

Privately owned **stately homes** tend to charge £5–12 for admission to edited highlights of their domain. Attractions owned by the local authorities – municipal galleries and **museums**, for example – charge lower admission or are free, while private collections always have fees. The **cathedrals** in Bath, Wells and Salisbury request a voluntary donation of £6–8 and may charge a small fee for a photographic permit.

Health

Although Somerset does not present particular **health hazards** that are exclusive to this region of the country, there are some tips that are worth remembering whether or not you are covered by health insurance. Remember that the sun can be deceptively strong in the South West, especially (but not only) in the summer months, and ensure that you use a suitable **sunscreen** (sun factor 30+ is recommended). On beaches, the wearing of "jelly shoes" – available at many seaside shops – is a good safeguard against the **weaver fish**, which lurk under the sand at low tide and can cause painful stings from the venomous spines along their dorsal fins.

On Exmoor and other areas where there is woodland and thick vegetation (for instance bracken), beware of **ticks**, which are brushed (or fall) onto exposed skin and burrow down to suck blood. Covering bare flesh on walks is the best protection; if you find ticks in your skin, seek professional advice – yanking them out can leave traces behind. Other possible hazards on moorland include **toxocara**, a small parasite carried in the faeces of some animals, and **adders** (or vipers), distinguished by a zigzag stripe along their backs; they're quite rare, and if you should be unlucky enough to be bitten, it is extremely unlikely to be fatal, though you should seek medical attention as soon as possible.

More generally, it's worth checking what your health insurance covers (if you have it) and packing any prescription medication that you normally take, as well as carrying contact details of your own doctor. Should non-emergency health issues arise, you can call ☎111, a 24-hour service offering limited advice for most problems; alternatively, consult the **NHS website** Ⓦnhs.uk, which is packed with information on the most common ailments and provides details of local doctors (GPs), dentists, pharmacies and walk-in centres, where you can receive attention on a first-come first-served basis. **Pharmacies** can also advise on a range of health topics.

Internet

Most hotels, B&Bs and hostels, and some campsites, have **internet** connections, usually using wi-fi – though connectivity may not be consistent in all areas, especially in older properties. **Public internet points** can be found in all towns and villages in Somerset where there are public libraries, offering free access at specific times, for which booking is advisable to avoid a wait. See ⓦsomerset.gov.uk/libraries, ⓦbeta. bathnes.gov.uk/library-and-information-services, ⓦbristol.gov.uk/libraries and ⓦn-somerset.gov.uk/libraries for lists of the region's libraries and opening times. Increasing numbers of pubs and cafés offer free wireless connections, as do some tourist offices. Larger towns have internet cafés, charging around £1 for twenty minutes.

Maps

The best general **map** of Somerset is Philip's Somerset Navigator, which reproduces the county at a scale of two miles to the inch (1:125,000), with town plans of Bristol, Bath and Taunton, and showing cycle tracks and major footpaths. **Walkers** and **cyclists**, however, should get hold of maps published by Ordnance Survey (ⓦordnancesurvey.co.uk), either the 1:50,000 Landranger series (pink covers) or the more detailed 1:25,000 Explorer series (orange covers), available in regular or more expensive weather-proof versions. You can also consult these maps online. AA (ⓦtheaa. com) and Geographers' A–Z (ⓦaz.co.uk) produce useful road atlases for drivers. Geographers' A–Z 1:25,000 and Harvey's (ⓦharveymaps.co.uk) 1:40,000 maps cover the South West Coast Path. All the above are on sale at outdoors stores and bookshops in the region or from dedicated **map outlets** such as Stanfords (see page 127), who offer a mail-order service. It's also worth checking online maps at ⓦisharemaps.bathnes.gov.uk, ⓦgoogle.co.uk/maps and ⓦstreetmap.co.uk.

Opening hours

Opening hours of all attractions, cafés, restaurants and pubs are given in the Guide, though as these change regularly it's recommended to check before making any long excursions. Many paying attractions stop admitting visitors 30 minutes or an hour before closing. Larger and more important **churches** are almost always open during daylight hours, but you'll often find country churches locked up unless they're particular tourist attractions – most in any case close at 4 or 5pm.

Shops generally open from 9am to 5.30pm Monday to Saturday, with many shops in Bath and Bristol open on Sunday as well, along with supermarkets and some bigger stores everywhere. When all else is closed, you can normally find a garage selling basic items. In summer, food shops in tourist areas often stay open until 10 or 11pm. **Banks** are usually open Monday to Friday from 9am to 4pm, and larger branches are also open on Saturday mornings; most **post offices** are open Monday to Friday from 9am to 5.30pm, Saturday 9am to 12.30 or 1pm, with main branches open on Saturday afternoons and smaller branches closed at lunchtimes and/or Wednesday afternoons. Banks, post offices and most shops close on bank holidays (see box).

Phones

Public telephone kiosks can be found in towns and villages throughout Somerset, though most do not accept coins; instead, swipe a credit or debit card, or use a phone card available from the post office (£5, £10 or £20), for which you must dial an access number followed by the card's PIN. **Mobile phones** are not always to be relied upon in rural areas – large parts of Exmoor and the Mendip and Quantock hills, for example, are out of range or have only a weak signal.

Dial ☏100 for the **operator**, ☏155 for the **international operator**. Calling **directory enquiries** (available at a variety of numbers, for example ☏118500) is expensive; you can find some numbers online at ⓦthephonebook.bt.com and ⓦyell.com.

Tourist information

County-wide **tourist information** can be found on the websites of the regional tourist bodies Visit

---

PUBLIC AND BANK HOLIDAYS

January 1
Good Friday (late March or early April)
Easter Monday (as above)
First Monday in May
Last Monday in May
Last Monday in August
December 25
December 26
Note that if January 1 or December 25 or 26 falls on a Saturday or Sunday, the next weekday becomes a public holiday.

EMERGENCY NUMBERS

For all **emergencies**, including police, fire, ambulance and coastguard, dial ☎999; to call the police when it's not an emergency, dial ☎101.

local attractions and accommodation. Much of the material on hand relates only to places that have paid for their entries and listings in the official brochures, but it's worth grabbing whatever free literature and maps are available and perusing the books and leaflets for sale.

Somerset (Ⓦvisitsomerset.co.uk) and Visit Wiltshire (Ⓦvisitwiltshire.co.uk). For maps and practical information, contact the local tourist offices listed in the Guide: staff are knowledgeable and helpful as a rule, and well supplied with details of public transport,

Opening hours for most tourist offices are Monday to Saturday 9am to 5pm; in high summer many are open daily, while in winter some are open at weekends only or else close altogether. Some offices will book accommodation for you, and many also sell tickets for tours, ferries and National Express buses.

Bath and around

CASTLE COMBE

1 | Bath and around

Water, stone and wool are the elements that have shaped the history and appearance of the city of Bath: the thermal waters that underpinned the city's growth; the soft oolitic limestone that fashioned its elegant Palladian architecture; and wool, the foundation of the region's wealth, without which the grand vision and ambitions of its leading personalities could not have been realized. Bath's hot springs alone set the city apart from anywhere else in the UK, but it is the aesthetic experience of its buildings and crescents that makes the greatest impression – the eighteenth-century city *par excellence*, Bath is in many ways a collection of urban set pieces, a visual feast best appreciated at a leisurely pace. And it's not just the buildings that appeal to the senses: the acres of parkland between the Georgian developments and the green landscape of the surrounding hills contribute equally to the spacious, measured feel of modern Bath, simultaneously soothing and exhilarating.

It is also a city that repays digging beneath its operatic surface, which you can do in some of the most rewarding **museums and galleries** to be found anywhere in the country. As well as the artistic attractions displayed in these, Bath offers a dynamic cultural life in other areas – in the arts **festivals** that punctuate the year, and in the diversity of **restaurants** and **bars** that cater more strictly to the flesh. In the world of retail too, Bath has a multitude of small **shops** and **markets** that distinguish it from the majority of Britain's mid-size towns.

On the flip side, Bath has never lost its exclusive air, and it ranks among the country's most expensive cities. This doesn't deter the constant flow of visitors who throng its attractions, hotels and restaurants year-round, however. While it's sometimes a challenge to rein in the expenditure, it's not hard to find respite from the hubbub, either in the parks or during walks outside the centre and further afield. Bath may have a veritable surfeit of attractions, but there is much to be seen and enjoyed within a short ride. Upstream, **Bradford-on-Avon** delivers further architectural delights and has a cluster of engrossing historical remains. To the northeast, you can get a taste of the Cotswolds in the villages of **Lacock** and **Castle Combe**, both oozing charm.

Any of these places would make less pricey alternatives to Bath when you're seeking **accommodation**, though **public transport** links to Lacock and Castle Combe are sketchy.

Bath

A glance at a map might suggest that the city of **BATH**, with a population of 88,000, has its identity completely submerged by that of metropolitan Bristol, England's sixth most populous city, just twelve miles away. Nothing could be less true, for Bath is distinctive and independent from its neighbour in every way – a harmonious, leisurely, compact, rather complacent city, richly endowed with historical and literary associations, its smart, prosperous centre abuzz with shops and cafés. While there's something undeniably patrician in Bath's prevailing tone, it lacks the snooty pretensions of that other great West Country spa town, Cheltenham, while the quirky details, architectural oddities and fragments of delicate rococo ornamentation

Highlights

❶ Roman Baths They're what Bath is all about – the source of its fame and fashionability – but this thermal complex is also an imaginative and engaging insight into Roman Britain. See page 46

❷ Thermae Bath Spa Relive the rituals of past generations in Bath while pampering your body with treatments and a rooftop bathe at this twenty-first-century spa establishment. See page 48

❸ Holburne Museum In a newly renovated Palladian mansion, this collection gathers together exquisite examples of ceramics, silverware and sculpture. See page 50

❹ Royal Crescent This graceful Palladian masterpiece is the most jaw-dropping of Bath's architectural highlights. See page 54

❺ Two Tunnels Greenway Cycle (or walk) this well-maintained thirteen-mile circular route that allows you to experience abundant wildlife as well as the long, eery ex-railway tunnels for which it is named. See page 62

❻ Corsham Court Hidden away in the winsome village of Corsham, this place is a wonderful find – a treasure-trove of European masterpieces from the sixteenth and seventeenth centuries. See page 77

❼ Lacock Abbey Not just an eighteenth-century manor house superimposed on sixteenth-century ruins, this was the home of "father of photography" William Fox Talbot, and holds an excellent museum of his work. See page 79

HIGHLIGHTS ARE MARKED ON THE MAP ON PAGE 42

1

you'll come across when you look closely undermine any overweening tendencies. In long shot, with its architectural integrity and amphitheatre-like setting, Bath is the most Italianate of British towns, with theatrical vistas at every turn. Jane Austen set *Persuasion* and *Northanger Abbey* here, it is where Gainsborough established himself as a portraitist and landscape painter, and the city's elegant crescents and Georgian buildings are studded with plaques naming the eminent inhabitants and visitors associated with the place from its heyday as a spa resort.

Inevitably it is the **Roman Baths** that make up the city's most essential sight, and one that lives up to the hype, but visually it is Bath's Georgian character that constitutes the real pleasure of a visit. The showpieces are the **Circus** and the **Royal Crescent**, intensely satisfying architectural ensembles, closely followed by **Pulteney Bridge** and **Pulteney Street**. You can absorb more of the same – but without the crowds – in the stately crescents of the aristocratic **Lansdown** neighbourhood, and learn how these projects were brought to fruition in the instructive **Museum of Bath Architecture**. Housed in a Neoclassical mansion, the **Holburne Museum** displays some of the artistic treasures of the period, while the **Herschel Museum of Astronomy**, dedicated to one of the outstanding scientists of the era, illuminates the scientific achievements of the time, as well as revealing aspects of ordinary life in the eighteenth century.

Offering relief from the city's insistent evocations of Georgian Bath are a couple of wildly differing collections: the **Museum of East Asian Art** and the **Museum of Bath at Work**, while, outside town, the **American Museum and Gardens** presents a thoroughly enjoyable slice of the history and culture of the USA from colonial times.

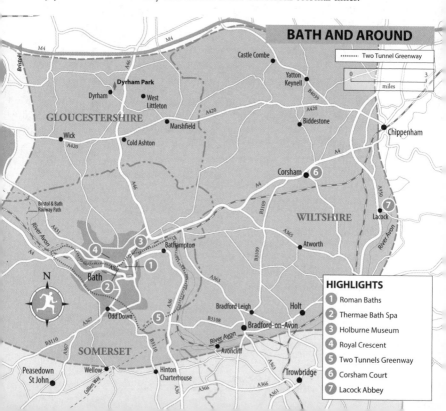

BATH AND AROUND

········ Two Tunnel Greenway

0   3
miles

HIGHLIGHTS

1 Roman Baths
2 Thermae Bath Spa
3 Holburne Museum
4 Royal Crescent
5 Two Tunnels Greenway
6 Corsham Court
7 Lacock Abbey

BATH'S LEGENDARY BIRTH

According to legend, Bath was founded by **Bladud**, a prince who suffered from some form of leprosy-like skin condition, for which he was banished from court by his father, Hudibras. Bladud survived by wandering from place to place and tending pigs, which themselves contracted the disease. Camped in what is now the Avon Valley, Bladud noticed that the lesions on their skins appeared to recede after his pigs wallowed in the warm mud in the valley, and he too was healed after wading in the mud. Returning to the court of Hudibras, he was accepted once more as his father's heir, and when he became king, Bladud formally recognized the sacred nature of the springs. His son, the legend goes, was Lear, Shakespeare's tragic hero.

Brief history

Bath owes its name and fame to its **hot springs** – the only ones in the country – which made it a place of reverence for the local Celtic population, the **Dobunni**, who dedicated the waters here to the goddess Sul. Numerous traces of Iron Age settlements have been found on the surrounding hills, including – east of the present city – on Solsbury Hill, the place immortalized in Peter Gabriel's eponymous song. But the place had to wait for Roman technology before a fully fledged bathing establishment could be created in the first century AD. The Romans identified the local deity Sul, or Sulis, with their own Minerva, and renamed the settlement **Aquae Sulis** ("Waters of Sulis"). Alongside the baths, a temple and probably a theatre and administrative buildings were established, the core of a thriving market town which was a stop on the great Fosse Way that ran between Lincoln and Exeter.

With the departure of the Romans, the baths quickly declined, but the town regained its importance under the **Saxons**, its abbey seeing the coronation of Edgar as king of all England in 973. All the same, a hundred years later, the Domesday Book recorded that Bath had a scarcely greater population than a large village today. The transfer of the seat of the bishopric of Somerset here (this was later reversed) and the Norman rebuilding of the Saxon cathedral 1090–1170 helped to stimulate the town, but in the centuries that followed it became increasingly overshadowed by the developing port and trading centre of Bristol.

A new bathing complex was built in the sixteenth century, popularized by the visit of Elizabeth I in 1574 and Anne of Denmark, James I's queen, in 1616, who came to find a cure for her dropsy. Following Charles II's visit in 1663, pumps were installed to encourage visitors to imbibe the waters, but it was not until after visits by Queen Anne in 1702 and 1703 and the reorganization of the town's social scene by **Beau Nash** (see page 57) that the city reached its fashionable zenith. And it was at this time – Bath's "**Golden Age**" – that the city acquired its ranks of Palladian mansions and townhouses, all of them built in the local **Bath stone**, which is still Bath's leitmotif today. The two John Woods – father and son – are the names most associated with the Georgian reconstruction of the city, but many other architects made significant contributions, among them Thomas Baldwin, John Eveleigh, John Palmer and John Pinch, whose works were predominantly Palladian and Neoclassical in style but made detours into the wilds of Georgian Gothic and Baroque.

Bath's heyday was over by the beginning of the **nineteenth century**. The currents of fashion had drawn people instead to such coastal resorts as Brighton and Weymouth, or to more exotic European climes, newly accessible following the end of the Napoleonic Wars. Now, elderly spinsters and retired military men made up the majority of the city's residents – none with much money to spend. The construction of the **Kennet and Avon Canal** in 1810 to link Bath with London via Newbury and the River Thames helped to revive the local economy, as did Brunel's extension of the Great Western Railway to Bath in 1841, but the Industrial Revolution largely passed the city

1

CENTRAL BATH

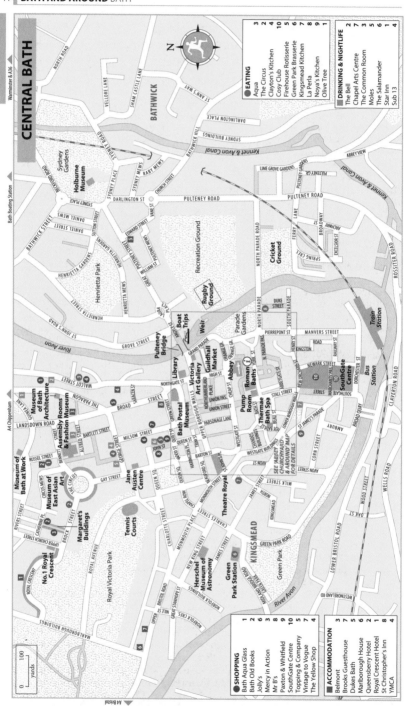

● EATING

Aqua	3
The Circus	2
Clayton's Kitchen	4
Cosy Club	10
Firehouse Rotisserie	6
Green Park Brasserie	7
Kingsmead Kitchen	8
La Perla	9
Noya's Kitchen	5
Olive Tree	1

● DRINKING & NIGHTLIFE

The Bell	2
Chapel Arts Centre	3
The Common Room	5
Moles	6
The Salamander	1
Star Inn	4
Sub 13	4

● SHOPPING

Bath Aqua Glass	1
Bath Old Books	2
Jolly's	6
Mercy in Action	3
Mr B's	9
Paxton & Whitfield	8
SouthGate Centre	10
Topping & Company	5
Vintage to Vogue	7
The Yellow Shop	4

● ACCOMMODATION

Belmont	3
Brooks Guesthouse	7
Dukes Bath	5
Marlborough House	6
Queensberry Hotel	2
Royal Crescent Hotel	1
St Christopher's Inn	8
YMCA	4

by, and it assumed the character of a slightly faded, slightly twee provincial resort that it has never entirely shaken off.

Spas were back in vogue in the late nineteenth century, and it was during a renovation of the King's Bath in 1878–79 that the remains of the old Roman Baths were discovered and excavated. The subsequent Victorian additions to the baths drew a new wave of tourism.

Bath didn't escape bombardment during **World War II**, with the Assembly Rooms among the buildings destroyed in 1942 (they were faithfully rebuilt). In 1964, the **University of Bath** was founded above the city on Claverton Down, bringing a much-needed infusion of youth culture to the staid city. The university has established a good reputation for its science and technology departments, while **Bath Spa University**, inaugurated in 2006, focuses on the humanities.

Bath Abbey

Abbey Churchyard • Mon 9.30am–5.30pm, Tues–Fri 9am–5.30pm, Sat 9am–6pm, Sun 1–2.30pm & 4.30–6pm; access may be restricted at short notice for special events • Requested donation £4 **Tower tours** Mon–Fri 10am–4pm hourly, Sat 10am–4pm every 30min • £8 • ☎ 01225 422462, ⓦ bathabbey.org

Dominating the pedestrianized **Abbey Churchyard**, whose two interlocking squares are usually a mêlée of buskers, tourists and traders, **Bath Abbey** commands attention. The site of a Roman temple and, in the seventh century, an Anglo-Saxon convent, the abbey is essentially a sixteenth-century replacement of a Norman construction erected between 1090 and 1170 and with a length of 348ft compared with 220ft today. This hugely overambitious Norman building ultimately turned out too big for the under-resourced monks to maintain adequately, and it was practically in ruins by the end of the fifteenth century when the new Bishop of Bath and Wells, Oliver King, in collaboration with Prior William Birde, commenced the formidable task of dismantling and rebuilding, incorporating the Norman foundations and much of the surviving stone. The bishop was said to have been inspired by a vision of angels ascending and descending a ladder to heaven, which the present **facade** recalls on the turrets flanking the central window. The west front also features the founder's signature in the form of carvings of olive trees surmounted by crowns, a play on his name.

King died shortly after work began, and the rebuilding project was further interrupted by the destruction of the abbey monastery in 1539 under Henry VIII, but significant restoration took place in the years following, with Henry's daughter, Elizabeth I, playing a large part in the repairs following her visit in 1574.

The interior

The abbey's **interior** is predominantly Perpendicular in style – this was in fact England's last major building to be built in this idiom – though much of it in a restrained manner, with relatively spare decoration. The glaring exception is the splendid **ceiling**, not properly completed until the nineteenth century when the great Victorian architect Sir George Gilbert Scott faithfully modelled the fan vaulting of the nave on the sixteenth-century ceilings of the choir and its aisles. The huge **east window** too, depicting 56 events in the life of Christ, is Victorian – it was restored after bomb damage during World War II.

Below the east window, to the right of the high altar, you can see traces of the grander Norman building in the **Gethsemane Chapel** (also called the Norman Chapel). Outside it, in a separate enclosure next to the altar, is the **chantry chapel of William Birde**, intricately decorated with its own little fan vault and carved with Birde's initials and, referencing his name, little birds. Elsewhere the abbey's floor and walls are crammed with elaborate monuments and memorials, including, in the **South Aisle** just before the transept, a wall tablet commemorating the renowned

1

Master of Ceremonies Beau Nash (see page 57). The **North Aisle** holds memorials to Thomas Malthus (1766–1834), the prophet of overpopulation, and shorthand pioneer Sir Isaac Pitman (1813–97).

On most days you can join a 45-minute **tower tour** to see the massive bells, clock and bell-pulling machinery, and to enjoy a bird's-eye view of Bath – but be prepared for the 212 spiral steps. MP3 downloads of various **audio tours** of the abbey on such themes as stonework and the "Bath Blitz" are available online (ⓦbathabbey.org/creatingvoices).

The Roman Baths

Abbey Churchyard • Daily: March to late June, Sept & Oct 9am–6pm, Easter until 8pm; late June to Aug 9am–10pm; Nov–Feb 9.30am–6pm; last entry 1hr before closing; free hourly tours • March–May Mon–Fri £18, Sat & Sun £20, June–Aug Mon–Fri £20, Sat & Sun £22; Nov–Feb Mon–Fri £16, Sat & Sun £18; £22 combined ticket with Fashion Museum and Victoria Art Gallery (all year); 10 percent discount if booked online • Ⓣ01225 477785, ⓦ romanbaths.co.uk

Even more than the abbey, the **Roman Baths** are the focal point of Bath, as they have been on and off since Roman times. Although ticket prices are high, there's two or three hours' worth of well-balanced, informative entertainment here, with hourly **guided tours** lasting about 45 minutes and audioguides available (both free) – the English version comes with three different commentaries, including one for kids and one by Bill Bryson, offering a more personal take. Allow up to three hours to get the most of this attraction, but come early in the day or in the evening – after 7pm between late June and the end of August – to avoid the crowds. Visiting after dark saves waiting time and gives the bonus of viewing the complex lit by flaming torches.

Check the website for dates of the thirty-minute **T'ai-Chi sessions** taking place on the outer terrace on selected Tuesdays at 8am (Ⓣ01225 477773; £4 per session); booking is not normally necessary – enter from Stall Street.

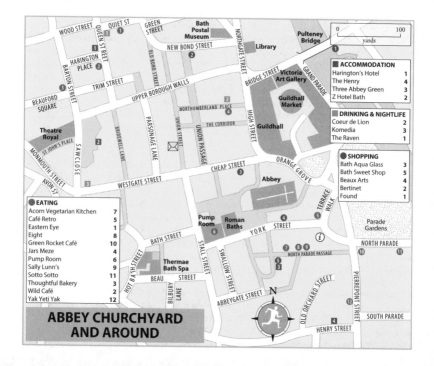

1

The architecture

Essentially, the baths complex visible today is the product of three eras – the Roman construction, originally much more extensive; the Norman-era reconstruction, when monks from Bath Abbey built a bathhouse on top of the Roman remains; and the Victorian additions, mostly in a cod-Roman style. The Roman structure dates from the mid-60s, just a few decades after the Romans first occupied the area, and remained in use for some 350 years thereafter, falling into disrepair in around 410. Successive constructions were erected over the rubble of the Roman site, by Saxon times buried some 15ft below. Saxon monks created a rudimentary bathing complex after the eighth century, which was augmented by Norman engineers. In subsequent centuries residential housing and even a tennis court were built over the site, but in the 1850s subsidence in the area led to investigations by city planners and the eventual discovery of the Roman site, far below street level. Excavations and restoration work continued until the grand opening of the Roman Baths to the public in 1897, since when there have been few alterations.

Visiting the baths

Among the highlights of a visit today is the **Sacred Spring**, part of the temple of the local deity Sulis Minerva, where water still bubbles up at a constant 46.5°C. The **Great Bath** is now open-air, but was originally covered by a barrel-vaulted roof. Its vaporous waters are surrounded by pillars, terraces and statues of Roman emperors and generals, all from the nineteenth-century restoration. Most of what you'll see at ground level is Roman, however, including a length of original lead piping and fragments of the arched roof showing the hollowed-out bricks. Following a conduit of iron-red water off one end of the bath brings you to the covered **Circular Bath**, where bathers cooled off, and, opposite, the open-air Norman **King's Bath**, placed over the hot spring and surrounded by original Roman arches and iron rings placed here in the sixteenth century to help bathers get in and out. This section was used for bathing up until 1978, when the waters were declared unsafe, mainly due to the presence of bacteria – much of it from the accumulation of pigeon droppings.

Throughout the complex, projections showing Roman-era characters help to re-create the atmosphere of the baths in use, and there are generally a few actors dressed up in Roman garb offering information and posing for photos. Look out for the fountain which will enable you to sample the filtered but still distinctly unpleasant spa waters.

The exhibits

The museum **exhibits** include a plethora of Roman finds, among them a quantity of coins, jewellery and sculpture. The most impressive items are a bronze head of Sulis Minerva and a grand, Celtic-inspired gorgon's head from the temple's pediment, but less ostentatious items such as the scraps of graffiti salvaged from the Roman era – mainly curses and boasts – give a nice personal slant on the range of people who frequented this antique leisure centre. There's plenty of background on the Roman Baths, their origins and their rediscovery and restoration, and models of the complex at its greatest extent give some idea of the awe that it must have inspired.

The Pump Room

You can get a free glimpse of the Roman baths from the next-door **Pump Room**, one of the social hubs of the Georgian spa community and still redolent of that era. Built in 1706, the Pump Room was enlarged and remodelled in the 1790s by Thomas Baldwin and John Palmer, two of the principal architects of Bath's Golden Age. Today, the building houses a formal tearoom and restaurant where lunches and teas are served in a period setting (see page 67). It's all a bit self-conscious and touristy, but the interior is worth a glance even if you don't want to order anything. Customers can also sample the filtered spa waters from a jug here (50p a glass for non-customers and non-ticket-

1

TAKING THE WATERS

"I assure you, Miss Woodhouse, where the waters do agree it is quite wonderful the relief they give. In my Bath life, I have seen such instances of it!" Mrs Elton, in Jane Austen's *Emma*

Bath's natural thermal springs are its *raison d'être*, an object of worship for the local Celtic population, a social ritual for the Romans and a fashionable fad for the Georgians, who congregated here by the carriage-load to "**take the waters**". The spa water was historically claimed to assuage gout and skin conditions as well as promote fecundity – hence the decision of Charles II to bring his queen, Catherine of Braganza, here in 1663, in the (vain) hope of producing a legitimate male heir. The most usual therapy consisted of immersion in the water, but drinking it became popular in the eighteenth century: "The water should always be drunk hot from the pump, or else at your lodgings as warm as it can possibly be procured," instructed the Bath Guide of 1800. "The water is generally drunk in the morning fasting, between the hours of six and ten, that it may have time to pass out of the stomach; though some drink a glass about noon. The quantity generally drunk in a day is from one pint to three, though some drink two quarts; few constitutions require more."

Health-giving properties are still attributed to the water, which mostly fell as rain 6000–10,000 years ago in the Mendip Hills, was warmed by geothermal heat and rose through fissures in the limestone beneath Bath. It contains some thirty different **minerals**, including sodium, calcium, magnesium, sulphate and iron – in fact it is slightly radioactive and, with so much dissolved lime, extremely hard. Today, various spa treatments are offered at some of Bath's swisher hotels such as the *Royal Crescent* (see page 64), but the only place to experience the natural thermal waters to the full is at the modern Thermae Bath Spa complex.

The tourist office (see page 63) offers a **Spas Ancient and Modern** package (W romanticbaths.co.uk) that includes a ticket to the Roman Baths, a voucher for a three-course lunch or champagne afternoon tea in the Pump Room, and a voucher for a two-hour spa session at Thermae Bath Spa, costing £86–90 per person.

holders for the Baths). Note the Greek quotation from Pindar picked out in gold lettering above the entrance, roughly translated as "Water is the greatest essence".

Thermae Bath Spa

Hot Bath St • Daily 9am–9.30pm, last entry at 7pm **New Royal Bath** £36 for 2hr (£40 Sat & Sun), £10 per additional hour (subject to availability); treatments range in price, starting from £49 for a 30min facial **Cross Bath** £18 for 90min (£20 Sat & Sun) • Children under 16 are not admitted into the New Royal Bath, under-12s cannot use the Cross Bath; each child aged 12–16 using the Cross Bath must be accompanied by an adult, and you must be 18 or over to book a spa treatment **Visitor Centre** April–Sept Mon–Sat 10am–5pm, Sun 11am–4pm • Free • ☎ 01225 331234, W thermaebathspa.com

At the bottom of the elegantly colonnaded Bath Street, **Thermae Bath Spa** allows you to take the local waters in much the same way that visitors to Bath have done since Roman times, but with state-of-the-art spa facilities. The complex is heated by the city's thermal waters and offers both pool and shower sessions and a variety of treatments from massages to dry flotation. The centrepiece is the **New Royal Bath**, a sleekly futuristic "glass cube" designed by Nicholas Grimshaw, incorporating the curving indoor Minerva Bath, fragrant steam rooms and a **rooftop pool** with glorious views.

Across from the entrance, the **Cross Bath** is in a separate building, a smaller, oval, open-air pool on a site once used by the Celts and Romans and rebuilt by Thomas Baldwin and John Palmer in the eighteenth century, when it was the most fashionable of the city's baths for its more intimate setting (bathers at the time were serenaded by musicians). The Cross Bath is open for spa sessions, though it has more rudimentary facilities than the New Royal Bath. All the baths have a depth of 4ft 5in and a water-temperature of around 33.5°C.

Note that treatments can (and must) be booked at the ticket desk or by phone, but pool sessions cannot be booked in advance. The queues can be frustrating – weekdays are the quietest time to visit (quietest of all Tues–Thurs). Towels, robes and slippers

1

are provided, but you'll need a bathing costume. You can also book a Roman Baths/ Thermae Bath Spa package (see box).

The main building also houses *Springs*, an excellent **café-restaurant** with nourishing (but fairly pricey) soups and salads. Next to the Cross Bath outside the entrance, a small **Visitor Centre** shows displays relating to Bath's thermal waters and a brief film. Audioguides (£2) in various languages can be rented from here to learn more about the complex and its environs.

The Guildhall

High St

Just north of Bath Abbey, the main part of the **Guildhall** was the work of Thomas Baldwin in 1775–78, though the Victorians made additions at each end and the dome is twentieth-century. The Guildhall's centrepiece is the grand **Banqueting Room**, adorned with ornate chandeliers and portraits of some of Bath's chief movers and shakers – including the local general and MP Marshall Wade and the quarry magnate Ralph Allen (see page 54) – as well as national figures such as George III, Frederick, Prince of Wales and Pitt the Elder. The room is now used for civic ceremonies and is one of the main venues of Bath's music and literature festivals.

The rest of the building holds the council chamber and register office, while adjacent is the **Guildhall Market**, a small indoor area mainly selling household goods, with another entrance on Grand Parade (ⓦbathguildhallmarket.co.uk).

Bath Postal Museum

27 Northgate St • Mon & Tues 11am–5pm, Wed–Sat 2–5pm; Nov–Feb closes 4.30pm • £5 • ☎ 01225 460333, ⓦ bathpostalmuseum.co.uk

Bath has a distinguished role in the history of Britain's postal system, largely due to the efforts of two Bathonians. Ralph Allen, later to become one of the city's great entrepreneurs, became Postmaster of Bath in 1712 at the age of nineteen, and introduced a series of reforms, notably the use of "cross" and "bye" posts to send mail on new delivery routes rather than going via London every time. John Palmer set up the first mail coach run in 1784, a system that was extended all over the country, greatly speeding up deliveries. Both men are celebrated in the **Bath Postal Museum**, in which you'll find examples of postboxes, stamps, stamp machines and post horns, with lots of buttons to press for recordings and quizzes.

Sally Lunn's

4 North Parade Passage • Museum daily 10am–6pm • Free • ☎ 01225 461634, ⓦ sallylunns.co.uk

One of Bath's oldest houses, **Sally Lunn's** is named after a Huguenot refugee – possibly Solange Luyon originally – who arrived in Bath in 1680, worked in this building and is said to have invented the Bath bun, a sort of soft-doughed brioche, here called the Sally Lunn bun. The building, which may date back to 1482 but incorporates remains of much earlier dwellings, now houses a rather twee tearoom and restaurant (see page 67) where various permutations of the bun take centre stage on the menu. In the basement (originally the ground-floor kitchen), a tiny **museum** reveals the Roman and medieval foundations of the various buildings that have occupied the site, and shows the reconstructed eighteenth-century kitchen and some bits and pieces unearthed during excavations.

Parade Gardens

Grand Parade • Daily: Easter–May & Sept 10am–6pm; June–Aug 10am–7pm; Oct–Easter 10am–4pm • £2, free in winter

Abutting the west bank of the Avon, the **Parade Gardens** were once an orchard belonging to the abbey's monks and were formally laid out as ornamental gardens by

1

John Wood the Elder in 1737. The tidy, flower-bordered lawns are furnished with deck-chairs and make a peaceful refuge from bustling Bath and a great picnic venue – not least when the traditional brass band strikes up from the bandstand (early May to early Sept most Sunday afternoons from 3pm). Among the gardens' numerous commemorative plaques and statues is the original "Angel of Peace" sculpture from c.1910, copied in parks and gardens all over the country, and an image of Bladud, Bath's legendary founder, with one of his pigs who helped reveal the presence of therapeutic springs here (see page 43). You'll also see a sundial from 1916 and a Victorian pet cemetery, and there's a café (usually closed Oct–Easter).

There are great views over the Avon and the two bridges – Pulteney Bridge and North Parade Bridge, an iron structure built in 1836 and encased in Bath stone a century later. Overlooking the gardens on the west is **The Empire**, a rather hideous Victorian hotel (now retirement flats) that was taken over by the Admiralty when the latter was relocated outside London at the start of World War II. Rather bizarrely, its roof is variously made up to resemble carved cottages, a townhouse, a gabled manor house and a castle – said to represent the different classes of Victorian customer who were apparently welcomed at the hotel.

Victoria Art Gallery

Bridge St · Daily 10.30am–5pm, last entry 4.40pm · £5, or £25 combined ticket with Roman Baths and Fashion Museum; 10 percent discount if booked online · ☎ 01225 477233, ⓦ victoriagal.org.uk

At the top of Grand Parade, the **Victoria Art Gallery**, built in the 1890s, has temporary exhibitions on the ground floor and two permanent exhibition spaces upstairs. In the latter you can see works by artists who worked locally, including Gainsborough. Beau Nash appears among the subjects of the numerous portraits, while twentieth-century works include Rex Whistler's *The Foreign Bloke*, John Nash's painting of Sydney Gardens, *Corsham Towers* by Peter Lanyon and Walter Sickert's *London Street, Bath*, as well as works by Chagall and Lowry. Look out too for the intricate Lichfield Clock, an eighteenth-century device encased in a miniature Gothic churchtower that plays five different tunes including a Handel minuet, and one of the gallery's most recent additions, *A Map of Days* – a typically unconventional self-portrait by Grayson Perry, depicting himself as a walled city.

Pulteney Bridge and Great Pulteney Street

The flow of the River Avon through Bath is interrupted by a graceful V-shaped weir, just below the Palladian, shop-lined **Pulteney Bridge**. This Italianate structure from around 1760, inevitably calling to mind Florence's Ponte Vecchio, was designed by the Scottish Robert Adam, best known for his work on house interiors, and is now one of Bath's most iconic landmarks.

On the far side of the bridge, the handsome, broad avenue of **Great Pulteney Street** was begun in 1788, planned to be the nucleus of a large residential quarter. The project ran into financial difficulties, however, which is why the roads running off it stop short after a few yards. Nonetheless, the street (the work of Thomas Baldwin) makes a striking impression, with Corinthian pilasters, impressive detail around the first-floor windows and a lengthy vista to the grand classical facade of the Holburne Museum at the end of the street.

Holburne Museum

Great Pulteney St · Mon–Sat 10am–5pm, Sun 11am–5pm · £11, free Wed 3–5pm · ☎ 01225 388569, ⓦ holburne.org

The imposing columned and pedimented Georgian mansion at the far end of Great Pulteney Street began life as Sydney House, a coffee house and ballroom that backed

A DIP IN CLEVELAND POOLS

A project to restore and reopen Britain's only surviving Georgian lido has received the green light, and work is currently under way to reveal this bathing spot in its full glory. Located just off the River Avon (and close to the Kennet and Avon Canal) to the northeast of the city in Bathwick, the **Cleveland Pools**, first built in 1817 in the shape of a small crescent, were one of the earliest examples of a "Subscription Pool" – built with private money for public use – and were a secret summer retreat for Bathonians and others for many years until their closure in 1984.

Restoration work is due for completion in 2021; keep up to date with developments at ⓦclevelandpools.org.uk. There are no parking facilities, though it is planned to make the pools accessible by ferry, and they are a fifteen-minute walk from Pulteney Bridge.

onto pleasure gardens where Bath's leisured classes were wont to promenade (Jane Austen, who lived at nearby 4 Sydney Place in the autumn of 1801, enthusiastically described the public breakfasts here). Started by Thomas Baldwin and finished by his pupil Charles Harcourt Masters, the building later became a hotel and hydropathic establishment, and since 1916 has housed the **Holburne Museum**, Bath's primary exhibition space for the fine arts. The core of the collection was created by Sir William Holburne (1793–1874), a naval officer who had fought at Trafalgar as an 11-year-old and whose private collection of paintings, silverware and porcelain was bequeathed to the city after his death. It has since been greatly augmented, and in 2011 the building acquired a startlingly modern extension at the back.

First floor

On the first floor, the regal **Ballroom** holds the kernel of Sir William Holburne's collection with numerous later additions: among the ceramics, silver, paintings and a rich collection of sixteenth-century Italian maiolica, highlights include the gracefully contorted *Crouching Venus*, a sculpture attributed to the Florentine Antonio Susini (1572–1608). Some treasures need to be sought out – in the room opposite, for example, drawers open to reveal a collection of miniature spoons and a miniature tea set.

The rest of the museum

The **mezzanine** floor displays items relating to Bath's eighteenth-century "consumer society" – statuettes, plates and some eye-catching vases suspended on cords – while the **top floor** has hilarious caricatures of some of the fashionable visitors to the city of the time, and an impressive gallery showing paintings by Stubbs, Angelika Kauffman and Gainsborough, among others. The latter's most famous work here is the *Byam Family*, his biggest portrait, which originally showed a typical well-to-do couple of the time but was later modified to include the addition of their daughter – her shy presence softening the haughty and slightly austere attitude of her parents. The gallery also includes works that formed part of Somerset Maugham's collection of theatrical paintings, bequeathed to the Holburne, among them a portrait of the eighteenth-century actor-manager David Garrick by Johan Zoffany. Look out too for some minor works by Turner, a couple of pieces by Pieter Brueghel the Younger and a miniature portrait of Beau Nash.

Sydney Gardens and the canal

Behind Holburne House, **Sydney Gardens** make a quiet, elegant and shady expanse in which to take a breather. Today, the gardens' slopes are cut through by both the railway and the **Kennet and Avon Canal**, whose towpath runs through a couple of short tunnels and beneath two ornate cast-iron bridges overhead. It's a pleasant 1.5-mile saunter east along the canal to *The George* pub (see page 68), beyond which you can walk or cycle the whole way to Bradford-on-Avon (see page 73), around ten miles in all. Alternatively, you can **rent a dayboat** for cruises along the canal from Sydney Wharf, near Bathwick Bridge (from £80 for half-day, £120–140 for full day; ☎01225 447276, Ⓦbath-narrowboats.co.uk).

Theatre Royal

Sawclose **Tours** Consult the website or call for dates and times · £6 · ☎ 01225 823475, Ⓦ theatreroyal.org.uk

West of the abbey, Westgate Street leads into the largely traffic-free **Sawclose**, once the site of a timber yard. The city's master of ceremonies, Beau Nash, had his first house in Bath here from 1743, in what is now the foyer of the **Theatre Royal**. Opened in 1805, the theatre is one of the country's finest surviving Georgian theatres; it was originally entered from round the corner in Beauford Square, where its monumental facade is preserved. You can join one of the occasional hour-long **tours** to view the interior, or book tickets for a play here (see page 69). Next door (now a restaurant) is the former home of Juliana Popjoy, mistress of Beau Nash, where he spent his last years.

Queen Square

North of Sawclose, Barton Street leads to the graceful **Queen Square** (1736), a fenced-in pocket of greenery holding a few gravelly areas for games of boules. Now rather besieged by the circulating traffic, the square was the first Bath venture of the architect **John Wood the Elder**, whose home at no. 9 (not no. 24, as a tablet there mistakenly asserts) afforded him a vista of the palatial northern terrace, with its pediment and Corinthian columns and pilasters. Wood had originally planned for the square to contain formal gardens, with a circular pool in the centre from which an obelisk rose; the pool is gone but the obelisk remains, erected in honour of a visit to Bath by Frederick, Prince of Wales in 1738, at the instigation of Beau Nash, who also persuaded Alexander Pope to write the rather lacklustre inscription (Pope was no fan of the Prince). The physician and philanthropist William Oliver (see page 54) lived on the square's west side, in a grand house that's now disappeared.

Jane Austen Centre

40 Gay St · April–June, Sept & Oct daily 9.45am–5.30pm; July & Aug daily 9.30am–6pm; Nov–March Mon–Fri & Sun 10am–4pm, Sat 9.45am–5.30pm · £12 · ☎ 01225 443000, Ⓦ janeausten.co.uk

North of Queen Square, the **Jane Austen Centre** helps to tie Bath's various Austen threads together with an overview of the author's connections with the city, illustrated by extracts from her writings, contemporary costumes, furnishings and household items. Visitors are given a useful fifteen-minute introductory talk before viewing the exhibits, which also include stills from films and TV adaptations. There's little here that Austen aficionados won't already know, but it's an entertaining whirl around life in Bath circa 1800, shedding light on the social and domestic context of the two Austen novels largely set in the city, *Persuasion* and *Northanger Abbey*.

The top floor holds the period-furnished *Regency Tea Room* (open to non-visitors to the museum), while the ground-floor shop has all the novels as well as lace, needlepoint and stationery for sale.

Herschel Museum of Astronomy

19 New King St · Feb to late July & Sept to early Jan Mon–Fri 1–5pm, Sat & Sun 10am–5pm; late July to Aug daily 11am–5pm; last admission 4.15pm · £6.70, or £16–19.50 combined ticket with No. 1 Royal Crescent, Museum of Bath Architecture and Beckford's Tower · ☎ 01225 446865, Ⓦ herschelmuseum.org.uk

JANE AUSTEN'S BATH

Jane Austen paid two long visits to Bath, at the end of the eighteenth century and between 1801 and 1806, setting most of **Northanger Abbey** and much of **Persuasion** here. In fact, Austen wasn't entirely enamoured of the city, expressing relief to be leaving in letters to her sister Cassandra, though it is thought that she fell in love while in Bath, possibly receiving her only known offer of marriage here.

The only place in the city devoted to the author is the **Jane Austen Centre** (see page 52), a Georgian house at 40 Gay Street a few steps up from no. 25, where the writer lived in 1805 – one of a number of places the Austen family inhabited while in Bath. You can learn more about the author and her life in Bath by downloading a free walking tour available in mp3 format from ⓦ visitbath.co.uk, including extracts from her novels and letters. The Jane Austen Festival (see page 69) in September features a procession through town in Regency costume led by a town crier, and there are banquets, country dances and readings.

Five minutes' walk west of Queen Square, a surprisingly modest Bath townhouse was the home of the astronomer Sir William Herschel (1738–1822), who, in collaboration with his sister Caroline, was the first to identify the planet Uranus. The building is now the **Herschel Museum of Astronomy**, celebrating this great achievement as well as the Herschels' other significant breakthroughs: the detection of two of Saturn's and two of Uranus's moons, the discovery of infra-red radiation in sunlight, the cataloguing of nebulae and of the behaviour of binary stars, and the discovery of the disc-like structure of the Milky Way itself. It's an absorbing collection, with knowledgeable and helpful staff ready to answer questions.

Formerly a German soldier in a Hannoverian regiment, and later an itinerant music teacher in the north of England, William Herschel arrived in Bath in 1766 to take up a post as organist at the Octagon Chapel, off Milsom Street. In 1772, he invited his sister Caroline to join him from Germany, and the couple moved into this building five years later. They left Bath when William Herschel was appointed "King's Astronomer" to George III in 1782, moving to Datchet, near Windsor. Although both Herschels earned their living in Bath primarily as music teachers, it was astronomy that claimed most of their free time, and was the field in which they made the most lasting impact. Accordingly the museum focuses mostly on their scientific careers, though you don't need to be an astronomy buff to appreciate the collection. The Georgian furnishings and personal knick-knacks of the Herschels in the ground-floor **dining room** give insights into life in contemporary Bath, while cartoons and pictures scattered around the house lend a flavour of the time.

The ground floor and basement

The former **drawing room** displays a replica of the 7ft telescope with which Uranus was identified in 1781, and more instruments are displayed in the basement of the building, where Herschel's preserved **workshop** holds the treadle lathe he used to make parts for his own home-made telescopes. Also here are the **kitchen** and a **cinema** that shows a ten-minute film of Herschel's life and career narrated by the astronomer Sir Patrick Moore. The tiny – once larger – back **garden** was where the telescopes were wheeled out and where the significant discoveries were made. Now it holds a Bath stone statue of William and Caroline from 1988 and a modern stainless-steel representation of Uranus.

The first floor

An amusing collection of satirical (and often outrageous) cartoons adorns the staircase leading upstairs, as well as a copy of the famous wildly dramatic photographic portrait by Julia Margaret Cameron of John Herschel, William's son and a renowned astronomer in his own right. At the top, the **Science Room** holds notebooks, examples of eyepieces

1

and such items as a brass orrery, or model of the solar system, and an Indian astrolabe. The adjacent **Music Room** displays a few musical instruments of the Georgian era and usually has a decorous soundtrack of pieces composed by William Herschel.

The Circus

Up from Queen Square, at the end of Gay Street, the elder John Wood created his masterpiece, **The Circus** (1754–67), Britain's first circular street. Consisting of three crescents arranged in a tight circle of three-storey houses, this architectural *pièce de resistance* has been compared to an inverted Colosseum and to Stonehenge (which shares roughly the same diameter). A closer look reveals a wealth of detail suggesting other influences, notably in the carved frieze running round the entire circle, where, among a range of arcane, possibly masonic symbols, acorns recall the mythical story of Bath's founding – how Prince Bladud discovered the health-giving waters here with the help of pigs rooting for acorns.

Wood died soon after laying the foundation stone for the "King's Circus", as it was then known, and the job was finished by his son. The centre was originally paved, and the elder Wood had planned for it to be occupied by an equestrian statue of George II, though this was never realized (the towering plane trees were first planted decades later). The painter **Thomas Gainsborough** lived at no. 17 from 1760 to 1774.

Royal Crescent and Victoria Park

The Circus is connected by Brock Street to the **Royal Crescent** (1767–74), Bath's grandest architectural statement, and said to be the country's first crescent. Built by the

1

younger John Wood, the design reflected the new taste for "picturesque" landscaping, with the stately arc of thirty houses set off by a spacious sloping lawn with a ha-ha (sudden drop), from which a magnificent vista extends to green hills and distant ribbons of honey-coloured stone. The houses themselves, embellished with 114 Ionic columns, are austere in their simplicity and almost indistinguishable from each other, even the house at the centre of the arc – marked by coupled columns – which now fronts the five-star *Royal Crescent Hotel* (see page 64), though lacking any outward advertising of the fact. According to some, the Royal Crescent's design may have been inspired by the older John Wood's belief in the existence of an arc-shaped Druid temple dedicated to the moon that once stood near Stonehenge, though there is no firm evidence for this link.

No. 1 Royal Crescent

Feb to early Jan daily 10am–5pm; last admission 4pm • £10.90, or £16–19.50 combined ticket with Herschel Museum, Museum of Bath Architecture and Beckford's Tower • ☎ 01225 428126, Ⓦ no1royalcrescent.org.uk

Though rigidly uniform in outward appearance, the interiors of the houses on the Royal Crescent reveal great variations in planning and decoration. You can get a close-up look at one of these, **No. 1 Royal Crescent**, on the corner with Brock Street. The first house to be completed on the crescent, when it was leased to John Wood and Thomas Brock (probably Wood's father-in-law), it has been restored to reflect as closely as possible its original Georgian appearance at the end of the eighteenth century. All furnishings, pictures and other items on display are authentic of the period or else – in the case of the wallpaper – faithful re-creations, as explained by the highly well-informed attendants providing commentaries in each room. Highlights are the golden-hued "Withdrawing Room" with its harpsichord and portraits, the secluded Gentleman's Retreat, the dining room with its mahogany table laid for dessert, the sepia-toned bedroom, the surprisingly cramped basement kitchen and the Servants' Hall, which shows an example of a dog wheel, in which a dog was made to run in order to turn a spit. Regular exhibitions are also held in an upstairs room.

Royal Victoria Park

At the bottom of the Royal Crescent, Royal Avenue leads onto **Royal Victoria Park**, the city's largest open space, containing copious flower displays, an obelisk dedicated to Victoria and Albert, an aviary and nine acres of **botanical gardens**, including a replica Roman temple that was the city's contribution to the British Empire Exhibition in Wembley in 1924. The western end of the gardens, alongside Upper Bristol Road, holds a large, well-equipped children's **play area**, with climbing apparatus, skateboard ramp, zip-lines and tyre-swings.

The park has an old-fashioned bandstand with performances by brass bands on occasional summer Sundays (early May to late July), and the lawns below the Royal Crescent and further west are used for balloon launches (around dawn and towards sunset) and events spilling over from Bath's various festivals. At its east end, the park has a bowling green, tennis courts and "adventure golf" course (see page 72 for details).

Museum of East Asian Art

12 Bennett St • Tues–Sat 10am–5pm, Sun noon–5pm; last admission at 4.30pm • £5 • ☎ 01225 464640, Ⓦ meaa.org.uk

The private **Museum of East Asian Art** is based on the collection of a retired solicitor who spent more than 35 years in Hong Kong. The displays are spread over three floors, with the **ground floor** taken up with wide-ranging exhibitions on such themes as Chinese calligraphy and the implements and vessels used in eating and drinking in China through the ages. Objects on the **first and second floors** (subject to a reorganization in 2020) include delicate ceramics, a diverse haul of snuff bottles, ivory figurines from the sixteenth century, bronze weaponry and, in a rare meeting between

1

THE PERFECT LOCATION: BATH IN THE MOVIES

Given their well-preserved state and theatrical panache, it's no surprise that the Georgian buildings and streets of Bath have been used for a plethora of **film locations**, including in such recent titles as *Persuasion* (1995 and 2007), *Vanity Fair* (2004), *The Duchess* (2008) and *The Other Boleyn Girl* (2008). Less predictably, episodes of *Buffy the Vampire Slayer* were filmed here in 2002. The most frequently used settings are the Assembly Rooms and Royal Crescent. Outside Bath, scenes from the Charles Darwin biopic, *Creation* (2009), were filmed in Bradford-on-Avon, while Castle Combe and Lacock have also been seen in a steady stream of films, notably *Dr Dolittle* (1967), *Stardust* (2007) and *War Horse* (2011) in Castle Combe, and the Harry Potter series (2001–09) and the BBC's *Cranford* in Lacock.

---

oriental craftsmen and Bath's high society, examples of armorial porcelain made in China for aristocratic families in England in the eighteenth century. There are also two themed collections: Stunning Craftsmanship, highlighting the work of anonymous artisans in various fields, and Dynamic World, illustrating the exchange of objects across cultural and trading networks. A ten-minute video explains the origins of the museum and the ideas behind its conception. Look out too for the small displays on the two staircase landings: a selection of some of the favourite items of the museum's founder on the first, examples of jade – for centuries one of the most highly valued materials in China – on the second landing.

Occasional **workshops** are held at the museum, for example on origami and ink painting (free or up to £40 for a full day; see website for details), and between September and June there are regular **talks** on East Asian themes connected to the current exhibitions, which usually take place at nearby 16–18 Queen Square on or around the first Friday of the month between 7 and 8pm (£6–8).

The Assembly Rooms

Bennett St • Daily: March–Oct 10.30am–6pm; Nov–Feb 10.30am–5pm; last entry 1hr before closing • Free • ☎ 01225 477789, ⓦ nationaltrust.org.uk

From the time they opened in 1771, the younger John Wood's **Assembly Rooms** were, together with the Pump Room, the centre of Bath's social scene. Here, subscription-holders gathered to play cards, drink tea and engage in polite conversation, no doubt spiced with generous helpings of flirtation and social climbing. The various rooms were used for specific activities, with the centrepiece being, naturally, the stately **Ball Room**, elegantly coved and chandeliered, and still the largest eighteenth-century room in Bath, where genteel minuets and more sprightly country dances were performed. The **Octagon and Card Rooms** were the venues for gambling and card-playing (and organ recitations on a Sunday), and the **Tea Room** for refreshment and music. Jane Austen described evenings in the Assembly Rooms in *Northanger Abbey* and *Persuasion*, while Dickens, another visitor to Bath, wrote in *The Pickwick Papers* how "the hum of many voices, and the sound of many feet, were perfectly bewildering. Dresses rustled, feathers waved, lights shone, and jewels sparkled".

The Assembly Rooms saw tough times in the nineteenth century, with competition from the newly enlarged Pump Room, and in the twentieth century they even briefly housed a cinema before suffering savage bombing in World War II, leaving the structure roofless. A faithful restoration eventually left the Rooms as we see them today, largely following the original eighteenth-century decor and colour scheme. The nine chandeliers are authentic, however, having been safely sequestered during the war. The Rooms are open to view whenever they are not in use for functions, and host **exhibitions and concerts** – ask at the desk about forthcoming events.

The Fashion Museum

Assembly Rooms • £9.50 (includes audioguide), or £25 combined ticket with Roman Baths and Victoria Art Gallery; 10 percent discount if booked online • ☎ 01225 477789, Ⓦ fashionmuseum.co.uk

The basement of the Assembly Rooms now houses the **Fashion Museum**, a well-presented and entertaining review of clothing from the Stuart era to the latest Milanese designs. Apart from anything, it's an excellent opportunity to see how the Georgians dressed, showing, for example, the hoops worn under the dresses of society ladies, which they were obliged to remove in designated apartments before joining in the dances at balls. Regular exhibitions focus on different aspects of dress through the ages – from the evolution of wigs to sportswear, while current and past "Dresses of the Year" are also displayed – a holder of this title has been acquired and shown every year since 1963.

Museum of Bath at Work

Julian Rd • April–Oct daily 10.30am–5pm; Nov & Jan–March Sat & Sun only; last entry at 4pm • £8 (including audioguide), or £7 Mon when top floor is closed • ☎ 01225 318348, Ⓦ bath-at-work.org.uk

This down-to-earth collection makes a refreshing antidote to Bath's prevailing tone of high-society hedonism. Installed in a Real Tennis court dating from 1777, the **Museum of Bath at Work** is largely given over to a re-creation of a soft drinks factory and engineering workshop that operated in Bath from 1872, and also includes material on different aspects of the city's industrial, manufacturing and mining history. The ground floor displays reconstructions of a cabinet-maker's workshop and a quarry face, together with an original manually operated crane and the various mining tools used for the extraction of Bath stone, while the top floor holds a pristine Horstmann car, made in Bath in 1914, a self-winding clock also invented by Gustav Horstmann, and a copy of *The Hound of the Baskervilles* written in Pitman shorthand (locally born Isaac Pitman lived on Royal Crescent in the 1890s). Also here is the "velocipede" – a sort of pedal-cart – belonging to entrepreneur J.B. Bowler, whose factory is reconstructed on the museum's middle floor. It features a crowded assemblage of bottling devices, carbonating machines for such fizzy concoctions as Cherry Punch and Orange

---

BEAU NASH

Bath's social renaissance in the eighteenth century was largely due to one man, **Richard "Beau" Nash** (1674–1761), a Welsh ex-army officer, ex-lawyer, dandy and gambler, who became Bath's Master of Ceremonies in 1704. Determined to rescue the city from the neglect and squalor into which it had fallen, Nash wielded dictatorial powers over dress and behaviour, for instance banning smoking in Bath's public rooms – an early example of health awareness at a time when pipe-smoking was a general pastime among men, women and children – and, most radical of all, forbidding the wearing of swords in public places. (This injunction was referred to in Sheridan's play *The Rivals*, in which Captain Absolute declares: "A sword seen in the streets of Bath would raise as great an alarm as a mad dog.") Less philanthropically, Nash encouraged gambling – in fact his wealth depended on his cut from the bank's takings. Nonetheless, he was generally held in high esteem, his influence even extending to cover road improvements and the design of buildings. Most important of all, the public balls he conducted were of an unprecedented splendour, though rigidly orchestrated – white aprons were banned, scandalmongers were shunned and each function had to begin at six (opening with a minuet "danced by two persons of the highest distinction present") and end at eleven. Nash also exercised his skills in the spa town of Tunbridge Wells, but his fortunes changed when new gambling restrictions were introduced in 1739 and 1745, and long before his death in Bath at the ripe age of 87 he had lost his influence and was reduced to shabby poverty. Buried in a pauper's grave, he was later recognized with a fine memorial in Bath Abbey.

Champagne, numerous lathes, a brass foundry and even the firm's office, together offering a fascinating insight into the working life of Bath, far removed from the flighty gossip of the Pump Room.

Museum of Bath Architecture

The Vineyards, The Paragon • Early Jan to late July & Sept to late Nov Mon–Fri 1–5pm, Sat & Sun 10am–5pm; late July to Aug daily 11am–5pm • £6.90, or £16–19.50 combined ticket with No. 1 Royal Crescent, Herschel Museum of Astronomy and Beckford's Tower • ☎ 01225 333895, ⓦ museumofbatharchitecture.org.uk

Accessed from a raised pavement, the graceful Georgian-Gothic Countess of Huntingdon's Chapel from 1765 now contains the **Museum of Bath Architecture**, an absorbing exploration of Bath's construction and design. This should ideally be an early stop on your wanderings around the city, with special appeal for anyone interested in the finer points of Palladian architecture. Explaining and illustrating the evolution of the city, the museum focuses on the architectural features that you'll see, with examples of everything from the kind of facades associated with the two John Woods, Baldwin, Palmer and others, to such details as balustrades, door designs and sash windows.

The exhibition also focuses on aspects of interior ornamentation, for example marbling, stencilling and japanning (European imitations of oriental lacquer-work). A huge 1:500 scale model of the city allows you to view Bath in long shot.

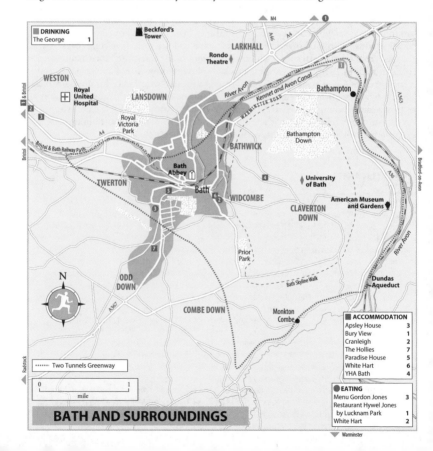

BATH AND SURROUNDINGS

1

BATH SKYLINE WALK

The streets and lanes of Bath are perfect for gentle ambling, but you can really stretch your legs on the heights to the east of the city by following the **Bath Skyline Walk**, a six-mile trail laid out by the National Trust. The waymarked circular route takes in woods, meadows and two of Bath's sights – Prior Park and the American Museum – as well as **Sham Castle**, a battlemented architectural folly erected in 1762 at the expense of local entrepreneur Ralph Allen, supposedly to improve the view from his townhouse; it's located below the university campus on Bathwick Hill. Needless to say, the vistas of the towers, spires and crescents of Bath from here and numerous other points on the route are superb.

The easiest access points for the Skyline Walk are Cleveland Walk, Bathwick (near the Holburne Museum and the canal), or, higher up, from the University of Bath campus at Claverton (bus #U1), from where it's signposted alongside a golf course. You can download a free route description and map from the National Trust website (ⓦ nationaltrust.org.uk).

Lansdown

North of the centre, Lansdown Road ascends to the salubrious heights of **Lansdown**, an aristocratic neighbourhood mostly laid out in the 1790s. Off the lower end of Lansdown Road, it's worth taking a look at **Camden Crescent**, designed by John Eveleigh and with a splendid prospect over city and valley. It's a typically Palladian composition, with Corinthian pilasters and a pediment with a tympanum displaying the arms of Lord Camden, lawyer, MP and Lord Chancellor – the elephant heads over the doorways are his Pratt family crest.

Lansdown's most pleasing groups of buildings, however, lie further up Lansdown Road. With its broad pavements and graceful iron lamp-holders, **Lansdown Crescent**, the work of John Palmer, is considered one of the city's greatest glories – William Beckford, the eccentric builder of Beckford's Tower (see page 60), lived at nos. 19 and 20. Close by, the quiet and secluded **Somerset Place** is another design by John Eveleigh; like Lansdown Crescent, it looks out over a fabulous skyline. West of Somerset Place, **Sion Hill Place**, a simple and elegant construction, was the work of one of the last of Bath's great Georgian architects, John Pinch the Elder, in around 1820. Bath Spa University has one of its campuses here.

Prior Park

Ralph Allen Drive • Feb–Oct daily 10am–5.30pm or dusk; early Nov to late Jan Sat & Sun 10am–4pm; last entry 1hr before closing • £7.50 • NT • ☎ 01225 833977, ⓦ nationaltrust.org.uk • Bus #2

One of the leading lights of Bath's Golden Age, Ralph Allen, who made his wealth by providing the stone for the city's rebuilding (see page 54), commissioned John Wood the Elder to construct a grand home for himself on a hill southeast of the centre in around 1738. The Palladian mansion, where he entertained such guests as Alexander Pope, Henry Fielding and Samuel Richardson, is now a school and closed to the public. You can, however, pass a pleasurable hour or two in the landscaped grounds, **Prior Park**, part-designed by Capability Brown and draped picturesquely along a valley that was chosen to provide the best views over the Georgian city. A circular path takes in wooded areas, cow pastures and the artificial lake that is the centrepiece of the ensemble, crossed by a perfect Palladian bridge, complete with columns and roof. There are benches for secluded panoramic picnics, and a pleasant garden tea-house halfway along the route.

Note that the walk from the centre is an uphill trudge or cycle ride along a busy road, and that the limited car parking is reserved for people with disabilities. Everybody else coming from town should consider either taking a taxi or bus from the bus station; Prior Park is also a stop on the hop-on hop-off City Sightseeing service (see page 70) and part of Bath's Skyline Walk (see box).

1

American Museum and Gardens

Claverton, 2 miles east of Bath centre • Mid-March to early Nov Tues–Sun 10am–5pm, daily in Aug; late Nov to mid-Dec Tues–Sun noon–4.30pm • £13, gardens only £7.50 • ☎ 01225 460503, ⓦ americanmuseum.org • University bus #U1 runs frequently every day to The Avenue (the stop at the entrance to the campus, then a 15min walk)

Built on a high wooded slope in the Greek-Revival style, the early nineteenth-century Claverton Manor was where Winston Churchill made his maiden political speech in 1897. Since 1961 it has been home to the highly engaging **American Museum in Britain**, the first collection of Americana to be established outside the US, with a particular focus on folk and decorative arts.

American culture from the seventeenth to the twentieth centuries is illustrated via a series of reconstructed rooms, such as a seventeenth-century "keeping room" (a "hearth" or family room off the kitchen) from Massachusetts and a richly red New Orleans bedroom from the 1860s. Special sections are devoted to textiles, whaling, Native Americans, the opening of the West and Hispano-American culture, while other galleries display rugs, quilts, porcelain and the minimalist furniture associated with the Shaker sect.

Even without the museum, the lovely **grounds** of Claverton Manor make the trek here worthwhile, with sweeping views across the Limpley Stoke valley. The gardens contain a **Folk Art Gallery**, as well as a replica of George Washington's garden at Mount Vernon, Virginia, a wigwam, an arboretum and assorted other relics resembling items from a movie set. A separate building houses America-themed **exhibitions**, ranging from history and popular culture to photography and sculpture.

Contact the museum or check the website for details of America-themed exhibitions, talks, workshops, fairs, concerts and other events taking place here throughout the year.

Beckford's Tower

Lansdown Rd, 2 miles north of Bath centre • Early March to Oct Sat & Sun 10.30am–5pm • £4.70, or £16–19.50 combined ticket with No. 1 Royal Crescent, Herschel Museum of Astronomy and Museum of Bath Architecture • ☎ 01225 460705, ⓦ beckfordstower.org.uk • Bus #31 from Milsom St

High above the city, aloof from its conventionalities, **Beckford's Tower** is the eccentric creation of one of England's true originals, a soaring flight of fancy concocted in 1827 in order to take advantage of "the finest prospect in Europe". William Beckford (1760–1844) was used to making grand statements: the traveller, collector and author, aged 21, of *Vathek* – an Oriental Gothic romance written in French – was previously known for his *grande folie*, Fonthill Abbey, a vast neo-Gothic palace built in Wiltshire in collaboration with the architect James Wyatt, whose central 280ft tower spectacularly collapsed in 1825. Beckford had already sold the ungainly building by this time, and, now a recluse, had moved to Lansdown Crescent in Bath. From here, working with the architect H. E. Goodridge, he directed the construction of his new project, a 120ft-tall Neoclassical tower, Italianate in style, and topped by a belvedere commanding distant views (according to legend, it was from here that Beckford discovered the collapse of Fonthill Abbey's tower, some 25 miles away).

Beckford passed most of his remaining life in this retreat, riding out from the city to spend his hours in solitary contemplation and study. Fire and rebuilding work have removed his Scarlet and Crimson drawing rooms, the Sanctuary and two libraries, but on the first storey of the tower you can view some of Beckford's preserved *objets* and furniture, along with paintings of the original rooms, a model of Fonthill Abbey and further items relating to Beckford's colourful life. An earthy-pink spiral staircase of 154 steps leads to a small viewing room at the top (the tower's highest section is closed to the public).

Beckford himself is buried in a raised and moated granite sepulchre in the **cemetery** that spreads around the base of the tower, an attractively overgrown site that also holds the tombs of Goodridge (who designed the cemetery's imposing gateway), Sir William Holburne (see page 51) and Beckford's dog.

1

THE TWO TUNNELS GREENWAY

Forming a misshapen circle to the east and south of Bath, the 12.5-mile **Two Tunnels Greenway** (ⓦ www.twotunnels.org.uk) provides a great opportunity to enjoy some of the choicest countryside around the city without enduring the steep gradients that characterize much of the landscape hereabouts. Bikers and walkers won't see very much of the natural world on the twin highlights of the route, however: the two disused railway tunnels (once part of the Somerset & Dorset Railway line) from which the shared-use path is named. The most striking is the **Combe Down Tunnel**, which at 1829yds is the UK's longest cycling tunnel, complete with piped classical music and an audio-visual artwork, *Passage*. Other noteworthy features of the Greenway include Dundas Aqueduct (see page 75) and the Georgian folly of Midford Castle. You could take a refreshment break at the *Hope & Anchor* pub at Midford, necessitating a half-mile diversion. Not all of the route runs around the city's outskirts – part of it passes over **Pulteney Bridge**. The route also links with the **Colliers Way** (see page 277) and Bristol–Bath cyclepaths (see page 116), and the **Kennet and Avon Canal** towpath. The tourist office can provide a map showing access points.

Dyrham Park

Dyrham, 7 miles north of Bath on the A46 **House** Daily: Mid-Feb to late Oct 11am–5pm; late Oct to mid-Feb 11am–4pm (Mon–Thurs by guided tour only) **Grounds** Daily: Mid-Feb to late Oct 10am–5pm; late Oct to mid-Feb 10am–4pm; last entry 1hr before closing • £13.50 house and grounds • NT • ☎ 0117 937 2501, ⓦ nationaltrust.org.uk

The landscape north of Bath is a scenic patchwork of verdant slopes, offering a far-reaching panorama at the top of Tog Hill, near the intersection of the A46 with the A420. A couple of miles north of here, **Dyrham Park** stands on the site of a calamitous defeat of the Celtic Britons by the Saxons in 577. While the extensive parkland affords grand vistas, the house – a late seventeenth-century Baroque mansion – shelters within a dip in the valley, its grand east front presenting a magnificent sight as it swings into view at the end of a long curving drive.

Within the house is a finely decorated but rather sombre succession of rooms panelled in oak, cedar, walnut and gilt leather or else draped in Flemish and English tapestries. Alongside furniture used by the diarists Pepys and Evelyn, many contents reflect the career of the first owner William Blathwayt, a diplomat who collected Delftware from Holland, and fine wood from North America for Dyrham's staircases and abundant panelling. Later additions include rows of portraits of the Blathwayt family, who occupied the house for nearly three centuries, and a good painting by Murillo, as well as a copy of the same by Gainsborough.

The name Dyrham means "deer enclosure", and the surrounding 268 acres of **parkland** are still grazed by fallow deer – and afford marvellous views as far as the Welsh hills. Garden and park **tours** take place in summer (see website for dates), and you can hear stories and myths connected to the house told by costumed story-tellers. From the entrance at the top of the drive, you can either walk downhill to the house (about 15min) or take the shuttle bus.

ARRIVAL AND DEPARTURE   BATH

By air Air Decker (☎ 01225 444102, ⓦ airdecker.com) provides a public transport link to Bristol Airport (see page 114), with departures from the bus station in Dorchester St and a few stops in town including Orange Grove; a one-way ticket is £14. A taxi to or from the airport costs around £55.

By train GWR (www.gwr.com) trains stop at Bath Spa station, a 5min walk from the centre at the bottom of Manvers St.

Destinations Bradford-on-Avon (Mon–Sat 2 hourly, Sun hourly; 15min); Bristol (Mon–Sat 3–5 hourly, Sun 2–3

hourly; 20min); Chippenham (every 30min; 10min); Frome (Mon–Sat 10 daily, Sun 4 daily; 40min); London Paddington (every 30min; 1hr 35min); London Waterloo (2–4 daily; 2hr 40min); Salisbury (1–2 hourly; 1hr); Trowbridge (Mon–Sat 2–3 hourly, Sun 1–2 hourly; 20min); Westbury (Mon–Sat 2–3 hourly, Sun 1–2 hourly; 30min).

By bus Bath's bus station is next to the train station on Dorchester St.

Destinations Bradford-on-Avon (Mon–Sat every 30min, Sun hourly; 25–40min); Bristol (every 15–20min;

55min); Corsham (Mon–Sat 3–4 hourly, Sun 1–2 hourly; 35–40min); Frome (Mon–Sat 2–3 hourly, Sun 5 daily; 40–50min); London Paddington (hourly; 2hr 40min–3hr 40min); Salisbury (Mon–Sat 1–2 hourly; 2hr 35min–2hr 50min); Wells (Mon–Sat every 30min, Sun hourly; 1hr 20min–1hr 40min); Westbury (Mon–Sat every 30min, Sun 4 daily; 1hr 20min).

By bike If you're coming from Bristol, you can cycle all the way along the Bristol and Bath Railway Path (see page 116), following the route of a disused railway line and the course of the Avon.

INFORMATION

Tourist office Bridgwater House, 2 Terrace Walk (Mon–Sat 9.30am–5.30pm, Sun 10am–4pm; ☎01225 614420, Ⓦ visitbath.co.uk). Tickets for some attractions and tours can be purchased here.

GETTING AROUND

There are few English cities in which **walking** is such an integral part of the experience as Bath. With architectural idiosyncrasies at every corner, walking allows you to take everything in at the pace for which the city was designed. However, to visit some of the more far-flung corners of the city – especially those lying at the top of steep hills – there are good local transport links. For Claverton (for the American Museum and the Bath Skyline Walk), Beckford's Tower and Prior Park, **bus services** are detailed in the Guide.

By bike Most of hilly Bath is not ideal for biking but the canal towpath is ideal for leisurely excursions. Yo Bikes (Ⓦ yobike.com) operates an app-based rental scheme costing from £1/hr to £5/24hr. Bike rental is also available from Bath Bike Hire, part of Bath Narrowboats (£15 for up to a full day: ☎01225 447276, Ⓦ bath-narrowboats.co.uk) at

Sydney Wharf, Bathwick Hill, and Brassknocker Basin on the Somerset Coal Canal, useful for the Colliers Way (see page 277).

By car Cars are simply a hindrance in Bath, and parking is expensive; drivers should use one of the Park-and-Ride car parks on the periphery of town at Newbridge, off the A4 Bristol road; Lansdown Rd, northeast of the centre, and Odd Down, southwest of town on the A367 Radstock road. Two of the most useful car parks in the centre are on Charlotte St, near Queen Square, and Green Park Rd, west of the stations. See Ⓦ beta.bathnes.gov.uk/find-car-parks-bath for all options.

By taxi Ranks at Orange Grove, near the abbey, Bath Spa train station and South Parade, or call Abbey Taxis ☎01225 444444 or V Cars ☎01225 464646.

ACCOMMODATION   SEE MAPS PAGES 44, 46 AND 58

Bath is chock-full of **hotels and B&Bs**, but they do fill up in busy periods. It's always worth booking early, especially at weekends when most places demand a two-night minimum – and prices rise. There's also a choice of good-value, centrally located **hostels**, and there's a decent **campsite** a short distance outside town. Note that the centre can get quite noisy at night, so choose a room away from the street for an undisturbed sleep. Unless otherwise stated, all places listed here have wi-fi available. Some of the establishments listed also offer **self-catering** options. For more choice, contact a dedicated agency such as Halcyon Apartments (☎01225 585100, Ⓦ thehalcyon.com); Bath Self Catering (☎01225 334466, Ⓦ bathselfcatering.com), or Queensberry Estates (☎07426 942408, Ⓦ queensberry estates.co.uk), which have properties sleeping between two and fourteen people; a week is the usual minimum stay, though some places are available for short breaks. As an alternative to staying in Bath, consider Bradford-on-Avon (see page 76), a brief train ride away, with generally lower rates and greater availability.

HOTELS AND B&BS

Apsley House 141 Newbridge Hill ☎01225 336966, Ⓦ apsley-house.co.uk. Expect extra helpings of old-

fashioned romance at this villa originally built for the Duke of Wellington, a 30min walk west of the centre. As well as the four-posters, swags and slipper baths, you'll find modern facilities and friendly, attentive service. Some rooms open directly onto the south-facing lawned garden. Breakfasts cover all tastes, and a bus stop is close by. **£155**

Belmont 7 Belmont, Lansdown Rd ☎01225 423082, Ⓦ belmontbath.co.uk. In the upper town, this simple Georgian B&B has six large doubles, most with tiny but clean and modern en-suite bathrooms. The house was designed by the younger John Wood. No credit cards. **£90**

Brooks Guesthouse 1 Crescent Gardens ☎01225 425543, Ⓦ brooksguesthouse.com. Capacious place on a fairly busy road near Royal Victoria Park, blending traditional and modern elements in stylish, mostly good-sized rooms (some rooms and bathrooms are cramped). There's a lounge, guests' fridge and honesty bar, and breakfasts are outstanding – abundant, with a huge variety of options. A parking permit is available for £10/day, though spaces are often scarce. **£110**

Cranleigh 159 Newbridge Hill ☎01225 310197, Ⓦ cranleighbath.com. Just over a mile west of the centre but close to a bus stop, this period Victorian house has spacious rooms – two with four-poster beds – and valley

1

views from the back. Multiple breakfast choices are offered, including delicious porridge, pancakes and smoked salmon, tea and cake are served in the afternoon, and there's a well-equipped honesty bar. There's limited free off-street parking, and usually spaces available close by. If you choose to have breakfast (it's optional), it will be brought to your room in a hamper. There's a bus stop outside for frequent services into the centre. **£98**

Dukes Bath 53–54 Great Pulteney St ☎01225 787960, �🌐dukesbath.co.uk. This classic Georgian lodging from 1789 provides lashings of period atmosphere, occupying a prime location on one of Bath's most characteristic boulevards. Some of the seventeen rooms have good views and the basement bar has a secluded patio. Breakfast is fresh and varied, and a parking permit is included in the room rate. **£110**

Harington's Hotel 8–10 Queen St ☎01225 461728, ⏦haringtonshotel.co.uk. Hidden away in the cobbled heart of Bath, this hotel in a converted townhouse has thirteen well-equipped rooms, mostly quite small, and some at the top of steep steps. Breakfasts are superlative, and you can order Bath Ales and snacks throughout the day. For further sustenance, book a session in the hot tub in the minuscule courtyard for £7.50. Service is friendly, parking costs £14 per day and there are also six stylish apartments for longer stays. Expect some street noise in front-facing rooms. **£124**

The Henry 6 Henry St ☎01225 424052, ⏦thehenry. com. Handy guesthouse for the stations and central sights, with seven large, clean rooms, all (except the one single room) with en-suite bathrooms. Cheaper rooms are at the top of the house, and there's a family room on the first floor. Special diets are catered for at breakfast, and there's a laundry service. **£100**

★ **The Hollies** Hatfield Rd ☎01225 313366, ⏦the holliesbath.co.uk. A brief bus ride or a 15min uphill walk south of the stations, off Wellsway (A367), this B&B from 1850 has three themed (English, Indian and Chinese), meticulously decorated rooms, an agreeably cluttered library and a lovely garden overlooked by the neighbouring church. Breakfasts around a communal table include delicious home-made jams. Free parking available. No under-16s. Two-night minimum stay. **£115**

Marlborough House 1 Marlborough Lane ☎01225 318175, ⏦marlborough-house.net. Close to the Royal Crescent, this Victorian B&B on a busy road has quiet and elegant air-conditioned rooms with period furnishings, fridges and complimentary sherry. The owner is extremely helpful and friendly and breakfasts are organic, vegetarian and gluten-free, with options for vegans. Drivers can park on the forecourt (two spaces) or on the street with supplied permits. There are discounts for longer stays on weekdays, and a small discount is offered if you mention this book when booking. **£105**

★ **Paradise House** 88 Holloway ☎01225 317723, ⏦paradise-house.co.uk. The inspiring views over the city justify the 10min uphill trudge from the centre to this Georgian villa, where three rooms have four-posters and three open straight onto the lush garden. New arrivals receive a complimentary drink, buffet breakfasts are superb, and there are Molton Brown products in the bathrooms. Open fires add atmosphere and warmth in winter. **£140**

★ **Queensberry Hotel** Russel St ☎01225 447928, ⏦thequeensberry.co.uk. Occupying four Georgian townhouses built for the eponymous marquis, this luxurious boutique hotel lays on the hipster charm with tastefully minimalist white-walled rooms, a walled garden, a sleek bar and a superb basement restaurant, the *Olive Tree* (see page 67). The staff are extremely professional, complimentary tea and coffee are available all day in the lounge, and there are Nespresso machines dotted throughout – though no tea/coffee-making facilities in the rooms. Valet parking costs £7 per day when rooms are booked through the hotel, otherwise £14. Avoid front-facing rooms at weekends. **£110**

Royal Crescent Hotel 16 Royal Crescent ☎01225 823333, ⏦royalcrescent.co.uk. For that special occasion, Bath's most palatial lodging – and at the most prestigious address – has rooms and suites with sofas, old paintings, fireplaces and bookcases. Bodily needs are taken care of in the spa and the top-notch *Dower House* restaurant, where evening set-price menus range from £50 to £78. **£264**

Three Abbey Green 3 Abbey Green ☎01225 428558, ⏦threeabbeygreen.com. Classy B&B in two beautifully renovated Georgian houses a stone's throw from the abbey. Rooms are airy and spotless; the larger ones overlooking a peaceful car-free square are more expensive but may suffer from street noise at night. There are a couple of spacious family suites, too. Breakfasts are outstanding. **£130**

Z Hotel Bath 7 Saw Close ☎01225 613160, ⏦the zhotels.com. It may not be everyone's cup of tea, but this functional lodging may particularly appeal to anyone who wants to stay centrally for a night or two while keeping to a budget. Rooms are decidedly small, some without windows, and en-suite bathrooms are separated off by frosted glass. On the plus side, everything is very clean, the location is right in the heart of the action, and rates are rock-bottom. Complimentary cheese and wine are doled out every evening – a nice opportunity to meet your fellow guests. Buffet breakfasts are £7/person extra (£9 if not pre-booked). **£55**

HOSTELS AND CAMPING

Bury View Corston Fields, on the A39 between Corston and Marksbury (bus to Newton St Loe, then walk 1 mile) ☎01225 873672, ⏦buryviewfarm.co.uk. The nearest campsite to the city lies on a working farm 5 miles west of the centre. It's small and quiet, with basic but clean facilities, and within walking distance of *The Wheatsheaf Inn* for meals.

(For a fancier "glamping" experience outside Bradford-on-Avon, see page 76.) No credit cards. Pitches **£16**

St Christopher's Inn 9 Green St ☎01225 481444, ⓦst-christophers.co.uk/hostels/uk/bath. Guests at this central, clean and modern hostel receive a 25 percent discount on food as well as drinks deals at *Belushi's* bar/restaurant downstairs, which is where you should check in. There are lockers and luggage storage, no curfew or lockout, and no kitchen – though a simple uncooked breakfast is included in the rate when rooms are booked through the hostel, otherwise it's £4. There's a chill-out room with kettle, fridge and TV, too. Beds are in six- or twelve-bed mixed or female-only dorms, or in private rooms. There's usually noise from the bar or street – ask for earplugs at reception if you're a light sleeper. Dorms **£15**, doubles **£77**

★ **White Hart** Widcombe Hill ☎01225 338053, ⓦwhitehartbath.co.uk. In the villagey Widcombe neighbourhood, the comfiest of Bath's hostels has dorm beds (in four- or six-bed dorms), singles, doubles and twin rooms (some en suite). There's a spacious kitchen where self-serve breakfasts of cereals and toast are provided, as well as a first-class bar-restaurant downstairs (see page 67). While being reasonably central, it's still fairly quiet. Closed Sun. Dorms **£20**, doubles **£50**

YHA Bath Bathwick Hill ☎0345 371 9303, ⓦyha.org.uk. An elegant Italianate mansion houses this hostel at the top of a steep hill a mile from the centre, with gardens and panoramic views. Most rooms are in a newly renovated back annexe. Evening meals, a bar and a kitchen available. It's close to the Bath Skyline walk, and there's a bus stop outside (buses #U1 and #U18). Dorms **£25**, doubles **£65**

YMCA International House, Broad St Place ☎01225 325900, ⓦymcabathgroup.org.uk. Nicely located on Walcot Street, this place offers a range of options, including dorms of varying sizes and private rooms (some en suite). All rates include a light breakfast, and you can also order a cooked breakfast (£4), packed lunch (£5) and evening meal (£10), but there's no kitchen. There's a reasonably priced laundry service, and guests get a discount in the attached gym. Rates increase at weekends. Dorms **£14**, doubles **£62**

EATING SEE MAPS PAGES 44, 46 AND 58

Bath has a huge range of places to eat, from relatively inexpensive **cafés** and **tapas bars** to pricey gourmet **restaurants**. Booking in the evening is advisable at most of them, essential at weekends. Many places offer excellent-value set-price meals at certain times, usually at lunchtime and before 7pm. Bath's dynamic restaurant scene is fast-changing, with places going in and out of fashion and business at a rate of knots; check out ⓦthepigguide.com for the latest news and reviews.

★ **Acorn Vegetarian Kitchen** 2 North Parade Passage ☎01225 446059, ⓦacornrestaurant.co.uk. One of the South West's top-flight vegan restaurants, this bijou place offers inventive and delicious dishes in an unruffled, elegantly arty environment. Fresh and locally produced ingredients such as cauliflower, kale and celeriac are subtly melded into delicate parfaits, sorbets and polenta dishes. Prices are high for the smallish portions, however, with set-price menus costing £21, £30 and £40 for one, two or three courses and taster menus at £45 for five courses, £54 for seven, though you can eat fairly economically at lunchtime when the menu features small plates for £4–7 each. The wine pairings are well chosen. Daily noon–3pm & 5.30–9.30pm.

Aqua 88 Walcot St ☎01225 471371, ⓦaqua-restaurant.com. In a converted Arts and Crafts church house, this convivial Italian eatery has chandeliers suspended from the high-beamed roof and a gallery. The menu ranges from sourdough pizzas (£9–12) and smoked haddock risotto (£12.50) to fillet steak (£25), and fixed-price deals are available, as are a selection of breakfasts and brunches. Mon–Fri 9.30am–10pm, Sat & Sun 9.30am–10.30pm.

Café Retro 18 York St ☎01225 339347, ⓦcaferetro.co.uk. This congenial spot near the abbey with a continental air is ideal for a lazy breakfast (American pancakes available), a proper cappuccino or a spot of lunch. Hot meals such as ratatouille and gourmet burgers cost £8–10. The *Retro-to-Go* takeaway next door sells fresh ciabattas, hot panini and breakfast butties. Daily 9am–4pm.

★ **The Circus** 34 Brock St ☎01225 466020, ⓦthecircusrestaurant.co.uk. Conveniently placed between the Royal Crescent and The Circus, this provides a welcome break from foot-slogging around the city's landmarks, open all day as a café as well as offering scrumptious meals. The seasonal menu features dishes such as lamb, braised rabbit, curried goat and fresh seafood, and such desserts as apricots poached in Muscatel wine; mains are around £15 at lunchtime, £18–25 in the evening. The creamy interior is elegantly soothing, and there's a more spacious dining area in the dark olive basement as well as some pavement seating. Mon–Sat 10am–late (last orders 10pm).

Clayton's Kitchen 15a George St ☎01225 585100, ⓦclaytonskitchen.com. Lively restaurant on two floors with unintrusive jazz background music and tables outside. Standouts on the menu include the whipped ewe's curd for starters and the Creedy Carver duck breast or cannon of lamb for main course. The quality of the food is matched by fairly high prices: expect to pay £80–100 for two excluding drinks. The basement cocktail bar *Circo* is handy for pre- or post-prandial refreshments. Mon–Thurs noon–2.30pm & 6–9.30pm, Fri noon–2.30pm & 6–10pm, Sat noon–3pm & 6–10pm, Sun noon–3pm & 6–9pm.

Cosy Club Southgate Place ☎01225 464161, ⓦcosyclub.co.uk/bath. Inauspiciously sited in the middle of the modern SouthGate shopping complex, this large, open-plan space reveals an unorthodox style that somehow

1

suggests 1920s decadence with its exuberantly mismatched decor – a jumble of lamps, mirrors, retro prints and deep sofas. Drop in for a game of Scrabble, brunch, coffee on the broad terrace, sandwiches (£8–10), a burger or fishcakes (£10–15) or an evening cocktail. There's plenty of choice for anyone on a special diet. Mon–Wed & Sun 9am–11pm, Thurs–Sat 9am–12.30am; food served 9am–10pm.

Eastern Eye 8a Quiet St ☎01225 422323, ⓦeasterneye. com. In true Bath style, this curry house in a former exhibition space from 1824 features huge frescoes and a spectacular domed and vaulted ceiling. The food doesn't quite live up to the grand setting, but the menu is wide-ranging and includes such dishes as Nowabdar, a North Indian dish of chicken or lamb cooked with cashew nuts and fennel seeds, and Sultan puri pillau, a mildly spiced lamb biryani with egg; most mains are £10–15, alternatively order three courses at lunchtime for £10. Daily 11.30am–2.30pm & 6–11.30pm.

Eight 3 North Parade Passage ☎01225 724111, ⓦeight inbath.co.uk. You'll find eight small main dishes on the frequently changing menu of this elegant little restaurant tucked away in a quiet alley near the Abbey, each priced at £11–15, with the aim of allowing you to sample two or more items. As the dishes are usually imaginatively and delicately prepared, for example lemongrass gazpacho, pan-seared pigeon breast and fillet of plaice with seafood risotto and lobster bisque, the formula works well. The small tables and minimalist dark grey decor make for a calm and romantic atmosphere. There's a cocktail bar in the basement and eight equally elegant guestrooms upstairs (£125–175). Tues–Fri 5.30–9.30pm, Sat & Sun 5.30–10pm.

Firehouse Rotisserie 2 John St ☎01225 482070, ⓦfirehouserotisserie.co.uk. Delicious, thin-crusted Californian pizzas, rotisserie free-range chicken and succulent burgers (all £11–14) are the mainstay of this busy place with a woody interior and excellent service. Upstairs is smaller and more subdued. Mon–Fri noon–2.15pm & 5.30–10pm, Sat noon–10pm, Sun noon–9.30pm.

Green Park Brasserie Green Park Station ☎01225 338565, ⓦgreenparkbrasserie.com. Spacious and laidback café-restaurant housed in the old ticket office of a restored train station, with a well-stocked bar, live jazz (Wed–Sat eves) and some outdoor seating. Panini, cakes and full meals are served (evening mains £12–18.50), and there are Deli Lunch (£10) and Early Diner (£14 and £18) menus. Alongside, and under the same management, *The Bath Pizza Co* serves wood-fired pizzas for around £10. Mon & Sun 10.30am–9pm, Tues–Fri 10.30am–11pm, Sat 10am–11pm; kitchen noon–2.45pm & Tues–Sat 5.30–10pm.

★ **Green Rocket Café** 1 Pierrepont St ☎01225 420084, ⓦthegreenrocket.co.uk. This bright, modern vegetarian and vegan café-restaurant offers amazing flavours in such dishes as *imam bayaldi* (baked aubergine stuffed with tomato and chickpea), ginger beer-battered

halloumi, and smoked mushroom and chestnut sausages. It's a mellow spot even if you're not dining here; the coffees are first-rate, as are the freshly squeezed juices. Mains cost £9–12, and breakfasts are served until 11.30am. Mon & Tues 9am–4.30pm, Wed–Sat 9am–4.30pm & 6–9.30pm, Sun 10am–4.30pm.

Jars Meze 6 Northumberland Place ☎01225 471434, ⓦjarsmeze.com. For a change from the usual fare, go Greek in this modest family-run taberna in an alley in the centre of the shopping quarter. You'll find all the classics: gyros (£12.50), moussaka (£14), *stifado* (£16) and *kleftiko* (£17.30), with an excellent selection of *mezedes* (£5–9). It's homely but fairly cramped, with seating on the ground floor, upstairs and outside. Tues–Sat 11am–3pm & 5–9pm, Sun 11am–3.30pm.

Kingsmead Kitchen 1 Kingsmead St ☎01225 329002, ⓦkingsmeadkitchenbath.co.uk. This locals' hangout with small marble tables is most renowned for its breakfasts, including *Shakshuka* (baked eggs in a spicy tomato sauce; £9) and the mammoth Kingsmead (£10.50), all made with free-range eggs (gluten-free also available). There are plenty of other choices on the menu, too – salads, toasted sandwiches, quiche (£10) and seasonal mezzes in two sizes (£8 and £9.50). Smoothies, beers, wines and spirits are sold, and there's some outside seating. Mon–Sat 8am–6pm, Sun 9am–5pm.

La Perla 12a North Parade ☎01225 463626, ⓦla-perla.co.uk. This Spanish restaurant and tapas bar occupies atmospheric vaults with outdoor seating below pavement level. Most dishes are £7–11, including *puntillitas* (deep-fried micro-squid), *presa Ibérica* (grilled pork) and *croquetas de queso* (goat's cheese croquettes), though the authentic paellas are £15 and should be booked 24 hours ahead. Even if you're not eating, it's a cool place to wind up the day over a glass of Sangria. Mon 6–10pm, Tues–Fri noon–3pm & 6–10pm, Sat noon–late, Sun noon–2pm & 6–10pm.

Menu Gordon Jones 2 Wellsway ☎01225 480871, ⓦmenugordonjones.co.uk. You never know what you're going to get in this award-winning restaurant as there's only a "surprise tasting menu" offered, but you can be confident that it will be inventively prepared, flavoursome and incorporating adventurous taste combinations. Dishes may include asparagus mousse, raw fish and ice cream, fried herring, rose veal – in short, a foodie's delight. Prices are £55 for six courses at lunchtime, or £60 for seven at dinner. The accompanying wine flight is £45 each. The atmosphere is casual and upbeat, but there are only ten tables so book ahead (there's always more availability at lunchtime). Tues–Sat 12.30–2pm & 7–9pm.

Noya's Kitchen 7 St James's Parade ☎01225 684439, ⓦnoyaskitchen.co.uk. This small and busy place showcasing Vietnamese cuisine has created a local sensation since it grew out of a pop-up restaurant. The small menu usually has pork dumplings and spring rolls for starters (£6 each) and chicken curry (£7.50 or £11.50) among the mains. and there's always a specials board worth investigating. Wednesday is *pho* (soup) night, and Fri, Sat and some Thurs eves are Supper Club nights (£45 per person), which are often booked weeks in advance. Wines and Vietnamese beers are available. Tues–Sat noon–3pm & 6–9pm (Supper Club 7.15–10pm).

★ **Olive Tree** Russel St ☎01225 447928, ⓦolivetree bath.co.uk. In the basement of the *Queensberry Hotel*, this iMichelin-starred restaurant offers a contemporary ambience, discreetly attentive service and original and toothsome combinations of dishes. The changing, set-price menus – £26 and £32.50 for lunch, £68–85 in the evening – might include smoked eels, duck and lamb rump, and there are some delectable desserts (there are also vegetarian, vegan and dairy-free menus). Tues–Thurs 6.30–9pm, Fri–Sun 12.30–2.30pm & 6.30–9pm.

Pump Room Abbey Churchyard ☎01225 444477, ⓦthepumproombath.co.uk. Splash out on a breakfast or brunch, sample the lunchtime menu of traditional English fare (£15, £21 or £27 for one, two or three courses) or succumb to a Champagne Tea or just a Bath bun, usually accompanied by the refined sounds of a pianist or classical trio. It's a bit hammy and overpriced, and you may have to queue, but it's appropriately theatrical, and you get a good view of the Baths. When they're available, evening menus list such dishes as grilled salmon and lamb shoulder for around £15 (book ahead for dinners). Daily 9.30am–5pm; Jan, Feb, Oct & Nov from 10am; July, Aug, Dec & major festivals 9.30am–9pm (last orders).

Restaurant Hywel Jones by Lucknam Park Colerne, 6 miles northeast of Bath, off A420 ☎01225 742777, ⓦlucknampark.co.uk/dining. Housed in a former ballroom in the Palladian-style *Lucknam Park* luxury hotel, this restaurant has scooped a Michelin star under the direction of chef Hywel Jones, who creates sophisticated dishes using the best of seasonal and organic produce, some of it from the hotel's own kitchen garden. The surroundings are sumptuous and smart dress is required; set-price menus are £87 for three courses (the separate vegetarian menu is also £87) or £110 for the expanded seasonal menu. There's also a less formal brasserie in a separate building offering a simpler range of dishes, including pizzas (around £11) and burgers (£18), with other mains costing £16–25, and has alfresco dining in summer. Restaurant Wed–Sat 6.30–10pm, Sun 12.30–2.30pm & 6.30–10pm; brasserie daily 10.30am–10pm.

Sally Lunn's 4 North Parade Passage ☎01225 461634, ⓦsallylunns.co.uk. Trading on the great age of its premises and on what is said to be the original Bath bun, this tearoom and restaurant gets packed (expect a queue in summer), but it's a good opportunity to sample the famous Sally Lunn bun, served here with a choice of more than twenty sweet and savoury toppings (£7–10). Buns are also incorporated into

ancient-recipe "Trencher" dishes such as steak and mushroom and vegetable (£12.50–15). In the evening, the menu lists such dishes as Lady Llanover's duck and braised beef (£12.50–15), and there are set-price deals. Daytime diners can view the small kitchen museum in the cellar (see page 49). Mon–Fri 10am–10pm, Sat 9am–10pm, Sun 9am–9.30pm.

Sotto Sotto 10 North Parade ☎01225 330236, ⓦsotto sotto.co.uk. Authentic Italian restaurant in cave-like, brick-vaulted subterranean rooms. The simple but usually heavenly dishes include risotto with salmon and asparagus (£11.50), polenta with creamed spinach and pecorino cheese (£11.50) and grilled swordfish (£17.50). Make sure you sample the excellent antipasti too (£6–10). It's always packed, so booking is essential. Daily noon–2pm & 5–10pm.

Thoughtful Bakery 19 Barton St ☎01225 471747, ⓦthoughtfulbakery.co.uk. Whether it's sourdough toast and jam (£2.40) you're after, or a filled croissant, a bacon sandwich (£4) or an oatmeal iced latte, everything in this artisan bakery and café with white walls, simple wooden tables and a bright, airy feel is lovingly prepared with the accent on quality and taste. Other breakfast options include eggs benedict (£7), and for lunch you can order sausage rolls (£3.50), a soup or stew (around £5) or a fantastic ploughman's board with local cheese (£6.50). Everything can be bought to take away, and breadmaking courses are also held here. Tues–Fri 8am–5pm, Sat 8am–4pm, Sun 9am–4pm.

White Hart Widcombe Hill ☎01225 338053, ⓦwhite hartbath.co.uk. Off the tourist track, this gastropub has a simple woody interior (enhanced with some nice art on the walls), a walled garden and a friendly atmosphere. The short menu has mains such as guinea fowl, sea bream and chickpea fritters at £17–22, there's a £15 two-course lunch (Mon–Fri), and they do a great Sunday roast, too. Leave room for the puds. Mon–Sat noon–2pm & 6–10pm (Mon & Tues until 9pm), Sun noon–2.30pm.

Wild Café 10a Queen St ☎01225 448673, ⓦwildcafe. co.uk. Relaxed, backstreet café-restaurant much favoured by locals for its fresh ingredients, friendly staff and good coffees. Among the food offerings are chunky sandwiches, halloumi wraps, bubble and squeak and hot smoked trout salad (all £6–8.50). There's a good choice of breakfasts amd brunches, too, including pancakes. Rooms are also available here. Mon–Fri 8am–4.30pm, Sat 9am–6pm, Sun 10am–5pm.

★ **Yak Yeti Yak** 12 Pierrepont St ☎01225 442299, ⓦyakyetiyak.co.uk. This highly regarded Nepalese restaurant occupies a series of cellar rooms whose authentic Kathmandu-style decor is dotted with photos and other mementoes of the owners' Himalayan ascents. Meat is stir-fried or slow-cooked, and there are some enticing vegetarian choices, all mains costing around £7 for vegetarian dishes, £9 for meat. Choose between sitting at a table or on floor cushions. Daily noon–2pm & 5/6–10/10.30pm.

1

DRINKING

SEE MAPS PAGES 44, 46 AND 58

★ **The Bell** 103 Walcot St ☎01225 460426, ⓦthebell innbath.co.uk. Community-owned, this easy-going, slightly grungy pub and social hub has a great juke box, wi-fi, bar billiards and a beer garden with table footy. There's always a good atmosphere, and at least seven real ales on tap, plus freshly made pizzas (Wed & Fri from 5pm, Sun from noon). It's also one of Bath's best venues for live music (Mon & Wed eves, plus Sun lunchtime) and vinyl DJs (Thurs–Sun eves). Mon–Thurs 11.30am–11pm, Fri & Sat 11.30am–midnight, Sun noon–10.30pm.

Coeur de Lion 17 Northumberland Place ☎01225 463568, ⓦabbeyinnsbath.co.uk. Centrally located tavern on a flagstoned shopping alley, with a few tables outside (and more upstairs), this is one of four pubs belonging to the local Abbey Ales brewery. It's also Bath's smallest boozer and a regular tourist stop, but persevere for the Victorian trappings – including some nice stained glass – a decent pint of bitter, and the house speciality: steak and Bellringer ale pie. Mon–Thurs 11am–11pm, Fri & Sat 11am–11.30pm, Sun noon–9pm, food served 11am–4.45pm.

The George Mill Lane, Bathampton ☎01225 425079, ⓦchefandbrewer.com. Popular canalside pub 20min walk from the centre, with local ales and plenty of outside seating. The location is the main draw: the bar food is mediocre at best and the service slow. By car it's off the Warminster Rd, at the bottom of Bathampton Lane. Mon–Sat 10am–11pm, Sun 10am–10.30pm; kitchen noon–9.30pm.

The Raven 7 Queen St ☎01225 425045, ⓦtheraven ofbath.co.uk. Civilized and traditional watering hole with first-rate local ales (try the Raven's Gold), served both downstairs and in the less crowded upstairs room. Superior snacks are available, most customers opting for the renowned Pieminister pies. Check the website for details of the regular talks and readings taking place here. Mon–Thurs 11am–11pm, Fri & Sat 11am–midnight, Sun 11am–10.30pm; food served Mon–Sat 11am–9pm, Sun 11am–8.30pm.

The Salamander 3 John St ☎01225 428889, ⓦbath ales.com. Bath Ales pub with woody decor and excellent food at the bar or in the upstairs restaurant. It's a smart but laidback kind of place, with a quiet local clientele – though gets quite merry on rugby match days. Mon–Thurs & Sun 11am–11pm, Fri & Sat 11am–1am; food served Mon–Fri noon–3pm & 6–9pm, Sat noon–9pm, Sun noon–6pm.

★ **Star Inn** 23 Vineyards, The Paragon ☎01225 425072, ⓦabbeyales.co.uk. First licensed in 1759, this Bath stalwart has a classic Victorian interior of four wood-panelled rooms uncompromised by modern intrusions. It's run by the local Abbey Ales, serving such beers as Bellringer and draught Bass straight from the cask, as well as a good range of whiskies. With an open fire in winter and a timeless, unflappable air, it's a place for lingering. Mon–Wed & Sun noon–midnight, Thurs noon–12.30am, Fri & Sat noon–1am.

NIGHTLIFE AND ENTERTAINMENT

SEE MAPS PAGES 44 AND 46

The two or three **theatres** in town often stage productions before or after their London run, but most of the fare is fairly mainstream. Little Theatre Cinema is Bath's only independent **cinema**, St Michael's Place (☎0871 902 5747, ⓦpicturehouses.com); there's also the Odeon, with eight screens, at James Street West, Kingsmead Leisure Complex (ⓦodeon.co.uk). Bath's **music scene** is lively, especially during the festival (see page 69), while its small but relaxed **clubbing scene**, overshadowed by the proximity of Bristol, takes place mostly in unventilated basements. See ⓦwhatsonbath.co.uk for listings and events.

Chapel Arts Centre St James Memorial Hall, Lower Borough Walls ☎01225 461700, ⓦchapelarts.org. Lovely little venue for all kinds of performing arts, with an emphasis on jazz, blues and folk. Arrive early to get one of the cabaret-style tables. Organic wines and ales are available at the bar, and there's an excellent vegetarian/vegan-friendly café too. Daily 9.30am–4.30pm & 7.30pm–late.

The Common Room 2 Saville Row ⓦcommonroom bath.co.uk. A bit like someone's front room, this is an intimate spot for late-night chat and chilled sounds, though things get a bit more raucous at weekends. There's a small dancefloor and a quieter room with sofas upstairs. Mon–

Thurs 5pm–2am, Fri & Sat 5pm–3am, Sun 10pm–2am.

Komedia 22–23 Westgate St ☎01225 489070, ⓦkomedia.co.uk/bath. Cabaret and burlesque, comedy, tribute acts and more are all staged at this venue. Saturdays see the popular Krater Comedy Club, after which you can stay on for club nights. Meals are available. Tues–Sat 10am–4pm & 6.30pm–late.

★ **Moles** 14 George St ☎01225 437537, ⓦmoles. co.uk. This Bath institution has been hosting both live music and DJs for more than 40 years. The cramped basement can get pretty hot and sweaty – not for claustrophobes. Usually 5pm–late.

Rondo Theatre St Saviour's Rd, off London Rd ☎0333 666 3366 (for tickets), ⓦrondotheatre.co.uk. You can get close to the action at this intimate place northeast of the centre, which hosts drama productions, comedy, burlesque and concerts. Buy tickets online, by phone or at the theatre 30min before start of show.

Sub 13 4 Edgar Buildings, George St ☎01225 466667, ⓦsub13.net. There's a gin bar on the ground floor, a garden and a dimly lit basement bar where you can order what are reputed to be Bath's best cocktails. The atmosphere modulates from chilled to party-central as the evening

BATH'S FESTIVALS

Bath has a rich range of **festivals** throughout the year, featuring talks, gigs, exhibitions and other events in often sumptuous surroundings. If you're visiting during one of these occasions, you'll find the city's mellow pace livened up a notch or two, but accommodation gets scarce and restaurants fill up. The main events are listed below, but there are a few others scattered throughout the year. For information, call ☎01225 614180, see ⓦbathfestivals.org.uk, visit the festivals office desk in the tourist office in Bridgwater House, or check out the individual websites. Tickets for events in most of the festivals can be purchased from the festivals office or the website ⓦbathboxoffice.org.uk.

Bath Comedy Festival ⓦbathcomedy.com. Stand-up routines from mainstream to left-field in various venues, plus walks and other events. Twenty days, usually starting on or near to April Fool's Day (April 1).

Bath Fringe Festival ⓦbathfringe.co.uk. Firmly puts the accent on art and performance at a range of venues. Two weeks from late May to early June.

Bath Festival ⓦbathfestivals.org.uk. Focusing on music and literature, Bath's major festival features a roster of literary stars together with big names in classical, jazz and global music, ending with a grand

open air gig at the Recreation Ground. There's plenty of activity on the streets, too. Ten days in late May.

Bath Mozartfest ⓦbathmozartfest.org.uk. Classical performances, mainly at the Guildhall and Assembly Rooms. Nine days in mid-Nov.

FilmBath Festival ⓦfilmbath.org.uk. Previews, shorts, talks, awards and new releases from around the world. Eleven days in Nov.

Jane Austen Festival ⓦjaneaustenfestivalbath. co.uk. Walks, talks, dances and a flamboyant promenade through the streets in Regency costume. Ten days in mid-Sept.

---

progresses. DJs Fri & Sat. There's a nice garden area too. Mon–Wed 5pm–midnight, Thurs 5pm–1am, Fri 3pm–3am, Sat 1pm–3am, Sun 5–11pm.

Theatre Royal Sawclose ☎01225 448844, ⓦtheatre

royal.org.uk. Theatre, opera and dance fans should check out what's showing at this historic and atmospheric venue. More experimental productions are staged in its Ustinov Studio. Book as early as you can.

SHOPPING

SEE MAPS PAGES 44 AND 46

In Bath, **shopping** has been a major pastime at least since Austen's day. As in every British town, **chain stores** are much in evidence, but Bath's strength lies in its range of independent, chic **boutiques**, speciality food shops and galleries. There's a concentration of these squeezed into the tiny lanes north of the abbey, and you'll find more clusters in and around Bartlett Street (near the Assembly Rooms) and Brock Street (near the Royal Crescent), while Milsom Street, where Austen's contemporaries once patronized millinery shops and dressmakers, holds some of Bath's smartest stores.

INDEPENDENT SHOPS

Bath Aqua Glass Abbey Churchyard & 105–107 Walcot St ☎01225 428146, ⓦbathaquaglass.com. Glass *objets* of every description are sold here, including delicate jewellery. There are nods to the locale in the addition of copper oxide to the molten glass to produce an aquamarine effect reminiscent of Bath's thermal waters and in the "Georgian Range" which includes Jane Austen goblets. You can watch the glass being blown in the Walcot Street branch, with demonstrations at 11.15am and 2.15pm (Sat just 2.15pm), and courses are available. Abbey Churchyard Mon–Sat 9am–7pm, Sun 10am–6pm; Walcot St Mon–Sat 9.30am–5pm.

Bath Old Books 9c Margaret's Buildings ☎01225

422244. Maps, prints and antiquarian books are sold at this classic old shop, one of very few of the kind remaining in the city. Bargains to be found. Mon–Sat 10am–5pm.

Bath Sweet Shop 8 North Parade Passage ☎01225 428040. The oldest sweet shop in town sells more than 250 varieties including all your granny's favourites – mint humbugs, dolly mixtures, lemon sherbets and liquorice. Sugar-free alternatives are available too. Mon–Sat 10am–5.30pm, Sun till 5pm.

Beaux Arts 12–13 York St ☎01225 464850, ⓦbeaux artsbath.co.uk. There's always plenty to admire among the contemporary sculptures and ceramics in this smart gallery near the abbey – thought-provoking canvases, beautifully executed bronze statuettes and richly coloured pottery by world-class artisans. It's the sister-gallery of Beaux Arts in Cork Street, London – the three- and four-figure price tags may daunt, however. Mon–Sat 10am–5pm.

★ **Bertinet** 1 New Bond St ☎01225 920069, ⓦbertinet.com. Widely acknowledged to be the best bakers in Bath, Bertinet bakes and dispenses buns, pastries, croissants and crusty artisan breads including sourdough, spelt and baguettes. Richard Bertinet, a Breton, also operates a cookery school. Mon–Fri 8am–5pm, Sat 8.30am–5.30pm, Sun 10am–4pm.

1

TOURS IN AND AROUND BATH

A **tour** with an informative and/or entertaining commentary can be the best way to take in a lot of Bath in a short time. For orientation and insider's knowledge, you can't beat the free **walking tours** conducted by the Mayor of Bath's Honorary Guides; these cover the main architectural sites, with heaps of historical detail and insight that reveal the guides' genuine passion for the city. The walks leave daily from Abbey Churchyard at 10.30am and 2pm (☎01225 477411, ⬡bathguides. org.uk; no 2pm tour on Sat; May–Aug also Tues & Thurs 6pm; 2hr). If you want to go at your own pace, you can **download** one or both of the two walking tours available in mp3 format from ⬡visitbath.co.uk, either in their entirety or individual chapters; the more general World Heritage Site tour takes in the city's main historical highlights, while In the Footsteps of Jane Austen focuses on the author's experience of Bath, including extracts from her novels and letters.

Bizarre Bath With the emphasis on entertainment rather than information, Bizarre Bath offers "comedy walks" around the city, offering an irreverent and idiosyncratic take on the city with magic tricks thrown in, taking place every evening from April to October (⬡bizarrebath.co.uk; 1hr 30min; £10); meet at 8pm outside the *Huntsman Inn* on North Parade Passage.

Ghost Walks For fans of the macabre and gruesome, ghost walks (1hr 30min) leave from outside the *Garrick's Head* pub next to the Theatre Royal at 8pm (☎01225 350512, ⬡ghostwalksofbath.co.uk; Thurs–Sat; £8).

Bus tours Open-top City Sightseeing bus tours with commentaries are available all year (☎01225 444102, ⬡city-sightseeing.com; all-day tickets £16.50), leaving from Grand Parade every 15min or so. Choose between city and skyline tours – the latter taking in the higher reaches of the city around Claverton Down.

Boat tours Between Easter and October, hour-long river trips run from Pulteney Bridge to Bathampton and back. Booking is not normally necessary; just turn up and pay on board. The main operators are Pulteney Cruisers (1–2 hourly; £10 return; ☎07810 837787, ⬡pulteneycruisers.com) and Avon Cruising (6 daily; £9 return; ☎07791 910650, ⬡pulteneyprincess.co.uk). One-way trips are also possible (around £6) and bikes can be carried free when there's space.

Outside Bath Mad Max Tours offers minibus excursions with commentaries to Wells, Glastonbury, Cheddar Gorge, Lacock, Castle Combe, Stonehenge, Avebury and the Cotswolds, as well as bespoke tours (☎07990 505970, ⬡madmaxtours.co.uk; £35–38), while Scarper Tours conducts daily trips (April–Oct 9.30am & 2pm; Nov–March 1pm) to Stonehenge lasting 4hr, including two hours at the site (⬡scarpertours.com; £40 including Stonehenge entry).

Found 17 Argyle St ☎01225 422001, ⬡foundbath. co.uk. As well as lovely views over the weir, this boutique on Pulteney Bridge offers a quirkily original selection of dresses, contemporary satchels and shoes, plus a range of gifts from prints to notebooks. Mon–Sat 10am–5.30pm.

Mercy in Action 12 Margaret's Buildings ☎01225 542095. Bath has no shortage of of second-hand outlets, but this one, calling itself a "boutique charity shop", is a cut above, specialising in vintage wear, exotic geegaws and quirky ornaments – worth a quick trawl. Mon–Sat 9am–5.30pm, Sun 10am–4pm.

★**Mr B's** 14–15 John St ☎01225 331155, ⬡mrbs emporium.co.uk. Captivating independent bookshop on three floors, with armchairs and fresh coffee for browsers. It's strong on fiction, travel writing and children's literature, and has an excellent local-interest section. Ask about the regular readings and book signings by authors. Mon–Fri 9.30am–6pm, Sat 9.30am–6.30pm, Sun 11am–5pm.

Paxton & Whitfield 1 John St ☎01225 466403, ⬡paxtonandwhitfield.co.uk. Cheeses galore, and everything to do with cheese, are available in this corner shop, where you'll encounter an array of goat's and

sheep's cheeses, Cornish blues, Somerset bries and French camemberts among the hundred-plus varieties, as well as local ciders and apple juices, and some very handsome olive-wood boards. Mon–Sat 9.30am–6pm, Sun 11am– 5pm.

Topping & Company The Paragon ☎01225 428111, ⬡toppingbooks.co.uk. This book-lover's bookshop has a huge range of titles, including a great travel section with an excellent selection of maps. Check the website for regular author talks. Daily 8.30am–7.30pm.

★**Vintage to Vogue** 28 Milsom St ☎01225 337323, ⬡vintagetovoguebath.co.uk. This tiny shop in an alley off Milsom St packs a lot in. The great choice of clothes and accessories runs from glamorous Charleston-era handbags to school satchels, from sequined dresses to tweed jackets, and from fascinators to top hats. Tues–Sat 11am–5pm.

Yellow Shop 72 Walcot St ☎01225 404001, ⬡yellow shop.co.uk. A happy miscellany of retro, vintage and new items are crowded into this shop, from 1960s silk scarves and dapper fedoras to leather and baseball jackets and chunky lumberjack shirts. Mon–Sat 10.30am–5.30pm, Sun noon–4pm.

1

MARKETS, DEPARTMENT STORES AND SHOPPING CENTRES

Green Park Station Green Park Rd ⓦ greenparkstation. co.uk. Formerly a terminus of the now-defunct Midland Railway, in use between 1870 and 1960, this refurbished station has a few permanent shops selling food and crafts Monday to Saturday, but is best known for its various markets, including Bath's farmers' market every Saturday morning, a general market all day Saturday, and a flea market, an artisan market and a vintage and antiques market on the first, second and last Sundays of the month respectively. The *Green Park Brasserie* provides refreshments (see page 66).

Guildhall Market Between High St and Grand Parade ⓦ bathguildhallmarket.co.uk. The dome of this indoor market, which has been in operation since 1770, is one of Bath's landmarks. It's worth a rummage for its delicatessens, craft shops and general bric-a-brac. Mon–Sat 8am–5.30pm.

Jolly's 13 Milsom St ☎ 0844 800 3704, ⓦ houseoffraser. co.uk. Bath's oldest department store is now part of the House of Fraser group, but hasn't lost its idiosyncratic style nor its maze-like layout. There's something for everyone among its gents' suits, ladies' wear, perfumes and handbags, with top brands represented. Mon–Wed 9.30am–5.30pm, Thurs & Fri 9.30am–6pm, Sat 9am–6pm, Sun 10.30am–4.30pm.

SouthGate Centre Between Southgate St and Manvers St ⓦ southgatebath.com. Part covered, part broad avenues, this modern precinct has big-name megastores including Debenhams and H&M as well as a few independent stores, brand outlets (Tommy Hilfiger) and refreshment stops (as well as a Sainsbury's supermarket). Mon–Sat 9am–6pm, Sun 11am–5pm.

ACTIVITIES

Adventure Golf You can try your hand at crazy golf at the eighteen-hole mini-course off Royal Ave, at the eastern end of Royal Victoria Park (£5.50; ☎ 01225 425066, ⓦ bathminigolf.com), open daily 10am–dusk.

Ballooning Get a dizzy new perspective of Bath from a hot-air balloon. Bath Balloons (☎ 01225 466888, ⓦ bathballoons.co.uk) launch from Royal Victoria Park or, depending on the wind, within a 15-mile radius of Bath. Flights take place March–Oct, with prices starting at £110 for a weekday dawn departure, rising to £145 for a champagne flight any day morning or evening. Flying time is about 1hr, but the round trip may be 3–4hr.

Boating Skiffs, punts and canoes for leisurely rides on the River Avon can be hired from Bath Boating Station at the end of Forester Rd, north of Sydney Gardens (Easter–Sept Wed–Sun 10am–5.30pm; £8 per person for 1hr, then £4 per hour, or £20 all day; ☎ 01225 312900, ⓦ bathboating.co.uk). At Brassknocker Basin, 3.5 miles southeast of the centre on the Somerset Coal Canal (an offshoot of the Kennet and Avon Canal, accessible on bus #D1 from bus station), electric-driven day-boats (from £40 for half-day, £60–75 for a full day) and canoes (£10 for 1hr, then £8 per hour, or £40 for a full day) can be rented from Bath Narrowboats (☎ 01225 447276, ⓦ bath-narrowboats.co.uk).

Rugby Bath's rugby club (☎ 01225 536900, ⓦ bathrugby. com) is one of the country's oldest, and still one of the most formidable, with a tally of championships to its name. It also has one of Britain's most evocative homes – its Recreation Ground stadium ("The Rec") lies right next to the River Avon in the centre of Bath. To see a match, book well ahead by calling ☎ 0844 448 1865, via the website or at the ticket office at 8 Pulteney Bridge; ticket prices start at around £30 for standing, £30–70 for seats. In summer the ground is adapted for cricket matches.

Tennis There are tennis courts on Royal Ave at the eastern end of Royal Victoria Park, both outdoor (£4 per person/hr) and indoor (£16–18). Racket hire costs £2. To be safe, an indoor or outdoor game should be booked a week in advance, but it's worth trying at shorter notice (☎ 01225 425066, ⓦ tennisintheparkbath.co.uk).

DIRECTORY

Hospital Royal United Hospital, west of the centre (Combe Park, ☎ 01225 428331, ⓦ ruh.nhs.uk) has an emergency department (for emergencies call ☎ 01225 824391). Bus #4 from the bus station.

Internet Computers are available at @ Internet & Luggage, 13 Manvers St, for £3/hr.

Laundry Coin-operated washers at Spruce Goose, 4 Margaret's Buildings, 8am–8pm daily.

Left luggage @ Internet & Luggage (see above) accepts bags for £2.50–3 each according to size, while *Bath Backpackers* (13 Pierrepoint St) charges £3 per item per day.

Post office Upstairs at WHSmith's, 6–7 Union St (Mon–Sat 8.30am–6pm, Sun 11am–3pm).

Around Bath

Bath has plenty to occupy your time, but it also makes a useful base or starting point for expeditions across the county border into Wiltshire. River, canal and train line

1

run together to **Bradford-on-Avon**, which, with its old tithe barn and rows of cloth-workers' cottages interspersed with handsome merchants' mansions, makes an enticing destination in its own right, and is also a viable alternative to staying in Bath itself. With its homogeneous pale stone architecture, Bradford has more than a whiff of the Cotswolds about it, a sensation that grows stronger in such meticulously preserved villages as **Lacock**, once home to the photography pioneer William Fox Talbot, whose work is showcased in the museum attached to local crowd-puller **Lacock Abbey**. Further off the beaten track, the villages of **Corsham** and **Castle Combe** are equally well preserved, and **Corsham Court** has an outstanding collection of Old Masters.

There are good **transport** connections from Bath to Bradford-on-Avon and Corsham, but nothing direct to Lacock or Castle Combe, for which it's easiest to take a train to Chippenham and catch a bus from there.

Bradford-on-Avon

Wedged in Wiltshire's northwest corner, eight miles east of Bath, **BRADFORD-ON-AVON** is a hugely appealing small town with buildings of mellow fawn-coloured stone, many in a striking style sometimes described as vernacular Baroque, and reminiscent of the architecture of Bath and the nearby Cotswolds. Sheltering against a steep wooded slope, Bradford made its living for six centuries from the mills that once lined the River Avon, powering its wool and cloth trade. The local textiles industry was revolutionized by the arrival of Flemish weavers in 1659, and much of the town's architecture reflects the prosperity of this period – both the splendid stone houses owned by the rich wool

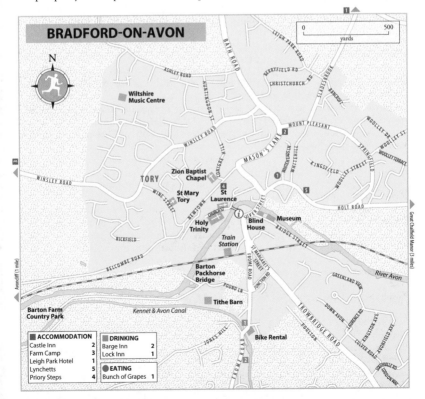

BRADFORD-ON-AVON

0   500
yards

N

Wiltshire Music Centre

Zion Baptist Chapel

TORY

St Mary Tory   St Laurence

Holy Trinity   Blind House   Museum

Train Station

Barton Packhorse Bridge

Tithe Barn

Barton Farm Country Park   Kennet & Avon Canal

River Avon

Bike Rental

ACCOMMODATION		DRINKING	
Castle Inn	2	Barge Inn	2
Farm Camp	3	Lock Inn	1
Leigh Park Hotel	1		
Lynchetts	5	**EATING**	
Priory Steps	4	Bunch of Grapes	1

THE WEALTH OF WOOL

The wealth of northeast Somerset and the Cotswold region was founded on the huge growth in England's **wool trade** and cloth industry in the Middle Ages. Compared to continental breeds, English sheep were small and neat, with long, soft fleeces, and they thrived on the verdant, well-watered uplands of the Cotswolds to the north. The proximity of these grazing pastures, combined with the abundant and fast-flowing rivers to power the fulling mills (where woven cloth was felted to make it thick and strong), generated a good deal of wealth in the area around Bath and Bradford-on-Avon. Much of the trade was owned and run by the great religious houses, such as Bath Priory, one of the richest houses in the southwest, while its beneficiaries embraced the whole gamut of society, including such people as Chaucer's Wife of Bath, who lived "bisyde Bath", probably in the important weaving village of Twerton, now a Bath suburb. Bradford's cloth industry flourished in the seventeenth and eighteenth centuries, dwindling to almost nothing by 1900, though, like nearby Castle Combe, the town preserves its picturesque rows of weavers' and cloth-workers' cottages.

manufacturers and the humbler cottages of the spinners and weavers working from home. The impact on the town of the gradual decline of Britain's cloth manufacture was partially offset in the last century by the growth of a rubber industry, with many of the tall mills adapted for use for the production of rubber components, though this too ended in 1992. More recently, Bradford has evolved as a local cultural and shopping centre, with a vibrant local arts scene and small independent stores in and around the pedestrianized **Shambles**, just up from the bridge off Silver Street.

The town's long history is reflected in its tithe barn and its rich heritage of churches, most significant of which is **St Laurence**, dating from Saxon times. A short distance outside town lies **Great Chalfield Manor**, a well-preserved fifteenth-century house.

The town bridge

Bradford's original fording place was replaced in the thirteenth century by a **bridge** that was in turn largely rebuilt in the seventeenth century, and which is still the focal point of the town. The small domed structure at its southern end, the **Blind House**, is a quaint old lock-up, or jail for the drunk and disorderly, converted from a chapel in the seventeenth century. Its weather vane is topped with a golden gudgeon, or fish, an early Christian symbol.

Looking west along the river from the bridge you'll see **Abbey Mill** from 1857, the last woollen mill to be built in Bradford and now containing retirement apartments.

Bradford-on-Avon Museum

Library, Bridge St • Easter–Oct Wed–Sat 10.30am–12.30pm & 2–4pm, Sun 2–4pm; Nov & mid-Jan to Easter Wed–Fri & Sun 2–4pm, Sat 10.30am–12.30pm & 2–4pm • Free • W bradfordonavonmuseum.co.uk

A brief walk east from the bridge along Bridge Street will bring you to Bradford's **museum**, housed above the library. It's a strictly local collection, an entertaining diversion worth a few minutes for its diminutive Roman sarcophagus, a reconstructed Victorian pharmacy and various war mementos. Among the curiosities are photographs of the underground mushroom crops that were once harvested from a nearby quarry, and a couple of **Moulton bicycles** – the revolutionary small-wheeled bike that was all the rage in the 1960s was designed and built in Bradford by Dr Alex Moulton, a local resident until his death in 2012.

Saxon church of St Laurence

Church St • Daily: April–Sept 10am–6pm; Oct–March 10am–4pm • Free • W saxonchurch.org.uk

Bradford's most significant building is the tiny church of **St Laurence**, an outstanding example of Saxon church architecture. Tall and narrow with small windows, its exact age is uncertain; though it has been suggested that it dates back to the eighth century, the architecture points to an early eleventh-century construction. Later used as a school and a simple dwelling, it was reworked by a local vicar in the 1860s and the west wall was rebuilt. Its only decoration is two carved angels flying across the nave's east wall. The north entrance has photographs and documents relating to the Saxon church.

Holy Trinity
Church St • Daily during daylight hours • Free

Tall as it is, St Laurence is almost dwarfed by the much larger medieval church of **Holy Trinity** standing below it. Originally twelfth-century, the parish church was much rebuilt in later times. Inside are various memorials and brasses connected to the wool industry, and what is claimed to be England's longest "squint", or opening through the wall allowing people in peripheral parts of the church a view of the altar.

St Mary Tory
38 Tory, off Newtown • Daily during daylight hours • Free • Ⓦ smallpilgrimplaces.org

From Holy Trinity, a steep uphill path brings you to the **Tory** neighbourhood (from *tor*, meaning "hill"), the loftiest part of Bradford with bird's-eye views over town and river stretching as far east as the Marlborough Downs. Nestled among the cottages, accessed along footpaths, the fifteenth-century chapel of **St Mary Tory** once served the needs of pilgrims en route to Glastonbury. Heavily renovated in the nineteenth century, it's a very simple affair, the interior illuminated by beautiful stained-glass windows from 1999. The adjoining former hospice is now a private dwelling.

Northeast of St Mary Tory, past prosperous houses once belonging to managers and high-ranking specialists in the cloth industry, **Zion Baptist Chapel**, dating from 1698, is worth a glance, though it's rarely open.

The Tithe Barn
Daily 10.30am–4pm • Free

Heading down narrow Barton Orchard from Holy Trinity church, or following the river southwest from Bradford's town bridge, you'll come to the medieval **Barton Packhorse Bridge** across the Avon, a pretty and serene sight, untroubled by traffic. East of the bridge stands Bradford's **Tithe Barn**, a magnificently preserved example of buildings used by religious houses to store food (a "tithe" was a tenth of a tenant's produce). This one, dating from the fourteenth century, was owned by Shaftesbury Abbey – once the richest nunnery in the country – and boasts a fine cruck roof, made from curved timbers extending to the ground, and the old threshing floor.

On the east side of the farmyard, the restored granary now holds a shop. Note the dovecote on the rear wall of the farmhouse, a source of meat during winter. The old cow byres surrounding the main building now house craft shops, workshops, galleries and a tea garden (Wed–Sun 11am–5pm; Ⓦ tithebarnartscrafts.co.uk).

Along the canal to Avoncliff

Extending west of the Tithe Barn, the **Barton Farm Country Park** offers wooded walks and picnic areas between the river and canal. The **Kennet and Avon Canal** towpath offers the possibility of easy walks or cycle rides, either thirteen miles east to Devizes, or a mile and a quarter west to **Avoncliff**, a lovely spot where the canal crosses the river on a graceful aqueduct, close to a pub with riverside seating. Continuing north will bring you to another aqueduct at **Dundas**, and eventually to Bath. You can **rent bikes** from TT Bikes, where Frome Road crosses the canal (☎ 01225 867187, Ⓦ towpathtrail.co.uk; £12 for 4hr or £18 per day; call ahead Nov–March); they also rent out **canoes**.

Great Chalfield Manor
Near Holt, 3 miles northeast of Bradford-on-Avon **House** Guided tours April–Oct Tues–Thurs 11am, noon, 2pm, 3pm & 4pm, Sun 2pm, 3pm & 4pm **Garden** April–Oct Tues–Thurs 11am–5pm, Sun 1–5pm • £10.60 house and garden, £6.60 garden only • NT • ☎ 01225 782239, Ⓦ nationaltrust.org.uk • Bus to Holt, then walk 1 mile

1

The splendid moated complex of **Great Chalfield Manor** consists of a house dating from about 1480, sensitively restored at the beginning of the twentieth century as a family home, plus an equally ancient church and outbuildings. The house has the typical exterior of a Cotswold manor, all gables and mullions, while its **Great Hall** is overlooked by a minstrels' gallery from which three gargoyle-like masks gaze down into the hall, the eyes cut away so that the womenfolk could inspect the proceedings below without jeopardizing their modesty. Briefly besieged during the Civil War, the modest but perfectly proportioned house has remained much as it was in the late fifteenth century, a rare survival of the period and genre. The interior of the pinnacled **church** features some fifteenth-century wall paintings depicting the martyrdom of St Katherine. Scenes from the television adaptation of Hilary Mantel's *Wolf Hall* were shot here.

ARRIVAL AND DEPARTURE   BRADFORD-ON-AVON

By train Bradford's train station, with regular connections to Salisbury, Dorchester, Bath and Bristol, is close to the town centre on St Margaret's St.

Destinations Avoncliff (Mon–Sat hourly, Sun 9 daily; 5min); Bath (Mon–Sat 2–3 hourly, Sun 1–2 hourly; 15min); Bristol (1–3 hourly; 25–40min); Chippenham (1–3 hourly with change; 30min–1hrn); Frome (Mon–Sat every 1–2hr, Sun 4 daily; 25min); Salisbury (hourly; 50min); Westbury (1–2 hourly; 15min).

By bus Most buses stop on Silver St, St Margaret's St and Frome Rd.

Destinations Bath (Mon–Sat every 30min, Sun hourly; 35–50min); Chippenham (Mon–Sat 1–2 hourly with change; 1hr–1hr 45min); Corsham (Mon–Sat 4 daily; 50min); Lacock (Mon–Sat hourly with change; 50min–1hr 10min); Salisbury (Mon–Sat 5 daily; 2hr).

By bike or on foot The canal towpath provides a level and rewarding route of about 9 miles between Bradford-on-Avon and Bath.

INFORMATION

Tourist office Westbury Gardens, 50 St Margaret's St (daily 10am–4pm; ☎01225 865797, ⓦbradfordonavon.co.uk).

Ask here about twice-monthly local walks.

ACCOMMODATION   SEE MAP PAGE 73

Castle Inn 10 Mount Pleasant ☎01225 865657, ⓦthe castleinnboa.co.uk. Four boutiquey rooms with thick carpets, contemporary designs and generous bathrooms are available at this excellent inn at the top of town. First-class food and real ales are served in the flagstone bar, and there's a large garden. **£100**

Farm Camp Church Farm, Winsley ☎01225 582246, ⓦthefarmcamp.co.uk. For a comfortable and satisfying "glamping" experience, try out one of the four bell-tents available at this site a couple of miles west of Bradford. The tents, which are well spaced from each other, sleep up to four and are equipped with wood stoves, "candeliers" and compost loos. There are good showers with plenty of hot water, free access to an indoor pool and a well-equipped kitchen, while the neighbouring farm shop and café sells home-grown vegetables and serves excellent breakfasts. Minimum two-night stay, 1-week mid-Oct to Easter. Two-people **£99**

Leigh Park Hotel Leigh Road West ☎01225 864885, ⓦleighparkhotel.co.uk. A mile northeast of town in a rural setting off the B3105, this Georgian country house hotel with a small vineyard attached is a bit dated but has character, extensive grounds, good views and reasonable rates. The restaurant is fairly nondescript, however, some

of the rooms are disappointing and it's a popular wedding venue, so call ahead if you want to avoid a possibly noisy stay. **£95**

★ **Lynchetts** 15 Woolley St ☎01225 866400, ⓦlynchetts.co.uk. This handsome Georgian B&B is in the centre of town, but you might as well be in the country for its peace and quiet, not least in the huge garden which includes a croquet lawn (mallets available) and orchards that provide the fresh fruits, jams and honey served at breakfast. If you don't mind the stairs and low ceiling, the attic room offers most space as well as seclusion. Parking, bike storage and a self-catering flat are also available. No credit cards. **£90**

★ **Priory Steps** Newtown ☎01225 862230, ⓦpriory steps.co.uk. Above the centre, with great views over the rooftops, this spacious family home was converted from seventeenth-century weavers' cottages. The five elegant rooms come with modern bathrooms and panoramic views, and the owners are friendly. There's a library, a garden, and candles and silverware are brought out for the gourmet dinners that are available with notice (£30). Breakfast is served at a communal table. Discounts are available for two or more nights, and there are also three self-catering apartments for three or more nights. **£128**

BOX TUNNEL AND CORSHAM'S QUARRIES

When **Isambard Kingdom Brunel** (see page 101) extended the Great Western Railway in the 1830s, he was confronted by a massive obstacle in the form of **Box Hill**, a couple of miles west of Corsham. His solution was simply to bore through it, creating what was then the longest **railway tunnel** in the world, at nearly two miles. In recognition of the achievement, the western entrance to the tunnel was given an imposing Neoclassical style (though the embellishment is invisible to rail passengers). The excavations revealed large new deposits of quality **limestone** (or Bath stone) which spurred the local underground quarrying business and boosted the local economy. The **quarries** were used in the 1930s and during World War II to store ammunition and even contained a munitions factory, and in the 1950s they were earmarked as a regional seat of government in the event of nuclear war, to accommodate up to four thousand people. The centre was decommissioned in 1991 and declassified in 2004.

EATING, DRINKING AND ENTERTAINMENT   **SEE MAP PAGE 73**

Barge Inn 17 Frome Rd ☎01225 863403, ⓦthe bargeinn.org. This freehouse has Melksham and other local beers on tap and tables by the canal. The menu includes sandwiches and ciabattas (around £7), salads (£7.50–12) and pizzas (£11–13) as well as such dishes as mushroom, walnut and spinach linguine (£8 or £12) and roast duck breast (£17). The pub has a spacious, modern feel, and exposed stone walls, a flagstone floor and log fires in winter add to the atmosphere, though service can be slow. Daily 7am–11pm, kitchen 7am–9.30pm.

★ **Bunch of Grapes** 14 Silver St ☎01225 938088, ⓦthebunchofgrapes.com. This upmarket pub and restaurant has probably the best food in Bradford, enhanced by an excellent selection of local beers and a friendly, modern feel. The kitchen uses quality produce for its well prepared and presented dishes, which might include chilli crab and pigeon breast for starters (£8–10) and duck breast, rack of lamb and hake among the mains (£17–25 each). There's also a seven-course tasting menu (£55). At lunchtime, choose between the bar menu (for example risotto, fish and chips or cheeseburger,

all around £13) or more substantial fare (on weekdays pay £19.50 or £22.50 for two or three courses). There's an upstairs dining area open in the evenings. Tues–Thurs 11am–3pm & 6–11pm, Fri & Sat 11am–11pm, Sun noon–6pm.

Lock Inn 48 Frome Rd ☎01225 868068, ⓦthelockinn. co.uk. This popular canalside pub and café has a motley collection of memorabilia hanging off its ceiling and various eating areas including a shed, a garden and a boat. The long menu includes the mighty Boatman's Breakfast (meat and veggie version, £8), ciabattas (£4–4.50), jacket potatoes (£2.50–5.50) and fairly standard pub grub (most hot dishes £9–10); enthusiastic carnivores will be drawn to the Boatman's Grill (£14). There's also a children's menu. Drinks include Bath Ales and local Iford Cider. Daily 8.30am–11pm, food till 9pm.

Wiltshire Music Centre Ashley Rd ☎01225 860100, ⓦwiltshiremusic.org.uk. High up on the outskirts of town (on the Bath side of Bradford), this arts centre hosts music and other cultural events throughout the year, specializing in world, folk, classical and jazz.

Corsham

Like Bradford-on-Avon, **CORSHAM**, about seven miles northeast of Bath and the same distance north of Bradford, grew rich on the manufacture of cloth, and its nearby quarries were also a source of building stone. It's a friendly, low-key village, thankfully free of traffic and bustle, with a concentration of well-preserved historic buildings as well as a good range of small, independent shops, pubs and cafés to amble around, all on or close to the central, part-pedestrianized High Street. The street holds buildings of every period, including Corsham's elegant **town hall** dating from 1783 (rebuilt a century later), and, at the bottom of the street, a row of **Flemish Buildings** where weavers fleeing Catholic persecution settled in the seventeenth century.

Corsham Court

Mid-March to Sept Tues–Thurs, Sat & Sun 2–5.30pm; Oct, Nov & Jan to mid-March Sat & Sun 2–4.30pm • £10, gardens only £5 • ☎01249 712214, ⓦcorsham-court.co.uk

Corsham's star attraction is unquestionably **Corsham Court**, accessible from Church Street off the High Street. Though the house dates from Elizabethan times, major rebuilding in the eighteenth century by Lancelot "Capability" Brown, John Nash and Humphrey Repton effaced most of the Tudor construction, and a further radical remodelling by Thomas Bellamy in the 1840s replaced most of Nash's work. The interior was furnished by Thomas Chippendale and Robert and James Adam among others, while the landscaped grounds, designed initially by Brown, were completed forty years later by Repton. House and gardens have featured in such films as *The Remains of the Day* and in the BBC adaptation of *Tess of the D'Urbervilles*.

For the Methuen family, who took possession of the property in 1745, the house was first and foremost a showcase for the magnificent collection of sixteenth- and seventeenth-century art originally assembled by Sir Paul Methuen, an ambassador to Portugal. The centrepiece is Capability Brown's long **Picture Gallery**, still covered in the original rich, red damask silk wall-hangings and topped by an unusually intricate plaster ceiling. Works displayed here include paintings by Van Dyck, Guercino and Guido Reni; other rooms contain pieces by Rubens, Andrea del Sarto, Turner, Lely and Reynolds. Among the stand-outs are an Annunciation by Fra Filippo Lippi in the **Cabinet Room** and, in the **State Bedroom**, an allegorical painting of Elizabeth I in old age and a pair of gaudy but gracefully carved eighteenth-century wall mirrors of English design.

After viewing these masterpieces, take time to stroll around the gardens, which include a Gothic Bath House (the joint work of Capability Brown and John Nash), a host of strutting peacocks and, in spring, a splendid display of magnolias. The six hundred acres of parkland include a lake created by Repton.

Hungerford Almshouses

Corner of Pound Pill & Lacock Rd • Feb, March, Oct & Nov Sat 1–3pm; April–Sept Wed, Fri & Sat 1.30–4pm • £3 • ☎ 01249 701414, ⓦ corshamalmshouses.org.uk

Opposite the original main gateway to Corsham Court, a brief walk from the High Street, **Hungerford Almshouses** is one of Corsham's most revered buildings, a heavily gabled complex built in 1668 for "6 poor people" and "10 needy scholars" by Lady Margaret Hungerford, wife of a commander of Parliamentary forces during the English Civil War who lived in Corsham Court. The well-preserved exterior displays the flamboyant Hungerford coat of arms, and at the back the Pentice, or cloister, still holds cottages for homeless or needy locals. Inside you can tour the original schoolroom, with a gallery, pulpit and seventeenth-century benches showing ancient graffiti, and an exhibition room with explanatory panels.

ARRIVAL AND INFORMATION
CORSHAM

By bus There are bus stops on Newlands Rd and Pickwick Rd, close to the High St.
Destinations Bath (2–4 hourly; 45min); Bradford-on-Avon (Mon–Sat 3 daily; 50min); Castle Combe (Mon–Sat 6 daily via Chippenham; 55min–1hr 10min); Chippenham (2–4 hourly; 25min); Lacock (Mon–Sat 2 hourly most via Chippenham; 35–55min).

Tourist office 31 High St (Tues–Sat 10am–4pm; ☎ 01249 714660, ⓦ corshamheritage.org.uk). The volunteer-staffed office may close when volunteers are unavailable.

ACCOMMODATION

Methuen Arms 2 High St ☎ 01249 717060, ⓦ the methuenarms.com. This inn offers chic, contemporary rooms in dark brown and grey tones, and bathrooms with rainforest showers and freestanding baths. Antique touches complement the modern facilities. Breakfasts include home-made granola, fresh fruit salad and fresh pastries and muffins, and quality food and drink are served in the bar. £140

21 Park Lane 21 Park Lane ☎ 01249 715677, ⓦ 21park lane.com. In a quiet neighbourhood a 20min walk west of the centre, this B&B offers three bright, good-sized en-suite doubles with modern bathrooms. There's a good choice of breakfasts including gluten-free and vegetarian options. £85

EATING AND DRINKING

Grounded Martingate Centre ☎ 01249 715555, ⓦ cafegrounded.co.uk. In a shopping precinct just off the High Street, an old chapel house from 1790 has been sympathetically converted into a modern café-bar and restaurant, serving breakfasts, panini, burgers, salads and pastas , as well as stone-baked and gluten-free pizzas in the evening – mains are £8–16. If you don't want to eat, come just for a coffee or beer. There's outdoor seating in a cosy patio, too. Daily 9am–10pm; kitchen 9am–9pm.

Mother & Wild 8 High St ☎ 01249 716777, ⊛ mother andwild.com. This ancient building with a cottagey interior and informal, intimate ambience makes an ideal stop at any time – breakfast, brunch, snack lunch or dinner, or just for an excellent coffee with a muffin. The menu offers tapas (£4.50–8), for example arancini and aubergine parmigiana with smoked mozzarella, as well as burgers, sautéed mushrooms and slow-cooked pork belly, but the restaurant is best known for delicious wood-fired sourdough pizzas (£8–12). There's an outdoor terrace too. Mon–Fri 8.30am–11pm, Sat & Sun 9am–11pm; kitchen 8.30/9am–10.30pm, noon–3pm & 5–10pm.

Lacock

With its lime-washed, half-timbered stone houses, **LACOCK**, four miles southeast of Corsham, is a perfectly preserved if highly gentrified version of an English feudal village. The National Trust owns all but three houses here – a curious state of affairs, but one that has ensured Lacock's survival in a relatively pristine and tack-free state. As an established coach stop, however, the village is besieged by tourists all summer, many of them here to view the settings of the various period dramas and movies that have been filmed in the village and its abbey, including scenes from the Harry Potter films and *Pride and Prejudice*. The wealth accumulated from the wool trade is still evident in Lacock's well-to-do houses and fine church, and some historic inns and excellent B&Bs provide added incentives for a detour here.

In the village, the Lady Chapel in the fifteenth-century church of **St Cyriac** contains Sir William Sharington's opulent tomb beneath a splendid lierne-vaulted roof where traces of paint testify to its once brightly coloured appearance. Three panels on the front of the tomb show Sharington's crest with a scorpion in each.

Lacock Abbey

Daily mid-Feb to early Nov 10.30am–5pm; early Nov to mid-Feb 11am–4pm • £14.50, including cloisters, museum & grounds • NT • ☎ 01249 730459, ⊛ nationaltrust.org.uk

Standing gracefully aloof within its grounds at the eastern end of Lacock village, **Lacock Abbey** consists mainly of an eighteenth-century neo-Gothic stately home, but a few monastic fragments survive from the nunnery founded in 1232 by Ela, Countess of Salisbury, including the original cloisters, chapter house and sacristy. The rest was levelled during and after the Dissolution of the Monasteries in 1539, when the abbey passed to Sir William Sharington. Ten years later Sharington was arrested for colluding with Thomas Seymour, Treasurer of the Mint, in a plot to subvert the coinage; Sharington narrowly escaped with his life by shopping his partner in crime – who was beheaded – and after a period of disgrace managed to buy back his estates. Furniture and paintings owned by later generations of the family are now displayed in a series of rooms, culminating in the lofty **Great Hall**, its walls studded with terracotta figures in niches (look out for the sugar lump on the nose of a goat, first placed here in 1919).

The Fox Talbot Museum

Appropriately for such a regular TV and film location, the grounds of Lacock Abbey hold a fascinating museum dedicated to the founding father of photography, **William Henry Fox Talbot** (1800–77), a scion of the Sharingtons and the first person to produce a photographic negative, in 1834 (five years before the announcement of the discovery of the daguerreotype process in France). The **Fox Talbot Museum**, in a sixteenth-century barn by the abbey gates, captures something of the excitement he must have experienced as the dim outline of an oriel window in the abbey's south gallery slowly imprinted itself on a piece of silver nitrate paper. A copy of the postage-stamp-sized result is on display in the museum (the original is in the National Science and Media Museum in Bradford, Yorkshire). Fox Talbot enjoyed a reputation in many other fields, and some of the exotic trees in the abbey were planted by him.

1

By bus Almost all bus routes go via Chippenham; Lacock's stop is outside *The George* pub on West St.

Destinations Bath (Mon–Sat every 30min with change; 1hr–1hr 20min); Bradford-on-Avon (Mon–Sat every 30min with change; 50min–1hr 15min); Castle Combe (Mon–Sat 5 daily with change; 1hr–1hr 25min); Chippenham (Mon–Sat every 30min; 20min); Corsham (Mon–Sat 2 hourly; with change; 40min).

ACCOMMODATION, EATING AND DRINKING

George Inn 4 West St ☎01249 730263, ⓦgeorgeinn lacock.co.uk. Dating from 1361, this Wadworth pub has beams, a fireplace, outdoor seating in the yard or a beer garden and a good range of ales, making it a popular stop for coach parties. The rather mediocre menu runs from from sandwiches (around £8) to parmesan-crusted chicken (£14.50). Look out for the dog-wheel opposite the bar, once used for turning a spit, and photos of the filming of *Harry Potter*, *Cranford* and other productions. Guest rooms are clean and functional. Mon–Sat 11am–11pm, Sun 11am–10.30pm; kitchen noon–2.30pm & 6–9pm (Sun 6–8pm). **£95**

★ **The Sign of the Angel** 6 Church St ☎01249 730230, ⓦsignoftheangel.co.uk. This upmarket hostelry has all the low ceilings, oak beams and sloping floors you could wish for, but the five guestrooms are tastefully converted with all modern conveniences, though unsuitable for anyone with mobility issues. The restaurant also has plenty of atmosphere, and there's garden seating amid an orchard and stream; food is traditional and highly rated – the set-price two- and three-course lunches cost £20 and £23, mains at dinner are around £21, and there are cream teas. Mon–Sat 10am–11pm, Sun noon–3pm & 7–10pm; kitchen Mon–Sat noon–2pm & 6–8.30pm (Fri & Sat till 9pm), Sun noon–2.30pm & 7–8.30pm. **£115**

Talbot House 7 Cantax Hill ☎01249 730568, ⓦtalbot houselacock.co.uk. Just one attic room is available at this period cottage a short walk outside the centre, but it's in a separate wing that includes a private sitting room and a fridge with juice, fresh milk and home-made fudge supplied. Locally-sourced produce is served at breakfast, and guests can use the garden with its lily-strewn fish pond. Two-night minimum stay at weekends. No credit cards. **£110**

Castle Combe

Set in a wooded valley four miles north of Lacock, **CASTLE COMBE** is a quintessential Cotswold village, all pale-gold houses grouped around a fourteenth-century market cross and an even older church largely financed by wealthy wool merchants. The church can also be accessed from the local manor house, which in the early fifteenth century was the property of Sir John Fastolf, on whom Shakespeare based his comically villainous character Falstaff. In fact, the real Fastolf – who never actually came to Castle Combe – was said to be a loyal and respected follower of Henry V, fighting with him at Agincourt. Hidden within its grounds, the house is now a swanky hotel with a Michelin-starred restaurant (see page 81).

Mills once lined the Bybrook stream running through the village, but the cloth industry folded in the eighteenth century after an unexplained drop in the river's level, the last mill closing in the early 1800s. The town, which had far outstripped nearby Chippenham in size and influence, dwindled to a set-in-aspic village, which now trades largely on the golf course attached to the hotel in the old manor house and the racetrack located a short distance outside.

St Andrew's

Dating back to the thirteenth century, the richly endowed church of **St Andrew's** shows traces from most subsequent periods, including examples of Early English, Decorated and Perpendicular windows. In the north aisle lies the effigy and tomb (from 1270) of the Norman baron, Walter de Dunstanville, who is said to have built the original castle from which the village takes its name. At the back of the church, at the base of the bell tower, you can admire the workings of a seventeenth-century faceless clock – now electrically powered.

Castle Combe Circuit

Three quarters of a mile southeast of Castle Combe on the B4039 • ☎01249 782417, ⓦ castlecombecircuit.co.uk

Back in the twenty-first century, Castle Combe is best known for the **Castle Combe Circuit** racing track, though it's well out of sight of the village, with noise levels rigidly controlled. Race days for Formula Fords, GTs, sports cars, classic saloons from the 1950s and 1960s, and motor bikes take place on selected Saturdays, Sundays and Mondays between April and October, with tickets at around £15. On Experience Days and Track Days you can take a turn at the wheel yourself or travel as a passenger in a white-knuckle ride, with prices ranging from £40 for a circuit to £200 for a full day.

ARRIVAL AND DEPARTURE   CASTLE COMBE

By bus The only bus services in Castle Combe are #35 and   #35A to Chippenham (Mon–Sat 4–5 daily; 25–45min).

ACCOMMODATION, EATING AND DRINKING

Castle Inn ☎01249 783030, ⊛thecastleinn.co.uk. In keeping with the dominant tone of the village, this is a romantic but posh bolthole, with small, smart rooms and modern bathrooms. Bar snacks, cream teas and full meals (£14–24) are available downstairs noon–3pm & 6–9pm (bar open all day until 11pm). **£116**

Manor House Hotel ☎01249 782206, ⊛exclusive. co.uk/the-manor-house. One of the most luxurious hotels in the region, this place wears its history on its sleeve, stuffed with oak panelling, antique furnishings and old paintings. Some of the rooms have Elizabethan fireplaces but the cheaper ones are in blander cottage annexes. The setting is magnificent, with a tennis court and golf course in the ample grounds. The Michelin-starred *Bybrook* restaurant, with chef Rob Potter at the helm, is well worth investigating if you're looking to splurge, at £75 for three courses. **£156**

Bristol and around

CLIFTON SUSPENSION BRIDGE

Bristol and around

The South West's de facto capital and one of the most vibrant urban centres outside of London, dynamic, cosmopolitan Bristol has harmoniously blended its mercantile roots and rich maritime history with an innovative, modern culture, fuelled by a lively arts and music scene. While it's not as immediately attractive as nearby Bath, a simple stroll round the medieval quarter, along the rejuvenated waterfront or through the gorgeous suburb of Clifton will gradually reveal the Bristol that John Betjeman once declared "the most beautiful, interesting and distinguished city in England".

Up snug against the borders of Gloucestershire and Somerset, Bristol is defined by the River Avon, which weaves through the centre and forms part of a system of waterways that once made the city a great inland port. The revitalized **Harbourside** remains a focal point and is home to heavyweight attractions such as M Shed and the SS *Great Britain*, part of Brunel's illustrious impact on the city's landscape and, along with his Suspension Bridge, one of its greatest monuments.

The tongue of land that juts out into the harbour holds picturesque Queen Square and historic King Street, the southern reaches of the compact **Old City**, a blend of medieval churches, merchants' houses and lively markets. A short walk from here leads to the celebrated religious sites of cockeyed **Temple Church** and striking **St Mary Redcliffe**, each the focus of its eponymous neighbourhood, or, in the other direction, Bristol Cathedral, at the foot of shop-lined **Park Street**. Some of the city's best restaurants and bars can be found here, towards the top of the hill, in the surrounding streets of the **West End** and on Whiteladies Road.

Whiteladies acts as the eastern boundary of **Clifton**, Bristol's most refined neighbourhood. Running west to the very edge of the Avon Gorge, it is famously home to some beautiful Georgian housing, as well as the Downs, trumped only by the estates of Ashton Court and Blaise Castle in the city's leafy ensemble of attractive parks and green spaces.

Conservative Clifton contrasts sharply with **East Bristol**, where the city's reputation for free thinking is alive and kicking in Stokes Croft, the artsy area of Montpelier and the slowly resurgent, West Indian-influenced district of St Pauls. Across the Avon in **South Bristol**, Southville – drolly referred to as "Lower Clifton'" due to its gentrification over the last decade or so – is centred around the hub of bars, delis and chilled-out cafés that is North Street, and has seen its fortunes revived by the Tobacco Factory, a neighbourhood-defining theatre and arts centre.

Somerset begins just beyond the suburbs, and it's a short hop down the A37 or A38 to the picturesque **Chew Valley**, a scenic taster of the verdant fields and rolling hills that await to the south.

Brief history

Legend points to Bristol being founded in the sixth century by **Brennus**, a descendant of Brutus, the mythical King of Britain, but the earliest known settlements here were the **Iron Age hillforts** at Blaise Castle and Stokeleigh (in Leigh Woods), and at Clifton Camp on the opposite side of the Avon Gorge.

The Anglo-Saxon trading centre of **Brycgstow** – the first recorded reference to the city we know today as Bristol – grew up around Bristol Bridge (*Brycgstow* means "Place of the Bridge"), on the high ground, away from the far-reaching tides of the River Avon, that is now Castle Park. The natural protection afforded by the Avon (and from the River Frome) was supplemented by stout city walls and, under the Normans, a castle, later enhanced with a huge keep.

SS GREAT BRITAIN

Highlights

❶ St Nicholas Market Browse for bargains at historical St Nick's, stock up on fresh produce at the Farmers' Market or catch the twice-weekly street-food fest. See page 91

❷ Street art Nelson Street showcases the work of some of the best street artists in the world, Stokes Croft's cityscape includes Banksy's most famous mural while North Street gets a host of new works each year. See pages 92 and 113

❸ SS Great Britain Moored in the dock in which she was built, the iconic ship is now an iconic museum, an interactive insight into life aboard a nineteenth-century steamer. See page 100

❹ Clifton Fine Georgian mansions and a buzzing café culture make the crescents of Clifton worth a prolonged wander. See page 108

❺ Clifton Suspension Bridge Brunel's "darling" soars above the ragged edges of the dramatic Avon Gorge. See page 109

❻ Eating out Bristol's restaurants are the best in the West, with "local" and "seasonal" the buzzwords on most of the city's menus. See page 118

❼ Bristol International Balloon Fiesta Memorable four-day festival held in the wooded grounds of Ashton Court Estate. See page 129

❽ The Chew Valley Attractive lakes, atmospheric pubs and a ring of ancient standing stones, in verdant countryside just a few miles from Bristol. See page 129

HIGHLIGHTS ARE MARKED ON THE MAPS ON PAGES 86 AND 88

The **diversion of the Frome** in the mid-thirteenth century increased the nascent harbour's capacity for trade, and the granting of a **Royal Charter** a hundred years later enhanced the city's power and widened its boundaries to include previously separate settlements such as Redcliffe. But it was the advent of **transatlantic trade** – sparked by John Cabot's discovery of America in 1497 – that helped Bristol really boom, the trading of tobacco, sugar and most notably **slaves** bringing enormous wealth and privilege to the city's merchant classes and making it the busiest commercial centre outside of London.

Much of this money helped fund the building of modern-day Bristol: Temple Meads station, the Suspension Bridge and the graceful Georgian houses that stagger down

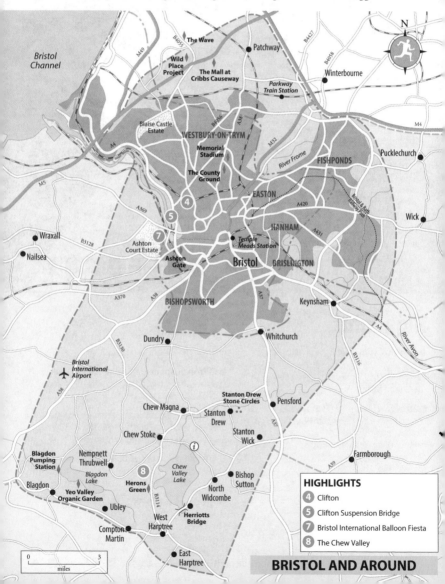

HIGHLIGHTS

4 Clifton

5 Clifton Suspension Bridge

7 Bristol International Balloon Fiesta

8 The Chew Valley

BRISTOL AND AROUND

ARK AT EE! THE RUFF GUYED TO SPEEKEN BRIZZLE

One of the warmest and most rhythmic of local dialects, **Bristolian** or Bristolese (or, to use the local lingo, Brizzle), is proudly spoken throughout the city, and particularly by *Bemmies* and *Meaders* – residents of Bedminster and Broadmead, respectively.

"Celebrated" by Little Britain's Vicky Pollard (Matt Lucas studied in Bristol), it can roughly be characterized by a confusion of **ownership** and the **first- and third-person singular**, and the **addition of an "l"** to words ending with a vowel – which is how the Anglo-Saxon city of Brycgstow ultimately became "Bristol".

The below words and phrases should start you off, but for a handy on-the-street **reference**, check out *A Dictionary of Bristle* by Harry Stoke and Vinny Green (Tangent Books).

2

BASIC WORDS AND PHRASES

Macky	*mack-ee*	Big
Gertmacky	*guRt mack-ee*	Very big
Gertmackybiggun	*guRt mack-ee big-uhn*	Enormous
Proper job	*pRah-peR jaahb*	Nice work
Gert lush	*guRt luush*	Very nice
Alright my lover?	*awlRite moi luvveR?*	How's it going?
How be on young 'un?	*ow bee-yon young uhn?*	How's it going?
Owbis me babber?	*ow biss mee babbeR?*	How's it going?
Where's ee to?	*wuRzee two?*	Where is he?
Cheers then drive	*chuRz en droive*	Thanks for the lift
Laters!	*lay-uRz!*	See you!
That's mint, innit?	*thas menn, en-et?*	It's good
Ark at ee!	*aRk at eeeee!*	Listen to you!
I'll have two of they	*oil aave tua they*	Two of those, please
Don't tell I, tell ee!	*doughn tell aye, tell ee!*	It's not my problem
Zider I up	*zydeR aye up*	A pint of cider please
Forn or fatch?	*fawRn oaR faatch?*	What kind of cider would you like, Dry Blackthorn or Thatchers?

Clifton, to name a few. The area around the Old City would be just as grand, were it not for the heavy bombing it sustained during **World War II**, a particularly brutal Blitz that wiped out more than a quarter of medieval Bristol. The rise of some hideous postwar architecture around Broadmead and Temple coincided with the commercial demise of the harbour, marking a shift towards technology-based businesses, such as the aerospace industry (**Concorde** was built at Filton), and the fields of computing, communications and design.

More recently, the city has developed a reputation as a testbed for **eco** entrepreneurs – it is home to the Soil Association and Sustrans, the charity behind the National Cycle Network – and its successful efforts in recycling, cutting carbon emissions and becoming increasingly energy efficient saw it named as the UK's first **European Green Capital** in 2015.

The Old City and around

The church-cluttered wedge that constitutes the **Old City** is a compact lesson in Bristol's history. Heading south from Castle Park, it starts at the centre of the initial Saxon settlement and leads to the historic buildings of cobbled **King Street** and grand merchants' houses of **Queen Square**, whose tranquil air belies its turbulent past.

The harbour may have brought much of Bristol's wealth, but trade was established here long before that. The church of St Mary le Port in **Castle Park**, one of the oldest in the city, was originally known as St Mary de Foro ("of the Market"), and the mercantile classes had been striking deals for centuries before they packed up their tables and

2

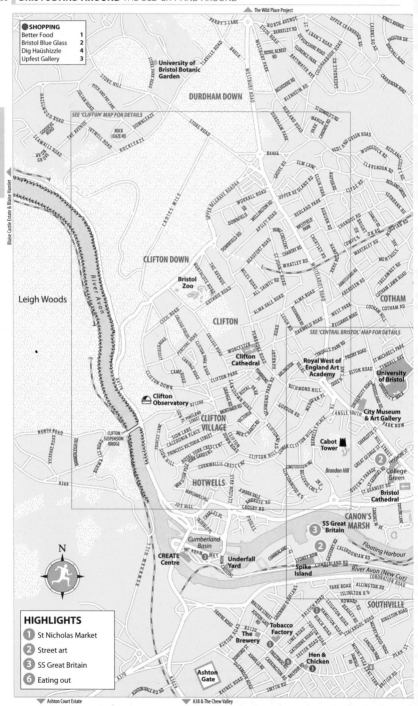

● SHOPPING

Better Food	1
Bristol Blue Glass	2
Dig Haüshizzle	4
Upfest Gallery	3

HIGHLIGHTS

1 St Nicholas Market

2 Street art

3 SS Great Britain

6 Eating out

2

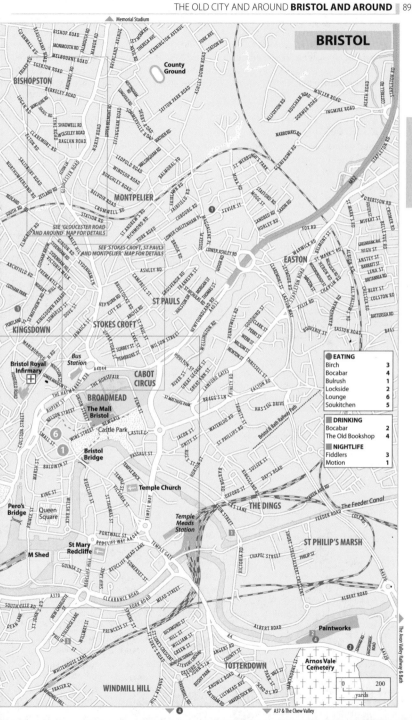

BRISTOL

Memorial Stadium

BISHOPSTON

County
Ground

MONTPELIER

SEE 'GLOUCESTER ROAD
AND AROUND' MAP FOR DETAILS

SEE 'STOKES CROFT, ST PAULS
AND MONTPELIER' MAP FOR DETAILS

EASTON

ST PAULS

KINGSDOWN

STOKES CROFT

Bristol Royal
Infirmary

Bus
Station

CABOT
CIRCUS

BROADMEAD

The Mall
Bristol

Castle Park

Bristol
Bridge

Temple Church

Pero's
Bridge

Queen
Square

M Shed

St Mary
Redcliffe

Temple
Meads
Station

THE DINGS

The Feeder Canal

ST PHILIP'S MARSH

Paintworks

TOTTERDOWN

Arnos Vale
Cemetery

0   200
yards

WINDMILL HILL

A37 & The Chew Valley

The Avon Valley Railway & Bath

● **EATING**

Birch	3
Bocabar	4
Bulrush	1
Lockside	2
Lounge	6
Soukitchen	5

■ **DRINKING**

| Bocabar | 2 |
| The Old Bookshop | 4 |

■ **NIGHTLIFE**

| Fiddlers | 3 |
| Motion | 1 |

moved into the grander surroundings of the Exchange – a practice that continues today in the form of **St Nicholas Market**. The Castle District, the biggest commercial centre of recent times, was all but flattened during World War II, though the shopping tradition survives in the ugly, postwar development of **Broadmead**, and the more recent, and more sympathetically designed, **Cabot Circus**, one of the largest inner-city retail centres in the South West.

Broad Street

Crowned with churches and leading down to the old city wall, condensed **Broad Street** gives perhaps the best impression of how medieval Bristol once looked – along

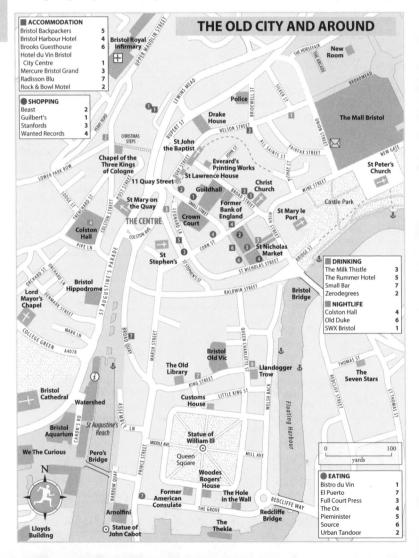

THE OLD CITY AND AROUND

ACCOMMODATION

Bristol Backpackers	5
Bristol Harbour Hotel	4
Brooks Guesthouse	6
Hotel du Vin Bristol City Centre	1
Mercure Bristol Grand	3
Radisson Blu	7
Rock & Bowl Motel	2

SHOPPING

Beast	2
Guilbert's	1
Stanfords	3
Wanted Records	4

DRINKING

The Milk Thistle	3
The Rummer Hotel	5
Small Bar	7
Zerodegrees	2

NIGHTLIFE

Colston Hall	4
Old Duke	6
SWX Bristol	1

EATING

Bistro du Vin	1
El Puerto	7
Full Court Press	3
The Ox	4
Pieminister	5
Source	6
Urban Tandoor	2

0   100
yards

with High Street, Wine Street and Corn Street, it is one of the city's four original thoroughfares. Interest today lies in its range of architectural styles, which run the gamut from the Greek Doric former **Bank of England**, at nos. 13–14, to the **Guildhall** next door, the earliest Gothic town hall in England.

Christ Church

Broad St • Wed 1.10–1.45pm • Free • ⓦ christchurchcitybristol.org

Standing at the very heart of the Old City, eighteenth-century **Christ Church** is most notable for its little tunic-clad quarter-jacks, who strike their bells outside the clock every quarter of an hour; at the time of writing, they had been removed for redecoration. Outside of services, you can only get a glimpse of the elaborate interior on Wednesday lunchtimes when the church is open for organ recitals, piano concerts and other musical events.

Everard's Printing Works

37–38 Broad St

The stunning English Art Nouveau facade of the former **Everard's Printing Works** can come as a bit of a shock, standing back from the street as it does, and hidden behind its neighbouring buildings. Designed by W. J. Neatby in 1901, and made using Carrara-Ware tiles, the lavish mural depicts Johannes Gutenberg (spelled "Gutenburg" here) and William Morris – the fathers of modern printing – separated by the Spirit of Literature and presided over by a woman holding a lamp (representing Light) and a mirror (Truth). Everard's name, spanning the two arches below, is written in a typeface he designed himself. The facade is now the rather grand entrance to a four-star hotel, though nothing survives of Henry Williams's original interior.

St John the Baptist

Broad St • Tues–Sat 11am–2pm • Free • ⓦ visitchurches.org.uk

The striking church of **St John the Baptist** is unique in Bristol, the last of five churches that were built into the city walls, its slim tower and spire straddling the archway of St John's Gate. The side passages were added in 1828, but the carved statues on either side of the gate are much older: Brennus, legendary founder of the city, and his brother Belinus.

It ceased to be a working church long ago, but it's worth venturing into what is effectively the city wall for a peek inside the spooky vaulted **crypt**, and to admire the rather grand **monument of Walter Frampton**, the three-time Mayor of Bristol who founded St John in the fourteenth century.

Corn Street

Running at a right angle to Broad Street, Corn Street is home to the excellent St Nicholas Market, the majority of it occupying John Wood the Elder's eighteenth-century **Exchange**, arguably his finest public building. It was designed specifically to house the merchants who were blocking up the surrounding streets – they settled their debts on the four flat-topped **Nails** (brass pillars) outside, hence the expression to "pay on the nail". The **clock** above the entrance has two minute-hands: "Bristol Time" and, just over ten minutes ahead, "Railway Time" (GMT), adopted by the city in 1852 following the advent of Brunel's London–Bristol line the decade before.

St Nicholas Market

Corn St • Mon–Sat 9.30am–5pm, also first Thurs of month 5–9pm • ⓦ stnicholasmarketbristol.co.uk

Bustling **St Nicholas Market** – more affectionately known as St Nick's – is the largest collection of independent retailers in the city, with over sixty traders peddling just about everything you might ever want to rummage through. Head to the **Exchange**

2

> ### SEE NO EVIL: THE RENAISSANCE OF NELSON STREET
>
> In August 2011, over 35 graffiti artists from around the globe descended on **Nelson Street**, just off The Centre, to turn its dreary, run-down office blocks and high-rises into a gallery of stunning street art. The phenomenal three-day-long event, dubbed **See No Evil**, created some of the largest murals in the world: **Nick Walker**'s banker still pours paint down the side of eleven-storey St Lawrence House, while **Aryz**'s wolf in a lumberjack shirt covers the entire length of Drake House. Partly funded by the city council, See No Evil's guest list read like a *Who's Who* of international graffers, with the likes of LA artist **El Mac** daubing a huge photo-realistic mural of a woman and baby on the side of 11 Quay St, and the **Tats Cru**, from the Bronx in New York, filling a wall above *Roll for the Soul* with their "Welcome to Bristol" aerosol sign. Many of the buildings daubed with smaller murals have since been redeveloped, but new works are regularly added.

and the **Covered Market** for clothes, jewellery, records (see page 127) and general gifts, and to the **Glass Arcade** for lunchtime snacks such as falafel wraps, pit-smoked BBQs and chunky pies (see page 118).

Corn Street and neighbouring Wine Street also play host to a number of other markets: the produce-laden **Bristol Farmers' Market** (Wed 9.30am–2.30pm); the **Bristol Indies' Market** (Fri & Sat 10am–5pm), specializing in arts, crafts and clothing; and a locally focused **Street Food Market** (Tues & Fri 11am–2.30pm).

The Centre and around

Away from the heart of the original settlement, **The Centre** links the Old City with the Harbourside and Park Street but is little more than a concrete island surrounded by a sea of traffic. The harbour once covered all this area, as evidenced by the name of the stout church on the western side of St Augustine's Parade: St Mary on the Quay.

Christmas Steps

Leading off the northern side of Colston Avenue, higgledy-piggledy **Christmas Steps**, "steppered done and finished September 1669", leaps straight off the pages of a Charles Dickens novel. The specialist little shops that line both sides help break the stiff climb, as does the sedilia near the top, moved here from the Chapel of the Three Kings of Cologne that stands in the grounds of nearby John Foster Almshouse.

St Stephen's

21 St Stephen's St · Mon–Fri 9.30am–2.30pm · Free · ⓦ saint-stephens.com

Hemmed in by public buildings, **St Stephen's** might easily be missed but for its slender spire towering over the surrounding office blocks. One of Bristol's oldest churches, it was established in the thirteenth century and has some flamboyant tombs inside, mainly of various members of the mercantile class who were the church's main patrons: look out for the Flemish mercer **Edmund Blanket**, in the north wall, who supposedly gave his name to the stitched woollen bedspread.

King Street

King Street, a short walk southeast from The Centre, was laid out on marshland in 1663 (the "King" in question being Charles II) and still holds a cluster of fine historic buildings, among them the **Old Library**, one of the first in England (now a Chinese restaurant), and the timber-framed **Llandoger Trow**, reputedly the meeting place of Daniel Defoe and Alexander Selkirk, the model for Robinson Crusoe, and allegedly the basis for the *Admiral Benbow* in Robert Louis Stevenson's *Treasure Island*.

Queen Square

South of King Street, **Queen Square** is an elegant grassy area with a statue of William III by Flemish sculptor John Michael Rysbrack at its centre, reckoned to be the best equestrian statue in the country. The square was home to some of Bristol's wealthiest merchants, including, on the site of nos. 33–35, **Woodes Rogers**, the privateer who rescued Alexander Selkirk from four years of solitude on the Juan Fernández Islands; many of these grand houses were targeted in the **Reform riots** (see box), during which much of the northern and western sides were razed. Further along the relatively untouched southern side, a plaque at no. 37 recalls how the first **American Consulate** in Britain was established here in September 1792.

The New Room

36 The Horsefair, Broadmead • Mon–Sat 10.30am–4pm • Chapel free, museum £7 • ☎ 0117 926 4740, ⓦ newroombristol.org.uk

One of the few buildings in Broadmead to have survived World War II, the **New Room** is the oldest Methodist chapel in the world, established by **John Wesley** in 1739. Access is from both the central strip of Broadmead and from the Horsefair, though the former gives a more immediate impression of this neatly austere but strangely captivating little place – bar the addition of pews, it is very much as Wesley left it, with a double-deck pulpit beneath a hidden upstairs window, from which the evangelist could monitor the progress of his trainee preachers.

The top-floor **preachers' rooms** are similarly perfunctory and are now part of a museum that contains Wesley's bedroom and study – he somehow managed to find time to publish over two hundred works between the estimated forty thousand or so sermons he delivered during his life.

The truly committed can also book tours of **Charles Wesley's house** at 4 Charles St here (ⓦ charleswesleyhouse.org.uk); Wesley's brother shared his appetite for hard work, penning over nine thousand religious poems and hymns, an obsessive feat that earned him the nickname of the "Poet Preacher".

Castle Park

The open expanse of **Castle Park** is effectively a grassy short-cut to the Harbourside. Crowded on sunny days with picnicking office workers, it can seem quite bleak otherwise, littered with the ghosts of Bristol past: the scant remains of the city's Norman **castle**, demolished after the Civil War; the ruined tower of **St Mary le Port**, abandoned behind a boarded-up 1970s eyesore; and the roofless shell of **St Peter's Church**, the city's oldest. Projects to regenerate the area are underway, though, with

---

I PREDICT A RIOT: QUEEN SQUARE, 1831

Bristol has a long history of **violent protest**, from the food riots of 1709 to the disturbances in Stokes Croft in 2011. None, however, has been quite as ferocious as the riots that erupted in genteel **Queen Square** in October 1831, which were some of the worst civil disturbances ever seen in England.

At the time, just five percent of Bristol's population was able to vote, and so when local magistrate **Sir Charles Wetherall** arrived to open the new Assize Courts – having just played a key role in initially overturning the **Reform Act** that would have brought greater democracy to the city – the touchpaper was lit. Angry mobs chased him to the **Mansion House** in Queen Square, and in the violence that followed over the next three days a hundred buildings were destroyed, including the Bishop's Palace, the Mansion House itself, the Custom House and most of the jail. It was eventually suppressed when the 3rd Dragoon Guards charged the square, their swords drawn, cutting down the rioters, driving them into burning buildings and killing and wounding 130 people in the process.

2

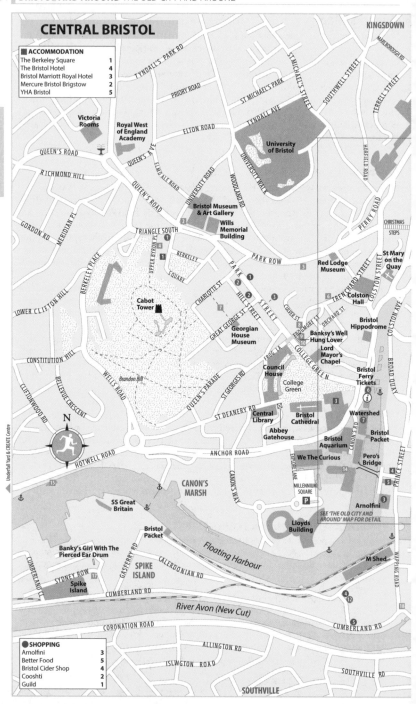

CENTRAL BRISTOL

■ ACCOMMODATION	
The Berkeley Square	1
The Bristol Hotel	4
Bristol Marriott Royal Hotel	3
Mercure Bristol Brigstow	2
YHA Bristol	5

● SHOPPING	
Arnolfini	3
Better Food	5
Bristol Cider Shop	4
Cooshti	2
Guild	1

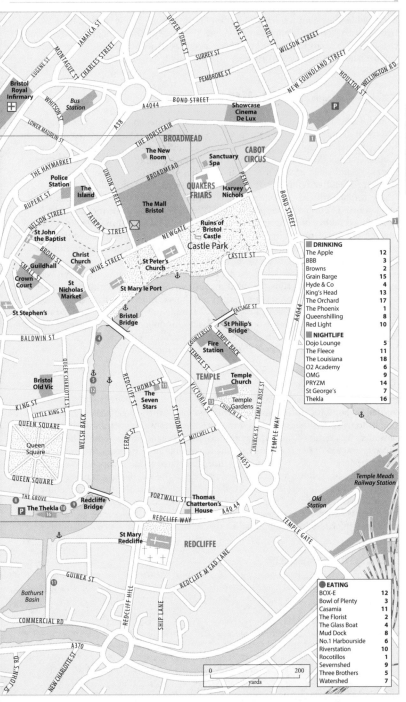

DRINKING

The Apple	12
BBB	3
Browns	2
Grain Barge	15
Hyde & Co	4
King's Head	13
The Orchard	17
The Phoenix	1
Queenshilling	8
Red Light	10

NIGHTLIFE

Dojo Lounge	5
The Fleece	11
The Louisiana	18
O2 Academy	6
OMG	9
PRYZM	14
St George's	7
Thekla	16

EATING

BOX-E	12
Bowl of Plenty	3
Casamia	11
The Florist	2
The Glass Boat	4
Mud Dock	8
No.1 Harbourside	6
Riverstation	10
Rocotillos	1
Severnshed	9
Three Brothers	5
Watershed	7

what will be the tallest residential building in the city scheduled to open here in 2022. Until German bombers came calling in late 1940 (see box), the medieval area formed part of the Old City and – hard as it is to imagine today – was a bustling network of narrow lanes that constituted Bristol's busiest shopping district.

Temple and Redcliffe

South of the Old City, just across Bristol Bridge, **Temple**'s blend of 1960s office blocks and modern quayside developments is a legacy of the pounding it received during the Blitz, the drab ensemble making for a rather ignominious introduction to the city for visitors emerging from Isambard Kingdom Brunel's **Temple Meads Railway Station**. German bombers destroyed most of the buildings around here, though the quirky fourteenth-century **Temple Church** just about survived the Luftwaffe.

Like Temple, which wasn't incorporated into Bristol until after the Reformation, neighbouring **Redcliffe** developed as a separate settlement outside the city walls, becoming a suburb of the city only by default, when Edward II included it as part of the new county of Bristol in 1373. Also like Temple, the one reminder of the area's medieval past is its church, magnificent **St Mary Redcliffe**, which is second only to Bristol Cathedral as the city's most beautiful place of worship.

Opposite the church, Redcliffe Parade leads down to the Floating Harbour, where you can best see the **red cliffs** that lend the district its name. The sandstone "**caves**" here, extending over a dozen acres underground, were quarried for use in Bristol's many glassworks; the skyline of both Redcliffe and Temple was at one time studded with conical glass kilns, though the only reminder of this once-thriving industry is the 25ft stub of the city's last remaining kiln, which has been converted into the restaurant of the nearby *DoubleTree by Hilton Bristol City Centre* hotel.

Temple Church

Temple St, Temple · Closed to the public · ⓦ english-heritage.org.uk

Gutted by bombing during World War II, **Temple Church** is still well worth a visit thanks to its extraordinary leaning tower – it seems to be slowly submerging into the pavement as a result of the soft clay foundations on which it was built. The 114ft tower was constructed in stages throughout the fourteenth and fifteenth centuries, the top added seventy years after the bottom, once it appeared to have stopped leaning; the additional weight, however, exacerbated the angle, and the tower was never finished.

You're restricted to peeking through the window-less frames, but you should be able to make out the circular plan of the original twelfth-century church built by the **Knights Templar**, the religious military order who gave the current church – and the area – its name. Its design matched that of the Church of the Holy Sepulchre in

---

BRISTOL IN THE BLITZ

The significance of Bristol's docks was not lost on Adolf Hitler, and between November 24, 1940 and April 11, 1941 the city was on the receiving end of six **major bombing raids**. Despite the best efforts of surrounding "Starfish" sites (see page 151), the Luftwaffe were able to navigate into the very heart of the city (using moonlight reflecting off the River Avon) and in five months of severe bombing put paid to the entire **Castle District**, including St Mary le Port and St Peter's Church, **Broadmead** and large parts of **Temple** and **Park Street**. Areas as far afield as **Filton** (targeted for its aircraft manufacturing industry) were also damaged – though, ironically, the docks were not. St Peter's now acts as a memorial to the 1500 civilians killed in the raids, the names of whom are remembered on a plaque outside the church's western entrance.

2

THOMAS CHATTERTON: THE MARVELLOUS BOY

Born in 1752, **Thomas Chatterton** grew up in the shadows of St Mary Redcliffe, where his family had held the office of sexton for nearly two hundred years – his childhood home still stands, isolated, on the opposite side of busy Redcliffe Way (with the facade of his old school clumsily tacked on to one end in 1939). He received a distinguished education at Colston's School, but there was nothing to suggest that the brilliant poems he "discovered" – distributed as the work of a fifteenth-century monk named **Thomas Rowley**, a chaplain of William Canynges – could be anything but authentic. They were, however, dazzling fakes, penned instead by the teenager himself.

Exposed and discredited, Chatterton committed suicide aged just 17 and was buried in an unmarked grave in the Shoe Lane Workhouse cemetery in London, thereby supplying English literature with one of its most glamorous stories of self-destructive genius and providing the inspiration for the **Romantic Movement** that followed – William Wordsworth, who described Chatterton as a "marvellous boy" and a "sleepless soul that perished in his pride", made pilgrimages to St Mary's; John Keats dedicated *Endymion* to him; while both Samuel Taylor Coleridge and Robert Southey chose to be married in the church, within six weeks of each other in 1795.

Jerusalem, which the knights were ordained to protect. The church's **cemetery** is today a tranquil public garden, from where you can get a real sense of just how far out the tower veers from the nave behind.

St Mary Redcliffe

Redcliffe Way, Redcliffe • Mon–Sat 8am–5pm, Sun 7am–8pm • Free • 📞 0117 929 1487, 🌐 stmaryredcliffe.co.uk

"The fairest, goodliest and most famous parish church in England."   Queen Elizabeth I

Dominating its eponymous parish, the richly decorated church of **St Mary Redcliffe** was largely paid for and used by merchants and mariners, who would pray to the Virgin Mary, and leave offerings for a safe voyage in its intricately carved north porch. The present building was begun at the end of the thirteenth century, though it was added to in subsequent centuries, much of it by **William Canynges**, a wealthy medieval shipping magnate and five times Mayor of Bristol who swapped commerce for the cloth and is buried in a canopied altar tomb in the south transept. The soaring spire, which provides one of the distinctive features of the city's skyline, dates from 1872, the original having been destroyed in a storm some four hundred years before.

The Handel Window and Penn Memorial

Of St Mary's many memorials and tombs, the **Handel Window** in the north choir aisle – installed in 1859 on the centenary of the death of Handel, who composed on the magnificent organ here – is perhaps the most interesting, and the funerary achievements of **Admiral Sir William Penn** the most dramatic. As reformer of the Royal Navy, Penn was arguably the instigator of what became the British Empire but is better known as the father of the founder of Pennsylvania.

St John's Chapel, the muniment room and the cemetery

William Edney's elegant wrought-iron gates, fashioned to separate the west end from the pews of the nave, open into **St John's Chapel**, which features St Mary's only remaining medieval stained glass and a striking modern "boat" altar. The wooden statue of Queen Elizabeth I here commemorates her famous admiration of the church.

Heading back through the north door leads to the inner porch, the oldest part of the church, from which a spiral staircase leads up to the **muniment room**, where **Thomas Chatterton** claimed to have found a trove of medieval manuscripts that were later revealed as forgeries (see box).

Chatterton is remembered by a memorial stone in the south transept, and there is another one to his family, who were long associated with the church, in the sparsely populated **cemetery**. The chunk of tramline up near the railings on Colston Parade was hurled here by a bomb explosion on Redcliffe Hill in 1941 and still protrudes from the grass like a rusting javelin.

Harbourside

The Old City may be the historical centre of Bristol, but the **Harbourside** is its heart. Lined with restaurants and bars and home to marquee attractions such as the **SS Great Britain**, the whole harbour area has undergone a remarkable transformation. Old warehouses, once crumbling and derelict, now boast arts centres and museums, cinemas and cafés, a trend that started with the conversion of Bush House into the **Arnolfini** in 1961 and continues today with **M Shed**, the city's innovative history museum.

Developed at the lowest bridging point on the River Avon, the harbour swelled the city's coffers with a wealth built on tea and tobacco, sugar and slaves. Goods were traded first with Ireland and the Severn ports, then Iceland and the Mediterranean, and ultimately – following John Cabot's discovery of America in 1497 and the subsequent expansion of the Atlantic slave trade (see page 107) – the colonies and the Caribbean.

The creation of the **Floating Harbour** extended Bristol's eminence, and in its heyday it was one of the busiest ports in the country, second only to London. The harbour ceased operating commercially in 1975, but its trading past is writ large in the names

PIRATES OF THE CARIBBEAN

"Fifteen men on the dead man's chest–
Yo-ho-ho, and a bottle of rum!
Drink and the devil had done for the rest–
Yo-ho-ho, and a bottle of rum!"   *Treasure Island*, Robert Louis Stevenson

In the early eighteenth century, Bristol was a hotbed of **piracy**. The burgeoning trade between Africa, the Caribbean and Europe meant rich pickings were to be had at sea, and the city's docks were rife with smugglers, pirates and privateers intent on getting their share of the spoils – it was no coincidence that when Robert Louis Stevenson penned his quintessential pirate tale, he made **Long John Silver** the landlord of a Bristol tavern (reputedly based on *The Hole in the Wall* pub on Queen Square) and had his characters set sail from the city's harbour.

The most famous Bristol pirate, indeed of all pirates, was Edward Teach, allegedly born in Redcliffe and better known as **Blackbeard**. Teach was feared across the Caribbean, a reputation he encouraged by tying lit cannon fuses to his hair so that his thick black beard fizzled "like a frightful meteor". Legend has it that he marooned a mutinous crew on Dead (Man's) Chest Island, in the British Virgin Islands, leaving them each with just "a bottle of rum" and a cutlass for company; pirates will be pirates, and by the time he returned, only a few ("fifteen") were still alive. Blackbeard's reign of terror caught up with him, however, and he was killed in a battle off Ocracoke Island, North Carolina, in 1718.

The most successful pirate in history also sailed from Bristol: Bartholomew Roberts, or **Black Bart**, who captured over 450 vessels in raids off the coasts of Brazil, West Africa and the Caribbean before his death in 1722.

Ironically, though, it was another Bristolian, **Woodes Rogers**, who proved instrumental in the ultimate demise of piracy. Rogers, who was born in Bristol in 1679 and lived on Queen Square (see page 93), was made Governor of the Bahamas with the sole mandate of ridding the islands of their two-thousand-strong pirate contingent. That he did, and his maxim "Piracy expelled, commerce restored" remained the motto of the Bahamas until they gained independence in 1973.

THE DISCOVERY OF "AMERYKA"

The Italian explorer **John Cabot** (Giovanni Cabboto), whose statue gazes wistfully across the water from outside the Arnolfini, set sail from Bristol in 1497 in the belief that a short cut to the East lay in fact to the West. He landed his ship, *The Matthew* (a replica of which is moored outside M Shed; see page 100), at Newfoundland, thus "discovering" North America in the process.

Of this, there is no doubt. More contentious, however, is the name his new continent acquired. History points to its stemming from **Amerigo Vespucci**, the Italian navigator who explored the New World at the end of the fifteenth century and whose name was marked on maps depicting the Americas. But records show that Cabot's transatlantic trip was mostly funded by one **Richard Ameryk**, Sheriff of Bristol and the King's Custom Officer, and who, as the principal patron of the voyage, was likely to have had any new-found lands named after him.

So is it, in fact, the Bristolian politician from whom "America" is derived? We'll never know for sure, but when weighing up the evidence consider this: the Stars and Stripes, the flag of the United States, is based on the design of Ameryk's coat of arms…

2

---

that adorn its quays: **Welsh Back**, the departure point for boats bound for Swansea and Newport; **Baltic Wharf**, whose warehouses once heaved with Russian timber; and **Bordeaux Quay**, where crates of fine wine arrived from the vineyards of western France.

Arnolfini

16 Narrow Quay • Tues–Sun 11am–6pm • Free • ☎ 0117 917 2300, Ⓦ arnolfini.org.uk

Occupying a former tea warehouse at the head of the Floating Harbour, the **Arnolfini** – named after Jan van Eyck's fifteenth-century painting, *The Arnolfini Portrait* – is Bristol's leading centre for contemporary arts, with a history of probing and sometimes controversial exhibitions, performance art, music, art-house films and talks.

The attached **bookshop** (see page 127) has an excellent range of arty books and magazines, and there's also a trendy little café-bar, with harbourside seating in summer.

We The Curious

Anchor Rd • Daily 10am–5pm, Sat, Sun & school hols till 6pm • £14.50 • ☎ 0117 915 1000, Ⓦ wethecurious.org

Although chiefly aimed at families, engaging **We The Curious** (former At-Bristol) packs in a good half-day's worth of wizardry for everyone. It's all very interactive and hands-on, and there are regular science shows and workshops.

Across more than 250 exhibits, you can dress up as bees to catch pollen, watch ice form, study bacteria and have a go at making fake blood. The brilliant **Animate It!**, made with input from Bristol-based Aardman Animations (*Wallace and Gromit, Shaun the Sheep*), gives you the chance to create your own short films, from storyboarding through to frame-by-frame shooting at touch-screen Animation Stations. With We The Curious' new commitment to sustainability, expect future exhibits and events to look at our impact on the environment and the science behind climate change.

The spherical, stainless-steel digital 3D **planetarium** attached to the complex, the first of its kind in the UK, has regular shows illustrating the night sky – make sure you book a slot when you buy your entry tickets (£3.50 extra).

Bristol Aquarium

Anchor Rd • Daily 10am–5pm • £16.50, 10 percent discount if booked online • ☎ 0117 929 8929, Ⓦ bristolaquarium.co.uk

The deceptively large **Bristol Aquarium** allows you to get face to fin with a fabulous array of native and tropical marine life, from sea horses to stingrays. Displays range from sunken ships to the Amazon, though the huge Coral Sea tank, with its underwater tunnel and circling sharks, is the most impressive. It's worth catching one or more of the feedings (you can return throughout the day), which feature piranhas and the resident giant octopus, and an educational talk or show at the Learning Lab, a sort of aquatic nursery.

M Shed

Princes Wharf, Wapping Rd • Tues–Sun (also Mon in school hols) 10am–5pm • Free • Guided tours Tues, Thurs & Fri 11.30am, Wed 2.30pm; 45min; free • Boat, train and crane rides on selected days throughout the year; £2.50–6 • ☎ 0117 352 6600, ⓦ bristolmuseums.org.uk

It's difficult to miss **M Shed**. Marked by four huge cargo cranes, the three-storey transit shed dominates the harbour, and is an altogether different beast to the city's other museums.

Its three galleries, spread across the first two floors (the top floor hosts changing exhibitions), are devoted totally to Bristol: its **people**, their **history**, their **common identity**, now and in the past. In a way, it's perhaps of most interest to locals – the first gallery is usually busy with residents trying to pick out their homes on the satellite map covering the floor – but the everyday details and the novel way in which they're delivered offer the best official insight into what makes Bristol Bristol.

Guided tours of neighbouring **L Shed** explore some of the museum's vast reserve collection of industrial machinery and maritime models that await their turn in the spotlight.

Bristol Places

On the ground floor, **Bristol Places** charts the city's changing face, from the Triassic period of Thecodontosaurus – or the "socket-toothed lizard", better known as the Bristol Dinosaur – through its development as a port and the hardships of World War II, epitomized by an old Anderson air-raid shelter, one of forty thousand erected across the city during the Blitz (see page 96).

Bristol People and Bristol Life

Bristol People, on the floor above, and the adjoining **Bristol Life**, look at the (often ordinary) folk who have shaped the city. There's an excellent – and long overdue – display on the slave trade in Bristol, where the copious visitor feedback can be equally as interesting, and others depicting music, art and protest in the city. The Bristol Life gallery is now also the home for Banksy's *Grim Reaper*, originally painted on the side of the *Thekla* nightclub.

SS Great Britain

Great Western Dockyard • **Museum** Daily 10am–6pm, Nov–March till 4pm • £17, 5 percent discount if booked online **Go Aloft!** Sat & Sun noon–4pm • £10, free for under-18s • ☎ 0117 926 0680, ⓦ ssgreatbritain.org

Harbourside's major draw, and one of Bristol's iconic sights, the **SS Great Britain** was the first propeller-driven, ocean-going iron ship in the world, built by Brunel in 1843. She initially ran between Liverpool and New York, then between Liverpool and Australia, chalking up more than a million miles at sea until she was caught in a storm off Cape Horn in 1886 and abandoned in the Falkland Islands. Salvaged and returned to Bristol in 1970, she is now berthed in the same dry dock in which she was built.

Dry Dock

Visits start in the mammoth **Dry Dock**, purpose-built to house the SS *Great Britain* during four years of construction. Enclosed under a striking "glass sea" that acts as a giant dehumidification chamber and keeps her iron panels from rusting any further, you can stand beneath the mighty hull and its enormous replica propeller – the original is in the Dockyard Museum – and admire the sheer scale of what was, in its time, the largest ship in the world.

ISAMBARD KINGDOM BRUNEL

"The commercial world thought him extravagant; but although he was so, great things are not done by those who sit down and count the cost of every thought and act."   The Diaries of Sir Daniel Gooch, 1892

The most celebrated of British engineers, **Isambard Kingdom Brunel** (1806–59) was a man who dealt in superlatives. During a prolific career of permanent planning and relentless construction, the "Little Giant" – a nickname bestowed on him thanks to his bold ideas but diminutive stature (he was just 5ft 3in tall) – built the first major railway in Britain, the fastest vessel to cross the Atlantic, record-breaking bridges and tunnels, and the world's largest ship, three times in a row.

Born in Portsmouth on April 9, 1806, the only son of a French engineer, Brunel was educated at the Lycée Henri-IV in Paris before joining his father on a project to link Rotherhithe with Wapping in East London. The **Thames Tunnel** was to set the tone for his career. A remarkable feat of engineering – it was described as the Eighth Wonder of the World when it opened in 1843 – the tunnel was beset by financial difficulties and took eighteen years to complete.

The project was hampered by a spate of accidents, and it was during a flood that destroyed part of the tunnel that Brunel himself was badly injured. He was sent to convalesce in the healing waters of **Hotwells** (see page 111) and so began a relationship with Bristol that was to last the rest of his life. Brunel's impact on the city was immense, but it was his first (and, ultimately, his last) design that remains his most iconic. Begun in 1831, the monumental **Clifton Suspension Bridge** (see page 109), which Brunel referred to as "my first child, my darling", soars over the River Avon, spanning the 702ft gap between the two sides of the Avon Gorge. It, too, was plagued with economic problems, and Brunel oversaw only the building of the towers at either end during his lifetime.

Within a couple of years of starting work in Clifton, aged just 27, Brunel was appointed chief engineer of the **Great Western Railway** (GWR), a train line conceived to connect London with Bristol and bring rail travel to the people. It was a project that would shape his career and leave his greatest legacy. Brunel designed the dramatic stations that bookend the line – **Temple Meads** in 1840 and **Paddington** in 1849 – and planned every inch of the 118-mile route, creating imposing viaducts at Hanwell and Chippenham, ground-breaking bridges at Maidenhead and Chepstow, and the unerringly straight, two-mile-long **Box Tunnel** outside Bath (see page 77), the longest in the world at the time.

Brunel married Mary Horsley in 1836, with whom he had three children (his son, Henry, was a structural engineer on Tower Bridge), but his focus remained resolute, and he worked eighteen-hour days in order to satisfy his increasingly ambitious plans. Despite the huge scale of the GWR, Brunel considered it only one stage in the linking of London and New York – his three "great" ships, two of them built in a harbour he helped design (see page 102), would provide the other. When the **SS Great Western** was launched in 1837, she was the largest steamship in the world and the first to provide a service across the Atlantic. The **SS Great Britain**, which followed six years later, was bigger and faster, making the journey to New York in just fourteen days. Brunel's final ship, the **SS Great Eastern**, was the largest of them all, but also the least successful. Designed in an unhappy alliance with John Scott Russell, the *Great Eastern* was easily the biggest ship ever built when she launched in 1859, but, like his most audacious assignments before, ran over budget and behind schedule. The project took its toll, and Brunel died of a stroke on board on September 15, 1859, shortly before her maiden voyage. He was buried, like his father, at Kensal Green Cemetery in London.

Dockyard Museum

The ship itself is accessed through the **Dockyard Museum**, which traces her history from ocean liner to emigrant clipper and finally windjammer through a variety of interactive exhibits and historical tidbits, including original tickets and a 140-year-old ship's biscuit.

Perhaps the most resonant displays are those on her salvage and ultimately triumphant **return to Bristol**: thousands lined the Avon to watch her stubby, mastless frame being towed up river – ironically, one of the trickiest stretches of her eight-thousand-mile journey home (see box) – and the attention this focused on the harbour was instrumental in its eventual regeneration.

2

THE FLOATING HARBOUR

For over five hundred years, Bristol's harbour flourished thanks to the ebb and flow of the Severn Estuary and the River Avon's tides. Ships used the extraordinary **tidal range**, the second largest in the world, to carry them the six miles between the mouth of the river and into the city's docks. But these same waters grounded them in the harbour when the tide went out – or worse, stranded them in the mud halfway up the receding Avon – often resulting in damaged hulls and ruined cargo. (The consequential custom of building the ships more robustly, and of carefully stowing their loads, led sailors elsewhere to regard them as being "**Bristol fashion**", a term that was later co-opted into the phrase "ship-shape and Bristol fashion" to indicate that everything was in good order.)

As trade increased, so did the number of ships waiting on each high tide. There was not enough room at the quay, and many had already turned to the larger and more accessible docks at Liverpool by the time the **Floating Harbour** opened in 1809. Eventually designed by William Jessop, the harbour was forty years in the planning but only took five years to build. It worked by trapping over eighty acres of river behind a system of **dams** and **locks** around the Cumberland Basin, the level of water maintained at first by a weir and then later by a set of Brunel-designed **sluices**; together, the locks and sluices enabled quayside ships to stay "afloat" at all times. The locks are still in use – though the current one dates to 1873 – and the gates and sluices are still operated from **Underfall Yard** (see page 103).

Two man-made waterways completed the Floating Harbour. The **New Cut**, which carries the River Avon south of the harbour, was dug so that smaller vessels could bypass the main locks and instead access the docks at Bathurst Basin, closer to their berths – the Bathurst lock was blocked during World War II to prevent the harbour from draining were it hit by a bomb. The **Feeder Canal**, east of Temple Meads, maintains its water level by "feeding" the harbour and provided a way for barges to rejoin the Avon above the weir at Netham Lock.

For 150 years after the Floating Harbour was built, the city's docks flourished again. The harbour, however, could do nothing about the navigability of the Avon, and as ocean-going ships grew ever bigger, they began to use the docks further out at **Avonmouth**, developed in the late nineteenth century. The harbour closed its lock gates to commercial shipping for the last time in 1975, and the closure two years later of Charles Hill & Sons, the oldest shipbuilders in the country, truly marked the end of an era.

The ship

The immersion in Victorian life continues on board, pepped by the smell of freshly baked "bread" and a smoky engine. Strolling the **Weather Deck** gives a good idea of her record-breaking 322ft length, while beneath the funnel you can peer into the immense **engine room** (with its working engine) and see the restored **cabins**, their bunks occupied by eerily breathing mannequins. Compact but comfortable, the cabins' contrast with the crowded steerage accommodation is reflected in the eating arrangements on board: pease soup and stale biscuits for the latter; grouse, pigeon and veal for the former, served in some style in the sumptuous first-class **dining saloon**.

If you've got a head for heights, then you can get an even better insight into the life of a Victorian sailor with **Go Aloft!**, where you're harnessed up before climbing the ship's rigging and inching out onto the main yard, some 100ft above the dock below.

Being Brunel

Opened in 2018, **Being Brunel** is a warts-and-all study of the man behind the most ambitious engineering projects of his day. Personal items, spread across a recreation of Brunel's London home and his original, restored Bristol dock office, include his last cigar (he got through 48 a day) and his sketchbook of ideas and plans for the construction of the SS *Great Eastern*. You can (literally) get inside Brunel's mind, too, stepping into an 8m-tall model of his head, à la *Being John Malkovich*, for an interesting audio-visual experience

Brunel Institute

Tues–Fri & first & second Sat of the month 10.30am–4.30pm • Free • ID required • ☎ 0117 926 0680, ⓦ ssgreatbritain.org/brunel-institute

For a detailed insight into Brunel's work – and of British maritime history in general – pop into the **Brunel Institute**, built on the site of his former steam-engine factory (its exterior is designed to look like the original) that adjoins the SS *Great Britain*. This research-centric library holds over seven thousand ship plans, a hundred ship models, Brunel's diaries and drawing instruments, and correspondence from the passengers and crew of the famous ship herself.

2

Spike Island

133 Cumberland Rd • Tues–Sun noon–5pm; café Mon–Fri 9am–5pm, Sat & Sun noon–5pm • Free • ☎ 0117 929 2266, ⓦ spikeisland.org.uk

There's a creative buzz about **Spike Island**, which enjoys a similar setup to the Arnolfini (see page 99) – a former tea-packing factory turned contemporary arts venue, with a relaxed café attached – but is also home to artists' studios and commercial workspaces. It's not as extensive as its forerunner, though the huge central galleries provide plenty of scope for the variety of (often left-field) exhibitions and events that run here throughout the year.

While you're here, it's worth hunting out Banksy's *Girl with a Pierced Eardrum* (see page 113), just behind Spike Island.

Underfall Yard

Cumberland Rd • **Boatyard** Daily: Easter–Oct 7.30am–9.30pm; Nov–Easter 9am–5pm **Visitor Centre** Tues–Sun 10am–5pm, till 4pm Nov–Easter • ⓦ underfallyard.co.uk

Built on land formed by the creation of the Floating Harbour in the early nineteenth century (see page 102), **Underfall Yard** offers a rare glimpse into the goings-on of a working boatyard. You can walk among the traditional boat-builders, blacksmiths and riggers that still operate out of their original workshops, and there's often some kind of historical vessel perched on top of the restored slipway awaiting repairs.

The yard is named after the **sluices**, or "underfalls", designed by Isambard Kingdom Brunel to control the level of water in the docks – exhibits in the Visitor Centre demonstrate exactly how they work – and its **engine house** continues to serve as the operational centre for the harbour's entire network of swing bridges and locks.

CREATE Centre

Smeaton Rd, Spike Island • **CREATE** Mon–Fri 9am–5pm • Free • **Ecohome** Mon–Fri noon–3pm • Free • ☎ 0117 922 4370, ⓦ createbristol.org

The **CREATE Centre**, at the western tip of Spike Island, is a neat little red-brick metaphor for Bristol. Occupying a former WD & HO Wills factory, it has effectively replaced tobacco production with environmental concerns and is now the city's hub for sustainable development. Bruges Tozer's low-impact **Ecohome** is the highlight, a poster child for sustainable living that covers the obvious points (low-energy light bulbs, solar panels), as well as more creative ways of cutting down your carbon footprint.

Park Street and the West End

Originally the preserve of monied merchants and the well-to-do, the graceful residential premises of **Park Street** gradually succumbed to traders, and since the 1820s it has been one of Bristol's most popular destinations for an afternoon's shopping. A few big names are creeping in, but it essentially remains an enclave of quirky boutiques and offbeat independents, an eclectic collection mirrored by the area's variety of cafés and bars.

Park Street climbs steeply from **College Green** and the medieval lines of **Bristol Cathedral**, on the way passing one of the more central of Banksy's works, *Well Hung Lover* (see page 113), unfortunately now partially vandalized. A stiff uphill hike from here leads to the traffic-ringed "**Triangle**", marking the move towards Clifton.

The surrounding Georgian streets loosely form what's known as the **West End**, more a marketing tag than any physically recognizable area; much of it forms the precinct of Bristol University, which stretches back behind the towering **Wills Memorial Building** and includes the **Victoria Rooms**, a dramatic-looking concert hall that hosts regular lunchtime recitals (ⓦbris.ac.uk/music).

Bristol Cathedral

College Green • Mon–Fri 8am–5pm, Sat & Sun 8am–3.15pm **Evensong** Mon–Fri 5.15pm, Sat & Sun 3.30pm • Free **Guided tours** Sat 11.30am & 1.30pm (also Tues 2.15pm during school term time) • Free, suggested donation £5 • ⓦ bristol-cathedral.co.uk

Founded around 1140 as an abbey on the supposed spot of St Augustine's seventh-century convocation with Celtic Christians, **Bristol Cathedral** became a cathedral church with the Dissolution of the Monasteries in the mid-sixteenth century. Among the many later additions are the two towers on the west front, erected in the nineteenth century, eleven years after the nave was rebuilt to its medieval design.

The choir and the Elder Lady Chapel

The cathedral's interior is a unique example among Britain's cathedrals of a German-style "hall church", in which the aisles, nave and choir rise to the same height; the immense **choir** – the highest in England – offers one of the country's most exquisite illustrations of the early Decorated Gothic style.

The adjoining thirteenth-century **Elder Lady Chapel** contains some fine tombs and eccentric carvings of animals, including (between the arches on the right) a monkey playing the bagpipes accompanied by a ram on the violin.

The Eastern Lady Chapel

At the far end of the cathedral, the **Eastern Lady Chapel** was restored in 1935 and gives a good indication of how the abbey would once have been decorated. Paul Bush, who in 1542 became Bristol's first bishop, is entombed here; he was expelled twelve years later for marrying and, as fate would have it, is buried near the grave of his wife.

The south transept and the Chapter House

The thousand-year-old stone bas-relief of the *Harrowing of Hell* in the **south transept** – showing Christ plucking Eve from the devil's clutches – is one of the world's most important Saxon sculptures; it was discovered under the Chapter House floor, where it was being used as a coffin lid. From the south transept, a door leads through to the **Chapter House** itself, a richly carved piece of late Norman architecture that, for the most part, is little changed from when it was built in 1160.

Around College Green

Dominated by the crescent-shaped 1950s **Council House**, the grassy expanse of **College Green** was created in the twelfth century, when pastoral land at the bottom of what is now Park Street was enclosed to form the precincts of St Augustine's Abbey – the later conversion of which into a collegiate church gives the green its name. Aside from the chapels inside Bristol Cathedral, the old **Abbey Gatehouse**, opposite, is one of the abbey's few remains that are accessible to the public, the rest being incorporated into the various buildings of Bristol Cathedral School.

Central Library

Deanery Rd · Mon, Wed & Fri 9.30am–5pm, Tues & Thurs 9.30am–7pm, Sat 10am–5pm, Sun 1–5pm · Free

The **Central Library**, adjoining the Abbey Gatehouse, was built in 1906 to house the collection of the Old Library on King Street, one of the first public libraries in the country and a frequent port of call for Samuel Taylor Coleridge and Robert Southey; it preserves one of the original rooms, complete with rich wooden panelling and period furniture.

Lord Mayor's Chapel

College Green · Sat 1.15pm & Sun 11am · Free

Opposite College Green from the cathedral, and conspicuous by its large Perpendicular window, the **Lord Mayor's Chapel** is crammed with a bewildering array of monuments and memorials, all painstakingly explained in some of the most enthusiastic signage in the city. The only civic church in England, the chapel's nave is lined with the **funeral hatchments** of six of the former mayors that lend it its name – the large wooden boards were hung outside the deceased's door before being carried to the church for burial.

Georgian House Museum

7 Great George St · April–Dec Mon, Tues, Sat & Sun 11am–4pm · Free · ☎ 0117 921 1362, ⊕ bristolmuseums.org.uk

Built in 1790, the deceptively large, six-storey **Georgian House Museum** is the former home of local sugar merchant John Pinney, its spacious and faithfully restored rooms filled with sumptuous examples of period furniture. The basement gives particular insight into domestic times past, with "speaking tubes" for summoning workers in the kitchen, and, in the room opposite, Pinney's colossal stone cold-water plunge bath.

Upstairs, illustrated panels tell the engrossing story of the family's dealings in the West Indies, including their involvement in **slavery** – Pinney's slave, Pero, was commemorated in iron in 1999 with the opening of the horned Pero's Bridge down in the harbour, a rare acknowledgement of the impact the slave trade had in shaping modern Bristol.

Brandon Hill and Cabot Tower

Daily dawn–dusk · Free

From Great George Street, or from Berkeley Square further up the hill, you can access the attractive parkland of **Brandon Hill**, a conservation area that's home to the landmark **Cabot Tower**, built in 1897 to commemorate the four-hundredth anniversary of John Cabot's voyage to America.

You can climb the 105ft tower for the city's best panorama, with far-reaching views over the cathedral and down across the harbour below.

Wills Memorial Building

Queen's Rd · Tours Sat 1pm, first Wed of month 12.30pm, first Sat of month also 11am · 1hr–1hr 30min · £5 · ☎ 0117 954 5219

The imposing neo-Gothic **Wills Memorial Building** that crowns the top of Park Street was built by George and Henry Wills in honour of their father, the tobacco magnate Henry Overton Wills, who founded the University of Bristol and was its first chancellor. Its bold, near-faultless design earned its architect, Sir George Oatley, a knighthood in 1925.

You can access the entrance hall, directly underneath the 215ft Wills Tower, to see the double staircase and lofty, ornate ceiling, while occasional **tours** take you into the heart of the building itself.

THE SLAVE TRADE IN BRISTOL

Over two hundred years after the abolition of the British **slave trade**, Bristol is still haunted by the instrumental part it played in the trafficking of African men, women and children to the New World – indeed, it was Bristol-born Sir John Yeamans, a Barbados planter, who effectively introduced slavery to North America.

The slave trade in Britain was monopolized by the London-based Royal African Company until 1698 when, following pressure from Bristol's powerful **Society of Merchant Venturers** (see page 109), the market was opened to all. For the next hundred years, the city's merchants were able to participate in the "**triangular trade**" whereby brass pots, glass beads and other manufactured goods were traded for slaves on the coast of West Africa, who were then shipped to plantations in the Americas, the vessels returning to Europe with cargoes of sugar, cotton, tobacco and other slave-labour-produced commodities. By the 1730s, Bristol had become – along with London and Liverpool – one of the main beneficiaries of the trade, sending out a total of more than two thousand ships in search of slaves on the African coast. The direct profits, together with the numerous spin-offs, helped to finance some of the city's finest Georgian architecture.

Bristol's primacy in the trade had long been supplanted by Liverpool by the time **opposition to slavery** began to gather force: first the Quakers (remembered in a plaque to Thomas Clarkson outside *The Seven Stars* pub on St Thomas Street) and Methodists, then more powerful forces, voiced their discontent. By the 1780s, the Anglican Dean Josiah Tucker and the Evangelical writer Hannah More had become active abolitionists, and Samuel Taylor Coleridge made a famous anti-slavery speech in Bristol in 1795.

The British slave trade was finally abolished in 1807, but its legacy is still felt strongly in the city, particularly in the divisive figure of **Edward Colston**. The eighteenth-century sugar magnate is revered by many as a great philanthropist – his name given to numerous buildings, streets and schools in Bristol – but reviled by more as a leading light in the Royal African Company. His statue in The Centre has more than once been the subject of graffiti attacks and calls for its removal, and Massive Attack (see page 124) refuse to play at the Colston Hall because of the connotations of its name.

Bristol Museum and Art Gallery

Queen's Rd · Tues–Sun 10am–5pm (also Mon in school hols) · Free · ☎ 0117 922 3571, ⓦ bristolmuseums.org.uk

The labyrinthine **Bristol Museum and Art Gallery** has the sections on local geology and natural history that you'd expect in a provincial museum, but its scope is occasionally surprising – it has some magnificent **Assyrian** reliefs carved in the ninth century BC, while the excellent **Egyptology** collection features a number of mummies and their elaborately decorated coffins.

Aptly enough, though, the piece that immediately catches your attention in the light-filled atrium is Banksy's *Paint Pot Angel*, donated from his pioneering **Banksy v Bristol Museum** exhibition in 2009, by far the most popular art exhibition ever held here (and for which he received a £1 fee).

It's worth a brief stop on the first floor to take in the series of **historical maps** that plot Bristol's growth as a port before heading up to the top floor, where **works** by the Bristol School of Artists and French Impressionists are mixed in with some choice older pieces.

Red Lodge Museum

Park Row · April–Dec Mon, Tues, Sat & Sun 11am–4pm · Free · ☎ 0117 921 1360, ⓦ bristolmuseums.org.uk

The **Red Lodge Museum** was a merchant's home when built in the sixteenth century, and was later England's first girls' reform school. Its undoubted highlight is the Tudor Great Oak Room, featuring a splendid carved stone fireplace and lavish oak panelling. From the Great Oak Room's windows, you can see Colston Hall, occupying the site of the "Great House" that the lodge was originally created for; the barn-like building in the Elizabethan-style knot garden below is the Wigwam, home of the Bristol Savages (see page 109).

Clifton

Perched on a hillside overlooking the Avon Gorge, elegant, leafy **Clifton** has always felt somewhat removed from the chaotic commerce of the city down below. Bristol's most attractive quarter, its slopes lined with honeyed Georgian terraces, Clifton started life as an aloof spa resort, and it wasn't until the late eighteenth century – when wealthy merchants started building mansions up here, away from the dirty and densely populated city centre – that Clifton became the desirable address that it remains today.

It's a sizeable suburb, spreading east to bar-laden **Whiteladies Road** and north to **Bristol Zoo**. But by far the most enjoyable area to wander is the select enclave of **Clifton Village**, centred on The Mall and close to **Royal York Crescent**, the longest Georgian crescent in the country. North of the Village lies Brunel's mighty **Clifton Suspension**

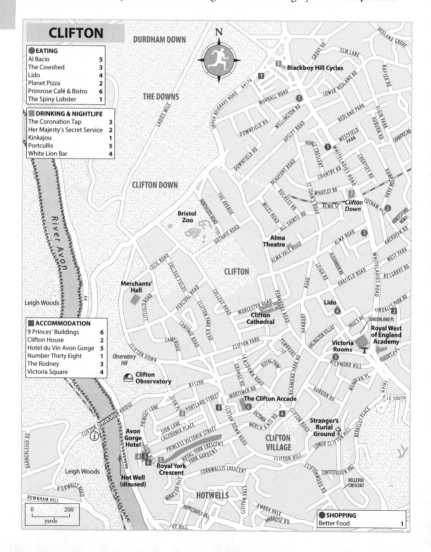

CLIFTON

DURDHAM DOWN

N

THE DOWNS

CLIFTON DOWN

Bristol Zoo

Alma Theatre

CLIFTON

Merchants' Hall

Leigh Woods

Clifton Cathedral

Clifton Observatory

Observatory Hill

Lido

Royal West of England Academy

Victoria Rooms

The Clifton Arcade

Stranger's Burial Ground

CLIFTON VILLAGE

Avon Gorge Hotel

Royal York Crescent

Hot Well (disused)

Leigh Woods

HOTWELLS

Blackboy Hill Cycles

Clifton Down

River Avon

ROWNHAM HILL

●EATING	
Al Bacio	5
The Cowshed	3
Lido	4
Planet Pizza	2
Primrose Café & Bistro	6
The Spiny Lobster	1

■ DRINKING & NIGHTLIFE	
The Coronation Tap	3
Her Majesty's Secret Service	2
Kinkajou	1
Portcullis	5
White Lion Bar	4

■ ACCOMMODATION	
9 Princes' Buildings	6
Clifton House	2
Hotel du Vin Avon Gorge	5
Number Thirty Eight	1
The Rodney	3
Victoria Square	4

● SHOPPING	
Better Food	1

0   200
yards

HIGH SOCIETY: MERCHANTS, RINGERS AND SAVAGES

The attractive **Merchants'** **Hall** on Clifton Down Road is home to arguably the most powerful organization in Bristol. Established by royal charter in 1552 to protect and promote trade in the city, the **Society of Merchant Venturers** (ⓦ merchantventurers.com) effectively controlled Bristol's docks (and therefore the city itself) for three hundred lucrative years, monopolizing trade with the New World and amassing a vast fortune from slavery.

Merchant money lay behind many of the city's major civic achievements – they helped finance Cabot's voyage to Newfoundland, established the Floating Harbour, set up the Great Western Railway, provided the means to build the Clifton Suspension Bridge and founded Bristol University and the University of the West of England. In 1686, the Merchants bought the manor of Clifton; Clifton Down, which the Hall overlooks, is still Merchant property. Merchants continue to dominate Bristol business, and the society remains an invite-only, predominantly male enclave, but it adopts a far more philanthropic approach these days, running almshouses and contributing to numerous community charities.

Membership of the Merchants historically overlaps with that of another, mysterious-sounding, group, the **Antient Society of St Stephen's Ringers** (ⓦ leftedge.co.uk/ saintstephensringers), dedicated to the upkeep of St Stephen's Church (see page 92). Starting out in 1620 as a collection of campanologists, the Ringers quickly progressed to secret drunken feasts and a bizarre procession featuring a stuffed fox and a model of Queen Elizabeth I's death mask, though nowadays they settle for a rather lively annual dinner instead.

That dinner is traditionally held in the Red Lodge Museum's Wigwam, the meeting place since 1904 of another invite-only (and male-only) society, the **Bristol Savages** (ⓦ bristol-savages.org). Essentially an elite art club, the twenty or so "Brothers of the Brush" meet once a week during winter, the Red Feathers (artists) sketching or painting before being entertained by the Blue Feathers (musicians).

2

Bridge, and above that, the vast expanse of **the Downs**, a popular spot for picnicking couples and kite-flying kids.

Clifton Suspension Bridge

Free, £1 for vehicles **Visitor Centre** Daily 10am–5pm • Free **Guided tours** Easter–Oct Sat & Sun 3pm • 45min • Free • ⓦ cliftonbridge.org.uk

Spanning the Avon Gorge, 702ft long and poised 245ft above the water, **Clifton Suspension Bridge** is Bristol's most famous symbol. Money was first put forward for a bridge to link Clifton with the opposite cliffs in 1754, though it was not until 1829 that a competition was held for a design, won by Isambard Kingdom Brunel (see page 101) on a second round, and not until 1864 that the bridge was completed, five years after Brunel's death. The tradition of illuminating the bridge at night dates back to its opening ceremony.

Hampered by financial difficulties, the Suspension Bridge never quite matched the engineer's original ambitious design, which included Egyptian-style towers topped by sphinxes on each end, although it was still ingenious in its execution – in 2002, the bridge's solid-looking abutments were revealed to be hollow, instead containing a latticework of vaulted chambers that reduced construction costs without weakening the bridge.

You can see copies of Brunel's drawings in the **Visitor Centre**, located at the far side of the bridge, alongside other designs that Brunel's rivals proposed, some of them frankly bizarre.

Clifton Observatory

Litfield Rd, Clifton Down • Daily 10am–5pm, Oct–Easter till 4pm • Camera obscura £2.50; Giant's Cave £2.50; entry to both £4 • No under-4s • ☎ 0117 974 1242, ⓦ cliftonobservatory.com

Set on the slopes of an Iron Age hillfort, the medieval-looking tower of **Clifton Observatory** is home to a **camera obscura**, one of only a handful in the country open to the public – it uses mirrors to reflect a panorama of the surrounding area, so achieves the best results in sunny weather.

From the tower, a passage leads down to the **Giant's Cave**, site of an ancient hermitage (it's also known as St Vincent's Cave), and to a viewing platform perched 250ft above the Avon, with giddy vistas of the Suspension Bridge and the gorge below.

Clifton Cathedral

Clifton Park • Mon–Fri 6.15am–7pm, till 6pm in winter, Sat 8am–7.15pm & Sun 7.15am–7.15pm • Free

The pink granite Roman Catholic Cathedral Church of Saints Peter and Paul, otherwise known as **Clifton Cathedral**, is unlike any other house of worship in the city. Described as "a sermon in concrete", it was completed in May 1973, its dramatically stark interior accommodating a thousand people around a hexagonal-shaped sanctuary, creatively designed so that it bathes in reflected natural light. Cutting-edge acoustics, one of the finest Neoclassical organs in Europe and a highly regarded cathedral choir (who normally sing at the 11.15am Sunday Mass) also make this a great place to catch **liturgical music**; see ⓦ cliftonms.com for details of concerts and other events.

Royal West of England Academy

Queen's Rd • Tues–Sat 10am–5.30pm, Sun 11am–5pm • £7.95 • ⓣ 0117 973 5129, ⓦ rwa.org.uk

The first art gallery in Bristol, the **Royal West of England Academy** (RWA) has amassed over 1700 pieces in its permanent fine-art collection, including works by Elizabeth Blackadder, Julian Trevelyan and Mary Fedden. But it's the wide-ranging and thought-provoking programme of temporary displays that is the real draw here, from photography and sculpture to woodblock prints and street art.

Bristol Zoo

Zoo Daily 9am–5.30pm • £12 or £17, depending on the date ZooRopia Sat, Sun & school hols 10am–4pm • £7.65 • ⓣ 0117 428 5300, ⓦ bristolzoo.org.uk

One of the oldest zoological gardens in the world, ever-popular **Bristol Zoo** is home to over 450 different species of squawking, swinging and slithering animals. The **enclosures** in its dozen acres of gardens range from the Monkey Jungle to the walk-through Butterfly Forest and from Gorilla Island to the Twilight World – an update of the world's first nocturnal house, featuring blind naked mole rats and other oddities – but it's hard to beat the Seal and Penguin Coasts, where underwater walkways prove just how much more adept African penguins are in the water than out of it.

The zoo is renowned for its animal **conservation** work and has a strong track record in breeding endangered species in captivity, including Asiatic lions, as well as providing a home to several slightly less glamorous critters (such as the Partula snail) that are now extinct in the wild. Numerous talks, feeds and animal encounters can easily extend your visit into a full-on day-trip, as can **ZooRopia**, a primate-themed aerial obstacle course that ends in a zip wire onto the main lawn.

University of Bristol Botanic Garden

Hollybush Lane, Stoke Bishop • Daily 10am–4.30pm • £6 • ⓣ 0117 331 4906, ⓦ botanic-garden.bristol.ac.uk

The **University of Bristol Botanic Garden** near Durdham Down cultivates some 4500 plant species, including several you won't see outside these walls. It's not your average botanical garden: science-centric displays trace the evolution of land plants and reflect modern theories on how different species are in fact related through their DNA. There are also Chinese and European medicinal herb gardens, a number of glasshouses that contain floral gems such as giant Amazon water lilies and South Africa *fynbos* and, closer to home, collections of threatened native species like the Bristol onion, the pinky-purple flowers of which you may see sprouting out of the rocks in the Avon Gorge.

SPA AND AWAY

It's strange to think that the rather nondescript area of **Hotwells** that lies at the base of Clifton is largely responsible for the affluent neighbourhood of sweeping crescents above. As early as the fifteenth century, people were drinking the **spring waters** that revealed themselves in the river here at low tide, but its potential was only realized in the late seventeenth century, when the Society of Merchant Venturers (see page 109) purchased the "hot wells", along with the manor of Clifton itself. Spring water was pumped into Hotwell House – and later to the Clifton Grand Spa and Hydropathic Institution, now the *Avon Gorge Hotel* – and **Hotwell Spa** took off, a smaller summer complement to Bath's winter season. Indeed, so popular was its water that Bristol's glass-making industry was born out of the demand for it to be bottled.

By the end of the eighteenth century, though, with prices (and pollution) on the rise, the spa went into decline and Hotwells became the preserve of the **terminally ill** seeking one last chance of a cure. Despite some "success" (the waters allegedly rid John Wesley of tuberculosis), the stay for the majority of visitors was a permanent one – with the church graveyards filled to capacity, many were interred in the **Strangers' Burial Ground** at the foot of Lower Clifton Hill.

2

East Bristol

Down at heel and rough around the edges, the vibrant areas that make up **East Bristol** are some of the most culturally diverse in the city. United by their resilient, resourceful communities (and historically by their less-than-savoury reputations), **Stokes Croft** and **St Pauls** are uncompromisingly creative quarters that are quite unlike anywhere else in the city – Clifton Village this is not.

North of Stokes Croft, The Arches mark the start of **Gloucester Road**, a buzzing stretch of independent shops, restaurants and bars; while heading east leads into the bohemian district of **Montpelier**, centred round foodie Picton Street and looking like a slightly wearier version of Clifton thanks to its shabby-chic Georgian terraces.

Stokes Croft

Fiercely independent **Stokes Croft**, the area (and road) immediately north of the bus station, is one of the most dynamic neighbourhoods in Bristol. An exercise in collective ownership, it owes much of its independent ethos to the **People's Republic of Stokes Croft** (⊕prsc.org.uk), a community-action group charged with promoting the area and protecting it from "the blandification of conventional development"; the PRSC has had a pretty significant impact judging by the number of cafés, restaurants and bars that have opened up in this once-neglected neighbourhood since it was formed in 2007.

Stokes Croft is also one of the best places to explore the city's thriving **street art** scene, most obvious on the **Outdoor Gallery**, which occupies a wall next to the headquarters of the PRSC and serves as a controlled canvas for local artists. Longer-lasting murals include *Tsunami of Roses*, on the corner of Jamaica and Hillgrove streets; *Boycott Tesco*, at the junction of Stokes Croft and Sydenham Road; and, of course, a number of **Banksys** – look out for the *Rose & Mousetrap*, on St Thomas Street North, now under protective plexiglass; *Take the Money and Run*, a collaboration that adorns a health-centre wall on Bath Buildings in nearby Montpelier; and, on Stokes Croft itself, the striking *Mild, Mild West* (see page 113).

St Pauls

The embattled neighbourhood of **St Pauls** still struggles to shake off the stigma of the 1980 riots. While its reputation for crime is hardly undeserved – it's not *that* long ago that even the police refused to venture beyond the notorious "Frontline" of Grosvenor Road – this is one of Bristol's most cosmopolitan neighbourhoods, with a very real and tangible community spirit, fostered here perhaps more than elsewhere as a direct result of over thirty years of social prejudice. St Pauls has been shaped by Caribbean migrants, whose lasting legacy is the hugely popular **St Pauls Carnival** (see page 129).

St Pauls Church

Portland Square

Standing proud over the eastern side of eighteenth-century Portland Square, **St Pauls Church** encapsulates the progress that's slowly changing the wider area – boarded up and abandoned in the 1990s, it has now been restored to its former glory, and thanks to a novel initiative with the Churches Conservation Trust, provides a dramatic home to Circomedia, one of only two circus schools in the country; you can see the elegant interior during one of their performances (see page 126). Designed by Daniel Hague

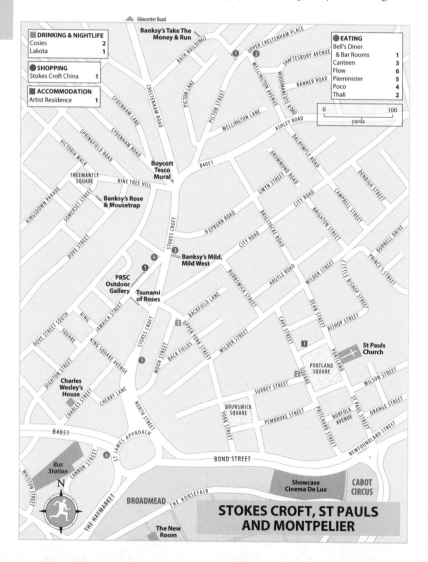

DRINKING & NIGHTLIFE
Cosies	2
Lakota	1

SHOPPING
Stokes Croft China	1

ACCOMMODATION
Artist Residence	1

EATING
Bell's Diner & Bar Rooms	1
Canteen	3
Flow	6
Pieminister	5
Poco	4
Thali	2

STOKES CROFT, ST PAULS AND MONTPELIER

THE BANKSY PHENOMENON

Shrouded in mystery despite his fame (his true identity is yet to be revealed) and dividing opinion because of his art, the street artist known as **Banksy** has spray-painted walls in London, Detroit, Melbourne and the Middle East, but it was in the graffiti hotbed of Bristol that he developed the stencil style that defines his work.

Street art comes and goes but several of Banksy's key murals remain, dotted around the city, all exhibiting the dry wit that undercuts his social message. The most iconic piece, and the first stop on any Banksy trail, is **Mild, Mild West** (1999), at the junction of Stokes Croft and Jamaica Street. Showing a wobbly white teddy bear pitching a Molotov cocktail at advancing riot police, it was seen by many as a reference to the St Pauls riots of 1980 (which were ignited by a police raid on a café in nearby Grosvenor Road), though is actually a reaction to the crackdown on the city's "free parties", a late twentieth-century Bristol phenomenon where scores of people broke into abandoned warehouses. The piece took three days to paint and even went through a couple of drafts – look closely and you can see the outlines of the policemen have been slightly adjusted.

Mild, Mild West was chosen as the city's alternative landmark in a local radio poll in 2007, and there's similar affection for Banksy's image of **Death** (2003), painted on the waterline of the *Thekla*, a nightclub boat moored in the harbour; the piece is now on display at the M Shed (see page 100) after fears that it was on the verge of deteriorating completely (Banksy's tag had already long since disappeared). His original work was removed by the city's harbourmaster (the nightclub wanted to keep it, and subsequently sued for criminal damage), prompting Banksy to return and paint a Grim Reaper figure rowing in the same spot.

Arguably the most famous of Banksy's works lies a short walk northwest from here, off the bottom of Park Street. Secretly created beneath sheet-covered scaffolding, **Well Hung Lover** (2006), an adulterous man hanging from a window, was saved thanks to a petition from a Lib Dem councillor. Finally acknowledging public opinion, it was the first official recognition of Banksy's rising role in the city's cultural profile and paved the way for his wildly successful exhibition in the Bristol Museum and Art Gallery in 2009.

Since then, Banksy has created several more satirical works on the walls of his hometown. His latest piece, *Girl with a Pierced Eardrum* (2014), decorates the side of a dockyard clocktower in Hanover Place, near the city's marina. A parody of Johannes Vermeer's famous *Girl with a Pearl Earring*, it is unerringly similar to the Dutch master's painting, except Banksy has replaced the earring with a burglar alarm that's fitted to the wall here.

in 1789, the church is thought to be the most important example of provincial Gothic architecture in Bristol.

Ashton Court Estate

Long Ashton • Daily 8am–dusk • **Arts Mansion** Sat & Sun 11am–4pm; ☎ 0117 973 8508, ⊛ artspacelifespace.com **Café** Daily 9.30am–5.30pm **Golf, Foot Golf & Disc Golf** Daily 7am–dusk, Jan & Feb from 8am; £7; ☎ 0117 973 8508 • Free • ⊛ ashtoncourtestate.com

Although it never feels crowded, the **Ashton Court Estate** attracts more visitors than anywhere else in the South West, welcoming over 1.75 million people into its landscaped grounds each year. Set around a rather grandiose Victorian mansion west of the city, the estate's 850 acres of woodland and open grassland – home to badgers, bats and, most noticeably, **deer** – make for one of the city's most enjoyable retreats. The park's foundations were laid as early as 1392, by Thomas de Lyons, but it was the wealthy Smythe family who, over four centuries of architectural tweaking, gave the focal **Ashton Court Mansion** its present appearance. The mansion is now an arts venue that hosts exhibitions and performances at the weekends; at other times, you can get an idea of its period decor from the *Courtyard Café*, located in the stables courtyard.

In addition to the variety of **festivals** that are held here each year (see page 129), there are numerous events and **activities**, as well as two eighteen-hole pitch-and-putt **golf courses** (which also used for foot golf and frisbee disc golf) and a mountain-bike trail.

Blaise Castle Estate

Henbury Rd • Park daily 7.30am–dusk; castle May–Oct third Sun of the month 2–4.30pm; museum Thurs–Sun 11am–4pm (also Tues & Wed in school hols) • Free • ⓦ bristol.gov.uk/blaisecastleestate • Entrance on Kings Weston Rd (B4057), 5 miles from the city centre (bus #1/#40/#76)

The varied grounds of **Blaise Castle Estate** have all the ingredients for a perfect sunny afternoon excursion, including woodland trails and picnic-friendly downs. The "**castle**" is actually a folly, and was used as a summer house; it's open when the flags are flying. Blaise House itself, built in 1796, now serves as a charming **museum** of everyday objects from Victorian Bristol, including kitchen equipment, clothing and toys.

Wild Place Project

Blackhorse Hill, off junction 17 of the M5 • **Wild Place Project** Daily 10am–5pm • £11 or £12.50, 10 percent discount if booked online **Leap of Faith** Daily 11am–4pm during school hols, rest of year weekends only • From £6 • ☎ 0117 980 7175, ⓦ wildplace.org.uk

An offshoot of Bristol Zoo (see page 110), **Wild Place Project** was set up as a low-key conservation park to harbour some of the endangered species they help protect abroad. Six areas run the range of habitats from the Edge of Africa (gelada baboons) to Bénoué National Park (cheetah and red river hogs). Bear Wood takes visitors back to Ancient Britain, its raised walkways snaking above woodland that's home to European brown bears, wolves, lynxes and wolverines. Among several outdoor activities, the **Leap of Faith** consists of a giant swing, climbing walls and the adrenaline-inducing leap itself.

Aerospace Bristol

Hayes Way, Patchway, off junction 17 of the M5 • Daily 10am–5pm, till 4pm in winter • £17 • ☎ 01179 315315, ⓦ aerospacebristol.org • Buses #75 and the T2 run from the city centre to Gipsy Patch Lane, 700yds from the museum

Set on an old airfield in Filton, the excellent **Aerospace Bristol** traces the city's substantial role in the development of flight, from the early pioneers through two world wars and on to the race into space. The exhibitions feature several locally made aircraft, but pride of place goes to the last ever Concorde to fly, which occupies its own purpose-built hangar – you can climb aboard and peer into the cockpit.

The Wave

Easter Compton, off junction 17 of the M5 • Daily 7am–8pm, surfing hours vary depending on daylight • £40, includes wetsuit and surfboard; lessons from £55 • ☎ 0333 016 4133, ⓦ thewave.com • Buses #411, #623 & #625 from the city centre drop off at Prospect Close, 500yds from the entrance

Bristol's surfing community received a major boost in 2019 with the opening of **The Wave**, an inland surfing complex northwest of the city. The centre's state-of-the-art technology produces up to a thousand waves an hour, particularly useful if you're learning the sport. Six different areas cater to all abilities of surfers and bodyboarders.

ARRIVAL AND DEPARTURE   BRISTOL

Bristol is the busiest **transport hub** in the South West: it has the region's biggest airport, a major train terminus and excellent bus links.

BY PLANE
Bristol Airport Bristol's international airport is at Lulsgate, 8 miles southwest of the city on the A38 (☎ 0871 334 4444, ⓦ bristolairport.co.uk); the Airport Flyer bus service runs to

and from Temple Meads and the Bus Station (#A1; every 10min; 30min; £7 single/£11 return). The airport also runs its own taxi and minibus service, Arrow Cars (☎ 01275 475000, ⓦ arrowcars.co.uk; around £30 to the city centre).

Destinations Aberdeen (6 weekly; 1hr 25min); Belfast (1–4 daily; 1hr 10min); Cork (daily; 1hr 20min); Dublin (4–7 daily; 1hr–1hr 15min); Edinburgh (1–5 daily; 1hr 10min); Glasgow (1–5 daily; 1hr 15min); Guernsey (1–2 daily; 1hr

5min–1hr 50min); Inverness (daily; 1hr 25min); Isle of Man (2 weekly; 55min); Jersey (daily; 1hr); Knock (3 weekly; 1hr 15min); Newcastle (1–3 daily; 1hr 5min).

BY TRAIN

Bristol Temple Meads is served by Great Western Railway (ⓦgwr.com) and is a 20min walk east of the city centre; buses #8, #9, #72 & #73 pass through the city centre, as does the m2 Metrobus. Alternatively, you can make use of the cycle-way into town or the river ferry (see page 116).

Bristol Parkway is in Stoke Gifford, 7 miles north of the city centre, off Junction 1 of the M32, and is much less convenient than Temple Meads; bus #73 runs into The Centre.

Destinations Regular services from: Bath (10–15min); Birmingham (1hr 25min); Bradford-on-Avon (25–35min); Bridgwater (45min); Cardiff (50min–1hr); Cheltenham (40min); Chippenham (25min); Exeter St David's (1hr 10min–1hr 30min); Gloucester (50min); London Paddington (1hr 40min–1hr 50min); Oxford (1hr 20min–1hr 40min); Plymouth (2–3hr); Portsmouth (2hr 30min); Reading (1hr 10min); Salisbury (1hr 10min–1hr 25min); Southampton (1hr 40min); Swindon (40min); Taunton (30min–1hr); Weston-super-Mare (25–35min); Weymouth (2hr 20min); Worcester (1hr 20min–1hr 35min); Yeovil (1hr 45min).

BY BUS

Bristol Bus Station is centrally located on Marlborough St and is the destination for National Express (ⓦnationalexpress. co.uk) services from London; Megabus (ⓦuk.megabus.com), whose departures invariably leave at antisocial hours, stops opposite the Colston Hall, off The Centre.

Destinations Bath (Mon–Sat every 20min, Sun every 30min; 50min–1hr); Birmingham (10 daily; 1hr 55min–2hr 55min); Camborne (daily; 6hr 20min); Cardiff (frequent; 1hr–1hr 25min); Coventry (daily; 3hr 55min); Exeter (hourly; 1hr 50min–2hr 30min); Glastonbury (every 30min; 1hr 30min); Leeds (6 daily; 5hr 10min–6hr 5min); London (frequent; 2hr 30min–3hr 5min); Manchester (6 daily; 4hr 35min–6hr 15min); Middlesbrough (4–5 daily; 7hr 35min–8hr 35min); Newcastle (4 daily; 8hr 35min–9hr 50min); Newquay (2 daily; 5hr 30min–6hr 15min); Nottingham (5 daily; 3hr 40min–5hr); Penzance (daily; 6hr 30min); Plymouth (hourly; 2hr 30min–3hr 45min); Redruth (2 daily; 6hr 5–6hr 45min); Rugby (daily; 4hr 5min–4hr 20min); Salisbury (hourly; 1hr 10min–1hr 25min); Sheffield (2 daily; 4hr 45min–5hr 55min); Sunderland (3 daily; 8hr 10min–9hr 10min); Swansea (11 daily; 2hr 5min–2hr 30min); Torquay (3 daily; 2hr 50min–3hr 45min); Wells (every 30min; 1hr 20min).

INFORMATION

Tourist information Bristol's Tourist Information Centre is in the E Shed on the Harbourside (daily 10am–5pm; ⓣ01179 929 9205, ⓦvisitbristol.co.uk) and provides bus timetables and cycling maps, sells City Sightseeing Bus and ferry tickets, and offers an accommodation booking service.

Useful websites Check out ⓦthebristolmag.co.uk (lifestyle and reviews) and ⓦwhatsonbristol.co.uk (events).

GETTING AROUND

Bristol is served by a comprehensive network of **buses**, with most stopping around The Centre (the name given to the busy intersection at the heart of the modern city) and Cabot Circus; conversely, local **train** services are infrequent and of only real use to suburban residents. The **ferry** is a nifty (and cheap) way of exploring the city's waterways and gives access to major sights such as M Shed and the SS *Great Britain*. **Driving** is fun if you like traffic jams, particularly around The Centre;

CITY TOURS

In addition to the recommended **tours** below, you can also download five **audio tours** from the Visit Bristol website (ⓦvisitbristol.co.uk), which explore the city's slave-trading past and literary connections, among others.

Bristol Packet ⓣ0117 926 8157, ⓦbristolpacket. co.uk. Cruises around the harbour (£6.75), through the Avon Gorge (£17.75) and along the river to Bath (£32). Check website for dates.

Bristol In-Sight ⓣ07422 963454, ⓦbristolinsight. co.uk. Hop-on, hop-off, open-top bus tour of the city's key sights, including the SS *Great Britain*, St Mary Redcliffe and the Clifton Suspension Bridge. Daily April–Oct; £15.50.

Haunted and Hidden Bristol ⓣ07766 258407, ⓦhauntedandhiddenbristol.co.uk. Spooky stories

of haunted inns, ghostly monks and other mysterious apparitions. Fri 8pm; £5.

Pirate Walks ⓣ07950 566483, ⓦpiratewalks. co.uk. Enthusiastic tours of Harbourside with Pete "The Pirate" Martin, covering the legend of Blackbeard, smuggling and Bristol's links with piracy. Sat & Sun 2pm; £12.50.

Walk Bristol ⓣ0117 968 4638, ⓦbristolwalks. co.uk. Two-hour guided walks, taking in either Bristol's highlights or the city's slave-trading past. March–Oct: Highlights Sat 11am, £6; Slave Trade Sun noon, £8.

2

THE BRISTOL AND BATH RAILWAY PATH

The UK's first off-road cycle route, the **Bristol and Bath Railway Path** (ⓦ bristolbathrailwaypath.org.uk) traces the former Midland Railway Line for 13 miles, cutting through the suburbs of Easton, Fishponds and Staple Hill before heading on past Warmley, Oldham Common, Bitton and Saltford. Sculptures by local artists line the route, and there are plenty of cafés and pubs along the way; short detours from the path lead to Willsbridge Valley Nature Reserve (ⓦ avonwildlifetrust.org.uk) and the restored Saltford Brass Mill (May–Oct second & fourth Sat of the month 10am–4pm; ⓦ tcsafety.co.uk). Moreover, it's a novel way of nipping between the two cities and is quite scenic in parts, particularly the final stretch, where it follows the River Avon as it meanders into Bath.

there are plenty of multi-storey car parks in central Bristol, though finding a place to park further afield, especially in Clifton, is notoriously difficult. The best way to see the city is by **bike** (Bristol is the UK's first Cycling City) or **on foot** – the major sights, perhaps with the exception of Clifton, are all within walking distance of each other.

BY BUS

Routes The majority of local services are run by First Group (see ⓦ firstgroup.com/bristol-bath-and-west for timetables and network maps); the most useful are the #8 and #9, which depart from Temple Meads and pass the city centre and Park Street on their way up to Clifton, and the m2 Metrobus (ⓦ metrobusbristol.com), with stops at Temple Meads, The Centre, Queen Square and SS *Great Britain*.

Travel cards and passes If you're going to be doing much travelling by bus, it makes sense to buy a FirstDay travel card (from £4.50). If travelling by train to Bristol, you can buy a PlusBus pass (ⓦ plusbus.info) at the same time as your train ticket, which gives you unlimited bus travel around Bristol from £4 a day.

Night buses At weekends, 11 services (12 on Sat) run hourly through the night, departing from The Centre.

BY FERRY

Bristol Ferry A daily ferry service (ⓣ 0117 927 3416, ⓦ bristolferry.com) connects the various parts of the Floating Harbour including Temple Meads, The Centre, SS *Great Britain* and numerous waterside pubs. Ferries leave every 20min between 9.55am and 6.15pm; buy tickets on board (from £1.80 single, £3 return; £6.60 all-day ticket).

BY CAR

Park & Ride Bristol has four Park & Ride locations that serve the city centre (ⓦ travelwest.info), with buses running from Long Ashton (15min), just off the A370 towards Weston-super-Mare; Portway (20min), just off the A4, near Junction 18 of the M4; Brislington (25min), just off the A4 towards Bath; and Lyde Green (30min), just off the A4174 towards Yate.

Parking There are large NCP car parks at Frogmore St and Nelson St, an underground car park at Millennium Square (convenient for Harbourside), plus a huge car park at Cabot Circus, linked to the city centre by a series of pedestrian bridges. Parking elsewhere, especially in Clifton, can be tricky (and expensive).

Taxis Reliable and reputable taxi firms include V Cars (ⓣ 0117 925 2626) and Yellow Cabs (ⓣ 0117 923 1515).

BY BIKE

Information See ⓦ bristol.gov.uk/streets-travel/cycling for information on cycling in the city, and ⓦ betterbybike.info/maps-and-rides for a range of downloadable route maps. You can stop by *Mud Dock* (see page 119) for repairs and a breather over a latte.

Bike rental Cycle the City, No.1 Harbourside, 1 Canon's Rd (Thurs–Sun 10am–5pm; ⓣ 07873 387167); Blackboy Hill Cycles, 180 Whiteladies Rd, Clifton (Mon–Fri 9am–6pm, Sat 9am–5.30pm, Sun 11am–4pm; ⓣ 0117 973 1420, ⓦ black-boy-cycles.co.uk). Yo Bikes (ⓦ yobike.com) operates an app-based rental scheme costing from £1/hr to £5/24hr. Bikes can be collected from, and returned to, designated parking spaces across the city.

ACCOMMODATION

With a few notable exceptions, quality **independent accommodation** in Bristol is surprisingly thin on the ground, and the emphasis at many of the big names is on **business** – although there are several, including the boutique Hotel du Vin chain, at which you'd feel equally at home as a tourist. Hotels in the **Old City** and on the **Harbourside** are ideally located for the majority of the city's sights, while the grand Georgian terraces around chic **Clifton Village** offer a different kind of stay. Note that

parking can be a problem, but most places can provide permits or offer discounts at a local car park.

THE OLD CITY AND AROUND
SEE MAP PAGE 90

Bristol Backpackers 17 St Stephen's St ⓣ 0117 925 7900, ⓦ bristolbackpackers.co.uk. Friendly, independent hostel with mixed and single-sex dorms, a decent kitchen and a bar that stays open late; the surrounding area can get noisy at night, though, especially at the weekend. Good discounts on both short- and long-term stays. Dorms £19

Bristol Harbour Hotel 55 Corn St ☎0117 203 4445, ⓦbristol-harbour-hotel.co.uk. Two former banks in an elegantly fronted building have been brilliantly converted into this Old City hotel and spa – it's on Corn Street, despite the name. Colourful rooms feature big beds, chaises longues and cut-glass decanters of free gin and sherry. The seafood grill is good, and there's more than a hint of speakeasy about the hotel's trendy Gold Bar. £125

★ **Brooks Guesthouse** St Nicholas St, entrance on Exchange Ave ☎0117 930 0066, ⓦbrooksguesthouse bristol.com. This charming boutique guesthouse, superbly located in the midst of bustling St Nicholas Market, was the first of its kind in Bristol when it opened in 2011. Compact rooms, done out in designer wallpaper and with natty little shutters, benefit from comfy beds and even comfier pillows; you can also stay in retro airstream trailers located on the roof (from £80). There's a good choice of organic breakfasts. £80

★ **Hotel du Vin Bristol City Centre** The Sugar House, Narrow Lewins Mead ☎0117 925 5577, ⓦhotelduvin. com. The city's best hotel is a stylish conversion of an eighteenth-century sugar factory, the last remaining one in Bristol. Contemporary decor (trademark *du Vin* dark woods and glinting chrome) is matched by modern comforts: hand-sprung mattresses, luxury linens, and a freestanding bath in every room. The plush Big Loft Suites (£234), some with private roof terrace, are stunners. The attached *Bistro du Vin* also happens to be one of the best places for fine dining in the Old City (see page 118). £109

Mercure Bristol Grand Broad St ☎0117 929 1645, ⓦmercure.accorhotels.com. Ornate Victorian hotel on historic Broad Street, set back from the road and lavishly designed in Venetian Quattrocento style. The crisp, modern rooms and funky public spaces are dotted with works from street-art gallery Upfest (see page 129). There's an indoor swimming pool, gym and spa. On-site car park. £118

Radisson Blu Broad Quay ☎0117 934 9500, ⓦradisson hotels.com. The city's tallest hotel, housed in a striking glass tower that dominates The Centre skyline. There's not that much difference between the rooms, so settle for a Standard; whichever one you chose, the floor-to-ceiling windows make the most of the spectacular views. Breakfast costs extra. £127

Rock & Bowl Motel 22 Nelson St ☎0117 325 1980. Basic, budget digs in a variety of dorm rooms (4 to 20 beds) and student accommodation-style doubles. Its location above The Lanes, a multi-purpose venue that is nominally a retro bowling alley, American diner and karaoke joint but also hosts live music and club nights, is a mixed blessing – the club doesn't close until 3am but you do get decent discounts on bowling and booths. Dorms £17

HARBOURSIDE
SEE MAP PAGE 94

The Bristol Hotel Prince St ☎0117 923 0333, ⓦdoyle collection.com. Deceptive hotel, with a Brutalist exterior that would have swept the board at architectural prize-givings in the former Soviet Bloc, but a swishly renovated interior that's surprisingly pleasant, its smart little rooms big on amenities. Its great location means it's probably worth paying extra for the rooms with harbour views. £98

Mercure Bristol Brigstow 5–7 Welsh Back ☎0117 929 1030, ⓦmercure.accorhotels.com. Rooms are bright but functional – this is another central Bristol hotel with the business traveller in mind – though the views along the eastern arm of the Floating Harbour are good and the location is difficult to fault: it rises directly over the restaurants and bars along Welsh Back, while the historical pubs of King Street are a few minutes' walk away and the buzzing Harbourside a minute or so more. £78

YHA Bristol 14 Narrow Quay ☎0800 191700, ⓦyha. org.uk. In a top location, occupying a refurbished grainstore right on the quayside, this relaxed hostel is almost as popular with families as it is with backpack-toting twenty-somethings. Most dorms have four beds, and there's a chilled-out café-bar attached. Dorms £15, doubles £49

PARK STREET AND THE WEST END
SEE MAP PAGE 94

The Berkeley Square 15 Berkeley Square ☎0117 925 4000, ⓦcliftonhotels.com. Set on a regal-looking square, just yards from the indie boutiques of Park Street, this "art hotel" in a smart Georgian building has two permanent exhibition spaces and rotating works displayed on each floor. Rooms are smallish but well appointed – avoid those near the noisy basement bar. Breakfast costs extra. £108

Bristol Marriott Royal Hotel College Green ☎0117 925 5100, ⓦmarriott.co.uk. Overlooking College Green and right next to Bristol Cathedral, this Italianate-style Victorian hotel is by far the more attractive of the city's two *Marriotts* (the other is at the northeast end of Castle Park), with spacious rooms, a bar and grill, and a lovely swimming pool. £127

CLIFTON
SEE MAP PAGE 108

★ **9 Princes' Buildings** 9 Princes' Buildings ☎0117 973 4615, ⓦ9princesbuildings.co.uk. A short walk from the Suspension Bridge and handily located for the pubs around Sion Hill, this five-storey Georgian B&B, lovingly cared for by its easy-going owners, enjoys a grand vista over the Gorge from its antique-filled rooms. Great breakfasts, too. £115

Clifton House 4 Tyndalls Park Rd, Clifton ☎0117 973 5407, ⓦcliftonhousebristol.com. Victorian villa in a handy location, down a quiet side street off the bottom of Whiteladies Road. Rooms vary in decor and size across the price ranges, so it probably pays to upgrade from a standard. £75

2

Hotel du Vin Bristol Avon Gorge Sion Hill ☎0117 973 8955, �🌐hotelduvin.com. Historic hotel, originally a spa fed by the spring waters of nearby Hotwells, given a Hotel du Vin revamp in 2018. Rooms are decorated in more contemporary version of the classic Hotel du Vin style, but what really counts are the views: close-up vistas of Brunel's mighty Suspension Bridge. If anything, they're even better from the terrace of the White Lion Bar (see page 124). Breakfast costs extra. **£99**

★ **Number Thirty Eight** 38 Upper Belgrave Rd, Clifton ☎0117 946 6905, ⍵number38clifton.com. Swish Georgian townhouse B&B, overlooking the Downs at the top of Clifton and offering 12 elegantly furnished rooms, most of them with enormous, deeply comfortable beds. The communal sitting rooms are stylishly done out, complete with vivid artwork, and there's an appealing summer terrace. No under-12s. **£115**

The Rodney 4 Rodney Place ☎0117 973 5422, ⍵clifton hotels.com. Occupying a Georgian terrace in the heart of Clifton Village, this hotel's rooms lack the historical grandeur of the exterior but have all the mod cons. Informed staff are extremely helpful. Sunday-night stays are a bargain. **£84**

Victoria Square 29–30 Victoria Square ☎0117 973 9058, ⍵victoriasquarehotel.co.uk. Some of the rooms in this Georgian hotel are on the petite side, though the interiors are subtly elegant and the location is great, on a leafy square near Clifton Village. **£79**

EAST BRISTOL
SEE MAP PAGE 112

Artist Residence 28 Portland Square, St Pauls ☎0203 019 8623, ⍵artistresidence.co.uk. Located in a former boot factory, this could be the best thing that's happened to St Pauls in a generation. Signs that it could kickstart a proper neighbourhood revival are strong, with the owners aiming to establish the residence as a neighbourhood hangout, with a coffee shop, kitchen, bar and event space. There's a Shoe Box, Boot Room and Factory Loft among the industrial-styled rooms and suites. **£75**

EATING

Eating out is one of the real pleasures of a visit to Bristol. There's a strong **café culture** that very much reflects the local, relaxed way of life, and watching the world go by over a flat white on the **Harbourside** or in one of the cosy cafés in **Clifton Village** is as quintessentially a Bristol experience as poking around the SS *Great Britain*. **Park Street**, too, has a number of good coffee shops, which provide a particularly welcome respite from scaling the city's steepest shopping street. It's the **restaurants**, though, that really deliver. Their range, scope and quality are easily the best in the South West, and with the city at the forefront of all things eco, it's no surprise that many of its menus are built around fresh **local**, **seasonal produce**.

THE OLD CITY AND AROUND
SEE MAP PAGE 90

CAFÉS AND SNACK BARS

Full Court Press 59 Broad St ☎07853 521955, ⍵fcp. coffee.com. The select menu of superb speciality coffees at this dinky joint near St Nick's Market has made it an instant hit with local connoisseurs. Try your single coffee served four ways. Mon–Fri 7.30am–5pm, Sat 9am–5pm, Sun 10am–4pm.

Pieminister The Glass Arcade, St Nicholas Market ☎0117 302 0070, ⍵pieminister.co.uk. The St Nick's outlet of this Bristol institution (see page 122) does a roaring lunchtime trade, with office workers and market browsers tucking into one of their dozen or so heart-warming pies (£5.95) around a couple of tile-topped benches. There's a third branch at the harbour, on Broad Quay. Mon–Sat 10am–5pm.

★ **Source** 1–3 Exchange Ave ☎0117 927 2998, ⍵source-food.co.uk. This beautiful Bath-stone building on the fringes of St Nick's Market houses a great concept: an airy, high-ceilinged café that uses ultra-fresh ingredients from the adjoining deli/butchers/fishmongers. Look out for salt-marsh lamb, a tender meat with a distinctly sweet flavour that's derived from their diet of low-tide grasses in the Severn Estuary. Lunchtime mains around £11. Mon–Sat 8am–3.30pm.

RESTAURANTS

★ **Bistro du Vin** Hotel du Vin, The Sugar House, Narrow Lewins Mead ☎08447 364252, ⍵hotelduvin. com. French bistro-style dining in the elegant surroundings of a former sugar factory, using good seasonal West Country produce in its Modern European menu; mains from £12.50. Wines from the extensive list are stored in the factory's old engine house. Mon–Sat noon–2.30pm & 5.30–10pm, Fri & Sat till 10.30pm, Sun 12.30–4pm & 6–9.30pm.

El Puerto 57 Prince St ☎0117 925 6014, ⍵el-puerto. co.uk. Authentic tapas bar, expertly covering all the essentials, as well as some more unusual dishes, such as *higaditos con cebolla* (pan-fried chicken liver with onions) and *alubias salteados* (plump alubia beans in a creamy tomato sauce); prices range between £4.45 and £7.95. Interesting Spanish wine list. Popular live flamenco on the first Sun of the month. Daily noon–midnight.

The Ox 43 Corn St ☎0117 922 1001, ⍵theoxbristol. com. Set in the basement of the Commercial Rooms, this upmarket steak restaurant has the vintage vibe of its sister bar *Hyde & Co* up on The Triangle (see page 123), but there's nothing old-fashioned about the cooking: roast bone marrow smeared on sourdough toast, a tempting charcuterie board and a range of deliciously smoky steaks, from the 6oz rump (£12.50) to a monster 30oz T-bone for two (£72). Mon–Fri noon–2.30pm & 5–10.30pm, Sat 5–10.30pm, Sun noon–4pm.

Urban Tandoor 13 Small St ☎ 0117 929 9222, ⓦ urbantandoor.com. Popular, classy Indian restaurant whose menu of authentic, expertly cooked dishes trots around the Subcontinent, taking in king prawn moilee, Goan fish curry and saag chicken, plus tender pieces from the Tandoor. Mains from £9.25. Daily 5–10.45pm, Sun till 9.45pm.

HARBOURSIDE
SEE MAPS PAGES 88 AND 94

CAFÉS AND SNACK BARS

★ **Lockside** 1 Brunel Lock Rd ☎ 0117 925 5800, ⓦ lockside.net. It's easy to miss this contemporary little diner, wedged under the Cumberland Basin flyover, although the excellent, generous breakfasts – of which there are over two dozen varieties – should ensure that you don't. Lunchtime is equally buzzing, with regulars cramming the circular tables for dishes such as chicken schnitzel with bubble and squeak (£12.75) and pan-fried calamari and chorizo salad (£11.95); offbeat desserts include a bowl of Maltesers. Daily 7am–4pm, Sat from 8am, Sun from 9am.

Mud Dock 40 The Grove ☎ 0117 934 9734, ⓦ mud-dock. com. A bike-shop-café combo sounds odd until you see it in action – the large, open dining space makes a chic setting for satisfying meals (ploughman's, burgers, blackboard specials; mains from £9), while pedal-pushers can get their bike checked at the downstairs Cycleworks. The south-facing terrace, with great views over the Floating Harbour, is a sunny-day hotspot. Daily 10am–10pm, Sat from 9am.

No.1 Harbourside 1 Canon's Rd ☎ 0117 929 1100, ⓦ no1harbourside.co.uk. This relaxed, great-value café-bar from the guys behind Canteen (see page 121) has established itself as a real Harbourside hub. The short but satisfying menu includes unusual dishes such as Cornish mussels in cider cream (£12.50); things really get going in the evening with a strong programme of events. Live music Fri & Sat. Mon & Tues 11am–11pm, Wed & Thurs 11am–midnight, Fri & Sat 10am–1am, Sun 10am–11pm; food served Mon–Fri noon–3pm & 5–9pm (Fri till 10pm), Sat 11am–10pm, Sun noon–5pm.

★ **Watershed** 1 Canons Rd ☎ 0117 927 5101, ⓦ watershed.co.uk. Cool café-bar in a respected arts complex at the head of the Floating Harbour, as great for people-watching on the harbourfront below as it is for grabbing a post-flick drink. Mon–Fri 9.30am–11pm, Sat 10am–11.30pm, Sun 10am–10.30pm; main meals served noon–9.30pm.

RESTAURANTS

★ **BOX-E** Unit 10, Cargo 1, Wapping Wharf ☎ 0117 329 6226, ⓦ flowbristol.co.uk. There are just 18 seats at this old shipping container in the buzzing harbourside hub of Wapping Wharf. Be sure to book in advance, so as not to miss the epicurean adventure that is Elliott Lidstone's short

BEST PLACE FOR...
Breakfast *Lockside* (see below)
Café lunches *Primrose Café & Bistro* (see page 120)
Close-up cooking *BOX-E* (see below)
Confirmed carnivores *The Ox* (see page 118)
Historic surroundings *Bistro du Vin* (see page 118)
Local legends *Pieminister* (see page 122)
Poolside dining *Lido* (see page 120)
Treating yourself *Casamia* (see below)
Veggies *Flow* (see page 121)

menu of beautifully balanced dishes (mains from £14). Tues 5.30–9.30pm, Wed–Sat noon–2.30pm & 5.30–9.30pm.

★ **Casamia** The General, Lower Guinea St ☎ 0117 959 2884, ⓦ casamiarestaurant.co.uk. Since coaxing his parents' trattoria in Westbury-upon-Trym into a select Modern Italian diner, the highly talented Peter Sanchez-Iglesias has been voted Gordon Ramsey's favourite restaurant in the UK and won his first Michelin star. Now in a former hospital on Bristol's waterfront, he continues to conjure up well-sourced seasonal dishes that sound simple – "parmesan", "lamb", "lemon" – but are anything but, their beautiful cooking often playing on all the senses. Try the Four Course tasting menu (£48) or push the boat out for the Full Menu (£118) extravaganza. Wed 6.15–9.30pm, Thurs–Sat noon–1.30pm & 6.15–9.30pm, also one Sun a month noon–1.30pm.

The Glass Boat Welsh Back ☎ 0117 332 3971, ⓦ glassboat. co.uk. This vintage barge, moored near Bristol Bridge, was the city's first upmarket floating restaurant. It's still going strong, thanks to a stylish makeover and a continued dedication to good Mediterranean cooking, particularly fish dishes. Mains, such as Cornish hake and smoked roe, cost around £18.50. Mon–Sat noon–2.45pm & 5.30–9.45pm, Sun noon–4pm.

Riverstation The Grove ☎ 0117 914 4434, ⓦ riverstation.co.uk. Two-storey former river-police station, with light bites at the relaxed ground-floor bar and kitchen and more refined dining upstairs, with mains such as fillet of Cornish hake and char-grilled pork skirt from £15.50. Bar Mon–Sat 10am–11pm, Sun till 8pm (food served Mon–Sat 10am–4pm & 5–10pm, Sun till 7pm); restaurant Mon–Sat noon–3pm & 6–10pm, Sun noon–3pm.

Severnshed The Grove ☎ 0117 925 1212, ⓦ severnshedrestaurant.co.uk. Housed in a former Brunel transit shed that dates to around 1865, with one half a restaurant serving grilled flatbread, hot sandwiches and a variety of mains (from £10), and the other a bar. Wall-length windows look out over the Floating Harbour. Mon–Thurs noon–11pm, Fri noon–1am, Sat 9am–1am, Sun 9am–11pm.

Three Brothers Welsh Back ☎ 0117 927 7050, ⓦ threebrothersburgers.co.uk. Winning combination of quality

2

burgers and craft beer. Their 28-day-aged Herefordshire beef patty in a brioche bun with smokey chilli is hard to beat (burgers from £6.25), but they also do other diner classics such as hot dogs and Philly cheese steaks. Mon–Thurs noon–11pm, Fri 11.45am–11pm, Sat 11.30am–11pm, Sun 11.30am–8pm.

PARK STREET AND THE WEST END
SEE MAP PAGE 94

CAFÉS
Bowl of Plenty 40A Park St ☎0117 908 5035, ⊚bowlof plenty.co.uk. Hearty, home-cooked soups and sandwiches in a friendly, no-frills café tucked down an alley halfway up Park Street; there's normally a good range of toasties, and most of the produce is organic. It's part of the Bristol Folk House (⊚bristolfolkhouse.co.uk), which hosts live music and runs workshops on everything from yogic medicine to hula hooping for beginners. Mon–Thurs 9am–8.30pm, Fri & Sat 9am–4pm.

Rocotillos 1 Queens Row, Triangle South ☎0117 929 7207. The huge breakfasts at this authentically furbished 1950s-style American diner put the "full" in "full English" and are reckoned by some to be the best in Bristol. But it's the legendary ice-cream milkshakes that really make this a must-visit: creamy concoctions that are big enough to share and come in a bounty of flavours, from peanut butter to Crunchie Bar and honey (from £4.25). Also club sandwiches, hot dogs and good old-fashioned, proper beefburgers. Mon–Sat 8am–6pm, Sun 10am–5pm.

RESTAURANT
The Florist 69 Park St ☎0117 945 1950, ⊚theflorist. com. Beautiful rambling Georgian building, decorated in floral wallpaper and festooned with bucketloads of flowers. Colourful, healthy dishes – steamed sea bass, teriyaki lamb cutlets – are influenced by Asia and the Mediterranean (mains from £10.50). There's also a great cocktail bar (its "Ale Anthology" stretches to nearly 90 pages), with live music and DJs at the weekend. Mon–Thurs 4.30pm–midnight, Fri & Sat 4.30pm–1am.

CLIFTON AND AROUND
SEE MAPS PAGES 88 AND 108

CAFÉ
★ **Primrose Café & Bistro** Boyces Ave, Clifton Village ☎0117 946 6577, ⊚primrosecafe.co.uk. Bustling, homely café at the entrance of Clifton Arcade, known for its excellent breakfasts but really a top spot at any time of day, especially if the sun is shining. Grab a brunch of bubble and squeak or one of the croques, or a tasty lunch including fishfinger stack, Cornish crab rarebit, halloumi burger and salads. Good range of teas and organic fruit juices. Mon–Sat 9am–5pm, Sun 9.30am–4pm.

RESTAURANTS
Al Bacio 95 Queens Rd ☎0117 973 9734, ⊚albaciobristol. co.uk. Slick, contemporary Italian with a warm and welcoming atmosphere. It'll take time to pick your way through the comprehensive menu, but you can't go far wrong with black-ink risotto with squid, lamb cutlets in saffron sauce or lobster linguine. Pasta dishes from £9.95. Mon–Thurs noon–2.30pm & 5.30–11pm, Fri & Sat noon–11pm, Sun noon–10pm.

The Cowshed 44–46 Whiteladies Rd, Clifton ☎0117 973 3550, ⊚thecowshedbristol.com. A proper temple to the tenderloin: *The Cowshed* is serious about its steak, sourcing quality cuts from local suppliers and dry-ageing them for thirty days. Take a deep breath and tackle the 900g T-bone, or order Steak on Stone, brought uncooked to your table so you can sear it yourself (from £22). Mon–Sat 8–11.30am, noon–3pm & 6–10pm, Sun 8–11am, noon–5pm & 6.30–8.30pm.

Bulrush 21 Cotham Road South ☎0117 329 0990, ⊚bulrushrestaurant.co.uk. You might not guess it from the relaxed setting and simple whitewashed walls, but chef-proprietor George Livesey has won a Michelin star for his exquisite dishes at this lovely little restaurant in Cotham. Try BBQ broccoli, highland grouse or pig's trotter and gooseberry (mains from £17.50) or indulge in the fantastic tasting menu (from £55). Tues & Wed 6.30–8.30pm Thurs–Sat 12.30–3pm & 6.30–8.30pm.

★ **Lido** Oakfield Place, Clifton; restaurant entrance on Southleigh Rd ☎0117 933 9533, ⊚lidobristol.com. Set-piece venue given a stylish new lease of life as a restaurant/bar and pool/spa complex. The glass-walled restaurant overlooks the heated outdoor pool, which makes dining on dishes like wood-roast venison and Basque fish stew (from £17), while others exercise, a deliciously guilty affair. Restaurant daily noon–3pm & 6–10pm; poolside tapas bar Mon–Sat 8am–11pm, Sun 9am–10.30pm.

Planet Pizza 187 Gloucester Rd ☎0117 944 4717, ⊚planetpizza.co.uk. Back in its old haunt on Gloucester Road and still serving a range of great, planet-christened pizzas: "Mars" (pepperoni, sausage and red onion) and the "Moon" (gorgonzola, feta and ricotta) neatly reflect their names; luckily, "Uranus" does not (it's chicken and smokey bacon). Twelve-inch pizzas average around £12.50, nine-inch £7.95; daytime deal of any nine-inch pizza for a fiver. Tasty salads, too. Daily 11am–11pm.

The Spiny Lobster 128 Whiteladies Rd ☎0117 973 7384, ⊚thespinylobster.co.uk. A rich, wonderful smell greets you at this upmarket but informal restaurant, owned by celeb chef Mitch Tonks and serving pricey but perfectly cooked fresh fish and seafood – the kitchen (and the adjoining fishmongers) get their delivery direct from the boats at Brixham each morning. Starters include fat scallops roasted with garlic butter (£12.50), while for mains it's worth trying the catch of the day cooked over a charcoal grill, a speciality of the restaurant that lends dishes like monkfish (£24) a lovely smoky Mediterranean flavour. Tues–Sat noon–2.30pm & 6–10pm.

GLOUCESTER ROAD AND AROUND
SEE MAP PAGE 121

CAFÉS
La Ruca 89 Gloucester Rd ☎0117 944 6810, ⓦlaruca. co.uk. Cosy Latin American organic health-food shop with a warm and welcoming upstairs café. Good-value home-cooked food includes *chimichangas*, bean enchiladas, hummus-topped spinach tortilla and other simple but tasty delights (mains around £5.50). Mon–Sat 9am–5.30pm.

RESTAURANTS
Greens' Dining Room 25 Zetland Rd ☎0117 924 6437, ⓦgreensbristol.co.uk. Elegant eatery at the bottom of Zetland Road, with a two-course lunch and dinner menus that consistently deliver cooking of the highest order. Expect an interesting choice of dishes such as octopus and *salsa macha* and lamb and apricot stew (lunch £14.50, dinner £18.50). Vegetarian menu also available. Mon–Thurs 6–9pm, Fri noon–2.30pm & 6–10pm, Sat & Sun noon–10pm.

★ **Koocha** 10 Zetland Rd, Redland ☎0117 924 1301, ⓦkoochamezzebar.com. Located at the junction of Zetland and Cranbook roads – *koocha* means "corner" in Persian – this homely restaurant serves up generous portions of delicious vegan mezze dishes (£3.50, 4 for £12), plus stews and kebabs. Daily noon–10pm.

Turtle Bay 221–223 Cheltenham Rd ☎0117 923 29532, ⓦturtlebay.co.uk. Colourful Caribbean restaurant that takes a more packaged approach to Bristol's West Indian heritage than the independent Jamaican place that used to occupy these premises. The food is good, though, and includes classic dishes like jerk chicken, babybacks (slow-roast pork ribs) and goat curry. Daily 10am–11.30pm, Thurs till 12.30am, Fri & Sat till 1.30am.

EAST BRISTOL
SEE MAP PAGE 112

CAFÉS
Canteen 80 Stokes Croft ☎0117 923 2017, ⓦcanteen bristol.co.uk. Overlooked by Banksy's famous *Mild, Mild West* mural, a drab 1960s office block now accommodates this incredibly popular artsy collective-style bar. Take a seat at a graffitied table for a coffee or a pint, or try something from the good, cheap menu that includes dishes such as roasted broccoli jambalaya (dishes from £6). Live music from 9.30pm most nights (from 4pm on Sun). Mon–Thurs 10am–midnight, Fri 10am–1am, Sat 11am–1am, Sun 11am–11pm.

Poco 45 Jamaica St, Stokes Croft ☎0117 922 2333, ⓦeatpoco.co.uk. Ethically conscious tapas bar serving

Moroccan and Spanish-influenced dishes with one foot firmly in Britain (tapas include Portland crab toast and Isle of Wight padron peppers; from £3). There's a popular brunch menu, plus lunch of salads and sourdough sandwiches (from £4.70). Mon–Fri 9am–midnight, Sat 10am–midnight, Sun from 10am–11pm

RESTAURANTS
Bianchis 1–3 York Rd, Montpelier ☎0117 329 4100, ⓦbianchisrestaurant.co.uk. This light-filled restaurant brings a touch of the Italian trattoria to East Bristol. Run by the cousins behind Cotham's ever-popular *Pasta Loco*, the food here has the same home-cooked quality at its heart but with more refined flair. Set lunches start at £15 for two courses; a la carte mains (from £13.50) range from artichoke stuffed with pine nuts to braised quail with pancetta. Mon & Tues 6–10pm, Wed–Sat noon–2pm & 6–10pm.

★ **Flow** 8A Haymarket Walk ☎0117 329 6226, ⓦflowbristol.co.uk. Chef-proprietor Jen Williams' ever-changing menus of sharing plates focus on incredible-

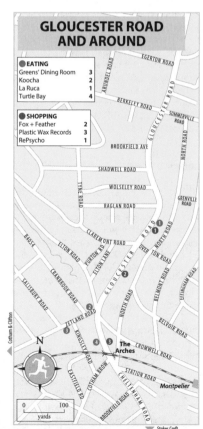

GLOUCESTER ROAD AND AROUND

● EATING	
Greens' Dining Room	3
Koocha	2
La Ruca	1
Turtle Bay	4

● SHOPPING	
Fox + Feather	2
Plastic Wax Records	3
RePsycho	1

2

looking (and even better-tasting) vegetarian dishes, using the best seasonal local ingredients but taking inspiration from further afield. Choose chive dumplings, chilli beet fava beans or halloumi with sticky dates. Or, with dishes costing from just £2.25, try all three. Wed–Sat 6–11pm.

★ **Pieminister** 24 Stokes Croft ☎ 0117 942 3322, ⓦ pieminister.co.uk. Headquarters of the Bristol-based pie empire that has rapidly been making their goody-filled pastries a lifestyle choice. Fresh, home-made pies (from £5.95) include Chicken of Aragon (with bacon and tarragon) and Saag Pie-Neer (pea, paneer, spinach and potato). Make it a meal by adding minted mushy peas, crispy shallots and a dollop of mash, then drench it all in rich gravy. There's also a branch on Broad Quay and a stall at St Nick's Market (see page 118). Daily 11.30am–10pm, Fri & Sat till 11pm, Sun till 9.30pm.

SOUTH BRISTOL
SEE MAPS PAGES 88 AND 112

CAFÉ
Lounge 227–231 North St, Southville ☎ 0117 963 7340, ⓦ thelounges.co.uk. The original *Lounge* (there are five others in Bristol, including one on Gloucester Road) is one of the mellowest joints around. It's pitched just right for trendy Southville, acting as a relaxed, family-friendly meeting place during the day and a chilled-out drinking destination come nightfall. Food is fairly classic – panini, wraps, salads and burgers, plus a decent range of tapas – though they also serve up a selection of Deep South-inspired mains such as jambalaya and beef chilli (mains from £7.95). Perfect weekend-brunch fodder. Daily 9am–11pm.

RESTAURANTS
★ **Birch** 47 Raleigh Rd, Southville ☎ 0117 902 8326,

ⓦ birchbristol.co. Bijou neighbourhood restaurant, simply set out and serving passionately cooked West Country produce. The superb seasonal menu might take in anything from guinea fowl to cauliflower fritters but will always include their signature braised pork belly with burnt apple purée and black pudding (£13.50). The Sunday roast is top notch. Tues–Fri 6–10pm, Sat noon–3pm & 6–10pm, Sun noon–4pm.

Bocabar Paintworks, Bath Rd, Arnos Vale ☎ 0117 972 8838, ⓦ bocabar.co.uk. Set in a huge, open warehouse at the heart of the Paintworks creative quarter, this art-filled café-restaurant and bar (see page 124) has a solid reputation for relaxed lunches and snazzy pizzas – authentic thin-crust beauties, nearly thirty to choose from (from £9.95), all made on site with Italian dough and stone-baked to perfection. Daily 9.30am–11pm, Fri & Sat till 1am (no entry after midnight), Sunday till 10.30pm.

Soukitchen 277 North St, Southville ☎ 0117 966 6880, ⓦ soukitchen.co.uk. Fairly stark decor, but the food does the talking at this incredibly successful merging of Middle Eastern and North African dishes, with a delicious range of hot and cold mezze (from £4.10) as well as more substantial mains that wander around Turkey (stuffed baked aubergine; £12.95) and Iran (*ghalieh mahi* fish curry; £13.95) among others. Mon & Tues 5.30pm–late, Wed–Fri noon–2.30pm & 5.30pm–late, Sat 10am–2.30pm & 5.30pm–late, Sun 10am–2.30pm.

Thali 12 York Rd, Montpelier ☎ 0117 942 6687, ⓦ the thalirestaurant.co.uk. Born in the fields of Glastonbury and the Big Chill, this eco-conscious concept first opened in Bristol in 1999. This Montpelier branch – there's another one in Easton – has the trademark splashes of deep-pink decor and range of tasty *thalis*, a balanced selection of dishes served on a stainless-steel platter (from £8.95), plus veggie dishes from South India. Daily 5–10pm, Sat & Sun from noon.

DRINKING

Bristol's repertoire of drinking dens is almost as varied as its restaurants: traditional **pubs**, most obviously around the Old City; cool **cocktail bars**, particularly up Park Street; and well-worn **cider houses**, spread throughout. Most areas are welcoming and relaxed, though The Centre is perhaps best avoided late at night, when worse-for-wear revellers descend on the area's taxi ranks. Many pubs and bars feature **live music**, and several of the latter host **club nights** throughout the week (see page 125).

THE OLD CITY AND AROUND
SEE MAP PAGE 90
The Milk Thistle Quay Head House, Colston Ave ☎ 0117 929 4429, ⓦ milkthistlebristol.com. Knock on the large wooden door (there's no sign) and enter a world of wood-panelled rooms and stiff leather couches, lifted straight out of a gentlemen's club in Mayfair. Friendly staff serve up top-quality cocktails – either from the lengthy list or to order – in

a setting that's as equally quirky yet relaxed as their sister establishment *Hyde & Co* up on The Triangle (see page 123). Mon–Thurs 5pm–1am, Fri 5pm–3am, Sat 6pm–3am.

The Rummer Hotel All Saints Lane ☎ 0117 929 0111, ⓦ therummer.co.uk. Historic but relaxed place, with sinking Chesterfields set around a roaring fire and an enclosed medieval bar that heaves with the weight of over four hundred spirits, over a quarter of them (unsurprisingly) rums. Book a gin tasting (Fri & Sat) to try some of the output from their own micro-distillery, which also makes vodkas and Aquavits. Mon–Thurs 10am–11pm, Fri 10am–midnight, Sat 11am–midnight, Sun noon–6pm.

Small Bar 31 King St ⓦ smallbarbristol.com. Riding the crest of Bristol's craft-beer craze, *Small Bar* stocks a superb selection of beers from the best independent breweries in the region. It's a mellow vibe, with a few table-topped barrels and bearded bartenders serving over thirty beers on tap. There's also over a hundred bottled varieties – from reds and stouts to sours and saissons. Daily noon–12.30am, Thurs–Sat till 1am, Sun till midnight.

Zerodegrees 53 Colston St ☎0117 925 2706, ⓦzerodegrees.co.uk. Huge stainless-steel vats take centre stage at this industrial-chic microbrewery at the top of Christmas Steps, which produces its own crisp pilsner, black lager, wheat beer, mango beer and vegan-friendly pale ale. Tables are arranged over a number of terraces, most looking down over the vast, very open central space – it's normally buzzing in here, but when it's quiet, it feels *really* quiet. Daily noon–1am, Sun till 11pm.

TEMPLE
SEE MAP 94

King's Head 60 Victoria St ☎0117 927 7860. Snug old pub, squished into a row of shops that partly hide Temple Church – it's very narrow, and there can't be room for much more than a dozen or so people in here at any one time. The ornate interior is modelled on an old Bristol tramcar, prints of which adorn the walls. The bar is equally decorative; you can get draught lagers and ciders, but it's more of a cask-ale kind of place, with Doom Bar and Betty Stoggs on tap. Daily 11.30am–midnight, Sat & Sun from noon.

HARBOURSIDE
SEE MAP 94

The Apple Welsh Back ☎0117 925 3500, ⓦapplecider. co.uk. No prizes for guessing what this converted Dutch barge specializes in, though you may be taken aback by the range: around forty ciders, perries and other alcoholic, apple-related drinks, from cocktails to brandies. Food is simple but unusual – build-your-own cheesy chips, from seven varieties of cheese and nine different sauces. Daily noon–midnight, Sun till 10.30pm.

Grain Barge Mardyke Wharf, Hotwell Rd ☎0117 929 9347, ⓦgrainbarge.com. Floating bar and restaurant near the mouth of the harbour, with a tranquil ambience and a dozen craft beers and real ales, half of them brewed at the Bristol Beer Factory just south of the river. Occasional exhibitions and live music. Daily 10am–11pm, Thurs–Sat till 11.30pm.

The Orchard 12 Hanover Place ☎07405 360994. This dinky former CAMRA National Cider Pub of the Year, tucked behind some dockyards on Spike Island, punches well above its weight, with over twenty ciders, including Black Rat, Wilkins and Hecks. There are Orchard Rolls (ham and chorizo salad, roasted pepper and hummus) to soak up the cider. Live music three or four times a week. Daily noon–11pm, Fri & Sat from 11am.

PARK STREET AND THE WEST END
SEE MAP 94

Browns 38 Queen's Rd ☎0117 930 4777, ⓦbrowns-restaurants.com. Spacious and relaxed place for an early

WHAT'S YOUR TIPPLE?

Cider *Coronation Tap* (see below)
Cocktails *Hyde & Co* (see below)
Craft beer *Small Bar* (see page 122)
Home brew *Zerodegrees* (see below)
Real ale *Portcullis* (see page 124)
Rum *The Rummer* (see page 122)

evening drink, housed in the Venetian-style former university refectory – some summer nights, with the squadron of ceiling fans whirring in unison and the piano player tinkling the ivories, it can feel like you've stepped into a Colonial bar at the height of the Empire. Plenty of choice on the drinks front, with over 25 wines and champagnes by the glass, the usual lagers on tap and a long list of very moreish cocktails. Daily 9am–11pm, Fri & Sat till midnight, Sun till 10pm.

★ **Hyde & Co** 2 The Basement, Upper Byron Place ☎0117 929 7007, ⓦhydeand.co. Stylish speakeasy – look for the bowler-hat sign next to the unmarked black door – with a mature but mellow ambience, just yards from The Triangle but feeling a world away. Moody lighting, tassel-fringed lampshades and dapper bar staff done up in 1920s vintage attire lend the place a Prohibition vibe, as do the classic (quality) American cocktails, from sours, swizzles and fizzes to highballs, juleps and smashes. Tues–Sun 6pm–late.

Red Light 1 Unity St ☎0117 929 1453. This trendy basement bar is hidden away near The Centre, with only a lit-up payphone – lift the receiver and they'll buzz you in – in front of a graffiti-covered door to show that you're in the right vicinity. Downstairs, bartenders in braces serve punchy cocktails in a speakeasy-style atmosphere. Mon–Thurs 7pm–1am, Fri & Sat 7pm–3am.

CLIFTON AND AROUND
SEE MAP PAGE 108

★ **The Coronation Tap** 8 Sion Place, Clifton ☎0117 973 9617, ⓦthecoronationtap.com. A legend in its own (long) lifetime, *The Cori Tap* is a proper cider house, producing its own Exhibition "apple juice", which is sold by the half-pint only, and stocking a wide range of locally produced ciders, from still to sparkling, clear to cloudy. Excellent live music saw it shortlisted for UK Music Pub of the Year three years running. Daily 5.30–11pm, Sat & Sun from 7pm.

Her Majesty's Secret Service 1 Whiteladies Gate, Whiteladies Road ☎0117 973 3926, ⓦhmssbristol. com. A gentleman's club meets the Cold War in this tongue-in-cheek bar that's a homage to British espionage. Old passports double as the cocktail list, and the decor is a mix of Winston Churchill paintings, Union Jack cushions and lots of references to James Bond. Mon–Thurs 4.30pm–midnight, Fri & Sat 4.30pm–1am.

Kinkajou 52 Upper Belgrave Rd, Clifton ☎0117 312 0086, ⓦkinkajoubar.co.uk. Sophisticated, darkly atmospheric basement-bar that reflects the characteristics of its namesake animal, a sociable, nocturnal creature. Expect quality cocktails from the highly knowledgeable bartenders. Tues & Wed 7pm–1am, Thurs & Sun 7pm–2am, Fri & Sat 6pm–2am.

Portcullis 3 Wellington Terrace, Sion Hill, Clifton ☏0117 973 0270. A CAMRA favourite, this tiny pub, wedged into a graceful terrace on swanky Sion Hill, is a bastion of real ales in Clifton, with up to nine on tap at any one time, including – as a Dawkins pub – Bristol Best and The Projectionist. The friendly landlords hold Monday-night Curry Nights and regular beer festivals. Mon–Fri 4.30–11pm, Sat noon–11pm, Sun noon–10.30pm.

White Lion Bar Hotel du Vin Bristol Avon Gorge, Sion Hill, Clifton ☏0117 973 8955, ⦿theavongorge.com. Located on the very edge of the Avon Gorge, this modern bar draws in the crowds thanks to the magnificent views from its expansive terrace, where it feels like you're almost sitting underneath the Suspension Bridge; it's a spectacular spot on a sunny day. Daily noon–11pm, Sun till 10.30pm.

EAST BRISTOL
SEE MAP PAGE 112

Cosies 34 Portland Square, St Pauls ☏0117 923 2886. Going strong for over thirty years, this bunker-esque basement bar comes into its own at night, when the pews quickly fill with drinkers who drop by for the intimate atmosphere or the top-drawer DJs spinning mostly hip-hop, drum'n'bass and dubstep. Wed 4pm–2am, Thurs & Fri 4pm–3.30am, Sat & Sun 10pm–3.30am.

SOUTH BRISTOL
SEE MAP PAGE 88

Bocabar Paintworks, Bath Rd, Arnos Vale ☏0117 972 8838, ⦿bocabar.co.uk. Breezy, easy-going warehouse hangout in the self-styled Paintworks creative quarter, which doubles as a café-restaurant (see page 122). Melt into a comfy sofa with one of their ever-changing bottled beers or try one of the mighty fine caipirinhas. Live music (from funk to blues) and DJs at the weekends. Daily 9.30am–11pm, Fri & Sat till 1am (no entry after midnight), Sun till 10.30pm.

The Old Bookshop 65 North St ☏0117 953 5222, ⦿theoldbookshop.co.uk. Buzzing little café-bar covered in street art and decorated with an assortment of knick-knacks – think trombone lightshades and stuffed foxes. Bristol Beer Factory and Arbor Ales are on tap, and there's a good selection of dishes on the food menu. They also own the cocktail bar next door at number 63. Mon–Wed 5–11pm, Thurs & Fri 4–11.30pm, Sat 11am–11.30pm, Sun 12.30–11pm.

MASSIVE ATTACK AND THE BIRTH OF TRIP-HOP

You could be forgiven for thinking that **music** didn't exist in Bristol until the 1990s. Despite a healthy history of establishment-shaking bands such as The Pop Group and Strangelove, it wasn't until the release in 1991 of *Blue Lines*, the stunning debut album of local collective Massive Attack, that the city forced itself upon the nation's musical psyche. And for the following decade, Bristol seemed to rule the urban music scene.

Massive Attack – essentially Grant Marshall (Daddy G), Andy Vowles (Mushroom) and former graffiti artist Robert del Naja (3D), with whispered rapping from Adrian Thaws (better known as Tricky) – were born out of the city's New York-influenced underground scene, and their work, marked by mesmeric beats and a laidback but highly worked hip-hop style, was unlike anything that had gone before. Music journalists called it **trip-hop**, a concept the group themselves have never bought into, but the tag stuck and was cemented as a genre with the release of **Portishead**'s *Dummy* in 1994. Coupling slow-burning beats with cinematic scores, Portishead's equally unique sound was underwritten by the fragile vocals of Beth Gibbons, a technique Massive Attack had so effectively used with Shara Nelson on *Blue Lines*, and did so again with Tracey Thorne on *Protection* (1994) and Elizabeth Fraser on *Mezzanine* (1998). No sooner had Portishead picked up the Mercury Music Prize for *Dummy*, than **Tricky** released his *Maxinquaye* (1995) masterpiece, an unexpectedly complex solo triumph that took dark and down-tempo to a whole new level.

Portishead gained further acclaim with the self-titled *Portishead* in 1997, but didn't produce their next album, *Third*, until 2008. Massive Attack, in turn, waited five years before releasing *100th Window* (2003), a far more experimental and electronic album that had only 3D at the helm. Compared to his peers, Tricky has been prolific, producing another 12 albums, with his most recent release, *ununiform*, in 2017, although none have come anywhere near to reaching *Maxinquaye*'s heights. Massive Attack themselves experienced something of a return to form with *Heligoland* (2010), their first album in seven years, which saw 3D and Daddy G united once more. Their long-awaited sixth album is still to materialise, though their EP *Ritual Spirit* (2016) included Tricky's first involvement with the group since 1994.

NIGHTLIFE

As you might expect, nightlife in Bristol is lively to say the least. Few places outside of London have as vibrant a **live music** scene, which runs the gamut from hip-hop and reggae to jazz and folk – though the city is particularly renowned for drum'n'bass and dubstep. The local **club** scene is equally dynamic, from old-timers *Lakota* and the *Thekla* to the newer breed of super-venues such as *Motion*. Several places host both live bands and club nights, as do some bars, including *Cosies* (see page 124); the *Coronation Tap* (see page 123) is also known for its live music.

Listings For the latest musical offerings and club happenings, check out ⓦ bristolinstereo.com, or consult ⓦ whatsonbristol.co.uk for details of events.

Tickets In addition to the venues themselves, you can buy tickets from the Bristol Ticket Shop at 41 High St (Mon–Sat 10am–6pm; ☎ 0117 929 9008, ⓦ bristolticketshop.co.uk).

CLUBS
SEE MAPS PAGES 88, 90, 94 AND 112

Dojo Lounge 12–14 Park Row ☎ 0117 925 1177. Intimate venue specializing in weekend all-nighters, where you can dance till dawn to house and techno at Deepmasters or 4ToTheFloor. Entry £5–6, some events free.

Lakota 6 Upper York St, Stokes Croft ⓦ lakota.co.uk. The *grande dame* of Bristol's club scene still serves up the goods, churning out jungle, psytrance and drum'n'bass. Entry £4–10.

Motion 74–78 Avon St, St Philips ⓦ motionbristol.com. It's worth the effort to reach this out-of-the-way warehouse near Temple Meads Station, for all-night raves and big-name acts pumping out dubstep, drum'n'bass and electro. Organizes regular DJ match-ups, plus the monumental In:Motion (ⓦ bristolinmotion.com), an underground music season from end Sept to the New Year. Entry £5–13.50, some events free.

PRYZM The South Buildings, Canons Rd ⓦ pryzm.co.uk/bristol. The Bristol franchise of this national chain occupies a foreboding black cube on the Harbourfront and has three "arenas" playing host to mash-up DJs and guest table-turners. Entry £2–5.

Thekla The Grove, East Mud Dock ☎ 0117 929 3301, ⓦ theklabristol.co.uk. Salvaged Baltic coaster that found a new calling as a live-music venue and club and has never looked back. It's much loved round these parts, mostly for the varied club-night line-up, and the consistently fine acts that belt out tunes in the bowels of the boat.

SWX Bristol 15 Nelson St ⓦ thesyndicate.com. A real super-club, the largest in Bristol, attracting big-name DJs and live-music acts to its three rooms. Expect plenty of pyrotechnics. Entry £7–25.

LIVE-MUSIC VENUES
SEE MAPS PAGES 88, 90 AND 94

Colston Hall Colston St ☎ 0117 203 4040, ⓦ colstonhall.org. Bristol's largest concert hall and probably the South West's premier venue, attracting major players in pop and classical music plus top emerging talent.

Fiddlers Willway St, Bedminster ☎ 0117 987 3403, ⓦ fiddlers.co.uk. Mainly live folk, world music and Afrobeat at this relaxed family-run venue south of the river, which began life as a jail in 1740.

The Fleece 12 St Thomas St ☎ 0117 929 450996, ⓦ thefleece.co.uk. Stone-flagged ex-wool warehouse, now a loud, sweaty pub for live rock, jazz, folk and more. An old-timer on the Bristol music scene but with a strong programme of quality touring acts.

The Louisiana Wapping Rd, Bathurst Terrace ☎ 0117 926 5978, ⓦ thelouisiana.net. Established music pub with a well-earned reputation for helping break bands (The White Stripes, Elbow, Florence and the Machine) and promoting local artists; more recent acts to have played the upstairs room include Outfit and The Script.

O2 Academy Frogmore St ☎ 0117 927 9227, ⓦ o2academybristol.co.uk. The Bristol branch of this national chain is a spacious, multi-level place that stages regular live gigs and regular club nights, indie and alternative at Ramshackle, in the main room, and harder sounds in the smaller Room 2 upstairs.

Old Duke 45 King St ☎ 0117 401 9661, ⓦ theoldduke.co.uk. Trad-jazz and blues pub with live music every night of the week, plus Sunday lunchtime. Plenty of real ales and ciders on tap, with seating on the historic cobbled street out front.

St George's Great George St ☎ 0845 402 4001, ⓦ stgeorgesbristol.co.uk. Elegant Georgian church with superb acoustics, staging a packed programme of lunchtime and evening concerts covering classical, world, folk and jazz. Hosts the Bristol Folk Festival in early May.

ENTERTAINMENT

CINEMA

Showcase Cinema De Lux Glass House, Cabot Circus ☎ 0871 220 1000, ⓦ showcasecinemas.co.uk. Vast multiplex at the heart of the Cabot Circus shopping centre, with thirteen screens (several of them 3D) showing the latest releases in suitable comfort.

Watershed 1 Canons Rd ☎ 0117 927 5100, ⓦ watershed.co.uk. A real Bristol landmark, delivering a consistently diverse programme of open-run films and one-off viewings across three screens, plus talks, Q&As and other events. The popular café-bar is worth a visit whether you're catching a movie or not (see page 119).

THEATRE

Alma Theatre The Alma Tavern and Theatre, 18–20 Alma Vale Rd, Clifton ☎ 0117 973 5171, ⓦ almatavern

2

LGBTQ BRISTOL

Bristol's dynamic gay scene is focused on **Old Market**, the area just east of Castle Park that was earmarked as a gay village by the city council a long time ago and is increasingly living up to the name – The Village is now home to a dozen or so gay bars and clubs. The area around **Frogmore Street**, sometimes referred to as Gay Central, is a smaller enclave. **Pride Week** (June/July; w pridebristol.co.uk), a varied programme of art, film and theatre that culminates in a parade and music festival in Castle Park, is the biggest LGBTQ event in the South West.

INFORMATION

LGBT Bristol w lgbtbristol.org.uk. Member-driven focus group concerned with local issues but also providing an up-to-date diary of regional LGBTQ events.
Out Bristol Magazine w outbristol.co.uk. Monthly mag for the LGBTQ community, covering the local bar and club scene.

BARS AND CLUBS   SEE MAP 94

BBB 2–4 West St, Old Market. The *Bristol Bear Bar* is the only one of its kind in the country, a cosy street-corner bar that provides a relaxed venue for both bears and non-bears alike. Tues–Thurs 7–11.30pm, Fri & Sat 7pm–2am, Sun 5–11pm.

OMG 4 Frogmore St. Lively club where the combination of a good sound system and great cocktails makes for a happy clientele and a busy dancefloor. Daily 8pm–2am, Sun till 3am.
The Phoenix 1 Wellington Buildings, Champion Square w phoenixbristol.com. Tucked away near Cabot Circus, at the entrance to Old market, this gay-owned, gay-friendly pub occasionally hosts Horseplay, the roaming "Homo Disco". Mon–Thurs 4–11pm, Fri noon–midnight, Sat noon–late, Sun 1–10pm.
Queenshilling 9 Frogmore St, w queenshilling. com. This scene-goers' stalwart hosts a variety of nights, from cabaret to karaoke. Entry £5, though some events are free.

---

andtheatre.co.uk. Intimate pub-theatre venue (there are fewer than fifty seats) that entertains local and touring companies, including the Bristol Old Vic Theatre School. Expect a broad range of productions, with lots of left-field, experimental theatre, from state-of-the-nation monologues to musical adaptations of Shakespeare.
Bristol Hippodrome St Augustine's Parade ☎ 08448 717615, w atgtickets.com/venues/bristol-hippodrome. Large traditional theatre that's been going strong for over a hundred years. It's the favoured port of call for big West End shows heading to the West Country, but is equally at home hosting opera, ballet, touring comedians and concerts.
Bristol Old Vic King St ☎ 0117 987 7877, w bristololdvic. org.uk. Highly respected historical complex, home to the company of the same name and centred around the Theatre Royal, a beautiful Georgian theatre that's the oldest in the country. A strong programme of new takes on old plays, spoken-word performances and outdoor events.
Tobacco Factory Raleigh Rd, Southville ☎ 0117 902 0344, w tobaccofactory.com. Neighbourhood-defining

theatre offering a broad spectrum of plays and other performing arts. Work from the much-admired theatre company Shakespeare at the Tobacco Factory (w stf-theatre. org.uk) is supplemented with comedy and theatre festivals.

COMEDY AND PERFORMANCE ART

Circomedia St Pauls Church, Portland Square, St Pauls ☎ 0117 924 7615, w circomedia.com. Gothic St Pauls Church is the unlikely but enlightening venue for this ground-breaking circus school, which runs classes and workshops and puts on a variety of performances that provide an unforgettable evening of Big Top tricks and physical theatre.
Hen & Chicken 210 North St, Southville ☎ 0117 966 3143, w henandchicken.com. The upstairs room of this big open boozer is home to The Comedy Box (w thecomedybox. co.uk), a popular comedy club that attracts an interesting range of local and national talent; bigger names that need a bigger venue play the Tobacco Factory or Bristol Old Vic (see above).

SHOPPING

The £500 million superstore "suburb" of **Cabot Circus** has bumped the city up the shopping charts, but while it offers all the convenience you'd expect from a one-stop retail centre, the real joy of shopping in Bristol is browsing its boutiques, at the harbourside hub of **Wapping Wharf** and particularly in **Park Street**, **Clifton** and along **Gloucester Road**, whose diverse selection of shops has earned it the moniker of Bristol's Independent High Street.

ARCADES, SHOPPING CENTRES AND MALLS SEE MAPS PAGES 86, 94 AND 112

Cabot Circus w cabotcircus.com. Ultra-contemporary shopping precinct filled with the usual big-name brands and a three-floor House of Fraser; the adjoining piazza-style Quakers Friars is home to the only Harvey Nichols in the South West. There's also an upmarket cinema (see page 125). Mon–Sat 10am–8pm, Sun 11am–5pm.

Clifton Arcade Boyces Ave, Clifton w cliftonarcade.com. Lovely little Victorian shopping arcade, refurbished to its original Venetian design – look out for the striking decorative window at its far end – and housing an eclectic collection of one-off shops, including antiques stores, an art gallery and a place selling refurbished furniture from rural China. Mon–Fri 10am–5.30pm, Sat 10am–6pm, Sun 11am–4pm.

Guild 68 Park St w bristolguildgallery.co.uk. Quality independent retailer that has been operating at the top of Park Street for over a hundred years. Various departments, from designer kitchen goods to a gourmet food hall, plus an outside terrace for a quick coffee break. Changing exhibitions from regional artists on the second-floor gallery. Mon–Sat 10am–5pm.

The Mall at Cribbs Causeway Off Junction 17 of the M5 w mallcribbs.com; bus #1, #3 & #4, plus Metrobus M1, from The Centre. Classic out-of-town, everything-under-one-roof retail destination, with over 150 big-name brands such as John Lewis, M&S, Apple and H&M. Over a dozen cafés and restaurants provide nourishment for a sustained bout of credit-card swiping. Mon–Wed 9.30am–8pm, Thurs & Fri 9.30am–9pm, Sat 9am–8pm, Sun 11am–5pm.

BOOKSTORES AND RECORD SHOPS
SEE MAPS PAGES 90, 94 AND 121

Arnolfini 16 Narrow Quay w arnolfini.org.uk. Small but very browsable arts-centric bookshop just off the main gallery, with one of the UK's best collections of contemporary-art titles, from situationism to stencil graffiti, plus magazines covering art, architecture and design. Daily 10am–6pm.

★ **Plastic Wax Records** 222 Cheltenham Rd w plastic waxrecords.com. This is Bristol's largest record dealer, and it's wall-to-wall vinyl (over 10,000 LPs, allegedly), across all genres, all of it crying out to be leafed through, pored over and ultimately added to your collection. Mon 9.30am–5.30pm, Tues–Fri 9.30am–7pm, Sat 9am–6pm, Sun noon–5pm.

Stanfords 29 Corn St w stanfords.co.uk. Dedicated travel bookshop stocking a good range of local-interest books, regional walking guides, and maps of the city and surrounding area. Mon–Sat 9am–6pm.

Wanted Records The Covered Market, St Nicholas Market w wantedrecords.co.uk. Compact, relaxed and strictly vinyl, with a little bit of everything, from folk and jazz to reggae and hip-hop. Mon–Wed 9.30am–5pm, Thurs–Sat 10.30am–5pm.

FASHION
SEE MAPS PAGES 90, 94 AND 121

★ **Beast** St Nicholas Market w beast-clothing.com. Amusing T-shirts, hoodies and hats emblazoned with snippets of the local lingo – "Job's A Good Un", "Ark At Ee" and "Gert Lush" among others. Possibly the most authentic souvenir of Bristol you can get. Mon–Sat 9.30am–5pm.

Cooshti 57 Park St w cooshti.com. A treasure-trove of trendy streetwear, stocking the latest labels such as Obey, By Parra, Nixon and Deus Ex Machina; it's usually a good bet if you're looking for old-school styles and limited-edition footwear. The regular sales make the price tags much more palatable. Mon–Sat 10am–6pm, Sun noon–5pm.

Fox + Feather 43 Gloucester Rd w foxandfeather. co.uk. Cool clothing, plus Nordic-style homeware items, all individually selected and sourced both locally and across Europe, from Goldie London to Madam Stoltz. Pop next door to sister store Ida for sustainable fashion and lifestyle goods. Mon–Sat 10am–6pm, Sun 11am–5pm.

RePsycho 85 Gloucester Rd. Great little "retro superstore" where you can wade through racks of vintage clothing (on the ground floor) or pick up a vintage piece of furniture (upstairs); Prime Cuts, in the claustrophobic basement down possibly the steepest stairs in Bristol, has plenty of old records, too. Mon–Sat 10am–5.30pm, Sun 11am–4pm.

FOOD AND DRINK
SEE MAPS PAGES 88, 90, 94 AND 108

★ **Better Food** 21 Sevier St, St Werburghs; 94A Whiteladies Rd, Clifton; 1–5 Gaol Ferry Steps, Wapping Wharf w betterfood.co.uk. Superb one-stop organic shop for local breads, cheeses, fruit and veg, and artisan wines and beers, plus other fresh produce from their own community farm based in the nearby Chew Valley. Mon–Sat 8am–8pm, Sun 10am–6pm.

Bristol Cider Shop Unit 4, Cargo, Gaol Ferry Steps, Wapping Wharf w bristolcidershop.co.uk. Welcoming store stocking over a hundred varieties of local cider and perry, with several on tap, including Rich's Farmhouse, Hecks and Burrow Hill. The knowledgeable staff organize talks and tastings. Tues–Sat 11am–7pm, Sun 11am–5pm.

Guilbert's 16–17 Small St w guilbertschocolates.co.uk. This little boutique is the last of its kind in Bristol, crafting luxury hand-made chocolates, many of which are based on the same recipes that Piers Guilbert used over a century ago at his store on Park Street. Decadent boxed collections, plus individual creams, fondants and truffles. Mon–Thurs 7.30am–4.30pm, Fri 7.30am–12.30pm.

MARKETS

As well as the markets listed below, there's a farmers' market on Corn Street every Wednesday (see page 92).

Harbourside Market Bordeaux Quay. Reliable market running outside *No.1 Harbourside* and the tourist office, with stalls selling food, books, clothes and crafts. Wed & Thurs noon–2.30pm, Sat & Sun 11am–4pm.

Tobacco Factory Market Raleigh Rd, Southville. Weekly community market, with over fifty stalls offering mostly organic and local goodies, from cakes to crafts, plus vintage and retro goods. Sun 10am–2.30pm.

2

2

MISCELLANEOUS
SEE MAPS PAGES 88 AND 112
Bristol Blue Glass 357–359 Bath Rd, Arnos Vale
ⓦ bristolblueglass.com. Glass-blowing studio and factory shop where you can watch craftsmen teasing the soft, deep-blue resin into intricate (and expensive) stemware, tableware and centrepieces. Studio closed on Sundays. Mon–Sat 9am–5pm, Sun 10am–4pm.

Dig Haüshizzle 141 St John's Lane ⓦ dig-haushizzle. co.uk. The unusual name befits an award-winning remit that spans a curious collection of antique, vintage and industrial furniture – all very much individual pieces – plus lighting and prints. Open by appointment only.

Upfest Gallery 198 North St ⓦ upfest.co.uk. Great little street-art gallery from the people behind the festival of the same name (see page 129), with prints from the city's top graffiti artists, plus paints and sprays if you fancy giving it a go yourself. Tues–Sat 9.30am–5.30pm, Sun 10am–3pm.

Stokes Croft China 35 Jamaica St, Stokes Croft ⓦ prcshop.co.uk. The headquarters of the People's Republic of Stokes Croft (see page 111), and as such less of a shop than a series of political statements. Posters, prints, T-shirts and postcards, but mostly a range of subversive china mugs and tableware, made on their own kiln next door and featuring work from local street artists. Mon–Sat 11am–6pm, Sun noon–5pm.

SPORT

Bristol is perhaps most famous in sporting circles for being the biggest city in England without a Premier League **football** team. The rivalry between its two clubs has waned since Rovers were relegated from Division Two in 2001, which was the last time they met in a league derby; City now play in the Championship, Rovers in League One. The city is also home to professional **rugby**, **cricket** and **basketball** teams.

FOOTBALL
Bristol City ☎ 0117 963 0600, ⓦ bcfc.co.uk. The Robins have played at Ashton Gate in South Bristol for over a century. Tickets start at £25.

Bristol Rovers ☎ 0117 909 6648, ⓦ bristolrovers. co.uk. The Pirates, or The Gas (Rovers' old ground, Eastville Stadium, was right next to Stapleton Gasworks, and their supporters are still known as Gasheads), play at Memorial Stadium in Horfield. Tickets cost from £19.

RUGBY
Bristol Bears ☎ 0117 963 0600, ⓦ bristolbearsrugby. co.uk. Bristol Bears share Ashton Gate with City; they play their rugby in the Premiership, with tickets starting at £30.

CRICKET
Gloucestershire County Cricket Club ☎ 0117 910 8000, ⓦ gloscricket.co.uk. GCCC play the majority of their County Championship and Vitality Blast home games at The Bristol County Ground in Bishopston. Tickets start at £10.

BASKETBALL
Bristol Flyers ☎ 0117 963 0600, ⓦ bristolflyers.co.uk. The Bristol Flyers played their inaugural season in the top-tier British Basketball League (BBL) in 2014/2015. Their home games are held at the SGS College Arena in Stoke Gifford. Tickets start at £7.50.

ACTIVITIES

Although navigating the steep hills around Clifton and Cotham is a workout in itself, there are plenty of other, more official, activities to engage in, from sailing around the harbour to soothing your aches away in a city **spa**. Given the city's connections to **ballooning** and its status as the home of the biggest hot-air balloon festival in Europe, taking to the skies in a gas-fired basket is a quintessentially Bristol experience.

Aerosaurus Balloons ☎ 01404 823102, ⓦ ballooning. co.uk. Run by the Flight Director of the Balloon Fiesta, Aerosaurus has a big fleet of balloons and offers Champagne balloon flights (from £110) from Ashton Court and the

chance to fly at the festival itself (£225).

Lido Oakfield Place, Clifton ☎ 0117 933 9530, ⓦ lido bristol.com. Stylishly renovated Victorian lido with an infinity lap pool, sauna, steam room and trendy spa, offering massages (from £35) and holistic treatments (from £65). Also home to a sleek café-bar and top-notch restaurant (see page 120). Spa daily; swimming Mon–Fri 1–4pm.

SUP Bristol ☎ 0117 422 5858, ⓦ supbristol.com. Try your hand at stand-up paddleboarding in the scenic surroundings of the harbour, either with a lesson on the basic strokes (£25) or on a tour of the Harbourside (£40).

CHILDREN'S BRISTOL

From the simple pleasure of kicking about in the fountains in Millennium Square to exploring the SS *Great Britain*, Bristol is an excellent city to discover with kids in tow. **Harbourside** is the principal destination, home to many of the city's top children's attractions, and with plenty of pirate folklore to spice up the walks between them. All of the city council's **museums** are free, meaning you can take

the family to half a dozen sights (including M Shed and the Bristol Museum and Art Gallery) without spending a penny. For more **information**, check out the Kids' Zone at ⓦ whatsonbristol.co.uk.

Bristol Aquarium Anchor Rd ☎ 0117 929 8929, ⓦ bristolaquarium.co.uk; see page 99. Sharks, rays, a giant octopus, and a walk-through underwater tunnel.

TOP 5 FESTIVALS

Bristol's calendar is packed with some outstanding **festivals and events** (see page 32), but the following five are not to be missed.

St Pauls Carnival St Pauls; free; ⓦ stpaulscarnival. net. Second only to London's Notting Hill Carnival for sheer Caribbean colour, this community carnival normally attracts over eighty thousand people to St Pauls for street parties, samba bands and sound systems, plus the legendary parade itself. Early July.

Bristol Harbour Festival Harbourside; free; ⓦ bristolharbourfestival.co.uk. Hundreds of sailing vessels fill the harbour for this weekend event, one of the biggest free festivals in the country, which also takes in music, street theatre, circus, cabarets and food markets in a variety of waterfront venues. Mid-July.

Upfest Southville; free; ⓦ upfest.co.uk/page/ upfest-festival. Street-art festival with workshops and music providing the background to some of the best

street artists in the world, many of them from Bristol, giving the buildings on and around North Street a fresh look for the year. Last weekend in July.

Bristol International Balloon Fiesta Ashton Court Estate, Long Ashton; free; ⓦ bristolballoonfiesta. co.uk. Unique four-day festival celebrating Bristol's ballooning heritage with twice-daily mass ascents of over a hundred balloons – an incredible sight – and a visually stunning "night glow" performed to music and topped off with a fireworks finale. Early Aug.

The Downs Festival Clifton Down; £55; ⓦ the downsbristol.com. Bristol's largest one-day music festival attracts some classic names to its three stages, such as Lauryn Hill, Grace Jones and local breakthrough act, the IDLES. Late Aug.

Bristol Museum and Art Gallery Queen's Rd ☎ 0117 922 3571, ⓦ bristolmuseums.org.uk; see page 107. Kids should love the Egyptian section, complete with ageing mummies, and there are a number of family areas, including the Dinosaur area and Curiosity, where they can play with puppets or dress up as a character from one of the paintings upstairs.

Bristol Zoo Clifton ☎ 0117 428 5300, ⓦ bristolzoo.org.uk; see page 110. As well as getting up close and personal with all creatures great and small, children can keep themselves busy at an activity centre, an adventure playground and a water play area. The aerial assault course, ZooRopia (Sat, Sun & school hols 10am–4pm; £7.65, under-14s £6.75, no under-5s), will appeal to older children and teenagers.

SS Great Britain Great Western Dockyard ☎ 0117 926 0680, ⓦ ssgreatbritain.org; see page 100. Plenty of interactive displays in the Dockyard Museum, and Go Aloft!, the chance to climb up into the rigging, is free for under-18s. Educational programmes in the adjoining Brunel Institute include "Sea Hear", storytelling for the under-5s (first Tues of the month; free).

We The Curious Anchor Rd ☎ 0117 915 1000, ⓦ wethecurious.org; see page 99. Addictive hands-on science centre with planetarium shows, Live Lab sessions and a bounty of thought-provoking and interactive exhibitions. There's also an inviting section just for the under-5s, plus weekly "Toddler Takeover" sessions.

DIRECTORY

Medical care Hospital: Bristol Royal Infirmary, Upper Maudlin St ☎ 0117 923 0000. Walk-in centres: 35 Broad St ☎ 0117 906 9610 (Mon–Sat 8am–8pm, Sun 10am–6pm); Boots chemist, 59 Broadmead ☎ 0117 929 3631 (Mon–Sat 8am–8pm, Sun 11am–5pm).

Police Bridewell Police Station, 1–2 Bridewell St ☎ 101.

Chew Valley

Just the other side of Dundry Hill from Bristol, eight miles south of the city centre, the swathe of bucolic countryside that stretches to the foothills of the Mendips constitutes the fertile **CHEW VALLEY**, a cluster of contented villages set around man-made **Chew Valley Lake**. Like nearby **Blagdon Lake**, it was built to provide Bristol with a much-needed water supply but has since become a scenic spot for lakeside walks, fishing and other activities.

The most notable of the valley's many pretty villages are **Chew Magna** – named the best village in the UK by *The Sunday Times* in 2011, a decision no doubt influenced by its bounty of appealing pubs – and **Stanton Drew**, home to an intriguing set of Neolithic **stone circles**.

2

FISHING ON THE LAKES

Experienced anglers go all misty-eyed at the mention of the Chew Valley, whose two lakes provide the setting for some of the best still-water fishing in the country. **Blagdon Lake** is the more famous of the two, a name resonant throughout the world of fly-fishing for its hefty brown and rainbow trout, though **Chew Valley Lake** is equally as popular, and is regarded as the UK's premier pike-fishing venue.

The trout-fishing **season** runs from mid-March to November, with fishing for pike allowed on certain dates within that period. **Permits** start at £19 for an afternoon of bank fishing at Chew Valley and are available at Woodford Lodge, on the B3114 between Chew Stoke and West Harptree (early March to Oct daily 8am–4.30pm; ☎01275 332339, 🄴woodford.lodge@ bristolwater.co.uk); the lodge also has a fully stocked **tackle shop**. For advice on which spots to fish and what tactics to use, contact John Horsey (🅦johnhorsey.co.uk), a former World Champion with over twenty years' experience as a professional fishing **guide**.

Chew Valley Lake

🅦 bristolwater.co.uk/activities

On sunny days, its sparkling waters dotted with the white specks of sailing boats, **Chew Valley Lake** is simply majestic. The largest lake in the South West, it was formed in 1956, flooding the village of Moreton in the process; during particularly dry summers, the arch of the old village bridge emerges, Excalibur-like, from the receding water, an occasional reminder of what lies beneath.

Two **picnic areas** on the road between Chew Stoke and Bishop Sutton – the first with a fish and chip restaurant (daily 8.30–11.30am, noon–3.30pm & 5.30–9pm, closed Sun eve) – provide great views across the water. The one furthest from Chew Stoke has access to **trails** that cut through the corner of a nature reserve, where it's possible to spot kingfishers, great-crested grebes and (occasionally) bittern.

Stanton Drew Stone Circles

Daily dawn–dusk • £1 • EH • 🅦 english-heritage.org.uk

The megaliths that dot a farmer's field on the fringes of **STANTON DREW** enjoy a wonderfully low-key location that is all the more surprising given their status as the third largest set of prehistoric standing stones in England. The collection of stones – actually three separate sets of circles, as there's another to the southwest – are not, as local legend may have it, the petrified members of a wedding party, punished for celebrating on the Sabbath, but are instead part of an ancient ritual site dating back some four thousand years to the late Neolithic–early Bronze Age. Geophysical research has revealed that the largest of these, **The Great Circle**, contains a number of burial pits, and is itself set within a larger enclosure, or henge.

Further along the main road through Stanton Drew, you'll find **The Cove**, three stones erected around the same time as the Great Circle that now huddle together in the back garden of *The Druids Arms*, and are accessible to patrons of the pub only.

Blagdon Lake and around

Blagdon Lake predates neighbouring Chew Valley by over half a century, and has been supplying much of Bristol's water since 1899. The original **pumping station** is still in good working order, and is open to visitors during the summer, though for many, the lake's chief attraction is its plentiful stocks of **trout**.

Blagdon Pumping Station

Station Rd, Blagdon • Closed for engineering works at time of writing but usually April–Aug Sun 2–5pm • Free

The two huge beam engines at the **Blagdon Pumping Station** are a reminder that the Victorians didn't do anything by half – the surviving set of four engines that operated under steam until 1949, they weigh 37 tonnes each, consumed nearly six tonnes of coal a day between them and took nine men to operate. One of them was given an electric motor in the 1980s, so you can now see it "in action".

The wildlife exhibit in the attached **visitor centre** is worth a look before heading out on one of the surrounding **trails**, though perhaps the most interesting nature experience is feeding the thousands of trout being bred in the two huge suction tanks outside.

Yeo Valley Organic Garden

Bath Rd, Blagdon • June–Sept Thurs & Fri 11am–5pm • £5 • ☎ 01761 462798, ⓦ yeovalley.co.uk/the-organic-gardens.co.uk

2

One of the first of its kind in the country, the creatively designed **Yeo Valley Organic Garden** has been over twenty years in the making and is still constantly evolving, with around a dozen different areas spread over five acres including meadows, a gravel garden and a willow garden that takes its inspiration from the Somerset Levels.

You can finish off your visit with tea and home-made scones (all organic, of course) on the attractive terrace that overlooks Blagdon Lake.

ARRIVAL AND GETTING AROUND   **THE CHEW VALLEY**

By bus The #672 bus (Mon–Sat 5 daily) runs from Bristol to villages within the Chew Valley, taking about 35min to get to Chew Stoke, the nearest stop to the Chew Valley Lake Visitor Centre, and another 10min to Stanton Drew.

By car Having your own wheels is by far the best way of getting around; you can reach the Valley on the B3114 via Bishopsworth and Dundry, or the A37 via Totterdown and Whitchurch.

ACCOMMODATION AND EATING

The Bear & Swan 13 South Parade, Chew Magna, on the B3130 ☎ 01275 331100, ⓦ ohhpubs.co.uk. Well-respected open-plan gastro pub with lots of distressed wood and a romantic little restaurant at one end. The daily changing blackboard is usually strong on fish and locally sourced meat (char-grilled sirloin steak £29; other mains from £14.95). There are also three attractive, homely doubles and a family/twin room upstairs. Daily 8am–11pm, Sat & Sun from 8.30pm; food served Mon–Thurs 8am–9.30pm, Fri 8am–10pm, Sat 8.30am–10pm, Sun 8.30am–9.30pm. **£130**
New Manor Farm North Widcombe, West Harptree, on the A368 near Herriots Bridge ☎ 01761 220172, ⓦ newmanorfarmshop.co.uk. Inviting farmyard tearoom that foregoes the frills for a focus on home-made soups, baguettes and panini (from £5.25), plus good-value Sunday lunches. Much of it is made using produce from their excellent farm shop just across the courtyard, which also stocks local cheeses, honey, smoked salmon and the like. Daily 9.30am–5.30pm, Sat & Sun till 5pm.
★**The Pig near Bath** Hunstrete House, Pensford

☎ 0345 2259494, ⓦ thepighotel.com. Superb country-house accommodation, closer to the Chew Valley than Bath but making a great base for both. Stylishly rustic rooms are done out in pastel shades with stripped-back floorboards and, in some rooms, claw-foot baths; there's a library and billiard room; and you can properly unwind in the cute "Potting Shed" spa. The hotel's kitchen garden provides much of the ingredients for the bustling restaurant; anything else – such as the pork in the char-grilled pork tomahawk (£22) – comes from nearby. Daily noon–2.15pm & 6.30–9.30pm. **£185**
The Pony and Trap Newton, Chew Magna, signed off the A368 ☎ 01275 332627, ⓦ theponyandtrap.co.uk. The creative cooking of patron chef Josh Eggleton has made this one of the most popular pubs in the Valley (sometimes a little too popular) and earned him a Michelin star in the process. The food – virtually all of it sourced locally and ranging from baked polenta and ewe's-curd stuffed courgette to Ston Easton lamb rack and belly – is decently priced considering, with mains from £18. Tues–Thurs noon–2pm & 7–9pm, Fri & Sat noon–2pm & 6–9pm, Sun noon–6pm.

BIRDWATCHING AT CHEW

Over 270 **bird species** have been recorded at Chew Valley Lake – including osprey, an occasional visitor – and the lake is the third most important site in Britain for wintering waterfowl. Popular bird-watching spots include **Herons Green**, on the B3114 between Chew Stoke and West Harptree, and **Herriotts Bridge**, on the A368 between West Harptree and Bishop Sutton. The glazed hide on the picnic area's Bittern Trail (see page 130) is free and open to all, but you'll need a permit (£5/day) to access the five **hides** at the lake's southern end (see ⓦ cvlbirding.co.uk/birdingmap.html for locations), which are available from Woodford Lodge (see page 130).

Wells
and the
Mendips

WELLS FARMERS' MARKET

Wells and the Mendips

The miniature cathedral city of Wells, 21 miles south of Bristol and the same distance southwest from Bath, has not significantly altered in eight hundred years. Charming and compact, it is eminently walkable, and a stroll around its tightly knit streets reveals a cluster of medieval religious buildings, archways and almshouses. This architectural ensemble – impressive in its own right – is capped by the city's stunning cathedral, its startling west front adorned with some of the finest medieval statuary in Europe.

From the first few years of the tenth century, the cathedral's bishops effectively ruled both the city and the greater portion of Somerset, their estates once extending as far south as Kingsbury Episcopi, between Taunton and Yeovil. It was these same bishops who created Wells as we know it today, building the walled **Bishop's Palace**, which houses the celebrated wells themselves, and the tidy **Vicars' Close** – the city's two other must-see sights – and establishing the oldest almshouses in the county.

Spreading northwest of Wells, the ancient woodland, exposed heaths and craggy limestone gorges of the **Mendip Hills** provide the perfect backdrop to some lovely **walks**, as well as caving and climbing in the potholes and ravines that give the area its distinct geological character. The main **A371** traces the Mendips' southern escarpment, linking Wells with Cheddar and Axbridge and running on to Weston-super-Mare. The region's famed outdoor activities lie to the north – indeed, this is real get-up-and-go country, and you haven't really experienced the Mendips until you've squeezed through a cavern in **Wookey Hole**, scaled the cliffs at **Cheddar Gorge** or **Burrington Combe** and hiked through some of the nature reserves encircling the former mining land at **Charterhouse**.

Wells

WELLS owes its celebrity entirely to its spectacular **cathedral**, the presence of which makes what would otherwise be a beautiful little town into a beautiful little city – the smallest, in fact, in England. Approaching from **Brown's Gate**, the thirteenth-century archway cut through the old city walls on Sadler Street, allows you to fully appreciate the cathedral's grandeur: its dazzling west front is one of the visual highlights of Somerset.

The clerical houses on the surrounding **Cathedral Green** are mostly seventeenth and eighteenth century, though one, the **Old Deanery**, shows traces of its fifteenth-century origins; the chancellor's house, further along, is now the **Wells and Mendip Museum**, beyond which a little arch marks the entrance to cobbled **Vicars' Close**, another of the city's architectural treasures. The archway on the green's southeastern corner, **Penniless Porch**, was built in the fifteenth century to provide alms for beggars and opens onto the attractive **Market Place**, the focal point of the city and still the site of a twice-weekly market. The **conduit** here is served by the springs that rise in the gardens of the **Bishop's Palace**, accessed through the **Bishop's Eye** archway, at the top of Market Place.

Many visitors – and there can be an awful lot at weekends in summer – are content with ticking off the big sights gathered together at this end of the city, but a leisurely stroll down the bunting-strung High Street will cover the rest of Wells in very little time, taking in Gothic **St Cuthbert's Church** and the dinky **almshouses** nearby.

Highlights

❶ Wells Cathedral The wow factor of the west front is continued on the inside, a combination that adds up to one of the finest cathedrals in the country. See page 137

❷ The Good Earth Something of a Wells institution, this easy-going and very enjoyable vegetarian restaurant has been serving up wholesome wholefood for decades. See page 142

❸ Walking in the Mendips Take your pick from hiking along the fringes of Cheddar Gorge, through the nature reserves around Charterhouse or up precipitous Crook Peak – or sling a pack on your back and visit the lot on the West Mendip Way. See page 144

❹ Cheddar Gorge A bounty of attractions, including the most remarkable cave system in the region, and, of course, the gorge itself – towering, craggy and with a brooding, elemental presence. See page 146

❺ Charterhouse Dotted with Roman remains, disused Victorian mines and a World War II decoy town, the area around Charterhouse is one of the most intriguing on the Mendips. See page 148

❻ Axbridge Diminutive medieval market town that makes a great base for exploring the western end of the Mendips. See page 150

HIGHLIGHTS ARE MARKED ON THE MAP ON PAGE 136

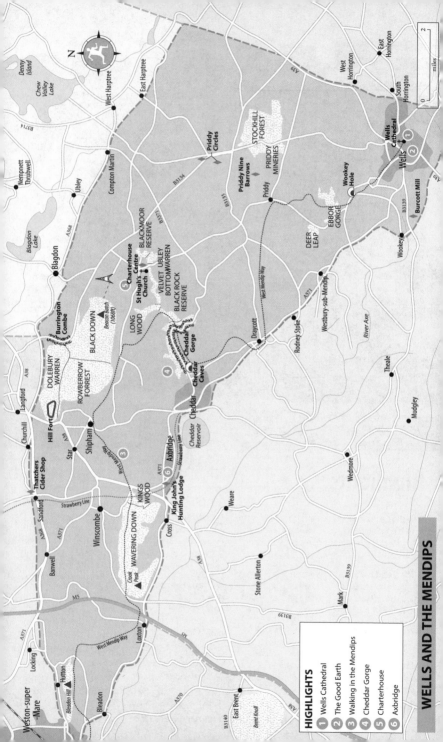

HIGHLIGHTS

1 Wells Cathedral
2 The Good Earth
3 Walking in the Mendips
4 Cheddar Gorge
5 Charterhouse
6 Axbridge

Brief history

People have been drawn to the city's **springs** (*wella* in Anglo-Saxon) since the Stone Age, although the earliest evidence of them assuming spiritual significance is a Romano-British mausoleum. The mausoleum was succeeded by a mortuary chapel, and the chapel by the **Saxon church of St Andrew**, founded in 705 AD by Ine, King of Wessex, in a spot that now lies in the gardens of the cathedral. In 909, St Andrew became the cathedral of the new diocese of Wells (which included all of Somerset), with Athelm its first bishop.

The city has been shaped by its **bishops** ever since. From 1245, they have held the powerful title of Bishop of Bath and Wells, a position that has historically enabled them to get things done, and much of Wells's appearance is owed to them: **Bishop Burnell** (1275–92) built the Great Hall at the Bishop's Palace and **Bishop Ralph** (1329–63) founded Vicars' Close, but it was **Bishop Bekynton** (1443–65) who was the busiest of the lot, building the city's three medieval gateways and the cathedral's Chain Gate bridge, and providing the precious water supply that is still pumped into the conduit on Market Place today.

Much more recently, Wells was the setting for the movie **Hot Fuzz**, the Simon Pegg/Nick Frost cult comedy directed by local lad and former Wells Blue pupil, Edgar Wright. The city fondly remembers its brush with fame, and several places proudly brandish their fifteen minutes' worth – the exterior of *The Crown*, an ancient coaching inn on Market Place, bears two historical plaques, one denoting the arrest of William Penn in 1685 for illegal preaching, the other recalling its role in the *Hot Fuzz* shootout scene of 2006.

Wells Cathedral

Cathedral Green • **Cathedral** Daily 7am–7pm, Oct–March till 6pm; library Mon–Fri 11am–1pm & 2–4pm, Sat 11am–1pm • Cathedral Tours Mon–Sat 10am, 11am, 1pm, 2pm & 3pm (Nov–March 11am, noon & 2pm); 1hr; free • High Parts Tours Mon–Fri 11am & 2.30pm, Sat 11am; 1hr 30min; £13 Café Daily 10am–4pm, Sun from 11am • Free (suggested donation £6); photography permit £4 • ☎ 01749 674483, ⓦ wellscathedral.org.uk

Revealing its full glory only when you pass into its spacious close, **Wells Cathedral** presents a majestic spectacle, the broad lawn of its former graveyard providing the perfect foreground. The **west front** teems with some three hundred thirteenth-century figures of saints and kings, once brightly painted and gilded, though their present honey tint has a subtle splendour of its own. The sensational facade was completed about eighty years after work on the main building was begun in 1175. The interior itself is a supreme example of early English Gothic, the long nave punctuated by dramatic and very modern-looking "**scissor arches**", constructed in 1338 to take the extra weight of the newly built tower.

The quire and the Lady Chapel

Beyond the arches, the **quire** is framed at its eastern end by a wonderfully vivid **Jesse Window**, a fourteenth-century stained-glass masterpiece that shows the family tree of Christ sprouting from Jesse's abdomen. The Bishops' Throne here (the *cathedra*, which gives this, and all cathedrals, their name) is backed by an embroidery of **St Andrew**, Wells's patron saint – his image crops up throughout the cathedral, most notably in the row of disciples that adorn the top of the west front (he's in the middle, bearing a cross).

The gnarled old tombs in the aisles of the quire include the **chantry chapel of Bishop Bekynton**, Chancellor of England and the man who changed Wells's fortunes when he gave the city a public water supply in 1451 – a gesture that is still acknowledged by the mayor each year.

At the far eastern end of the cathedral is the light-filled **Lady Chapel**, a star-shaped room dating to the fourteenth century. Its stained-glass windows, visible from the quire, were smashed during the Civil War, but the resulting collage of richly coloured pieces is mesmerizing nonetheless.

The transepts

The capitals and corbels of the **south transept** hold some amusing narrative carvings – look out for the man with toothache (on the first column on the right) and the old man caught pilfering an apple (on the next one along). The stout-looking **font** is from the Saxon church that once occupied the site of the present-day Camery Garden (see page 139), and as such is the oldest object in the cathedral.

In the **north transept**, the 24-hour astronomical **clock** is almost as ancient, dating from 1390. From his seat high up on the right of the clock, a figure known as Jack Blandifer kicks a couple of bells every quarter-hour, heralding the appearance of a pair of jousting knights charging at each other – a little routine they haven't tired of in over six hundred years – and on the hour, he strikes the bell in front of him.

The Chapter House

Beyond the North Transept, a doorway leads to a graceful, much-worn flight of steps rising to the **Chapter House**, an octagonal room elaborately ribbed in the Decorated style. It was here that the members of the clergy met to discuss cathedral affairs and, from time to time, carry out legal proceedings. The door at the top of the steps (usually closed) leads to the Vicars' Hall and the **Chain Gate**, a covered walkway that bridges St Andrew Street before descending into Vicars' Close (see page 139), thus ensuring that the clergy could commute to work untempted by the distractions of a "sinful" city.

Below the Chapter House, the **undercroft** built to support its considerable weight now houses an **interpretation centre** covering the building's history and its life as a contemporary church.

The cloisters

The tranquil **cloisters**, laden with monuments, were substantially remodelled in the fifteenth century, when an extra storey was added to both the west (for a school)

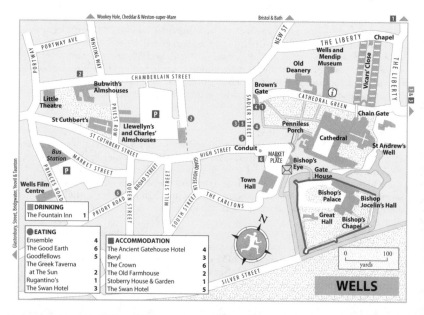

HEAVENLY MUSIC

Regarded as one of the finest choirs in the world, **Wells Cathedral Choir** has been singing hymns here for over 1100 years – although it wasn't until 1994 that they welcomed girl choristers into their ranks. Hearing their voices soaring through the vast, echoing nave is seemingly paramount to a divine experience: during term times, the traditional performance to catch is **Evensong** (Mon–Fri 5.15pm, Sun 3pm), though they also sing at the Sunday **Eucharist** (9.45am) and **Matins** (11.30am) services.

In addition to its choir, the cathedral also serves as the occasional venue for evening **concerts**, orchestral performances and opera (box office ☎01749 672773), while local schools and visiting choirs regularly perform lunchtime concerts throughout the year (check 🌐 wellscathedral.org.uk/whats-on for details).

Each year, the cathedral hosts the **new music wells festival**, a retrospective of choral and organ music held over five or six days.

and east (a library) cloisters. The collection in the library features ancient tomes on theology, of course, but also science and mathematics – the library's set of Aristotle's works, published in 1497, has been uniquely annotated by Erasmus.

Just off the east cloister, the fifteenth-century foundations of **Bishop Stillington's Lady Chapel**, commissioned mainly to house his own tomb, poke through the grass of the Camery Garden; the chapel was itself built on the site of an earlier Saxon church.

Wells and Mendip Museum

8 Cathedral Green • Mon–Sat 10am–5pm, Nov–Easter till 4pm • £3 • ☎01749 673477, 🌐 wellsmuseum.org.uk

The former chancellor's house, adjacent to the cathedral, is now home to a tourist information centre (see page 141) and the **Wells and Mendip Museum**, displaying some of the cathedral's original statuary, fossils from the surrounding area and a steady stream of changing exhibitions from local artists. The displays charting the history of caving – including the bones of the Witch of Wookey Hole (see page 145) – are a nod to the museum's founder, Herbert Balch, who was something of a potholing pioneer, opening up several of the area's complex cave systems.

Vicars' Close

The word "quaint" might have been invented for **Vicars' Close**, two symmetrical rows of impossibly picturesque clergymen's cottages that constitute the oldest continuously inhabited medieval street in Europe. The cottages were built in the mid-fourteenth century to house the Vicars' Choral (the men of the choir), and its members still make up most of their inhabitants today. A chapel was added to the northern end in the early fifteenth century, and the cottages themselves have undergone various alterations over the years – small front gardens created, chimneys extended into their current distinctive forms – though you can get a good idea of the street's initial appearance at no. 22, which was restored to its original proportions in 1863.

The Bishop's Palace

Palace Daily: Jan–March, Nov & Dec 10am–4pm; April–Oct 10am–6pm; free tours daily: April–Oct Palace & Chapel 11am & 2pm, Grounds noon & 3pm; Nov–March Palace & Gardens noon **Restaurant** Daily 9.30am–6pm, end Oct–March till 4pm • £8.05 • ☎01749 988111, 🌐 bishopspalace.org.uk

The residence of the Bishop of Bath and Wells since 1206, the **Bishop's Palace** was walled and moated as a result of a rift with the borough in the early fourteenth century, and the imposing gatehouse still displays the grooves of the portcullis and a chute for pouring oil and molten lead on would-be assailants. The **moat**, fed by the springs from which the city takes its name, makes for a short but pleasant walk, with views over the Palace Fields; the bishop's **swans** that circuit it have learnt to feed on demand, ringing the little bell that hangs next to the drawbridge when it's time for more grain.

Bishop Jocelin's Hall and the Bishop's Chapel

The oldest part of the palace, **Bishop Jocelin's Hall**, or the Jocelin Block, contains the Palace Rooms and the Long Gallery, hung with portraits of former bishops. Among these, Bishop Mews (1673–84), easily identified by the circular black patch on his left cheek, pleaded the case of the Monmouth rebels at Judge Jeffries' Bloody Assizes (see page 209), and owed his nickname, "The Bombardier Bishop", to the fact that he fought in various conflicts, including the English Civil War (the patch covers an injury sustained during a campaign in the Low Countries).

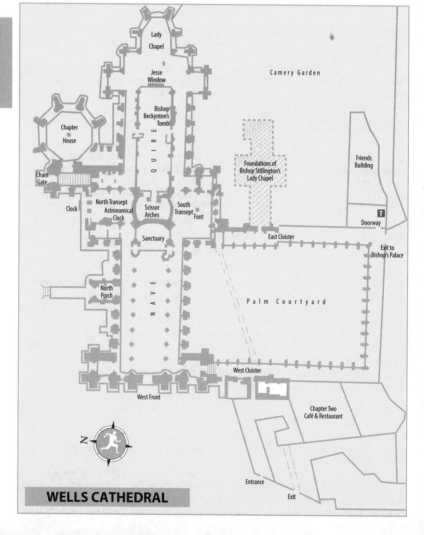

WELLS CATHEDRAL

An annex of the palace proper, the thirteenth-century **Bishop's Chapel** (weekly service Tues noon) was built by Bishop Burnell, a vastly wealthy landowner who also funded the addition of the Great Hall.

The Great Hall and the gardens

Adjacent to the Bishop's Chapel and facing the gatehouse across a well-trimmed croquet lawn, stand the scant but impressive remains of the **Great Hall**, built at the end of the thirteenth century and despoiled during the Reformation.

The tranquil **gardens** predate the palace itself and contain the wells that give the city its name. Despite its placid appearance, **St Andrew's Well** – set in the shadow of the cathedral just behind – is swollen by some 3.5 million gallons of spring water each day.

St Cuthbert's Church and around

A short walk down the High Street from Market Place leads to Gothic **St Cuthbert's Church**, its lengthy spire visible above the rooftops from some way off. Despite its location at the opposite end of Wells to the cathedral, this was once the focus of city life – workers in the wool trade lived in nearby Tucker Street, and St Cuthbert's was the parish church of the trade guilds. The attractively carved ceiling is worth a fleeting glance, but otherwise the church's main interest today lies in its starring role in *Hot Fuzz* – it was a falling pinnacle from St Cuthbert's that squished over-inquisitive local journalist Tim Messenger at the film's characteristically gory church fete.

Old almshouses

Facing St Cuthbert's across its cemetery, compact **Bubwith's Almshouses** are the oldest in Somerset, having been founded by the eponymous bishop in 1436. A chapel and guildhall, both still in use, make up the miniature complex, which fronts Chamberlain Street just behind.

The nearby **Llewellyn's and Charles' Almshouses**, on Priest Row, are even more petite, two opposing rows of traditional-looking almshouses that actually date from 1887.

ARRIVAL AND DEPARTURE   WELLS

By bus Buses (ⓦfirstgroup.com) pull in at the station on Princes Rd, off Market St.

Destinations Axbridge (Mon–Sat 11 daily, Sun 4 daily; 40min); Bath (Mon–Sat every 20min, Sun 14 daily; 1hr 20min); Bridgwater (Mon–Fri 6 daily, Sat 5 daily; 1hr 40min); Bristol (daily every 30min; 1hr 20min); Cheddar (Mon–Sat 11 daily, Sun 4 daily; 30min); Glastonbury (Mon–Sat every 30min, Sun 7 daily; 15min); Street (Mon–Sat every 30min, Sun 7 daily; 25–30min); Taunton (Mon–Fri 6 daily, Sat 5 daily; 1hr 40min); Weston-super-Mare (Mon–

Sat 11 daily, Sun 4 daily; 1hr 25min); Wookey Hole (Mon–Fri 7 daily; 15min); Yeovil (Mon–Sat 7 daily; 1hr 20min).

By train The nearest train station is at Castle Cary, 13 miles away (see page 182), which serves London Paddington, Birmingham and stations across the West Country. Bristol Temple Meads and Bath Spa have more regular services, and frequent bus connections on to Wells.

By car Wells is 21 miles from both Bristol (A37/A39) and Bath (A367/A362/A39), and 6 miles from Glastonbury (A39). There are a couple of long-stay car parks, both west of the cathedral.

INFORMATION AND TOURS

Wells Visitor Information Service 8 Cathedral Green (Mon–Sat 10am–5pm; Nov–Easter till 4pm; ⓣ01749 671770, ⓦwellssomerset.com). Offers an accommodation-booking service, discounted tickets to Wookey Hole and a *Hot Fuzz* trail for film enthusiasts.

Wells Walking Tours ⓣ01749 672438 or ⓣ07961

159122, ⓦwellswalkingtours.co.uk. Historical tours depart from outside *The Crown* on Market Place (Easter to mid-Oct Wed 11am; 1hr 30min; £7; no booking required); check the website for dates of other walks (ghost, *Hot Fuzz*-themed) plus tailor-made tours of the surrounding countryside.

ACCOMMODATION   MAP PAGE 138

The Ancient Gatehouse Hotel Sadler St ⓣ01749 672029, ⓦancientgatehouse.com. This fourteenth-

century hostelry has a range of Laura Ashley-designed rooms, some more boldly furnished than others – only take

3

WELLS MARKET

Market Place still fulfils its historical role twice a week, when around eighty stalls form the city's thriving **market** (Wed & Sat 9am–4pm). Part of the general market is given over to a **farmers' market**, selling a variety of local produce, such as honey, cheese, breads and organic fruit and vegetables.

---

the pink four-poster bedroom if you've brought your eye mask with you – and several have views across the green to the cathedral. Also home to a good Italian restaurant (see below). Minimum two-night stay at weekends. **£115**

Beryl Hawkers Lane, 1 mile northeast of Wells ☎01749 678738, ⓦberyl-wells.co.uk. Luxury country-house B&B, a former hunting lodge, set in lovely gardens with a children's play area and pool (May–Sept). Decor varies among the fourteen rooms – some quite twee, others stylishly understated – though all enjoy great views. If you're after more room, opt for the spacious (self-catering) garden apartment (minimum three-night stay). **£110**, apartment **£150**

The Crown Market Place ☎01749 673457, ⓦcrownat wells.co.uk. Fifteenth-century inn enjoying a very central location, with fifteen en-suite bedrooms, some of them four-posters. It's kiddy- and canine-friendly (extra £5 per dog), and there's a popular bar and restaurant fronting Market Place. (Limited) free parking. **£95**

The Old Farmhouse 62 Chamberlain St ☎01749 675058, ✉theoldfarmhousewells@hotmail.com. Highly regarded B&B, opening onto an attractive walled garden

and draped with wisteria. There are just two en-suite rooms (a double and a twin), each with a flat-screen TV, so you'll probably need to book well in advance. The entertaining hosts (a retired diplomat and a Cordon Bleu-trained chef) create an amiable atmosphere, and there's home-made bread and jam included in the breakfast spread. Two-night minimum stay. **£90**

★ **Stoberry House & Garden** Stoberry Park, off College Rd ☎01749 672906, ⓦstoberryhouse.co.uk. The five beautifully furnished rooms, superb breakfast and immaculate gardens make this gorgeous B&B the top choice in Wells. The attentive owner can also provide Afternoon Tea (from £11.25) in the grounds, with their stellar views down over the cathedral. **£95**

The Swan Hotel Sadler St ☎01749 836300, ⓦswan hotelwells.co.uk. Rambling old coaching inn full of antique atmosphere, with stylish rooms and a lavish Cathedral Suite (£300), complete with freestanding brass bath. The warm interior – oak beams, open fires – is reflected in the friendly service. There's a restaurant in the hotel itself, and a terrifically positioned terrace just over the road (see below). **£114**

EATING AND DRINKING

MAP PAGE 138

★ **Ensemble** 12 Sadler St ☎01749 676246, ⓦensemble wells.co.uk. Beautifully presented Mediterranean-influenced dishes in a classy but casual setting. The restaurant is tucked into the corner of the cathedral green, so you can enjoy spectacular views of the west front while you tuck into salt and pepper squid, seam bream and the like (mains from £12), all made using local produce. Set lunches (from £9.50 for one course), evening a la carte (except Tues). Tues 6–9pm, Wed–Sat noon–2.30pm & 6–9pm.

The Fountain Inn 1 St Thomas St ☎01749 672317, ⓦthefountaininn.co.uk. Leave the touristy pubs of High Street Wells behind and head under the Chain Gate to this rustic-chic gastropub northeast of the cathedral. Good food, with an interesting menu that includes an excellent confit of duck and aubergine chermoula (mains from £12.95). Mon 6–10pm, Tues–Sat noon–2pm & 6–10pm, Sun noon–5pm.

★ **The Good Earth** 4–6 Priory Rd ☎01749 678600, ⓦthegoodearthwells.co.uk. Lovely wholefood restaurant that was making a name for itself with its delicious home-made quiches long before eco food was in vogue. Soups, salads, veggie pizzas (from £3.95) and other organic goodies (mains from £6.95), plus Fair Trade coffee, available to eat in

or take away. Mon–Fri 9am–4.30pm, Sat 9am–5pm.

Goodfellows 5 Sadler St ☎01749 673866, ⓦgood fellowswells.co.uk. Top-notch diner specializing in innovative but pricey seafood on its evening menu and a range of pastries and lighter bites at lunchtime; seafood mains, such as hake and pan-fried scallops from £19; five-course tasting menu £50. There's also a patisserie serving a short but decadent selection. Mon & Sun noon–3pm, Tues 10am–3.30pm, Wed–Sat 9am–3.30pm & 6–10pm (Thurs & Fri from 10am, Wed & Sat till 9.30pm).

The Greek Taverna at The Sun 20 Union St ☎01749 939533, ⓦsungreektaverna.co.uk. Welcoming family-run restaurant, where the traditional recipes for tasty shared plates, salads and grilled meats served at lunch and dinner – including *loutza* (smoked pork loin and *mizithra* cheese; £5.50) and *loukanika* (Greek sausages; £11.90) – have been passed down through the generations, and are still usually cooked by the Greek owners' mother. There's an onus on good produce and simple, authentic dishes – and it's all the better for it. Mon–Sat noon–2pm & 6–9pm.

Rugantino's The Ancient Gatehouse Hotel, Sadler St ☎01749 672029, ⓦancientgatehouse.com. Long-running restaurant serving quality Italian cuisine in

gorgeous medieval surroundings. Choose from a wide-ranging menu of antipasti, pizzas, risottos and mains (from around £17), or push the boat out for the seven-course tasting menu (including excellent home-made pasta) at £32.50. Takeaway also available (daily 6.15–9.30pm). Daily noon–2.30pm & 6.30–10pm.

The Swan Hotel Sadler St ☎01749 836300, ⓦswan hotelwells.co.uk. Tuck into Modern British dishes such as venison Wellington in the handsome surrounds of the oak-panelled *15c A.D.* restaurant (two-course menu £25, three-course menu £32), or alfresco in the *Walled Garden Café* out back or the *Swan Terrace*, facing the cathedral's west front (mains from £8.50). Daily: lounge noon–9pm, Sun from 2pm; restaurant 7–9pm, Sun also 12.30–2pm.

ENTERTAINMENT

Little Theatre Chamberlain St ☎01749 672280, ⓦlittletheatrewells.org. Local players and enthusiastic amateurs come together for a variety of short-run plays, musicals and pantomimes.

Wells Film Centre Princes Rd ☎01749 673195, ⓦwellsfilmcentre.co.uk. Independent cinema showing mostly mainstream movies plus the odd arthouse flick on its three screens.

DIRECTORY

Banks Several, including an HSBC on the corner of Market Place and Sadler St and a NatWest diagonally opposite, on the High St.

Post office In Market Place (Mon–Fri 9am–5.30pm, Sat 9am–12.30pm).

The Mendips

Rising abruptly between the fertile fields of north Somerset and the marshy Levels to the south, the rolling **MENDIP HILLS** – commonly shortened to the Mendips (or just Mendip) – forge a plateau of gorges, dry valleys and collapsed caverns that runs for 22 miles across the centre of the county.

Designated an Area of Outstanding Natural Beauty in 1972, the Mendips are a haven both for wildlife and walkers. Even on the shortest of jaunts, though, it's worth packing a fleece (it can get windy up here) and a rain jacket – as the local saying goes, "If you can see the Welsh hills, it's going to rain; if you can't see them, it's raining."

Aside from the medieval town of **Axbridge**, the best place to base yourself outside of Wells, settlements are few and far between, and only in **Cheddar Gorge** do you really encounter significant numbers of visitors.

Brief history

The Mendips were formed around 280 million years ago, when they were folded into their characteristic whaleback shape – though the coral-rich limestone that makes up Cheddar Gorge and **Burrington Combe** predates that by some eighty million years. As meltwaters bored through this rock during the last Ice Age, they left behind them a

---

THE WEST MENDIP WAY

There are a lot of good walks on the Mendips, but none more so than the **West Mendip Way**, a thirty-mile hike that heads inland from the coast at Uphill, near Weston-super-Mare, and camelbacks the hills to Wells. Along the way, it serves as a vigorous dot-to-dot, connecting many of the area's best individual walks. The route's first proper climb is up **Bleadon Hill**, with good views back across the Bristol Channel, before it summits **Crook Peak** (see page 151). Cutting through the reserves around **Charterhouse** (see page 148), it then links up with the walk fringing **Cheddar Gorge** (see page 146); the last leg threads through **Ebbor Gorge** (see page 145) before finishing in style at the west front of **Wells Cathedral** (see page 137).

Tourist offices in Wells and Weston-super-Mare can provide you with details of the route, and sometimes stock **guides** such as *The West Mendip Way*, by Derek Moyes (£5.95); two OS Explorer **maps**, 141 (*Cheddar Gorge & Mendip Hills West* 1:25,000) and 153 (*Weston-super-Mare & Bleadon Hill* 1:25,000), cover the route.

CAVING IN THE MENDIPS

The Mendip Hills are riddled with sinkholes and underground caverns, and the variety of complex cave systems in a relatively small area makes this one of the best **caving** destinations in the country, with plenty of boulders, waterfalls and canyons to negotiate. **Priddy Caves** alone contain over ten miles of passages, including **Swildon's Hole**, a phreatic cave (meaning it was carved out by water pressure), and **Eastwater Cavern**, Britain's first swallet cave (a depression formed by water washing soil through a cave system), discovered by Herbert Balch (see page 139) in 1902.

Several companies run beginners' **caving trips** around Priddy, as well as to Burrington Combe (see page 150) and Cheddar Gorge (see page 146) – try the Bristol Exploration Club (☎ 01749 672126, 🌐 bec-cave.org.uk), Rocksport (☎ 01934 742343, 🌐 cheddargorge.co.uk/rocksport/adventure-caving) or Adventure Caving (☎ 07971 621946, 🌐 adventurecaving.co.uk).

network of caves, which sheltered hyenas, mammoths, woolly rhinos – the remains of which have been found in **Ebbor Gorge** and in caves in **Long Wood** – and, eventually, man. Settlements were established on the spring lines at the foot of the hills, then up on the plateau, at first in the area around modern-day **Priddy** and then further afield. **Charterhouse** developed with the discovery of lead, and **mining**, first by the Romans and later the Victorians, has left a lasting legacy on the hillsides – the very word Mendips is thought to stem from the medieval term for its deep mines, or "Myne-deepes".

Wookey Hole and around

Daily 10am–5pm, Nov–March till 4pm • £19.95, 15 percent discount if booked online • ☎ 01749 672243, 🌐 wookey.co.uk

Hollowed out by the River Axe a couple of miles outside of Wells, **Wookey Hole** is a cave complex of deep pools and intricate rock formations, but it's folklore rather than geology that takes precedence on the guided tours. The highlight is the alleged petrified remains of the Witch of Wookey, a "blear-eyed hag" who was said to turn her evil eye on crops, young lovers and local farmers until the Abbot of Glastonbury Abbey intervened; a monk, dispatched from the abbey, sprinkled the witch with holy water, turning her to stone.

Aside from the tour, you can also visit a functioning Victorian paper mill and rooms containing speleological exhibits. Indeed, for families, the caves are likely to be just the start of the "Wookey Hole Experience", a mishmash of attractions that range from King Kong and the Valley of the Dinosaurs to a 4D Cinema, a Magical Mirror Maze and a Pirate Circus Show. But no Chewbacca-themed displays – as yet.

Burcott Mill

On the B3139 • Tours July–Sept Wed–Sat 3pm; 45min; £3.50 • ☎ 01749 673118, 🌐 burcottmill.com

One of only a handful of traditional flourmills still working in the West Country, **Burcott Mill**, two miles from Wells, hasn't changed its methods or machinery – including an immense waterwheel, powered by the River Axe – in over a century and a half. The mill makes a pleasant diversion from Wells, especially if you stop by the tearooms after the tour for a scone or cake, made with their own organic, stone-ground flour, of course.

Ebbor Gorge and around

Cutting into the very edge of the Mendips, 2.5 miles northwest of Wells, **Ebbor Gorge** offers a wilder, smaller-scale alternative to the more famous Cheddar Gorge, with tranquillity guaranteed on the wooded trails that follow its ravine to the Mendip plateau. The mixture of ancient woodland and rocky cliffs, cloaked in unusual mosses, liverworts and lichen, attracts a variety of wildlife, including an abundance of butterflies. Lesser horseshoe bats roost in the gorge's caves, which – as fossil remains have revealed – sheltered reindeer and arctic lemming during the Ice Age. The main trails can be bumpy and quite steep in parts, but a two-mile loop near the car park is accessible to pushchairs and wheelchairs.

Deer Leap

Half a mile or so up the road from Ebbor Gorge, a kissing gate leads to **Deer Leap**, an open-access site that rewards a short ramble with some staggering views: Glastonbury Tor, emerging from the Somerset Levels; the Quantocks; and, in the distance to the west, Brean Down, Steep Holm island and the end of the Mendip Hills as they slip into the Bristol Channel.

Priddy

The rich agricultural land surrounding the dinky settlement of **PRIDDY**, five miles from Wells, has provided summer pasture to shepherds working the Mendip plateau for eight hundred years, and its village green hosted an annual **Sheep Fair** for almost as long. The traders' fair, which dated back to 1348, ran until as recently as 2013; the tradition is commemorated by a **hurdle stack** on the focal green. The well-respected **Priddy Folk Festival** (July; ⓦ priddyfolk.org) is still going strong, though, mixing a couple of dozen live acts with Ceilidhs, step clogs and Morris dancing.

Priddy Circles and Priddy Nine Barrows

The whole Priddy area was of ritual significance to tribal Britons, and two intriguing Neolithic monuments lie just northeast of Priddy village itself. **Priddy Circles**, four henge-like enclosures believed to be contemporary to Stonehenge, are spread across private land, but you can wander among the dumpy mounds of **Priddy Nine Barrows**, an eyebrow-shaped row of Bronze Age tumuli; the latter are accessed from a public footpath off the B3135, or off Nine Barrows Lane, northeast of Priddy Green.

Priddy Pools and Priddy Mineries

Behind Priddy Nine Barrows, and just off the B3134, the varied habitat of **Priddy Pools** supports a range of wetland wildlife, including dragonflies and all three species of British newt; pond-dipping for little sticklebacks is particularly fun. The pools were used in the nearby St Cuthbert's lead works, which now make up **Priddy Mineries** nature reserve, home to grass snakes, adders and a number of unusual plants that thrive in the lead-rich soil.

Cheddar Gorge

The deep fissure of **CHEDDAR GORGE** cuts a jagged gash across the Mendips, at times squeezing the road that bisects it through the narrowest of gaps. The first few rocky curves, with the cliffs towering almost 500ft above, hold the gorge's most dramatic scenery, though each turn of its two-mile length presents new, sometimes startling, vistas.

CLIMBING IN THE MENDIPS

The limestone cliffs of Cheddar Gorge are one of the most popular places in the Mendips for **climbing**, its granite-grey walls laced with the coloured ropes of rock-hugging mountain types as they scale Acid Rock, Freaky Wall or any other of its four-hundred-odd routes. If you fancy having a go yourself, contact Rocksport (☎ 01934 742343, ⓦ cheddargorge.co.uk/rocksport) or Cave Climb (☎ 01934 741623, ⓦ caveclimb.com), who can also take you up (and down) the equally impressive cliffs at nearby Burrington Combe (see page 150).

CHEDDAR'S CHEDDAR

The legacy of the rather mundane village of Cheddar, about a mile south of the gorge, is to have given its name to Britain's most famous cheese. **Cheddar cheese** has been handcrafted here for nearly 850 years; Henry II was pretty partial to the stuff, ordering 10,000lb of Cheddar in 1170 (its earliest recorded reference), as was Charles I, under whose reign the cheese was the preserve of the king's court only.

Several factors determine whether a cheese can be Cheddar, including the amount of fat and protein it contains and the level of moisture – lower than 39 percent, according to law. But the thing that really makes Cheddar Cheddar is the practice of cutting the cheese into "bricks", stacking them and then turning them every ten minutes or so to squeeze out the whey – a process, understandably enough, known as **Cheddaring**. Slowly maturing the cheese (traditionally done in muslin cloth, and for up to eighteen months in some cases) hardens it and allows the strong, tangy flavour to develop.

Originally, cheese had to be made within thirty miles of Wells Cathedral to be called Cheddar. While only cheese made in Somerset, Dorset, Devon and Cornwall can be called West Country farmhouse Cheddar, its name has not been protected to the same degree that, say, Melton Mowbray pork pies or Arbroath Smokies have, and most "Cheddar" is now mass-produced far from here. Two companies can still claim to make authentic Cheddar cheese, though. The **Original Cheddar Cheese Co** (daily 10am–5pm; W originalcheddargorgecheese.co.uk), established in 1870 and owners of the first shop in the gorge, use milk from their nearby farm to produce their Cheddars, while the **Cheddar Gorge Cheese Company** (daily 10am–5pm; W cheddaronline.co.uk) age one of their varieties for around a year in Gough's Cave; you can watch part of their seven-hour Cheddar-making process from a viewing gallery in a visitor centre behind their shop (daily 10am–3pm; £1.85). While the output from both includes several quality cheeses, aficionados tend to rate the Cheddars produced by Montgomery's and Kean's, down in South Somerset, as the finest in the country – and therefore, arguably, the world.

3

The gorge, the largest in Britain, was carved out by successive glacial meltwaters over a million years ago, and its toothy limestone crags are now the precipitous domain of primitive **British goats** (the archetypal Billy Goat Gruff) and feral **Soay sheep**, introduced a couple of decades ago to keep invasive plants from killing off rare local wildflowers such as the Cheddar Pink.

Striking though it is, the gorge's natural beauty is undermined somewhat by the mile of tea shops, trinket stores and car parks at its lower end, which cater for the half-million or so visitors that funnel through each year and give this area a slightly nagging theme-park feel, enhanced by the branded bins that run along the pavement.

Cheddar Caves

Daily: Easter, May, mid-July to Sept & school hols 10am–5pm, rest of year from 10.30am • £19.95, 15 percent discount if booked online; combined ticket includes entry to the Museum of Prehistory, Beyond the View and Jacob's Ladder • 01934 742343, W cheddargorge.co.uk

The network of caverns that lies beneath the gorge can be explored to some extent in the **Cheddar Caves**, which were scooped out by underground rivers in the wake of the Ice Age and subsequently occupied by primitive communities. Several important Stone Age discoveries have been made here, including the nine-thousand-year-old skeleton known as **Cheddar Man** – spookily, DNA tests have proved that a local schoolteacher is his direct descendant.

Gough's Cave

Discovered in 1890, **Gough's Cave** burrows deep into the Somerset countryside, following the former route of the River Yeo through a sequence of extravagantly gouged chambers. Just inside the entrance – where Cheddar Man was found – you're immediately swallowed up by the dank, dripping underground world that Richard Gough painstakingly revealed during eight years of exploration. The exhaustive audio tour, narrated by "Gough" in a thick West Country burr, does a good job of rekindling the excitement he must have felt emerging for the first time into caverns such as **St Paul's Cathedral** and **King Solomon's Temple**, their floors arrayed with tortuous rock formations and their walls "flowing" with banoffee-coloured calcite – it's easy to see how, after visiting on honeymoon in 1916, the caverns provided J. R. R. Tolkien with the inspiration for Rohan's Glittering Caves in *The Lord of the Rings*.

Dreamhunters

Further down the main drag, the much smaller **Cox's Cave** was discovered by George Cox (Richard Gough's uncle) in 1837, and now provides the backdrop to **Dreamhunters**, a multimedia walk-through that charts the ascendency of early man. Film projections and lighting effects cleverly recreate the life of cavemen – look out for cackling "fires" flickering on the chamber walls, wolves and a woolly mammoth as you squeeze between crevices and under rock ledges.

Museum of Prehistory

Daily: Easter, May, mid-July to Sept & school hols 10am–5pm, rest of year from 10.30am • £19.95, 15 percent discount if booked online; combined ticket includes entry to the Cheddar Caves, Beyond the View and Jacob's Ladder • ☎ 01934 742343, ⓦ cheddargorge.co.uk

The **Museum of Prehistory** charts Cheddar Gorge's forty thousand years of human occupation, exploring the hunter-gatherer lifestyles of Mesolithic man with displays on tools, religion, sex and cannibalism – five skeletons from Gough's Cave showed signs of butchering – as well as plenty of background information on Cheddar Man. Children will also enjoy the "cave-painting" section and the outdoor demonstrations of flint-knapping, fire-lighting and other Stone Age survival skills (most days in summer).

Beyond the View

Daily: Easter, May, mid-July to Sept & school hols 10am–5pm, rest of year from 10.30am • £19.95, 15 percent discount if booked online; combined ticket includes entry to the Cheddar Caves, the Museum of Prehistory and Jacob's Ladder • ☎ 01934 742343, ⓦ cheddargorge.co.uk

For anyone not tackling Jacob's Ladder and the Gorge Walk, the next best way of appreciating this magnificent landscape (now that open-top buses no longer ferry visitors up and down the gorge) is **Beyond the View**, a 270-degree cinema in the arcade near Gough's Cave. Starting in Cheddar Village, the fifteen-minute film heads up to the highest point on Cheddar Gorge, with asides on local history and wildlife along the way.

Jacob's Ladder and the Gorge Walk

Daily: Easter, May, mid-July to Sept & school hols 10am–5pm, rest of year from 10.30am • £19.95, 15 percent discount if booked online; combined ticket includes entry to the Cheddar Caves, the Museum of Prehistory and Beyond the View • ☎ 01934 742343, ⓦ cheddargorge.co.uk

The best way to experience Cheddar Gorge is from above. Climbing the 274 steps of **Jacob's Ladder** leads to a lookout tower offering vistas towards Glastonbury Tor and occasional glimpses of Exmoor and the sea. From the tower, the three-mile **Gorge Walk**, a public footpath that circuits the summit, provides close-up views over the Pinnacles, the highest point in the gorge; distinctive Horseshoe Bend; and, further down the gorge towards Cheddar, the sheer cliff face of High Rock. A marked path at the top of the loop branches off to Black Rock reserve and, beyond that, Velvet Bottom, Blackmoor and Black Down (see page 149).

Charterhouse and around

The fascinating former mining area of **Charterhouse** lies at the centre of a patchwork of nature reserves that, linked together, provide enough varied walks to keep even the most jaded of ramblers entertained. Long ago reclaimed by nature, this one-time industrial wasteland still bears the scars of nearly two thousand years

A WALK AROUND CHARTERHOUSE

You could spend days following the trails around Charterhouse, though the following six-mile circular **walk** (around 2hr 15min) is as good an introduction to the area as any, traversing four nature reserves and taking in Roman lead workings, World War II remains and the highest point in the Mendips along the way.

Starting from the car park at **Blackmoor Reserve**, follow the footpath as it curves around the site of the **Roman fort**, then head down the steps to the left and across the dam that bridges a slag-fringed pond, where the path traces a dry-stone wall up to the main road. Turn right onto the main road, then take the first left, Rains Batch. The sign at the corner here ("Town Field") refers to the **Roman settlement** that once occupied this entire area – recent surveys indicate that the town was up to five times bigger than Roman Bath, though little archeological evidence has survived the ravages of mining. Where the road levels out at the top of Rains Batch, the fenced-off depression in the field to the left marks the site of Town Field's **amphitheatre**.

At the **radio masts** at the top of the hill, follow signs to the left along a rutted bridleway. After about a quarter of an hour, the landscape opens out into the far-reaching blanket of heather and gorse that constitutes **Black Down**. Following the footpath (not the bridleway) straight ahead leads to the trig point at **Beacon Batch** – at 1068ft, the highest point on the Mendips, with dazzling panoramas of rolling fields, distant villages and the sliver of steely grey water that forms the Bristol Channel.

The path continues down the other side of the hill to **Burrington Combe** (see page 150), but return instead along the narrow trail due south (to the right of the one you came up when looking back at it from Beacon Batch) that runs directly through the heather – the exposed path is a perfect sunbathing spot for adders, so watch your step. Believe it or not, the stone cairns, or "tumps", dotted along either side of the trail here are actually **anti-glider landing obstructions**, which, together with the remains of a **bunker** in the next field to the south (reached by turning left at the fence at the end of the trail and then crossing the first stile on the right), formed part of the decoy town complex constructed on Black Down during World War II (see page 151).

The path eventually runs to the bottom left-hand corner of this field; first, though, it cuts diagonally across to the stile halfway along the fence on the right, before following the fence downhill and then turning left, running parallel to the row of bushes that mark the field's southern boundary. At the bottom left-hand corner of the field, follow the trail south through a wooded coppice and then turn right at the stile on the road, shortly forking left down Fir Lane; taking the first left (before Lower Farm) picks up a trail as it wends through **Long Wood**, dappled on sunnier days and carpeted with bluebells in the spring – the little "gates" in the stone walls here enable badgers to move freely around the reserve.

Shortly after emerging from the woods, the path forks. Right leads to **Black Rock Reserve** and **Cheddar Gorge** (see page 146), left (which is the route to take) through **Velvet Bottom**, where the soft ground staggers up over a series of settlement dams, remnants of the area's Victorian lead-mining industry. The trail runs past a number of large **buddles** and then some seriously bobbly **"gruffy" ground**, before rejoining the main road; turn left and, shortly after passing the old miners' church of **St Hugh's** (May–Sept Sun afternoons only), turn right at the crossroads to return to the Blackmoor Reserve car park.

of mining – within a few years of conquering Britain, the Romans were dispatching pigs of Mendip lead across the Empire, with lead mined at Charterhouse shaping the water pipes of Pompeii and, closer to home, lining the Roman Baths just up the road (see page 46).

The legacy left on the landscape – and by the Victorian miners who followed them – is best seen at **Blackmoor Reserve** and the adjoining reserves of **Velvet Bottom** and **Ubley Warren**, where the swathes of furrowed ground are eerily treeless. From Blackmoor, paths lead north to **Black Down**, a gorse-covered heathland offering wonderful rural views, and on to **Rowberrow Forest** and **Dolebury Warren**, the latter a medieval rabbit keep and home to the earthen ramparts of an enormous Iron Age hillfort.

Blackmoor Reserve

Charterhouse itself is little more than a quiet crossroads and the Charterhouse Centre, an old school that now serves as a base for outdoor activities. Beyond this, **Blackmoor Reserve**, like much of the surrounding area, is covered with grassy humps known as "grooves" or **gruffy ground**, the result of lead ore being cut from veins directly beneath the surface. Blackmoor is the site of an old **Roman fort** – little more than a tussock-clumped bowl today – and, further along the path to the right (and much more noticeable), the remains of two Victorian **lead-condenser flues**. The glassy slag heaps nearby date from around this time, when the increasingly desperate miners resorted to re-smelting slag from earlier operations to try and draw out the residual lead.

Velvet Bottom and Ubley Warren

The terrain at **Velvet Bottom**, accessed from the main road just south of the Charterhouse Centre, is the sort of spongy, rabbit-trimmed surface that characterizes much of the walking on the Mendips. The narrow reserve is dotted with circular pits known as **buddles**, settling beds that were used for washing the impurities out of lead ore.

Nearby **Ubley Warren** harbours similar reminders, including, at Banwell's Shaft, a series of **rakes**, lines of mineral veins that have been hacked into what look like rocky gullies, and the remains of a **horse whim**, a horse-drawn winch that was used to haul buckets full of ore to the surface.

Axbridge

Set at the foot of the Mendips' southern escarpment, sleepy **AXBRIDGE** still retains the look of a medieval market town, though the heady days it enjoyed when the town was important enough to have its own mint are long gone. A number of attractive, ancient-looking houses line the High Street, including the **old drugstore** and, diagonally opposite, the **old butcher's shop**, its studded wooden door making for a "magnificent entrance", as so aptly described by John Betjeman.

Axbridge's mercantile tradition continues on the first Saturday of the month, when a dozen or so stallholders congregate in the pretty little central square for the local **farmers' market** (9am–1pm).

King John's Hunting Lodge

April–Oct daily 1–4pm, first Sat of the month from 11am • £2.50 • ☎ 01934 732012, ⓦ kingjohnshuntinglodge.co.uk

Sitting on the corner of The Square, the beautifully restored timber-framed **King John's Hunting Lodge** is home to Axbridge's local-history museum, whose focus includes minor exhibits on the town's wool-trading past, the geology of the Mendips and scattered finds from a Saxon site at Brent Knoll (see page 236).

Although the king used to hunt in the Royal Forest of Mendip (modern-day Axbridge and Cheddar), the building was actually built around 1460, a good two and a half centuries after John's reign, for a wealthy wool merchant – note the wooden arch braces that support the vertical beams, a structure found only in Somerset timber-framed houses, and the decorative upstairs windows, known as ogee-headed windows. The crowned figurehead on the corner is a remnant of the days when the house served as *The King's Head Inn*.

Burrington Combe

Dotted with billy goats skittering about its upper ledges, **Burrington Combe** (pronounced *coom*) is a smaller version of nearby Cheddar Gorge, popular with cavers, climbers and walkers seeking a quieter alternative to its more famous neighbour. The limestone has been worn into sharp, serrated crags, most significantly at a crevice in the

OPERATION STARFISH

Thanks to their network of old mines, underground caverns and hidden gorges, the Mendips assumed an unusual role during **World War II**. The Home Guard stored weapons in caves at Burrington Combe, the Special Operations Executive had a secret hideaway in Ebbor Gorge, and St Hugh's Church at Charterhouse doubled as an anti-gas centre. But nothing was quite as elaborate as the **decoy town** on Black Down.

An important part of **Operation Starfish** – a countrywide system of dummy towns that distracted night-time German raids away from their intended targets – Black Down was one of a dozen sites set up around the region to protect the docks at Bristol. The scaled-down city was a remarkable feat. Hundreds of lights were strategically placed across the hilltop to mimic key areas of Bristol, turning a bit of the Somerset countryside into Temple Meads Railway Station, for example, or the Pyle Hill Goods Yard. The whole system was carefully manipulated to resemble the comings and goings of "trams" and "trains" far below – an old **control bunker**, one of the complex's few surviving remnants, can still be seen in a field just south of Black Down (see page 149). To further hoodwink the Luftwaffe, when bombs *were* dropped on the area, ground crews would ignite fire baskets, giving the impression to the pilots above that the "city" was ablaze.

Despite the ingenuity of the system – and the occasional "success", as scattered bomb craters testify – the decoy ultimately did little to protect Bristol, and the city was on the receiving end of some of the severest bombing of the Blitz (see page 96).

lower end of the combe (on the left if you're coming down from Wells), known as the **Rock of Ages**. It was here in 1763 that the Reverend Augustus Toplady sought refuge from a storm, inspiring him to pen the famous hymn ("Rock of Ages, cleft for me, let me hide myself in thee…"), though judging by the size of the crack, it can't have been much more than a damp drizzle.

About 275yds back up the combe, on the same side, an unmarked trail leads 50yds or so to **Aveline's Hole**, the site of the oldest cemetery in Britain (its incumbents perished nearly 8500 years ago) and home to one of the UK's few examples of prehistoric cave art. The cave belongs to the University of Bristol Speleological Society, and only experienced cavers can go beyond the gate two-thirds of the way in.

At the top of the combe, a path from the lay-by on the right weaves up heather-clad **Black Down** to Beacon Batch, the highest point on the Mendips (see page 149).

Crook Peak

The Mendips tail out as they approach the Bristol Channel, but rocky **Crook Peak**, two miles west of Axbridge and one of the last hills in the range, rewards hikers who struggle up its steep summit with great views over Brent Knoll and Brean Down (and the M5) and across the water to Wales. The shortest route to the top (about a mile one-way) starts from a path just opposite the car park on Webbington Road; the longer approach from the car park on Winscombe Hill, just off the A38 (around 2.5 miles one-way), follows the West Mendip Way (see page 144) through **King's Wood** and across **Wavering Down** before climbing up to the barrelling wave of rock that marks the peak itself.

GETTING AROUND   **THE MENDIPS**

By bus Public transport is essentially limited to First Group's (w firstgroup.com) #126 service from Wells (for Axbridge and Cheddar); some of the smaller destinations are walkable from stops along this route.
Destinations Axbridge (Mon–Sat 11 daily, Sun 4 daily; 40min); Cheddar (Mon–Sat 11 daily, Sun 4 daily; 30min).
By bike Wookey Hole, Ebbor Gorge, Priddy and Charterhouse are on the West Country Way (National Cycle Route 3). The Strawberry Line (National Cycle Route 26; w thestrawberryline.co.uk) follows the old GWR branch route that was used to ship strawberries to London from the fields of the Cheddar Valley; it currently connects Cheddar with Axbridge and Kings Wood, and passes through the orchards of Thatchers cider farm in Sandford (see page 152).

THERE'S GOLD IN THEM THAR HILLS

Thatchers Gold, that is. Plus Old Rascal, Cheddar Valley and the dozen other varieties of **cider** that **Thatchers** produce at their farm in Sandford, four miles north of Axbridge on the A368. It's a big operation, capable of fermenting a million litres of apple juice at a time; on a more personal scale, you can taste their cider straight from the barrel at their shop (Mon–Sat 9am–6pm, Sun 10am–1pm; ☎01934 822862, ⊛thatcherscider.co.uk), or take a walk through their orchards nearby.

INFORMATION

National Trust Office The Cliffs, Cheddar (10am–5pm: mid-March to Oct daily; Nov–Feb Sat & Sun only; ☎01934 744689, ⊛nationaltrust.org.uk/cheddar-gorge). Information point and outdoor centre, the first of its kind in the country when it opened in 2010.

Useful websites Mendip Hills AONB (⊛mendiphillsaonb.

org.uk) has details of events in the area and a number of downloadable walking routes.

Maps OS Explorer 141 (*Cheddar Gorge & Mendip Hills West* 1:25,000) and 153 (*Weston-super-Mare & Bleadon Hill* 1:25,000) cover the area.

ACCOMMODATION

Compton House Townsend, Axbridge ☎01934 733944, ⊛comptonhse.com. Georgian country-house hotel, whose five lovely bedrooms – two with tremendous four-poster beds and stylish rolltop or claw-foot iron bath, all with flat-screen TVs and reading matter – offset the fact that it's located just off the A371, a walk west of town. The amiable host can whip up home-cooked evening meals (from £18.50). **£110**

The Oak House Hotel The Square, Axbridge ☎01934 732444, ⊛theoakhousesomerset.com. Right in the heart of medieval Axbridge – and dating back to the eleventh century itself – the friendly *Oak House Hotel* has a variety of smartly designed modern en suites, including good-value family rooms, and a great little restaurant (see below). **£94**

★ **The Wookey Hole Inn** Wookey Hole ☎01749 676677, ⊛wookeyholeinn.com. Just down the street from the caves, this excellent inn has contemporary, fully equipped rooms – with low-slung beds, matt flooring and swish bathrooms – that belie its traditional exterior. And you get your continental breakfast delivered to your room.

The restaurant and bar are also top choice (see below). **£110**

YHA Cheddar Hillfield, Cheddar ☎0845 371 9730, ⊛yha. org.uk. Clinically refurbished Victorian house in Cheddar village, not too far from the gorge but far enough to be away from the hustle and bustle. It's all very spick and span, with modern, spacious rooms – dorms, private rooms, en-suite doubles and family rooms – and a decent kitchen. There's an on-site laundry and a cycle store – the Strawberry Line cycle route to Axbridge passes nearby. Dorms **£15**, doubles **£39**

CAMPING

Wookey Farm Campsite Monks Ford, Wookey ☎01749 671859, ⊛wookeyfarm.com. Relaxed family-run campsite set on a small working farm. It's simple (composting loos and no showers, yet) but all the better for it – entertainment comes around the campfire or down on the rope swings along the River Axe. The cute honesty farm shop (in an old horse box) sells milk and cheese from the farm's goatherd. Minimum two-night stay at weekends & during July/Aug. Closed Nov to mid-March. Pitches **£18.50**

EATING AND DRINKING

Frank's Restaurant The Bays, Cheddar ☎01934 742761, ⊛franksrestaurant.co.uk. Upmarket restaurant, with candlelit tables come dinner, tucked away off the main drag at the bottom of Cheddar Gorge. The mostly Modern British dishes are, for the majority, based around locally sourced products such as rump of Somerset lamb and sirloin steaks from a farm in nearby Priddy. Mains from £18.95, plus two- and three-course set lunches (£17.95/22.50). Tues, Wed & Sat 6–9pm, Thurs & Fri noon–2pm & 6–9pm, Sun noon–2pm.

The Lamb The Square, Axbridge ☎01934 732253, ⊛lamb.butcombe.com. Traditional fifteenth-century coaching inn, with oak-beamed ceilings, a striking "bottle bar" and a pleasing pub-grub menu that features steak and

Butcombe pie (£13). Butcombe's own cask ales dominate, including Bitter and Gold. Outside seating, on the square, looks directly across to King John's Hunting Lodge. Mon–Thurs 11.30am–11pm, Fri & Sat 11.30am–midnight, Sun noon–11pm; food served Mon–Fri noon–3pm & 6–9pm, Sat noon–9pm, Sun noon–8pm.

The Oak House Hotel The Square, Axbridge ☎01934 732444, ⊛theoakhousesomerset.com. A simple setting – just half a dozen tables, nicely spaced out in the hotel's red-brick restaurant – but with a good menu that changes regularly and includes some lip-smacking dishes such as slow-cooked cider chorizo (mains from £11.95; seasonal tasting menu £49). There's a chilled little lounge bar next door for an after-dinner drink, with Thatchers Old Rascal and their own Oak House Ale on tap. Daily 8am–11pm, food served noon–9pm.

The Queen Victoria Inn Pelting Drove, Priddy ☎ 01749 676385, ⓦ thequeenvicpriddy.com. Cosy, characterful Butcombe pub, just off Priddy Green, with low ceilings, stone walls and a light, flagstone-floored restaurant (char-grilled meats a speciality; from £9.25). There's also a little children's playground. Daily noon–11pm, Sun till 10.30pm, food served Mon–Fri noon–3pm & 5–9pm, Sat noon–9pm, Sun noon–8pm.

The Wookey Hole Inn Wookey Hole ☎ 01749 676677, ⓦ wookeyholeinn.com. Consistently good cooking and a fairly wide-ranging menu of interesting dishes such as herb-crusted cod with samphire, and a hit-list of tempting desserts (mains from £13.50). The bar serves a great selection of Belgian beers, plus local ales and ciders (including Wilkins); in fine weather, you can quaff them in the quirky sculpture garden. Daily noon–11pm, Sun till 3pm, food served Mon–Sat noon–2pm & 7–9pm.

3

Glastonbury and the Somerset Levels

THE AVALON MARSHES

Glastonbury and the Somerset Levels

In a county laden with legends, Glastonbury is king. For centuries a site of pilgrimage, its historical guestbook reads like a Who's Who of ancient mythology and religious lore, with everyone from St Patrick and King Arthur to Jesus Christ himself alleged to have passed through at some point; some say the Holy Grail is here, others that the Lord of the Underworld resides just outside of town. There's no disputing, however, the status of Glastonbury Abbey: the cradle of Christianity in the UK and the supposed final resting place of Arthur and Guinevere, its ruins make up one of the most evocative sights in Somerset. There are a couple of good regional museums in town – scattered among the sanctuaries and shops that form the country's most enthusiastic centre of New Age cults – though the other must-see sight, the humpback hill of Glastonbury Tor, lies just to the southeast, where more folklore (and fine views) await. The cluster of houses that almost runs into Glastonbury from the south is Street, a town whose link with Clarks shoes is the focus of a worthwhile little museum.

4

Beyond here spread the **Somerset Levels**, a curious patchwork of rivers, rhynes (pronounced *reens*), drains and ditches that constitute the largest area of low-lying wetlands in Britain. Topping out just a few feet above sea level, they are under constant threat of **flooding**, though plans are gradually being put in place to prevent a repeat of the disastrous floods that beset the region in late 2013 and early 2014 (see page 169). Even then, for lengthy periods of the year vast areas will still be submerged beneath several feet of water – when the floodwaters rise and the fields go under, the countryside can resemble a disjointed lake, with the spindly silhouettes of pollard willows appearing to float above the surface. The area's original settlers deserted the Levels during winter, prompting the Saxons to label them the *Sumorsaete*, or **Land of the Summer People**, a name that over time has been co-opted to cover the entire county.

Some of Somerset's earliest signs of settlement have been found here, in the so-called **lake villages** preserved in peat bogs near Glastonbury and Meare, and in the wooden walkways that carried tribal Britons across the marshes, most famously on the **Sweet Track**. Sections of this ancient footpath are preserved under **Shapwick Heath Nature Reserve**, the largest in a system of wildlife reserves that attract myriad birdlife to their shallow pools and densely packed reedbeds.

Most of the man-made sights – such as the assorted ruins of **Muchelney Abbey**, near the regional hub of **Langport** – are set on higher ground, though much of the area's appeal lies in simply ambling through its sweeping lowlands, the gentle rhythm of rhyne and river slowly ingraining itself until you can no longer imagine a horizon that isn't endless.

Glastonbury and around

Six miles south of Wells, **GLASTONBURY** lies at the centre of the so-called **Isle of Avalon**, a region rich with mystical associations. At the heart of it all is the early Christian legend that the young Jesus once visited this site, a story that is not as far-fetched as it sounds. The Romans had a heavy presence in the area, mining lead in the Mendips,

GREY HERON CHICKS, SWELL WOOD NATURE RESERVE

Highlights

❶ **Glastonbury Abbey** Thanks to King Henry VIII, Somerset's most spectacular abbey is now the county's most spectacular ruin. See page 159

❷ **Glastonbury Tor** Steeped in legend and mired in myth, and offering views fit for a (legendary) king. See page 164

❸ **Glastonbury Festival** Buy your ticket eight months in advance, pack your wellies and enjoy the ride that is simply Britain's biggest, boldest and best music festival. See page 168

❹ **The Avalon Marshes** A magical wetland wilderness, home to some of the best birdwatching in the country. See page 169

❺ **Muchelney** Dinky village with a trio of fine medieval buildings, capped by the prominent remains of Muchelney Abbey. See page 176

❻ **Swell Wood Nature Reserve** Make a beeline for the southwest's largest heronry, where spiky-feathered chicks take their first tentative flights from the treetops in spring. See page 177

❼ **Smoked eels** A Somerset Levels delicacy, and at their tastiest when they've been whipped hot out of the smokery and plonked straight onto your plate. See page 178

HIGHLIGHTS ARE MARKED ON THE MAP ON PAGE 158

and one of these mines was reportedly owned by **Joseph of Arimathea**, a well-to-do tin merchant said to have been related to Mary. It's not *completely* unfeasible that the merchant took his kinsman on one of his many visits to his property, in a period of Christ's life of which nothing is recorded – it was this vague possibility to which William Blake referred in his *Glastonbury Hymn*, better known as *Jerusalem*: "And did those feet, in ancient times/Walk upon England's mountains green?".

Glastonbury's legends are much larger than the town itself, a few streets focused around Market Place and the walled square of grassy parkland that houses the **abbey** ruins. New Age mystics and spiritual healers dominate the esoteric **High Street**, running shops with names like Cat & Cauldron, Natural Earthling and The Wonky Broomstick, and selling more crystals than you can shake a shaman stick at.

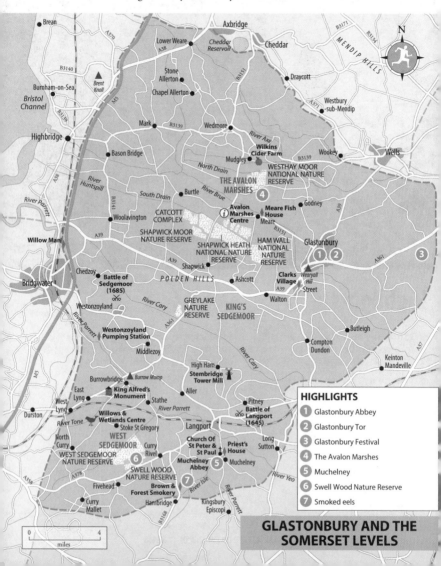

HIGHLIGHTS

1. Glastonbury Abbey
2. Glastonbury Tor
3. Glastonbury Festival
4. The Avalon Marshes
5. Muchelney
6. Swell Wood Nature Reserve
7. Smoked eels

GLASTONBURY AND THE SOMERSET LEVELS

For a bit of a breather, away from the pungent waft of incense, head up nearby **Glastonbury Tor** and **Wearyall Hill**, both rich in folklore themselves and offering, particularly in the case of the Tor, superlative panoramas of the surrounding Levels.

Brief history

It's difficult to separate fact from fiction in Glastonbury's past. Its history – a complex interweaving of ancient Celtic myth and religious legend – begins around 150 BC, when tribal Britons lived in the marshland huts that made up the **Glastonbury Lake Villages**. At that time, Glastonbury was surrounded by water and was known as *Ynis Witrin*, the Isle of Glass, or **Avalon**, the Island of Apples – though other myths link this name to the Celtic underworld (see page 161).

The lake villages were abandoned around the same time that **Joseph of Arimathea** allegedly landed here to convert the country in 63 AD, establishing with his disciples – who according to some eighth-century chroniclers included Mary, her sister Martha and Mary Magdalene – the first church in Britain. **St Patrick** was believed to have been made abbot of a Celtic monastery here in 443 (later visited by **St David**), and in the eighth century, Ine, the Anglo-Saxon king of Wessex, built the stone church around which the abbey later grew.

Glastonbury was briefly awoken from the slumber that followed the abbey's demolition in the mid-sixteenth century when the waters of the **Chalice Well** were discovered to have curative properties – the **Old Pump House** was fashioned in a hurry in the early 1750s to deal with the influx of visitors – but has since relied on trade brought in first on the **Glastonbury Canal** and then on the **Somerset & Dorset Railway**, and more recently a burgeoning tourist industry founded on its mystical past.

Glastonbury Abbey

Abbey Gatehouse, Magdalene St • Daily 9am–6pm June–Aug till 8pm, Nov–Feb till 4pm • £8.25, discount if booked online • ☎ 01458 832267, ⓦ glastonburyabbey.com

Aside from its mythological origins, **Glastonbury Abbey** can safely claim to be the country's oldest Christian foundation, dating back to the seventh century and possibly earlier. Three kings (Edmund, Edgar and Edmund Ironside) were buried here, and in the tenth century, funded by a constant procession of pilgrims, the Anglo-Saxon church was enlarged by St Dunstan (later archbishop of Canterbury), under whom it became the richest Benedictine monastery in the country. Further expansion took place under the Normans, though most of the additions were destroyed by fire in 1184. Rebuilt, the abbey was the longest in Europe when it was destroyed in the Dissolution of the Monasteries in 1539, and the ruins, now hidden behind walls and nestled among acres of well-tended grassland, can only hint at its former extent.

The Lady Chapel

The most complete set of remains is the shell of the **Lady Chapel**, at the west end of the abbey, with its carved figures of the Annunciation, the Magi and Herod. The chapel was built on the site of the wooden Anglo-Saxon church, itself believed to have been erected around the Vetusta Ecclesia or "**Old Church**", the small wattle and daub construction allegedly built by Joseph of Arimathea and his disciples in 63 AD, on a spot subsequently known as the "Holiest Earthe of England". With that legend in mind, venturing down into the now-open crypt below the chapel can make for a momentous few steps.

The choir

The abbey's **choir** – announced by the photogenic remains of the transept piers – introduces another strand to the Glastonbury story, for it holds what is alleged to be the **tomb of Arthur and Guinevere** (see page 161). The discovery of two bodies in an ancient **grave** south of the abbey in 1191 was taken to confirm the popular identification of Glastonbury with Avalon; in 1278, the bones were transferred to the abbey but disappeared after the Dissolution of the Monasteries – a plaque near the **High Altar** marks the spot where their black marble tomb lay.

The rest of the grounds

The fourteenth-century **Abbot's Kitchen** is the only monastic building to survive intact, with a great central lantern that funnelled smoke away from the four huge corner fireplaces. Henry III ate here in 1497, dining on fish that were dried and salted at

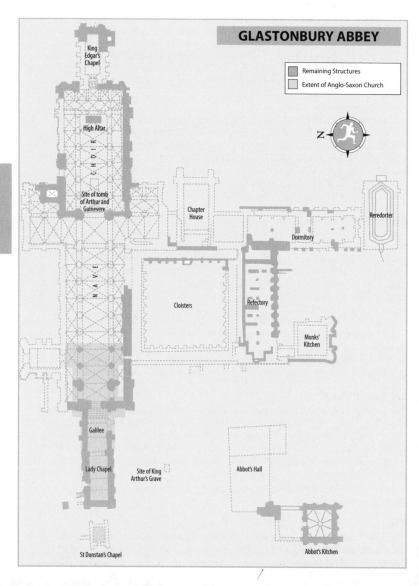

GLASTONBURY ABBEY

King Edgar's Chapel

Remaining Structures

Extent of Anglo-Saxon Church

N

High Altar

CHOIR

Reredorter

Site of tomb of Arthur and Guinevere

Chapter House

Dormitory

NAVE

Cloisters

Refectory

Monks' Kitchen

Galilee

Lady Chapel

Site of King Arthur's Grave

Abbot's Hall

St Dunstan's Chapel

Abbot's Kitchen

4

KING ARTHUR AND THE ISLE OF AVALON

The West Country is sprinkled with sites relating to the legendary **King Arthur**, but only in Glastonbury do you get the feeling that some of these tales might not be so tall. Arthur's name appears in historical texts as early as the ninth century, in the Welsh poem *Y Gododdin*, the *Historia Brittonum* (*History of the Britons*) and the *Annales Cambraie* (*Welsh Annals*), which tell of an Arthur (or Arturius) defending his lands against the Anglo-Saxons in the mid-sixth century. Flesh was added to these bones by **Geoffrey of Monmouth** in the mid-twelfth century, whose embellished *Historia Regum Britanniae* (*History of the Kings of Britain*) established most of the Arthurian legend that we know today, while the French writer **Chretien de Troyes** later added Lancelot and Camelot to the mix.

The bastard child of Uther Pendragon, King of Britain, Arthur was raised by the wizard **Merlin**, and was crowned king himself aged just 15, a feat preordained when he pulled the sword **Excalibur** from its seemingly immovable position, wedged deep into a stone. Arthur married **Guinevere** and ruled his kingdom from **Camelot** (believed to be the sixth-century fort at Cadbury Castle; see page 187) but spent much of his time on a fruitless quest with his **Knights of the Round Table** to find the **Holy Grail** – though it would seem that they didn't have too far to look (see page 163).

Returning to England to quell a rebellion led by his nephew **Mordred**, Arthur was mortally wounded at the **battle of Camlann**; Excalibur was subsequently thrown into a lake – supposedly from Pomparles (or Pons Perilis) Bridge, which crosses the River Brue just south of Glastonbury – and his dying body brought to the **Isle of Avalon**. He lay buried at **Glastonbury Abbey** until the late twelfth century, when, shortly after its gutting by a great fire, monks "discovered" his body, along with Queen Guinevere's, under a leaden cross bearing the inscription "Here lies the renown King Arthur in the Isle of Avalon". Experts argue over how old the writing style is, and the cross itself was lost centuries ago, but there's no doubt that the resulting **influx of pilgrims** provided the finance necessary for the abbey's restoration. The bones were lost after the Dissolution of the Monasteries and have never been seen again.

the fish house in Meare (see page 170) and produce stored in barns throughout the abbey's estates, like the one at the Somerset Rural Life Museum (see page 162).

Behind the main entrance, look out for the **Glastonbury Thorn** that is supposedly from the original thorn tree on Wearyall Hill (see page 164); only at Glastonbury do they flourish, it is claimed – everywhere else they die within a couple of years.

Glastonbury Lake Village Museum

9 High St • April–Sept daily 10am–5pm, Sun till 5.30pm; Oct–March Mon–Thurs 10am–4pm, Fri & Sat till 4.30pm • £3.50 (free for EH members) • ⓦ glastonburyantiquarians.org/site

The bulging fifteenth-century **Tribunal** – long thought to be the abbots' court but actually a merchant's house – provides an atmospheric setting for the small but interesting **Glastonbury Lake Village Museum**, with displays from the Iron Age settlements that grew up in the former marshland northwest of Glastonbury. Discovered by Arthur Bulleid in 1892, the villages consisted of conical wattle houses that were consistently rebuilt on layers of clay as they slowly submerged into the marshes – the finds, which were perfectly preserved in peat after the villages were abandoned in 53 AD, include jewellery made from animal bones, carbonized cakes and a 3000-year-old wooden canoe.

St John the Baptist

High St • Usually Mon–Sat 10.30am–4pm, but times vary throughout the year • Free

The fifteenth-century church of **St John the Baptist**, halfway up the High Street, is worth a quick glance. The tower is reckoned to be one of Somerset's finest, and the interior has a fine oak roof from the period of the church's construction. Modern stained glass depicts the legend of St Joseph of Arimathea, but more interesting are the medieval windows to the right of the altar, illustrating St Dunstan (in the middle), abbot of Glastonbury Abbey; the vessels in the bottom right-hand pane of the window to his right are cruets, a variation of the Grail tale – one contained the blood of Christ, the other his sweat.

For the last 450 years or so, a sprig has been cut each winter from the **Glastonbury Thorn** that grows in the churchyard, and sent to the reigning monarch to place on the royal table come Christmas Day.

Somerset Rural Life Museum

Abbey Farm, Chilkwell St • Daily except Mon 10am–5pm, Nov–Easter also closed Sun • £7.50 • ☎ 01458 831197, ⓦ swheritage.org.uk/somerset-rural-life-museum

Centred round the fourteenth-century Abbey Barn, the engaging **Somerset Rural Life Museum** focuses on a range of local rural occupations, from cider-making to willow growing, with further galleries exploring regional festivals (such as wassailing) and folklore. Temporary exhibitions cover work from local artists, and there are regular themed arts and crafts activities for kids. The barn itself, once a produce storehouse for the abbey's 524 acres of arable estates, has been preserved in its original (atmospheric) state and backs onto an orchard that holds twenty different types of cider-apple trees, including Gennet Moyle, a local variety once thought extinct.

4

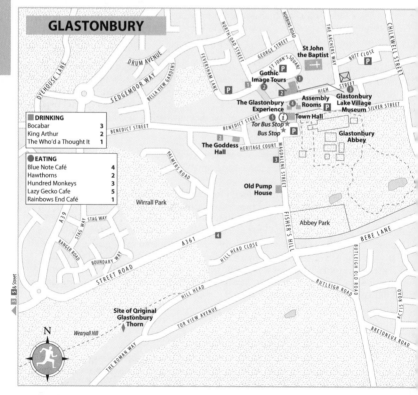

GLASTONBURY

DRINKING	
Bocabar	3
King Arthur	2
The Who'd a Thought It	1

EATING	
Blue Note Café	4
Hawthorns	2
Hundred Monkeys	3
Lazy Gecko Cafe	5
Rainbows End Café	1

Chalice Well

Chilkwell St • Daily 10am–6pm, Nov–March till 4.30pm • £4.50 • ☎ 01458 831154, ⓦ chalicewell.org.uk

Standing amid a tranquil garden intended for quiet contemplation, the fabled **Chalice Well** is fondly alleged to be the hiding place of the Holy Grail. Legend has it that Joseph of Arimathea buried the Grail (the chalice from the Last Supper, in which the blood was gathered from the wound in Christ's side) at the foot of Glastonbury Tor; the spring of blood that miraculously flowed forth is now marked by the well, though the water's red colouring has more to do with its rich iron content than any sacred symbolism.

You can **sample the spring waters** at the Lion's Head fountain, towards the top of the gardens – it's akin to sucking on a copper coin, and quite a different taste to the water flowing from the White Spring – or from the tap around the corner in Well House Lane.

White Spring

Well House Lane • Mon, Tues & Fri–Sun 1.30–4.30pm • Free • ⓦ whitespring.org.uk

Around the corner from the Chalice Well, the Well House, a vaulted Victorian reservoir, has been converted into a shrine-filled temple in order to protect the **White Spring**, a natural well that drops 15ft into a series of pools. Legend links this place with the entrance to Gwyn Ap Nudd's Underworld in Glastonbury Tor (see page 164); less controversial is the fact that the reservoir itself was never used – the very waters it was built to store, sweet-tasting and tinged white with calcium, saw to that.

4

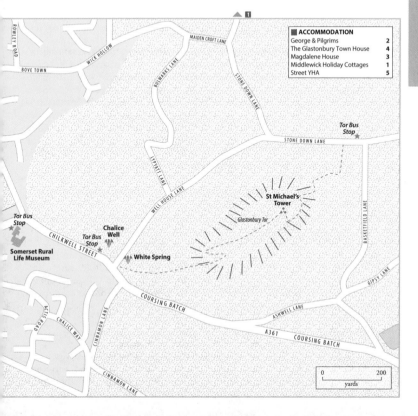

> **PARADISE LOST?**
>
> One of Glastonbury Tor's earliest mythic incarnations is as a magic mountain that was home to **Gwyn ap Nudd**, the Celtic Winter King and Lord of the Underworld, and in later legends the King of the Fairies. As the **Winter King**, Nudd rode through the sky each autumn, leading his pack of phantom hounds (the *Cŵn Annwn* in Celtic mythology, known locally as the Gabble Ratchet) in the "Wild Hunt", seen as a sign of imminent death – more likely a primitive explanation for storms, or the night-time honking of migrating geese. Likewise, it was his Tor-top battle with the Summer King each year that represented the changing of the seasons.
>
> As the **Lord of the Underworld**, Nudd protected the dead on their way to *Gwynfa*, or Paradise – the road just north of the Tor is called Paradise Lane – and ruled over the inner realm of *Annwn*, or Avalon, the Meeting Place of the Dead. To this day, some people still believe that the Tor is hollow, though no one knows what exactly lies inside.

Wearyall Hill

A five-minute walk up Hill Head leads to **Wearyall Hill**, with good views of Glastonbury Tor and across the surrounding Levels to the Mendips and the Polden and Quantock hills. It was here that a tired Joseph of Arimathea, with his disciples ("Weary, All"), was said to have stuck his thorn staff into the ground to rest; by morning, it had taken root. Descendants of this original **Glastonbury Thorn** are dotted about town and still bloom twice a year (Easter and around Christmas); the thorn on Wearyall itself was vandalized in 2010, its stump lingering forlornly for nearly a decade until it was removed entirely in 2019.

Glastonbury Tor

From Chilkwell St, turn left into Well House Lane and immediately right for the footpath that leads up to the Tor; the shorter, steeper path is accessed from the top of Well House Lane and is served by the Tor Bus (see page 165) • Free • NT • ⓦ nationaltrust.org.uk/glastonbury-tor

Towering over the Somerset Levels, a lone pinnacle in an open expanse of marshland, the 521ft-high conical hill of **Glastonbury Tor** has invited myth and conjecture for centuries, serving (allegedly) as everything from the Land of the Dead (see box) to a meeting point for UFOs. Topped by the dilapidated **St Michael's Tower**, sole remnant of a fourteenth-century church, it is visible for miles around and commands stupendous views, encompassing Wells, the Quantocks, the Mendips and, on very clear days, the mountains of South Wales. Pilgrims once embarked on the stiff climb here with hard peas in their shoes as penance – nowadays, people come to picnic, fly kites or feel the vibrations of crossing ley lines.

Street

The one-road town of **STREET**, two miles south of Glastonbury, could only be better named if it was called Clarksville, such is the impact the shoemaking magnates **C. & J. Clark** have had on its fortunes since they first started stitching soles here in 1825. Clarks stopped making shoes in Street in the early 1990s, but their headquarters are still here, and their legacy lives on: in the **Shoe Museum**, the **Clarks Village** shopping centre and the focal **Crispin Hall**, built by the Quaker brothers in 1885 as a community centre and named after the patron saint of – yep, you guessed it – shoemakers.

Shoe Museum

40 High St • Mon–Fri 10am–4.45pm, Sat 10am–4pm • Free • ☎ 01458 842243, ⓦ the-shoe-museum.org

The old Clarks factory clock-tower now houses the quirky **Shoe Museum**, whose dazzling collection of slip-ons, knee-highs and strap-up sandals, dating back to Roman times, would make Imelda Marcos blush – compare the extravagant diamante-studded 1930s evening wear with the comfy-looking sheepskin slippers that got the ball rolling over a century before. Such is the bond between company and town that the displays of clunky foot measurers, fashion plates and sepia photographs make this as much a history of Street as it is of shoemaking.

Clarks Village

Farm Rd • Mon–Sat 9am–7pm (Thurs till 8pm), Sun 10am–5pm • ☎ 01458 840064, ⓦ clarksvillage.co.uk

When shoe manufacturing in Street ended in 1993, the derelict warehouses were transformed into **Clarks Village**, the first discount shopping outlet in the UK. The "village" – a clever concept at the time but one that has since snowballed into the scourge of small-town stores across the country – is home to over ninety shops, including GAP, Barbour, The North Face, Superdry and, of course, Clarks (the biggest of the lot), several coffee and food outlets, as well as a tourist information centre (see below) and a children's play area.

ARRIVAL AND DEPARTURE

By bus National Express (ⓦ nationalexpress.com) runs a daily service each way between London Victoria and Glastonbury (4hr 20min), while Berry's Coaches (ⓦ berryscoaches.co.uk) run to and from London Hammersmith (Mon–Sat daily, Sun 2 daily; 3hr 10min). Local First Group (ⓦ firstgroup.com) services drop you off outside the abbey on Magdalene St.

Destinations Bridgwater (Mon–Fri 7 daily, Sat 5 daily; 1hr 15min); Bristol (daily every 30min; 1hr 30min); Street (Mon–Sat every 15min, Sun every 30min; 10min); Taunton (Mon–Fri 6 daily, Sat 4 daily; 1hr 15min); Wells (Mon–Sat every 30min, Sun 7 daily; 15min); Yeovil (Mon–Fri 8 daily,

GLASTONBURY AND AROUND

Sat 7 daily; 1hr 5min).

By train The nearest train stations are Bridgwater, on the Bristol–Exeter line, and the more useful Castle Cary, which serves London Paddington, Birmingham, Weymouth and Plymouth among others (both are about 15 miles away), though Bristol Temple Meads, Bath Spa and Taunton have more regular services and better bus connections.

By car Glastonbury is 29 miles from both Bristol (A37/A39) and Bath (A367/A362/A39), 8 miles from Wells (A39) and 22 miles from Taunton (A39). There are several car parks in town, one right next to the abbey.

GETTING AROUND

By bus The Glastonbury Tor Bus runs from in front of the Glastonbury Tourist Information Centre (see below) to the base of the Tor every 30min, stopping at the Somerset Rural Life Museum (when open) and Chalice Well (April–Sept

daily 10am–5pm; £3, ticket valid all day).
By taxi AJ Taxis ☎ 07877 886797.
Bike rental Available at Glastonbury TIC (see below) for £20 per day.

INFORMATION AND TOURS

Glastonbury TIC St Dunstan's House, 1 Magdalene St (Mon–Sat 10am–5pm, Sun 11am–4pm; ☎ 01458 832954, ⓦ glastonburytic.co.uk). Plenty of info on Somerset in general, plus discounted tickets to the Cheddar Caves, Wookey Hole and other local attractions.
Street TIC Clarks Village, Farm Rd (daily except Wed 10am–4pm; ☎ 01458 447384, ⓦ glastonburytic.co.uk).
Gothic Image Tours Half-day tours of the Ancient Isle of

Avalon and the labyrinth that runs around Glastonbury Tor with the guys behind the Gothic Image Bookshop at 7 High St (£80, much cheaper if you can get a few people together; ☎ 01458 831281, ⓦ gothicimagetours.co.uk).
Tor's Tours Weekly full-day tour that takes a mystical look at Glastonbury's legends with Tor Webster (£95, cheaper if you can get a group together; ☎ 01458 899428, ⓦ torstourofthetor.com).

BY HECKS: CIDER IN STREET

Street might not seem like the kind of place you'd find **traditional farmhouse cider**, but that's exactly what **Hecks** have been producing here since 1841. Stop by the family's cider barn, on the corner of Middle Leigh and Ivythorn Road (it's signed down Stone Hill off the High Street), and sample some straight from the barrel (Mon–Sat 9am–5pm, Sun 10am–12.30pm, Sat till 4.30pm in winter; ☎ 01458 442367, ⓦ hecksfarmhousecider.co.uk).

They're particularly noted for their **Kingston Black** (medium sweet), a former CAMRA National Gold Winner, but also produce several other single-variety ciders, including the smokey Red Jersey from nearby Shepton Mallet. There's also a choice of their own **Torside apple juice** (18 varieties in total), plus a perry or two.

HEALING HANDS

It can seem that every other shop in Glastonbury offers some sort of crystal healing or shamanic training, but if you're interested in developing your soul armour, want to find out more about runic sound work or just fancy getting your chakra balanced, then drop into **The Glastonbury Experience**, a New Age hub at the bottom of the High Street that's home to some of the town's longest-established practitioners. Try the **Isle of Avalon Foundation** (☎01458 833933, ⊛isleofavalonfoundation.com) for an away-day with the faeries; **The Bridget Healing Centre** (☎01458 833317, ⊛bridgethealingcentre.co.uk) for rune reading and shamanic healing; or **The Goddess Temple** (☎07760 775733, ⊛goddesstemple.co.uk) for worshipping the Divine Feminine (Dan Brown would have a field day), and whose temple, behind St Benedict's Church, hosts regular drop-in healing days. Only the truly committed, though, sign up for their Priestess of Avalon training, an in-depth course that takes around three years to complete.

ACCOMMODATION

SEE MAPS PAGES 162 AND 170

George & Pilgrims 1 High St ☎01458 831146, ⊛historicinnz.co.uk/Glastonbury. Built by Abbot Selwood in the fifteenth century, this oak-panelled inn brims with medieval atmosphere, though unless you go for a frilly four-poster (from £107.10) – from which Henry VIII is rumoured to have watched the abbey burn – the rooms themselves are less characterful than the public areas downstairs. **£80.10**

The Glastonbury Town House Street Rd ☎01458 831040, ⊛glastonburytownhouse.co.uk. Three light and airy en-suite rooms – one a double, the others slightly larger twins – in a welcoming B&B a short walk from the centre of town. Breakfast includes a very good full English, taken overlooking the south-facing garden. **£86**

Magdalene House Magdalene St ☎01458 830202, ⊛magdalenehouseglastonbury.com. Grade II-listed former convent directly opposite the abbey, whose three stylish but homely rooms (one with views over the abbey itself, the others to Wearyall Hill) make a great place to retreat to at the end of the day. Comfy beds and a generous breakfast. No children under 7. **£95**

Middlewick Holiday Cottages Middlewick Farm, Wick Lane, 1.5 miles north of Glastonbury ☎01458 832351, ⊛middlewickholidaycottages.co.uk. A dozen self-catering cottages converted from old outbuildings on a farm in nearby Wick, sleeping two to six people – Meadow Barn is the finest, with stone walls, oak floors and a wood burner – plus a beautifully refurbished shepherd's hut and some funky domed glamping cabins. There's an indoor pool and steam room. Some cottages have minimum-night stays. **£70**

Street YHA The Chalet, Ivythorn Hill, Street ☎0845 371 9143, ⊛yha.org.uk. Quirky Swiss-chalet-style accommodation a couple of miles south of Glastonbury. It's the oldest operational YHA in the country but has brightly decorated rooms, including a few for families. Camping pitches also available, plus pre-erected bell tents and camping pods. Dorms **£16**, rooms **£45**, bell tents **£49**, pods **£59**

CAMPING

Isle of Avalon 1 Godney Rd ☎01458 833618. Clean, friendly campsite, a 10min walk from Northload St and within sight of the Tor. The pitches are spacious, and there's a well-stocked shop, plus decent washing facilities and a freezer for cool-box ice-packs. Two-night minimum stay. **£19**

EATING AND DRINKING

SEE MAP PAGE 162

Blue Note Café 4A High St ☎01458 832907. A relaxed place to hang out over inexpensive coffees and cakes or such satisfying veggie bites as falafel and halloumi burgers (burgers around £7). It backs on to The Glastonbury Experience (see box), with some seating in the shared courtyard. Daily 9am–4pm, Sun from 10am.

Bocabar The Red Brick Building Centre, Morland Rd ☎01458 440558 ⊛https://glastonbury.bocabar.co.uk. The younger sibling of Bristol's long-running social hub, this laidback place brings the same popular blend of good food and music to the Somerset Levels. The veg-focused menu works well for a relaxed lunch or an evening out, when there

are regular live bands and DJ sets. Mon 9.30am–4pm, Tues–Thurs 9.30am–11pm, Fri & Sat 9.30am–1am, Sun 10am–5pm.

Hawthorns 8–12 Northload St ☎01458 831255, ⊛hawthornshotel.co.uk. Homely bar and restaurant whose main draw is its eastwards-looking menu: daily ethnic specials (from £12.95) and a variety of quality curries chalked up on the blackboard. Daily 6–11pm, Thurs–Sun till 11.30pm.

Hundred Monkeys 52 High St ☎01458 833386, ⊛hundredmonkeyscafe.com. Mellow contemporary café-restaurant whose wholesome snacks include a

4

GLASTONBURY FESTIVAL

Glastonbury Festival of Contemporary and Performing Arts (ⓦ glastonburyfestivals.co.uk) takes place over four days in late June, with happy campers braving the predictable mudfest at Worthy Farm, outside Pilton, six miles east of Glastonbury itself. Having started as a small hippy affair in the 1970s, "Glastonbury" has become the biggest and best-organized festival in the country, without shedding too much of its alternative feel. It's much more than just a music festival: large parts of the sprawling site are given over to themed "lifestyle" areas, from the meditation marquees of Green Fields to campfire-filled Strummerville and futuristic Arcadia. Bands cover all musical spectrums, from up-and-coming grime acts to international superstars – recent headliners have included Arcade Fire, The Foo Fighters and Stormzy. Despite the steep price (£248), tickets are invariably snapped up within hours of going on sale around mid-October of the previous year.

renowned seafood soup, as well as gourmet sourdough tartines (from £10) and varied salads (from £9.50). Try one of their thirty different varieties of tea with a home-made cookie. Take-away available. Daily 9am–6pm, Thurs–Sat till 8.30pm, Sun till 5pm.

King Arthur 31–33 Benedict St ☎ 01458 830338, ⓦ thekingarthurglastonbury.com. Wood-floored free house near St Benedict's Church, known for its crusty rolls, stuffed with roast pork, roast beef or falafel (£6.50), and its hearty Sunday lunches. Drinks are reassuringly local: beer from Glastonbury Ales, cider from Orchard Pig. Live music most nights. Mon–Thurs 3pm–midnight, Fri–Sun from noon.

Lazy Gecko Cafe 8 Magdalene St ☎ 01458 835624. Directly opposite the abbey gatehouse, this bustling, funky café has an eclectic menu that runs from salads to sardines, via seafood chowder and spicy Moroccan lamb

burger (£9.85). Local art (for sale) provides the decor. Daily 10am–4.30pm.

★ **Rainbows End Café** 17B High St ☎ 01458 833896, ⓦ rainbowsendcafe.com. Classic Glastonbury café, accessed down a narrow arcade and through a vintage clothes shop. Very laidback and very appealing, serving huge wedges of cheese and broccoli quiche, Cajun lentil bake, mushroom and cashew-nut flan and other assorted mains (around £7.95), topped up with heaps of unusual salads (£1.60 a pop). Cute garden out back. Daily 10am–4pm.

The Who'd a Thought It 17 Northload St ☎ 01458 834460, ⓦ whodathoughtit.co.uk. Quirkily decorated dining pub (think along the lines of a mannequin in a phone box and assorted farming implements nailed to the ceiling) with a bijou garden, specializing in meaty mains, such as steak and kidney pie (£9.50). Daily 11.30am–late; food served noon–2pm & 6–9pm.

ENTERTAINMENT

Assembly Rooms High St ☎ 01458 834677, ⓦ assembly rooms.org.uk. Regular talks and musical and theatrical performances.

Chalice Well Chilkwell St ☎ 01458 831154, ⓦ chalice well.org.uk. Various events (concerts, meditations, healings

and the like) throughout the year.

Glastonbury Abbey ☎ 01458 832267, ⓦ glastonbury abbey.com. Big-name concerts, miracle plays, film festivals and exhibitions staged in the abbey grounds.

DIRECTORY

Banks Several on the High St, including a Lloyds and a Barclays.

Markets There's a small monthly farmers' market in Market

Place on the last Sat of the month (9am–2pm).

Post office At the eastern end of the High St (Mon–Sat 9am–5.30pm).

The Somerset Levels

Stretching over 250 square miles from the Mendips to the Quantocks, the vast marshy flatness of the **SOMERSET LEVELS** is a region apart: sparsely populated, flooded in winter (see box) and characterized by the silvery fingers of **rhynes** (drainage ditches) that chase the horizon. The natural area of the **Somerset Levels and Moors** (to give them their full, seldom-used, title) is defined by a huge basin, marked in the east by a zigzagging depression that runs between Nailsea, Weston-super-Mare, Cheddar, Glastonbury and Langport, and to the west by the Bristol Channel. The "**Levels**" part actually refers to the clay areas along the coast; the peat-heavy, lower-lying area inland that makes up most of the region covered in this chapter is technically the "**Moors**" but is almost never referred to as such.

The Levels were created – and the area given its crazy-quilt pattern – in the eighteenth and nineteenth centuries, when the River Brue was irrigated and the fields were drained for peat-digging and enclosed for farming; this system of "wet fencing" is still in use today, though the government is intent on phasing out peat extraction completely by 2030. The result is a highly distinctive landscape, at its most evocative around the old peat workings of the mist-draped **Avalon Marshes**, which have been carefully converted into a series of precious nature reserves. There are a few breaks in the flatness, most obviously at **Burrow Mump**, but also at elevated outcrops like the **Isle of Wedmore** and the **Isle of Athelney**, which were once islands surrounded by impenetrable marshes. In some cases, you can plot the lie of the land simply by the names on a map: villages containing the word "zoy" (such as **Westonzoyland**, where the Duke of Monmouth's attempted rebellion was emphatically crushed at the **Battle of Sedgemoor**) denotes that they too were formerly islands, as were places ending in "ey" – **Muchelney**, for example, is Anglo-Saxon for "Great Island", an obvious setting for a religious building on the scale of **Muchelney Abbey**.

Perhaps as a result of the demands such a landscape places on its populace, the area remains one of Somerset's most traditional. Eels are still fished from the Parrett using hand-held dip-nets, as they have been for centuries, and withies harvested by hook and trussed into bundles for use at basket-making workshops like the one at the **Willows and Wetlands Centre** in Stoke St Gregory. The local importance of this time-honoured industry, a quintessentially Somerset craft, was recognized in 2001 with Serena de la Hey's 40ft-tall **Willow Man**: chest puffed, pointy arms outstretched as he strides beside the M5 near Bridgwater, the wicker figure has become something of an *Angel of the South*.

The Avalon Marshes

The curve of the A39 around Glastonbury effectively marks the eastern boundary of the **Avalon Marshes**, a broad wedge of wetlands rich in wildlife and currently conserved in a patchwork of **nature reserves** that stretches for several miles to the west. Cut through by forgotten roads edged with the occasional pile of freshly dug peat, it's a quite magical landscape, at its most beguiling in the first rays of sunlight, when cotton-budded wisps of mist hang lazily above the waters.

The area's few scattered villages are set on higher ground, either on the **Polden Hills**, which divide the Levels cleanly in half, or on what were once "islands" within the

---

A DISASTER WAITING TO HAPPEN?

Winter flooding is a part of life on the Somerset Levels, but between December 2013 and March 2014, following some of the heaviest rainfall Somerset has ever seen, great swathes of the region were submerged under water. In the worst recorded case of **flooding** in the UK, some 17,000 acres of farmland were swamped, entire villages cut off and nearly two hundred people evacuated from their homes.

Local residents blamed the disaster on the **Environment Agency**'s ongoing refusal to dredge the area's rivers and rhynes, so it was no surprise that the first part of the **Somerset Levels and Moors Flood Action Plan**, a twenty-year project drawn up as soon as the waters receded, was to dredge the crucial first five miles of the rivers Parrett and Tone.

The £100m plan also includes building new pumping stations, creating a tidal barrier on the River Parrett and increasing the capacity of the River Sowy and King's Sedgemoor Drain, but with only a fifth of the project's cost being footed by the government, it remains to be seen exactly where the rest of the funds will come from.

marshes themselves. Nearly six thousand years ago, when this low-lying area was under water, Neolithic man fashioned some of Europe's first **wooden walkways** to connect the communities at what are now Shapwick, Westhay and the Isle of Wedmore (see page 169); the "**lake villages**" that were later established near Glastonbury and Meare remain the best-preserved prehistoric villages ever discovered in the UK.

Meare Fish House

St Mary's Rd, Meare • Key available at any reasonable time during daylight hours from Manor House Farm, 350yds up the road, just behind the church • Free • EH • ⓦ english-heritage.org.uk

The B3151 shadows a rhyne for 3.5 miles west of Glastonbury to the strung-out village of Meare, where the **Meare Fish House** once provided a bounty of roach and pike for the monks of Glastonbury Abbey. Built in 1330 by Abbot Adam of Sodbury (whose figure stands above the front door of the nearby Manor House), it was gutted by a fire in the nineteenth century but remains the only surviving monastic fishery building in England, with a central storage area, used for drying and salting fish, and an upstairs bedroom where the abbot's water bailiff slept. Up to 25,000 fish and 5000 eels were netted each year in a vast **pool** – the "mere" that gave the village its name – which stretched for four miles beyond what is now the River Brue.

Shapwick Heath National Nature Reserve

Entrances on the Westhay–Shapwick and Meare–Ashcott roads • Daily dawn–dusk • Free • ☎ 01458 860120, ⓦ naturalengland.org.uk

The former commercial peat bogs of **Shapwick Heath National Nature Reserve**, four miles west of Glastonbury, make up the largest reserve in the Somerset Levels, its trails cutting through a variety of hay meadow, reedbed and marshy fen. Together with adjacent Ham Wall (see page 171), Shapwick forms a near-unbroken block of superb

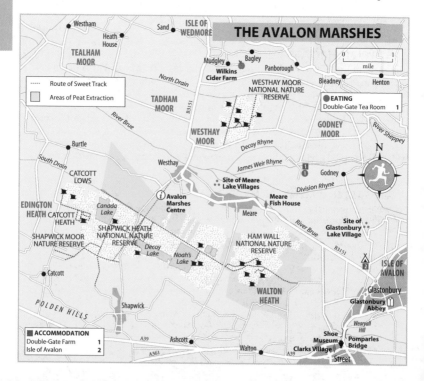

BIRDWATCHING ON THE LEVELS

One of the most ecologically important wetlands in the world, the waterlogged expanse of the Somerset Levels is simply *the* finest place in the country for inland **birdwatching**, its dykes and ditches, seasonal lakes and sodden fields providing a vast haven for countless bird species. A network of excellent **nature reserves** (five in the Avalon Marshes alone) not only preserves their habitat but in many cases has extended it, returning abandoned peat workings and former farmland back into flooded meadows or boggy mire.

Spring and early summer are the **best times** for birding in the Levels: the vegetation isn't too thick, the courtship season is in full swing, and you can see stellar species such as hobby at **Shapwick Moor** (see below), marsh harrier at **Catcott** (see page 172) and the rare bittern at **Ham Wall** (see below). In April and May, herons and their young gather in the treetops of **Swell Wood Nature Reserve** (see page 177), and you may even catch a glimpse of a reintroduced crane at **Greylake** (see page 174). Winter, though, can be equally rewarding, with migrants from Northern and Eastern Europe such as redwings and fieldfares holing up here. Wildfowl are abundant at this time of year, and you'll probably see hen harriers at Greylake (see page 174), but the big event is the arrival of the starlings in November (see page 172); although their major roosting sites vary from year to year, **Westhay Moor** (see page 172) is more often than not *the* place to be.

You'll be able to tick off a fair few species with just a pair of binoculars, a field guide and a bit of patience, but you'll get much more out of birding here if you can tell your warblers from your wigeons – check the relevant reserve websites for details of **guided walks** and birdwatching introductions throughout the year.

birding country: it's home to over sixty species of **birds**, including marsh harriers, lapwing and water rail, easiest to see around the open waters of Noah's Lake and Canada Lake, as the woodland enclosing the meadows gives that part of the reserve a much denser feel.

The otherwise elusive **otter** is common here, and you've got a very good chance of spotting one from the lakeside hides in the early morning. Look out, too, for the unusual **hairy dragonfly**, a chunky insect with a furry thorax.

Shapwick also includes the site of **The Sweet Track**, an ancient wooden walkway that once connected the area's dry high points (see page 172); a modern replica gives you a good insight into the simple but ingenious Neolithic engineering that kept the track from sinking into the marshes.

Ham Wall National Nature Reserve

Entrances on the Meare–Ashcott road and from Sharpham village • Daily dawn–dusk • Free • ☎ 01458 860494, ⦿ rspb.org.uk

Directly opposite the eastern entrance to Shapwick Heath, the more compact **Ham Wall National Nature Reserve** is a good place to spy great-crested grebes and kingfishers feeding among the reedbeds of Walton Heath and Loxton's Marsh, which vibrate with the rasping croak of **marsh frogs** in summer. Its most prized resident, however, is the **bittern**. Thanks to some sterling conservation work (in the mid-1990s, only 11 males were left in the whole of the UK), Ham Wall now hosts the country's largest breeding population of this cautious bird, but even here they can be difficult to spot, so well do they blend in with the surrounding reeds – their fog-horn "boom", though, is a familiar sound in spring and can be heard up to a mile away.

Shapwick Moor Nature Reserve

Entrance on the Westhay–Shapwick road; also accessed via a trail from the Canada Lake hide in Shapwick Heath National Nature Reserve • Daily dawn–dusk • Free • ☎ 07919 095705, ⦿ hawkandowltrust.org

Since 2007, acres of former arable land at the southwestern fringe of Shapwick Heath have slowly been returned to their natural state in order to create **Shapwick Moor Nature Reserve**, one of only three in the country that's dedicated specifically to **birds of prey**. You can observe the action from two hides, from which you might see barn

---

THE SWEET TRACK

One of the oldest roads in the world lies hidden a few feet beneath Shapwick: the **Sweet Track**, a timber routeway built in 3806 BC to cross the mile or so of marsh that lay between the Polden Hills and Westhay. Named after Ray Sweet, who discovered it in 1970, the walkway was made by driving pairs of slanted stakes diagonally into the ground and then resting oak planks on the resulting V-shaped cradle; about 550yds of the track is preserved today, buried in the peat under a boggy trail to keep it from drying out and ultimately disintegrating.

The Sweet Track, the most famous of at least forty ancient tracks that crisscrossed the Levels, was believed to be the oldest in Britain until another wooden walkway (the **Post Track**) was discovered beneath it – its timber predated the Sweet Track's by just thirty years. The Post Track itself lost that title, though, when a causeway dating from around 4000 BC was unearthed in the grounds of London's Belmarsh Prison in 2009.

---

owls, buzzards, kestrels or (in summer) hobbies; the tussocked ridge of grass that parallels the reserve's southern boundary is a good place to spot sparrowhawks hunting for bullfinches.

Catcott Complex

Entrance on the Burtle–Catcott road • Daily dawn–dusk • Free • ☎ 01823 652400, ⓦ somersetwildlife.org

Two reserves make up the **Catcott Complex**: the grazing marshes of **Catcott Lows** – which, as the name implies, occupies one of the lowest parts of the Brue Valley – and the more varied habitat of **Catcott Heath**, to the southeast. The seasonal changes at Catcott are perhaps even more defined than those of its neighbours, the wafting summer grasslands here deep under water come winter.

There are four hides in the Catcott Complex (two on both the Lows and the Heath), with the 13ft Tower Hide providing brilliant panoramic views, but even if you don't see anything (**whimbrels** are fairly common), you might still be able to pick out the distinctive "ping" of a **bearded tit**. Panicky **water voles** are also sometimes seen, though that often amounts to little more than a quick glimpse of fur as the startled critter scurries across the track in front of you and hurls itself into the nearest rhyne.

Westhay Moor National Nature Reserve

Entrance on the Westhay–Godney road, signed off the B3151 between Westhay and Wedmore • Daily dawn–dusk • Free • ☎ 01823 652400, ⓦ somersetwildlife.org

The flagship **Westhay Moor National Nature Reserve** is something of a celebrity in the birdwatching world: old-time twitchers whisper its name in reverential tones and Chris Packham and Kate Humble are regulars down here, scanning the skies for their seasonal series on the BBC. Even for the uninitiated, Westhay can be quite enchanting, especially in summer, when the sun glints off the pools and the dried reeds crackle in the breeze; it's in winter, though, that the reserve really comes into its own, when the

---

MURMUR ON THE DENSE MOOR

Seeing a couple of **starlings** squabbling in your back garden might not be the most thrilling of wildlife encounters, but watching millions of them come together in an orchestrated swarm above the Somerset Levels is one of Britain's great natural spectacles. From November to February, the starlings gather in great cacophonous clouds (known as a **murmuration**), swirling back and forth before darting down to roost among the reeds. Local populations are swollen by migrants from as far afield as Russia, with half a dozen or more birds often clinging to a single reed.

The best places to see this phenomenon are usually **Westhay Moor** or **Shapwick Heath**, but check the **Starling Hotline** (☎ 07866 554142) to find out exactly where they're roosting at any given moment. And wait for sunny weather – the birds go straight to roost on rainy days.

skies literally darken with millions of **starlings** returning to the reedbeds to roost (see box). There are six hides from which you can watch the action, including one perched on its own island and another up a rickety tower, with views across the bulrushes.

ARRIVAL AND DEPARTURE   THE AVALON MARSHES

By bus From Glastonbury, First Group's (ⓦfirstgroup. com) fairly regular #75 to Bridgwater runs via Ashcott (for Shapwick Heath and Ham Wall; 25min) and Catcott (for the Catcott Complex; 35min).

By bike National Cycle Route 3 traces the old Somerset and Dorset Railway through Shapwick Heath and Ham Wall.

INFORMATION

Avalon Marshes Centre On the road between Westhay and Shapwick (daily 10am–5pm; ⓦavalonmarshes. org). The Visitor Information Point, located in the Craft Gallery (daily 10am–5pm), has info on events and activities in the reserves, particularly at Shapwick Heath; there's also an eco-friendly café (same hours).

ACCOMMODATION AND EATING   MAP PAGE 170

In addition to the places listed below, there are plenty of options in Glastonbury itself, just a few miles to the east; for the *Isle of Avalon* campsite, see page 166.

Double-Gate Farm Godney ☎01458 832217, ⓦdouble gatefarm.com. Traditional farmhouse offering traditional B&B: cute rooms, a communal lounge and a generous breakfast spread (sausage, kippers, pancakes) that will set you up for the day. Free wi-fi, and a well-equipped games room with snooker and table tennis. Accessible riverside rooms (£99) would also suit families. **£85**

Double-Gate Tea Room Godney ☎01458 832217. The Riverside Dining Room at Double-Gate Farm B&B provides the perfect pit stop for a lunch (noon–3pm) of wholesome sandwiches, home-made quiches or Sunday roast, or a cream tea and cake after a walk in nearby Westhay Moor, looking over the farmhouse gardens and the River Sheppey. 10.30am–4pm: March Sat & Sun; April Fri–Sun; May Thurs–Sun; June–Sept Wed–Sun (Sat & Sun till 5pm).

4

Westonzoyland and around

The biggest village hereabouts, **WESTONZOYLAND** lies at the westerly end of what was once an island in a sea of peaty marsh – with Middlezoy and Chedzoy to the east. It secured its place in the annals of English history on July 6, 1685, when the Duke of Monmouth's rag-tag rebels were routed by James II's Royal Army in the fields a few hundred yards to the north: the **Battle of Sedgemoor** turned out to be the last fought on English soil.

Battle of Sedgemoor Visitor Centre

St Mary's Church, Main Rd • Daily 9am–4pm • Free • ☎01278 691722, ⓦzoylandheritage.co.uk

After the Battle of Sedgemoor, some five hundred rebel prisoners were held in central **St Mary's Church** while they awaited trial and, more often than not, punishment at the end of a rope, a particularly severe retribution that came to be known as the **Bloody Assizes** (see page 209). The church is now home to the **Battle of Sedgemoor Visitor Centre**, which features detailed displays on the costumes and weapons used and touch screens that chart the course of the battle.

Sedgemoor Inn

19 Main Rd • Mon–Wed 4–11pm, Thurs 10am–11pm, Fri noon–midnight, Sat noon–11pm, Sun noon–10pm • ☎01278 691382

CIDER ON THE EDGE

Up on the Isle of Wedmore's southern edge, **Roger Wilkins** has been making cider at his suitably named Land's End Farm for over sixty years. More than a local legend, his simple attitude to the apple – pick it, press it, taste it, sell it – has seen him become one of the best-known traditional cider-makers in the country. Stop by his cider barn (daily 10am–8pm, Sun till 1pm; ☎01934 712385, ⓦwilkinscider.com) for a (generous) tasting or two: no fuss, no frills, just good old-fashioned farmhouse cider from a barrel (from £1.60 for one litre).

Rich in battle lore, the **Sedgemoor Inn**, just down the road from St Mary's Church, hosted Lord Faversham, commander of the Royal Army, the night before Monmouth's attack. It was a popular drinking den for Royalist troops – the stone on the left-hand side of the fireplace was allegedly used to sharpen their swords. You can sup on a pint (see page 175) amid a wealth of "memorabilia", including a *List of Rebels*, which details the four hundred or so men who were subsequently executed and hung from gibbets throughout the West Country.

Battle of Sedgemoor Memorial

Information panels around Westonzoyland culminate in a **memorial** in the middle of the battlefield, dedicated to those who "doing the right as they saw it" were killed on July 6, 1685, executed or later transported as slaves to the West Indies. A waymarked "Family Activity Trail", dotted with rubbing plates, leads from St Mary's Church to the battlefield; to reach it by car, head up Standards Road, on the corner by the post office, then turn right into Broadstone and right again into Monmouth Road; after half a mile, a drove (track) on the left leads to the memorial.

Westonzoyland Pumping Station

Hoopers Lane, signed from Westonzoyland • Sun 1–5pm, in steam on various dates throughout the year (check website for details) • Free; steam days and other events £8 • ☏ 01278 691595, ⓦ wzlet.org

Standing on the banks of the River Parrett just southwest of Westonzoyland, a red-brick chimney visible for miles around houses Somerset's first steam-driven pumping station. Now the Soviet-sounding **Westonzoyland Pumping Station Museum of Steam Power and Land Drainage**, the station was built in 1830 when Westonzoyland became part of a Parliament-instigated "drainage district", set up to try and stem the perpetual problem of flooding. The station is still home to the old racing-green Easton Amos drainage machine that served the area until its closure in 1951, as well as a large collection of various other steam engines – the best time to visit is when the Easton is "in steam", when it's quite literally all hands to the pump.

Greylake Nature Reserve

Signed off the A361 between Greinton and Othery • Daily dawn–dusk • Free • ☏ 01458 252805, ⓦ rspb.org.uk

Like Shapwick Moor to the north, **Greylake Nature Reserve** was arable farmland not so long ago, and the gradual reversion of this small wildlife sanctuary into seasonally flooded marshes, fringing reedbeds and water-filled "scrapes" has provided the ideal habitat for a host of waders and other wildfowl. A short (accessible) boardwalk leads to the comfy modern hide, where you're likely to tick off lapwing, snipe, yellow wagtail

---

THE BATTLE OF SEDGEMOOR

Cornered at Bridgwater, his rebellion in tatters (see page 209), the **Duke of Monmouth**'s only hope of escape lay in taking the fight to the Royal Army, camped outside **Westonzoyland**, five miles to the southeast. But only in an ambush, and at night, when the greater size of Monmouth's forces might just outweigh their inferior organization and experience. Monmouth's guide lost his way trying to lead the rebels across **Langmoor Rhine**, the alarm was sounded and the Royal Army drove them back into the cornfields around **Chedzoy**, slaughtering them as they went. Over 1300 of the 3500-strong rebel force were killed.

Some of the rebels escaped, including Monmouth (and a certain Daniel Defoe, who had joined the rebellion with a few of his old colleagues from Morton's Academy for Dissenters in London – most of whom were not so lucky). Monmouth himself was captured in a field in Hampshire two days later and beheaded in London on July 15. His hapless executioner, **Jack Ketch** – who famously delivered five blows to the duke with his axe, asked for help from the crowd and then had to finish the job with his knife – is remembered as the Hangman in Punch and Judy shows throughout the land.

and maybe even a crane or two – in an effort to re-establish these graceful waterbirds back into Britain's wetlands after an absence of nearly four hundred years, a hundred or so cranes were released into the protected environment of the Somerset Levels over a five-year period from August 2010 (⦻ thegreatcraneproject.org.uk).

Burrow Mump and King Alfred's Monument

Rising up by the side of the A361 at Burrowbridge, just before it crosses the River Parrett, **Burrow Mump** looks much like a miniature Glastonbury Tor, a conical hill topped by a ruined church of St Michael – though unlike the Tor, not one that you can venture inside. Burrow Mump translates as "Hill Hill", an emphasis that's easy to understand after making the short walk to the top, such are the views of pancake-flat farmland for miles around.

The mump acted as an outpost of the nearby fort at the Isle of Athelney, now **Athelney Hill**, at the end of the ninth century. King Alfred is said to have sheltered here from the Danes in 878 (it was in the Athelney marshes that he famously burnt his cakes), before repelling them at the Battle of Ethandun and signing the subsequent peace treaty that effectively saved the Anglo-Saxon kingdom of Wessex. A **monument** to Alfred on the hill (now private land) marks the site of the abbey he founded in thanks.

Willows and Wetlands Visitor Centre

Meare Green Court, Stoke St Gregory **Visitor centre** Mon–Sat 9.30am–5.30pm • Free **Tours** Mon–Fri 11am & 2.30pm • £4.50 • ☎ 01823 490249, ⦻ englishwillowbaskets.co.uk

The countryside around Stoke St Gregory, south of Athelney, is prime willow-growing territory, perfect fodder for a deeply traditional Somerset skill that you can explore in more depth at the engaging **Willows and Wetlands Visitor Centre**. The Coates family have been growing willow here since 1819 and teasing it into baskets for almost as long. There's an **exhibition** on the history of the industry, and their **museum** – containing wicker beehives, eel traps (known as kypes), a child's potty and a coffin among others – is well worth a wander. Try and coincide your visit with one of their hour-long **tours** where you get to watch the experts at work, deftly twining and weaving the withy sticks into a range of log baskets, picnic hampers and desk tidies ready for the on-site **shop**.

ARRIVAL AND DEPARTURE

By bus Hatch Green Coaches' (⦻ hatchgreencoaches. co.uk) #51 from Taunton (Mon–Sat 5 daily) passes North Curry (25min) and Athelney Bridge (30min) on its way to

WESTONZOYLAND AND AROUND

Stoke St Gregory (40min). From Westonzoyland, their #16 runs to and from Bridgwater (Mon–Sat 5 daily; 25min) and Langport (Mon–Sat 6 daily; 30min).

ACCOMMODATION AND EATING

The Coffee Shop Town Farm, North Curry ☎ 01823 491411. Welcoming café-cum-craft-shop in a restored stable at the western end of North Curry, serving home-made soups, jacket potatoes, cakes and, of course, coffee. Tues–Sun 10am–5pm, Jan & Dec till 4.30pm.

Rose and Crown Woodhill, Stoke St Gregory ☎ 01823 490296. Light, airy, modern-looking place, completely renovated after a fire, with just one simple but pretty en-suite double decked in bright cushions and comfy throws. The downstairs pub does very good food, including a pie and a pint for £10. **£70**

Sedgemoor Inn 19 Main Rd, Westonzoyland ☎ 01278 691382. Historic boozer (see page 173) that played a central role in the Battle of Sedgemoor and is now decorated with tidbits from the time, including a proclamation from the King rewarding £5000 for "whoever shall bring in the person of James, Duke of Monmouth". Local ales, and a skittle alley out the back. Mon–Wed 4–11pm, Thurs 10am–11pm, Fri noon–midnight, Sat noon–11pm, Sun noon–10pm.

Langport and around

The self-proclaimed "heart" of the Somerset Levels, **LANGPORT** fans out from a nook in the languid River Parrett, broadened here by its tributaries, the Sowy, Isle and Yeo, either side of town. Focused around the neat strip of houses that fall back from Bow Street, today's town seems a world away from the busy river port that once operated its own customs house and needed a good twenty inns to cater for the number of crews that ran barges here from Bridgwater.

The town was torched by retreating Royalists after the **Battle of Langport** in 1645, and a short stroll up the hill from central Cheapside will tick off the two main sights. Langport's real appeal, however, lies in its location: there's pleasant walking in the surrounding countryside – you can follow the bucolic **River Parrett Trail** (see page 199) two miles south to the medieval ruins of **Muchelney Abbey** – and a smattering of fine traditional **pubs** and a fantastic little **smokery** nearby.

All Saints Church

The Hill • Key available from Langport Information Centre (see page 177) • Free

Crowning the top of the steep hill that slopes up from Cheapside, disused **All Saints Church** is decorated with contorted gargoyles (known locally as "hunky punks") and, in its glorious east window, houses the finest collection of medieval stained glass in Somerset: some remarkably well-preserved fifteenth-century work that depicts Joseph of Arimathea and other saints.

Hanging Chapel

The Hill

Just beyond All Saints Church and bridging the road down to Muchelney, the distinctive **Hanging Chapel** is set on top of a fourteenth-century gateway that was once part of Langport's old town wall; the chapel is now home – as the square and compasses on the wall outside testify – to a Masonic lodge.

Muchelney

The teeny village of **MUCHELNEY**, two miles south of Langport, punches way above its diminutive weight. Within a few yards, it has some of the finest medieval buildings in the area: an unusual priest's house, a distinctive parish church and the atmospheric ruins of Benedictine Muchelney Abbey, second only to Glastonbury until Henry VIII flattened it in the 1530s. The road from Langport to Muchelney was completely submerged by floods in early 2014 (see page 169), cutting off the village for three months and briefly returning Muchelney to the island it once was.

Muchelney Abbey

Muchelney • Daily: April–June, Sept & Oct 10am–5pm; July & Aug 10am–6pm • £6 • EH • ☎ 01458 250664, ⓦ english-heritage.org.uk

Founded in 939 by Athelstone on the remains of an Anglo-Saxon church, **Muchelney Abbey** mostly dates to the mid-twelfth century. Start in the **south cloisters**, one of only three sections to survive the Dissolution, where exhibitions chart the story of the abbey and the well-preserved **Abbot's House**. Just inside the Abbot's House itself, worn steps lead up to the lodge's late fifteenth-century **Abbot's Great Chamber**. The intricately carved grapes hanging from the lion-topped medieval fireplace denote its use as a room for entertaining, while the small but beautifully rich stained glass – which bears the signature of former abbot Thomas Broke – is an indication of the abbey's wealth. The expensive white oak beams here hint at the lodge's esteem, an impression further enhanced in the **Painted Chamber** next door, where the pomegranates on the wall and the barrel-vaulted ceiling depict the coat of arms of Catherine of Aragon, and the spider-like symbols (actually ermine) represent the king. The adjoining **East Room** has a patch of very faded wall painting, though it's still possible to get an idea of its quality.

Downstairs, the thirteenth- and fourteenth-century **kitchens**, once one room – look up between the two to see the blackened chimney soaring towards the open sky – lead to the **Stewards Room**, accessed via an impressive medieval door, and a display of ornamental gargoyles (or "hunky punks") carved in local hamstone.

Outside the Abbots' House, and originally joined to the abbey, the thatched **reredorter** (monastic latrine) is the most complete example of its kind in the country; it was built in 1256 and still clearly features the close-knit cubicles that the monks once lined up in, cheek by jowl.

St Peter and St Paul

Muchelney • Daily 10am–6pm, till dusk in winter • Free

Though just yards from the ruins of Muchelney Abbey, the village's fifteenth-century church of **St Peter and St Paul** fares well in comparison, thanks mostly to its unusual painted Jacobean ceiling, each panel bursting with bare-chested angels and arch-winged cherubs. The church, unusually, was built by the abbey and now houses some of its earliest decorated tiles, moved here from the Lady Chapel and relaid around the altar. They date back to the twelfth century but are still quite vivid – look out for knights on horseback, howdah-backed elephants and, near the bottom left-hand corner of the altar, the two west towers of the abbey itself.

Priest's House

Muchelney • Mid-March to Sept Mon & Sun 2–5pm; admission by guided tour only, last tour at 4.30pm • £4 • NT • ☎ 01458 253771, ⓦ nationaltrust.org.uk

Squatting opposite the church of St Peter and St Paul, the sweet-looking **Priest's House** was built of local blue lias stone in 1308 for Muchelney's parish priest, who certainly didn't have too far to walk to work. One of the National Trust's first projects when they requisitioned it in 1911, the medieval hall-house is now a private home; a tour reveals a huge fifteenth-century hamstone fireplace and other aspects of an interior that has barely changed in over four hundred years.

Swell Wood and West Sedgemoor nature reserves

Swell Wood Daily dawn–dusk • Free • **West Sedgemoor** Access by guided walks in spring, summer & winter only; book well in advance during peak winter times • Free • ☎ 01458 252805, ⓦ rspb.org.uk

Few places in spring can top **Swell Wood Nature Reserve**, when the treetops reverberate with the squabbling of baby grey herons in what is one of the UK's biggest heronries. Over a hundred pairs nest here, with the bristle-covered chicks emerging in early April (visible from the hide); little egret chicks follow in late May.

You're free to walk the trails and visit the hide at Swell Wood, but access to the adjoining **West Sedgemoor Nature Reserve** is limited to pre-booked guided walks – well worth doing, especially in winter, as these wet meadows are home to the largest population of wading birds in southern England. Alternatively, you can get good views across the meadows from the **footpath** that runs west from Curry Rivel, further up the A378 towards Langport.

ARRIVAL AND INFORMATION

By bus Langport has fairly decent bus connections with the main towns in the regional.

Destinations Bridgwater (Mon–Sat 4 daily; 40min); Taunton (Mon–Sat 8 daily; 35min); Westonzoyland (Mon–

LANGPORT AND AROUND

Sat 4 daily; 30min); Yeovil (Mon–Sat 8 daily; 30min).

Langport Information Centre Bow St (Mon–Fri 10am–3pm; ☎ 01458 253527). Helpful advice on accommodation and attractions in Langport and the surrounding area.

ACCOMMODATION

As well as those below, places listed around Martock (see page 197) and Somerton (see page 190) are also within reach, as is *The Pilgrims* in Lovington (see page 188).

The Devonshire Arms Long Sutton, 3.5 miles from Langport on the A372 ☎ 01458 241271, ⓦ the

devonshirearms.com. Slick, contemporary gastropub-with-rooms – all creams and beiges, with dark-wood furnishings (including canopied four-posters in some rooms) and wide-screen TVs. The special rates, including dinner for two in the quality restaurant (see below), can be

EEL BE BACK: THE GREAT ELVER MIGRATION

Each spring, thousands of baby **eels** (elvers) wriggle their way up through the rhynes and ditches of the Somerset Levels, having spent the previous year drifting across the Atlantic Ocean from their breeding grounds in the Sargasso Sea near Bermuda. No one really knows why they make such a mammoth journey, only to return when fully mature, to spawn and die; or indeed what triggers the transformations on the way that take them from larvae to "glass" eel to elver. In fact, not much is known about this mysterious creature at all, other than that they don't half taste good – eels have been a central Somerset delicacy for hundreds of years, covered in flour and deep-fried, cooked with bacon and served in an omelette or, best of all, smoked.

a good deal if you're in one of the larger, more expensive rooms. Proper full English breakfasts. No singles Fri & Sat nights. **£100**

★ **Gypsy Caravan** Marsh Farm, Pitney, 3 miles from Langport on the B3153 ☏ 01458 274944, ⊛ gypsycaravanbreaks.co.uk. Thoroughly romantic gypsy wagons, lovingly restored and beautifully finished, set in an old cider apple orchard and an open meadow on a farm just outside Pitney. You'll need a hearty supper, cooked over the open fire (you can stock up on organic goodies at nearby Pitney Farm Shop; see below), to tackle the scramble up into the bow-top beds. Don't forget the folk guitar and Tarot cards. Two-night minimum stay. Closed Oct–March. **£82**

The Parsonage Muchelney, 2 miles south of Langport ☏ 01458 259058, ⊛ theparsonagesomerset.co.uk. Perfectly located for Muchelney Abbey – it's just 300yds from the ruins – this top B&B ticks all the boxes: welcoming, committed owners; three light and lovely rooms; and an inglenook fireplace so large that it's effectively another room. Generous breakfasts are served in the oak-beamed and antique-stuffed dining room, and there's also a little library for the evenings. **£95**

EATING AND DRINKING

In addition to the following places, it's also worth travelling a little further to enjoy a meal at *The Pilgrims* (see page 189) or a pint at the *Wyndham Arms* in Kingsbury Episcopi (see page 198).

Art Tea Zen 105 Cheapside, Langport ☏ 01458 250635, ⊛ artteazen.co.uk. There's art on the wall, tea on the shelves (several teapigs varieties) and plenty of good karma running through this chilled-out café at the top of Langport's high street. The distressed-textile armchairs and benches are perfect for relaxing over a chicken and avocado toastie (£4.70) or home-made tart and salad (£8.95), while making the most of the free wi-fi. Mon–Sat 9am–5pm.

★ **Brown & Forrest** Bowdens Farm, Hambridge, 4 miles southwest of Langport on the B3168 ☏ 01458 250875, ⊛ brownandforrest.co.uk. Tuck into succulent Somerset eels (see box), hot-smoked over beech (to bring out their delicate flavour) and apple wood (which gives them a mellow sweetness) and served straight from the smokery. Starters include smoked eel on rye bread (£6.50) and mains smoked lamb fillet (£9.95), though there are no smoked puddings as yet. Add a pinch of pepper – or, for the smoked-eel aficionado, a dash of horseradish. You can pick up some vacuum-packed smoked goodies at the next-door deli (open until 4pm). Mon–Sat 9–11.30am & 11.45am–3pm.

The Devonshire Arms Long Sutton, 3.5 miles east of Langport on the A372 ☏ 01458 241271, ⊛ the devonshirearms.com. Beautiful pub – a former hunting lodge, lording it over Long Sutton green – that runs a stylish (and busy) restaurant serving original, well-presented dishes, such as slow-cooked pork belly in a cider cream sauce (mains from £12.50). Relax among the scatter cushions in the bar next door with a pint of draught Moor Revival or a shot of local Somerset Cider Brandy. Daily noon–2.30pm & 7–9.30pm, Sun till 9pm.

★ **The Halfway House** Pitney Hill, Pitney, 2.5 miles northeast of Langport on the B3153 ☏ 01458 252513, ⊛ thehalfwayhouse.co.uk. This low-lit, flagstone-floored village pub, "halfway" between Langport and Somerton, is the sort of place you'd love to call your local. Music is a no-no and there's little in the way of decor, but it oozes character, with the lengthy list of real ales – sometimes ten or more at any one time, including Butcombe Rare Breed and Otter Bright – drawn from barrels out the back. Plenty of lagers, too, plus Ashton Press, Hecks and Wilkins for cider-drinkers. Big open fires and simple, honest pub grub. Mon–Fri 11.30am–3pm, Sat & Sun 11.30am–11pm.

Rose and Crown Huish Episcopi, half a mile east of Langport on the A372 ☏ 01458 250494. Don't be put off by the "seems to be shut" exterior. This friendly, flagstone-floored local legend – universally known as *Eli's* – is a great place for a drink, with a "walk-through" bar connecting the appealing front parlours. The range of real ales on tap includes a couple of Teignworthys, while local cider comes from nearby Burrow Hill (see page 196). One of the two back gardens has a children's play area. Mon–Thurs 11.30–2.30pm (Thurs till 3pm), Fri & Sat 11.30am–11.30pm, Sun noon–10.30pm.

SHOPPING

★ **Muchelney Pottery** Muchelney, 2.5 miles south of Langport ☎01458 250324, ⓦjohnleachpottery. co.uk. Quality stoneware from John Leach, a master potter with over fifty years' experience, hand-crafted at his pretty thatched workshop in Muchelney. There's usually something going on – throwing, glazing or regular exhibitions at the next-door John Leach Gallery. Tues–Sat 10am–1pm & 2–4pm.

★ **Pitney Farm Shop** Glebe Farm, Woodbirds Hill Lane, Pitney, 3 miles northeast of Langport, off the B3153 ☎01458 253002, ⓦpitneyfarmshop.co.uk. Highly acclaimed organic farm shop selling freshly picked veg, dry-cured meats from their own herd of saddleback pigs, and home-made cakes, plus Somerset cheeses, local ciders and beers, and organic fruit wines. Walk or cycle over here to take advantage of the five percent "green" discount. Mon–Sat 9am–5.30pm.

4

South Somerset

DLE STREET | THE BOROUGH

MONTACUTE VILLAGE

5

South Somerset

Framed by its borders with Wiltshire, Dorset and Devon, verdant South Somerset matches the county's rural image more than any other region. Rolling fields are broken by the occasional isolated farm, while the backcountry lanes that link them are plied by tractors loaded with hay. This is an area of hamstone hamlets and "Honey for sale" signs, where villages bearing names like Haselbury Plucknett and Hardington Mandeville have barely changed in centuries.

The region's towns developed on the back of flourishing textile trades, first wool and then later flax, linen and lace, prosperity that endowed places like **Crewkerne, Bruton** and **Ilminster** with the kind of handsome, grandiose churches for which Somerset has become renowned. There is much more appeal in wandering the streets of towns such as **Somerton** and **Castle Cary** than there is in the bigger, more industrial sprawls of **Yeovil** and **Chard**, though even these find it hard to compete with South Somerset's glorious **hamstone villages**, built of a beautiful soft limestone quarried locally from Ham Hill and which glows the colour of flapjacks in the late afternoon sun.

Similar in size to some of the smaller villages in the region, the destination museums of **Haynes International Motor Museum** in Sparkford and the **Fleet Air Arm Museum** at Yeovilton hold hours of interest for younger travellers, while South Somerset's numerous National Trust properties – from antiques-heavy **Lytes Cary Manor** to **Montacute House**, the most magnificent of manor houses – will keep their parents (and grandparents) happy for even longer.

ARRIVAL AND INFORMATION

By bus Berry's Coaches (☎01823 331356, ⓦ berryscoaches. co.uk) run to and from London Hammersmith and Ilminster, South Petherton, Wincanton and Yeovil.

Tourist offices In addition to the local information centres listed with the relevant town accounts, there's a regional

tourist information centre at Cartgate Picnic Site, off the A303/A3088 near Stoke-sub-Hamdon (Easter–Oct daily 9am–4pm; Nov–Easter Mon & Fri 10am–3pm; ☎01935 829333).

GETTING AROUND

By car Having your own wheels is by far the best way to see South Somerset, and the ever-present A303 can make getting between places quicker than you might think.

By bus Services run by South West Coaches (☎01935

475872, ⓦ southwestcoaches.co.uk) connect many of the region's towns and villages, but the majority of them depart just one afternoon a week and make dozens of stops.

Castle Cary and the east

Set on the main rail routes from Bristol, Bath and London, the pretty little market town of **CASTLE CARY** makes an attractive (and fairly authentic) introduction to South Somerset, with its neat ensemble of mustard-coloured buildings and minor historical sights. "Cary" means "castle", but despite the double emphasis, nothing remains of the twelfth-century stronghold, though the hill on which it was set, to the south of town, offers pleasant enough views.

Cary was awarded its market charter by Edward IV in 1468; the stalls moved to the high street's distinctive **Market House** in 1855, a practice that continues today with the town's weekly **market** (Tues 9am–2pm). Up behind Market House, the dinky pepper-pot **Round House** was used as a lock-up for a short time at the end of the eighteenth

PLEASE RING FOR CIDER ←

BURROW HILL CIDER FARM

Highlights

1 Hauser & Wirth Somerset Thought-provoking contemporary art gallery in the unusual setting of a former farmhouse outside Bruton. See page 186

2 Country cooking South Somerset is blessed with some quality places to eat – *At The Chapel, The Pilgrims* and *Little Barwick House* in particular will do your palate proud. See pages 189 and 195

3 Montacute House A stately home worthy of the title, stuffed with fine furniture and tapestries and housing an impressive collection of paintings from the National Portrait Gallery. See page 191

4 Hamstone villages Nothing says South Somerset quite as much as a hamlet of houses carved from golden stone – Martock and Montacute are two of the most harmonious. See pages 191 and 195

5 Fleet Air Arm Museum Step inside Concorde or take a "ride" on a helicopter at this brilliant interactive aircraft museum. See page 193

6 Cider farms South Somerset is real cider country: work your way through the vintages at Bridge Farm, Burrow Hill and Perry's. See pages 195, 196 and 198

7 River Parrett Trail Follow the Parrett as it meanders for fifty bucolic miles across South Somerset and beyond. See page 199

HIGHLIGHTS ARE MARKED ON THE MAP ON PAGE 184

5

century. Several **walking routes** run through and around Cary: the local Leland Trail and the much longer Monarch's and Macmillan ways, the latter named after the cancer charity's founder, who was born here in 1884.

Castle Cary and District Museum

Market House, Market Place • April–Oct Mon–Fri 10.30am–12.30pm & 2–4pm, Sat 10.30am–12.30pm • Free • ⓦ castlecarymuseum.org.uk

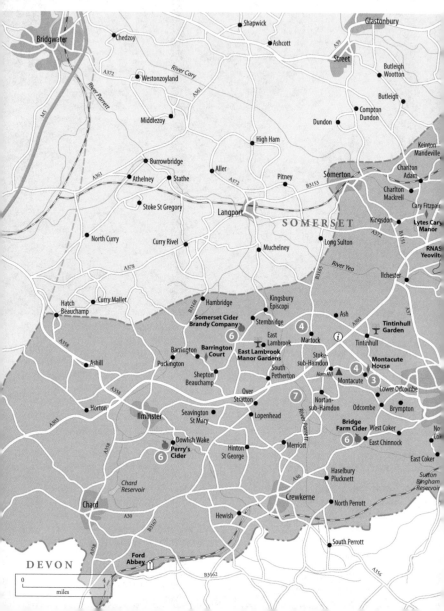

The two-floor **Castle Cary and District Museum** is most notable for its striking setting, the mid-Victorian Market House that's propped up at the front by an arch-lined colonnade, under which the town's traders used to go about their business. Displays depict the local industries of rope-making and **horsehair weaving**, a tradition that survives at John Boyd Textiles, whose work has graced Number 10 Downing Street and the White House. Displays chart the lives of local lads **Douglas Macmillan**, the founder of Macmillan Cancer Support, and the diarist **Parson James Woodforde**, whose father was vicar of Castle Cary.

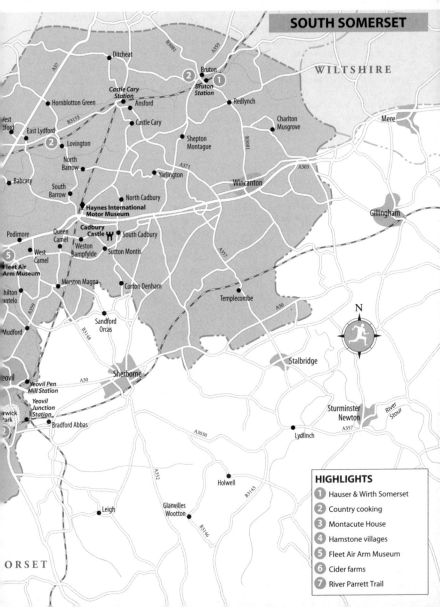

SOUTH SOMERSET

WILTSHIRE

Ditcheat

Bruton ❶

Bruton Station ❷

Castle Cary Station

Hornblotton Green

Ansford

Redlynch

Mere

West ...dford

East Lydford ❷

Lovington

Castle Cary

Charlton Musgrove

Shepton Montague

North Barrow

Yarlington

Wincanton

A303

Babcary

South Barrow

North Cadbury

Haynes International Motor Museum

Gillingham

Podimore

Queen Camel

Cadbury Castle

South Cadbury

❺

West Camel

Weston Bampfylde

Sutton Montis

Fleet Air Arm Museum

...hilton ...antelo

Marston Magna

Corton Denham

Templecombe

...Mudford

Sandford Orcas

Stalbridge

...eovil

Yeovil Pen Mill Station

Sherborne

Yeovil Junction Station

...rwick ...ark ❷

Bradford Abbas

A3030

Sturminster Newton

River Stour

Lydlinch

A357

Holwell

B3143

HIGHLIGHTS

❶ Hauser & Wirth Somerset

❷ Country cooking

❸ Montacute House

❹ Hamstone villages

❺ Fleet Air Arm Museum

❻ Cider farms

❼ River Parrett Trail

Leigh

Glanvilles Wootton

...ORSET

5

Bruton

By some calculations the smallest town in England, tranquil **BRUTON**, four miles northeast of Castle Cary, has been making a name for itself in recent years, with a clutch of hip little restaurants and a new **contemporary art gallery** leading *The Sunday Times* to declare the town the coolest place to live in England in 2015.

After stopping by the one-room **Bruton Museum** (Mon–Fri 11am–1pm, Sat 11am–3pm; free; ⊛brutonmuseum.org.uk), which charts the town's thousand-year history, it's worth also popping into two-towered **St Mary's Church**, notable for the striking eighteenth-century Rococo plasterwork in its chancel, and, a much more recent addition to the town, **Make Hauser & Wirth Somerset** (Wed–Sat 10am–1pm & 2–4pm; free; ⊛hauserwirthsomerset.com), an offshoot of the gallery just outside of Bruton, which showcases bespoke works in a range of changing exhibitions. Most appeal, though, lies in simply wandering. Duck into the courtyard of **Sexey's Hospital**, an attractive quadrangle of Jacobean almshouses founded by the auditor to both Elizabeth I and James I, follow one of the narrow alleyways, known as "bartons", that run down to the river – winding Elliotts Barton pops out at the fifteenth-century **Packhorse Bridge** – or head up Park Road (on the left just after the railway bridge) to the hilltop **dovecote**, the town's most notable landmark.

Hauser & Wirth Somerset

Durslade Farm, Dropping Lane • Tues–Sun 10am–5pm, Nov–Feb till 4pm • Free • ☏ 01749 814060, ⊛ hauserwirthsomerset.com

Housed in a seventeenth-century farmhouse on the fringes of Bruton, **Hauser & Wirth Somerset** is the highly unlikely but highly successful fourth branch of Iwan Wirth and his wife Manuela Hauser's cutting-edge contemporary art galleries. The risk of following London, New York and Zürich with rural Somerset has been handsomely rewarded, with the former threshing barn, stables and other outbuildings providing a sublime setting for Hauser & Wirth's fifty-strong stable of artists.

The gallery was inaugurated in 2014 with a solo show by **Phyllida Barlow**, and exhibitions since have ranged from **Susan Philipsz**'s sound installations to abstract sculptural works by **Berlinda Bruyckere**. Pieces on regular display include **Smiljan Radić**'s egg-shaped pavilion, a modern-day folly in the gardens – themselves designed by **Piet Oudolf**, the man behind New York's High Line.

The gallery doubles as an education centre, with a library, excellent bookshop and a calendar of events that include talks and workshops, and is also home to a **restaurant** and suitably innovative **bar** (see page 189).

Wincanton

Sitting virtually atop the A303, near the border with Wiltshire and Dorset, **WINCANTON** shows few signs of its former life as an important staging post on the road from London to the west, and is regularly dismissed as a bit of a peculiar place – thanks, in no small part, to its twinning with a city that doesn't even exist. In 2002, Wincanton's town council took the unusual decision to officially twin with **Ankh-Morpork**, the fictional city-state of the late Sir Terry Pratchett's fantasy Discworld novels.

Discworld Emporium

41 High St • Mon, Tues, Fri & Sat 10am–4pm • ☏ 01963 824686, ⊛ discworldemporium.com

Lovingly assembled into a one-stop-shop for Terry Pratchett memorabilia, Wincanton's unique **Discworld Emporium** is chock-full of artefacts, mementoes and trinkets. There are Discworld-themed models and stamps (accepted by Royal Mail, so you can use them to send letters from the on-site Ankh-Morpork Post Office), Assassins' Guild college scarves and even Ankh-Morpork passports – which you can get stamped here, this being the official **Ankh-Morpork Consulate** and all.

KING ARTHUR'S CAMELOT?

"At the very South Ende of the Chirch of South-Cadbyri standith Camallate… The People can telle nothing ther but that they have hard say that Arture much resortid to Camalat."
The Itinerary of John Leland the Antiquary, 1542

At least half a dozen places in the UK claim to be the site of **Camelot**, the legendary court of King Arthur, but Cadbury Castle is the most convincing of the lot. The connection was first established by the antiquarian John Leland in the mid-sixteenth century, but it wasn't until the 1950s that there was any form of physical evidence to support it, when pottery shards similar to those found at Tintagel, Arthur's reputed birthplace, were unearthed within its enclosure. These finds were sufficient enough for further excavations to be carried out in the late 1960s, and the **Camelot Research Committee** – with a name like that, clearly a group confident of finding *something* – uncovered a gatehouse, and a wooden hall that also dated to the sixth century. More importantly, it was found that the hilltop bank at Cadbury had been refortified on a scale that only a king could command, and that the enclosure within once housed a thousand-strong army. Whether the king was Arthur and the army his, is anybody's guess. But there could be a further clue in the names of nearby villages, for just a few miles down the road lie the hamlets of Queen Camel and West Camel…

Cadbury Castle

South Cadbury • South West Coaches' #19 from Bruton to Yeovil

Occupying a prominent hill just half a mile south of the A303, **Cadbury Castle** is actually a hillfort dating from around 500–200 BC, although there is evidence of earlier occupation stretching back to the Neolithic period. All that remains today are the concentric rings of earthen ramparts that protected a settlement of the Iron Age Durotriges tribe. The site was refortified around 470 AD following attack by the Romans, but it's Cadbury's role as a Saxon fort – which lends some credence to its claim of being the site of King Arthur's **Camelot** – that draws people to this windswept hilltop.

Arthurian legends (see page 161) originate from a mid-sixth-century Briton who battled with invading Anglo-Saxons, and Cadbury certainly enjoys a strategic military position; following the uppermost ring around its perimeter, it's obvious why this spot was chosen, with its commanding 360-degree views of central Somerset. The remnants of the complex – a central **timber hall** and a 16ft-thick **dry-stone wall** – lie buried beneath the turf, though the original entry to the fort, marked by a break in the earthworks' southwest side, is easy enough to make out; in a legend not too dissimilar to the Wild Hunt (see page 164), folklore has it that once a year the sound of galloping horses fills the air as Arthur and his Knights of the Round Table ride down through the gateway and into the village of Sutton Montis below.

Haynes International Motor Museum

Sparkford, just off the A303 • Daily 9.30am–5.30pm, Nov–Feb till 4.30pm • £15 • ☎ 01963 440804, ⊕ haynesmotormuseum.com • South West Coaches' #1/1A/1B/1C from Castle Cary to Yeovil

Every petrol-head's dream, the **Haynes International Motor Museum** opened in 1985 with the private collection of John Haynes, the man behind the *Haynes Owners Workshop Manual*, the amateur car mechanic's Bible. It now houses over four hundred gleaming automobiles, with some of the classiest cars in history – the **Lamborghini Countach**, with its gullwing "coleopter" doors (found in the Supercar Century), the **Rolls-Royce Silver Shadow**, the **Jaguar XJ220** – interspersed with oddities like the Heinkel Cabin-Cruiser, a *Ghostbusters*-style Pontiac ambulance and the Sinclair C5, perhaps motoring's most famous flop. Among the fifteen halls, a few of which are given over entirely to British cars and motorbikes, it's worth seeking out the **1905 Daimler**

5

limousine, whose one careful owner was Edward VII, and the rare **1931 Duesenberg**, elevated on a podium and worth a cool $10 million.

Kids are kept entertained with an outdoor play area, an interactive garage and a Top Trumps Trail; to see some of the cars in action, try and coincide your visit with one of the many themed **events** detailed on the website.

ARRIVAL AND DEPARTURE

CASTLE CARY AND THE EAST

BY TRAIN
Castle Cary Station is just north of town, on the B3153, and served by trains on both the "Heart of Wessex" line and the main route from London.

Destinations Bath Spa (Mon–Sat 10 daily, Sun 5 daily; 55min); Bradford-on-Avon (Mon–Sat 10 daily, Sun 5 daily; 45min); Bristol Temple Meads (Mon–Sat 10 daily, Sun 5 daily; 1hr 15min); Bruton (frequent; 5min); Dorchester (Mon–Sat 10 daily, Sun 5 daily; 50min); Exeter St David's (6–10 daily; 45min); Frome (Mon–Sat 10 daily, Sun 5 daily; 20min); London Paddington (5 daily; 1hr 40min–2hr); Plymouth (5–6 daily; 2hr 5min); Reading (9 daily; 55min–1hr 20min); Taunton (6–10 daily; 25min); Weymouth (Mon–Sat 10 daily, Sun 5 daily; 1hr 5min); Yeovil Pen Mill (Mon–Sat 10 daily, Sun 5 daily; 15min).

Bruton Station is a few minutes' walk southeast of town, off the B3081; the "Heart of Wessex" line runs here from Bristol to Weymouth (Mon–Sat 10 daily, Sun 5 daily).

Destinations Bath Spa (50min); Bradford-on-Avon (35min); Bristol Temple Meads (1hr 10min); Castle Cary (frequent; 5min); Dorchester (55min); Frome (10min); Weymouth (1hr 10min); Yeovil Pen Mill (20min).

BY BUS
Wincanton Bus Station is served by Berry's Coaches' twice-daily service to and from London Hammersmith (2hr 15min), which also stops at Ilminster (1hr 15min), Taunton (1hr 40min) and Yeovil (45min).

INFORMATION

Castle Cary Market House, Market Place (Mon–Fri 9.30am–12.30pm, Sat 9am–noon; ☏ 01963 351763).

Bruton 26 High St (Mon–Fri 9.30am–12.30pm; ☏ 01749 813014).

Wincanton Town Hall, Market Place (Mon–Thurs 9am–1pm & 2–4pm, Fri 9am–1pm; ☏ 01963 31693).

ACCOMMODATION

At The Chapel High St, Bruton ☏ 01749 814070, ⓦ atthechapel.co.uk. The eight stripped-back and stylish rooms at this brilliantly converted chapel all have king-sized beds; several have views towards Bruton's iconic dovecote and one even has its own garden terrace. Breakfast includes freshly baked croissants from their own bakery, which forms part of a superb restaurant (see below). **£125**

High House Bruton 73 High St, Bruton ☏ 01749 813015, ⓦ highhousebruton.co.uk. Centrally located Victorian townhouse B&B – a short walk from the river and an even shorter walk from Bruton's cafés and restaurants – with two tastefully furnished rooms, both with flat-screen TVs, DVD players and wi-fi. Breakfast features lots of home-made goodies, plus a "full Somerset" of local produce. **£80**

★ **The Newt in Somerset** Just off the A359, 3.5 miles southwest of Bruton ☏ 01963 577777, ⓦ thenewtinsomerset.com. This fabulous Georgian country-house retreat was named *The Sunday Times* Newcomer of the Year within a few months of opening in 2019. You can tour the gardens (£15, free for guests), watch them press their own "cyder" (it's still a working farm), or just relax in one of the sumptuous rooms or in the designer spa. Much of the produce at the hotel's excellent *Botanical Rooms* restaurant (daily: lunch from noon, dinner from 6.30pm) is sourced from the expansive estate. **£80**

The Pilgrims Lovington, 4.5 miles west of Castle Cary, off the B3153 ☏ 01963 240597, ⓦ pilgrimsrestaurant.co.uk. Three modern rooms in the pub's high-ceilinged old cider barn, all with good-sized beds (one with a French sleigh bed, another with a leather double), flat-screen TVs and DVD players and big bathrooms with sleek bathtubs and a wet-room shower. A great breakfast served in the adjoining restaurant (see below), a meal at which is worth an overnight stay on its own. No under-14s. **£130**

The Queens Arms Corton Denham, about 2.5 miles southeast of South Cadbury ☏ 01963 220317, ⓦ thequeensarms.com. This lovely pub (see below) on the edge of the border with Dorset has a range of chic twins and doubles, all individually styled and all, bar the "Classic Room", big enough to include their own seating areas; two of the "Luxury" rooms (£109) have lovely baths, either slipper or deep, cast-iron tubs. A former nearby piggery has been brilliantly converted into a couple of semi-detached cottages, sleeping up to 8 people (from £400 for a three/four-night stay), which come with their own gardens and bucolic countryside views. **£95**

Yarlington Yurt Yarlington, signed off the A371 between Castle Cary and Wincanton ☏ 0117 204 7830, ⓦ canopyandstars.co.uk. Glamp it up at this very spacious yurt in the grounds of Yarlington House, whose period

5

decor – Victorian luggage cases, globes, rugs and paintings – has come from the Georgian manor house itself. There's a king-size double in the main dome and two singles in a connecting pod; the kitchen and bathroom are set in a

neighbouring tent. Guests have use of the family pool. Breakfast £10 extra. Minimum stay in high season: three nights at weekends, four nights midweek. Three nights **£450**

EATING AND DRINKING

★ **At The Chapel** High St, Bruton ☎01749 814070, ⓦatthechapel.co.uk. Contemporary gem in sleepy Bruton, making the most of its spacious setting with seating around the gallery, spread-out refectory tables and a cocktail bar where the altar used to be. Tuck into quality dishes such as watercress risotto with dolcelatte (mains from £9), or try one of their tempting wood-fired pizzas (from £8.50), served all day – the chefs perfected their skills in Venice. Artisan breads baked on site. Daily 8am–9.30pm (food served 8am–11am, noon–3pm & 6–9pm), Sun till 8pm (food served from noon).

The Bakehouse High St, Castle Cary ☎01963 350067, ⓦcastlecarybakehouse.co.uk. Unusual but successful combination of coffeehouse and Thai restaurant, with lattes and the like served all day and authentic pad Thai and chili-packed pad ka-ree spicing up the lunch menus (served noon–2pm; mains from £12). No under-11s. Tues–Sat 9.30am–4pm.

The Camelot Chapel Rd, South Cadbury ☎01963 441685, ⓦcamelotpub.co.uk. A good place to grab a bite to eat after circuiting Cadbury Castle, with a pretty, ivy-clad exterior and various cubbyholes leading off the main bar. Honest, tasty food includes sausage bubble and squeak (£12.95). Daily noon–11pm, Fri & Sat till midnight, Sun till 10.30pm; food served Mon–Sat noon–3pm & 6–9pm, Sun noon–7pm.

Matt's Kitchen 51 High St, Bruton ☎01749 812027, ⓦmattskitchen.co.uk. Novel little restaurant serving authentic home-cooked food (*Matt's Kitchen* is in Matt's house) to a few in-the-know diners. The ad-hoc menu revolves around a single dish of the day, such as rosemary lamb with colcannon or pork shoulder in cider with smokey mash (around £15), plus a choice of starters (from £8). Bring your own alcohol. No credit cards. Wed–Fri 6.30–10.30pm.

★ **The Pilgrims** Lovington, 4.5 miles west of Castle Cary, off the B3153 ☎01963 240597, ⓦpilgrims restaurant.co.uk. A real find, this fantastic place combines the relaxed atmosphere of a country pub with the elegant cooking of a fine-dining restaurant. The commitment to quality (local) cuisine is evident in dishes such as the Langport duck confit with pink-roasted breast in a Cognac sauce (mains from £19); just make sure you leave room for the superb Somerset cheese board. Thurs–Sat 7–11pm.

The Queens Arms Corton Denham, about 2.5 miles past South Cadbury ☎01963 220317, ⓦthequeensarms. com. Hidden away in the back roads south of Cadbury Castle, this attractive former AA Pub of the Year is extremely popular thanks to its solid but sophisticated food, from (wild) beer-battered haddock and chips through to white truffle gnocchi (mains from £14 at lunch, £17 at dinner); there are normally some great fruity desserts on the pudding menu, too. Excellent selection of bottled beers (around 45 in total) and ciders. Daily 8am–11pm, Sun till 10pm; food served 7.30–9.30am (Sat & Sun from 8.30am), noon–3pm & 6–9.30pm (Sun till 9pm)

★ **Roth Bar & Grill** Hauser & Wirth Somerset, Durslade Farm, Dropping Lane, Bruton ☎01749 814700, ⓦrothbarandgrill.co.uk. The former cowshed at this contemporary art gallery (see page 186) makes a suitably cool venue for flavour-packed dishes ranging from home-made Merguez sausages with harissa mayonnaise (£9) to dry-aged lamb chop from their own salt room (£20). Huge photographic prints and other works adorn the walls, and the bar is a work of industrial art in itself, with salvaged drums finding a new life as bar stools. There are fireside feasts every Thursday through summer, plus monthly Friday-night live music and DJ sets. Tues–Sun 9am–3.45pm, Fri & Sat till 11pm; food served 10am–3pm (Sat & Sun till 3.30pm), Fri & Sat also 6–9pm.

Somerton and around

It's difficult to picture quiet, unassuming **SOMERTON** as a county town, let alone the ancient capital of Wessex, but it has been both, the latter allegedly for a short period in the seventh century, when King Ina's royal council met here – it is in Somerton that Ina reputedly drew up the oldest written laws in English.

The town's spell as an important crossroads on the road to London and the south coast bequeathed it a number of fine seventeenth- and eighteenth-century buildings, most notably its **church** and **Market Cross**, which was built by Sir Edward Hext from local blue lias stone. Hext also gave Somerton its oldest **almshouses**, the ancient-looking building down West Street, established in 1626 and still in use today.

5

St Michael and All Angels

Market Place · Free · ⓦ stmichaelssomerton.co.uk

The stout octagonal tower of **St Michael and All Angels** shelters one of the finest Jacobean altars in the country, but it's the church's sixteenth-century oak roof that catches the eye. Constructed from some seven thousand different pieces, its elaborate carvings include a pair of dragons at each spandrel, mouths agape and growing ever bigger as they approach the altar. Among the many motifs – including a devil with a pig's nose – look out for the full-relief cider barrel in the north aisle; it's lying on a leaf on the fourth horizontal beam above the second window from the left.

Lytes Cary Manor

About three-quarters of a mile from the A372, near the A37/A303 junction · **House** March–Oct daily 11am–5pm · **Gardens** March–Oct daily 10.30am–4.30pm · £11.50 · NT **Estate** Daily dawn–dusk · Free · ☎ 01458 224471, ⓦ nationaltrust.org.uk

Of the many stately homes in South Somerset, **Lytes Cary Manor** offers perhaps the most personal insight into period country living: a private, unpretentious home that just happens to have belonged to particularly wealthy owners. Built for William le Lyte in 1286, it bounced between the Lyte family members for five hundred years until it was sold to an MP in the eighteenth century; the house fell into disrepair, and when Sir Walter Jenner bought the house in the early 1900s, the Great Hall was being used as a cider press.

Each room at Lytes Cary is stuffed with Dutch paintings, Flemish tapestries and period furniture, much of it – including the mahogany bed of William Pitt the Elder – purchased by Sir Walter. The entrance room, the **Great Hall**, has the rarest exhibit in the house, a first edition (1578) of the *Niewe Herball*, an updated translation of the Flemish *Cruydeboeck* by botanist Henry Lyte. The pair of creepy mannequins in the **Great Parlour** next door were known as "Good Companions", as they were believed to have bumped up "unlucky" dinner parties that would otherwise have numbered thirteen.

Outside, beyond the topiary of the trim Arts and Crafts **garden**, several **walks** lead round the wider estate and along the river.

ARRIVAL AND INFORMATION

By bus The First Bus #54 service (Mon–Fri 8 daily) links Somerton with Langport (15min), Taunton (50min) and Yeovil (35min).

SOMERTON AND AROUND

Tourist office Somerton Local Information Centre, The Library, Cox's Yard, West St (March–Oct Mon, Tues, Thurs & Fri 10am–4pm, Sat 10am–noon).

ACCOMMODATION AND EATING

As well as the below, there's also accommodation at *The Devonshire Arms* in Long Sutton (see page 178) and *The Pilgrims* at Lovington (see page 188). Both do good food, while *The Halfway House* at Pitney (see page 178) is the most atmospheric drinkers' pub for miles.

Cary Fitzpaine House Cary Fitzpaine, 4 miles southeast of Somerton, off the A37 ☎ 01458 223250, ⓦ caryfitzpaine.co.uk. Attractive farmhouse B&B, with three sweet bedrooms, one with a four-poster that can sleep up to four, and a homely drawing room in the main house, plus a tastefully converted self-catering barn (weekly rental), with its own private garden. The considerate owners can provide storage for wet walking/cycling kit and have repair equipment for bikes. Pet-friendly – and not just dogs and horses, either. B&B **£80**, self-catering per week **£850**

The Courtyard Café West St, Somerton ☎ 01458 273101. Occupying the back of a gift shop in central Somerton and opening out onto a tidy courtyard, this relaxed spot does delicious soups, and panini, toasted teacakes and the like, but is mostly known for its selection of scrumptious cakes and cookies. Mon–Sat 9.30am–4.30pm.

Lynch Country House Hotel Somerton ☎ 01458 272316, ⓦ thelynchcountryhouse.co.uk. Archetypal Georgian country house, with cropped ivy hugging the walls, and pretty grounds; it's in a residential area on the fringes of Somerton but overlooks the Cary Valley. The rooms – particularly the first-floor "Premiere" ones – are equally classic, with plenty of floral furnishings; the cheapest are in the eaves of the main house, while there are four more in a converted coach house. **£80**

The White Hart Market Place, Somerton ☎ 01458 272273, ⓦ whitehartsomerton.com. Made from the same handsome blue-lias stone as the church it faces, the beautifully renovated and relaxed White Hart scores highly for its innovative pub grub, such Cornish plaice with

5

MANORS FROM HEAVEN

While it's all very enlightening to spend a few hours nosing around stately homes such as Lytes Cary Manor, it's not quite the same as **staying the night** – but that's exactly what you can do at some of the National Trust's finest mansions in the area (☎0344 335 1287, ⓦnationaltrustcottages.co.uk). The period properties can be rented for between two nights and two weeks, with lets starting on a Thursday (Friday for Lytes Cary Manor). The prices given below are for July and August; they're significantly cheaper at other times of the year.

1 Strode House Barrington Court. The rooms in this red-brick former stables overlook Barrington Court (see page 197) and were built a century after the house itself; the bedrooms are quite plain, though the sitting room is grander. The gardens here are some of the most attractive in the county. Sleeps 5. Two nights **£589**

Lytes Cary Manor Charlton Mackrell. The best choice if you really want to feel like the lord of all you survey. Set in the west wing, authentically baronial rooms – one with a four-poster bed – look out over the well-kept gardens; the surroundings of the fantastic wood-panelled dining room, heavy with portraiture, can make dinner a very grand affair. There's a private terraced garden, plus croquet lawn and grass tennis court (June–

Sept). Sleeps 14. Three nights **£2099**

South Lodge Montacute House, Montacute. This sixteenth-century lodge stands at the entrance to Montacute House (see below), and so enjoys easy access if not the *exact* same setting. It's built from the same lovely hamstone, though, and has a slate-floored dining room (with piano), very big (if sparsely furnished) bedrooms and a private rear garden. Sleeps 6. Two nights **£919**

Tintinhull House Farm St, Tintinhull. Beautiful seventeenth-century manor house with antique beds and original roll-top baths, a cosy lounge with monumental open fire and a lovely country kitchen. Best of all, you can have Tintinhull Garden (see page 193) to yourself come closing time. Sleeps 8. Three nights **£1179**

chorizo, fennel and capers (mains from £13.50). The eight individually styled rooms all have deep, comfy beds, but it's worth pushing the boat out for Room 3, with its open four-poster and cast-iron bath (£130). Breakfast is officially (according to the 2019 National Breakfast Awards) the best in the South West. Daily 9am–11pm; food served 9–11am, noon–3pm & 6–9.45pm. **£85**

SHOPPING

★ **ACEarts** The Old Town Hall, Market Place, Somerton ☎01458 273008, ⓦacearts.co.uk. Excellent gallery that hosts monthly-changing exhibitions, plus various events, from Meet the Artist events to drawing days, plus a shop full of exquisite locally made works. Tues–Sat 10am–5pm, exhibition space closed 1–2pm.

Yeovil and around

The largest town in South Somerset by some way, **YEOVIL** disproves the theory that appearances can be deceptive, its fringe of humdrum suburbs and business parks giving way to a uniformly bland central shopping precinct. Consequently, it does have the best facilities in the area, which, combined with its central location, can make it a fairly convenient base for exploring the region, particularly **Montacute House**, four miles to the west, and the excellent **Fleet Air Arm Museum**.

In town itself, the fourteenth-century church of **St John the Baptist**, known as the Lantern of the West due to its abundance of windows, is quite a sight when the sun streams through its (modern) stained glass. Yeovil's main attraction, though – ironically, given the surrounding countryside – is the sizeable **Yeovil Country Park**, the Ninesprings area in particular providing plenty of trails and a children's playground.

Montacute House

Montacute • **House & gardens** House March–Oct daily 11am–4.30pm; Nov & Dec daily 11am–3pm • Gardens March–Oct daily 10am–5pm; Nov–Feb daily 10am–4pm • £13.80 • NT **Parkland** March–Oct daily 10am–5pm; Nov–Feb daily 10am–4pm • Free • ☎01935 823289, ⓦnationaltrust.org.uk • South West Coaches' #81 from Yeovil to South Petherton

5

Set in the picture-postcard hamlet of the same name, majestic **Montacute House** still makes the striking statement that Sir Edward Phelips intended when he built it from local hamstone in the late sixteenth century. The mansion, a beautifully designed and lavishly filled status symbol, was intended to help further Phelips's progress at court and deliver him his dream of entertaining Elizabeth I – an ambition he never achieved as the queen died just two years after the house was completed.

Phelips would have appreciated the attention his mansion attracted in 1995, when it was used as the Palmer residence in Ang Lee's adaptation of *Sense and Sensibility*, and again in 2015, when it stood in for Greenwich Palace in the BBC drama *Wolf Hall*.

The house
Among the assorted period furniture and paintings that decorate the first-floor rooms (including pictures by Gainsborough and Reynolds), there's an interesting frieze in the **Great Hall** depicting the public humiliation of a cuckolded husband, and several vibrant tapestries, most significantly *The Hunter*, in the **Parlour**, a late eighteenth-century piece based on a set woven for Louis XIV.

Upstairs, the windows in the grand **Library**, originally the Great Chamber, showcase the stained-glass coats of arms of the Phelips family and their well-to-do associates. The centrepiece of the neighbouring **Crimson Bedroom** is its four-poster, richly carved with foliage and figures and surrounded by embroidered bed hangings; the bed was built in 1612, hence the royal arms of James I above its headboard, showing a lion (for England) and a unicorn (for Scotland), the first time the supporters of the United Kingdom had appeared together in a monarch's coat of arms.

Fifty or so of the National Portrait Gallery's vast collection of Tudor and Jacobean portraits are on permanent loan in the top-floor Elizabethan **Long Gallery**, the longest of its kind in the country. Admittedly, most are by unknown artists or are copies of more famous works, but there are still some fine pieces here, particularly John de Critz's seventeenth-century portrait of a luxuriously dressed James I.

The gardens and parkland
The formal **gardens** are most notable for their bulbous hedges, while a couple of waymarked walks lead through the estate's three hundred acres of **parkland** to a tower on St Michael's Hill that marks the site of a motte and bailey castle. **Events** in the grounds include the monthly Levels' Best farmers' market (last Sat of the month except Aug 10am–2pm) and an annual wassail; the pleasant **courtyard café** uses fruit and vegetable from the kitchen gardens at Tintinhull (see page 193) and Barrington Court (see page 197).

Montacute TV, Radio and Toy Museum
1 South St, Montacute • Open selected dates in Easter, May half term, Summer & October half term holidays; check website for details • £9.99 • ☏ 01935 823024, ⓦ montacutemuseum.co.uk

Just a few yards from Montacute House but an altogether different proposition, the **Montacute TV, Radio and Toy Museum** provides a nostalgic trip down memory lane, as much perhaps for its curator as for the parents who try to kid themselves that they're only here for the children. The collection started with a few vintage radios and TVs (which now number over six hundred) and today features a labyrinth of display cases crammed with annuals, games and all the other associated memorabilia that has sprung up over the last eighty years around programmes ranging from *Dixon of Dock Green* and *Dad's Army* to *The Simpsons* and *CSI*.

Stoke-sub-Hamdon Priory
North St, Stoke-sub-Hamdon, 8 miles northwest of Yeovil • March–Sept Mon & Sun 2–5pm • Free • ☏ 01935 823289, ⓦ nationaltrust.org. uk • South West Coaches' #81 from Yeovil to South Petherton

THE FOLLIES OF BARWICK PARK

Marking the boundaries of Barwick House estate, just south of Yeovil, the four whimsical and triumphantly pointless **follies of Barwick Park** were built in the 1770s for no reason other than as a bit of decadent decoration – an easy one-and-a-half-mile walk along public footpaths leads past three of the follies, with views across an open field to the fourth.

From Barwick Village Hall (to get here, follow signs for *Little Barwick House* off the A37, a mile south of Yeovil), turn left into Rex's Lane and head up past Barwick House and through an "avenue" of high-banked trees until you come to an overgrown byway on your left. Not far along here, on the left, stands **Jack the Treacle Eater**, an arch of ragged stones topped by a round lock-up tower with a conical roof; the statue of Hermes at its tip recalls the eponymous messenger whose journeys to and from London were allegedly sustained only by tins of the sticky stuff. Follow the byway for three-quarters of a mile to Two Tower Lane, turn left, and after a while you'll see **The Fish Tower** on your left-hand side; it originally peaked with a fish-shaped weather vane but now looks more like a bung-topped test tube. Beyond here, through a gate signed "Barwick Park", a path cuts diagonally across the field, giving good views of the **Rose Tower**, which appears on the ridge to the right like a pock-marked pixie hat; in the distance, in the line of trees just up from the A37 and almost behind Barwick House, **The Needle** is a much less fanciful obelisk. Follow the path to the driveway of Barwick House, turn left past the house – looking up to see Jack the Treacle Eater from its western side – and then right at the end of the driveway back onto Rex's Lane; Barwick Village Hall is a third of a mile down the road.

The attractive but crumbling hamstone ensemble of **Stoke-sub-Hamdon Priory** sees few visitors bar the house martins that nest in the drafty rafters of its hall. The buildings were erected around the chantry of the Beauchamp family, the thirteenth-century lords of Stoke Manor who gave their name to some of the villages around here. The barn and its bulging, thatch-roofed stables are well and truly closed, and the ruined dovecote and granary are off limits and awaiting funds for restoration, but you can poke around the Great Hall, kitchen and what appears to be a small larder while enjoying the likely solitude.

Tintinhull Garden

Farm St, Tintinhull, 5 miles northwest of Yeovil on the A3088 and half a mile south of the A303 • Mid-March to Sept daily 11am–5pm • £7.10 • NT • ☎ 01458 224471, ⓦ nationaltrust.org.uk

The half-dozen interconnecting "outdoor rooms" that make up orderly **Tintinhull Garden** are largely the work of Felicity (Phyllis) Reiss, who spent nearly thirty years tweaking its aesthetics after moving into the seventeenth-century manor house in 1933. Avid gardeners will find interest in the careful combinations of colour and texture, and in the busy kitchen garden (which provides fruit and veg for the restaurant at nearby Montacute House), but you don't need green fingers to appreciate the overriding air of tranquillity here – Tintinhull is a place to unwind, and it's not uncommon to see people idling through a paperback at the edge of the Pond Garden's lily pool.

Fleet Air Arm Museum

RNAS Yeovilton, on the B3151 near the junction of the A303 and the A37 • April–Oct 10am–5.30pm; Nov–March Wed–Sun (also Mon & Tues in school hols) 10am–4.30pm • £17, 20 percent discount if booked online • ☎ 01935 840565, ⓦ fleetairarm.com

Set on RNAS Yeovilton, Europe's busiest military air base, the **Fleet Air Arm Museum** boasts one of the largest collections of naval aircraft in the world, as well as the first Concorde ever built in Britain. But despite the superlatives, it's the interactive displays throughout – from touch-screen simulations to mini-wind turbines that show how an aircraft banks, pitches or yaws – that set this museum apart.

5

The halls

Hall 1 deals with over a century of British naval aviation, from the bullet-ridden first plane to take part in a naval battle to a Search and Rescue Sea King helicopter, while the exhibits in **Hall 2** span World War II and Korea, with a separate exhibition on the Women's Royal Naval Service. It's the last two halls, though, that elevate the Fleet Air Arm from an interesting museum to an excellent one: in the Aircraft Carrier Experience in **Hall 3**, a noisy Phantom fighter launch from the plane-packed flight deck is followed by the chance to "land" an F35B stealth fighter on to one of the Fleet Air Arm's carriers that are currently under construction. **Hall 4** features six aircraft that were used in the Falklands campaign, though the biggest draw (literally) here is a climb-aboard Concorde, a test prototype that was used to run experiments before the first commercial models could roll off the production line.

ARRIVAL AND INFORMATION

YEOVIL AND AROUND

BY TRAIN

Yeovil Junction is in Stoford, 2 miles south of the centre.
Destinations Basingstoke (every 30min–1hr; 1hr 25min); Crewkerne (hourly; 10min); Exeter St David's (hourly; 1hr 5min); London Waterloo (every 30min–1hr; 2hr 25min); Salisbury (every 30min–1hr; 45min).
Yeovil Pen Mill is 1 mile east of town, just off the A30 and on the "Heart of Wessex" line that runs here from Bristol to Weymouth.
Destinations Bath (Mon–Sat 10 daily, Sun 5 daily; 1hr 25min); Bradford-on-Avon (Mon–Sat 10 daily, Sun 5 daily; 1hr 10min); Bristol (Mon–Sat 10 daily, Sun 5 daily; 1hr 45min); Bruton (Mon–Sat 10 daily, Sun 5 daily; 20min); Castle Cary (Mon–Sat 10 daily, Sun 5 daily; 15min); Dorchester (Mon–Sat 10 daily, Sun 5 daily; 35min); Frome (Mon–Sat 10 daily, Sun 5 daily; 35min); Weymouth (Mon–

Sat 10 daily, Sun 5 daily; 50min).

BY BUS

Yeovil Bus Station is on several national routes: Berry's Coaches operates a twice-daily service to and from London Hammersmith (2hr 50min), while National Express runs daily services to and from Bristol (1hr 30min); Bournemouth (2hr 5min); Dorchester (35min); Poole (1hr 45min); and Weymouth (55min). The First Bus #54 service (Mon–Fri 8 daily) links Yeovil with Langport (45min), Somerton (35min) and Taunton (1hr 25min).

INFORMATION

Yeovil Information Centre Petters House, Petters Way (Mon–Fri 9am–4pm; ☎ 01935 8293331).

ACCOMMODATION

The Lanes High St, West Coker, 2 miles southwest of Yeovil ☎ 01935 862555, ⓦ laneshotel.net. Enclosed by walled gardens, the soft hamstone exterior of this former rectory belies the boutique hotel within. The rooms are suitably contemporary, as are the public spaces – the restaurant is pretty much a glass cube. Facilities include a gym, sauna, Jacuzzi and "experience shower", with plenty of treatments available at the on-site spa (ⓦ spatherapyatlanes.com). There are also one- and two-bedroom apartments, with stylish stand-alone baths (from £160). **£140**

Little Barwick House Rex's Lane, Barwick, signed off the A37 1 mile south of Yeovil ☎ 01935 423902, ⓦ littlebarwickhouse.co.uk. Intimately grand Georgian dower house set in attractive grounds. The eight rooms are individually furnished in a country-house style and enjoy nice touches such as home-made shortbread – but you're really here for the divine three-course dinner at the downstairs restaurant (see below), included in the rate – along with afternoon tea. Occasionally two-night minimum stays at weekends. Closed Mon & Sun & first 3 weeks in Jan. No children under 5. **£250**

The Masons Arms 41 Lower Odcombe, about a mile off the A3088 west of Yeovil ☎ 01935 862591, ⓦ masonsarmsodcombe.co.uk. The oldest building in the hamstone village of Lower Odcombe, with spacious modern rooms (doubles and family rooms) in an extension off the back of the pub (see below), overlooking the pub garden. The good breakfast includes eggs from their own chickens. Camping is also available in the field behind, with sparkling facilities, plus a cosy shepherd's hut; there's also a lovely one-bedroom cottage nearby. Doubles **£98**, shepherd's hut **£80**, cottage **£130**, pitches **£15**

Slipper Cottage 41 Bishopston, Montacute ☎ 01935 823073, ⓦ slippercottage.co.uk. Seventeenth-century hamstone cottage in the charming village of Montacute, a few hundred yards from Montacute House itself, thoughtfully renovated and still with plenty of low beams and open fireplaces, plus a lovely long cottage garden. There are just two rooms, both with inviting double beds and, of course, slipper baths. Good-value single rates (£45). No debit or credit cards. **£65**

HOW DO YOU LIKE THEM APPLES?

There are several low-key cider producers in the deep south of Somerset, pressing apples on a smaller scale than neighbouring Perry's (see page 198) and Burrow Hill (see page 196) but still crafting a quality traditional farmhouse cider or two. One of the best is **Bridge Farm Cider**, on the A30 just out of East Chinnock, on the way from Yeovil to Crewkerne (9.30am–6.30pm: May–Sept daily; Oct–April Fri, Sat & Sun only; ☎01935 862387, ⊛bridgefarmcider.co.uk). The owner, Nigel Stewart, makes excellent dry, medium and sweet cider (from £5.50 for 2l), a bottle-fermented sparkling cider, cider brandy and perry, plus ten types of single-variety apple juices.

EATING AND DRINKING

Cow & Apple 8–10 Church St, Yeovil ☎01935 433292, ⊛cowandapple.co.uk. Great little burger joint overlooking St John the Baptist church, whose menu includes their signature Gurt Burger, a double patty with pulled pork, bacon, cheese, onion rings and BBQ sauce, plus a decent selection of vegetarian options (burgers from £9.50). Wash them down with over 50 varieties of cider. Tues–Fri 11.30am–late, Sat 9am–late, Sun 9am–4pm.

★ **Little Barwick House** Rex's Lane, Barwick, signed off the A37 1 mile south of Yeovil ☎01935 423902, ⊛littlebarwickhouse.co.uk. Whitewashed Georgian restaurant with rooms (see above), run by a family team whose enviable skill is to provide quality cooking in a refreshingly relaxed environment – locally sourced produce makes up the majority of a tastebud-teasing menu, featuring the likes of lobster cannelloni and saddle of wild roe deer. Very good (and very good-value) wine list, too. Lunch: two courses £28.95, three courses £31.95. Dinner: two courses £49.95 (available Tues–Thurs), three courses

£54.95. Tues 7–9pm, Wed–Sat noon–2pm & 7–9pm.

The Masons Arms 41 Lower Odcombe, about a mile off the A3088 west of Yeovil ☎01935 862591, ⊛masonsarmsodcombe.co.uk. Lovely-looking thatch-roofed inn whose friendly owners keep their regulars coming back for more thanks to a combination of classic pub grub, pizza from their own wood-fired pizza oven and an a la carte menu (mains from £13.75) – all served in generous portions. The pub's own microbrewery produces three real ales, including the deep, dark Roly Poly. Daily 8am–midnight; food served Mon–Sat 8am–11am, noon–2pm & 6.30–9.30pm, Sun 8am–11am & noon–9pm.

The Winking Frog 17 Princes St, Yeovil ☎01935 508151. Relaxed, brightly decorated trust-run coffee shop that provides employment opportunities to people with learning difficulties – and also happens to do the best home-made cakes in town. Hearty breakfasts and a reliable lunchtime (11.30am–3pm) menu of paninis, sandwiches and baps. Mon–Fri 8.30am–4pm, Sat 9am–2.30pm.

Martock and around

Set around Church Street and its continuation, North Street, the grand village of **MARTOCK** is chock-full of pretty hamstone buildings. Many date from the sixteenth and seventeenth centuries, literally the town's golden age, when it prospered thanks to the fertile fields nearby – according to one seventeenth-century writer, Martock was "seated in the fattest place of the Earth of this Countie". Any walk around the village should start at the **Treasurer's House** and the church, just opposite, but it's also worth exploring North Street, where you'll find the eighteenth-century **Market House** (Mon–Fri 10am–1pm), which used to shelter the village's horse-drawn fire engine and is still in use as the local tourist information centre.

Treasurer's House

Church St, Martock • Mid-March to Sept Mon & Sun 2–5pm • £4 • NT • ☎01935 825015, ⊛nationaltrust.org.uk

The oldest inhabited private house in Somerset, the **Treasurer's House** was built for Hugh, Treasurer of Wells Cathedral, not long after the Bishop of Bath and Wells had acquired the village in 1226; up until then, Martock had belonged to the Abbot of Mont St-Michel in Normandy. In 1293, John de Langton, at that time Chancellor of England, tagged the high-ceilinged **Great Hall** onto its northern end; among several later alterations, a medieval **kitchen** was constructed alongside.

5

The manor house itself later became a vicarage and then, by the mid-nineteenth century, a series of individual tenements. Its oldest part is the upstairs **solar block**, the Treasurer's private apartment, one side of which is covered with a rare wall painting depicting the Crucifixion (with St Mary, St John – clasping his gospel inside his robe – and Christ); the picture dates to around 1262 but was only discovered in 1995, when the whole house was extensively restored.

All Saints

Church St, Martock • Free

The thing that grabs your attention most as you enter **All Saints**, the second-largest church in Somerset, is its bold and beautiful oak nave **ceiling**, dating to 1513 and exquisitely carved with open-winged angels hovering from its cross beams – if it's dark, switch on the light by the pulpit to illuminate the work. Musket shot found embedded in the wood dates to when Cromwell and his Parliamentarian troops were billeted here after the battle for Bridgwater in 1645; it's alleged that they were trying to pick off the angels.

Almost as striking as the ceiling are the canopied **niches** spaced among the aisle windows, which contain seventeenth-century paintings of (uniquely) all twelve apostles. They're believed to have been based on contemporary bigwigs, with St James the Less – the right of the two figures directly opposite the church door – bearing an uncanny resemblance to Charles I.

Somerset Cider Brandy Company and Burrow Hill Cider

Pass Vale Farm, Burrow Hill, signed from Kingsbury Episcopi, about 3 miles northwest of Martock • Mon–Sat 9am–5pm • Free • Tours by arrangement; £5 • ☎ 01460 240782, ⓦ somersetciderbrandy.co.uk

Lying at the foot of Burrow Hill, a local landmark topped by a single sycamore, the **Somerset Cider Brandy Company** is the only one of its kind in the county. Its varieties of smooth, rich cider brandy are produced in old French copper stills before being aged in oak barrels for between three and twenty years.

Their dry and medium **Burrow Hill Cider** is pressed from around forty varieties of cider apple but is perhaps eclipsed by their two single-variety, bottle-fermented sparkling ciders – a punchy Kingston Black and bone-dry Stoke Red – produced using the *méthode champenoise*, whereby the cider is matured within the bottle, its sediment frozen in the neck and then removed.

Pre-arranged **tours** among the vast cider vats (some holding up to eighty thousand pints) and copper stills add insight into the workings of a 150-year-old cider farm, as does the thirty-minute **self-guided walk** around the sheep-grazed orchards. The old, dark **ciderhouse**, crammed with oak barrels, is as atmospheric a place for tasting as any, though you'll need a designated driver if you want to sample the full range of ciders, aperitifs, eaux de vie, pomonas and apple brandies on offer (cider from £8.50 for 4l, brandy from £17 for a half-bottle of three-year-old).

East Lambrook Manor Gardens

East Lambrook, near South Petherton, 2 miles north of the A303 • 10am–5pm: Feb, May, June & July Tues–Sun; March, April & Aug–Oct Tues–Sat • £6 • ☎ 01963 240328, ⓦ eastlambrook.co.uk

The busy terraces of charming, Grade-I-listed **East Lambrook Manor Gardens** are the country's finest example of a cottage-style garden, mainly because this is where it all began. In 1938, when **Margery Fish** moved here from London with her husband, the editor of *The Daily Mail*, she had no experience of gardening whatsoever, just a notion that it needn't be the preserve of the wealthy few whose huge landscaped grounds required tending by paid gardeners.

5

After thirty years of fine-tuning and innovation – and a writing career that included the cottage-garden classic *We Made a Garden* (see page 323) – Margery Fish died a gardening icon in 1969. The garden today is essentially the same one she left behind, and now serves as a sort of pilgrimage site for pruners. Themed areas include the Scented Garden, the White Garden and the Ditch, where you'll find East Lambrook's famous hellebores and snowdrops (there are over eighty varieties on show in spring), plus hardy geraniums, a Fish favourite. You can pick up some of the plants you'll see at the **Margery Fish Plant Nursery**; the great lady was also a pioneer of commercial plant sales.

Barrington Court

On the B3168 in Barrington, signposted from the A303 and the A358 • Mid-Feb to Oct daily 10.30am–5pm; Nov to mid-Feb Mon & Fri–Sun 10.30am–3pm • £13.80, £11.20 Nov to mid-Feb • NT • ☎ 01460 241938, ⓦ nationaltrust.org.uk

In 1907, sixteenth-century **Barrington Court** became the first major manor-house project of a fledgling National Trust, but it was in such disrepair that it nearly ruined the organization. Only the intervention of Colonel Arthur Lyle (of Tate & Lyle fame) in 1920 saved Barrington – within five years, he had completed the restoration of the focal Court House. The house served as the Lyle family home until 1991, and the rooms, now empty of furniture again, are filled with the history of three generations, their memories brought to life in occasional audio snippets. The Great Hall and the Master Bedroom, with its 1625 Strode fireplace, are highlights, though the most notable feature throughout is the Colonel's collection of delicately carved wood panelling, salvaged from historic houses across the country.

Outside, you can wander the varied Gertrude Jekyll-inspired **gardens** and the estate's **orchards**; produce from the sizeable **Kitchen Garden** is used in the restaurant in **Strode House**, a later red-brick building that makes a vivid contrast to the muted hamstone of Court House itself.

ARRIVAL AND INFORMATION   MARTOCK AND AROUND

By bus Berry's Coaches' twice-daily service runs between London Hammersmith and South Petherton (3hr 20min); local South West Coaches' #52 links Martock with Yeovil (Mon–Sat 7 daily; 30min).

Martock LIC Market House (Mon–Fri 10am–1pm; ☎ 01935 310040).

ACCOMMODATION

As well as the places below, there are also some good accommodation options in the villages around Yeovil (see page 194), as well as *The Devonshire Arms* in Long Sutton (see page 177).

Burrow Hill B&B Orchard View, Burrow Way; follow the "Distillery & Cider Mill" signs from Kingsbury Episcopi ☎ 01460 240288, ⓦ burrowhillbandb.co.uk. Pretty little Grade II-listed cottage with just two doubles, one of which (Hill View) has a gorgeous double-ended bath and, unsurprisingly, views over Burrow Hill itself. As an added bonus, the B&B is right next door to the Somerset Cider Brandy Company (see page 196). Keen single rates (£60). No debit or credit cards. **£80**

New Farm Over Stratton, just off the A303 near South Petherton ☎ 01460 240584, ⓦ newfarmrestaurant. co.uk. Three airy, floral rooms (one twin and two doubles)

prettily done out in single tones. There's free tea and scones and Somerset apple cake to keep you going in between meals at the farm's excellent restaurant (see below). **£85**

★ **The Wheelhouse** Gawbridge Mill, Kingsbury Episcopi ☎ 01935 825783, ⓦ thewheelhousebandb.co.uk. Extremely friendly B&B set in an eighteenth-century mill atop the River Parrett, with double and twin rooms that can be combined to make a family suite. The generous breakfast spread includes home-made bread and jam, and the hosts can also provide packed lunches. Keen single rates. **£85**

The White Hart Hotel Over Stratton, Martock ☎ 01935 822005, ⓦ whiteharthotelmartock.co.uk. Good-value, spacious rooms in a Grade II-listed former coaching inn, now a friendly village pub, slap bang in the middle of Martock. There's great food downstairs, and a bar serving local ales and ciders. **£80**

EATING AND DRINKING

In addition to the places below, *The Devonshire Arms* in Long Sutton (see page 178) does good meals, while some

of the best food in the area is to be found at the delightful *Lord Poulett Arms* (see page 200); few pubs can better *The*

Halfway House at Pitney (see page 178) for character.

★ **New Farm Restaurant** Over Stratton, just off the A303 near South Petherton ☎ 01460 240584, ⓦ newfarmrestaurant.co.uk. A converted hamstone barn makes a great setting for this award-winning family-run restaurant, where global starters are followed by mostly Modern British mains (from £15.50) and finished off with one of "Jane's delicious desserts". Wed–Sat 6.30–9pm, Fri also noon–2pm, last Sun of the month noon–2pm.

Wyndham Arms Kingsbury Episcopi ☎ 01935 823239, ⓦ wyndhamarms.com. Attractive local, both outside and in, with a warm welcome and a decent range of regional brews – Butcombe and Otter for ale drinkers, Burrow Hill and Ashton Press Still for cider lovers. Also does comfortable pub staples such as (handmade) steak and ale pie, scampi and chips and sausage and mash (from £11.50). Daily noon–11.30pm, Thurs–Sat till late; food served Mon–Thurs noon–2pm & 6–9pm, Fri & Sat noon–3pm & 6–9.30pm, Sun noon–8.30pm.

SHOPPING

The Trading Post The Old Filling Station, Lopenhead, just off the A303 near South Petherton ☎ 01460 241666, ⓦ tradingpostorganics.co.uk. Well-stocked farm shop, selling their own organic veg, pork sausages and eggs, and trading various goodies from over eighty local suppliers, including Burrow Hill cider vinegar and Sharpham Park spelt. Mon–Sat 8.30am–6pm, Sun 10am–2pm.

Crewkerne and the west

The ancient market town of **CREWKERNE** (pronounced "crook-un", from *crug*, meaning "hill") still retains many of its fine hamstone buildings, the majority of them huddled around Market Square and adjoining Market Street. The town's original wealth was earned through wool, its prosperity reflected in the size and splendour of fifteenth-century **St Bartholomew's church**, at the end of Church Street. The subsequent success of its textile industry brought a second wind of prosperity and added a Georgian flavour to its architectural ensemble.

The old part of town is a pleasant place to wander, with a cluster of attractive townhouses up **Court Barton** and on Abbey Street, where the **Church Hall** (in its former life as Crewkerne Grammar School) educated Sir Thomas Masterman Hardy, Nelson's flag-captain, to whom the admiral turned during his dying moments at the Battle of Trafalgar and uttered the immortal line "Kiss me, Hardy".

Crewkerne Museum

The Heritage Centre, Market Square • April–Oct Wed–Fri 10am–4pm, Sat 10am–1pm • £1 • ☎ 01460 77079, ⓦ crewkernemuseum.co.uk

Housed in a noble Georgian building, the diminutive **Crewkerne Museum** charts the town's two boom periods, particularly the growth enjoyed by the flax and linen industries during the eighteenth and nineteenth centuries – aside from Sir Thomas Hardy hailing from Crewkerne, the town's flax mills also produced the sails for HMS *Victory*, Nelson's flagship at Trafalgar. Hardy's school is also covered; one of the earliest grammar schools in England, it was founded in 1499 and also counted the explorer William Dampier, the first Englishman to set foot in Australia, among its pupils.

Perry's Cider

The Cider Mills, Dowlish Wake, signed from Crewkerne, Ilminster and Chard • Mon–Fri 9am–5.30pm, Sat 9.30am–4.30pm, Sun 10am–1pm; café Mon–Fri 10.30am–4.30pm, Sat 10.30am–4pm • Free • ☎ 01460 55195, ⓦ perryscider.co.uk

The apple harvest at **Perry's Cider** is still pressed in the farm's creaking thatched barn, just as it has been since the sixteenth century. Now in their fourth generation of cider-makers since starting in 1920, the Perry family craft eight farmhouse and single-variety ciders, available from the farm shop – either straight from the barrel (from £7.50 for 2l) or, for the single varieties such as Dabinett, Tremlett, Redstreak and Morgan, in bottles. The small rural **museum** in the barn is packed with old cider-making

5

THE RIVER PARRETT TRAIL

The fifty-mile-long **River Parrett Trail** traces the route of the river from its source at Chedington in Dorset, just southeast of Crewkerne, to where it finally spills into the Bristol Channel near Steart. It's an easy amble, much of it across the flat Somerset Levels, and can be tackled in one four- or five-day hike or broken down into a series of shorter walks. As a snapshot of Somerset, it's difficult to beat, traversing apple orchards, running through hamstone villages and crossing withy beds and wetlands before ending at a nature reserve in Bridgwater. **Attractions** along the way include Ham Hill, East Lambrook Manor Gardens, Muchelney Abbey (see page 176), Burrow Mump (see page 175), Westonzoyland Pumping Station (see page 174) and the Bridgwater and Taunton Canal (see page 210), which the trail follows for a few miles towards its end. OS Explorer **maps** 116, 129 and 140 cover the route.

---

equipment and farm tools, as well as a working cider press and mills, which are in action in the autumn; a short video and display boards chart the process involved.

Ilminster

For its compact size, modestly handsome **ILMINSTER** is quite a social hub, with a vibrant arts centre and a number of independent shops along Silver Street. The central **Market House**, rebuilt in the early 1800s, still holds Ilminster's weekly market (Thurs 9am–1pm), though the main site is, of course, **The Minster**, which – along with the River Isle – gives the town its name. The tourist information centre can provide leaflets on local walks, some passing tank traps and pill boxes that formed part of the **Taunton Stop Line**, a coast-to-coast defensive system that was built in 1940 to hinder a potential German invasion of the South West.

The Minster

Silver St, entrance on Court Barton • Free

Raised above Silver Street, the golden, fifteenth-century church of St Mary's, better known as **The Minster**, is architecturally one of the finest in Somerset, cathedral-like in appearance and dominated by its fine Perpendicular tower. The Duke of Monmouth attended services here in 1690 as part of a recruitment drive ahead of his failed rebellion – over fifty Ilminster men fought with Monmouth five years later, an action that was later to cost a dozen of them their lives at the hands of the infamous Judge Jeffreys (see page 209). Today, the Minster is most notable for its elaborate **reredos** (behind the High Altar), carved from Caen stone and covered in statues of religious figures (and little critters); look out for the snail eating a grape just to the right of Moses.

Forde Abbey

Signed off the B3162, 5 miles southwest of Crewkerne and 3 miles southeast of Chard • **House & gardens** April–Oct Tues–Fri & Sun noon–4pm; gardens daily 10am–5.30pm, last admission 4.30pm • £13, gardens only £10, 10 percent discount if booked online **Tearoom** March–Oct daily 10.30am–4.30pm **Fruit farm** April–Oct daily 9.30am–6pm **Nursery** March–Oct daily 10am–5pm • ☎ 01460 220231, ⓦ fordeabbey.co.uk

Lying right on the border with Dorset, **Forde Abbey** was founded as a Cistercian monastery in 1148 and remained a place of worship until Edmund Prideaux, Oliver Cromwell's Attorney General, turned it into a private home in the middle of the seventeenth century. Of the so-called State Rooms, the Saloon is the main draw, with its colour-saturated **Mortlake Tapestries**, "woven frescoes" that were made in London in 1620; based on cartoons that Raphael created for the Sistine Chapel, they show vivid scenes from the lives of St Peter and St Paul.

5

The surrounding **grounds** contain a rockery, a bog garden, a huge arboretum and numerous ponds, one of which is dominated by the Centenary Fountain, at 160ft the highest in England (it's switched on daily at noon, 1.30pm & 3pm). The estate also runs a seasonal pick-your-own **fruit farm** and a **nursery**, and keeps herds of Red Ruby Devons and milking goats – produce from all these, and from the walled kitchen garden, is served in the vaulted *Undercroft Tearooms*.

Chard

The sizeable town of **CHARD** clings onto the last mile of the county before it slips into Dorset and Devon. Its long history dates back nearly eight hundred years – which is plenty of time for it to have lost any charm it may have once had. There are several survivors of the town's lace-making past – including Holyrood Lace Mill, on Holyrood Street – but other than its enjoyable little **museum**, the most intriguing aspect of Chard today is the pair of streams on its High Street, one of which flows north into the Bristol Channel, the other south into the English Channel.

Chard Museum

Godworthy House, High St • April–Oct Mon–Fri 10.30am–3.30pm, Sat 11am–2pm • £4 • ☎ 01460 65091, 🖥 chardmuseum.co.uk

Staffed by enthusiastic volunteers, the Tardis-like **Chard Museum** is a rabbit warren of rooms, its main displays focusing on **John Stringfellow**, who invented powered flight when his 9lb aircraft flew 22yds in an old lace mill here in 1848. It's also worth venturing into the barn out back for the exhibition on his fellow Chardian **James Gillingham**, a shoemaker who used his skills to better the lives of local amputees at the end of the nineteenth century. Recent displays focus on Chard-born Margaret Bondfield, the UK's first female cabinet minister, while the carnival costumes upstairs in the New Inn building, collected over 35 years, give a flavour of the pageantry if you're not around for the real thing in autumn (see page 217).

ARRIVAL AND INFORMATION

CREWKERNE AND THE WEST

By train Crewkerne Station, a mile south of town on the A356, is served by regular trains from Basingstoke (1hr 40min); Exeter St David's (55min); London Waterloo (2hr 30min); Salisbury (1hr 5min); and Yeovil Junction (10min).

By bus Berry's Coaches runs a twice-daily service between London Hammersmith and Ilminster (3hr 30min).

Crewkerne LIC Town Hall, Market Square (Mon, Wed & Fri 9am–3.30pm, Tues 9.30am–3.30pm, Thurs 9.30am–12.30pm; ☎ 01460 75928).

Ilminster LIC The Meeting House, East St (Easter–Oct Mon–Sat 10am–1pm; ☎ 01460 57294).

Chard LIC The Guildhall, Fore St (Mon–Sat 10am–1pm; ☎ 01460 260051).

ACCOMMODATION

As well as the places below, *New Farm* in Over Stratton (see page 197) is just over 5 miles up the B3168 from Ilminster, while the places southwest of Yeovil (see page 194) are within 6 or so miles of Crewkerne.

The Five Dials Hanning Road, Ilminster ☎ 01460 55359, 🖥 thefivedials.co.uk. Half a dozen tastefully furnished, contemporary rooms, a little on the small side (bar the garden unit, which has its own separate kitchen) but still light and airy, and with smart bathrooms. Welcoming owners and good food and local brews at the downstairs pub to boot (see below). **£85**

★ **Lord Poulett Arms** High St, Hinton St George ☎ 01460 73149, 🖥 lordpoulettarms.com. Set in the drop-dead gorgeous hamstone village of Hinton St George, the *Lord Poulett Arms* has the kind of rooms you'd want to live in: classy but comfortable, with antique beds, seagrass floors and gilded mirrors set against exposed brick and Osbourne and Little wallpaper. Room 6, with built-in bunkbeds (£160), makes a luxurious bolt hole for a family weekend getaway. What's more, there's a fantastic pub-restaurant at the bottom of the stairs (see below). **£85**

EATING AND DRINKING

Celandines 11 West St, Ilminster ☎ 01460 259393, 🖥 celandines.com. Intimate Mediterranean-style restaurant

with a bare-brick interior and an interesting menu of very well-cooked dishes that include slow-braised pork belly and vegetable tagine with Moroccan-spiced couscous (mains from £10.95). There's an attractive little garden out back. Wed–Sat 10am–3pm & 6.30–9pm, Sun 10am–3pm.

The Five Dials Hanning Road, Ilminster ☎01460 55359, ⓦthefivedials.co.uk. Smart, modern pub with a choice of tables either round a buzzing Shaker-style bar up at the front or in the more open (and less atmospheric) restaurant behind. There's a strong specials board, featuring fresh fish from Brixham, but you can't go far wrong with the slow-cooked lamb shank with rosemary jus (£16.50). Draught Otter Ale and Perry's cider, from just down the road (see page 198). Tues–Thurs 11am–3pm & 5–11pm, Fri–Sun noon–11pm; food served noon–2pm & 6.30–9pm, Sun till 8.30pm.

★ **Lord Poulett Arms** Hinton St George ☎01460 73149, ⓦlordpoulettarms.com. Fantastic pub restaurant – one half bare flagstones, the other polished wooden floorboards – serving game from Exmoor and fish from Dorset, with dishes running along the lines of pan-roasted pork fillet with salt-baked celeriac and black garlic ketchup (mains from £13). The cosy bar, decked in dried hops and lit with flickering candles, serves their own ale from the barrel and, in season, home-made mulled cider. In summer, regulars play boules on the lavender-fringed piste out back; in winter, open fires crackle with contentment. Daily 11am–11pm, Sun till 10.30pm; food served noon–2.15pm & 6–9.15pm.

Number 7 The Café 7 Market St, Crewkerne ☎01460 74194. Chose from nearly forty sandwiches – home-cooked gammon, ox tongue, and Somerset Brie and cranberry among them – plus a range of lighter bites and, on Friday evenings, home-made pizzas (from £7.75). Everything that goes into their breakfasts and lunches (from 11.30am) is freshly sourced their own deli. Mon–Thurs 9am–5pm, Fri 9am–5pm & 6–9.30pm, Sat 9am–4pm.

ENTERTAINMENT

Arts Centre at the Meeting House East St, Ilminster ☎01460 54973, ⓦthemeetinghouse.org.uk. Housed in a former chapel, this is a great little venue, with changing exhibitions in its gallery, plus regular music sessions (mainly jazz and classical), and craft workshops and demonstrations. Mon–Fri 9.30am–4.30pm, Sat 9.30am–2.30pm.

Taunton, Bridgwater and the Quantocks

PONIES ON THE QUANTOCKS

Taunton, Bridgwater and the Quantocks

The two major towns of western Somerset, Bridgwater and Taunton, offer a few specific attractions, notably Bridgwater's Blake Museum and the Museum of Somerset housed in Taunton's castle, but few people linger long in either place, and they are primarily useful as transport hubs and bases for excursions to the nearby Quantock Hills. Covered by heathland, woods and steeply sloping meadows, this wedge of uplands slanting northwest towards the Bristol Channel is home to snug villages nestled among scenic wooded valleys or "combes".

Designated England's first AONB (Area of Outstanding Natural Beauty) in 1956, the Quantocks offer an alluring alternative to the more famous expanses of Exmoor – less dramatic perhaps, but with equally panoramic views. The hills hold literary interest in the home of Samuel Taylor Coleridge, who lived in **Nether Stowey** for three years, but the main recreation hereabouts lies in the great outdoors, specifically hiking, biking and riding. The best areas, however, are remote from the public transport network, which sticks to the main A39, running west from Bridgwater, and A358 from Taunton, the two roads meeting near the northwestern end of the range at Williton. You can get a taster, though, on the private, steam-hauled **West Somerset Railway** between **Bishops Lydeard**, a village north of Taunton, and the coastal resort of Minehead (see page 240), with stops close to some of the thatched, typically English hamlets along the west flank of the Quantocks.

If you're not tempted by the **accommodation** choices at Bridgwater and Taunton, you'll find good options in the smaller centres, such as Nether Stowey, **Combe Florey** and **Crowcombe**, while refreshment is provided at some excellent pubs tucked away in these and other unspoiled rural outposts. There are **horseriding** facilities at many local farms, and a good network of bridleways and walking routes throughout the hills.

GETTING AROUND

Bridgwater and Taunton are both on the main **train** line between Bristol and Exeter. Apart from the steam and diesel trains of the private **West Somerset Railway**, however, **public transport** in the Quantocks area is limited to **bus** services running along the A39 between Bridgwater and Minehead and A358 between Taunton and Minehead, with stops at or near the main Quantock villages. Traveline (☏ 0871 200 2233, ⊛ travelinesw.com) has full **schedules** for the whole region.

By train Trains link Taunton and Bridgwater (hourly; 15min). Wellington has no station. Between late March and October (plus some dates in Dec), the West Somerset Railway (☏ 01643 704996, ⊛ west-somerset-railway. co.uk; see page 222) plies between Bishops Lydeard (with bus connections with the main-line station at Taunton) and Minehead, with stops at Crowcombe Heathfield, Stogumber, Williton, Doniford Halt, Watchet, Washford, Blue Anchor and Dunster.

By bus The major bus company in these parts is First, operating locally under the name Buses of Somerset (☏ 0345 646 0707, ⊛ firstgroup.com), but Hatch Green Coaches (☏ 01823 480338, ⊛ hatchgreencoaches.co.uk) and Dartline Coaches (☏ 01392 872900, ⊛ dartline-coaches.co.uk) also operate some routes. Taunton is the main hub for the region, and most services between Wellington and Bridgwater require a change there. There are good connections between Taunton and Minehead on service #28, with stops at Bishops Lydeard, Combe Florey, Crowcombe and Watchet (note that the village centres are sometimes a short walk from the stops). From Bridgwater, services #14 (Mon–Fri) runs infrequently from Bridgwater to Nether Stowey, but almost all services for Minehead and the coast go via Taunton.

BRIDGWATER AND TAUNTON CANAL

Highlights

1 Museum of Somerset The county's history – and plenty more – is imaginatively encapsulated in this eclectic collection housed in Taunton's old castle, especially strong on the Roman and pre-Roman eras and the seventeenth century. See page 207

2 Bridgwater and Taunton Canal Walk or cycle along the fourteen or so miles of this tranquil waterway to explore a range of wildlife, with pubs and other refreshment stops along the way. See page 210

3 Bridgwater Carnival There's not a lot of action on show in this small provincial town unless you come at Carnival, when the whole

place explodes in an exuberant outburst of sound and spectacle. See page 217

4 Coleridge Cottage, Nether Stowey Once home to Samuel Taylor Coleridge, this modest dwelling in the Quantock Hills is now an absorbing museum devoted to the poet and the birth of the English Romantic movement. See page 219

5 The walk to Wills Neck The Quantock Hills offer quiet, undemanding hikes in secluded combes, but the payback is immensely satisfying, with steep, scenic dips and folds, and stunning vistas. See page 221

HIGHLIGHTS ARE MARKED ON THE MAP ON PAGE 206

Taunton and around

Somerset's county town of **TAUNTON** lies in the fertile Vale of Taunton, watered by the surrounding Quantock, Brendon and Blackdown hills. The region is famed for its production of cider, while Taunton itself is host to one of the country's biggest cattle markets. The town's much restored castle holds the thoroughly engaging **Museum of Somerset**, while, a few steps from the county cricket ground and the **Cricket Museum**, are the pinnacled and battlemented towers of the town's two most important churches: **St James** and **St Mary Magdalene**, both fifteenth century though remodelled by the Victorians. A well-subscribed **literature festival** is held every November (St James is one of the venues; see ⓦtauntonliteraryfestival.co.uk), and a new motor museum is planned for the centre.

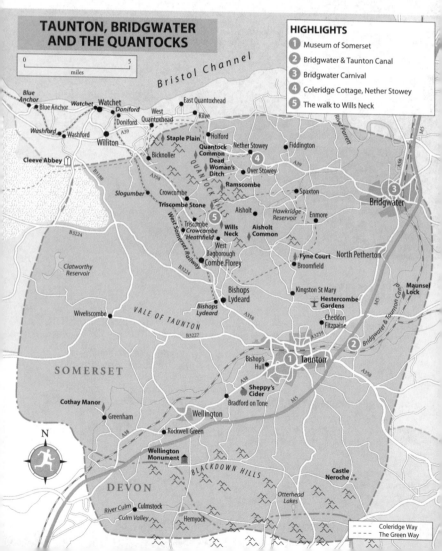

TAUNTON, BRIDGWATER AND THE QUANTOCKS

0 ____ 5
miles

HIGHLIGHTS

1️⃣ Museum of Somerset
2️⃣ Bridgwater & Taunton Canal
3️⃣ Bridgwater Carnival
4️⃣ Coleridge Cottage, Nether Stowey
5️⃣ The walk to Wills Neck

Bristol Channel

Blue Anchor · Blue Anchor · Watchet · Watchet · Doniford · Doniford · West Quantoxhead · East Quantoxhead · Kilve

Washford · Washford · Williton · A39 · Staple Plain · Holford · Nether Stowey · Fiddington

Cleeve Abbey · Bicknoller · Quantock Common · Dead Woman's Ditch · Over Stowey · River Parrett

Slogumber · Crowcombe · Ramscombe · Spaxton · Bridgwater

Triscombe Stone · Triscombe · Aisholt · Hawkridge Reservoir · Enmore

B3224 · Crowcombe Heathfield · Wills Neck · Aisholt Common · Maunsel Lock

Clatworthy Reservoir · West Bagborough · Combe Florey · Fyne Court · Broomfield · North Petherton

Wiveliscombe · Bishops Lydeard · Bishops Lydeard · Kingston St Mary · Hestercombe Gardens · Cheddon Fitzpaine

VALE OF TAUNTON · A358 · B3227

SOMERSET · Bishop's Hull · 1️⃣ Taunton · 2️⃣ Bridgwater & Taunton Canal · A358

Cothay Manor · Greenham · Sheppy's Cider · Bradford on Tone

Wellington · Rockwell Green

N · Wellington Monument · BLACKDOWN HILLS · Castle Neroche

DEVON · River Culm · Culmstock · Culm Valley · Hemyock · Otterhead Lakes

- - - Coleridge Way
- - - The Green Way

Out of town, both **Hestercombe Gardens** and **Fyne Court** would make splendid spots for a picnic, while you can delve into the finer points of cider-making at **Sheppy's Cider**.

Taunton Castle

Castle Green

Started in the twelfth century, **Taunton Castle** became one of the most important strongholds in the county. Here was staged the trial of royal claimant Perkin Warbeck, who in 1490 declared himself to be the Duke of York, the younger of the "Princes in the Tower" (the sons of Edward IV, who had been murdered seven years earlier). It was also the venue of one of the bloodiest of Judge Jeffreys' assizes following the Duke of Monmouth's rebellion (see page 209), at which 514 prisoners were tried for treason, of whom 144 were sentenced to be hanged, drawn and quartered. Some of the structure was demolished in 1662, and much of the rest has been altered, but you can still get a good idea of its once-imposing keep and inner bailey (courtyard).

6

Museum of Somerset

Taunton Castle • Tues–Sat 10am–5pm, daily during school summer hols • Free • 📞 01823 255088, 🖥 museumofsomerset.org.uk

The castle building now houses the **Museum of Somerset**, a well-organized and creatively displayed collection enhanced by hands-on activities and multimedia presentations. Centring on the castle's original Great Hall, the museum focuses mainly on the history, prehistory and geology of the county, starting with one of the largest ammonite fossils found in Britain and a complete plesiosaur skeleton discovered by fishermen in 2003. The human presence is represented by such items as the **Shapwick Canoe** (c.350 BC), suspended from the ceiling and made from a hollowed-out tree trunk preserved in peat; a wooden toy axe (possibly Britain's earliest-known toy), and the "**God dolly**" from around 2500 BC, showing both male and female characteristics (and claimed to be the country's oldest carving of a human figure).

The most spectacular Roman exhibits include the **Shapwick hoard** of 9,238 silver coins from the third century AD, the even greater **Frome hoard** of more than 52,000 coins unearthed in 2010, and the magnificent **Low Ham mosaic**, from around 350 AD, depicting the story of Dido and Aeneas. Exhibits from Somerset's Middle Ages include the vivid **Congresbury carving**, probably from the shrine of St Cyngar dating from around 1000, and a graphic collection of church carvings, but it is the seventeenth century that receives most attention, not least in the world's largest collection of cauldrons and skillets – many of them dangling overhead. There are arms and armour from the Civil War, and the Monmouth Rebellion is brought to life in the very room that held captured rebels before their execution. Modern times are sparsely covered, but a separate section houses the **Somerset Military Museum**, which tells the story of Somerset regiments in combat in the Zulu and Boer wars, the Afghan War of 1919 and World War II. Elsewhere in the museum you can view and listen to recordings of various local figures – such as Glastonbury Festival organizers Michael and Emily Eavis – talking about their experience of Somerset life, and there's a room dedicated to the great folklore revivalist Cecil Sharp, who in the early twentieth century spent five years travelling through the county collecting and transcribing traditional folk songs.

St Mary Magdalene

Church Square • Mon–Fri 9.30am–4pm (9.30am–3pm in winter), Sat 9.30am–2pm, Sun for services • Free •
🖥 stmarymagdalenetaunton.org.uk

Grandly set at the end of the Georgian-era Hammet Street, the church of **St Mary Magdalene** has seen many changes over a period of some 1300 years. An Anglo-Saxon church here was replaced in the thirteenth century by a more solid construction, which became the parish church of Taunton in 1308, but was itself much altered and rebuilt in the Perpendicular style between 1480 and 1514. In this form, with its four aisles giving it a width almost as great as its length, the church became the model for others throughout this part of Somerset. When this structure in turn was deemed unsafe, the church was completely rebuilt in 1858–62, though faithfully in keeping with its previous appearance. Thus, the richly sculpted **tower**, an iconic image in Taunton and at 163ft the highest church tower in Somerset, is a replica of the original tower of around 1510, while the roof, walls and pillars of the church are the main features surviving from the sixteenth century.

The interior

The earliest survivors of its previous history lie inside on the north aisle: two pink columns from the church's thirteenth-century construction. Below lie the foundations of the even earlier wooden church probably built by King Ine of the West Saxons in the eighth century. The hammer-beam roof and roof-bosses carved with medieval masks have survived more or less intact from the sixteenth century. Looking around, you'll see angels everywhere – 133 in all, on the roof, the capitals and the walls.

St James

Coal Orchard • Mon–Sat 9am–4.30pm, Sun for services, usually 9.30am–11.30am & 7–8pm • Free • ⓦ stjamestaunton.co.uk

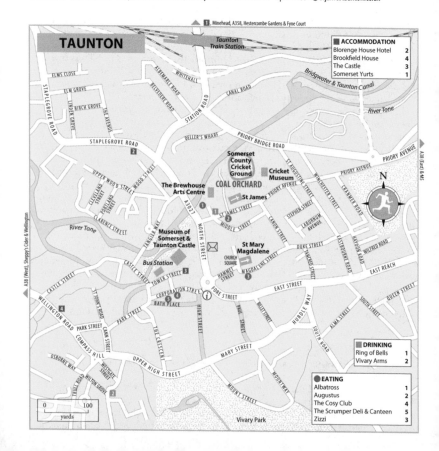

THE MONMOUTH REBELLION

Somerset and Dorset were the scene for one of England's last significant threats to the established monarchy. Having landed in Lyme Regis from his base in Holland in June 1685, the Protestant **Duke of Monmouth**, an illegitimate son of Charles II, was proclaimed king in Taunton's Market Square followed by an equally enthusiastic reception in Bridgwater. Resentment against the Catholic James II at this time was high, and Monmouth knew that if he could take Bristol, a potential source of mass support, the campaign could swing in his favour. However, in a botched night attack on the royal forces at Westonzoyland, near Bridgwater, his untrained rebel army was routed at the **Battle of Sedgemoor** – the last pitched battle to be fought on English soil (see page 174). Monmouth himself was later captured while trying to escape the country in the guise of a shepherd, and beheaded on London's Tower Hill. Meanwhile, a period of savage repression was unleashed in the West Country under the infamous Judge Jeffreys, whose **Bloody Assizes** resulted in gibbets and gutted corpses displayed around Somerset.

6

A less ambitious structure than St Mary Magdalene, the church of **St James** was rebuilt around 1840 but still retains its medieval lines and barrel roof, and has remnants of the early fourteenth-century building that stood on the site. At the front of the church, the elaborate, fifteenth-century font is probably the single most interesting feature, with carved panels on its eight sides showing figures of Christ and his disciples. The wooden pulpit, carved with mermaids and suns, dates from 1633, and the chancel holds a copy of a Rubens painting on its north side. Soaring above the adjacent cricket ground, the **tower** (120ft) is smaller and slightly older than that of St Mary Magdalene, and was replaced – again, in the original style – in the 1870s. If you stand by it while the bells are rung for services, you can feel the structure actually rocking.

Somerset County Cricket Ground

7 Priory Ave • **Match tickets** One-day matches £18–22 in advance, £27 on the day; international matches £25–125 per day; County Championship matches £13 in advance, £18 on the day • Advance ticket purchase ☎ 01823 425301, or visit ⓦ somersetcountycc.co.uk **Museum** Erratic opening, call to check • Closed to non-spectators on match days • £1 • ☎ 01823 275893, ⓦ somersetcricketmuseum.co.uk

Somerset is one of England's great cricketing counties, and it's particularly hard to escape some reference to the game in Taunton, home to Somerset County Cricket Club, which has numbered Ian Botham and Viv Richards among its members. Located just north of the centre of town, the **County Ground** is open to view on non-match days, and includes a **museum** dedicated to the sport, housed in what was once part of Taunton Priory, dissolved in the sixteenth-century. Here you can feast on ancient equipment, black-and-white photos of players, examples of the evolution of the cricket bat and a plethora of caps, badges and blazers, among other memorabilia. There are a few non-cricket oddities, but first and foremost the museum is a celebration of the game, and an opportunity for non-fans to dip into the arcane world of cricket.

Hestercombe Gardens

Cheddon Fitzpaine • Daily: April–Oct 10am–6pm; Nov–March 10am–5pm; last admission 1hr before closing • £12.50 • ☎ 01823 413923, ⓦ hestercombe.com • By car or bike, head north of the town centre along Cheddon Rd to Rowford and Cheddon Fitzpaine, following the brown signs; by public transport, take bus #21 from Taunton to Monkton Heathfield and walk a couple of miles northwest or bus #23 (Mon–Fri) from Taunton to Kingston St Mary and walk a couple of miles southeast towards Cheddon Fitzpaine

Three miles north of Taunton, **Hestercombe Gardens** grew from a Georgian landscape garden laid out along a combe in the eighteenth century by Hestercombe's then owner, the extravagantly named soldier and artist Coplestone Warre Bampfylde. Later additions were made on the south side of the house: a Victorian Terrace from the

6

ALONG THE BRIDGWATER AND TAUNTON CANAL

Opened in 1827, the **Bridgwater and Taunton Canal** was the only section to be completed of a major complex of waterways planned to reach as far as Bristol, a scheme abandoned with the advent of the railways. Today, the well-maintained 14.5-mile stretch makes a splendid walking or biking route (part of National Cycle Route 3), taking in some pubs along the way. You can access the canal from the River Tone that runs through Taunton's centre, for example near the Brewhouse arts complex at Coal Orchard – the canal runs off the river at Firepool Lock, a short way northeast past the cricket ground. Refreshments are available between Easter and October from *Maunsel Lock Tea Rooms* at **Maunsel Lock**, halfway along (☎ 01278 238220, 🖥 maunsellock.co.uk; closed Mon Oct–June), and nearby Somerset Boat Centre offers boat trips and paddle board, kayak and boat hire (☎ 07508 959996, 🖥 somersetboatcentre.co.uk).

1870s, and the Edwardian Formal Garden designed by Edwin Lutyens and Gertrude Jekyll in 1904–08; both these areas provide sublime views over to the Blackdown Hills.

Hestercombe House, which following the estate's sale to the council was occupied by the local fire brigade until 2006, now holds an excellent gallery showing exhibitions of mainly modern art. Apart from a majestic central staircase, the building itself is not particularly attractive, though the upstairs rooms afford a grand vista over the terrace and garden. There's an elegant tea room and restaurant and a good secondhand bookshop here too.

Behind the house, the **landscaped park** was discovered in its overgrown state in 1992 and subsequently restored. It repays a lingering stroll, taking in ponds, a cascade, a Chinese bridge, a temple arbour, a "Witch House" and a Gothic alcove; look out for fleeting glimpses of roe deer. Near the entrance you'll find a **bat roost**, viewable through a video link, where rare lesser horseshoe bats congregate in summer. Consult the website for outdoor performances, gardener talks, butterfly walks and other **events** in summer.

Fyne Court

Broomfield • Daily dawn–dusk • Free • NT • ☎ 01823 451587, 🖥 nationaltrust.org.uk • To reach Broomfield by public transport from Taunton, take bus #23 to Kingston St Mary (Mon–Fri), from where it's a 3-mile walk north on Lodes Lane

On the southern edge of the Quantock Hills, five miles north of Taunton, stands **Fyne Court**, famous as the home of Andrew Crosse (1784–1855), a child prodigy who had mastered ancient Greek at the age of eight and became a pioneer in the new science of electricity. Crosse first became obsessed with the potential of electricity while at school in Bristol, and on inheriting the family estates and fortune in 1805 he set up a laboratory in Fyne Court – much to the consternation of the local yokels, for whom he became the "Wizard of Broomfield" and the "Thunder and Lightning Man" on account of his noisy experiments. Crosse's renown grew, and it has been suggested that the seeds of the Frankenstein story were first planted when Percy Bysshe and Mary Shelley attended one of his lectures in London. He continued his electrical studies until the end; his last reported words were: "The utmost extent of human knowledge is but comparative ignorance."

The grounds

Of Fyne Court itself there are scant remains – the building was mostly destroyed by a fire in 1894. A former barn next to the courtyard café displays some of Crosse's notes and items from his laboratory, as well as information about the Quantocks, with examples of the rocks that make up the range. The main attraction, however, is Fyne Court's former leisure gardens, now largely overgrown and consisting of woodland and meadows. You can follow various trails around the park (pick up pamphlets at the café); look out too for details of open-air drama productions held here every summer.

A left turn out of Fyne Court brings you to the local churchyard, which has an obelisk in memory of Crosse. The church itself, **St Mary's and All Saints**, dates in parts from 1320, and has a table supposed to have come from Crosse's laboratory, along with some good specimens of the carved bench-ends that are so characteristic of Quantock churches.

Sheppy's Cider

Three Bridges, Bradford-on-Tone • Mon–Sat 8.30am–6pm, Sun 10am–4pm Mon–Sat 9.30am–4.30pm, Sun 10.30am–3pm • Museum £3 • **Tours** March–Nov Sat 2pm, Sun 11am, July & Aug also Sat 11am • £15 • ☎ 01823 461233, ⓦ sheppyscider.com

Here in the heart of cider country, you can explore the process of cider-making at **Sheppy's Cider**, 3.5 miles southwest of Taunton (and the same distance northeast of Wellington) on the A38. The complex combines a shop, restaurant, museum and orchards. You can taste the apple juices and ciders while pondering a purchase in the farm shop, stroll around the orchards to view the resident herd of pedigree longhorn cattle as well as other farm animals, and learn the nuts and bolts of cider-making in the **museum**, which shows the tools and equipment not only for producing the stuff – wooden presses and mills – but those used in farming, blacksmithing, thatchering and coopering. There's also a replica of a typical farm kitchen of former days and a film of the cider-maker's year. It's worth booking a place on one of the ninety-minute **tours** for deeper insights into the world of cider, and the Apple Bay **restaurant and bar** provides food and drink (there's also a deli for picnic ingredients).

ARRIVAL AND DEPARTURE
TAUNTON AND AROUND

By train Taunton's station lies a few minutes' walk north of town on Kingston Rd. There are good services between Taunton and Bridgwater (Mon–Sat hourly, Sun 11 daily; 15min), Bristol (Mon–Sat 2–3 hourly, Sun 1–2 hourly; 40min–1hr 10min) and Weston-super-Mare (Mon–Sat 1–2 hourly, Sun 12 daily; 20–35min) to the north, and Exeter St David's (Mon–Sat 2–3 hourly, Sun 1–2 hourly; 25min) to the southwest. There's also the West Somerset Railway (see page 222), which leaves from Bishops Lydeard, 5 miles northwest of Taunton.

By bus Taunton's bus station is off Castle Green. National Express (ⓦnationalexpress.com) and Berry's Coaches (ⓦberryscoaches.co.uk) operate a fast service to and from London (8–9 daily; 3hr 30min–4hr 30min). National Express and Megabus (ⓦuk.megabus.com) also operate buses to Exeter (8 daily; 40–55min). Within the region, there are services to and from: Bishops Lydeard (Mon–Sat 2–3 hourly, Sun 7 daily; 25min); Bridgwater (Mon–Sat 2–4 hourly, Sun 1–2 hourly; 40min); Burnham-on-Sea (Mon–Sat every 30min, Sun hourly; 1hr 20min); Dulverton (Mon–Sat 5–7 daily; 1hr 25min); Glastonbury (Mon–Sat 6 daily; 1hr 20min); Minehead (Mon–Sat every 30min, Sun 7 daily; 1hr 20min); Watchet (Mon–Sat every 30min, Sun 7 daily; 50min); Wells (Mon–Sat 5 daily; 1hr 40min); and Yeovil (Mon–Sat 10 daily, Sun 2 daily; 1hr 20min).

INFORMATION AND GETTING AROUND

Tourist information Market House, Fore St (Mon–Sat 9.30am–4.30pm; ☎ 01823 340470, ⓦvisitsomerset.co.uk/taunton). Provides information and publications on the whole area, including the Quantocks. Pick up guides for the Taunton Heritage Trail and circular walks in and around town from here.

By bus Buses of Somerset runs almost all local bus services, including the cheap and frequent service (not Sun) between Taunton's two Park-and-Ride car parks (at Silk Mills, west of town, and Taunton Gateway, near the M5 on the east side of town) and the centre.

By bike On the outskirts of town, Somerset Bike Hire rents out bikes from £17/day. You'll find them at Unit 14b, Creech Mill Industrial Estate, Mill Lane, Creech St Michael, about three miles east of the centre (Mon–Fri 9.30am–5/5.30pm; ☎ 01823 444246, ⓦ somersetbikehire.co.uk); call a day or two in advance to be sure of availability.

Taxi TLC ☎ 01823 444444; A1 Ace ☎ 01823 332211; Taunton Taxi Services ☎ 01823 248248.

ACCOMMODATION
MAP PAGE 208

Blorenge House Hotel 57–59 Staplegrove Rd ☎ 01823 283005, ⓦblorengehouse.co.uk. A 10–15min walk from Taunton's station and centre, this Victorian hotel is convenient and clean, with functional rooms and friendly staff. Though it's on a main road, you won't be bothered by traffic noise, and there's a garden with a heated outdoor

6

pool at the back (summer only). Single and family rooms and apartments are also available. **£115**

Brookfield House 16 Wellington Rd ☎01823 272786, ⓦbrookfieldguesthouse.uk.com. A smart, professionally run B&B dating from the eighteenth century, this provides a handy base close to the centre of town. Rooms are plain but clean and modern, and there's limited off-road parking. Noise from the busy road outside doesn't impinge too much, but light sleepers should choose rooms at the back. No under-12s. **£120**

The Castle Castle Green ☎01823 272671, ⓦthe-castle-hotel.com. The town's most atmospheric hotel, a wisteria-clad 300-year-old mansion next to Taunton Castle, exudes an old-fashioned baronial flavour. The rooms are mostly spacious and plush, but all different, so worth viewing

before booking. It's ultra convenient for the museum, though extras are pricey. **£132**

★ **Somerset Yurts** Hill Farm, West Monkton ☎07811 350176, ⓦsomersetyurts.co.uk. You can savour the authentic glamping experience on this working dairy farm 5 miles north of Taunton, and within walking distance of Hestercombe. Each of the five Mongolian yurts has a double bed and can additionally accommodate two to three children – bring your own sheets and blankets or rent them here (£5/100 per single/double bed). There's a wood burner inside and a barbecue and gas stove outside the yurt, while a nearby barn holds bathrooms and a communal kitchen and dining area. Minimum two-night stay at weekends (four nights during the week). "Safari yurts", with two bedrooms and a kitchen, and a geodesic dome are also available. Closed early Nov to late March. **£150**

EATING, DRINKING AND ENTERTAINMENT

MAP PAGE 208

Local produce is sold at the **farmers' market** in the High Street (Thurs 9am–3pm; ⓦtauntonvalefarmersmarket. wordpress.com).

Albatross 2 Riverside Place, off North St ☎01823 278000, ⓦalbatrosstaunton.co.uk. The best seafood in Taunton is served at this light and airy riverside restaurant on two floors, with relaxing, modern decor and big windows overlooking the River Tone. Try Brixham fish soup, Porlock Bay oysters or calamari fritters for starters (£7.50–9), *fritto misto* or baked megrim sole for mains (around £18.50). Fish and chips are £13, and there's a "little nibblers' menu" too. It's open in the mornings for breakfasts and coffees. Tues–Sat 10am–2.30pm (lunch from noon) & 6–9.30pm.

Augustus 3 The Courtyard, St James St ☎01823 324354, ⓦaugustustaunton.co.uk. Tucked away in a quiet corner of the town centre, this bistro has won plaudits for its elegant blends of Mediterranean and Asian cuisine. The menu might include seared Brixham scallops with cauliflower purée or smoked eel with scrambled egg for starters (£6–10), followed by breast of guinea fowl with basil mousse or turbot fillet with potato galette or Provençale vegetable tart (most mains £18–26). There are a few tables outside for fine weather. Tues–Sat 10am–3pm (kitchen noon–3pm) & 6–9.30pm.

The Brewhouse Coal Orchard ☎01823 283244, ⓦthebrewhouse.net. This arts centre by the river is Taunton's main venue for theatre presentations, concerts, comedy, cabaret and dance events.

The Cosy Club Hunts Court, Corporation St ☎01823 253476, ⓦcosyclub.co.uk. This converted ex-art college was the first location for what was to become a West Country chain of flamboyantly eccentric bar-restaurants. This one occupies several rooms on two floors, with comfy chairs and sofas, distressed brick walls and quirky bits and pieces scattered about. Come for a coffee or tea during the day, or tuck into a brunch, salad or sandwich; tapas

are £14 for three, and burgers (£10–15) and full meals are available all day. It makes a lively venue for evening cocktails too. Mon–Wed & Sun 9am–11pm, Thurs–Sat 9am–12.30am; kitchen daily 9am–10pm.

Ring of Bells 16–17 St James St ☎01823 259480, ⓦtheringofbellstaunton.com. Next to St James' church, this country-style free house has more character than most of Taunton's pubs, serving a range of West Country ales which you can enjoy in the beer garden. Top-quality pub nosh is available, from sausages and mash to Exmoor venison steak (£12–20). Daily 11am–11pm; kitchen Mon noon–2.30pm, Tues–Sun noon–2.30pm & 6–9pm (Sun till 8.30pm).

The Scrumper Deli & Canteen 19b Bath Place ☎01823 337234, ⓦthescrumper.com. In a tiny lane off the main shopping street, this modern place with small wooden tables inside and out makes a great stop for breakfasts, coffees or teas with cakes, a fresh and crusty sandwich or a full lunch, which might be an antipasto longboard, a quiche, or one of the daily specials, such as baked stuffed aubergine (most dishes £6–8). Beers, ciders and wines are also available, and there are deli items to take away, including superb sausage rolls. Mon–Sat 8.30am–4pm, Sun 9.30am–3pm.

Vivary Arms Wilton St ☎01823 272563. Said to be Taunton's oldest pub, this traditional place in the Wilton neighbourhood – once a rural settlement – has a suitably villagey feel, complete with nooks, crannies and quirky memorabilia on the walls. There's a good selection of cask beers, unpretentious bar food and Sunday roasts are served (£10), and there's a small beer garden. Daily noon–2/2.30pm & 5–11pm; kitchen Mon–Sat noon–1.30pm & 6–8pm, Sun noon–2.30pm & 6–8.30pm.

Zizzi Magdalene St ☎01823 617199, ⓦzizzi.co.uk. One of a chain of Italian eateries, this has a decent menu of Mediterranean staples, including a range of pizza rusticas

(£12–14), including "skinny" and gluten-free options, plus pastas and risottos (£10–14), but its main selling point is the setting, in a Tudor-era schoolhouse once associated with St Mary Magdalene opposite. There are fabulous views of the church, and the whole place has a lively, pleasantly airy feel. If it's too noisy in the main room, choose a spot in one of the quieter, smaller side rooms; there are also a few tables outside. Booking at weekends recommended. Mon–Sat 11.30am–11pm, Sun noon–10.30pm.

Wellington and the Blackdown Hills

6

Six miles southwest of Taunton, **WELLINGTON** has an appealingly sleepy, old-fashioned air, almost detached from modern life. It merits a glance for its town museum, and makes a useful base for visiting nearby attractions. The Duke of Wellington who triumphed at the Battle of Waterloo took his title from this town in 1809, though he had no obvious link with it; apparently, he chose the place as it sounded like his family name, Wellesley. More recently, the top-drawer Wellington School, founded in 1837, has produced such alumni as the chef Keith Floyd, the actor David Suchet and the author, ex-Tory MP and ex-con Jeffrey Archer.

Heading west from Wellington, in one of the remotest corners of the Vale of Taunton, you can step back in time at the perfectly preserved **Cothay Manor**. To the south, the **Blackdown Hills** form an enticing yet much-overlooked area, well furnished with walking routes.

Wellington Museum

28 Fore St • Easter–Sept Mon–Fri 10am–4pm, Sat 10am–1pm; Oct Mon–Fri 11am–3pm, Sat 10am–1pm; early to end Nov Sat 10am–1pm • Free • ☏ 07971 242904, ⊛ wellingtonmuseum.org.uk

Run by enthusiastic volunteers of the local history society, **Wellington Museum** squeezes plenty into its one room, a mix of diverse mementoes and historical relics, all carefully labelled. As such, it provides a nice insight into how small provincial centres in the West Country were touched and occasionally buffeted by the tides of national history. The earliest items include an axehead from the area's prehistory, and there are finds from skirmishes that took place during the Civil War. The Duke of Wellington's tangential and tenuous links with the town are summarized – the victor of Waterloo is thought to have visited once, if at all – and there is some background to the monument erected outside town in his honour (see box). More recent times are covered by a then-and-now photo gallery, a cabinet of relics of the two world wars including a French helmet, plumed and spiked, and a scale model of the town's Art Deco Wellesley Cinema from 1937 (still operating on Mantle Street). The stewards are more than

---

THE WELLINGTON MONUMENT

You don't even need to venture into the Blackdown Hills to view their most prominent feature: the soaring **Wellington Monument**, 2.5 miles south of Wellington. The 175ft obelisk, which celebrates the Iron Duke's rather arbitrary link with the town, was initiated in 1817, two years after the Battle of Waterloo, but not completed until 1854, two years after the Duke's death. However, funded by public subscriptions and consequently built on the cheap, the monument required drastic repairs and didn't assume its present form until the 1890s. Even then, it continued to suffer from structural problems – indeed, it's currently closed until the money is stumped up for a further major renovation. When it's open to the public, a **viewing platform** near the top affords dizzying views across Somerset and Devon, taking in the Blackdown and Quantock hills, Taunton Deane and Exmoor. The steps to reach the platform are steep and extremely tight. The walk from town is fairly straightforward, with a steep final approach through woods (by car or bike, take South Street, then Hoyles Road and Monument Road). The website ⊛ nationaltrust.org.uk details a mile-long circular walk around the site.

214 TAUNTON, BRIDGWATER AND THE QUANTOCKS WELLINGTON AND THE BLACKDOWN HILLS

> **BLACKDOWN HILLS BEER & MUSIC FESTIVAL**
>
> Held over two days in early or mid-August (ⓦ blackdownbeerfestival.co.uk; £12–15 per day),
> the volunteer-run **Blackdown Hills Beer & Music Festival** takes place in a huge field at
> Cherry Hayes Farm, near Smeatharpe, 10 miles south of Taunton, and brings together a range
> of ales, mostly from Devon and Somerset, and music ranging from folk to funk. Camping
> facilities are on hand at £5 per person per night.

6

willing to provide the back story of each item, and there are pamphlets and books
available for sale.

Cothay Manor

Near Greenham, 5 miles west of Wellington • **Gardens** Early April to Sept Tues–Thurs & Sun 11am–5pm, last entry at 4.30pm • £7.80 **House
tours** Early April to Sept Sun 11.45am & 2.15pm (but check first) • £14.75 including gardens ☎ 01823 672283, ⓦ cothaymanor.co.uk

Well off the beaten track, reached by winding country lanes, **Cothay Manor** for once
merits the term "hidden gem". Little altered since its construction in the late fifteenth
century, the building is privately owned and occupied, hence the restricted opening
hours, but it's worth going out of your way to join a house tour on a Sunday to appreciate
the eclectic range of treasures within, where highlights include the Great Hall with
wingless angels on the corbels of its massive roof trusses, the exquisitely carved chimney
pieces, the tiny oratory and the authentic period furnishings. At other times, only
the terraced gardens are accessible, but these too are remarkable: a highly photogenic
succession of hedged "rooms" running off a yew walk, with ponds and the occasional
sculpture to add interest. Delicious home-made cakes are served in the tea room.

You'll need your own transport and good navigational skills to get here, turning right
off the A38 westward from Wellington, signposted Greenham.

The Blackdown Hills

Straddling the border with Devon, the **Blackdown Hills** are a sparsely populated region
between Wellington and Honiton, largely wooded with oak, ash and beech. The hills,
which rise to 1033ft, are ideal for aimless wandering, though there are numerous
opportunities for more targeted walks along the Herepath Trails – old military roads
dating from the wars between Anglo-Saxons and Vikings. Some of these bring you
to archeological sites, for example **Castle Neroche**, a late Iron Age hillfort on the
northeastern edge of the range south of Taunton. Individual beauty spots include the
Culm Valley, five miles south of Wellington, and the **Otterhead Lakes** off the B3170
south of Taunton, part of a Local Nature Reserve that centres on the River Otter. The
lakes are much prized for their fishing, wildlife and general air of tranquillity; dippers,
kingfishers, grey wagtails, moorhens and herons are among the birds to be spotted.

ARRIVAL AND DEPARTURE

WELLINGTON AND THE BLACKDOWN HILLS

By bus Services #22 and #22A run by Buses of Somerset connect Wellington with Taunton (Mon–Sat every 15min, Sun hourly; 25min). For onward travel to Exeter (1hr 45min–2hr 20min in all), it's easiest to go to Taunton and take a bus or train from there. Public transport links with the Blackdown Hills are sketchy; bus #20 from Wellington goes to Culmstock, for the Culm Valley (Mon–Sat 4 daily; 20min), and #99 goes from Taunton to Castle Neroche (Mon–Sat 6 daily; 25min).

INFORMATION AND ACTIVITIES

Tourist information 30 Fore St (Mon–Fri 9.30am–4pm; ☎ 01823 663379, ⓦ visitsomerset.co.uk).
Walking in the Blackdown Hills OS Explorer 115 and 128 are the best maps for the Blackdown Hills area, while ⓦ blackdownhillsaonb.org.uk has downloadable hiking, biking and horseriding routes and maps. You can also pick up itineraries from the tourist offices at Wellington and Taunton, as well as lists of stables and riding schools.

ACCOMMODATION

★ **Bowhayes Farm** Park Lane, Culmstock ☎ 01823 680321, ⓦ bowhayesfarmculmstock.co.uk. Nestled in a tranquil rural setting close to the Blackdown Hills, this traditional thatched longhouse offers beamed, spacious and tastefully furnished bedrooms with modern bathrooms and views over the garden and the Culm Valley. Guests also have access to a private sitting rooms and kitchen facilities, and there's a family suite. The outstanding breakfasts use locally-sourced produce including home-made jams, and various bodily treatments such as shiatsu and acupuncture are available by appointment. The steep steps may pose difficulty for anyone with mobility issues. **£120**

The Blue Mantle 2 Mantle St ☎ 01823 662000, ⓦ thebluemantleguesthouse.co.uk. Good-value, no-frills B&B in the centre of town. It's friendly and clean, with eight en-suite rooms, a guests' lounge and excellent breakfasts provided in the large bay-windowed front room, including veggie and vegan options. A popular stop on the Land's End–John O'Groats route, it also has bike storage. **£45**

The Cleve Mantle St ☎ 01823 662033, ⓦ clevehotel. com. Guests at this country house hotel can take full advantage of its main attractions – the gym, the indoor pool, various spa and beauty treatments, and a decent restaurant. Despite some modern touches, the rooms are a bit outdated, and it's worth paying extra for a more spacious premier room. It's out of town, half a mile west off the A38, next to the BP garage (bus #22). **£90**

The Green Dragon 23 South St ☎ 01823 669650, ⓦ greendragon.southcoastinns.co.uk. Handy and reasonably priced accommodation can be found behind this pub in the centre of town. The modern rooms set around a courtyard are quiet and comfortable with good showers, and room 14 even has its own patio. Singles and a family room are also available. Breakfast is in the pub, where meals are also served. **£74**

Greenham Hall Greenham ☎ 01823 672603, ⓦ greenhamhall.co.uk. This castle-like Victorian lodging feels miles from anywhere but lies just a few minutes from the motorway and close to Cothay Manor. There are views of the beautiful gardens with a stream at the bottom from the bedrooms and breakfast room, and a couple of pubs are nearby. Discounts are given for bookings of three or more nights. **£100**

EATING AND DRINKING

Café Licious 15 South St ☎ 01823 663095. Handy place for a snack in the centre of town, offering big portions and very reasonable prices. If you want something more than toasties, salads or a fry-up, opt for a fish burger, pan-fried lamb's liver, grilled salmon or cottage pie. It's functional, but warm and friendly, and gets very busy (there's a room upstairs too). Mon–Sat 8am–5pm, Sun 9am–3pm.

★ **The Cheese and Wine Shop** 11 South St ☎ 01823 662899, ⓦ thecheeseandwineshop.co.uk. There's a great choice of goodies sold at this top-quality deli and café – not just delicious pies, pastries, artisan breads and local cheeses, but also Belgian chocolates, fruit smoothies and ice cream in such flavours as stem ginger, Kenyan coffee and mango sorbet. The café at the back serves brilliant breakfasts (including vegan) and the lunch menu lists such delights as haddock and plaice fishcake, mushroom risotto and grilled goat's cheese with toasted walnuts (all £8–10), as well as salads and sandwiches. Shop Mon–Sat 9am–5.30pm; café Tues–Sat 9am–4.30pm.

The Dolphin 37 Waterloo Rd ☎ 01823 665889, ⓦ thedolphinwellington.co.uk. With its eye-catching fishy exterior, this laidback pub stands out in every way. A great range of real ales and ciders is available (Otter Ales usually present), and there are some excellent veggie and vegan items on the menu as well as superb pizzas (cooked in the garden in summer, and also available to take away), with most dishes £5–10. Further inducements are books and games, live acoustic music on Thursdays, an open fire in winter and a garden for fine weather. It's a 10min walk from the centre up North St. Mon–Fri 4–11pm, Sat noon–11pm, Sun noon–10pm; kitchen Mon–Sat until 9pm, Sun noon–6pm.

Rule 7 Bar and Bistro 21 High St ☎ 07879 813062, ⓦ rule7barandbistro.co.uk. Relaxed basement bar for a drink or snack, offering a good range of bottled beers, ciders and gins (but nothing on draught). As well as tapas, platters and pizzas, the menu also has nachos, burgers, Indonesian rendang and smoked fish chowder (£10–11). You can spend an intimate hour or two in one of the nooks here, and open mic sessions are held on some Sundays (usually the first of the month). Wed–Sat 5pm–late.

Bridgwater

Sedate **BRIDGWATER** has seen little excitement since the seventeenth century, when it was first besieged then almost completely destroyed by Parliamentary forces during the Civil War, lying derelict for almost a century afterwards. What little of the town survived was then embroiled in the events surrounding the Monmouth Rebellion of 1685 – the Duke of Monmouth and his army spent their last night here before their

6

BLAKE IN BRIDGWATER

Bridgwater's most feted native son is **Robert Blake** (1598–1657), a swashbuckling soldier and naval hero who won glory during the English Civil War and then against the Dutch and Spanish fleets. Fighting on the Parliamentary side, he distinguished himself as a commander in the field during the defence of Bristol in 1643 and in subsequent engagements in Lyme Regis and Taunton. In 1649, Blake was appointed General-at-Sea, in which role he created a permanent, well-disciplined navy, adept in such techniques as blockades and amphibious landings. Blake went on to win outstanding victories in the English Channel and the Mediterranean, and at his death he was afforded the rare privilege of a state funeral and burial in Westminster Abbey. A **statue** of Blake surveys the modern shopping centre on Cornhill – one of the country's very few monuments to a Republican.

catastrophic defeat at the Battle of Sedgemoor (see page 174). The nineteenth century saw a partial revival of fortunes when the town became a centre for roofing tiles and brick production, but the Industrial Revolution largely bypassed Bridgwater, and recent times have seen the town further marginalized in the life of the county and country. Nowadays, the place is most associated with the **Bridgwater Carnival**, though this also takes in other Somerset towns (see page 217).

Bridgwater's major attractions are the excellent **Blake Museum** on Blake Street and the magnificent church of **St Mary's** in the centre. Less essential but equally absorbing, Bridgwater's **Brick and Tile Museum** throws light on this once-thriving local industry. Elsewhere, much of the town has a run-down look, and is overrun with traffic, though traces of its eighteenth-century prosperity are visible in some handsome architecture around East Quay and West Quay (alongside the River Parrett), in King Square and in Castle Street, where every entrance of the otherwise uniform row of early Georgian houses is different. On Dampiet Street, the red-brick Unitarian **Christ Church** is where Coleridge preached in 1797 and 1798, while nearby on Cornhill (at the top of Fore Street), the elegantly colonnaded **Rotunda** dates from 1844, originally part of the old market hall and now a restaurant (see page 218).

Bridgwater lies at one end of the **Bridgwater and Taunton Canal** (see page 210), and on the River Parrett Trail, a fifty-mile route from the river's source in the Dorset hills to its mouth at Stert Point on the Bristol Channel.

Blake Museum

Blake St • Early April to early Nov Tues–Sat 10am–4pm, last entry at 3pm • Free • ☎ 01278 456127, ⊛ bridgwatermuseum.org.uk

Beside the River Parrett, the probable birthplace of local hero Robert Blake (see box) is a sixteenth-century building now housing the **Blake Museum**. Most of the ground-floor exhibits are related to him, or place him in context with such items as model ships and a contemporary sea chest. Other rooms show local fossils, including a large ichthyosaurus, and illustrate the town's Roman and medieval history. Upstairs, the Battle Room focuses on the Monmouth Rebellion and the Battle of Sedgemoor, while the Maritime Room displays shipbuilding and rope-making artefacts. Lastly, the Bygones Room brings together everything from agricultural tools to an old boneshaker bicycle, and has a section devoted to the local brick and tile industry.

St Mary's

St Mary St • Tues & Wed noon–2pm, Thurs & Fri 10am–4pm, Sat 10am–2pm, Sun 8am–noon • Free • ⊛ stmarysbw.org.uk

Bridgwater's most striking monument is the thirteenth- to fourteenth-century church of **St Mary's**, immediately identifiable by its polygonal, slightly angled, red-sandstone steeple, soaring 175ft above the town centre like a medieval rocket. Much of the interior was rebuilt in the 1840s and 1870s, but there is plenty to admire here, including a black oak pulpit from 1490 and a seventeenth-century Italian altarpiece – the impressive hammer-beam roof, however, was added in the 1850s. Sadly, the church is often locked up outside service times, though you can gain access by calling one of the numbers pinned up outside, and it's occasionally used for concerts and other events.

Somerset Brick and Tile Museum

East Quay • Tues & Thurs 10am–4pm • Free • ☎ 01278 426088

Bridgwater's brick- and tile-making industry petered out in the 1960s, but this former mainstay of the local economy is celebrated at the **Somerset Brick and Tile Museum**, housed in the county's only surviving industrial kiln on the banks of the Parrett. Formerly one of six kilns at this site, it was last fired in 1965. The various stages of the manufacturing process are explained, from excavation through to weathering, pugging, extrusion, moulding, drying and finally firing. You can view numerous examples of the bricks and tiles, enter the "pinnacle" kiln and, under instruction, try your hand at tile-making. Call before visiting, as the museum can sometimes close without notice.

ARRIVAL AND DEPARTURE

BRIDGWATER

By bus From the bus station on Watson's Lane, National Express (☎ nationalexpress.com) and Berry's Coaches (☎ berryscoaches.co.uk) operate services to and from London (7–8 daily; 3–4hr). There are also services to: Burnham-on-Sea (Mon–Sat every 30min, Sun hourly; 30min); Glastonbury (Mon–Sat 6 daily, Sun 2 daily; 1hr–1hr 15min); Taunton (Mon–Sat every 30min, Sun 1–2 hourly; 45min); and Wells (Mon–Sat 6 daily; 1hr 30min). For the northern Quantocks and Minehead, services are extremely infrequent, just buses #14 and #15 stopping at: Holford (Mon–Fri 1 daily on college days; 35min); Kilve (Mon–Fri 1 daily on college days; 40min); Nether Stowey (Mon–Fri 3 daily; 30min); and Watchet (Mon–Fri 1 daily on college days; 1hr). For Watchet (2hr) and Minehead (2hr 25min), the most frequent services require a change at Taunton.

By taxi ☎ 01278 332211.

ACCOMMODATION

Admiral Blake 58–60 Monmouth Rd ☎ 01278 456424, ☎ admiralblakegh.com. This is a useful if unremarkable B&B, well placed for the centre and with reasonable rates, though subject to some traffic noise. Single, double and family rooms are basic but clean, with private or shared bathrooms, and there's a communal kitchen and a small courtyard garden. Breakfast is self-service. **£70**

Gurney Manor Mill Gurney St, Cannington ☎ 01278 653582, ☎ gurneymill.co.uk. Just outside the village of Cannington, 3 miles northwest of Bridgwater, a sixteenth-century watermill has been converted into this upmarket B&B with loads of character. The four spotless rooms have their own entrances and include a family room (£100). Breakfast is taken in a huge beamed hall with paintings, classical sculpture and antique furniture, and the garden has a stream and duck pond. A self-catering cottage is also

---

THE BRIDGWATER CARNIVAL

In a country that has never made a big deal about **carnival**, Bridgwater puts on a pretty spectacular show. The **Bridgwater Carnival** (☎ bridgwatercarnival.org.uk) claims to be the largest illuminated procession in Europe, attracting up to 150,000 people and traffic queues for miles around. Dating from 1605, when local people celebrated the failure of **Guy Fawkes** to blow up the Houses of Parliament in the Gunpowder Plot (one of the Catholic conspirators hailed from nearby Nether Stowey), the Carnival has expanded in recent years and now takes in various other local towns and villages, including Glastonbury and Wells. In Bridgwater, the festivities usually take place on the first Saturday of November, the procession starting at 6 or 7pm and taking more than two hours to trundle past on its 2.5-mile route. The grandly festooned floats belonging to Somerset's seventy-odd carnival clubs are accompanied by samba bands, majorettes and masqueraders. Festivities kick off the evening before, with a grand fireworks display at 7pm; there are more fireworks for the finale, when, following an age-old tradition, the High Street is lined with "squibbers" who set off their "squibs" (fireworks) simultaneously – a spectacular sight worth sticking around for. Visitors to the area in early November should book way ahead for accommodation and be prepared for massive crowds in Bridgwater itself.

6

available. **£75**

The Old Vicarage 45–51 St Mary St ☎01278 458891, ⓦtheoldvicaragebridgwater.com. This central choice right opposite St Mary's church is one of Bridgwater's oldest buildings (you can see a section of its wattle-and-daub fabric on the left of the archway). With creaky corridors and sloping floors, it has plenty of character, though would also benefit from an update. Rooms range from small to spacious, the most sumptuous being a grand, beamed chamber complete with four-poster bed, at around £110. There's a restaurant

and a garden for an evening drink. Opt for a room away from the street to avoid the noise of weekend carousers. **£75**

Tudor Hotel 21 St Mary St ☎01278 422093, ⓦtudorhotel.co.uk. Having started life as a bakery in the seventeenth century, this hotel has shed most of its historic character and is primarily used by business folk. It's not exactly over-modernized, however, its fifteen rooms furnished in a low-key, traditional style. There's a little more atmosphere in the bar and restaurant (closed Sun eve) where the menu includes Cypriot dishes. **£75**

EATING, DRINKING AND ENTERTAINMENT

Bridgwater Arts Centre 11–13 Castle St ☎01278 422700, ⓦbridgwaterartscentre.co.uk. Worth seeking out for exhibitions, concerts, films, plays and comedy, as well as the agreeable bar which on Thursdays hosts music sessions as well as a quiz. Wed, Thurs & events nights 10am–3pm & 7–11pm, Fri 10am–3pm, Sat 10am–1pm.

★**Green Olive** 5 Fisherman's Wharf, West Quay ☎01278 238565, ⓦgreenolivebridgwater.co.uk. This Turkish restaurant by the river is a welcome exotic injection to Bridgwater's parochial restaurant scene. The extensive menu includes spicy kebabs and *kuzu guvec* (lamb casserole), and there are separate vegan and gluten-free menus with such dishes as *imam bayildi* (sautéed vegetables on a bed of aubergine). A hot meze platter costs £13 and mains are £10–18, or you can opt for one of the set-price deals: two courses for £13/16, three for £16/20 for lunch/evening. Portions are large and the atmosphere is warm and friendly. Booking recommended at weekends, takeaways always available. Mon–Thurs & Sun noon–2pm & 5.30–9pm, Fri & Sat noon–2pm & 5.30–10pm.

The Nutmeg Angel Crescent ☎01278 457823, ⓦnutmeghouse.co.uk. Behind the shopping centre off Fore St, this spacious café-restaurant with a few outdoor tables offers coffees and cakes, as well as all-day breakfasts, baguettes, toasties, jacket potatoes, cottage pie and

gammon steak. Carveries are served at Sunday lunchtimes, and it opens on Friday and Saturday evenings for steak nights. Most hot dishes are £6–7.50. Mon–Sat 8am–4pm, Fri & Sat also 6–10pm, Sun 10am–4pm.

Prezzo 30 Cornhill, off Fore St ☎01278 433600, ⓦprezzorestaurants.co.uk. Though this restaurant is part of a so-so chain of Italian eateries, the location alone makes eating here something of an event, in the Victorian Rotunda building of the old Corn Exchange, with grand views from the tall windows. Stonebaked pizzas in two sizes, pastas and grills dominate the menu, all around £10–13, and you can come here for just coffees and teas during the day. Mon–Thurs & Sun 11.30am–10pm, Fri & Sat 11.30am–11pm.

The River Parrett 11 Salmon Parade ☎01278 451807, ⓦtheriverparrett.co.uk. Gourmet dining French-style is available at this semi-formal restaurant with exposed brick walls. Artfully presented mains, which include such dishes as caramelized venison loin (£21) and fish of the day with lobster and caviar bisque (£17), and such desserts as vegan chocolate mousse with beetroot and blackberry sorbet, use local ingredients wherever possible. There's a five-course tasting menu (£49) and good-value set menus: two/three courses for £15/£18. Tues–Thurs noon–3pm & 6–9.30pm, Fri & Sat noon–3pm & 6–10pm; closed 3 weeks Aug–Sept.

The Quantock Hills

West of Bridgwater, crossed by clear streams and grazed by red deer, the **Quantock Hills** measure just twelve miles in length and are mostly 800–900ft high. Most of the secluded settlements lie on the edges of the range, linked by a tangle of narrow lanes and connected to Bridgwater and Taunton by regular **bus** services, and with a restored **steam railway** tracking the western flank of the range. Many of the Quantock villages – notably **Bishops Lydeard**, **Combe Florey** and **Crowcombe** – boast beautifully preserved churches with superb examples of medieval wood-carving.

The Romantic poets Coleridge and Wordsworth were famous denizens of the area around 1800, and they brought with them such celebrated acquaintances as Hazlitt, with whom they trudged indefatigably over the hills. Today, the Quantocks are notorious for confrontations between hunting parties and anti-hunt activists, but if you want to indulge in less contentious **pony-trekking**, the tourist office in Taunton can supply a list of stables.

THE COLERIDGE WAY

Nether Stowey is the starting point of the **Coleridge Way** (ⓦ coleridgeway.co.uk), a walking route that supposedly follows the poet's footsteps on his hikes between Nether Stowey and Lynmouth on the Exmoor coast. Waymarked with quill signs, the 51-mile trail takes you through some of the most scenic parts of the Quantocks and Exmoor, though it takes in some pretty severe gradients too. The website has a detailed route itinerary with good maps, and also provides information on the 33-mile **Coleridge Bridleway** for horseriders, stretching between Nether Stowey and Exford in Exmoor.

6

Nether Stowey

On the northeastern edge of the hills, eight miles west of Bridgwater on the A39, the pretty village of **NETHER STOWEY** is best known for its association with **Samuel Taylor Coleridge**, who walked here from Bristol at the end of 1796 to join his wife and child at their new home, soon to be joined by William and Dorothy Wordsworth (see page 220). The core of the village hasn't much changed since then, and it makes an attractive and convenient base for visiting the whole Quantocks region.

Coleridge Cottage

35 Lime St • Early March to early Nov daily 11am–5pm; early Dec to late Dec Sat & Sun 11am–4pm • £7 • NT • ☎ 01278 732662, ⓦ nationaltrust.org.uk

Disparagingly called a "miserable cottage" by Sara Coleridge, the rather nondescript-looking house at the top end of the village now known as **Coleridge Cottage** was inhabited by the poet, Sara and their son Hartley for three years from December 1797. In fact only the front rooms of the house existed at that time – the building was later enlarged and even served as an inn during the later nineteenth century. Despite the changes it has been sympathetically restored, and it's easy to get a real feel for the poet, his straitened family life and his literary endeavours. After touring the parlour, kitchen, bedroom and an exhibition room containing letters, early editions and various locks of the poet's hair, you can clamp on some headphones in the reading room to hear readings of his work while browsing books on Romanticism and the Quantocks, and in the garden you can sit in the re-creation of the "lime-tree bower prison" that inspired his lines lamenting a time when an injury forced him to stay behind while Sara, the Wordsworths and Charles Lamb went rambling.

The eastern Quantocks

From Nether Stowey, a minor road winds west off the A39 through **Quantock Common**, a Site of Special Scientific Interest on account of its maritime heath – an endangered habitat mainly composed of heather, gorse and whortleberry (better known as bilberry) – and the wildlife that resides here. Among the species that may be spotted are Dartford warblers, nightjars, adders and red deer. An Iron Age earthwork runs across **Dead Woman's Ditch** – despite the name, a lovely open space for a picnic. From here, paths trail off, including one leading eventually to the highest point on the Quantocks, **Wills Neck** (1260ft). Drivers can most easily access this point by parking at **Triscombe Stone**, on the edge of Quantock Forest, from where a footpath leads to the summit about a mile distant.

Stretching between Wills Neck and the village of Aisholt is the bracken- and heather-grown moorland plateau of **Aisholt Common**. The best place to begin exploring this central tract is near **West Bagborough**, where a five-mile path starts at Birches Corner. Lower down the slopes, outside Aisholt, the banks of **Hawkridge Reservoir** make another scenic picnic stop.

Bishops Lydeard and the western Quantocks

The terminus for the West Somerset Railway (see page 222), the relatively large village of **BISHOPS LYDEARD** is worth a wander, not least for the church of **St Mary**. Built in the local

6

COLERIDGE AND WORDSWORTH IN THE QUANTOCKS

Shortly after moving into their new home in Nether Stowey, the Coleridges were visited by William Wordsworth and his sister Dorothy, who soon afterwards moved into the somewhat grander Alfoxden House, near Holford, a couple of miles down the road. The year that **Coleridge and Wordsworth** spent as neighbours was extraordinarily productive – Coleridge composed some of his best poetry at this time, including *The Rime of the Ancient Mariner* and *Kubla Khan*, and the two poets in collaboration produced the *Lyrical Ballads*, the poetic manifesto of early English Romanticism. Many of the greatest figures of the age made the trek down to visit the pair, among them Charles Lamb, Thomas De Quincey, Robert Southey, Humphry Davy and William Hazlitt, and it was the coming and going of these intellectuals that stirred the suspicions of local authorities in a period when England was at war with France. Wordsworth's previous support for the French Revolution, and his penchant for taking nocturnal walks on the hills – conceivably to communicate with French agents, it was thought – only encouraged these suspicions. Spies were sent to track them and Wordsworth was finally given notice to leave the area in June 1798, shortly before *Lyrical Ballads* rolled off the press.

Scenes from Julien Temple's film *Pandaemonium*, narrating a version of Coleridge and Wordsworth's poetic relationship, were shot hereabouts.

---

red sandstone, the church has a splendid, pinnacled tower in the Perpendicular style from around 1450, with five carved dragons on the corners, one with a stone in its mouth – these decorative gargoyles are known as "hunky punks" in Somerset. Inside is a renowned set of carved bench-ends, the work of itinerant Flemish craftsmen in the sixteenth century; look out for Green Men, a ship, a windmill and a pelican feeding its young with blood from its own breast – a symbol of the redemptive power of Christ's blood. Victorian renovation accounts for the appearance of much of the rest of the church, including all the stained glass.

Combe Florey

The pretty village of **COMBE FLOREY**, a couple of miles northwest of Bishops Lydeard, is almost exclusively built in the local red sandstone. Its centrepiece, fronted by a neat lawn, is the beautifully preserved church of **St Peter and St Paul**, originating in the thirteenth century, though it was largely rebuilt in around 1480, from when the tower, windows, roof and carved pews date. Some of the effigies and memorials lining the aisles date back to 1300. For over fifteen years (1829–45), the rector here was the unconventional cleric **Sydney Smith**, called "the greatest master of ridicule since Swift" by the essayist Macaulay, and who famously defined heaven as "eating pâté de foie gras to the sound of trumpets". He was also a champion of parliamentary reform and at one time Canon of St Paul's Cathedral. More recently (1956–66), Combe Florey House was home to **Evelyn Waugh**. He and his wife are buried near the northeast side of the church, and his son, the journalist Auberon Waugh, is also buried in the churchyard. Last on the literary roster, the playwright Terence Rattigan lived in the village as a boy.

Crowcombe

CROWCOMBE, a little over three miles along the A358 from Combe Florey, is another typical cob-and-thatch Quantock village, with a well-preserved Church House from 1515. Opposite, the red-stone parish church of the **Holy Ghost** has a superb collection of pagan-looking carved bench-ends from around the same time, intricately woven with vines, leaves and Green Men – well worth a look. The tower and part of the northern wall date from the fourteenth century.

GETTING AROUND | THE QUANTOCK HILLS

The cycle, hike or drive across the Quantocks from Crowcombe to Nether Stowey takes in some of the range's loveliest wooded scenery, including some very steep stretches.

By bus Buses of Somerset services #14 and #15 connect Bridgwater with Nether Stowey (Mon–Fri 1–2 daily; 40min); and #15 (Mon–Fri 1 daily on college days) also carries on to

Holford (7min from Nether Stowey), Kilve (15min), Watchet (30min), Dunster (50min) and Minehead (1hr). From Taunton, Hatch Green Coaches runs service #23 (Mon–Fri 1 daily) to Nether Stowey (1hr), Holford (1hr 15min), Kilve (1hr 20min) and Watchet (1hr 25min), and Buses of Somerset operates service #28 (Mon–Sat every 30min, Sun 7 daily) to: Bishops Lydeard (30min); Combe Florey (35min); Crowcombe (45min); Bicknoller (50min); Watchet (1hr); Dunster (1hr 20min); and Minehead (1hr 25min).

By train Vintage steam and diesel trains of the West Somerset Railway run between Bishops Lydeard and Minehead up to 6 times a day from late March to October; stops include Crowcombe Heathfield on the edge of the Quantocks, a ride of 15–20min. Note that the station of Crowcombe Heathfield lies 1.5 miles south of Crowcombe (see page 220).

INFORMATION AND ACTIVITIES

Tourist information There are no tourist offices in the Quantock Hills, but the office in Taunton (see page 211) can provide information, maps and advice. You can also find out about organized walks and other events, and download walking itineraries at ⓦquantockhills.com and ⓦquantockonline.co.uk.

Riding The Quantocks are superb trekking country, with views at every turn. Novices and experienced riders alike can explore the area on horseback with Quantock Trekking, West Bagborough (☎01823 431713, ⓦquantocktrekking.co.uk); prices range from £45 for a 2hr ride to £90 for an all-day ride including a pub stop for lunch. Two-day breaks with accommodation are also available.

ACCOMMODATION

BISHOPS LYDEARD

The Mount 32 Mount St ☎01823 431897, ⓦthemount-accommodation.co.uk. Just two rooms are available in this B&B in the centre of the village (and near some good pubs), but they're spacious, include a seating area where breakfasts using locally sourced ingredients are served, and one has its own entrance. No credit cards. **£75**

CROWCOMBE

Quantock Orchard Caravan Park Flaxpool, just off the A358 and a few minutes' walk from the West Somerset Railway stop at Crowcombe Heathfield ☎01984 618618, ⓦquantock-orchard.co.uk. This small, neat site is convenient for walks around Wills Neck. It offers a gym and heated outdoor pool (May–Sept), and has static caravans to rent (from £65 per night or £455 per week in high season). There's a small shop but no restaurant facilities. The "backpacker rate" for those arriving without a car is £12. Bike rental available. Pitches **£29.50**

FIDDINGTON

Mill Farm Caravan and Camping Park Signposted outside the village of Fiddington 2 miles east of Nether Stowey, ☎01278 732286, ⓦmillfarm.biz. Popular with families, this site has indoor and outdoor pools, a boating lake, a gym, a BMX track and a playground. The bar, restaurant and evening entertainment (late July to Sept) meet all other needs, and facilities are clean. It can get crowded, though, and booking is essential at peak times. Pitches **£25.50**

HOLFORD

Combe House Hotel ☎01278 741382, ⓦcombehouse.co.uk. Well off the beaten track, this place nestled in a combe a few minutes' walk above the village offers a serene, pampering experience, with a range of health and beauty treatments on offer, plus a classy restaurant. It's full of character, rooms are quietly luxurious, and trails lead directly into the hills. **£89**

WALKING IN THE QUANTOCKS

The Quantocks offer some great walks of differing lengths and terrain. The well-marked track running along the spine of the moorland ridge provides a comparatively effortless way of getting magnificent views towards south Wales and Exmoor from the high ground, with road access from a number of points including from the lane running over the top between Crowcombe and Nether Stowey. Of a clutch of waymarked trails, the most ambitious is the **Quantock Greenway**, which traces a figure of eight that takes in the Quantock villages of Holford, Crowcombe and Triscombe. The route can be tackled in two-day-long circular walks, or sampled on shorter sections. Alternatively, head for such specific areas as **Lydeard Hill**, southeast of Wills Neck and surrounded by woods and heathland, with far-reaching views across the Vale of Taunton; **Staple Plain**, for access to Beacon Hill and the northern end of Quantock Common; **Holford Combe**, thickly wooded with protected sessile oaks; and **Ramscombe**, north of Triscombe Stone, with barbecues and picnic tables in the midst of woodland.

THE WEST SOMERSET RAILWAY

The main road route fringing the western side of the Quantocks – the A358 heading northwest from Taunton – is accompanied for most of the way by the **West Somerset Railway** (☎01643 704996, ⬤west-somerset-railway.co.uk), a restored branch line that is claimed to be the UK's longest heritage railway, running some twenty miles between Bishops Lydeard, five miles out of Taunton (the station lies outside the village), to Minehead on the Somerset coast.

The original Taunton–Watchet line opened in 1862, and was operated by the Bristol and Exeter Railway; it was later absorbed into the Great Western Railway, became part of the nationalized British Rail and closed in 1971, only to reopen five years later as a heritage railway. The stations have often been used as locations in films, including the Beatles' *A Hard Day's Night* (in which Ringo memorably rode a bike along the platform at Crowcombe Heathfield), *The Lion, The Witch and the Wardrobe* and *Land Girls*.

Between late March and October (plus some winter dates), up to six steam and diesel trains depart daily from Bishops Lydeard terminus, stopping at renovated stations on the way. The total journey to Minehead takes around 1hr 20min, for which one-way **tickets** cost £14.60, and one-day Rover tickets, allowing multiple journeys, are £22; two-day Rovers cost £39; bikes travel for £2.50 each way. A discount is applied for Rover tickets bought online by midnight on the preceding day. See page 257, for visitors using the WSR to visit Dunster Castle. The station outside Bishops Lydeard can be reached on bus #28 from Taunton's centre and train station; a rail connection is being trialed at time of writing, worth checking out.

NETHER STOWEY

The Old Cider House 25 Castle St ☎01278 732228, ⬤theoldciderhouse.co.uk. Four fully equipped rooms are available at this central B&B, which also offers tasty evening meals (£15–25) and has a microbrewery on site. The owners are particularly welcoming to walkers, bikers and dog-owners, and run beer-brewing workshops. **£85**

★**The Old House** St Mary's St ☎01278 732392, ⬤theoldhouse-quantocks.co.uk. Once owned by the printer Thomas Poole, this house in the centre of the village accommodated Coleridge in 1807. The two rooms – Sara's Room and the huge Coleridge Suite – are furnished with antiques, and the fresh fruit salad at breakfast makes an invigorating start to the day. There's an acre of well-tended garden for relaxing with a book after tramping the Coleridge Way, and three cosy self-catering cottages are also available. **£90**

OVER STOWEY

★**Parsonage Farm** Over Stowey, about a mile south of Nether Stowey ☎01278 733237, ⬤parsonagefarm. uk. Set next to a lovely old Quantock church, this B&B with its own orchard and walled kitchen garden has three rooms and heaps of personality. Run organically and sustainably by a native of Vermont, it offers a Vermont breakfast among other options (all including garden produce), simple candlelit suppers are available for £12, and on Fridays in summer pizzas are cooked in the on-site pizza oven. There's a 5 percent discount for guests arriving without a car. **£70**

TRISCOMBE

The Blue Ball Inn Triscombe ☎01984 618242, ⬤blue ballquantocks.co.uk. This secluded inn located below Wills Neck has two comfortable rooms – one with a gorgeous bathroom up a spiral staircase in the attic – but breakfast is not available. There's also a self-catering cottage that can accommodate up to six. Meals, good ales and a pleasant pub garden are on hand. **£60**

EATING AND DRINKING

BICKNOLLER

The Bicknoller Inn Three miles northwest of Crowcombe ☎01984 656234, ⬤thebicknollerinn. co.uk. Traditional rustic pub with flagstone floors, low ceilings and open fires, serving Palmer's ales (from Dorset) as well as baguettes, ploughman's lunches, light bites, hot dishes (mains £11–16) and Sunday carveries in a separate restaurant. There's a patio and garden, a skittles alley used in winter, a boules court for summer, and occasional live music evenings. Tues–Fri noon–3pm & 6–11pm, Sat noon–11pm, Sun noon–6pm; kitchen Tues–Sat noon–2.30pm & 6–9pm, Sun noon–3pm.

COMBE FLOREY

The Farmers Arms Signposted off the A39 just south of Combe Florey ☎01823 432267, ⬤farmersarms atcombeflorey.co.uk. This is a lovely old place, tidily thatched, with log fires, a garden and a good menu that's strong on venison, lamb, poultry and charcoal-grilled steaks (main dishes £13–20). Booking is advised at peak times.

Mon–Sat noon–11pm, Sun noon–7pm; kitchen Mon–Sat noon–2.30pm & 6.30–9pm, Sun noon–3pm.

CROWCOMBE

★ **The Carew Arms** ☎ 01984 618631, ⓦ thecarew arms.co.uk. Don't be put off by the stags' heads covering the walls and the riding boots by the fire – this is a classic rustic pub with a skittles alley and a spacious garden. Local ales are served as well as generous portions of standard pub food (mains around £10 at lunchtime, £!6 at dinner). Friday is fish and chips night. Rooms are also available (from £50). Daily noon–11pm; kitchen Mon–Thurs noon–2pm & 7–9pm, Fri noon–2pm & 6–9.30pm, Sat noon–2.30pm & 7–9.30pm, Sun noon–2.30pm; reduced hours in winter.

HOLFORD

The Plough Inn On the A39 5 miles west of Nether Stowey (a stop on the #16 bus route) ☎ 01278 741652. This place was the unlikely setting for Virginia and Leonard Woolf's honeymoon in 1912 (before they travelled to Spain). Today it serves simple pub grub in large helpings (mains around £10), local beers and ciders, and there are various veggie/vegan choices. There's a nice beer garden too. Mon–Sat 11am–11pm, Sun noon–10.30pm; kitchen March–Oct noon–9pm, Nov–Feb noon–3pm & 6–9pm.

NETHER STOWEY

The Ancient Mariner 42 Lime St ☎ 01278 733544, ⓦ marinernetherstowey.co.uk. Named after Coleridge's seafaring yarn, and right opposite the poet's house, this rustic-looking tavern has a range of bar food, from halloumi and mushroom burgers and fisherman's pie to grills, bangers and mash and beef curry. Take advantage of the £15 deal for two courses at lunchtime (not Sun). You'll find a roaring log fire in winter, a gravelly beer-garden and good local ales. Nine rooms are also available in a separate building (from £70), including a family suite. Daily 11am–11.30pm, Fri & Sat 11.30am–midnight; kitchen Mon–Sat noon–2.30pm & 6–9pm, Sun noon–3pm & 6–8pm.

WEST BAGBOROUGH

★ **The Rising Sun Inn** Two miles northeast of Combe Florey ☎ 01823 432575, ⓦ therisingsunbagborough.co.uk. It's rather remote, but this classic Quantock inn is worth tracking down for its good range of local ales and its refined dining. The menu includes such expertly prepared dishes as seafood broth, katsu chicken curry, pork belly, vegetable platter and herb-crusted cannon of lamb. It's not particularly cheap, though – a three-course meal for two with drinks won't leave much change from £100. Booking recommended. B&B is available for £85. Mon–Fri 11am–3pm & 6–11pm, Sat 11am–11pm, Sun noon–10.30pm; kitchen Mon–Fri noon–2.30pm & 6–8.30pm, Sat & Sun noon–3pm & 6–9pm.

The coast

CLEVEDON PIER

The coast

Somerset's coast is dotted with Victorian resorts from the heyday of seaside holidaymaking, and though these have been brought up to date to greater or lesser degrees, they preserve a prosaic, old-fashioned air. The chic makeover that has given a fashionable edge to such resorts as Brighton and Falmouth has yet to happen here. Nonetheless, there is much to like about these time-warped towns, and a certain frisson in the collision between the holiday culture concentrated on their seafront esplanades and the more reserved, essentially staid life of the calmer neighbourhoods away from the sea. You don't have to go far along the coast to discover, in between the resorts, unspoilt and genuinely picturesque bays and beaches that most people never see, with long views across the Bristol Channel to Wales.

Of the resorts, **Weston-super-Mare** is the brashest, a full-on bucket-and-spade affair with two piers (one derelict) and acres of sand – though this turns into endless mud when the tide's out. On either side are two much lower-key towns: to the north, **Clevedon**, armed with a much more traditional pier, and **Burnham-on-Sea**, set in an especially atmospheric stretch of coast. Clevedon also boasts a fourteenth- and fifteenth-century manor house, **Clevedon Court**, a couple of miles inland, and is within easy reach of the much more flamboyant **Tyntesfield**, a Victorian-Gothic mansion, beautifully restored by the National Trust and surrounded by gorgeous parkland.

The coast turns a sharp corner westward at the River Parrett estuary, from where it extends along a tract of bleak flatlands, rising to low cliffs around **Kilve Beach**, part of the Quantock Hills AONB (Area of Outstanding Natural Beauty). **Watchet** is the first settlement of any size along this section of coast, a low-key fishing port that makes a nice place to hole up for a few days. Inland are a couple of intriguing distractions from the sea: the quirky **Bakelite Museum** at Williton and the medieval remains of **Cleeve Abbey**.

To the west, **Minehead** has all the trappings of the quintessential British seaside resort, whose proximity to both Exmoor and the medieval wool town of Dunster (see page 257) makes it a useful base for its accommodation and transport links. Minehead also marks one end of the **South West Coast Path**, Britain's longest national trail, which follows the southwest peninsula's coast to end up in Dorset.

The **Bristol Channel**, which separates the Somerset coast from Wales, has the second-highest tidal range in the world (up to 49ft; the highest is the Bay of Fundy in eastern Canada), with the result that half the time what was a beach becomes an extensive mud flat with the sea a distant ribbon up to a mile out. Given this, the grey-brown Channel doesn't always inspire great enthusiasm for anyone wanting a dip, though there are a few appealing sandy **beaches** which are good for a picnic or just a runaround, even if you're not tempted to take to the water.

Accommodation is abundant in Weston and Minehead, surprisingly scarce in Clevedon and Burnham, with much of it falling into the tired and dreary seaside-resort category. There are a few gems, though, which we've recommended in the listings.

GETTING AROUND

By train Some trains between Bristol and Exeter run through Weston-super-Mare and Highbridge & Burnham (outside Burnham-on-Sea). Heritage trains of the private West Somerset Railway (see page 222) stop at Williton, Watchet, Washford, Blue Anchor and Minehead between late March and October. The eastern terminus is Bishops Lydeard, outside Taunton on the edge of the Quantock Hills. For all stations and a full schedule, see ⓦ west-somerset-railway.co.uk.

By bus Weston-super-Mare, Clevedon and Burnham-on-

SAND BAY

Highlights

❶ Clevedon Court On the outskirts of Clevedon, this well-preserved manor house merits a lingering visit, as much for its fine collections of glassware and pottery as for the Tudor architecture and seventeenth- and eighteenth-century furnishings. See page 229

❷ Tyntesfield This Victorian mansion is a repository of aesthetic delights – every detail is a masterpiece of art and craftsmanship, and there are terrific walks in the grounds. See page 230

❸ Sand Bay The next bay up from Weston-super-Mare presents a calm contrast to that bustling resort, with a broad sandy beach and bracing panoramic walks. See page 233

❹ Kilve Beach One of the most atmospheric stretches of Somerset's coast centres on this foreshore embellished with beautiful rock formations; it's a good starting point for coastal walks and fossil hunts along the beach. See page 237

❺ Watchet Coleridge's Ancient Mariner supposedly set off from this unspoiled harbour town, a peaceful spot with a couple of great museums and within easy reach of some absorbing sights inland. See page 238

❻ Cleeve Abbey Largely intact, this Cistercian house has afforded valuable insights into medieval monastic life; its showpieces are the vaulted refectory and polychrome tiled floor. See page 239

HIGHLIGHTS ARE MARKED ON THE MAP ON PAGE 228

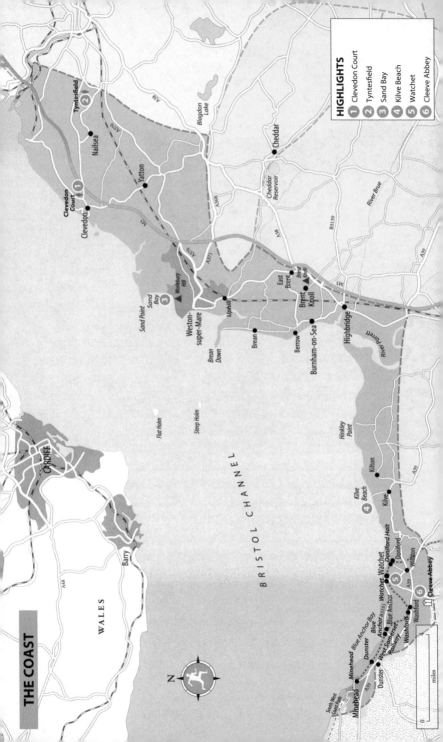

THE COAST

HIGHLIGHTS
1 Clevedon Court
2 Tyntesfield
3 Sand Bay
4 Kilve Beach
5 Watchet
6 Cleeve Abbey

WALES

CARDIFF

Barry

BRISTOL CHANNEL

Flat Holm

Steep Holm

Hinkley Point

Kilton

Kilve Beach

Kilve

Watchet

Doniford Halt

Doniford

Watchet

Washford

Wilton

Cleeve Abbey

Washford

Blue Anchor Bay

Blue Anchor

Blue Anchor

Dunster

West Somerset Railway

Dunster

Minehead

Minehead

South West Coast Path

N

miles

Sand Point

Sand Bay

Worlebury Hill

Weston-super-Mare

Uphill

Brean Down

Brean

Berrow

Burnham-on-Sea

East Brent

Brent Knoll

Brent Knoll

Highbridge

River Parrett

River Brue

Cheddar

Cheddar Reservoir

Blagdon Lake

Nailsea

Tyntesfield

Yatton

Clevedon Court

Clevedon

River Axe

Sea have direct National Express connections to London (wnationalexpress.com); travellers to Minehead should change at Taunton, from where service #28 stops at Williton, Watchet, Washford and Minehead. Local buses link Weston, Clevedon and Burnham to each other and to Bristol. The main operator is First, sometimes operating locally under the names Buses of Somerset and Badgerline (☎0345 646 0707, wfirstgroup.com). Ridlers (☎01398 323398, wridlers.co.uk) and Atwest (☎01643 709701, watwest. org.uk) also operate limited services from Minehead.

Clevedon and around

Fifteen miles west of Bristol, **CLEVEDON** is centred on hills slightly inland from the sea, but its jaunty seafront promenade is the most compelling part of town, with wind-bent trees and views across the Bristol Channel to the isles of Steep Holm and Flat Holm, and beyond to the coast of Wales. The focal point is its elegant Victorian **pier** – the country's only intact Grade 1-listed pier – but the whole beachfront invites a stroll, not least the promontory at its southern end, which shelters **Clevedon Marine Lake**, an open-air seawater pool (wclevedonmarinelake), and from where the **Poet's Walk** offers pleasant perambulations round the headland. The path, which was supposed to have provided inspiration for Tennyson and Coleridge, winds round Church Hill, passing St Andrew's churchyard and climbing Wain's Hill, taking in some bracing views en route – about a mile in all. There's a panel at the beginning of the walk providing a bit of background, and leaflets are sometimes available at the pier's Tollhouse.

7

Away from the sea, the higher reaches of Clevedon exude a genteel and prosperous air, not least around **Hill Road**, where there are rows of salubrious villas as well as trendy shops and the town's best choice of eateries (see page 231); head up Alexandra Road or Marine Parade from the pier to reach the area. The main shopping zone lies around the Triangle, marked by its clock-tower, located at the bottom of Chapel Hill from the southern end of Hill Road. Clevedon's prevailing air of nostalgia is once more evident on Old Church Road, west of the Triangle, where the local picture house, the **Curzon**, which first opened in 1912, is claimed to be the oldest continuously used cinema in Europe.

Clevedon Pier

The Beach • Daily 10am–sunset • £3 • ☎01275 878846, wclevedonpier.co.uk

Opened in 1869, **Clevedon Pier** is one of the best-preserved of Britain's 78 seaside piers and one of the most graceful, stretching 850ft into the Bristol Channel with an elegant pavilion at its end. Its construction was spurred by the arrival of the railway and the possibility of a faster route to South Wales than the route via Gloucester allowed before the construction of the Severn Tunnel in 1886: passengers would travel by train to Clevedon's station (now gone), and from the pier board a paddle steamer to cross the Bristol Channel. The sides of the pier are studded with more than ten thousand brass plates inscribed with the names of individual sponsors of the restoration following the collapse of part of the structure in 1970. Gracefully perched at the pier's end, the Edwardian-style *Pagoda* tea room serves teas and cakes. The pier was used to great effect as the setting for a scene from the 2010 film *Never Let Me Go*.

Clevedon Court

Tickenham Rd • April–Sept Wed, Thurs & Sun 2–5pm • House & garden £9, garden only £5.40 (cash only) • NT • ☎01275 872257, wnationaltrust.org.uk • Buses #X6 and #X7 from Clevedon (Old Street) or Bristol

Clevedon's greatest treasure is **Clevedon Court**, a fourteenth- and fifteenth-century manor house lying less than two miles inland. Since 1709 it has been the property of the Elton family, who continue to live in it. At the centre of the house is the **Great Hall**, its walls plastered with family portraits and with a curious Elizabethan carved stone doorway in one corner, created from old fireplaces. Other rooms contain some fine furniture spanning three hundred years, as well as portraits of and drawings by William Makepeace Thackeray, who, as a guest here in the 1840s, embarked on a platonic affair with one of the Elton daughters who was already married (as was Thackeray). The author used the house as the model for Castlewood in his novel *Henry Esmond*.

Elsewhere in the house you can see the tiny chapel whose window with reticulated tracery is a feature of the house's south front, while the Justice Room (or Glass Room) displays a collection of Nailsea glassware, multi-coloured and fashioned in the shapes of pipes and rolling pins. The Old Great Hall holds "Eltonware", the distinctive and internationally renowned pottery created by Edmund Elton (1846–1920), using unusual shapes and techniques such as platinum glazing. Outside, the terraced gardens give good views seaward, but suffer from traffic noise from the nearby M5 motorway.

Another offspring of the Elton family was Arthur Henry Hallam – the bosom friend of Tennyson who died aged just 22 while travelling in Austria, and the subject of the poet's grief-stricken elegy, *In Memoriam*. Hallam is buried in the family vault in St Andrew's church, off Old Church Road in the west end of Clevedon.

Tyntesfield

Wraxall • **House** Jan to mid-March & early Nov to late Nov Mon–Fri tours only, Sat & Sun 11am–3pm; mid-March to early Nov daily 11am–5pm; Dec Mon–Tues 11am–3pm, Wed–Sun 11am–7pm (Fri until 8pm before Christmas) • **Gardens & grounds** Daily: March–Oct daily 10am–6pm or dusk if earlier; Nov–Feb 10am–5pm or dusk if earlier (late opening Fri–Sun in Dec); last entry 1hr before closing • £16.50 house, gardens and grounds, £10.20 grounds only • NT • ☎ 01275 461900, ⊕ nationaltrust.org.uk • Buses #X6 and #X7 from Clevedon (Old Street) or Bristol, or #X9 from Bristol

Seven miles east of Clevedon and about the same distance west of Bristol, **Tyntesfield** represents one of the National Trust's most triumphant renovations, made possible by a huge fundraising campaign in 2002. The restoration of this mansion is ongoing, with meticulous efforts being made to present the house according to its final appearance, the fruit of four generations of the Gibbs family faithfully following a single aesthetic vision.

Largely with the profits of their business importing guano (seabird droppings) for use as fertilizer, William Gibbs bought the house in 1843 and set about its complete rebuilding in a florid Gothic Revival style, which was completed in 1865. The structure was embellished with towers, turrets and gargoyles, while the interior was given high Gothic ceilings, copious oak panelling and grand staircases, and was filled by successive members of the family with a treasure-trove of decorative artwork, making this a must-see for Arts and Crafts fans. Every detail is eye-catching, from the ornate fireplaces of Venetian marble and exuberantly carved doorways to the intricate cabinets and statuettes liberally sprinkled around. The library and drawing room have vaulted ceilings, and the billiards room impresses with its tiger-skin rug and numerous stag-head trophies. The upstairs bedrooms are less opulent, as are, of course, the servants' quarters.

Alongside the house, the imposing High Victorian **chapel** is also worth a look, while you could spend a pleasurable day traipsing over the 500-acre **estate**, spread over a ridge with marvellous views over the fertile Yeo Valley, and including a fine set of landscaped gardens and a croquet lawn.

Consult the website for news of talks, tours and concerts that take place throughout the year. Note that timed tickets available on a first-come-first-served basis soon sell out – so get here early. Mondays and Tuesdays are the least busy days.

ARRIVAL AND DEPARTURE   CLEVEDON AND AROUND

By bus Services #X6 and #X7 connect Bristol with Clevedon, both with stops at or near Clevedon Court and Tyntesfield. Service #X5 runs to Weston-super-Mare.

Destinations Bristol (Mon–Sat every 30min, Sun hourly; 35–50min); Weston-super-Mare (Mon–Sat hourly, Sun 5 daily; 30min).

ACCOMMODATION

Rooms at the Cellar 51 Copse Rd ☎01275 873444, ⊚roomsatthecellar.co.uk. Two spacious rooms adjacent to and run by *The Cellar* wine bar (see below) have been handsomely converted to provide sumptuous accommodation with modern bathrooms. One room has a sideways sea view, and both have a tiny kitchen area where a self-serve Continental breakfast is taken, including smoked salmon, cheese, bread and croissants. **£98**

★**Taggart House** Outside Walton-in-Gordano, 2 miles northeast ☎01275 316970, ⊚taggarthouse. co.uk. Given Clevedon's dearth of decent accommodation, this rural B&B offers an excellent alternative. The stylish modern bungalow is located on a secluded country lane and surrounded by an acre of woodland garden, providing peaceful views from the two rooms which have contemporary bathrooms and underfloor heating. Breakfast features local produce. Book early. A self-catering "luxury shepherd's hut" in the garden is also available for stays of two or more nights (£95/night). **£99**

Walton Park Hotel Wellington Terrace ☎01275 874253, ⊚waltonparkhotel.co.uk. Old-fashioned and rather posh, this central hotel occupies a prime clifftop position with great views over the sea from its bar, restaurant, garden and back bedrooms. It needs an overhaul but it's fine for a night or two, and the online rates can be quite reasonable. **£90**

EATING AND DRINKING

The Cellar 36 Hill Rd ☎01275 340340, ⊚thecellar winebar.co.uk. Located in a former pharmacy, with the old labelled drawers in the counter, this wine bar and bistro with a warm ambience has a range of tapas (mostly around £4, or three for £10 at lunchtime) to nibble while you sample the generous selection of beers, ciders, whiskies and wines. More substantial, Mediterranean-inspired dishes such as *boeuf bourguignon* and Moroccan spiced lamb are also on the menu (£10–16). There's live music on Tuesdays from 7.30pm. Bar Tues–Thurs 10am–10pm, Fri & Sat 10am–midnight; kitchen Tues–Fri noon–2.30pm & 6–9pm, Sat noon–9pm.

★**Murrays** 91 Hill Rd ☎01275 341222, ⊚murrays ofclevedon.co.uk. This light and airy Italian deli/café/ restaurant is a great place for picnic goodies – olives, home-made bread, wines and cheeses – as well as snacks and main meals to be eaten on the premises. The coffee is authentically zingy, the sandwiches are fresh and delicious (£5.50–8.50), and the menu includes first-class pizzas in two sizes (£8.50–13), lasagne (£12) and monkfish wrapped in pancetta (£19.50). Booking advised in the evenings. Tues–Sat 10am–5pm & 6–10pm (last orders 9.15pm).

Puro 32–34 Hill Rd (entrance at rear) ☎01275 217373, ⊚purorestaurant.co.uk. Tucked away behind Hill Street, this elegant place with wooden floors and modern art on white walls has an impressive menu that includes Cornish mussels and rabbit terrine for starters and pan-seared duck breast, butter-poached guinea fowl, and wild garlic gnocchi for the main course. Most mains in the evening cost £18, and there's a five-course tasting menu for £40. The Sunday roasts are outstanding (around £15). Wed & Thurs 5–11pm, Fri & Sat noon–3pm & 5pm–midnight, Sun noon–10pm (last orders 9.30pm, Sun 9pm).

Scoozi 18 Hill Rd ☎01275 877516, ⊚scooziclevedon. co.uk. Buzzy modern Italian with a dozen or so pizzas to choose from (£9–13), pastas and risottos (£11–15) and grills such as veal escalopes and tuna steak (around £15). The *pollo porcini* (chicken breast in a mushroom and marsala wine sauce) is amazing. There's a separate gluten-free menu. Mon–Sat noon–2pm & 6pm–late.

Weston-super-Mare

Eight miles south of Clevedon, and the major resort on this coast, **WESTON-SUPER-MARE** was a tiny fishing village at the beginning of the nineteenth century, but boomed after the arrival of the Great Western Railway in 1841 to become one of the West Country's chief seaside resorts of the Victorian and Edwardian eras. Much of the town is rather moth-eaten today, and the dramatic retreat of the sea at low tide to more than a mile out from Marine Parade creates a forlorn, sometimes surreal, picture, but with the tide in, its sandy beaches can look positively Mediterranean, and the town, with its shiny new **pier**, continues to attract busloads of trippers.

Traditional seaside amusements are still very much in evidence on the beach, such as donkey rides and Punch and Judy puppetry, and cockles and whelks on sale at stalls. There's a **Sand Sculpture Festival** every summer (see page 232), and the **Eat Weston Food Festival**, currently taking place over one day in mid-April and late September in the Italian Gardens, adjacent to High Street. If you're looking for entertainment, you can take a turn on the **Sky View**, a giant Ferris wheel, while indoor attractions include

> **WESTON'S SAND SCULPTURE FESTIVAL**
>
> Forget puny sand castles; if you don't want sand kicked in your face, aim high and try your hand at sand-sculpting. You can find inspiration at Weston-super-Mare's **Sand Sculpture Festival** (ⓦ westonsandsculpture.co.uk), an annual event taking place between mid-April and September on Weston's main beach (£10am–6pm; £4). The festival follows a theme every year; recent ones have been fairy tales, with evocations of Cinderella and Snow White among other tales, and Great Britain, which included everything from London's Tower Bridge to Henry VIII. The ideal ratio is roughly eight parts sand to one part water, but different sand requires different mixes. If you're intrigued; join a workshop; see ⓦ sandinyoureye.co.uk.

the **Weston-super-Mare Museum**, the **Lambretta Museum** and, some way inland, the **Helicopter Museum**.

North of the pier, you can take in the views from Knightstone Island, which once held public baths, and stroll beside the Marine Lake beyond, a sheltered, non-tidal, salt-water swimming spot. A short walk up to the point brings you to Weston's second pier, the ruined **Birnbeck Pier**, looking like a shamefully neglected poor relation of the comparatively glamorous Grand Pier.

The town is sandwiched between two hills that offer possibilities for more adventurous walking. To the south, **Uphill** has views over the cliffy promontory of Brean Down (see page 236), a spindly finger of land pointing towards the isle of Steep Holm. Uphill marks one end of the **West Mendip Way** (see page 144), a long-distance trail which follows the Mendip Hills for thirty miles to Wells (take bus #5 from the train station or Regent St to Links Rd for the start of the route, which can be viewed at ⓦ mendiphillsaonb.org.uk). North of town is **Worlebury Hill**, with some Iron Age remains and thick woods crossed by trails. Beyond Worlebury Hill, the wide arc of **Sand Bay** provides a quiet tonic to Weston's exuberance, ideal for a picnic or a nap.

Grand Pier

Marine Parade • Daily 10am–dusk • Pier £1, amusements £1–5 • ☎ 01934 620238, ⓦ grandpier.co.uk

The single object that for decades drew the crowds from London and Birmingham to Weston – almost its *raison d'être* – is its **Grand Pier**. It's had a chequered history: built in 1904, it burned down in 1930 and again in 2008, after which the resort was almost ready to close down. However, the pier was rebuilt and, following its reopening in 2010, has restored the fortunes of this grand-aunt of resorts. Weston-super-Mare's Grand Pier can now boast a gleaming new fun palace, all twenty-first-century glass, steel and wavy lines of blue neon, within which there are attractions ranging from the traditional (mirror maze, dodgems, ghost train, helter-skelter, shooting galleries and penny arcades) to up-to-date thrills (a Robocoaster, which thrashes passengers around at high speed in a giant claw; a split-level go-kart circuit; a laser maze, involving retrieving jewels without crossing laser beams; and a 4-D cinema, in which you're sprayed by rain and lashed by wind). Concerts and other events are held in the **Great Hall** and the pirate-themed *Captain Jack's* bar.

If the cacophony and crowds don't appeal, content yourself with simply treading the boards – following the length of the pier deck promenade. If it's windy or wet, you can use a central covered walkway.

Sky View

Beach Lawns • Mid-March to late-Oct daily 10am–6pm, Fri 10am–8pm, Sat 10am–9pm, Sun 10am–7pm; daily during school hols 10am–late • £5, family of four £15 • ⓦ facebook.com/skyviewwheel

A hundred and thirty feet tall, with thirty air-conditioned glass pods, Weston's giant Ferris wheel, **Sky View**, affords lofty views over the town, coast and across the Bristol Channel to Wales.

Weston Museum

Burlington St • July & Aug daily 10am–5pm; Sept–June Tues–Sun 10am–4.30pm, daily during school hols • Free • ☎ 01934 621028, Ⓦ westonmuseum.org

Housed in an old gasworks plant, the **Weston Museum** takes you on a whirlwind tour of the town's history, natural history and geology, including local prehistoric finds, Roman and medieval knick-knacks, and material on life during World War II. A brief survey of seaside culture includes an entertaining selection of still-operating vintage penny arcade machines, one of them with the self-explanatory title "American Execution". **Clara's Cottage**, a separate building at one end of the museum, holds a reconstructed front parlour, kitchen and bedroom from around 1900. The William Mable Gallery holds temporary exhibitions on such themes as "Punch and Judy Through the Ages".

Lambretta Museum

77 Alfred St • Mon–Sat 11am–2pm • Free • ☎ 01934 417834, Ⓦ facebook.com/lambrettamuseum

Back in the day, Weston, like other English seaside resorts, had a thriving mod scene, and ancient mods, scooterists and other nostalgia fans will be enthralled by the collection of scooters from the 1960s displayed at the **Lambretta Museum**, housed in a former community hall. Many of the exhibits are vintage and rare models, one or two of them preserved in the "mod" style from the 1960s, glistening with chrome and dripping with mirrors. As well as scooters you'll find badges, posters and other memorabilia. The staff are friendly and passionate about scooters and scooter culture, and there's a well-stocked shop.

Helicopter Museum

Locking Moor Rd • Wed–Sun: April–Aug 10am–5.30pm, Sept–March 10am–4.30pm; last admission 1hr before closing • £7.50 • ☎ 01934 635227, Ⓦ helicoptermuseum.co.uk • Bus #126 from Marine Parade

Every shape and size of whirlibird is represented at the **Helicopter Museum**, on the corner of an old airfield three miles inland of Weston. The country's only helicopter museum is claimed to be the world's largest, and among more than 100 helicopters and autogyros here are Eastern European, US and veteran models. Air Experience flights are offered on specified dates with prior booking (£50 including museum entry) – a memorable way to view the coast on a fifteen-mile excursion lasting around eight minutes – as well as numerous other shows and events throughout the year (see website for details).

Worlebury Hill and Sand Bay

Bus #1 from Regent St (near train station)

If Weston's crowds get oppressive, you can always climb up to **Worlebury Hill**, a breezy, much quarried and mined limestone elevation to the north of the main beach, reachable from around the point on Kewstoke Road. Here you can see the scant remains of an Iron Age hillfort and hut circle, and there are numerous trails running through **Weston Woods**, which thickly cover a large part of the hill. Continuing further north will bring you to **Sand Bay**, virtually undeveloped and a nice contrast to the bustle of Weston Bay. The beach here is bounded to the north by Sand Point, a headland maintained by the National Trust.

ARRIVAL AND DEPARTURE   **WESTON-SUPER-MARE**

By train Weston's train station lies a 10min walk from the seafront on Station Rd.

Destinations Bridgwater (Mon–Sat hourly, Sun 10 daily;

20min); Bristol (2–3 hourly, Sun 1–2 hourly; 30min); Taunton (Mon–Sat hourly, Sun 12 daily; 30min).

By bus Most buses arrive at and depart from Marine

FLAT HOLM AND STEEP HOLM

Looming up out of the sea, the two isles of **Flat Holm** and **Steep Holm** are a constant feature of the view across the Bristol Channel around these parts. Circular **Flat Holm** is the larger of the two, measuring less than half a mile across and consisting mainly of gently sloping rock and maritime grassland. The island is the most southerly point of Wales and was a smuggling base in the eighteenth century; today, apart from some rare flora found here – rock sea lavender and wild leek among them – you can see four gun emplacements dating from the 1860s, a derelict isolation hospital, a lighthouse and a handful of Soay sheep. As its name implies, **Steep Holm** is, at 256ft, the taller island, and forms part of England. Like its sister isle, it has a few Victorian gun batteries to explore and is a similarly protected nature reserve, with Muntjac deer among its denizens, and there's a visitor centre in the Victorian barracks.

Boats to Steep Holm are operated from Knightstone Harbour between spring and autumn by Bay Island Voyages (☏ 07393 470476, ⓦ bayislandvoyages.co.uk; £40). Depending on the tides, the whole excursion takes around eleven hours, including around ten hours ashore; see ⓦ steepholm.org.uk for more on the island. The regular boat service from Weston to Flat Holm (ⓦ flatholmisland.wordpress.com) was suspended at time of writing – contact the website or Weston's tourist office for an update. Light refreshments are available on both islands, but you should bring a packed lunch, as well as non-slip shoes, waterproofs and woollies, and, ideally, binoculars.

Parade, Regent St, Oxford St and Alexandra Parade. Buses #X1 and #X2 run to Bristol (Mon–Sat 4–5 hourly, Sun 2 hourly; 1hr–1hr 30min); bus #20 runs to Burnham-on-Sea (Mon–Sat every 30min, Sun hourly; 1hr); bus #X5 runs to Clevedon (Mon–Sat hourly, Sun 6 daily; 40min).

INFORMATION

Tourist office *Tropicana*, Beach Lawns, near the pier (Easter–Sept & Oct half-term daily 10am–4pm; ☏ 01643 888877, ⓦ visit-westonsupermare.com). Information is available year-round by phone or email.

ACCOMMODATION

Beachlands Hotel 17 Uphill Rd North ☏ 01934 621401, ⓦ beachlandshotel.com. Away from the seafront hubbub at the southern end of Weston, this family-run hotel opposite a golf course has a calm ambience, a good restaurant and an indoor pool and sauna. Some of the rooms are bright and exuberantly furnished, others are poorly maintained – check first. Rooms at the back giving onto the garden are quietest. **£122**

★ **Church House** 27 Kewstoke Rd ☏ 01934 633185, ⓦ churchhousekewstoke.co.uk. With grand views over Sand Bay, this elegant Georgian rectory offers five airy and spacious rooms with minimalist decor and smart modern bathrooms. You can soak up the panorama from the conservatory or patio, perhaps while savouring the complimentary home-made cake or muffins. Breakfasts are first-class and include fresh orange juice. It's on the #1 bus route, and a pick-up can be arranged from Weston's station. **£100**

Country View Sand Rd, Sand Bay ☏ 01934 627595, ⓦ cvhp.co.uk. Just 5min walk from the beach at Sand Bay, this small, clean campsite has a heated outdoor pool, a bar (but no food), wi-fi, spotless facilities and abundant hot water. Four-night minimum stay in peak season. Closed Nov–Feb. Pitches **£25**

Goodrington Guest House 23 Charlton Rd ☏ 01934 623229, ⓦ goodrington.info. This Victorian B&B close to the beach at the quieter, southern end of town has three spacious and spotless rooms, one for families with a separate (but private) bathroom. The hostess is friendly and breakfasts are fine. It's a 15min walk to the centre, and there's a bus stop at the end of the road. **£65**

Moorlands Country Guest House Main Rd, Hutton ☏ 01934 812283, ⓦ moorlandscountryguesthouse. co.uk. As the name implies, this place is in a quiet nook in a village three miles inland of the seafront. The homely Georgian building has bright, spacious rooms with an eclectic mix of decor, and there's an extensive garden with lawns and flowerbeds at the back. Breakfasts are excellent, and you'll find a pub with good food and beer just across the road. **£95**

EATING AND DRINKING

Demetris Taverna 18 Richmond St ☏ 01934 620187, ⓦ demetristaverna.co.uk. This long-established Greek restaurant has the smack of authenticity, with refreshingly few trappings of holiday kitsch. *Kleftiko* and souvlaki are on the menu, of course (£14–16), but the grilled chops, seafood and daily specials are also noteworthy, and portions are generous. Book ahead for Fridays and Saturdays, when there's often a bit of music and dancing. Tues–Sat 6.30–10pm (last orders).

Dr Fox's Tearoom Knightstone Causeway ☎01934 707411, ⊛drfoxstearoom.co.uk. On a promontory north of the Grand Pier, this place occupies one of the best vantage points in Weston, with views from the outdoor tables straight across to the pier and beyond. It's a great spot for breakfasts, freshly-baked scones (sweet or savoury), or a cream tea (£5). Cakes include vegan options. Tues–Sun 10.30am–6pm, daily in summer, until 4pm in winter.

★**Hadleys at Number One** 1 The Boulevard, an extension of South Parade and Waterloo St ☎01934 614416, ⊛www.hadleysatnumberone.co.uk. A cut above most of Weston's culinary establishments, this restaurant has a plush but relaxed ambience and a menu that focuses on traditional English cuisine. Dishes such as duck breast, rump of lamb, pork tenderloin and sea-bass fillets cost £17–19, and two-course lunches are £12. Breakfasts and coffees are also served. Ask to sit in the brighter and quieter room upstairs when it's open. Tues–Thurs 9am–2.45pm, Fri & Sat 9am–2.45pm & 6.30–9pm, Sun 10am–2pm.

Meze Mazi 45 Oxford St ☎01934 626363, ⊛meze maziweston.co.uk. The extensive menu of some fifty meze items at this Cypriot restaurant – including lots of salads and veggie and vegan options – makes for a difficult choice when ordering. All dishes are £5–8, and stand-outs include fish souvlaki and octopus; alternatively go for a selection on a meat, fish or vegetarian set menu for £19 (minimum two people), available Tues–Thurs & Sun. Wash it down with Greek beer and wine. Service is friendly and fast. Tues–Fri 5–10pm, Sat & Sun noon–3pm & 5–10pm.

Yo-Ji 25–27 St James St ☎01934 620800, ⊛yo-ji. co.uk. Top-notch Japanese restaurant where you can order a sushi platter or tempura scallops (£16), and pork, tuna and tiger prawns are cooked in front of you (£15–18). The menu is long, portions are large and the staff are helpful. Mon–Thurs & Sun 11am–3pm & 5–10.30pm, Fri & Sat 11am–11pm.

7

Burnham-on-Sea and around

Weston seems almost metropolis-like when compared with **BURNHAM-ON-SEA** eight miles south, a rather neglected resort in need of a charm injection. The seafront is the most appealing part of town, where the Esplanade offers views over a long, flat expanse of sand, stretching north as far as **Brean Down** and west along Somerset's north coast. Immediately south of the town is the estuary of the River Parrett, where, in the river mouth, tiny **Stert Island** is the nesting place for innumerable seabirds, and is also the halfway point of the annual **Stert Island Swim**, when around eighty intrepid swimmers race from Burnham's beach to the island and back, a distance of around 1.5 miles; the swim usually takes place on the third or fourth Sunday of July.

Like other resorts along this coast, Burnham's seafront can look delightful or depressing, according to the state of the tide in the Bristol Channel and the weather. Even in the worst conditions, though, the view across the sands to Wales has an intensely still, almost mesmerizing quality. The Esplanade itself is nothing special, though it does boast what is claimed to be Britain's shortest pier, dating from 1911–14, now entirely occupied by an amusement arcade. Further up the beach, you'll spot what is Burnham's oddest feature, the Low Lighthouse, also known as the Lighthouse-on-the-Sands or the **Lighthouse-on-Legs** due to its construction on stilts on the beach.

HAILE SELASSIE IN BURNHAM

Apart from the supposed arrival of Joseph of Arimathea with the young Jesus at Burnham-on-Sea before their legendary journey to Glastonbury (see page 156), the seaside town's most unlikely visitor was the **Ethiopian emperor Haile Selassie** in 1936. Having been ejected from his native land by Mussolini, the "Lion of Judah" stayed in a guesthouse on Berrow Road soon after his arrival in Britain, before moving on to set up home in Bath, where he lived before finally returning to Ethiopia in 1941.

St Andrew's

Victoria St • Free • ⓦ standrewsbos.co.uk

Burnham has little of any great age, one notable exception being **St Andrew's church**, right by the seafront, dedicated in 1316 but remodelled in subsequent centuries. Its showpiece is a marble altarpiece carved in 1686 by master-carver Grinling Gibbons, originally intended for the chapel at Whitehall Palace, later transferred to Westminster Abbey, and finally installed here in 1820. Other sculpted figures by Gibbons are in the nave windows and in the baptistery. Outside the church, note the distinct slant of the square, castellated tower, the result of faulty foundations.

Brean Down

Bus #20 from Burnham-on-Sea or Weston-super-Mare to Brean, then a 30min walk

North of Burnham, an unbroken succession of bungalows and caravan parks trails through Berrow and Brean. The beach, though, preserves an appealingly wild feel, backed by miles of grassy dunes – especially grand at **Berrow Dunes** – and ending at a car park and the cliffy peninsula of **Brean Down**. Maintained by the National Trust, this outcrop of the Mendips has steps leading up to the ridge, from where there are splendid coastal views taking in Steep Holm, Flat Holm, south Wales, the Mendips and Exmoor (and sometimes even extending to the Brecon Beacons). There are Iron Age remains and an abandoned Palmerston Fort (one of the defences thrown up around Britain's coasts under prime minister Lord Palmerston), dating from 1865. North of Brean Down, a saltmarsh spreads soupily around the mouth of the River Axe, cutting off access to Weston's beach. The currents around the headland can be ferocious, so don't attempt a swim.

Brent Knoll

A couple of miles northeast of Burnham, the round elevation of **Brent Knoll** appears more interesting the closer you get to it. Though not particularly high at around 450ft, it rears imposingly above the surrounding flatlands, and was an island before the Somerset Levels were drained. Its geographical prominence has given it a recurring role in history: Iron Age remains lie on the summit; for the Romans it was the "Mount of Frogs"; it was a refuge from invading Vikings; and it may even have been the site of a significant victory by Alfred the Great over the Danes.

A walk to the top is strongly recommended, which can be tackled from either of the two villages at its base, **East Brent** and **Brent Knoll**. While you're in the area, take a few minutes to look at the churches in both of these villages, which sport some remarkable examples of bench-carving. The bench-ends in **St Mary's** in East Brent are in better condition, and the church also has a graceful seventeenth-century plaster ceiling over the nave, a timber one over the north aisle and a gallery from 1637. The fourteenth-century carvings at **St Michael's** in Brent Knoll include a darkly amusing sequence showing the local abbot as a fox being arrested and hanged by his geese parishioners.

ARRIVAL AND INFORMATION

By train Highbridge & Burnham train station lies a couple of miles south of Burnham-on-Sea's seafront, linked by frequent local buses.

Destinations Bridgwater (Mon–Sat hourly, Sun 9 daily; 10min); Bristol (Mon–Sat hourly, Sun 11 daily; 35–50min); Weston-super-Mare (Mon–Sat hourly, Sun 11 daily; 10min).

By bus Most buses arrive at and leave from The Esplanade, Seaview Rd and Berrow Rd. Burnham is connected by services #20 with Brean and Weston-super-Mare and #21

with Bridgwater.

Destinations Brean (Mon–Sat every 30min, Sun hourly; 25min); Bridgwater (Mon–Sat every 30min, Sun hourly; 35min); Weston-super-Mare (Mon–Sat 3 hourly, Sun hourly; 40min–1hr).

Tourist information The website ⓦ burnham-on-sea. com has information on accommodation, eating out and local attractions.

ACCOMMODATION

Cheriton Lodge 4 Allandale Rd ☎01278 781423, ⓦcheritonlodge.com. Late Victorian B&B located in one of Burnham's most agreeable neighbourhoods, where the three light and airy rooms have en-suite or private, separate facilities. There's a good choice of breakfasts, and the beach is right at the end of this quiet cul-de-sac. No credit cards. No under-12s. Closed Oct–April. **£70**

Yew Tree House Hurn Lane, Berrow, 3 miles north ☎01278 751382, ⓦyewtree-house.co.uk. Parts of this house date back to the seventeenth century, but the seven rather dated rooms – some in converted stables in a courtyard garden – are spacious with modern en-suite bathrooms. It's on a secluded lane a few minutes' walk from the dunes. Bus #20 from Burnham and Weston stops nearby. **£80**

EATING AND DRINKING

Chandni 50–52 High St ☎01278 773844. This beats the opposition for miles around with its smart decor and crisp, white table covers, not to mention its classic Indian cuisine, including delicious pakora starters and such dishes as garlic chilli chicken, prawn Madras and Karachi king prawn. A Chandni Burnham-on-Sea Special (£10) is a mixed tikka and tandoori chicken and lamb dish. Most mains are under £8, and there are set-price lunch and evening deals (and takeaways). Daily noon–2pm & 5.30–11pm, but closed Fri lunch.

La Vela 4 Abingdon St ☎01278 782707, ⓦlavela.co.uk. Burnham has no shortage of cafés and fast food outlets, most a bit downbeat, but little in the way of decent restaurants. This one is not exactly cutting edge, but you'll find satisfying and well-presented versions of all your old favourites in this Italian eatery, including risottos, pastas and pizzas (around £12), with some gluten-free options. The antipasti and bruschettas are worth sampling, and there are succulent, flame-grilled steaks too (around £20). Service is friendly and there's usually a lively atmosphere. Mon–Thurs 5–10.30pm, Fri & Sat 5–11pm, Sun 5–10pm.

The Red Cow 134 Brent St, Brent Knoll ☎01278 760234, ⓦtheredcowpub.com. At the base of the Brent Knoll elevation, this pub with a skittle alley and gardens to front and rear has Butcombe ales and a full menu ranging from ploughman's lunches (£10) to generously filled steak and kidney pies (£12.50). Pub Mon & Tues 11am–2.30pm & 6–9pm, Wed–Sat 11am–2.30pm & 6–11pm, Sun 11am–3pm & 6–9.30pm; kitchen daily noon–2pm & 6–9pm (Sun until 8.30pm).

7

Kilve and around

An alien presence hangs over the otherwise flat and featureless landscape west of the Parrett estuary, lending it a spooky air of menace – **Hinkley Point**, a complex of nuclear power stations (Hinkley A and Hinkley B, with a third under construction). The installations dominate the coast west of Steart Point, though with your back to them, following the coast path west, the shore assumes a more benign air, with modest cliffs rising above the sea.

A WALK FROM KILVE BEACH

From Kilve Beach, you could make an easy **circular walk** of five miles or so, that takes in a couple of attractive Somerset churches. Head east along the coast, following the clifftop path for around 1.5 miles towards the distant, rather sinister landmark of Hinkley Point power station. At Lilstock Beach, at the end of a stretch of loose, sharp-edged stones, a gravel track heads inland to meet a tarmac road. Past Lilstock Farm, look out on the left for **St Andrew's chapel**, a small, simple and much restored fourteenth-century structure topped by a bellcote. The derelict and deconsecrated church was saved from demolition and restored by a local rector in 1993, and is now almost empty save for a pair of elegant stone memorials from the early eighteenth century, one carved from slate. Further up the road, easily visible on the brow of the hill, lies the much larger church of **St Nicholas**, mostly Victorian though sections (the chancel arch and lower part of the tower) date back to the fourteenth century. Among the curiosities within is a dusty collection of fossils and oddments picked up from the coast. Carry on through the scattered hamlet of Kilton; just before Hilltop Lane look out for a signposted footpath on the right leading through fields. Following the path westwards for a mile or so will bring you back to Sea Lane, at the bottom of which is the car park at Kilve Beach.

There's an especially atmospheric stretch of sand and rock at **Kilve Beach**, where the strata of shale and lias (limestone) form beautiful geometric patterns and it's not hard to spot ammonites and other fossils (see box). The beach here was once much used for conger-eel hunting, or "glatting", which took place during the low spring tides. The remains of a brick retort stand behind the beach, once used to extract oil from the shale, and a defunct lime kiln and stone jetty are nearby. The West Somerset Path provides easy walking here along the cliffs overlooking the shore; don't, however, be tempted to walk for any length along the beach itself at low tide – there are few opportunities to reach higher ground when the tide comes in.

KILVE itself lies a mile or so inland, little more than a huddle of shops on the A39, linked to Kilve Beach by an easily missed turn-off, Sea Lane. On the way to the beach, you'll pass the propped-up ruins of a **chantry** built in 1329 for the recitation of prayers for the local squire. Legend has it that it was used to store contraband liquor landed nearby.

<table>
<tr><td>**ACCOMMODATION AND EATING**</td><td>**KILVE AND AROUND**</td></tr>
</table>

★**Chantry Tea Gardens** Sea Lane, Kilve Beach ☎01278 741457. After exploring the coast, you'll find restorative refreshments at this tea garden beside the ruin of Kilve chantry, just up from the car park at Kilve Beach. Refuel with soups, sandwiches, quiches, salads and ploughman's lunches (mostly £5–7.50), or treat yourself to home-made cakes, a cream tea (£5–7) or seven flavours of Somerset ice cream. Gluten-free options are available. Late Feb to late Oct daily 10.30am–5pm, last orders 4.15pm.

Hood Arms Kilve ☎01278 741114, ⓦthehoodarms. co.uk. Although it's right on the A39, this seventeenth-century coaching inn in the village has quiet rooms, all different, some with modern showers. The bar area is bedecked with hunting jackets and boots, and offers local beers and ciders and a full menu (evening mains £11–16). There's a large garden, and bike storage too. Tues–Sat noon–3pm & 6–11pm, Sun noon–3pm; kitchen Tues–Sat noon–2pm & 6–9pm, Sun noon–3pm. **£95**

Watchet and around

Two miles northwest of Williton, Somerset's only port of any size, **WATCHET**, seems to have little in common with the coast's other holiday-focused centres, though it too gets its share of tourism. There has been a town here since at least 988, when a Viking raid was recorded, and it later became a highly active smuggling centre. **Samuel Taylor Coleridge**, on his perambulations around this area from his base in the Quantock village of Nether Stowey (see page 219), supposedly modelled the port from which his Ancient Mariner embarked on his doomed voyage on Watchet, an association recalled by the modern statue on the Esplanade of the Mariner himself, gazing out over a harbour now filled with yachts.

Seated close by the Ancient Mariner is a second statue that portrays another renowned local figure, that of John Short, or **Yankee Jack**, as he was known (1839–1933), a sailor famed for his powerful voice with which he sang rousing sea shanties. He was interviewed and recorded by the great collector and transcriber of English folk songs, Cecil Sharp, and had a colourful career, sailing the world and running the blockade during the American Civil War before becoming Watchet's town crier in his retirement.

Watchet has a couple of small but absorbing **museums**, and makes a good base for visiting **Cleeve Court**, outside the inland village of Washford, and the unique **Bakelite Museum**, near Williton. You could also make an easy excursion three miles west along the coast to one of Somerset's best beaches, the broad, sandy **Blue Anchor Bay**, a stop on the West Somerset Railway and reached by road from Watchet on the B3191.

Watchet Boat Museum

Harbour Rd • April–Sept Mon & Wed–Sun 10am–4.30pm, daily during school hols; Oct–March Mon & Thurs–Sat 10am–3pm • Free • ☎01984 632101

Outside Bristol, Somerset may not be immediately associated with maritime traditions, but Watchet has been a fishing and trading port for centuries, while the Levels have seen constant boat activity inland. The **Watchet Boat Museum**, housed in an old goods shed next to the WSR station, presents an overview of life afloat in times gone by, illustrated by an absorbing collection of old photographs, models and full-size examples of boats: coracles; punts; "flatners", the flat-bottomed vessels used for fishing on Somerset's inland waters; turf boats, for carrying the cut and dried blocks of peat; and withy boats, for carrying young willows. Other curiosities include a salmon butt (basket) for catching salmon, and a "mud-horse", a sort of barrow for use on mud flats, alongside an array of net-making and boat-building tools. It's a fascinating collection, and worth the donation visitors are asked to make. Watchet's visitor centre is housed in the same building.

Market House Museum

Market St • Easter to early Nov daily 10.30am–4.30pm • Free • ⓦ watchetmuseum.co.uk

Just up from the harbour, Watchet's old market building from 1820 now houses a chapel upstairs, and on the ground floor an old lock-up at one end and the **Market House Museum** at the other. This low-key but engaging display of local mementoes in one large room includes fossils and molluscs from the surrounding shores, fragments of tools and weapons from the Paleolithic, Neolithic and Bronze ages and Romano-British pottery shards. From more recent times are navigational instruments, a "glatting" spear for the hunting of conger eels, and dozens of black-and-white photos of the local fishing population.

Cleeve Abbey

Abbey Rd, Washford • Daily: April–June, Sept & Oct 10am–5pm; July & Aug 10am–6pm • £6.20 • EH • ☎ 01984 640377, ⓦ english-heritage.org.uk • Bus #28 to Shepherd's Corner then a 5min walk, or West Somerset Railway to Washford and walk 10–15min

Signposted off the A39 at Washford, three miles southwest of Watchet, the ruins of **Cleeve Abbey** are remarkable for the extent to which the monks' living quarters have survived (usually the part of the monastery to have disappeared), the source of much information about pre-Reformation monastic life. Founded as an abbey in the late twelfth century, this was Somerset's only Cistercian monastic house until the abbey church was razed during the Dissolution of the Monasteries in the 1530s and the remaining buildings adapted for domestic and farm use. Beside a stream, the tall arched **gatehouse** is particularly well preserved, as are the monks' **dormitory**, the low-roofed **chapter house** and part of the **cloisters**. Highlight of the site is the superb fifteenth- and sixteenth-century **refectory**, its lofty wagon roof carved with angels. There are also remains of an earlier, thirteenth-century refectory, paved with delicate polychrome **tiles** showing heraldic shields, foliage and combat scenes. Staff are on hand to answer questions, and open-air plays are occasionally staged here in summer.

FOSSICKING

In geological terms, the coast around **Kilve Beach** and **Watchet** is where sedimentary beds of the Jurassic period merge with those of the Upper Triassic, and has proved a fertile spot for "**fossicking**" (the word is probably Cornish in origin). Daniel Defoe, journalist and author of *Robinson Crusoe*, spent time on the fossil trail at Watchet in 1724, and countless others have followed in his footsteps. If you're interested in doing the same, be aware that the crumbly cliffs on this coast pose a threat, and hard hats are recommended. The best time is after a high tide or a stormy sea. See ⓦ www.kilve.ukfossils.co.uk, and enquire about occasional guided excursions at Watchet's tourist office.

ARRIVAL AND DEPARTURE

By train Trains of the West Somerset Railway (see page 222) stop at Williton, Watchet, Washford and Blue Anchor on their run between Bishops Lydeard and Minehead (late March to Oct plus some winter dates; ⓦwest-somerset-railway.co.uk). Watchet's station is on Harbour Rd, 5min from the seafront.

WATCHET AND AROUND

By bus Buses pull in outside Watchet's WSR station on Harbour Rd. For Bridgwater change at Taunton.

Destinations Minehead (Mon–Sat every 30min, Sun 7 daily; 25min); Taunton (Mon–Sat every 30min, Sun 7 daily; 50min); Washford (Mon–Sat every 30min, Sun 7 daily; 7min).

INFORMATION

Tourist office Part of the Boat Museum, Harbour Rd (April–Sept Mon & Wed–Sun 10am–4.30pm, daily during school hols; Oct–March Mon & Thurs–Sat 10am–3pm; ⓣ01984 632101, ⓦlovewatchet.co.uk).

ACCOMMODATION

Georgian House 28 Swain St, Watchet ⓣ01984 639279, ⓦgeorgian-house.info. Centrally positioned, a few minutes from the WSR station and the seafront, this handsome B&B offers comfortable accommodation including a huge four-poster room. It's quite cluttered, but with stylish touches in keeping with its Georgian heritage. **£70**

★ **Swain House** 48 Swain St, Watchet ⓣ01984 631038, ⓦswain-house.com. More than a cut above your average B&B hereabouts, this stylish and modern luxury pad has got the wow factor – from wall-size classical art to contemporary bathrooms with slipper baths and double showers. Rooms have real coffee and milk, and breakfast might include smoothies and American pancakes. Light suppers (£12) and picnic baskets can also be arranged. **£135**

Warren Bay Holiday Village On the B3191 ⓣ01984 631460, ⓦ warrenbayholidayvillage.co.uk. A mile or so west of Watchet on the coast road, this campsite overlooking the sea is set in a large, sloping field (though some flat pitches can be found), with an indoor pool (very limited hours; £1) and access to a muddy, pebbly beach with rock pools. Watchet is a 25min walk along the coastal path, Blue Anchor Bay about twice that. Closed Nov–March. Pitches **£22**

White House Hotel 11 Long St (A39), Williton ⓣ01984 632306, ⓦwhitehousewilliton.co.uk. Within the imposing white Georgian exterior are chic, modern rooms, some (costing less) in an old stables block, with modern bathrooms. There's a guests' lounge bar and restaurant (£19.50 for two courses). Aga-cooked breakfasts include veggie options, and packed lunches and a luggage-transfer service are available. **£85**

Wyndham House 4 Sea View Terrace, Watchet ⓣ01984 631315, ⓦwyndhamhouse-bb.co.uk. Tucked away in a quiet spot between the WSR station and the seafront, this elegant Georgian B&B offers accommodation in two comfortable rooms (one with sea views) and an excellent breakfast. There's a sward of lawn behind the house, and the friendly hosts are helpful with local tips. **£95**

EATING AND DRINKING

★ **Pebbles Tavern** 24 Market St, Watchet ⓣ01984 634737, ⓦpebblestavern.co.uk. This is an essential stop for anyone with a hankering for real ciders and ales served straight from the cask, with tastings encouraged (a range of spirits is also available). It's tiny and gets crowded, not least on one of the regular music or poetry evenings. There's no kitchen, but the chilli pickled onions are worth sampling, and plates and cutlery are provided for takeaways from the chippie next door, or ask the bar staff to call the local deli to send over a snack. No credit cards. Mon, Tues & Thurs 11am–11pm, Wed 5–11pm, Fri & Sat 11am–midnight, Sun noon–11pm.

Star Inn Mill Lane, Watchet ⓣ01984 631367, ⓦstarinn watchet.co.uk. This is the best option in town for a hearty pub meal accompanied by a range of well-kept Exmoor and Butcombe ales. Pies, burgers, vegetable lasagne and Exmoor steaks go for £9–15. There's a log fire in winter and a beer garden. Pub daily noon–3pm & 6.30–11pm; kitchen noon–2.30pm & 6.30–9pm.

★ **Somerset Farmhouse** North St, Williton ⓣ01984 632450. Drop into this quality deli for everything you might need for a snack on the go. You'll find wholesome pies, pasties, meats, cheeses and olives in abundance. It's on the corner of the A39. Mon–Fri 7.30am–5pm, Sat 7.30am–4pm.

Minehead

West Somerset's chief resort, **MINEHEAD**, is a smaller, more relaxed and genteel version of Weston-super-Mare, though equally devoted to holiday-making. The presence here of one of the country's three remaining Butlin's holiday parks seems only natural, but

Minehead's traditional bucket-and-spade character is also flavoured by its proximity to Exmoor and the wild coastline extending west from here.

Minehead certainly doesn't have Weston's expanses of mud, and its wide, sandy beach even at low tide makes an attractive sight. Backing the beach is a jaunty promenade, which can become frantically busy in the holiday season. Away from the sea, the town preserves some residue of its Victorian character in the well-to-do area of **Higher Town** on the slopes of North Hill, holding some of the oldest houses and offering splendid views across the Bristol Channel. Steep lanes link the quarter with **Quay Town**, the harbour area at Minehead's western end, where a few fishing vessels still operate. Science fiction fans may be interested to know that the author Arthur C. Clarke hails from these parts, born at 13 Blenheim Gardens, off The Parade.

Though this traditional family resort has little in common with the windswept uplands of Exmoor, the moor is only a hop away, accessible from North Hill, and the town's good range of shops, services and accommodation makes it a useful base for excursions. Minehead is also a terminus for the West Somerset Railway (see page 222), with a station practically on the seafront. If you're here for the **South West Coast Path** (see page 242), head west to Quay Street, where huge sculptured hands holding a map stand on the seafront; opposite the sculpture, a path between cottages ascends North Hill onto the coast path.

7

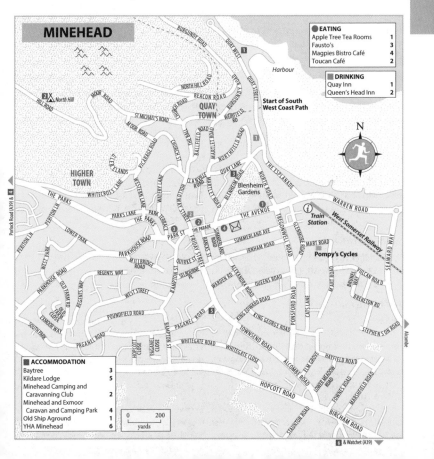

MINEHEAD

Harbour

Start of South
West Coast Path

North Hill

QUAY
TOWN

HIGHER
TOWN

Blenheim
Gardens

Train
Station

West Somerset Railway

Pompy's Cycles

N

0   200
     yards

7

The visitor centre housed within the *Beach Hotel* on the seafront incorporates a small **museum** (Tues–Sun 10am–4pm, daily during school hols; free), giving an overview of the town's history and showing regular exhibitions.

ARRIVAL AND DEPARTURE   MINEHEAD

By train Heritage trains of the West Somerset Railway (see page 222) connect Minehead with Bishops Lydeard in the Quantock Hills (late March to Oct; ⚉ west-somerset-railway.co.uk). The station is just off The Esplanade.

By bus Most bus stops are on or around The Parade, at the southern end of The Avenue.

Destinations Dunster (Mon–Sat every 30min, Sun 7 daily; 10min); Lynmouth (mid-July to early Sept 2 Mon–Fri; 1hr 5min); Porlock (Mon–Sat 7 daily; 15min); Taunton (Mon–Sat every 30min, Sun 7 daily; 1hr 10min); Watchet (Mon–Sat every 30min, Sun 7 daily; 25min).

GETTING AROUND

Bike rental Pompy's Cycles, Mart Rd ☎ 01643 704077, ⚉ pompyscycles.co.uk (£18 per day). Helmet and Exmoor route map included in price.

Taxis Rank outside the town hall on The Parade, or call Abi Cars ☎ 01643 709777 or Minehead Taxis ☎ 01643 704123 or 07919 892676.

INFORMATION

Tourist office *Beach Hotel*, The Avenue, on the seafront opposite the West Somerset Railway station (Easter–Oct Tues–Sat 10am–4pm, Sun 11am–4pm, daily during school hols; Nov–Easter Thurs–Sun noon–3pm; ☎ 01643 702624, ⚉ mineheadbay.co.uk).

ACCOMMODATION   MAP PAGE 241

★ **Baytree** 29 Blenheim Rd ☎ 01643 703374, ⚉ baytreebandbminehead.co.uk. This Victorian B&B facing public gardens near the centre of town offers three spacious rooms with private bathrooms, including a single. A good breakfast is served at a long communal table. Closed late Dec to mid-March. No under-10s. No credit cards. **£70**

Kildare Lodge Townsend Rd ☎ 01643 702009, ⚉ kildarelodge.com. This small hotel has more character than most in Minehead: a reconstructed faux-Tudor inn designed by a pupil of Edwin Lutyens and strongly influenced by him. It's got an impressive, high-ceilinged bar, a restaurant, a courtyard and garden. There are a few single rooms, but book early for a double, as there are only three (two with four-poster beds). **£70**

Old Ship Aground Quay St ☎ 01643 703516, ⚉ theoldshipaground.com. Rooms at this seafront inn close to the start of the coast path are modern and clean, and a couple have sideways views over the harbour. The more expensive ones are huge, but bathrooms are on the small side. There's a good range of beers and decent pub food to be had downstairs, and live music on Friday evenings and Sunday lunchtimes. **£88**

YHA Minehead Midway between Minehead and Dunster, signposted from the A39 at Alcombe ☎ 0345 371 9033, ✉ minehead@yha.org.uk. This well-run hostel is beautifully situated in a secluded combe on the edge of Exmoor. Most rooms have four beds, and there are family rooms as well as a kitchen, restaurant and a nice garden. There's a bell tent that's sometimes available too, kitted out with a double bed and sleeping up to five people – check on the website. Buses from Minehead, Dunster and Taunton stop a mile away at Alcombe. Dorms **£24**, doubles **£69**

CAMPING

★ **Minehead Camping and Caravanning Club** North Hill (go up Martlet Rd off Blenheim Rd) ☎ 01643 704138, ⊛ campingandcaravanningclub.co.uk. High above town

on the edge of Exmoor, this clean and well-equipped site is well placed for hiking excursions. Pitches are slightly sloping, but it's reasonably well sheltered, surrounded by trees with the occasional glimpse of Blue Anchor Bay and the town below. Two pre-erected safari tents sleeping up to six are also available, with self-catering facilities (£172 for three nights). A footpath leads through trees to town in 30min or less. Closed Oct to mid-April. Pitches **£21**

Minehead and Exmoor Caravan and Camping Park Porlock Rd (A39) ☎ 01643 703074, ⊛ minehead andexmoorcamping.co.uk. A mile or so west of town on the A39 (look out for the sign, on the right-hand side heading west, as it's tricky to see), this is a small but fully equipped site arranged in a series of "bays", or woody glades. There's some traffic noise from the adjacent main road, but it's quiet enough at night. Closed Nov–March. Per person **£10**

EATING AND DRINKING
MAP PAGE 241

Apple Tree Tea Rooms 29 The Avenue ☎ 01643 706090, ⊛ appleontheavenue.co.uk. Minehead's quainter side is shown at its uncloying best at this traditional venue for a snack lunch or afternoon tea that has all the right trimmings – armchairs, sofas, Beardsley prints and dozens of books – but with a touch of humour. As well as breakfasts, the menu has freshly made sandwiches, ploughman's lunches, and of course cream teas. There's a peaceful paved garden at the back too. No credit cards. Daily 10am–5pm.

Fausto's 16 Park St ☎ 01643 706372, ⊛ faustos.co.uk. With its low prices and friendly staff, there's usually a crowd at this rather cramped Italian restaurant adorned with Venetian masks and musical instruments. Pizzas, pastas and risottos (all around £10) are on the menu, as well as seafood and such dishes as *pollo e miele* (chicken with honey and mustard sauce, £17). Lunchtime prices are £2–3 cheaper. Service can be slow, however. Mon 6.30pm–late, Tues–Sat noon–3pm & 6.30pm–late.

Magpies Bistro Café 6 The Avenue ☎ 07731 851360. For a vegan or vegetarian snack, a great freshly ground coffee, or tea from a pot, drop into this relaxed café on the main street. Savoury dishes include soups, salads, quesadillas and black bean burgers (all £7–8). There's a children's menu, and the home-made scones are worth sampling, too. Mon–Fri 9am–4/5pm, Sat 9.30am–4pm; last orders 1hr before closing.

Quay Inn Quay St ☎ 01643 702839, ⊛ thequayinn

minehead.co.uk. On the seafront, this free house has a traditional bar serving cask ales, and a range of bar food. Baguettes and baked spuds are served at lunchtime, there are burgers, curries and steaks in the evening (around £10), and in fine weather you can take advantage of the large grassy garden. B&B is also available (£78). Bar Mon–Sat 11am–11pm, Sun noon–11pm; kitchen noon–1.45pm (Sun till 2.45pm) & 6–8.45pm.

Queen's Head Inn Holloway St ☎ 01643 702940, ⊛ queensheadminehead.co.uk. West Country ales are dispensed at the bar of this large central tavern, which also has darts, skittles and pool. There's the usual selection of burgers, seafood and curries (£9–13), steaks (£13–17), as well as a menu of Thai dishes (around £9–12). You'll find a good-value lunchtime carvery on Wednesdays (£8) and Sundays (£11) that's popular and worth booking. Bar Mon–Tues & Sun 11am–11pm, Wed–Sat till midnight; kitchen Mon 6–9pm, Tues–Sat noon–2.30pm & 6–9pm, Sun noon–3pm.

★ **Toucan Café** 3 The Parade ☎ 01643 706101. In a mustard-coloured room above a natural food store, with mellow background music, you can tuck into great veggie food – including falafels, bean burgers, curries and quesadillas (all around £8) – or just a Fair Trade tea or organic coffee. Also offered are healthy smoothies and fruit juices with names like Kale Thrill and Broccoli Boost (£3). Mon–Sat 10.30am–4pm.

Exmoor

DUNSTER CASTLE AND VILLAGE

Exmoor

A high, bare plateau sliced by wooded combes and splashing streams, Exmoor boasts tracts of wilderness every bit as forbidding as the South West's other national park, Dartmoor, but is smaller, with greater expanses of farmland breaking up the bare moorland. Its long seaboard, from which mists and rainstorms can descend with alarming speed, adds to its distinctive character, affording compelling views over the Bristol Channel. Most of the park is privately owned, but there's an extensive network of footpaths and bridleways, and you can walk at will in countryside held by the National Trust and in designated access areas.

Apart from around the moor's famed beauty spots, you'll generally find complete isolation here – with the exception of the occasional group of hikers, photographers, and hunting and shooting folk who often descend at weekends. The low population density has also attracted stargazers; in 2011 the national park became Europe's first International Dark Sky Reserve, and there are regular talks, films and organized events connected with viewing the galaxy and beyond. Back on the ground, drivers should beware of sheep and ponies straying over Exmoor's roads, including the relatively fast coastal A39; after dark, you may even come across sheep lying down on the tarmac.

Inland Exmoor lacks any major road running through it, though you'll almost certainly make use of the B3223, B3224 and B3358, traversing the moor in an east–west direction and providing access to some of the best walking country. Basing yourself at **Dulverton**, on the moor's southern edge and site of the park's main information office, or at **Exford**, at the centre of the moor, you'll be well placed for some of the choicest areas, including such celebrated beauty spots as **Tarr Steps** and the moor's highest point of **Dunkery Beacon**. The hamlets of **Winsford** and **Simonsbath** are smaller, less frequented starting points for excursions.

The **Exmoor coast**, which includes the tallest sea cliffs in England and Wales, is more easily accessible for visitors, with the A39 running parallel to the sea to link the pretty small towns and villages nestled between the steep bluffs. Consequently, you'll find more tourist activity here, not least around the well-preserved medieval village of **Dunster** with its impressive castle, on the northeastern edge of the moor. Nearby **Minehead** marks one end of the **South West Coast Path**, which offers the best way to get acquainted with Exmoor's seaboard.

Working west along the coast, a string of coastal villages, including **Porlock**, **Lynmouth**, **Lynton** and **Oare**, makes up part of what's known as "**Doone Country**", an indeterminate area that includes some of Exmoor's wildest tracts, and which is now inextricably tied to R.D. Blackmore's tale, *Lorna Doone*. Following its publication in 1869, this romantic melodrama based on local outlaw clans in the seventeenth century quickly established itself in Exmoor's mythology, and is still frequently recalled today, despite the fact that the book is not as widely read as it once was.

Exmoor is heaven for **outdoors** enthusiasts (for an overview of some of the options, see page 256). Be aware, however, that weather conditions are famously fickle on the moor, and you should prepare for all eventualities. Note too that winter, especially, is the time when you'll run into the **organized hunts** for which this part of the country is well known – despite the current statutory restrictions on hunting with dogs (the law is due to be reviewed at time of writing).

8

WATERSMEET

Highlights

① Riding on the moor Discover the moor on horseback for a memorable and exhilarating experience. Stables are plentiful, catering to all ability levels. See pages 250, 268 and 271

② Exford This tranquil village deep in the national park makes a great base for moorland excursions, not least the ascent of Dunkery Beacon, Exmoor's highest point. See page 254

③ Dunster Castle Looming above Dunster's tapering main street, this romantic castle is filled with sixteenth- and seventeenth-century furnishings and works of art. See page 258

④ Coast walking The hogback cliffs at Exmoor's northern edge can be tough going, but the ever-changing views more than compensate. See page 264

⑤ Valley of Rocks West of Lynton, this area is overlooked by crags and inhabited by feral goats – a wild spot for a wander. See page 264

⑥ Watersmeet Two rivers merge at this renowned beauty spot, from where paths radiate in every direction. See page 269

HIGHLIGHTS ARE MARKED ON THE MAP ON PAGE 248

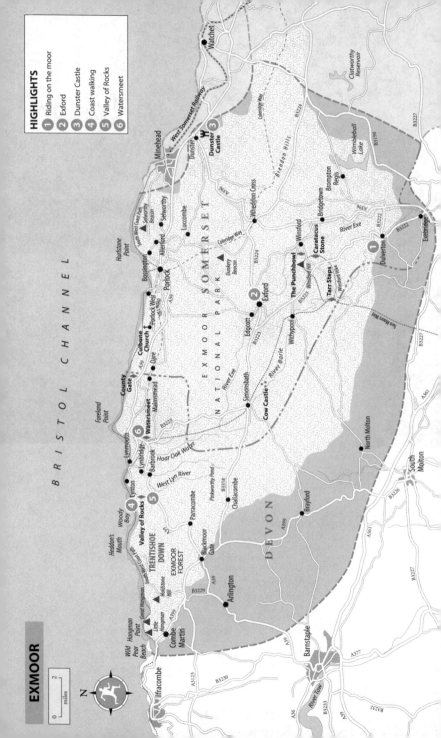

EXMOOR

N

0 ——— 2
miles

B R I S T O L   C H A N N E L

Watchet

West Somerset Railway

Minehead

Dunster

Dunster Castle 3

Wheddon Cross

Brendon Hills

Clatworthy Reservoir

Wimbleball Lake

Hurlstone Point

Selworthy Beacon

Selworthy

Luccombe

Allerford

Bossington

Porlock

Porlock Weir

Culbone Church

Oare

County Gate

Watersmeet 6

Malmsmead

Brendon

Lynmouth

Lynton

Lynbridge

Valley of Rocks 5

Woody Bay

Heddon's Mouth

Foreland Point

Hoar Oak Water

West Lyn River

Pinkworthy Pond

Parracombe

Challacombe

Trentishoe Down

Exmoor Forest

Blackmoor Gate

Holdstone Down

Hangman Point

Wild Pear Beach

Great Hangman

Little Hangman

Combe Martin

Ilfracombe

Arlington

Brayford

North Molton

South Molton

Barnstaple

River Taw

E X M O O R   S O M E R S E T

N A T I O N A L   P A R K

Dunkery Beacon

Coleridge Way

Winsford

Caratacus Stone

The Punchbowl

Winsford Hill

Withypool

Tarr Steps

Exford 2

Edgcott

Simonsbath

Cow Castle

River Exe

River Barle

Brompton Regis

Bridgetown

River Exe

Dulverton

Riding on the moor 1

Exebridge

Two Moors Way

D E V O N

Coast walking 4

INFORMATION

VISITOR CENTRES

Dulverton National Park Visitor Centre at 7–9 Fore St (April–Oct daily 10am–1.15pm & 1.45–5pm; Nov–March Mon–Wed, Fri & Sat 10am–2pm; ☎ 01398 323841, ⓦ exmoor-nationalpark.gov.uk) provides information on the whole moor. Other visitor centres are at Dunster (see page 260) and Lynmouth (see page 268).

USEFUL WEBSITES

ⓦ **atwest.org.uk** The Atwest accessible transport scheme operates two of the main bus services, #10, between Minehead and Porlock Weir, and #198 between Minehead and Dulverton.

ⓦ **everythingexmoor.org.uk** Wide-ranging, community-based directory and encyclopedia on all things

Exmoor, from adders to wild swimming – though not always up to date.

ⓦ **exmoor-accommodation.co.uk** Efficient directory of all types of accommodation, including campsites and self-catering.

ⓦ **exmoor-nationalpark.gov.uk** Official national park website – comprehensive and reliable.

ⓦ **visit-exmoor.co.uk** Official tourist website, useful for all aspects of Exmoor. The Active Exmoor pages are a useful resource for activities, from coasteering and mountain-biking to fly-fishing.

ⓦ **whatsonexmoor.com** Not so much a guide to events as a compendium of information on the moor, including accommodation, activities, transport, places to visit, disabled access, books to read and weather forecasts, with plenty of links.

GETTING AROUND

Apart from the steam and diesel trains of the **West Somerset Railway**, public transport around Exmoor is limited to a sketchy **bus** network. You can flag down a bus anywhere in the national park, providing it can safely stop. If you're planning to use bus services on Exmoor, it's worth checking routes beforehand, as services can be withdrawn or changed, depending on annual local transport budgets. Consider buying a money-saving **Travel Anywhere pass**, valid for travel on services operated by Buses of Somerset for one or seven days, available from bus drivers (see page 25). Traveline South West (ⓦ travelinesw.com) has full **schedules** for the whole region.

BY TRAIN

The nearest main-line stations for Exmoor are Taunton and Tiverton. Barnstaple, on a branch line from Exeter, could be a useful access point for access to the western part of the region, and there's also the West Somerset Railway (see page 222), a heritage line operating from late March to October between Bishops Lydeard (near Taunton) and Minehead, with a stop near Dunster.

BY BUS

Connections between Exmoor's coastal centres are fairly regular, but services to small inland villages are sporadic at best. Some lines run in the summer only; all services are greatly reduced in the winter months, and few buses run on

Sundays at any time. From Taunton train station, bus #28 goes to Dunster, and #25 goes to Dulverton; from Tiverton station, bus #398 links with Dulverton; from Barnstaple, buses #309 and #310 go to Lynton and Lynmouth.

The main bus companies operating in these parts are Quantock Heritage (☎ 01984 624906, ⓦ quantockheritage.com), Filer's (☎ 01271 863819, ⓦ www.filers.co.uk), Ridlers (☎ 01398 323398, ⓦ ridlers.co.uk), Atwest (☎ 01643 709701, ⓦ atwest.org.uk) and Dartline Coaches (☎ 01392 872900, ⓦ dartline-coaches.co.uk).

Bus #10 (Ridlers and Atwest) runs along the coast between Minehead, Selworthy, Allerford, Porlock and Porlock Weir throughout the year (not Sun).

Bus #28 (Buses of Somerset) runs daily between Minehead and Dunster, continuing on to Watchet, Bishops Lydeard and Taunton.

Bus #198 (Somerset County Council/Atwest) runs between Minehead, Dunster, Wheddon Cross, Exford, Winsford and Dulverton throughout the year (not Sun).

Bus #300 (Quantock Heritage), featuring heritage buses, runs along the coast between Minehead and Lynmouth, with stops at Selworthy, Allerford and Porlock, operating weekdays only in summer (mid-July to early Sept).

Buses #309 and #310 (Filer's) connect Lynton and Lynmouth with Barnstaple (not Sun).

Bus #398 (Dartline Coaches) links Dulverton, Exebridge and Tiverton throughout the year (not Sun).

8

Inland Exmoor

Watered by 325 miles of river, the upland plateau of inland Exmoor reveals a rich spectrum of colour and an amazing diversity of wildlife. The cheapest and best way to appreciate the grandeur of the moor is on foot, and endless permutations of **walking routes** are possible along a network of some six hundred miles of public footpaths and bridleways. **Pony trekking** is another option for getting the most out of Exmoor's desolate beauty, and stables are dotted throughout the area. **Kayaking** and **mountain biking** are also increasingly popular pursuits. Whichever of these you are pursuing, bear in mind the restrictions in place; special permission should certainly be sought before doing anything like camping or fishing.

There are four obvious bases for excursions: **Dulverton**, in the southeast and connected by good bus services to Taunton, Tiverton and Minehead, makes a good starting point for visiting the seventeen-span medieval bridge at Tarr Steps, about five miles to the northwest; you could also reach the spot from **Winsford** via a circular walk that takes in the prehistoric Wambarrows on the summit of Winsford Hill, and the ancient Caratacus Stone; on the B3224, **Exford** makes a useful base for the heart of the moor; and further west, **Simonsbath** is an excellent starting point for hikes in the Barle valley, despite holding only a couple of hotels. Dulverton and Exford have most of inland Exmoor's accommodation – and it's not uncommon for all of this to be filled by the various walkers, hunters, shooters and anglers who frequent these parts.

Dulverton

On the banks of the River Barle on Exmoor's southern edge, **DULVERTON** is one of the main gateways to the moor, and, as home to the National Park Authority's headquarters, makes a useful port of call before further explorations. The village is grouped around Fore Street and High Street, which run parallel from the river towards the hilltop parish church, and has an appealingly lively but low-key air. Fore Street has most of the shops and pubs, plus the post office, a bank with an ATM and the Exmoor Visitor Centre.

Guildhall Heritage and Arts Centre

Fore St • Easter–Oct Mon–Fri 10.30am–4.30pm, Sat 10.30am–1pm • Free • ☎ 07969 243887, ⓦ dulvertonheritagecentre.org.uk

Behind the visitor centre, and accessible from it, the **Guildhall Heritage and Arts Centre** has an absorbing museum of the village, including a reconstructed Victorian kitchen in "Granny Baker's Cottage", a room devoted to red deer on the moor, lots of knick-knacks relating to Dulverton's former station, which closed in the 1960s, and an archive room holding tapes of oral history and an extensive photographic collection which is displayed in a slideshow. There's also an exhibition space focusing on subjects of local interest such as the novel *Lorna Doone*.

ARRIVAL AND DEPARTURE   DULVERTON

By bus Buses run to and from: Dunster (Mon–Sat 2–3 daily; 45min–1hr); Exford (Mon–Sat 2 daily; 35min); Minehead (Mon–Sat 2–3 daily; 55min–1hr 10min); Taunton (Mon– Sat 5–6 daily; 1hr 30min); and Winsford (Mon–Sat 1–2 daily; 15min).

INFORMATION AND ACTIVITIES

Exmoor Visitor Centre Shares premises with the public library at 7 Fore St (daily: April–Oct daily 10am–1.15pm & 1.45–5pm; Nov–March Mon–Wed, Fri & Sat 10am–2pm; ☎ 01398 323841, ⓦ exmoor-nationalpark.gov.uk). The centre has information on the whole moor and a small exhibition on life on Exmoor with a film showing aspects of moor management.

Horseriding Moorland horseriding is offered year-round at West Anstey Farm (☎ 01398 341354), a couple of miles west of Dulverton.

ACCOMMODATION

★ **Exe Valley Caravan Site** Bridgetown ☎ 01643 851432, ⓦ exevalleycamping.co.uk. This clean and spacious adults-only site sits by the Exe, some 5 miles north of Dulverton on the A396. It's a peaceful, sheltered and picturesque spot, with a mill stream running to one side; pitches are a generous size, wi-fi is free and the *Badgers Holt* pub is just a 2min walk away. Closed mid-Oct to mid-March. Pitches **£22**

Lion Hotel Bank Square ☎ 01398 324437, ⓦ lionhotel dulverton.com. This family-run inn should suit anyone hankering for beams and four-posters, though it's a bit run-down in places. Rooms 9 and 11 have a nice prospect over the street, and there are several single rooms and a family room too. Two-night minimum stay at weekends. **£88**

Northcombe Farm A mile north of Dulverton, past the Rock House Inn ☏ 01398 323602, ⓦ northcombe campingbarns.co.uk. There are two camping barns here with cooking facilities, hot showers and bed mats (but no bedding), available for individuals Sun–Thurs, and for groups at weekends. Logs for the woodburner and electricity cost extra. Dorms **£10**

★ **Tongdam** 26 High St ☏ 01398 323397, ⓦ tongdam

thai.co.uk. Above a well-regarded Thai restaurant (see below), you'll find excellent accommodation: two doubles with shared bathroom, and a suite with a separate sitting room and balcony. The modern rooms are tastefully decorated with Far Eastern elements. Breakfast kicks off with a refreshing fruit salad. **£60**

★ **Town Mills** High St ☏ 01398 323124, ⓦ townmills dulverton.co.uk. A burbling stream runs through the garden of this elegant Georgian millhouse at the bottom of the High Street. The good-size, pine-furnished bedrooms include a suite with access to the pretty garden, and all are spotlessly clean. No under-10s. **£105**

EATING AND DRINKING

Bridge Inn 20 Bridge St ☏ 01398 324130, ⓦ thebridge inndulverton.com. This busy pub at the bottom of the village has a friendly atmosphere, a great selection of ales and bottled beers from around the world, and a garden. The food is excellent, with a sensibly priced menu ranging from light bites (£5–8) and baguettes (around £8) to "grazing plates" (£11–15), burgers (£11) and Pieminister pies (£9.50), including veggie and vegan choices. Daily noon–11pm, reduced hours in winter; kitchen noon–2.30pm & 6–9pm.

Mortimer's 13 High St ☏ 01398 323850. This classic Exmoor tea room serves hot and cold snacks, including a range of rarebits made with ham, mushrooms and blue cheese (around £7), and "moo burgers" (£9). There are traditional cream teas, of course, with home-made scones and cakes and a choice of leafy infusions, and there's a courtyard garden. Thurs–Tues 9.30am–5.15pm, daily during summer school hols.

Tongdam 26 High St ☏ 01398 323397, ⓦ tongdamthai. co.uk. Take a break from English country cooking at this Thai outpost, where dishes such as *massaman gae* (braised

marinated lamb with sweet potatoes and shallots, topped with cashews) and stir-fried prawns go for around £16, while vegetable mains are about £12. Mediterranean dishes are included on the menu at lunchtime, or pick the £11.50 Thai set menu. In warm weather eat alfresco on the small patio. There's a takeaway service too. Mon, Wed, Thurs & Sun 6–10.30pm, Fri & Sat noon–3pm & 6–10.30pm.

★ **Woods** 4 Bank Square ☏ 01398 324007, ⓦ woods dulverton.co.uk. With exposed stone walls, wooden furniture and floor, and a scattering of antlers, boots and riding whips, this gastropub has a smart-rustic feel. The menu features a mix of traditional English and French-influenced dishes, such as pan-fried fillet of stone bass, slow-roast shoulder of guinea fowl and wild mushroom linguine (mostly £14–17 in the evening, £11–14 at lunch), using local ingredients. There's a great selection of wines and the bar dispenses real ales. There are a few tables in the small garden too. Daily noon–3pm & 6pm–late; kitchen Mon–Sat noon–3pm & 6–9.30pm, Sun noon–2pm & 7–9.30pm.

Tarr Steps and around

Nestling in the deeply wooded Barle valley seven miles northwest of Dulverton, the **Tarr Steps** clapper bridge is one of Exmoor's most popular beauty spots. Many prefer to walk here (from Dulverton Bridge, simply follow the riverside track upstream); by road it's a left turn from Dulverton's Fore Street, and another left five miles along the B3223. If you're driving, leave your vehicle in the car park and walk the final 500yds downhill, or else you can follow a tributary of the Barle to the bridge signposted from the car park.

The ancient **woodland** around Tarr Steps largely consists of sessile oak – formerly coppiced for tan bark and charcoal production – and a sprinkling of beech, but you'll also see a mix of downy birch, ash, hazel, wych elm and field maple, often with a thick covering of lichen. The hazel coppice forms an important habitat for dormice, and you may spot red deer on the riverbanks. Birds breeding hereabouts include redstart, wood warbler and pied flycatcher, and you'll probably catch sight of dippers, grey wagtails and kingfishers. There's a choice of **walks** to embark upon, either onto Winsford Hill (see page 253); upstream of the river as far as Withypool (4 miles); or downstream along the Exe Valley Way (above the river for the first section) to Dulverton. The visitor centre at Dulverton sells itineraries for waymarked circular walks taking in Tarr Steps.

A WALK FROM TARR STEPS

Tarr Steps makes a great destination on foot from Dulverton or Winsford, and you can extend the trip by combining it with this exhilarating five-mile circular walk, which takes in Winsford Hill, near Winsford. It's not excessively challenging, and you should be able to complete the circuit in around four hours.

Follow the riverside path upstream from Tarr Steps, turning right about half a mile along Watery Lane, a rocky track that deteriorates into a muddy lane near Knaplock Farm. Stay on the track for three-quarters of a mile until you reach a cattle grid, on open moorland. Turn left here, cross a small stream and climb up **Winsford Hill** for the 360-degree moorland views and the group of Bronze Age burial mounds. If you want a refreshment stop, descend the hill on the other side to the village of Winsford (see below).

A quarter of a mile due east of the Barrows, via any of the broad grassy tracks, the ground drops sharply by over 190ft to the **Punchbowl**, a bracken-grown depression resembling an amphitheatre. Keep on the east side of the unfenced B3223 which runs up Winsford Hill, following it south for a mile to the Spire Cross junction, where you should look out for the nearby **Caratacus Stone** (see page 253), partly hidden among the gorse. Continue south on the east side of the road, cross it after about a mile, and pass over the cattle grid on the Tarr Steps road, from where a footpath takes you west another one-and-a-half miles back to the river crossing.

The bridge

Positioned next to a ford, the ancient **bridge** is said to be the finest of its type in Britain, constructed of huge gritstone slabs that are fixed onto piers by their own weight – which can be as much as two tons. Over 180ft long with seventeen spans, it's normally about 3ft above water level – much lower than when originally built due to the river silting up. Floodwaters now frequently cover the bridge, often causing damage – all but one of the slabs were washed away on the night of the 1952 Lynmouth deluge (see page 267). When this happens, however, the stones seldom travel far, and they are now numbered for easy repair; they're also protected by upstream cables that help to arrest flood debris charging down.

The bridge's age has been much disputed, with some claiming prehistoric origins, apparently backed up by the Bronze Age tracks found converging on the crossing, and its name, derived from the Celtic *tochar* meaning causeway. But there's no proof of a previous construction to this one, the earliest record of which is from Tudor times. Most now agree that, like the clapper bridges on Dartmoor, it is likely to be medieval. According to legend, however, the bridge was made by the devil as a place to sunbathe. The Prince of Darkness vowed to destroy any creature attempting to cross, and when a parson was sent to confront him he was met by a stream of profanities. The abuse was returned in good measure, however, whereupon the devil was so impressed he allowed free use of the bridge.

ACCOMMODATION AND EATING   TARR STEPS AND AROUND

Tarr Farm Inn ☎01643 851507, ⓦtarrfarm.co.uk. Above the Steps, this much restored sixteenth-century tearoom, pub and restaurant provides an excellent spot to contemplate the river, and also serves light lunches and cream teas, as well as evening meals (mains £15–24), for which you should book. The burgers are recommended. There's a garden, and upmarket accommodation is available in modern, fully equipped rooms. Daily 11am–11pm; kitchen noon–3pm & 6.30–9pm (winter noon–2.30pm & 7–9pm). **£160**

Winsford

Five miles north of Dulverton, and signposted a mile west of the A396, **WINSFORD** lays good claim to being the moor's prettiest village. A scattering of thatched cottages ranged around a sleepy green, Winsford is watered by a confluence of streams and rivers – one of them the Exe – giving it no fewer than seven bridges. Dominated, as it has been for centuries, by the rambling, thatched *Royal Oak Inn*, the village was the childhood home of the great trade union leader and Labour politician Ernest Bevin (1881–1951).

Winsford Hill

Once you've admired the village's obvious charms, the best plan is to abandon them in favour of the surrounding countryside. The obvious walking excursion from the village is the climb up **Winsford Hill**, a heather moor cut through by the B3223 that's reached on foot by taking the Tarr Steps road past the *Royal Oak*; turn off onto the moorland where it turns sharp left after about three-quarters of a mile. About the same distance further west, the hill's round 1400ft summit is invisible until you are almost there, but once you're at the top, your efforts are repaid by views as far as Dartmoor, and you can clamber around three Bronze Age burial mounds known as the **Wambarrows**.

The Caratacus Stone

A mile southeast of the summit, near the turning for Tarr Steps, the B3223 runs close to the **Caratacus Stone**, an inscribed monolith thought to date from between 450 and 650 and referred to in medieval documents as the Longstone. It is not immediately easy to spot among the vegetation, though you'll probably pick out the roof of the comic "bus shelter" canopy built over it in 1906. The damaged inscription on the greyish-green monolith, four feet high, reads "Carataci Nepos" – that is, "kinsman of Caratacus", the last great Celtic chieftain who was defeated by the Romans in 46 AD. It's an easy walk from here to Tarr Steps (see page 252).

ARRIVAL AND DEPARTURE WINSFORD | 8

By bus Buses run to and from: Dulverton (Mon–Sat 3 daily; 25min); Dunster (Mon–Sat 2–3 daily; 45min); Exford (Mon–Sat 2–3 daily; 15min); and Minehead (Mon–Sat 2–3 daily; 50min).

ACCOMMODATION AND EATING

Halse Farm Campsite A mile southwest of the village, reached from Halse Lane ☎01643 851259, ⓦhalsefarm.co.uk. Not very well sheltered and with fairly basic but clean facilities, this smallish site is located on the edge of the moor, convenient for walkers. Pitches are level and the owners, who run a livestock farm, are friendly. There's a laundry, a children's play area and free wi-fi. Closed Nov to mid-March. Pitches **£15**

Royal Oak Village centre ☎01643 851455, ⓦroyaloak exmoor.co.uk. This picturesquely thatched and rambling old inn offers Exmoor ales, snacks and full restaurant meals, for which advance booking is recommended (mains £15–18). Rooms are generally large and comfortable, and include four-posters. Daily noon–3pm & 6–11pm; kitchen noon–2pm & 6–9pm (till 8pm in winter). **£100**

EXMOOR WILDLIFE

The establishment of the national park has done much to protect Exmoor's diverse **wildlife**, from dormice and fritillary butterflies to otters and buzzards. The management of the coastal heath that makes up most of the terrain has allowed certain species of bird to thrive, while the gorse covering large parts of it has especially favoured the diminutive blue Dartford warbler and the orange-breasted stonechat. Most celebrated of the moor's mammals, though, are **Exmoor ponies**, a unique species closely related to prehistoric horses. Most commonly found in the treeless heartland of the moor around Exmoor Forest, Winsford Hill or Withypool Common, these short and stocky animals are not difficult to spot, though fewer than twelve hundred are registered, and of these only about 170 are living free on the moor. You probably won't get close to them, but if you do, don't try to feed them, and bear in mind that their teeth are sharp enough to tear up the tough moorland plants. Much more elusive is the **red deer**, England's largest native wild animal, of which Exmoor supports the country's only wild population. Over the centuries, hunting has accounted for a drastic depletion in numbers, but red deer have a strong recovery rate – some 2,500–3000 are thought to inhabit the moor today, and their annual culling by stalking as well as hunting is a regular point of issue among conservationists and nature-lovers.

8

HUNTING ON EXMOOR

For many, outdoor sports on Exmoor means hunting and shooting, practices which have been at the heart of local communities for centuries. Shooting mainly takes place between September and January, but **hunting** can go on all year – though mostly in winter – and plays a large part in the lives of many of Exmoor's inhabitants. Socially, too, the institution is central, since most hunts have full calendars of events. The voice of local hunt supporters is loud and clear: the **Countryside Alliance** (ⓦcountryside-alliance.org) pro-hunting lobby has strong support and "Fight Prejudice" stickers are evident everywhere,

In contrast, the true number of local **opponents** to the hunt will never be known – few want to risk taking a stand in Exmoor's close-knit communities. Alongside the cruelty argument, the two reasons most often cited for opposing hunting are the damage caused to farmland and gardens by dogs and horses, and the chaos created by the hunt followers – many of them city-folk – whose cross-country manoeuvrings can block up roads and show scant regard for either countryside or property. The National Trust's ban on stag-hunting on its land has added more fuel to the debate, since it has virtually ended the practice in many places.

What cannot be denied is the heavy dependence of Exmoor's economy – more than most other hunting areas in Britain – on the sport, not least in such villages as Exford, home to the kennels and stables of the Devon and Somerset Staghounds. If you're looking for a quiet time in these parts, you're best off keeping your views on the matter to yourself, since feelings run high.

You can find out about meets of the Devon and Somerset Staghounds in the local press or at ⓦdevonandsomersetstaghounds.net, alongside news of the hunt's puppy and horse shows, point-to-point races and other summer events. For the case against hunting, see the **League Against Cruel Sports**' website ⓦleague.org.uk.

Exford

At an ancient crossing point on the River Exe, **EXFORD**, four miles northwest of Winsford, preserves an insular air, its sedate cottages ranged around a tidy village green. A part of the Royal Forest of Exmoor from Saxon times until the early thirteenth century, the village prospered as a junction for packhorse trains carrying wool and cloth. During the nineteenth century, it grew as a **sporting centre**, and today, as the base of the Devon and Somerset Staghounds, local life is intimately involved with the **hunt**, particularly during the long season, which lasts from early August to late April.

Dunkery Beacon

Exford is a popular starting point for the hike to **Dunkery Beacon**, Exmoor's highest point at 1704ft. A four-mile hike to the northeast, the route is clearly marked along a track that starts from Combe Lane (off the green). The bridleway here eventually becomes a rough track, which winds slowly round to the summit of the hill – a steady uphill trudge. A substantial cairn sits at the top, from where a majestic vista unfolds, with lonely moorland all about and South Wales often visible across the Severn Estuary; there's also easy access by car, with a road passing close to the summit.

ARRIVAL AND DEPARTURE   EXFORD

By bus Buses run to and from: Dulverton (Mon–Sat 2–3 daily; 25–40min); Dunster (Mon–Sat 2–3 daily; 30min); Minehead (Mon–Sat 2–3 daily; 40min); and Winsford (Mon–Sat 2 daily; 15min).

ACCOMMODATION

Crown Hotel ☎01643 831554, ⓦcrownhotelexmoor.co.uk. With hunting pictures and a log fire in the lounge, this elegantly old-fashioned, rather upper-crust inn is at the heart of local sporty life. The quiet rooms are decorated in a plush country style and some have views over the green – view first, and try negotiating for the best rate. **£130**

Exmoor Lodge Chapel St ☎01643 831694, ⓦexmoor-lodge.co.uk. Small, plain and friendly B&B backing onto the village green, with most rooms en suite, a guest lounge, wi-fi and plenty of local information on hand. The garden overlooking the green serves teas in summer, and packed lunches can be prepared for walkers. Free transfers are offered to those on the Two Moors Way. **£80**

Westermill Farm Edgcott ☎01643 831238, ⓦexmoor

camping.co.uk. Located 2.5 miles northwest of Exford and at the centre of Exmoor's Dark Sky Reserve, this tranquil campsite has grass pitches on the banks of the Exe. There's wi-fi, free hot showers, waymarked walks over the five-hundred-acre farm and a small, seasonal shop selling local meat. Six self-catering chalets are also available. Per person **£8**

White Horse Inn ☎01643 831229, ⒲exmoor-white horse.co.uk. Large, impressively timbered and creeper-covered coaching inn right by the bridge, less exclusive than the *Crown* (see above) but similarly traditional in style, and with the huntin' and shootin' crowd equally in evidence (the local hunt's stables are right next door). Some rooms are on the small side, and some have four-posters. **£200**

YHA Exford ☎01643 831229, ⒲yha.org.uk or ⒲exfordhostel.co.uk. Exmoor's main hostel continues to be affiliated to the YHA but is now run by the *White Horse Inn* (see above) which has undertaken a general refurbishment of this gabled Victorian house on the banks of the Exe. Most rooms have four to six beds, and there's a two-bunkbed room with shared facilities, en-suite family rooms and facilities for campers (Feb–Nov; £12) are also available, along with a bell-tent (June–Oct; £95). There's a kitchen and restaurant – breakfast at the *White Horse Inn* across the road is £10. Dorms **£23**, doubles **£54**

EATING AND DRINKING

Crown Hotel ☎01643 831554, ⒲crownhotelexmoor. co.uk. You can choose between baguettes and snacks at lunchtime or menus that include beef and ale pie (£16) grills (£17–27) and classic local favourites such as roast loin of venison and braised lamb (£12–22) are offered. It's also a pleasant spot for afternoon tea, and the bar serves Exmoor ales which you can drink in the garden. Mon–Thurs 3–11pm, Fri–Sun noon–11pm; kitchen Mon–Thurs 6.30–9.15pm, Fri–Sun noon–2.15pm & 6.30–9.15pm; reduced hours in winter.

White Horse Inn ☎01643 831229, ⒲exmoor-white horse.co.uk. Basic bar meals popular with walkers, hunters and hostellers are offered here, with baguettes and sandwiches at £6–9, and a ploughman's costing £9–12. Alternatively, choose the ever-popular venison pie (£13) or a dish of locally-caught trout (£16). The carvery (£12) available on Wednesday evenings and all day Sunday is worth booking for. They also serve afternoon teas and some 150 malt whiskies, and there are tables outside by the river. Daily 11am–11pm; kitchen 8–9.30am, noon–2.30pm & 6–9pm.

8

Exmoor Forest and Simonsbath

At the centre of the national park, **Exmoor Forest** is the barest part of the moor, scarcely populated except by roaming sheep and a few red deer – the word "forest" denotes simply that it was formerly a hunting reserve. It's also one of the moor's wettest and boggiest zones – walkers should carry waterproofs whatever the weather, and take note of local weather reports.

In the middle of the area, and just over five miles west of Exford on the B3223, the village of **SIMONSBATH** (pronounced "Simmonsbath") consists of little more than a couple of hotels, a pottery and a sawmill at a crossroads between Lynton, Barnstaple and Minehead on the River Barle. The village was home to Midlands ironmaster John Knight, who purchased the forest in 1818 and, by introducing tenant farmers, building roads and importing sheep, brought systematic agriculture to an area that had never before produced any income. The Knight family also built a wall around their land – parts of which can still be seen – as well as the intriguing dam at Pinkworthy (pronounced "Pinkery") Pond, part of a scheme to harness the headwaters of the River Barle, though its exact function has never been explained.

Many of the estate's agricultural and management operations were based at **Simonsbath Sawmill**, below *Simonsbath House*, which has been restored and can be visited on one of the open days, usually taking place on the third Monday of the month (10am–4pm; free, but donations welcomed; ☎01643 831202, ⒲simonsbathsawmill.org.uk). The Victorian mill also generated power locally by means of a water turbine, which you may see in operation when there is sufficient flow in the River Barle.

Located on the Two Moors Way (see page 265), Simonsbath makes a useful first or last overnight stop for those on the trail. It's also a useful hub for hikers: **paths** radiate across epic moorland, for which park visitor centres can supply walking itineraries. An easy, waymarked route starts from opposite the *Exmoor Forest Inn* (see page 256) and leads through Birchcleave Wood, running more or less parallel to the Barle for a

8

EXMOOR ACTIVITIES

Outdoors enthusiasts, adventure-seekers and wildlife-spotters will find a range of organized activities available on Exmoor. **Walking** is the most popular pastime: you can pick up good, simple route cards of "Golden Walks" (£1), "Archaeology Walks" (£1) and footpath maps (£2–4) from visitor centres, while the National Park Authority has a wide programme of **guided walks** aimed at all abilities, graded according to distance, speed and duration, and either free or costing £3–5 per person depending on the length of the walk, and sometimes as much as £25 per person with refreshments provided. For more details contact any of the Exmoor visitor centres or see the *Exmoor Visitor* free newspaper or ⓦ exmoor-nationalpark.gov.uk.

The moor also provides exhilarating terrain for **riding** – again, park visitor centres can supply a full list of riding centres, and we've listed some of the best in this chapter.

Despite some serious-looking hills, there are also excellent **cycling** possibilities: see ⓦ visit-exmoor.co.uk/active-exmoor for details of the sixty-mile on-road **Exmoor Cycle Route**. Biketrail Cycle Hire, based at Fremington, near Barnstaple (☎ 01271 372586 or ☎ 07788 133738, ⓦ biketrail.co.uk), and Exmoor Adventures at Porlock (☎ 07976 208279, ⓦ exmooradventures. co.uk) rent out bikes and provide a delivery and collection service, plus luggage transfer and free route maps.

For those keen to focus on the moor's animal life, an appealing alternative is to join one of the local **Land Rover tours** to view Exmoor ponies, red deer and other wildlife. The main operators are: Exmoor Wildlife Safaris (☎ 07977 571494, ⓦ exmoorwildlifesafaris.co.uk), which leave from Dulverton, Exford and Dunster; Red Stag Safari (☎ 01643 841831, ⓦ redstagsafari. co.uk), leaving daily from various departure points; and Discovery Safaris based in Porlock (☎ 01643 863444, ⓦ discoverysafaris.com), leaving from the village hall car park off the High Street (or any other prearranged spot). Excursions generally last 2.5–4 hours and cost £25–50 per person.

Walkers and other outdoor enthusiasts may want to make use of one of the **luggage transport** services, such as Luggage Transfers (☎ 01326 567247, ⓦ luggagetransfers.co.uk).

couple of miles to **Cow Castle**, site of an Iron Age hillfort, and four miles further to Withypool. In the opposite direction, you can follow the River Barle upstream from Simonsbath for about four miles to the dark, still waters of **Pinkworthy Pond** – keep a lookout for red deer drinking here in summer. If you don't want to walk all the way, the B3358 passes within a couple of miles of the lake.

ACCOMMODATION
EXMOOR FOREST AND SIMONSBATH

Exmoor Forest Inn ☎ 01643 831341, ⓦ exmoorforest inn.co.uk. This down-to-earth, family-run inn has plain but clean, comfortable and good-sized rooms with decent bathrooms. It's worth paying a bit more for superior rooms – 3, 8 and 9 are airy and large, with excellent moorland views. There's a self-catering cottage and a garden for camping (but no camping facilities). The bar and restaurant are popular with locals (see below). **£84**

★ **Simonsbath House** ☎ 01643 831259, ⓦ simons bathhouse.co.uk. Former home of the Knight family and now a cosy, upmarket bolt hole offering plush, spacious rooms with glorious views, crackling log fires in the reception rooms, a sociable bar and a good restaurant (see below). Four self-catering cottages are also available, three of them in a converted 300-year-old barn. **£120**

EATING AND DRINKING

Black Venus Challacombe (5 miles west of Simonsbath) ☎ 01598 763251, ⓦ blackvenusinn.co.uk. In a sixteenth-century building, this traditional pub with pool, darts and a garden has two or three changing cask ales on tap and a range of excellent food – from ciabattas and ploughman's lunches to hot dishes costing £10–15. Daily noon–2.30pm & 5.30–11pm, closes 10.30pm Sun, open all day during school hols; kitchen until 9pm.

Exmoor Forest Inn ☎ 01643 831341, ⓦ exmoorforest

inn.co.uk. With its log fire and functional furnishings, the bar serving Exmoor ales and snacks is the hub of this scattered community, while the restaurant offers jacket potatoes and ploughman's lunches (£7–9), as well as local classics such as steak and ale pie, hunter's chicken and beef-burgers (all £12–13). Daily 11am–11pm, Nov–Feb Tues–Sun 11am–2.30pm & 6–10.30pm; kitchen noon–2.30/3pm & 6–8pm.

Poltimore Arms Yarde Down, 2 miles southwest of

Simonsbath off the Brayford road ☎01598 740338, ⒲poltimorearms.co.uk. This classic country pub has excellent beers, while steaks, pies, chips cooked in duck's fat and a renowned fish pie are served in a dining area with views over fields. It's on a tiny lane, and not easy to find. Daily 11am–11pm; kitchen noon–2pm & 6–9pm.

Simonsbath House ☎01643 831259, ⒲simonsbath house.co.uk. Treat yourself to a quality dinner in a romantic, refined setting at this restaurant, where set-price three-course dinners cost £24.50, and three courses a la carte will set you back £25–35. The menu is local, seasonal and imaginative, and might include rack of lamb, turbot and venison, followed by some fabulous puddings. Booking essential. Food served 6.30–8.30pm.

The Exmoor coast

The thirty-odd miles between Minehead and Combe Martin form England's highest section of **coastline**, with cliffs rising to 1043ft. With gentle upper slopes, the hogbacked hills still make for some fairly strenuous hiking if you're following the **South West Coast Path**, and long stretches of woodland add variety to an already diverse landscape. The narrow, stony strips of beach here don't compare with those in other parts of the West Country, but the **sea** is still the central attraction, with an ever-changing shoreline and constant views across the Bristol Channel to the Welsh coast. Tracking the coast, the A39 frequently affords sublime sea views, especially between Porlock and Lynmouth.

Though a couple of miles inland, **Dunster**, a typically genteel and quaint Somerset village crowned by a flamboyant castle, is an unmissable stop for anyone travelling along the coast and makes a more appealing place to stay than Minehead, three miles northwest (see page 240). Travelling west on the A39, Selworthy and Allerford score highly on the charm scale, and the latter has a diverting museum of rural life. **Porlock** has a stronger flavour of Exmoor and also makes a great base for excursions to places such as **Culbone Church**, deeply hidden in the woods west of the village, and around the so-called Doone Country south of Oare and Malmsmead. West of Foreland Point, there are more terrific walks to be enjoyed from **Lynton** and **Lynmouth** – sibling villages which occupy a niche in the cliff wall with woodland and moorland on all sides. Two of the easiest excursions present Exmoor's most contrasting faces: west to the dramatic **Valley of Rocks** and inland to **Watersmeet**, where two of the moor's rivers merge. Nine miles west, **Combe Martin** marks the edge of the moor and the end of one of the toughest sections of the coastal walk.

8

Dunster

On the northeastern edge of the moor, **DUNSTER** has a very separate identity from most Exmoor settlements, closer to the classic medieval Somerset village with its broad main thoroughfare. The well-preserved High Street is dominated by the towers and turrets of **Dunster Castle**, the main attraction here, but there is plenty else to see in and around the village to justify a leisurely wander before or after a tour of the castle.

As an important cloth centre, Dunster reached its peak of wealth in the sixteenth century, and the octagonal **Yarn Market** in the High Street, dating from 1609, is the

VISITING DUNSTER ON THE WEST SOMERSET RAILWAY

Between April and October, passengers on the West Somerset Railway (see page 222) on Wednesdays and Saturdays can buy an inclusive train-plus-castle ticket for £32. The ticket is valid for the "Dunster Castle Express" mid-morning departure from Bishops Lydeard (check the exact time), arriving at Dunster station about seventy minutes later and departing from there about five hours after that, and includes a bus connection between the station and castle – alternatively, it's a twenty-minute level walk.

most evocative of a handful of relics of its wool-making heyday, with a conical roof supported by hefty oak rafters.

Sprouting out of the woods at the northern end of Dunster's High Street, the hilltop folly, **Conygar Tower**, dating from 1776, is worth the brief ascent from the Steep for the excellent views. There are also longer walks from here, for which you can get route maps from the tourist office: **Grabbist Hill**, a mile or so west from the village via a path that starts near the school opposite St George's, or eastwards for about a mile to the sandy and rocky **Dunster Beach** – not great for swimming but with a long foreshore that makes an attractive spot for a picnic.

Dunster Castle

Castle Daily: Jan to mid-Feb & early Nov to mid-Dec tours only; mid-Feb to early Nov daily 11am–5pm; late Dec daily except Wed 11am–4pm • **Grounds** Daily 10am–5pm or dusk • £12.20 including grounds and watermill (see below) • NT • ☎ 01643 821314, ⓦ nationaltrust.org.uk

The site of **Dunster Castle** was once a Saxon frontier post against the Celts and was rebuilt by the Normans, but almost nothing of these earlier constructions survived the thorough pasting the building received during the Civil War. Inherited by Lady Elizabeth Luttrell in 1376, the property remained in her family for six hundred years until the National Trust took over in the 1970s. It owes its present castellated appearance to a drastic remodelling it received around 1870, though this itself was little more than a veneer on what remains essentially a stately home, predominantly Jacobean within. Dating back to 1420 and flanked by a pair of squat towers that formed part of the Norman construction, the formidable battlemented **gatehouse** smacks of authenticity, while beyond here, the irregular design of the main building reflects the various changes it has undergone over the years.

The interior

The highlights of the interior are all seventeenth century: most obvious is the grand oak and elm **staircase**, magnificently carved with hunting scenes – a recurrent theme throughout the house. Alongside the stags' heads, numerous portraits of the Luttrells gaze across the rooms, including one showing the sixteenth-century John Luttrell wading Triton-like across the Firth of Forth. Much of the furniture and artwork dates from the sixteenth and seventeenth centuries, such as the odd "thrown" chairs of ash, pear wood and oak in the Inner Hall, and the rare **gilt-leather hangings** in the upstairs Gallery, which vividly depict the story of Antony and Cleopatra.

The gardens

Outside, it's well worth a stroll round the sheltered terraced **gardens**, where oranges and lemons have been growing since 1700 (including what is claimed to be Britain's oldest lemon tree), and there's a renowned collection of strawberry trees. Mimosas and palm trees contribute a subtropical ambience, and picturesque paths lead down to the River Avill.

St George's

Church St • Daily 9am–5pm • Free • ☎ 01643 821812

Originally a Norman priory church, **St George's** has a fine, bossed wagon roof and a magnificent rood screen (said to be the longest in the country) from about 1500 with its own miniature fan vaulting. Among the tombs of various Luttrells, look out for a group at the top of the south aisle which includes the alabaster floor slab inscribed to Elizabeth Luttrell, from 1493. The sloping chest here is thought to be unique, and was probably used by the Benedictine monks of the priory in the fifteenth century.

Behind St George's church, the sixteenth-century **Tithe Barn** has been renovated as a community centre. The **Priory Garden** next to it would make a pleasant spot for a

picnic, and opposite you can peek into the circular **dovecote** that may date back to the fourteenth century. Doves damaged farmers' crops, so monks were the only people allowed to keep these birds.

Dunster Water Mill

Mill Lane, off West St · Daily 10am–5pm or dusk · £12.20 including castle (see above) · NT · ☎ 01643 821759, ⓦ nationaltrust.org.uk

A few yards beyond St George's on West Street, turn down Mill Lane to reach the three-hundred-year-old **Dunster Water Mill**, still used commercially for milling the grain that goes into the stoneground wholemeal flour sold in the shop along with porridge oats and muesli. The mill usually operates on Wednesdays and Saturdays (not in winter). Once you've absorbed the mysteries of milling and viewed the small array of agricultural tools, there isn't a great deal else to see or do here, but the riverside café and garden make a good spot for refreshment.

A path along the Avill from the mill soon brings you to **Gallox Bridge**, a quaint packhorse bridge from the eighteenth century surrounded by woods.

ARRIVAL AND DEPARTURE

DUNSTER

By train and bus Although Dunster is a stop on the West Somerset Railway, its station is inconveniently located a mile north of the village, near Dunster Beach, though the Dunster Castle Express offers a bus connection during the summer (see page 257). Minehead is the nearest transport hub, connected to Dunster by buses #198 and #467 from the High St and (most frequently) #28 from Marsh St, the A39 (Mon–Sat 2–3 hourly, Sun 7 daily; 10min). Bus #28 has direct connections with Taunton (Mon–Sat every 30min, Sun 7 daily; 1hr 10min), while #198 and #467 also provide direct bus links with Exford (Mon–Sat 2–3 daily; 35min), Winsford (Mon–Sat 3 daily; 25min) and Dulverton (Mon–Sat 3–4 daily; 50min–1hr 10min).

INFORMATION

Exmoor Visitor Centre By the main car park at the top of Dunster Steep (Easter–Oct daily 10am–5pm; Nov to early Dec & mid-Feb to Easter Sat & Sun 10am–2pm; ☎ 01643 821835, ⓦ exmoor-nationalpark.gov.uk). Has information on Exmoor generally, including details of guided walks on the moor, and a leaflet for a self-guided walk around the village. The centre also houses a free exhibition focusing on the peculiarities of the moor, with hands-on activities and background on the local wool and timber industries, and conservation issues. To find the Centre, follow the High St round to the north. Information on Dunster is also available at ⓦ visitdunster.co.uk and ⓦ discoverdunster.info.

ACCOMMODATION

Exmoor House 12 West St ☎ 01643 821268, ⓦ exmoor housedunster.co.uk. This elegant Georgian B&B offers six airy, refreshingly untwee en-suite rooms in pastel colours. Those at the back overlook a pretty garden. Guests get their own front-door key, and there's a large lounge, wi-fi, fresh milk on the landing and snack suppers of ham, cheese and pickle with a fresh baguette. The choice of breakfasts stretches to smoked trout. Minimum two-night stay at weekends & June–Aug. **£78**

Luttrell Arms 25–31 High St ☎ 01643 821555, ⓦ luttrellarms.co.uk. Right by the Yarn Market, this traditional and atmospheric fifteenth-century inn has open fires and beamed rooms, five with four-posters and some with views towards the castle. Standard rooms are more ordinary and lack views. **£145**

★ **Old Priory** Priory Green ☎ 01643 821540, ⓦ theold priory-dunster.co.uk. Parts of this B&B behind St George's church date back to the twelfth century, otherwise it's mainly from 1660, when it was converted into a farmhouse. It's all immaculately preserved (there's no TV anywhere), including the gigantic fireplace in the guests' sitting room. The three bedrooms are all different; one has an arched roof and a four-poster. You'll find local and organic ingredients at breakfast, and the pretty garden has its own door to the next-door church garden. No credit cards. **£110**

Yarn Market Hotel 25–33 High St ☎ 01643 821425, ⓦ yarnmarkethotel.co.uk. Traditional, family-run hotel overlooking the Yarn Market, offering fairly bland but clean and comfortable rooms (some with four-posters). There's a restaurant, and a range of themed short breaks for guests, from walking and garden visits to murder weekends. The owners are full of information about local excursions. **£120**

EATING AND DRINKING

Cobblestones 24 High St ☎ 01643 821595, ⓦ cobblestones dunster.co.uk. Friendly and unpretentious little restaurant with a nice walled garden and a fairly basic menu including baguettes, beef and mushroom ale stew, and burgers, with the occasional exotic foray (vegetable tagine with couscous). Prices are relatively low for Dunster, with all mains costing under £10. Local brews such as Exmoor Rebel cider and Dunster Beach Ales are also served. Daily 11am–3pm.

Luttrell Arms 25–31 High St ☎01643 821555, ⓦluttrellarms.co.uk. Serving Otter and other West Country ales, the bar here once served guests of the local abbot and oozes medieval atmosphere, with black-framed windows and huge fireplaces. The bar menu includes sandwiches (£7–8; served until 5.30pm) and ploughman's lunches (£11; served until 5.30pm), as well as fishcakes, burgers (£12–14) and vegetarian choices. The more formal *Psalter's* restaurant features locally sourced English classics such as poached

fillet of turbot and pan-fried duck breast (£23/28 for two/ three courses), and Sunday roasts are £20/23 for two/three courses. Daily 11am–11pm; kitchen 11.30am–9.30pm.

Reeves 20 High St ☎01643 821414, ⓦreeves restaurantdunster.co.uk. Fine dining is available at this atmospheric bistro with a low beamed ceiling and smart wooden tables. The menu offers such starters as scallops and mussels from Devon and Cornwall (£10–15), and mains including pork tenderloin (£20) and roast rump of Exmoor lamb (£21). Raspberry and dark chocolate mousse bombe features among the outstanding desserts. You can sit in the garden in summer. Advance reservations essential. Tues–Sat 7–9pm, Sun noon–2pm.

Selworthy

The National Trust-owned village of **SELWORTHY**, five miles west of Dunster, is a sequestered nook of custard-coloured thatched cottages and a church with a notable barrel-vaulted ceiling. The limewashed cottages were originally built in the 1820s for retired workers of the local Holnicote Estate, which was taken over by the National Trust in 1944. Predictably it's all very syrupy and picturesque, and a bit too Hansel-and-Gretel to swallow whole, but there's genuine charm in the tidy dwellings with their immaculate gardens, and the views across to Dunkery Beacon are undeniably lovely.

Downhill from the church stands a fourteenth-century **tithe barn** (now holiday accommodation) and paths through to the enclosed village green. There are walking routes everywhere, including a signposted path leading through thick woods from the village green to **Selworthy Beacon** (1012ft); the Macmillan Way (see page 278) and Coleridge Way (see page 219) also pass through the estate.

All Saints church

Daily 9am–8pm • Free

Crowning the village, Selworthy's church of **All Saints** is unusual for Somerset in being limewashed a brilliant white, and its square battlemented tower has little in common with the elaborate church towers elsewhere in the county. Most of the building dates from the fifteenth century, with the large windows, slim pillars and airy interior of the late Perpendicular style. Apart from its striking barrel roofs over the nave and aisles, the church is full of interest. The graceful south, or Steynings, aisle is the most impressive section, its roof decorated with angels and bosses carved with symbols of the Passion. Dominating the west end of the nave, the classically inspired gallery was designed in 1750 to hold musicians but now holds a massive organ. The wooden structure projecting like a theatre box above the church's entrance was installed at the start of the nineteenth century as a balcony pew for the local Acland family, former lords of the manor. At the east end, behind the high altar, is a reredos (ornamental screen), fashioned from leather in 1900.

ARRIVAL AND DEPARTURE
SELWORTHY

By bus There's a stop on the #10 and #300 bus routes at the turn-off for Selworthy on the A39, from which it's a 10min walk to the village. Services operate to and from: Allerford (Mon–Sat 5–7 daily; 2min); Lynmouth (mid-July to early Sept Mon–Fri 2 daily; 1hr); and Porlock (Mon–Sat 5–7 daily; 5–10min).

EATING AND DRINKING

Periwinkle Tea Rooms Selworthy Green ☎01643 829111, ⓦperiwinkletearooms.co.uk. This National Trust tearoom ticks all the boxes, not least for its cream teas made with locally renowned scones (£5–6). There are also

sandwiches, toasties (both around £5) and Ploughman's Platters (£7), not to mention a great selection of cakes. Daily: April–Oct 10am–5pm; Nov–March 11am–4pm.

8

> ## A WALK AROUND ALLERFORD
>
> The much-photographed packhorse bridge at **Allerford** makes a starting point for a varied
> five-mile circuit. A path leads northwest through the Allerford Plantation and later emerges
> into the open before reaching **Hurlstone Point**. From there, the coast path climbs southeast
> onto the rolling moor, reaching its highest point at Selworthy Beacon (1010ft), with sweeping
> views across to Wales and far inland. From there, a choice of tracks leads down into a wooded
> combe and into the village of **Selworthy**, at the bottom of which a track leads west back
> down to Allerford.

Allerford and around

The centrepiece of the unspoiled village of **ALLERFORD**, just off the A39 a mile or so
west of Selworthy, is its pretty, cobbled packhorse bridge next to a ford across Aller
Brook. Old school buildings now hold a museum of local memorabilia. Following the
minor road through the village will bring you eventually to another picture-postcard
hamlet, **Bossington**, and beyond to **Bossington Beach**, a shingle beach backed by salt
marshes where you may spot egrets and peregrine falcons.

West Somerset Rural Life Museum

The Old School • Easter–Oct Tues–Fri 10.30am–4pm, Sat 11am–3pm, Sun 1.30–4.30pm • £2 • ☎ 01643 862529, ⓦ allerfordmuseum.org.uk

An absorbing collection of domestic and farming knick-knacks fills two former
schoolrooms in Allerford's **West Somerset Rural Life Museum**. Don't expect spectacular
displays – this focuses on the nitty-gritty of everyday life, from a crib from around
1850 to an array of typewriters and a wall of equestrian accessories. There's plenty
here for a nostalgic wallow, and some of it is genuinely intriguing, particularly those
objects that have no modern equivalent such as a foot-warmer for carriage passengers,
lawnshoes worn by horses and a knife-cleaning drum. Other items are more pedestrian:
displays of teapots, police truncheons and carpenter's tools. There's a fascinating
photo archive, and one of the rooms has been restored to its Victorian appearance as
a schoolroom. In the yard are reconstructions of a dairy and a cobbler's workshop,
complete with glassy-eyed dairy maid and cobbler.

ARRIVAL AND DEPARTURE   ALLERFORD

By bus Buses #10 and #300 stop at Allerford. Services run
to and from: Lynmouth (mid-July to early Sept 2 Mon–Fri;
55min); Porlock (Mon–Sat 5–7 daily; 5min); and Selworthy
(Mon–Sat 5–7 daily; 2min).

Porlock and around

The real enticement of **PORLOCK**, a mile or so west of Allerford, is its extraordinary
position in a deep hollow, cupped on three sides by Exmoor's hogbacked hills.
The thatch-and-cob houses and dripping charm of the village's long High Street,
with its succession of hotels, cafés, antique shops and stores selling outdoor gear,
have always attracted droves of tourists. Some are also drawn by the place's literary
links: according to Coleridge's own less than reliable testimony, it was a "person on
business from Porlock" who broke the opium trance in which he was composing
Kubla Khan, while the High Street's ancient *Ship Inn* prides itself on featuring
prominently in the Exmoor romance *Lorna Doone* and, in real life, having sheltered
the poet Robert Southey, who staggered in rain-soaked from a ramble on Exmoor,
and wrote a sonnet here ("Porlock, thy verdant vale so fair to sight..."). Aside from
its atmosphere and charm, the village has some specific attractions, spaced along its
winding High Street, in the form of its fifteenth-century church, St Dubricius, and
an engaging museum collection. The High Street itself, which forms part of the A39
coast road, is somewhat blighted by the continuous procession of vehicles crawling
along it.

Porlock also stands on the **Coleridge Way**, a 51-mile route that takes in a good stretch of the Quantock and Brendon Hills and Exmoor from Coleridge's former home in Nether Stowey to Lynmouth (see page 267). A leaflet describing the walk is available at the tourist office.

Dovery Manor Museum

Doverhay • May–Sept Mon–Fri 10am–5pm, Sat 10.30am–4.30pm • Free • ⓦ doverymanormuseum.org.uk

Porlock's main appeal is its atmosphere and charm, but it does have a specific attraction at the eastern end of the High Street in the form of the volunteer-run **Dovery Manor Museum**, housed in a fifteenth-century cottage. A couple of cramped rooms show traditional domestic and agricultural tools of Exmoor – including a mantrap – together with some material on the local wildlife and a few photos and portraits, though the most impressive items here are the building's beautiful mullioned window and huge fireplace on the ground floor.

Porlock Weir

Porlock gets very busy in high season, but you can escape the crush by heading two miles west along reclaimed marshland to the tiny harbour of **PORLOCK WEIR**, whose sleepy air gives little inkling of its former role as a hard-working port trading with Wales. With its thatched cottages and lovely stony foreshore, it's a peaceful, atmospheric spot, giving onto a bay that enjoys the mildest climate on Exmoor and which produces some of the country's cleanest **oysters** (available from October). A rambling old pub and a couple of restaurants (see page 265) share prime position, while in the car park a room attached to the public toilets houses the **Natural History Society Field Centre** (early May to Sept Wed & Thurs 2–5pm), with informative pictures and panels showing the local fauna and flora.

An easy two-mile stroll west from Porlock Weir along the South West Coast Path brings you to **Culbone Church** (always open), sheltered within woods once inhabited by charcoal burners and claimed to be England's smallest church.

8

Oare and Doone Country

West of Porlock, the A39 climbs over 1300ft in less than three miles – cyclists and drivers might prefer either of the gentler and more scenic **toll roads** to the direct uphill trawl, one from Porlock (a right turn off the A39, after the *Ship Inn*; cars £2.50, bikes £1), the other narrower and rougher going from Porlock Weir (cars £2, bikes free), both passing mainly through woods. Just before the Devon–Somerset border at **County Gate** (site of a café and car park), the hamlet of **OARE** shelters a minuscule church that's famous in the annals of Lorna Doone as being the scene of the heroine's marriage, and where she was shot. R.D. Blackmore's grandfather was rector here, and it's likely that the author derived much of the inspiration for his border tale from the local stories told to him on his visits. Accordingly, the surrounding area, particularly Badgworthy Water and the valleys of Lank Combe and Hoccombe Combe, identified as the heart of "**Doone Country**", is rich with echoes of Blackmore's fictional Doone Valley. If you want to explore further, head three-quarters of a mile west to the hamlet of **Malmsmead**, from where you can follow the Badgworthy Water river upstream; Porlock's tourist office can supply a detailed route.

ARRIVAL AND INFORMATION

PORLOCK AND AROUND

By bus Service #10 connects Porlock and Porlock Weir with Minehead (not Sun), and #300 runs Mon–Fri in summer between Porlock, Allerford, Selworthy, Lynmouth and Minehead.

Destinations Allerford (Mon–Sat 5–7 daily; 6min); Lynmouth (mid-July to early Sept Mon–Fri 2 daily; 50min); Minehead (Mon–Sat 5–9 daily; 15min); Porlock Weir (Mon–Sat 5–7 daily; 10min); Selworthy (Mon–Sat 5–9 daily; 6min).

Tourist office Helpful spot at West End, High St (April–Oct Mon–Sat 10am–3.30pm; Nov–March Mon–Sat 10am–12.30pm; ☏ 01643 863150, ⓦ porlock.co.uk). There's a free booking service.

WALKS FROM LYNTON AND LYNMOUTH

The major year-round attraction in these parts is **walking**, not only along the coast path but inland. Most trails are waymarked, and you can pick up walkers' maps of the routes from the tourist office or Park Visitor Centre. One of the most popular walks is about two miles eastward, either along the banks of the River Lyn or high up above the valley along the Two Moors Way to **Watersmeet** (see page 269), itself the starting place for myriad trails; from Lynmouth, the path starts from the Lyndale car park opposite *Shelley's Hotel*. An easy expedition takes you west out of Lynton along the North Walk, a mile-long path leading to the **Valley of Rocks**, a steeply curved heathland dominated by rugged rock formations. The poet Robert Southey summed up the raw splendour he found here when he described it as "the very bones and skeleton of the earth, rock reeling upon rock, stone piled upon stone, a huge terrific mass". At the far end of the valley, herds of wild goats range free as they have done here for centuries; a short climb up Hollerday Hill yields a terrific view over the whole area.

Lynmouth is the best starting point for coastal walks eastwards, including to the lighthouse at **Foreland Point**, a little over two miles away, via a fine, sheltered shingle beach at the foot of Countisbury Hill – one of a number of tiny coves that are easily accessible on either side of the estuary – while the route west towards Combe Martin (see page 270) traces some of Devon's most majestic and unspoiled coastline.

The deep, wooded **Heddon Valley**, halfway between Lynton and Combe Martin, is another focus for scenic walks. The coast path crosses the River Heddon a short way upstream of **Heddon's Mouth**, site of an old lime kiln and ringed by treacherous rocks. By road you can reach the spot from the *Hunter's Inn*, signposted off the A399 and offering good refreshments. Either direction along the coast path is amply rewarding for views. Eastwards it contours halfway up the coastal slopes to Woody Bay, where you can climb up and return on a parallel path that wiggles its way round a higher contour. Westwards you can head to Trentishoe Down and the summit of **Holdstone Hill** for a breezy all-round view.

ACCOMMODATION

Burrowhayes Farm West Luccombe, off the A39 1 mile southeast of Porlock ☎01643 862463, ⍵burrowhayes. co.uk. Next to Horner Water, this well-equipped rural campsite has pitches for tents and motorhomes, and static caravans to rent. There's a shop and a laundry, and escorted pony treks are available for all abilities (£25 for 1hr; not Sat). Closed Nov to mid-March. Pitches **£19**

The Gables Doverhay ☎01643 863432, ⍵thegables porlock.co.uk. Classically thatched seventeenth-century cottage near Porlock's museum, with four restful rooms, including a family suite, all with bathrooms, and there's a lawned garden with table and chairs. Abundant breakfasts include muesli, yoghurt and fruit, and packed lunches can be provided. Self-catering accommodation is also available. Closed Nov–Easter. **£70**

★ **Glen Lodge** Hawkcombe, up Parson's St from the High St ☎01643 863371, ⍵glenlodge.net. You'll find perfect seclusion plus comfort and character at this beautifully furnished Victorian country B&B a few minutes from Porlock's centre. There are distant sea views from the rooms and access to the moor right behind. Guests can use the hot tub in the garden, breakfasts include waffles, pancakes, muffins and home-made organic jams, and two self-catering flats are also available. **£100**

Locanda on the Weir Porlock Weir ☎01643 863300, ⍵locandaontheweir.co.uk. Run by a husband-and-wife team, this "restaurant with rooms" offers five spacious bedrooms furnished with eclectic art and antiques, most with magnificent sea views and one with a four-poster. Among breakfast choices are Bircher muesli and avocado on sourdough toast, and first-class dinners are available (see below). Closed Jan to mid-Feb. **£115**

Lorna Doone Hotel High St ☎01643 862404, ⍵lorna doonehotel.co.uk. Conspicuously sited on the main drag, this thoroughly Victorian lodging retains its period atmosphere and has friendly owners. Named after characters in the book *Lorna Doone* (R.D. Blackmore is said to have written sections of the novel in the building that previously occupied the site), rooms come in various sizes (some in converted stables) but all are clean, comfortable and en suite. There's a good restaurant, too (see below), breakfasts are plentiful and packed lunches can be ordered. **£70**

Sparkhayes Farm Sparkhayes Lane, signposted off High St near Lorna Doone Hotel ☎01643 862470 or 07721 045123, ⍵sparkhayes.co.uk. This small campsite is little more than a level field with basic facilities (including a laundry, fridge, kettle and microwave), but it's extremely tidy, handy for the village, and has seaward views and a friendly and helpful owner. Hook-ups £5. No caravans. Closed Jan. Per person **£9**

Sparkhayes Farmhouse Sparkhayes Lane ☎01643 862765. Handsome, centrally located seventeenth-century lodging offering two tastefully furnished rooms with en-suite facilities. There's a charming guests' sitting room with a log fire in winter, and breakfasts – which include fresh fruit – are taken around one large table. No credit cards. Closed early Nov to March. __£75__

EATING AND DRINKING

The Big Cheese High St ☎01643 862773, ⓦthebig cheeseporlock.co.uk. This deli near the church provides everything you need for a hearty picnic as well as excellent teas, coffees and cakes for a sit-down. Over fifty varieties of cheese (from cows, ewes, goats and buffalos) are stocked, with an emphasis on local producers, and you can also pick up jams, chutneys and local gins, beers and ciders (including Porlock-produced Ex-Press cider). The cream teas are fabulous, with fresh and fluffy scones. Mon, Tues & Thurs–Sat 9am–4.30pm, Wed 9am–3.30pm.

Bottom Ship Porlock Weir ☎01643 863288, ⓦshipinn porlockweir.co.uk. Crab sandwiches are a lunchtime favourite at this thatched and oak-beamed pub by the harbour at Porlock Weir, with outdoor tables and a range of other bar food at around £12 for hot dishes. Local and guest ales are served, and three guestrooms are also available (£75). Booking for meals is recommended in high season. Daily 8.30am–11.30pm (closes earlier in winter); kitchen noon–2.30pm & 6–8.30pm.

★ **Locanda on the Weir** Porlock Weir ☎01643 863300, ⓦlocandaontheweir.co.uk. With its Neapolitan owner-chef, this restaurant brings top-flight Mediterreanan cuisine to this sleepy backwater, offering Italian takes on such local dishes as roasted shoulder of Exmoor lamb (£26) as well as full-on Italian classics, for example *linguine alle due sicilie* (with tuna, olives, capers and mint; £20) and *baccalà alla livornese* (lightly salted cod; £24.50). Pizzas are also available. Mid-Feb to Dec Thurs–Sat 6.30–9pm

Lorna Doone Hotel High St ☎01643 862404, ⓦlornadoonehotel.co.uk. This hotel's restaurant is open to all and has a menu that lists such dishes as Cajun cod (£15) and "lamb three ways" (£18), and desserts such as a delicious raspberry and cream cheesecake. Late July to early Sept Mon–Sat 6–8.30pm; early Sept to late July Thurs–Sat 6–8.30pm.

Ship Inn High St ☎01643 862507, ⓦshipinnporlock. co.uk. Bar billiards, darts, skittles, a garden and occasional folk evenings are the main attractions of this old tavern, also known as the *Top Ship*. Exmoor and Cornish ales and Porlock's own Ex-Press cider are served, while the menu lists fairly standard pub grub available all day, including sandwiches (£5–7) and hot dishes such as lasagne and chicken schnitzel (around £12). A Sunday roast is £9 or £11, according to size. Accommodation is also available (£75). Daily 8.30am–midnight; kitchen noon–8.30pm (Fri & Sat till 9pm).

Whortleberry Tearoom High St ☎01643 862891, ⓦwhortleberry.co.uk. Cream teas are the speciality here, with whortleberry (bilberry) jam thickly spread on home-made scones and muffins (gluten-free also available). It makes a great breakfast venue, too, and for lunch you can order a "soup and sandwich combo" for £9, or a quiche (£8) or fish pie (£9). The courtyard garden is open in summer. Tues–Fri 10am–4.45pm, Sat 9am–4.45pm, Sun 9.30am–4.45pm; till 4pm and closed Sun in winter.

Lynton and Lynmouth

On the Devon side of the county line, eleven miles west along the coast from Porlock, the Victorian resort of **LYNTON** perches above a lofty gorge with dramatic views over the sea and its sister resort of **LYNMOUTH**, down at sea level. Encompassed by cliffs, both places were pretty isolated for most of their history, but struck lucky during the Napoleonic Wars when frustrated Grand Tourists unable to visit their usual continental haunts discovered here a domestic piece of Swiss landscape. Coleridge and Hazlitt trudged over to Lynton from the Quantocks, but the greatest spur to the area's popularity was the 1869 publication of *Lorna Doone*, which led to swarms of literary tourists in search of the book's famous settings. Most of the present-day visitors are

THE TWO MOORS WAY

Lynmouth is the start (or end) of the **Two Moors Way** (ⓦtwomoorsway.org) a 103-mile walking route which runs to Ivybridge in South Devon thereby linking Exmoor with Dartmoor, and also running along part of North Devon's Tarka Trail (the walking and cycling route that follows the travels of Tarka the Otter in the book of the same name). Leaflets and other publications on both routes are available at tourist offices. Lynmouth also marks one end of the Coleridge Way, winding east across Exmoor to the Quantock Hills (see page 219).

similarly attracted by the natural beauty of the place, while the existence of a number of walks radiating out from here onto Exmoor and along the coast is a major bonus.

Lynton

A prosperous Victorian-Edwardian air imbues **Lynton**, epitomized by the imposing faux-medieval **town hall** from 1900 on Lee Road. It was the gift of publisher George Newnes, who also funded the nearby **cliff railway**, and today holds the local tourist office.

Cliff railway

Daily: early Feb to March 10am–5pm; early April to mid-April, early May to late May & mid-Sept to late Oct 10am–6pm; mid-April to early May, early June to late July & early Sept to mid-Sept 10am–7pm; late Oct to early Nov 10am–4pm; school hols 10am–8pm • £4 return, or £5 valid all day • ☎ 01598 753486, Ⓦ cliffrailwaylynton.co.uk

Opened in 1890, the **cliff railway** is the most practical way of moving between Lynton and Lynmouth, some 500ft below. The ingenious hydraulic system consists of two carriages on separate rails, counterbalanced by water tanks which fill up at the top from a natural water supply (piped from the West Lyn River). As the bottom carriage empties its load (sometimes the weight of passengers at the top makes this unnecessary), the water-powered brakes are released and the top carriage descends. Requiring no external power source, it's fast, scenic, virtually noise-free and completely eco-friendly. An outdoor café at the top serves snacks and teas.

Lyn and Exmoor Museum

Market St • Easter–Oct Mon, Thurs & Sat 10.30am–1.30pm, Tues & Wed 10.30am–1.30pm & 2–5pm • £2

A short distance below Lee Road, opposite the school, one of Lynton's oldest houses – probably from the early eighteenth century – holds the **Lyn and Exmoor Museum**, a must for fans of small and quirky local collections. The whitewashed cottage is stuffed to the gills with a miscellany of relics from the locality, and has a reconstructed Exmoor kitchen from around 1800 on the ground floor. Upstairs you'll find displays

8

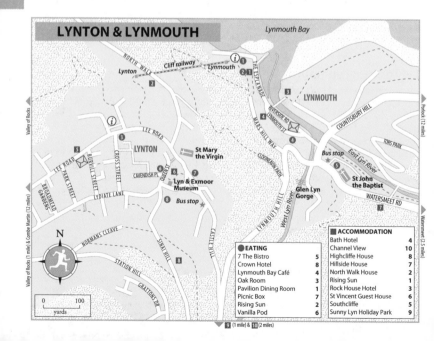

● EATING		■ ACCOMMODATION	
7 The Bistro	5	Bath Hotel	4
Crown Hotel	8	Channel View	10
Lynmouth Bay Café	4	Highcliffe House	8
Oak Room	3	Hillside House	7
Pavilion Dining Room	1	North Walk House	2
Picnic Box	7	Rising Sun	1
Rising Sun	2	Rock House Hotel	3
Vanilla Pod	6	St Vincent Guest House	6
		Southcliffe	5
		Sunny Lyn Holiday Park	9

9 (1 mile) & 10 (2 miles)

SHELLEY IN LYNMOUTH

In the summer of 1812, **Percy Bysshe Shelley**, aged 20, stopped in Lynmouth in the company of his 16-year-old bride Harriet Westbrook, Harriet's sister Eliza, and Dan Healy, their Irish servant. This, Shelley decided, would be the place to establish the commune of free-thinking radicals that he had long contemplated. Although this vision never materialized, Shelley used his nine-week stay – allegedly in what is now *Shelley's Hotel* – to work on his polemical poem *Queen Mab* and to compose his seditious manifesto, or *Declaration of Rights*, which declared, among other things, that "titles are tinsel, power a corrupter, glory a bubble, and excessive wealth a libel on its possessor". Copies of the *Declaration* were attached to balloons, inserted into bottles launched from Lynmouth's harbour and distributed in nearby Barnstaple (for which Healy was arrested and imprisoned). Now under observation, Shelley and his entourage took flight soon after, hiring a boatman to ferry them to Wales, where the poet continued to work on *Queen Mab*.

of history, geology and wildlife, including samples of local rocks, fossils and minerals, stuffed birds and small animals. Old paintings and prints illustrate the domestic and social life of former times, and agricultural tools recall how most locals made a living before the advent of tourism. There's also an illuminating section dedicated to the 1952 Lynmouth flood.

Lynmouth

Directly below Lynton, **Lynmouth** lies at the junction and estuary of the East and West Lyn rivers, in a spot described by Gainsborough as "the most delightful place for a landscape painter this country can boast". Shelley spent his honeymoon here (see box) – two different houses claim to have been the Shelleys' love nest – and R.D. Blackmore, author of *Lorna Doone*, stayed in **Mars Hill**, the oldest part of the town, whose creeper-covered cottages are framed by the cliffs behind the Esplanade.

Lynmouth's peace was shattered in August 1952 when nine inches of rain fell onto Exmoor in 24 hours and the village was almost washed away by **flood waters** raging down the valley. Huge landslips carried hundreds of trees into the rivers, all the bridges in the area were swept away, houses were demolished and 34 people lost their lives. Since the disaster, rumours have circulated regarding one possible cause of the inundation, in particular that secret tests were then being carried out by the Ministry of Defence in the Exmoor area, which involved sending pilots to "seed" clouds with dry ice to make them rain. The story has been denied by the MOD, but the suspicions remain.

Glen Lyn Gorge

Easter–Oct daily 10am–6pm; Nov–Easter call to check • £7 • ☎ 01598 753207, ⓦ www.theglenlyngorge.co.uk

Of numerous reminders of the 1952 flood around Lynmouth, the most vivid are the boulders and other rocky debris still strewn about the **Glen Lyn Gorge**, a steep wooded valley through which the destructive torrent took its course. Entered from the main road at the back of the village, the gorge has a deeply tranquil air, making it difficult to imagine the fury of that stormy night. The walks and waterfalls upstream make ideal picnic spots, and there are also displays on the uses and dangers of water power, including a small hydroelectric plant which provides electricity for the local community.

ARRIVAL AND DEPARTURE   LYNTON AND LYNMOUTH

LYNTON
By bus There are bus stops at Castle Hill car park and on Lee Rd, with services to and from Barnstaple (Mon–Sat 10–11 daily; 1hr).

LYNMOUTH
By bus The main bus stop is at Lyndale car park, with services to and from: Allerford (mid-July to early Sept Mon–Fri 2 daily; 55min); Barnstaple (Mon–Sat 4–5 daily;

1hr); Minehead (mid-July to early Sept Mon–Fri 2 daily; 1hr 5min); Porlock (mid-July to early Sept Mon–Fri 2 daily; 50min); and Selworthy (mid-July to early Sept Mon–Fri 2 daily; 55min).

INFORMATION AND ACTIVITIES

National Park Visitor Centre The Esplanade, Lynmouth (daily 10am–5pm; ☎01598 752509, ⓦ exmoor-national park.gov.uk). Three 10min films can be viewed here, focusing on the immediate area.

Tourist office Town Hall, Lee Rd, Lynton (late July to early Sept Mon–Sat 10am–4pm, Sun 10am–2pm; early Sept to late July Tues & Wed 10am–1pm, Thurs–Sat 10am–3pm; ☎01598 752225, ⓦ visitlyntonandlynmouth.com).

Horseriding and cycling A range of moorland rides for novices and experienced riders is offered by Exmoor Coast Holidays at Caffyns Farm, off the A39 2 miles southwest of Lynton, where camping and B&B accommodation are also offered (☎01598 753967, ⓦ exmoorcoastholidays.co.uk). A one-hour escorted ride costs £30, 3hr is £75, and anyone camping here gets a discount. Bikes for rent cost £7/2hr, or £14/day.

ACCOMMODATION   SEE MAP PAGE 266

LYNTON

Channel View Manor Farm, on the A39 east of Barbrook ☎01598 753349, ⓦ channel-view.co.uk. Useful campsite 2 miles south of Lynton (linked by a footpath through woods). A café serves all-day breakfasts and there's a shop, laundrette and wi-fi. Caravans available for weekly rent. Closed mid-Nov to mid-March. Pitches **£17**

★ **Highcliffe House** Sinai Lane ☎01598 752235, ⓦ highcliffehouse.co.uk. Perched on a steep hill above the village, this boutique B&B has terrific views over the valley and towards the sea. The dominant flavour is high Victorian, with sumptuous furnishings, high ceilings and heavy drapes, and the rooms are elegantly romantic. There's an honesty bar, and fresh juices, fruit and home-made granola are served at breakfast in the conservatory – again, with stunning views. Minimum two-night stay at weekends. No under-18s. **£130**

★ **North Walk House** North Walk ☎01598 753372, ⓦ northwalkhouse.co.uk. Top-quality B&B in a panoramic position overlooking the sea, and convenient for the coast path. The spacious, stylish rooms have rugs, wooden floors and sea views and there's a guests' lounge with an open fire in winter. Breakfasts around one large table are filling and delicious, and candlelit organic dinners are available for £33 per person. Discounts are given for stays of two or more nights. There are self-catering apartments, too. **£150**

St Vincent Guest House Castle Hill ☎01598 752720, ⓦ stvincentlynton.co.uk. This whitewashed, Georgian guest-house has elegantly furnished, light and airy rooms, all en suite. Breakfast includes free-range eggs, smoked salmon and vegetarian options, and the cosy lounge is full of books and games. **£85**

Southcliffe 34 Lee Rd ☎01598 753328, ⓦ southcliffe. co.uk. One of a row of guesthouses near the centre, this has clean and crisp rooms (each with a teddy bear), a lounge, on-site parking and helpful owners. It's worth paying a little extra for one of the two balcony rooms, slightly larger than the others. Breakfast is a lavish spread, including waffles, muffins and vegetarian options. **£80**

★ **Sunny Lyn Holiday Park** Lynbridge ☎01598 753384, ⓦ sunnylyn.co.uk. You can camp next to the West Lyn River at this tranquil spot halfway between Lynton and Barbrook off the B3234, but it's small so booking is essential. There's an on-site shop and café (closed in low season), a pub within walking distance and lodges that are available all year to rent. Internet access is via a pre-paid online portal. Camping closed Nov to mid-March. Pitches **£20**

LYNMOUTH

Bath Hotel The Harbour ☎01598 752238, ⓦ bathhotel lynmouth.co.uk. This central choice has oodles of old-fashioned character, quite grand in places but also rather dated (it's in process of a gradual refurb). Rooms come in four categories – some are small, and more expensive ones have great sea views. There's limited parking, but at £10 it's cheaper to use one of the public car parks. **£95**

Hillside House 22 Watersmeet Rd ☎01598 753836, ⓦ hillside-lynmouth.co.uk. This simple, spotless B&B is refreshingly free of the tweeness that affects many Lynmouth establishments. Most rooms are spacious, and all but one enjoy views over the East Lyn River. Packed lunches

---

HARBOUR BOAT TRIPS

Look out for boards at Lynmouth's harbour advertising **boat trips** with Exmoor Coast Boat Cruises (Feb–Oct; ☎01598 753207), or ask at Glen Lyn Gorge. Usually setting off at 11am or noon, depending on the tides, the 45-minute excursions go to Lee Bay and back (£10), while longer excursions (£20) go as far as Heddon's Mouth – both allowing you to view the abundant birdlife on the cliffs.

and a luggage transfer service are offered. Parking may be a problem. No under-15s. **£70**

Rising Sun Harbourside ☎ 01598 753223, ⓦ risingsun lynmouth.co.uk. Rooms in this fourteenth-century inn have all the requisite beams, oak panelling and sloping floors. It's touristy and expensive but steeped in atmosphere and with a superb location by the harbour. If you don't fancy relaxing in the bar there's a quiet guests' sitting room and a terraced garden. **£153**

Rock House Hotel Harbourside ☎ 01598 752251, ⓦ rockhouselynmouth.co.uk. Splendidly sited by the beach and river mouth, this has wonderful views from its smart but smallish rooms. The pub, restaurant and garden here are popular, so don't expect seclusion. **£99**

EATING AND DRINKING

SEE MAP PAGE 266

LYNTON

Crown Hotel Market St ☎ 01598 752253, ⓦ thecrown lynton.co.uk. Former coaching inn that's still at the heart of local life, good for a selection of St Austell ales or a very acceptable pint of Guinness. Bar snacks, stir-fries, pizzas and other diverse dishes (mostly £5–9) are served in the restaurant at the back, and there are a few tables on the front patio. You can play scrabble or other board games here and catch occasional live music – look out too for the murals by local artist Mick Cawston. Mon–Thurs 6–11pm, Fri–Sun 11.30am–11pm; kitchen summer Mon–Fri 12.30–3pm & 6pm–8.30pm, Sat noon–9.30pm, Sun noon–8pm, winter daily 4–9pm.

★ **Oak Room** 14 Lee Rd ☎ 01598 753838, ⓦ theoak roomlynton.co.uk. This Spanish-style restaurant opposite the town hall has small wooden tables and a sofa or two. Such tasty dishes as meatballs or pan-fried king prawns can be served as tapas (mostly £5–8) or as a main course (around £12 at lunchtime, £15 at dinner). The melon and chilli ice cream is worth sampling. Baguettes are also sold at lunchtime (£7–8), and the morning coffees and cream teas are good too. Mon & Thurs–Sun 10.30am–2.30pm (lunch noon–2pm), also March–Oct daily except Tues 6–9pm; closed Dec to mid-Feb.

Picnic Box 1 Castle Hill ☎ 01598 753721. This should be your first stop for superior picnic food, all fresh and locally produced. The sandwiches and baguettes are made to order, and there's a range of pasties, pies and quiches, as well as jams, Exmoor ice cream, smoothies and flagons of cider. Tues–Sat 8.30am–5pm, Sun 8.30am–4pm.

★ **Vanilla Pod** 10–12 Queens St ☎ 01598 753706, ⓦ thevanillapodlynton.co.uk. Wholesome and tasty meals with Mediterranean and Middle Eastern flavours are served at this friendly, modern eatery. The large choice of daily specials might include lamb tagine, Cornish mackerel, hake bake, pigeon breast, chicken and mushroom risotto, falafel, and pig cheeks – mostly £12–17. Vegan and gluten-free diets can be accommodated. Book. Daily 10am–4pm, also 6–9pm for bookings, mid-June to Sept daily 10am–10pm; reduced hours and closed Sun in winter.

LYNMOUTH

7 the Bistro 7 Watersmeet Rd ☎ 01598 752159, ⓦ 7thebistro.com. This small, traditional place has a good menu that takes in both fresh fish, including plaice and sea bass (£18), and meatier options, including pork medallions (£16) and steaks (from £18.50). Vegetarian dishes include mushroom stroganoff (£16). No under-10s. Tues–Sun 6.30–8.30pm (last orders); may close in winter.

Lynmouth Bay Café 18 Lynmouth St ☎ 01598 753337, ⓦ lynmouthbaycafe.co.uk. A perfect stop for a snack lunch or cream tea, with panini, pies, pasties, home-made soups, cupcakes and chocolate brownies on the menu. The decor is bright and modern, the service friendly, and prices are reasonable – the range of teas cost £4.50–6, pasties £5–6. It's on the small side, and can get busy, but there are tables in a small garden too. Packed lunches available. Daily except Fri 10.30am–4.30pm, winter till 3.30pm and closed Mon & Fri.

Pavilion Dining Room Lynmouth Pavilion, The Esplanade ☎ 01598 753484, ⓦ thepaviliondiningroom. co.uk. At various times, this building facing the sea has been a steamboat terminal, dancehall and theatre. It now holds the tourist office on the ground floor, and upstairs this sleek and airy café-restaurant which enjoys the best possible sea views. The food is fairly unadventurous, however, ranging from baguettes, toasties (around £7) and burgers (around £10) to seafood chowder (£8.50). Daily 10am–5pm.

Rising Sun Harbourside ☎ 01598 753223, ⓦ risingsun lynmouth.co.uk. Ancient and atmospheric inn with local ales and a great range of food. You can have sandwiches at lunchtime (a ploughman's is £12) or sample classic, expertly prepared and locally sourced English dishes: lamb, roast guinea fowl, duck breast and seafood are all available for £20–24, with a few vegetarian options (around £18). Eat in the bar rather than the more formal restaurant if there's a choice – it's the same menu. Daily 11am–midnight, kitchen noon–2.30pm & 6–9pm.

Watersmeet and around

The East Lyn River is joined by Hoar Oak Water 1.5 miles east and inland of Lynton and Lynmouth at **Watersmeet**, one of Exmoor's most celebrated beauty spots. To

---

WALKS AROUND WATERSMEET

Watersmeet is surrounded by signposted **paths**, many of which were established as donkey tracks when the local charcoal and tanning industries flourished in the nineteenth century. One short route from the bridge takes you south up Hoar Oak Water to **Hillsford Bridge**, the confluence of Hoar Oak and Farley Water, while the Fisherman's Path leads east along the East Lyn River, climbing and swooping through the woods above one of the river's most dramatic stretches. Another marked route strikes off from the Fisherman's Path after only a few hundred yards, zigzagging steeply uphill to meet the A39, about a mile north of Watersmeet and 100yds east of the *Sandpiper Inn*. Opposite the pub, a path leads a quarter-mile north to meet the coast path and gives access to **Butter Hill** which, at nearly 1000ft, affords stunning views of Lynton, Lynmouth and the North Devon coast. You can pick up pamphlets with full details about all the various routes at Watersmeet House.

---

see this thickly wooded location at its best, try to avoid visiting in peak season or at weekends. Even if you have the place to yourself, the tranquillity can be utterly transformed after a bout of rain, when the rivers become roaring torrents and the water that is usually crystal clear is stained brown with moorland peat. The walk from Lynmouth along the banks of the East Lyn takes around an hour. Drivers can leave vehicles at a car park off the A39, and follow the path down through oak woods to the two slender bridges where the rivers merge.

Watersmeet House

Tea-garden Daily: Mid-Feb to Sept 10.30am–5pm, Oct 10.30am–4pm • **Shop** Daily: March–Sept 11am–5pm • Free • NT • ☎ 01643 841831, ⓦ nationaltrust.org.uk

On the far side of the bridges, the only building in sight is **Watersmeet House**, a Victorian fishing lodge now owned by the National Trust, which operates a tearoom and shop in summer. You can view a small exhibition of photos of the 1952 Lynmouth floods in the back, and consume teas, salads and soups in the pleasant lawned garden.

Combe Martin

At the western edge of Exmoor's seaboard, **COMBE MARTIN** has little of the spirit of the moor but has some diversions that merit an hour or two of your time. Sheltered in a fertile valley, the village is famous for its prodigiously long and straggling main street, which follows the combe for about a mile down to the seafront, and holds the unusual *Pack o' Cards Inn* (see page 271), supposed to have been built by a gambler in the eighteenth century with his winnings from a card game. Originally possessing 52 windows (some were later boarded up), the building has four storeys – decreasing in size as they get higher – each with thirteen doors, and chimneys sprouting from every corner; it's now a pub.

Follow the High Street down to reach Combe Martin's **beach**, a good swimming spot which is sandy at low tide, with rock pools and secluded coves on either side. A spectacular stretch of coast extends east of Combe Martin, notably round Wild Pear Beach to Little Hangman and Hangman Point, part of the **Hangman Hills**. The waymarked path – a section of both the South West Coast Path and the Tarka Trail – is signposted off the north end of the car park behind the *Foc's'le Inn* (see page 271). It's a gruelling route, involving a two-mile uphill slog, with no refreshment stops on the way, to the great gorse-covered headland of **Great Hangman** – at 1043ft, the highest point on the South West Coast Path. The payback is the astonishing panorama, occasionally taking in glimpses of the Gower peninsula in Wales. From here you can retrace your steps back or complete a circle by veering inland round Girt Farm and west down Knap Down Lane to Combe Martin, the whole well-marked circuit adding up to about six miles.

Combe Martin Museum

Cross St • Late March to Oct Mon–Fri 10.30am–5pm, Sat & Sun 11am–3pm; Nov to late March Tues–Thurs 10.30am–3pm • £2.50 •
🕿 01271 889031, 🅦 combemartinmuseum.co.uk

Just behind the seafront, the **Combe Martin Museum** is more modern and child-friendly than most collections on Exmoor. Distributed on three floors is a diversity of items that illustrate the silver-mining that has taken place here since Roman times, as well as displays on lime-quarrying, agriculture, horticulture and maritime history. There are some nostalgic old photos of the local rabbit-catcher, and snaps of tourist charabancs and paddling holiday-makers from the 1920s and 1930s. Elsewhere you'll see items from the arcane (a "seed-fiddle" for scattering seeds) to the banal (fishing rods).

ARRIVAL AND DEPARTURE

COMBE MARTIN

By bus Bus #301 plies to and from Barnstaple (Mon–Sat 7 daily; 55min) and Ilfracombe (Mon–Sat 11 daily, Sun 2 daily; 20min). Stops are on the High St and near the seafront.

INFORMATION AND ACTIVITIES

Tourist office Housed within the museum on Cross St (late March to Oct Mon–Fri 10.30am–5pm, Sat & Sun 11am–3pm; Nov to late March Tues–Thurs 10.30am–3pm; 🕿 01271 889031, 🅦 visitcombemartin.co.uk).

Riding Dean Riding Stables, Dean, near Parracombe 🕿 01598 763565, 🅦 deanridingstables.co.uk. Instruction and escorted hacks (£30/hr) are provided at this riding centre 4 miles southeast of Combe Martin, with novices welcome. B&B and self-catering accommodation also available. No credit cards.

ACCOMMODATION, EATING AND DRINKING

Foc's'le Inn Off Cross St 🕿 01271 883354, 🅦 focsleinn.co.uk. Overlooking the beach, this is the top choice for a drink, with Devonian and Doom Bar ales on tap. It's also a good spot for snacks and hot meals, including ploughman's lunches and burgers (£8–15), which you can eat in the outdoors area adjacent to the beach. Seven clean and modern rooms are available, one of them a family suite. Daily noon–11pm, till 10pm in winter; kitchen noon–3pm & 6–9pm. **£75**

Harbour Deli Borough Rd, on the main road near the seafront 🕿 01271 883688. Drop in to this deli, with a bright interior and modern art on the walls, for huge breakfasts (£7), excellent baguettes made to order, plus quiches and home-baked bread, scones, cakes and pasties to eat in or take away, including gorgeous raspberry scones. It's the sort of place you could bring your gran. Mon–Sat 9am–5pm, Oct–Easter till 4pm.

Mellstock House Woodlands 🕿 01271 882592, 🅦 mellstockhouse.co.uk. Just a couple of minutes from the beach and coast path, and much favoured by walkers, this Edwardian guesthouse has lofty views from some of its rooms, an honesty bar and a garden with a veranda. A free pick-up service between Woolacombe and Lynmouth is offered to guests staying more than one night. **£88**

Pack o' Cards Inn 🕿 01271 882300, 🅦 packocards.co.uk. Despite its eccentric appearance, this pub and B&B has fairly conventional accommodation, including a family room and one with a four-poster – rooms at the back are quieter. A varied menu of bar meals is available, with mains at around £15; the Sunday carvery is £12. There's a large riverside garden and a skittle alley with a small exhibition of the history of the building. It's half a mile from the seafront. Mon–Sat 11.30am–11pm, Sun noon–10.30pm; kitchen Mon–Sat noon–3pm & 5.30–9pm, Sun noon–8pm. **£85**

8

East Somerset

STOURHEAD

9

East Somerset

The East Somerset region covers a disparate mix of historical themes and styles, from prehistoric burial sites to eighteenth- and nineteenth-century sophistication, and from ruined medieval castles to the whimsical trappings of the Italian Renaissance. What ties it all together is the hilly green landscape, whose deeply rural appearance belies its industrial past. Coal was discovered here in 1763, and the area was soon transformed by pitheads and "batches", or slagheaps. The coalmining centre was Radstock, in and around which some thirty pits were operating in 1900, though, due to the technical difficulties of coal extraction – the narrow seams and other local geological peculiarities – these had dwindled to fourteen in the 1930s, and the five remaining collieries in 1960 had been abandoned fifteen years later. Radstock's excellent mining museum tells the story and illustrates the reality of life underground.

Northeast of Radstock are a pair of sights evoking the area's remoter past: **Stoney Littleton**, one of the country's best-preserved Neolithic long barrows, and the ruins of fourteenth-century **Farleigh Hungerford Castle**. From the latter it's an easy walk to one of East Somerset's hidden surprises: **Iford Manor Gardens**, where an Italian Renaissance garden has been lovingly and convincingly created on a series of terraces.

The region is crossed by the **Fosse Way**, the Roman thoroughfare that traversed England from Lincoln to Exeter, running through the agricultural centre of **Shepton Mallet**, south of Radstock. Though Shepton's medieval layout can still be discerned, you'll find more historic character at **Frome**, which has recently become a thriving centre for arts and crafts, chic shopping and trendy hotels. The town lies at the hub of a handful of engaging sights, most notably **Stourhead** across the county boundary in Wiltshire, and the brasher stately home at **Longleat**, an unlikely hybrid of safari park and exquisitely furnished Elizabethan palace. Both feature first-rate landscaped parks – artificially improved versions of nature that became a favoured mode of display among the grandest landowners of the eighteenth century.

West of Frome, the unsung, pretty villages of **Nunney** and **Mells** strike a humbler note, the former holding a small but highly romantic ruined castle, the latter harbouring one of Somerset's loveliest churches. To the east of the region, one of Wiltshire's trademark white horses is carved into a hillside outside **Westbury**, also the site of an Iron Age hillfort.

GETTING AROUND

By train Frome and Westbury are served by trains on the London–Reading–Taunton line, and Westbury is also on the Bath–Salisbury line.

By bus There are good bus connections to Radstock, Shepton Mallet and Frome from Bath, but you'll normally have to change if you're arriving from Bristol. Almost all local services are operated by First (☎0345 602 0121, ⓦfirstgroup.com).

By bike or on foot You can take advantage of a couple of sections of the National Cycle Network: Route 24, of which the Colliers Way (see page 277) forms a part, connects the Kennet and Avon Canal at Dundas with Stoney Littleton, Radstock, Frome and Longleat, where it links with Route 25 going south to Stourhead. See ⓦsustrans.org.uk for further details. Two long-distance walking trails also pass through the region: the Macmillan Way (ⓦmacmillanway. org), connecting Bradford-on-Avon, Iford Manor, Farleigh Hungerford and Castle Cary, and the Mendip Way, from Weston-super-Mare through Cheddar, Wells, Shepton Mallet and Frome.

Highlights

❶ Stoney Littleton Long Barrow It takes some effort to reach, but the journey along narrow lanes and across fields is half the fun, and its remoteness from modern life is entirely appropriate for this site, one of the country's best-preserved Neolithic burial chambers. See page 277

❷ Farleigh Hungerford Castle Much of this classic old castle is in ruins, but there's enough here to evoke its glory days, and a well-presented museum fills out the picture. See page 277

❸ Iford Manor Gardens You don't need to be a gardening nut to be smitten by the charms of this patch of paradise on the Somerset–Wiltshire border. Inspired by Italy, the steep grounds

have been fashioned into terraces, rockeries and walks, all with vistas over the gorgeous countryside. See page 278

❹ Longleat There's a feast of rollicking entertainment to suit all tastes in the range of attractions here, as well as a taste of the savannah in the attached safari park, but beyond all this is one of the country's finest Elizabethan mansions. See page 286

❺ Stourhead Eighteenth-century landscape gardening reached its apogee in this meticulously planned park, whose studied harmonies are matched by the fine furnishings and art displayed inside the house. See page 288

HIGHLIGHTS ARE MARKED ON THE MAP ON PAGE 276

9

Radstock and around

The centre of the Somerset coalfield was at **RADSTOCK**, but long before the last pit closed in 1973 the place had lost much of its sense of identity beyond the label of "ex-mining town". The mining heritage of Radstock and the surrounding area is fully explored in its museum, though apart from this there's little else to detain you here. Even the shops are all in **MIDSOMER NORTON**, its more attractive sister village a mile and a half west (reachable via a riverside track), which also hosts a **farmers' market** on the first Saturday morning of every month (in Hollies Garden, off the High Street). The town lies within a short distance of a trio of more alluring, if rather remote, sights, for which you'll need your own transport or some stout walking shoes.

Radstock Museum

Waterloo Rd • Feb–Nov Tues–Fri & Sun 2–5pm, Sat 11am–5pm • £6 (valid 1yr) • ☎ 01761 437722, ⓦ radstockmuseum.co.uk

Housed in the town's Victorian market hall, **Radstock Museum** is East Somerset's major museum collection, mainly dedicated to the local **mining industry**. One of the highlights is the re-creation of a pit, showing the appalling conditions that miners had to endure, including dragging carts laden with rocks through passages that were too

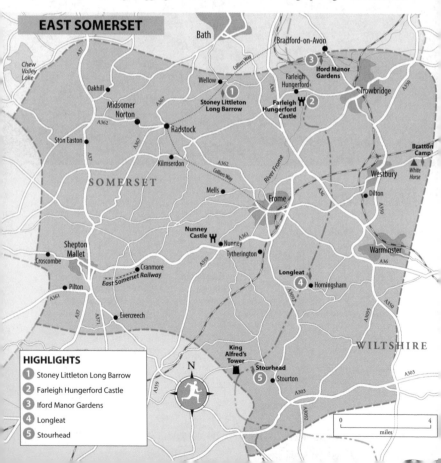

EAST SOMERSET

HIGHLIGHTS
1. Stoney Littleton Long Barrow
2. Farleigh Hungerford Castle
3. Iford Manor Gardens
4. Longleat
5. Stourhead

9

THE COLLIERS WAY

One of the most pleasurable ways to experience the rolling landscape of East Somerset is on foot or by bike along the **Colliers Way** (ⓦcolliersway.co.uk), part of Route 24 of the National Cycle Network. The route partly follows the disused Somerset and Dorset Railway, which itself was built over the Somerset Coal Canal, and extends for eighteen miles between Dundas, on the Kennet and Avon Canal (and therefore within easy distance of both Bath and Bradford-on-Avon), and Frome, passing close to the site of Stoney Littleton Long Barrow (see below) and through Radstock en route. Eleven miles are completely traffic-free, and most of the remainder is on country lanes. Route 24 continues on southeast from Frome to Longleat, Warminster and Salisbury.

Bike rental is available at the start of the route, by the bridge at Dundas, from Bath Narrowboats ⓣ01225 447276, ⓦbath-narrowboats.co.uk), which charges £15/day.

narrow and uneven for ponies to negotiate – a job usually undertaken by boys as young as 12 years old. The museum encompasses much more than just the mining industry, however, casting an eye over the culture and social life of the area and the wider activities of the mining families. There are reconstructions of a miner's cottage kitchen and scullery, a grocery and a blacksmith's workshop. Besides the collieries, other local employers in the town were boot manufacturers, brewers and foundries, all catering to the workers and their families and all represented here. Space is also given to such leisure pastimes as rugby, quoits and pigeon-racing, as well as brass bands, ale jugs and Methodism.

Volunteers and staff are on hand to add personal reminiscences, and the museum shop sells leaflets outlining four self-guided **heritage walks** that can be followed to the pit sites and quarries around Radstock.

Stoney Littleton Long Barrow

One mile south of Wellow, off A367 • Free • EH • ⓦenglish-heritage.org.uk • Bus #757 (Wed only) to Wellow

One of Britain's finest examples of a Neolithic long barrow – a prehistoric chambered grave or shrine – lies on a peaceful hillside 3.5 miles northeast of Radstock as the crow flies, about twice that by road. Covered by a grassy mound, **Stoney Littleton** is thought to date from around 3500 BC, and probably served as both a burial site and a place of worship. Following its discovery by a farmer in 1760, most of its contents disappeared, though excavations in 1816 yielded human bones, some burnt. The interior stretches for 42ft, with a height of about 4ft, necessitating some awkward stooping for exploring within, but it's worth the effort even if there's little specific to see. A torch will allow you to peer into the three pairs of chambers leading off the main passage and one at its end, all probably once containing bodies. In any case, it's the place itself that constitutes the real pleasure here, reached via a narrow lane between Wellow and Shoscombe, then across a bridge and up through fields (all well signposted).

Cyclists or walkers on the Colliers Way pass right by the path leading up to the barrow. It's not straightforward to arrive by **public transport**, however: unless you can use the weekly #757 service between Radstock and Bath, which stops nearby on Wellow Road, the best bet is to take any bus to Peasedown St John and walk 2.5 miles east.

Farleigh Hungerford Castle

Farleigh Hungerford • April–Sept daily 10am–6pm; Oct daily 10am–5pm; Nov–March Sat & Sun 10am–4pm • £5.70 • EH • ⓣ01225 754026, ⓦenglish-heritage.org.uk

Nine miles northeast of Radstock, the ruins of **Farleigh Hungerford Castle** strike a discordant note, incongruously evoking the threat of war amid the unruffled

9

valleys and meadows of deepest Somerset. The castle was the abode of the mighty Hungerford dynasty until 1686, abandoned soon after, and ruined by the early 1700s. The original structure, dating from around 1380, was enlarged in the following century with a ring of outer walls, where the **East Gatehouse**, the main entry to the site, still bears the sickle insignia of the Hungerfords and the family's coat of arms. Inside, an expanse of green leads to the flattened remains of the **Inner Gatehouse**, giving access to the castle's original core. On either side two towers still stand, but its counterparts on the northern wall have long since disappeared. Within this area you can discern traces of the inner courtyard, the great hall, kitchen and garden.

But the most impressive surviving parts of the complex lie between the East and Inner gatehouses, chiefly the **chapel**, dating from the original fourteenth-century construction of the castle and later enclosed within the new walls. The interior is full of interest, holding well-preserved Hungerford tombs to the right of the altar and a set of **wall paintings** probably dating from the 1440s, the most vivid showing a giant figure of St George slaying the dragon. The side chapel to the left of the altar also holds paintings of cherubs and flowers on the walls, commissioned by Lady Margaret Hungerford – connected with Corsham (see page 77) – in the mid-seventeenth century and once covering the entire side chapel. Below the chapel, accessed by a separate entrance, the **vault** holds the unusually shaped lead coffins of various Hungerfords, probably including Lady Margaret herself.

Behind the chapel, the **Priests' House**, built in 1430 and later converted into a dairy, and later still a farmhouse, holds displays relating to the site, including a model of the castle as it once looked, seventeenth-century arms and armour, and pictures. To immerse yourself in the day-to-day life of the castle as it once was, pick up a free audioguide at the ticket office.

Iford Manor Gardens

Off the A36 and B3109 1.5 miles north of Farleigh Hungerford • April–Sept Wed–Sun 11am–4pm; Oct Sun 11am–4pm • £7.50 • ☎ 01225 863146, ⓦ ifordmanor.co.uk

Set alongside the Somerset–Wiltshire border, **Iford Manor Gardens** occupy an idyllic corner of the English countryside just steps away from the River Frome where a statue of Britannia stands sentinel atop a pretty stone bridge. All the more surprising, then, to find transposed here an outpost of Italy, in the form of a Roman or Tuscan garden, rising on terraces up the hillside behind the Palladian-fronted house. The **Peto Garden** is named after its creator, Harold Peto, an architect (Lutyens was briefly his pupil) and garden designer who was besotted with the Italian Renaissance and lived here from 1899 to 1933. A strong believer in the importance of architecture in garden design, Peto set about re-creating an amalgam of the finest Italian Renaissance gardens he had seen while living and working abroad. Rather than herbaceous borders and gaudy colours – though the luxuriant swathes of wisteria in May and June are a brilliant exception – the emphasis here is on gravel walks, classical statuary and fountains splashing into lily-strewn ponds, amid Mediterranean herbs, junipers and statuesque cypress trees.

The house and gardens lie on the **Macmillan Way** cross-country walking route (ⓦ macmillanway.org), a useful link between the garden and Farleigh Hungerford Castle (see page 277). They lie about 1.5 miles' steep but delightful walk from Avoncliff train station. You can pick up superb scones and garden-produced jam in the **tearoom** (open April–Sept at weekends), where you can also sample the highly regarded **Iford Cider**, which is made on the estate and can be found in pubs across Somerset (also available for sale in the shop here).

There's an exhibition space, too, and the website has details of the various **workshops** held at Iford Manor, for example on photography, wildlife, wellbeing and gardening.

The gardens and the cloisters

On entering the garden, the Mediterranean theme is evoked straightaway by the **Loggia** that Peto added to the side of the house (which is far older than its eighteenth-century facade). From here paths ascend to the **Conservatory Terrace**, adorned with marble lions and columns from around 1200, and the **Great Terrace**, with its bronze wolf suckling Romulus and Remus (made from a mould of the original sculpture in Rome's Capitol Museum) and a Greek sarcophagus from the second or third century AD.

The gardens, which feature in the film *The Secret Garden* and the Jane Austen TV adaptation *Sanditon*, form the highly atmospheric setting for informal classical and jazz **concerts**, theatre productions and cinema screenings taking place on various dates throughout the summer – see the website for dates.

Past the eighteenth-century Garden House are the **Cloisters**, completed by Peto in 1914 in the style of an Italian Romanesque cloister of around 1200, very authentic in feel, and filled with antique fragments.

ARRIVAL AND DEPARTURE

RADSTOCK AND AROUND

By bus Most buses arrive at and depart from The Street, Wells Rd and Kilmersdon Rd, near the museum. Some of the routes below may involve a change.

Destinations Bath (Mon–Sat every 15min, Sun every 30min; 25min); Bristol (Mon–Sat hourly; 1hr 30min); Frome (Mon–Sat 7 daily; 35min); Midsomer Norton (Mon–

Sat every 5–15min, Sun every 30min; 10–15min); Shepton Mallet (hourly; 40min); Wells (Mon–Sat every 30min, Sun hourly; 50min1hr).

By bike or on foot Radstock lies on the Colliers Way between Dundas (between Bath and Bradford-on-Avon) and Frome (see page 277).

ACCOMMODATION

★ **Babington House** Babington, 3.5 miles south of Radstock ☎01373 812266, ⓦbabingtonhouse.co.uk. You'll feel properly pampered at this exclusive bolthole set in eighteen acres of grounds that include indoor and outdoor pools, tennis courts, a cricket pitch a spa centre and a lake. Accommodation ranges from quirky attic rooms to self-catering lodges and sumptuous suites, and guests can enjoy a cinema, a library and fine dining. **£360**

The Fromeway 62 Frome Rd ☎01761 432116, ⓦfrome way.co.uk. This is Radstock's best overnight option in the town itself – or at least on its outskirts, a 10min uphill walk from the museum. Above an elegant, well-maintained pub, and with a separate entrance, the three en-suite rooms are smallish, neat and quiet. Breakfasts are made using quality ingredients, and the bar serves excellent meals and real ales. **£80**

★ **Old Vicarage** Church St, Kilmersdon, 1.5 miles south of Radstock ☎01761 436926, ⓦwww.theoldvicarage somerset.com. Two luxurious suites are available at this guesthouse, with freestanding baths and views of the garden and adjacent church. The slap-up breakfasts include home-produced eggs, sourdough bread, yoghurt and jams, and can be served in the family kitchen or in your room – you choose. **£100**

Ston Easton Park Hotel Ston Easton, 3 miles west off the A37 ☎01761 241631, ⓦstoneaston.co.uk. The perfect spot for a secluded, old-fashioned country-house splurge, this Regency mansion has grand drawing rooms and guest rooms, with swags and swirls, antique furnishings and log fires. The extensive grounds were landscaped by Humphry Repton. **£159**

EATING

The Holy Cow Manor Farm, Church Lane, Lower Chilcompton ☎01761 410497, ⓦtheholycow chilcompton.com. This cosy café is situated in a remote rural spot, part of a farm that's a few minutes' drive southwest of Midsomer Norton. Breakfasts (till 11.30am) include American-style pancakes (£6–8) and smoked salmon with poached or scrambled eggs (£8.25), and salads, sandwiches, burgers and pies are served at lunchtime (£5–10), with good veggie options. In fine weather you can sit outside at tables overlooking St John's church. Mon–Fri 8.30am–3.30pm, Sat 9am–2pm, 1st and 3rd Sun of month 9am–2pm.

The Redan Inn Fry's Well, Chilcompton ☎01761 258560, ⓦtheredaninn.com. With few decent options for a good meal in Radstock itself, it's worth venturing 3.5 miles southwest to this excellent pub and restaurant with tables inside or in the garden. The wide-ranging menu ranges from burgers (£14) to barbecued steaks (around £20), also taking in such dishes as braised pork belly (£13.50) and goat's cheese dumplings (£15.50). Real ales are on tap and seven smart rooms are available for B&B (from £90). Mon–Sat 11am–11pm, Sun 11am–10.30pm; kitchen noon–3pm & 6–9.30pm (Sun till 8pm).

9

Shepton Mallet and around

Today a sleepy market town, **SHEPTON MALLET** has a rich industrial history, with some thirty mills once operating along the banks of the River Sheppey, producing wool and silk, while nearby quarries provided stone for Glastonbury Abbey and Wells Cathedral. In the nineteenth century, when two railways intersected here, the town was a brewing centre – its Anglo-Bavarian Brewery is claimed to be the first in the country to brew lager. Shepton's brewing days are not over, and cider continues to be produced in the brewery in the monumental, tall-chimneyed Anglo Trading Estate on Commercial Road, including the local Pilton Cider.

Shepton Mallet is still known as an agricultural centre, the home of the **Royal Bath and West Show**, held in late May/early June – primarily an agricultural fair but now catering to all tastes (see box). The **Mid-Somerset Show** is a more local and more strictly farming affair, taking place on the third Sunday of August, while a more workaday weekly market is held on Fridays at Market Place at the bottom of the partly pedestrianized High Street. Market Place is also the site of a hexagonal **Market Cross** (fifteenth century, but rebuilt in 1841) and the remains of the wooden **Shambles**, where butchers once displayed their wares. Following the failure of the Duke of Monmouth's rebellion in 1685 (see page 209), twelve men were hung, drawn and quartered here in one of Judge Jeffreys' Bloody Assizes.

Shepton Mallet is just three miles northeast of Pilton, the site of Glastonbury Festival (see page 168), making it a useful stop before or after the festival, or a base for festival-goers unable or unwilling to camp.

St Peter and St Paul

Church Lane • Daily 9am–5pm • Free • ⓦ sheptonbenefice.org

Shepton Mallet's jewel is its parish church of **St Peter and St Paul**, accessed from the High Street but mostly hidden behind an ugly 1970s development. With giant gargoyles around its exterior, its most distinctive feature is the **tower**, dating from the late fourteenth century though never completed, explaining its oddly truncated appearance. The church's airy **interior** is the real highlight, flooded with light from its large Perpendicular windows topped by a clerestory added in around 1500. Statues that originally stood in the clerestory's niches were destroyed by Puritans, as was the stained glass in the windows. Soaring above it all is the nave's intricate **wagon roof** made up of 350 oak panels, each different, and interspersed by an array of bosses. The octagonal stone **pulpit**, from around 1550, is also outstanding, carved with classical and Gothic motifs. Effigies of two knights, probably killed while crusading, have been laid on windowsills on the church's north aisle.

Fans of Somerset churches should also seek out the one at **Evercreech**, three miles south of Shepton, whose slender pinnacled tower is one of Somerset's best examples of the genre.

Kilver Court Gardens

Kilver St • April–Oct Mon–Sat 10am–5pm, Sun 10am–4.30pm; Nov–March daily 10am–4.30pm; last entry 1hr before closing • £7.50 • ☏ 01749 340410, ⓦ kilvercourt.com

Shepton Mallet has two areas of greenery close to the centre, ideal for a picnic or a runaround: **Collett Park**, a spacious public garden accessed from Park Road or Charlton Road, east of the High Street, and **Kilver Court Gardens**, a more formal space with a delightful parterre, rockery, waterfalls, a lake and the dramatic backdrop of the curved, 26-arch, 67ft-high Charlton railway viaduct slicing across. The gardens were laid out in the 1880s for factory workers, remodelled in 1960–61 by local entrepreneur Francis Showering (who owed his fortune to Babycham) and reopened by the founders of the

THATCHED HOUSE, NUNNEY

9

ROYAL BATH AND WEST SHOW

One of the foremost agricultural shows in the West Country, the **Royal Bath and West Show** was created by the Royal Bath and West of England Society in 1780, and first held at Weston, outside Bath. Since 1965 it has had a permanent home outside Shepton Mallet, regularly attracting some 160,000 visitors over three days in late May/early June. Pigs, livestock and cider are very much to the fore, and dog-handling, sheep-shearing and champion beef competitions attract the farming folk, but there are also air displays, live music and such crowd-pullers as the smelliest cheese competition. Ticket prices are around £20–22 in advance, £25 at the gate; camping pitches are available for £15/night.

The showground, located three miles south of Shepton on the A371, hosts numerous other events, from car boot sales and antiques fairs to the National Gardening Show in early September. In 1970, it was the venue of the famed Bath Blues and Progressive Music Festival, whose stellar line-up included Pink Floyd, Led Zeppelin, the Byrds, Santana and Frank Zappa. For information on current events, call ☎01749 822200 or see ⓦbathandwest.com.

Mulberry clothing and accessories brand, whose headquarters are in Shepton. As well as a nursery and café, the site includes a farm shop, with organic local produce, and the Emporium, selling designer brands at discounted prices, while the Mulberry factory shop is 200yds away on Kilver Street.

ARRIVAL AND DEPARTURE

SHEPTON MALLET AND AROUND

By bus Most buses stop on Paul St and by the Cenotaph at the southern end of the High St. Some of the routes below necessitate a change.

Destinations Bath (hourly; 1hr 10min); Bristol (1 daily; 50min); Frome (Mon–Sat 5 daily; 45min); Glastonbury (Mon–Sat 8 daily, Sun 3 daily; 20min); Wells (hourly; 20min); Yeovil (Mon–Sat 7 daily, Sun 1 daily; 45min–1hr 25min).

INFORMATION

Tourist Information and Heritage Centre 70 High St (Mon–Fri 10am–4pm, Sat 10am–1pm; ☎01749 345258, ⓦvisitsheptonmallet.co.uk). The annexed Heritage Centre — just one room — has a few local history displays, including a child's coffin from the fourth century and collections of cider tankards and Babycham glasses.

ACCOMMODATION

★ **Bowlish House** Corner of Coombe Lane and Wells Rd ☎01749 342022, ⓦbowlishhouse.com. An old cloth merchant's house from 1732 has been adapted to provide spacious accommodation that retains its Georgian elegance but comes with contemporary bathrooms and minibars. Smaller, cheaper rooms are available in the attic. There's a good restaurant too (booking required). **£95**

Charlton House Charlton Rd (A361), 1 mile east of centre ☎01749 342008, ⓦcharltonhouse.com. Owned by the Bannatyne health club chain, this "style hotel" set in its own grounds caters mainly to urban refugees or anyone else seeking a posh but informal country-house retreat. Service is attentive and friendly, the contemporary rooms (some with balconies) are well equipped, and guests have free use of the indoor/outdoor pool, spa facilities and gym – though these are on the small side – and the beautiful grounds. **£149**

Longbridge House 78 Cowl St ☎01749 572311, ⓦlongbridgehouse.co.uk. Somewhat marooned amid a 1960s housing estate at the north end of town, this B&B occupies a building with a long and eventful history, including accommodating the Duke of Monmouth before his defeat at the Battle of Sedgemoor in 1685 and subsequent execution. Three en-suite rooms are available, with the ornate Monmouth Room especially grand (with a roll-top bath), and breakfast includes good vegetarian options. **£90**

Maplestone Hall Quarr ☎01749 938356, ⓦmaplestonehall.co.uk. There's more than a dash of historic character in this wisteria-draped B&B with an attractive cottage garden and genial hosts, located in a quiet neighbourhood a short walk from the centre. The en-suite rooms are tastefully furnished, one has a four-poster and a separate garden entrance and there's also accommodation in a separate cottage annexe. Breakfast includes muesli, fresh fruit salad and Greek yoghurt. **£95**

Thatched Cottage 63–67 Charlton Rd ☎01749 342058, ⓦthethatchedcottageinn.co.uk. Dating from the seventeenth century, this inn on the outskirts of town (a fifteen-minute walk from the centre) has been extensively renovated, but its beams and open fireplaces still provide a cosy atmosphere. Rooms and bathrooms are modern, spacious and mostly quiet, despite the proximity of the main road – ask for a room at the back if available. **£89**

EATING AND DRINKING

Blostin's 29–33 Waterloo Rd ☎01749 343648, ⓦ blostins.co.uk. Shepton's finest dining can be found in this intimate and relaxed restaurant with warm orange walls and bright modern paintings, run by a husband-and-wife team five minutes' walk from the High Street. Dishes such as salmon baked in filo pastry and slow-roasted belly and fillet of pork are expertly prepared, and the good vegetarian menu includes Provençal vegetable strudel. The inventive desserts include iced ginger meringue with cappuccino cream. Mains cost around £24, otherwise set price menus are £24 for two courses, £28 for three. Thurs–Sat 7pm–late.

George Inn Long St, Croscombe, 2 miles west on the A371 (Wells road) ☎01749 342306, ⓦ thegeorgeinn. co.uk. This classic village pub has inglenook fireplaces in its hop-draped interior, a range of real ales – try the zesty King George the Thirst and George and Dragon beers, brewed exclusively for this establishment – and ciders. The menu is also worth sampling, from fresh baguettes to pies, burgers and steaks (£13–19). There's a beer garden at the back, and B&B is available too (from £90). Mon–Thurs 7.30am– 11pm, Fri 7.30am–midnight, Sat 8am–midnight, Sun 8am–11pm; food served Mon–Fri 7.30am–2.30pm & 6–9pm, Sat 8am–9pm, Sun 8am–8pm.

Mendip Inn Oakhill, 3 miles north on the A37 ☎01749 841703, ⓦ mendipinn.co.uk. This country pub outside Gurney Slade offers local ales in its smart-rustic bar, an open fire in winter and a courtyard garden for fine weather. Ciabattas are available at lunchtime, and the separate restaurant has a menu which includes such dishes as Mendip Trio of beef, pork and lamb, Thai green monkfish curry and vegan mushroom risotto (most dishes £12–16) – Wednesdays are steak nights and Fridays are seafood. Finish off with a Somerset cider brandy. Stylish double rooms are also available (from £80). Mon–Fri noon–2.30pm & 6–9pm, Sat & Sun noon–9pm.

Orelogio 6 Town St ☎01749 938090. Members of the local Portuguese community congregate at this authentic family-run café with warm orange and lime green walls and news from Lisbon on a TV set in the corner. Have a glass of wine or caipirinha, a Sagres beer, or a strong coffee with a home-made pastry. *Bolo do caco com manteiga de alho* (madeira bread with garlic butter) and *bitoque* (beef steak with chips, rice, egg and salad) feature on the menu, and there are daily specials (most mains around £10). Mon– Thurs 3–6pm, Fri 10am–9pm, Sat 10am–8pm.

★**Peppers** 2–4 Town St ☎01749 346640. This wholefood shop and café-restaurant offers the best local, seasonal produce, either to take away – crusty rolls, cheeses, hams, fruits and juices – or to eat in the adjoining restaurant, where the menu includes salmon fishcakes and brie and mushroom pancake (around £8.50) as well as a wholesome selection of cheese scones, salads and sandwiches (there are also gluten-free options). The coffee is the best in Shepton, and the scones with clotted cream are an additional draw. Mon 9am–2pm, Tues–Fri 9am– 3.30pm, Sat 9am–noon.

Frome and around

Combining a traditional, mainly unspoiled aspect with a lively, happening vibe, **FROME** (pronounced "Froom"), about seven miles northeast of Shepton Mallet, is one of Somerset's most attractive towns, with yellow-stone weavers' cottages and Georgian

EAST SOMERSET RAILWAY

The time when this area of Somerset was crisscrossed by railway lines is long past, but you can relive this golden era on the small **East Somerset Railway** (☎01749 880417, ⓦ eastsomersetrailway.com), based in the village of Cranmore, three miles east of Shepton Mallet. The line, with a length of just 2.5 miles, extends west to Mendip Vale station. The steam-driven trains operate March–Oct on Saturdays, Sundays and bank holidays; they also run on Wednesdays between June and Oct, on Thursdays during the summer school holiday, and on some dates in December. There are at least four departures a day (currently at 11am, 12.30pm, 2pm & 3.30pm from Cranmore); the five-mile round trip takes around forty minutes, and tickets (£10) are valid all day; one-way tickets from Cranmore cost £6. There are stops at Mendip Vale and, on the return journey, at Cranmore West station, where you can visit the workshop and Engine Shed, providing an insight into the amount of work it takes to keep these grand old locomotives running. The broad-gauge line continues east of Cranmore, eventually meeting the main line between Frome and Castle Cary, though this stretch is now only used for freighting stone from Merehead Quarry. The village of Cranmore is served by bus #162 bus between Frome and Shepton Mallet (Mon–Fri 5 daily); the station is a few minutes' walk from the stop.

rows above a bustling centre. There's not much in the way of specific sights, but plenty of scope for exploring the town's steep cobbled lanes and getting lost in its quaint nooks and alleys. In particular, seek out **St Catherine's Quarter**, an area of winding cobbled streets flanked by old stone buildings and pastel-painted antiques shops with nary a chain store in sight. At its centre is pedestrianized **Catherine Hill**, with its vintage stores and shops selling "upcycled" furniture. Across Market Place from here, you'll find narrow **Cheap Street**, with a leat (water channel) flowing through its open conduit, and cafés and delicatessens to either side.

The town has a number of **art** and **live music** venues, notably the Cheese and Grain (⍵ cheeseandgrain.com), Rook Lane Chapel on Bath Street (⍵ rooklane.org.uk) and Black Swan Arts on Bridge Street (⍵ blackswanarts.org.uk). All three places are among the chief venues of the **Frome Festival**, a wide-ranging cultural jamboree over ten days in July (⍵ fromefestival.co.uk).

The tourist office and the town museum can provide a Heritage Trail pamphlet and map for discovering Frome's many historical buildings on a circular walk (£3). The town has a good selection of lodgings, eateries and atmospheric pubs too, making this a great base for excursions to such nearby attractions as Nunney Castle, Longleat and Stourhead.

Frome marks the eastern end of the **Mendip Way**, a fifty-mile trail extending to Uphill, near Weston-super-Mare, and connecting with the cross-country Macmillan Way.

St John the Baptist

Church St • Mon–Sat 9.30am–3.30pm, Sun for services • Free • ⍵ stjohnsfrome.co.uk

Perched above Cheap Street, Frome's tall-steepled parish church of **St John the Baptist** is a grand affair, mostly a Victorian replacement of a twelfth- to fifteenth-century structure that itself stood on the site of a Saxon church. Unusually for an Anglican church, it has a Via Crucis, depicting the Stations of the Cross, leading uphill to the north porch, and roundels above the nave arches based on Christ's parables and

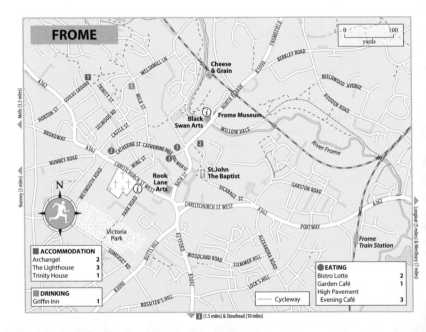

FROME'S MARKETS

In the context of the general decline of English market towns, Frome has proved an amazing success story, attracting regular crowds to its calendar of weekly and monthly **markets**. The hall inside the **Cheese & Grain** in Market Yard is the venue for most of these: flea markets on Wednesdays, country produce on Thursdays, vegan food on the first Saturday of the month (every two months), farmers' markets on the second Saturday of the month, and vintage items, crafts and gifts at the Magpie Market on the first Sunday of the month (March–Dec), while the car park outside hosts a cluster of stalls selling food and knick-knacks every Saturday and a car boot sale on Sundays. The most colourful and flamboyant of Frome's markets, though, is the **Frome Independent**, which takes over the whole town centre on the first Sunday of the month (March–Dec; ⓦ thefromeindependent.co.uk). Here you'll find crafts, clothing, local produce and streetfood as well as live music and other entertainments.

miracles. The tomb of the hymn-writer and ecclesiastic Bishop Thomas Ken (1637–1711) lies in a curious cage-like crypt outside the east end of the church.

Frome Museum

1 North Parade • Mid-March to mid-Nov Tues–Sat 10am–2pm • Free • ☎ 01373 454611, ⓦ fromemuseum.wordpress.com

Just over the town bridge from Market Place (at the bottom of Cheap Street), **Frome Museum** crams into two rooms exhibits illustrating local history, geology, archeology and industry, with a generous helping of those random items that are a staple of small-town museums everywhere. The collection has more of a bias towards technology than most, with a significant proportion devoted to the local firm of J.W. Singer, whose heyday was in the late nineteenth and early twentieth centuries, specializing in ornamental statuary and monuments. Their biggest customers were churches, but their productions included such iconic pieces as the statue of Boudicca on London's Victoria Embankment and "Justice" on the Old Bailey, and their commissions extended to South Africa.

Other items on display include a selection of old maps of the town and surrounds, rocks from the Mendip Hills, fossils found in local quarries (including bison teeth), a push-barrow fire engine and an equally ancient penny-farthing. All in all, it's an enjoyable diversion for half an hour or so.

Nunney Castle

Nunney • Free • EH • ⓦ english-heritage.org.uk

Well hidden in the pretty village of **NUNNEY**, three miles southwest of Frome off the A361, is Somerset's finest castle ruin, rearing dramatically over the surrounding cottage gardens. Dating from the late fourteenth century and modernized two hundred years later, **Nunney Castle** still stands within its moat, its exterior in remarkably good condition, all things considered, with the four corner turrets and three walls still presenting a formidable sight, though the north-facing wall has collapsed and the interior is gutted. The castle was constructed in the 1370s by the local baron, Sir John de la Mere (or Mare), who had gained favour fighting for Edward III in the Hundred Years' War and later became Sheriff of Somerset. During the Civil War it was besieged by Cromwell's forces who pounded it with cannon, destroying the interior and generally weakening the structure, though the north wall did not finally collapse until Christmas Day, 1910. You can still see traces of some of the original rooms: on the ground floor was a kitchen, above were a hall and private chambers, with a chapel leading off these.

Across a footbridge from the castle, Nunney's **All Saints** church holds tombs belonging to John de la Mere's family, the effigies of knights and their consorts laid out serenely in the northeast corner.

JACK, JILL AND LITTLE JACK HORNER

The hazy origins of most nursery rhymes are lost in centuries-old folklore, but two of the best-known rhymes have been linked to the parishes of **Mells** and **Kilmersdon** (south of Radstock). "**Little Jack Horner**" is said (probably wrongly) to have been a member of the Horner family whose Elizabethan manor neighbours Mells church; according to this version, the "plum" that he extracted from a Christmas pie turned out to be the house deeds – the gift of Richard Whiting, last Abbot of Glastonbury. Kilmersdon is said to be where **Jack and Jill** came to a sorry end while going to fetch water. There is no evidence for why Kilmersdon should be the site of this drama, but the steep hill behind the village is now called Jack and Jill Hill and is waymarked with lines from the rhyme.

Mells

Roughly 2.5 miles north of Nunney and 3.5 miles west of Frome, the dreamy, unspoiled village of **MELLS** is worth a brief diversion, most of all for the beautiful old church standing at the end of a row of medieval cottages. The mainly fifteenth-century **St Andrew** has a yellowy, pale-grey exterior, a superb pinnacled and battlemented four-decker tower, and a fan-vaulted porch. The interior is less striking but holds a memorial by Edward Burne-Jones under the tower, and an equestrian statue by Alfred Munnings honouring his close friend Edward Horner, killed in World War I. The local Horner family, who occupied the Elizabethan manor adjacent to the church, was claimed to be associated with the nursery rhyme *Little Jack Horner* (see box).

The churchyard holds the graves of a clutch of early twentieth-century celebrities, including Violet Bonham-Carter, Liberal politician, diarist and grandmother of Helena Bonham-Carter; the Roman Catholic priest and crime writer Ronald Knox; and the World War I poet Siegfried Sassoon, who had asked to be buried close to Knox, an influence in Sassoon's decision to convert to Catholicism.

Mells also has a fine old tavern, the *Talbot Inn* (see page 290), good for a drink, meal or sleepover. The village lies just over a mile from the Colliers Way (see page 277), and about the same distance east of Vobster, an old mining settlement whose quarry has been turned into the region's best inland **diving** centre (⊛vobster.com).

Longleat

Off the A362 5 miles southeast of Frome • Mid-Feb to late March Fri–Mon 10am–4pm (school hols daily till 6pm); late March to mid-July daily 10am–5pm (school hols till 6pm); mid-July to early Sept daily 10am–7pm; early Sept to Oct Mon & Wed–Fri 10am–5pm, Sat & Sun till 6pm (school hols daily); Nov–early Jan Thurs–Sun 10am–7.30pm; last entry to house 30min before closing; last entry to safari park 1hr before closing (but 2pm Nov & Dec); check winter opening • House and grounds £19; multiple entry to all attractions including safari park £35 for one day, £45 for two days; house, grounds, safari park and Cheddar Caves (see page 147) £47; 10–15 percent discount if booked online; safari bus £5 • ☏ 01985 844400, ⊛ longleat.co.uk • Frome's station is the closest for train travellers. Bus #53 (not Sun) shuttles mostly hourly between Warminster and Frome train stations, both 4–5 miles from Longleat – though the stop at Picket Post lies 2.5 miles from the entrance to the grounds; National Cycle Routes 24 and 25 meet at Longleat

One of the country's most magnificent stately homes, joined improbably to a safari park, lies just over the Wiltshire border. Apart from the house and park, **Longleat** offers a huge range of entertainment for all ages, in addition to its formal gardens and acres of grounds – enough to fill at least one full day. In fact, given its combined attractions, you might consider one of the ticket options allowing entry over more than one day.

The Great Hall

The **house**, an imposing three-storey construction topped with a panoply of ornamental statuary and cupolas, has been owned by the Thynne family since the site of an Augustinian priory was bought in 1541 by Sir John Thynne, steward to the Duke of Somerset. The house was more or less complete by Sir John's death in 1580, though it was further altered and embellished by succeeding generations. The **Great Hall** is the least changed part of the building, a lofty, cavernous space with a hammerbeam roof, galleries and enormous canvases showing hunting scenes above a grand Elizabethan fireplace, and wood panelling from which giant prehistoric antlers from Ireland are hung. A waistcoat worn by Charles I at his execution is displayed in one corner.

The rest of the house

The rest of the house is a dizzying succession of fine furnishings and works of art. The central **staircase** was added, like much else here, by Jeffrey Wyatville in the early eighteenth century, while the state rooms were altered beyond recognition in the 1870s and 1880s when the fourth marquess, returned from a tour of Italy, employed the celebrated designer J.D. Crace and a team of Italian craftsmen to create painted ceilings, gilded cornices and other extravagances that really elevate Longleat's interior to a palatial level. There are paintings everywhere, many of them family portraits, but the best works are reserved for the **State Drawing Room** where a range of Old Masters is displayed, including Titian's *Rest on the Flight into Egypt* and a scene from Ovid's *Metamorphoses* painted by Tintoretto. The works here are poorly displayed, however, not helped by the dim lighting (most of the state rooms are heavily curtained to limit damage from daylight).

Various **tours** costing extra. are offered every day, for example a General House Tour, a Rooftop Tour, a Butler and Housekeepers Tour and a Scandalous History Tour, details of which will be posted at the entrance; they normally start at 11am and last 45 minutes. You can also join one of the private **Chattels Tours** of rooms not normally open, scheduled once or twice a month during the main season, usually on a Thursday or a Friday and lasting up to two hours (book at least 24hr ahead by calling ☏01985 845420; £23.50) – check the website for dates.

The grounds and safari park

The magnificence of the house is complemented by the 900 acres of **grounds**, largely created in 1758–62 by Capability Brown, who installed the walled kitchen garden and the Pleasure Walk, planted prolifically (giving the park its heavily wooded appearance) and enhanced the lakes fed by the serpentine river, or "leat", from which the house takes its name. In 1966, the sixth marquess of Bath (father of the present Lord Bath), who had already raised eyebrows among his peers twenty years earlier by opening his house to the paying public (the first stately home owner to do so on a regular basis), caused even more amazement when he turned Brown's landscapes into a drive-through **safari park** – again, the first in the country. Today, this features lions, giraffes, rhinos, elephants, wildebeest, zebras and famously meddlesome monkeys, among other animals, which you can view at close quarters from your car or in a Safari Bus (places on this can be booked at the ticket booths at the entrance or in the Main Square).

Main Square

Once set on the commercial route, the bosses of Longleat knew no limits: the **Main Square** behind the house includes such attractions and curiosities as a hedge maze, the Bat Cave, the Monkey Temple, Koala Creek, an adventure castle and a miniature railway. Look out too for regular **seasonal events** such as fireworks in late October and early November, and ice-skating and other Christmassy activities between mid-November and early January.

Westbury

The Wiltshire village of **WESTBURY**, seven miles east of Frome, is best known for the **white horse** etched into a nearby hillside, and as a railway junction where the Bath–Salisbury line meets the line between Reading, Taunton and Exeter. But Westbury itself deserves a brief stop for a flavour of its attractive old centre, with Georgian houses

9

WILTSHIRE'S WHITE HORSES

Wiltshire's chalk downs have proved ideal for large and vivid hill-carvings, so much so that the county holds eight of Britain's 24 **white horses**, with several more overgrown and now invisible. The practice of carving figures into English hillsides is an ancient one, as the priapic Cerne Giant in Dorset testifies, but Wiltshire's white horses were probably all carved within the last three hundred years, as were all the rest in the country with the one exception of the sinuous horse at Uffington, Oxfordshire, thought to be 3000 years old. The background and purpose of the authentically old hill carvings has never been established – and probably never will be – but the more recent creations were usually the fruit of whimsy and fashion. Apart from Westbury's, some of the best examples can be seen outside Cherhill, Broad Town (outside Wootton Bassett) and Marlborough; the newest is outside Devizes, carved in 1999 to mark the millennium. For background on all of Wiltshire's carved horses, see Ⓦ wiltshirewhitehorses.org.uk.

around its Market Place and circling its handsome, fourteenth-century (though much restored) church of **All Saints**, which holds a chained copy of the Paraphrase of the New Testament by Erasmus.

There's another, more compelling, church a couple of miles southwest of Westbury in the hamlet of **Dilton** (also known as Old Dilton), signposted off the A3098. **St Mary's**, which has not been in use since 1900, feels as if its Georgian congregation has only just left. Probably dating from the fourteenth or fifteenth century, the church is preserved in immaculate condition, with a white-painted interior, galleries, a triple-decker pulpit and tall box pews crowding the small space.

Westbury White Horse

Perfectly positioned for maximum visibility on Westbury Hill, a couple of miles east of town, the **Westbury White Horse**, one of several in Wiltshire (see box), probably has its origins in the late seventeenth or early eighteenth century, though there are suggestions that there was a carved horse in Saxon times, possibly cut to commemorate Alfred the Great's victory over the Danes at Ethandun in 878. The carving we see today, however, is quite a different creature, as the original horse was judged to be a poor work and redesigned in 1778 by one G. Gee, a local steward. The figure was enlarged and possibly turned to face in the opposite direction, then further modified a hundred years later, and in the twentieth century it was stabilized with concrete and painted white.

The result is a vivid but rather inert affair, lacking the dynamic grace of some of Wiltshire's other hill carvings, though it still presents a strange and wonderful apparition when seen from afar (you'll get a glimpse of it from the train between Westbury and Trowbridge). The best view is from the B3098, where a parking area has been cleared for taking in the scene. If you want to get closer, follow the minor road signposted for Bratton Camp. Just above the carving, **Bratton Camp** is an Iron Age hillfort, one of a series of fortified encampments edging Salisbury Plain. Enclosed within the deep ditches and banks is a substantial **long barrow** (burial mound) some 5000 years old.

Stourhead

Stourton • **House** Daily: March to early Nov 11am–4.30pm; late Nov to late Dec 11am–3.30pm • **Grounds** Daily: April–Sept 9am–6pm or dusk, Oct–March 9am–5pm or dusk • House and grounds £17.50 • **King Alfred's Tower** Early March to early Nov Sat & Sun noon–4pm • £4.80 • NT • ☎ 01747 841152, Ⓦ nationaltrust.org.uk • Stourton is just over a mile's walk from Zeals, a stop on buses from Frome and Shaftesbury; the nearest train stations are at Gillingham, over 6 miles away, and Bruton, 7 miles

Ten miles south of Frome, off the B3092, **Stourhead** initially resembles a slimmed-down version of Longleat, though here the style of the house is predominantly Georgian and formal rather than Elizabethan and flamboyant, and instead of a safari park Stourhead is best known for its landscaped grounds, among the most accomplished surviving examples of the eighteenth-century craze for landscape gardening.

The grounds

The Stourton estate was bought in 1717 by Henry Hoare, who commissioned Colen Campbell to build a new villa in the Palladian style. Hoare's heir, another Henry, returned from his Grand Tour in 1741 with his head full of the paintings of Claude and Poussin, and determined to translate their images of well-ordered, wistful classicism into real life. In the **grounds**, he dammed the Stour to create a lake, then planted the terrain with blocks of trees, classical temples and statues, all mirrored vividly in the water of the lake, which is crossed by a modest, grass-carpeted **Palladian bridge** modelled on one in Vicenza. The most impressive of the lakeside monuments is the **Pantheon**, a domed and porticoed structure originally named the Temple of Hercules for the muscly statue that dominates the interior – a masterpiece by the Flemish sculptor John Michael Rysbrack. The whole park forms a kind of travel scrapbook, with an assortment of eye-catching features poetically jumbled together: a grotto built of volcanic rock imported from Italy; a soaring obelisk at the end of an avenue of firs; and a "Gothic cottage". In 1772, the folly of **King Alfred's Tower** was added at the far western end of the park (nearly three miles from the house), and today affords fine views across the estate and into neighbouring counties. The rhododendrons and azaleas that now make such a splash in early summer are a later addition to this dream landscape. A circuit around the lake and woods (not including King Alfred's Tower) adds up to around two miles.

The house

In contrast to the magnificent grounds, the exterior of the **house** is fairly run-of-the-mill, though the artistic treasures inside more than compensate. The spacious **Entrance Hall** makes a fitting introduction, a 30ft cube with regal doorways and fireplace, and walls decked with a parade of family portraits. The **Library** is just as imposing, a long, barrel-ceilinged room furnished with rare volumes on the shelves and more work by Rysbrack on show: two busts of Milton as a youth and an old man, and a terracotta model of the Hercules statue in the Pantheon, displayed on a magnificent Chippendale desk carved with the heads of philosophers and ancient Egyptians. This room survived a fire that devastated much of the house in 1902 – though most of the works of art and furnishings were rescued.

There's more fine furniture in the other rooms, notably the **Music Room**, with another exuberant chimneypiece, and the ornately plastered **Dining Room** and **Saloon**, the latter once used for theatrical performances, balls and other social occasions. The last stop on a tour of the house is the **Picture Gallery**, another room that escaped the 1902 conflagration, displaying a mix of Old Masters and landscapes.

ARRIVAL AND DEPARTURE — FROME AND AROUND

By train Frome's station is at the eastern end of town.

Destinations Bath (Mon–Sat 8 daily, Sun 3 daily; 40–50min); Bradford-on-Avon (Mon–Sat 7 daily, Sun 3 daily; 20–35min); Bruton (Mon–Sat 9 daily, Sun 5 daily; 12min); Castle Cary (Mon–Sat 9 daily, Sun 5 daily; 15min); Westbury (Mon–Sat 13 daily, Sun 9 daily; 10min).

By bus Stops are on Market Place, Cork St and Christchurch St West.

Destinations Bath (Mon–Sat 3 hourly, Sun every 2hr; 40–50min); Mells (Mon–Sat every 2hr; 10min); Nunney (Mon–Fri 4 daily; 10min); Shepton Mallet (Mon–Fri 4 daily; 50min); Radstock (Mon–Sat 7 daily; 35min); Westbury (Mon–Sat 5 daily; 35min).

Taxis ABC ⊕01373 452211; Arrow Taxis ⊕01373 470110.

INFORMATION

Tourist office Frome Town Hall, Christchurch St West (Mon–Fri 9am–5pm; ⊕01373 465757, ⊕discoverfrome.co.uk). There's also a handy information point in Black Swan Arts, Bridge St (Tues–Sat 10am–4pm, 1st Sun of month 10am–4pm).

9

ACCOMMODATION

FROME
SEE MAP PAGE 284

Archangel 1 King St ☎01373 456111, ⓦarchangel frome.com. Converted from an old coaching inn in a contemporary industrial style, this central lodging has ten boldly coloured rooms, some of which feature gigantic Renaissance murals and freestanding zinc baths. Staff are smiley and there's a courtyard garden, though noise from the buzzing café, bar and restaurant (as well as creaky floorboards) can intrude into the rooms. **£85**

★ **The Lighthouse** Tytherington, 1.5 miles south of Frome ☎01373 453585, ⓦlighthouse-uk.com. If you're looking for a wholesome country retreat, this laidback place outside town is just the ticket, offering modern B&B rooms opening onto a central patio. Guests can take advantage of the dairy- and gluten-free breakfasts, thirty acres of parkland that include play areas, woodland walks and a lake, and Café Nouveau on the same premises, for excellent coffees, cakes and takeaway sandwiches. There's a pub across the road and use of an indoor pool just next door. **£105**

★ **Trinity House** Goulds Ground ☎01373 451547, ⓦthepaintedhome.co.uk. Self-catering accommodation is available in this former Victorian schoolhouse, with its own entrance and private garden. Steps lead up from the well-equipped kitchen to the bedroom with its French king-size bed (but the bathroom is downstairs). A complimentary breakfast hamper is provided on your first night. No credit cards. **£120**

AROUND FROME

Chalford House Hotel 114 Warminster Rd, Westbury ☎01373 822753, ⓦchalfordhousehotel.co.uk. A 10min walk from Westbury's centre, this family-run hotel makes for a handy local stopover, offering twenty clean and spacious rooms, though the decor of some is slightly oppressive. Staff are attentive and friendly, and the garden offers a peaceful spot to sit. Breakfast is served in a conservatory and there's a bar-restaurant with good food and drink. **£105**

★ **Stay at Penny's Mill** Horn St, Nunney ☎01373 836210, ⓦstayatpennysmill.com. This delightful B&B in a converted watermill just up from Nunney Castle has three rooms – two of them interconnecting for family use – all with a light, airy feel and lovely garden views. Breakfast in the conservatory is a communal affair, and includes freshly baked bread and home-made jams. **£95**

Talbot Inn Mells ☎01373 812254, ⓦtalbotinn.com. Wonderful old coaching inn near Mells church, full of character, offering traditional-style rooms named after local figures. Two more luxurious rooms (costing more) have four-posters, and family rooms are also available. There's Butcombe beer and locally brewed Talbot Ale in the bar, along with an impressive collection of gins, as well as top-quality food (the Sunday carvery is renowned, and worth booking), making this an excellent refreshment stop too. **£100**

EATING AND DRINKING

FROME
SEE MAP PAGE 284

Bistro Lotte 23 Catherine St ☎01373 300646, ⓦbistro lottefrome.co.uk. You'll find this lively, French-style café and bistro at the top end of the trendy St Catherine's Quarter, housed in a former grocer's shop and decked out with panelled walls and low-hanging lamps. The short lunch menu features galettes (buckwheat crêpes, around £7.50), such as Chèvre Provençal (£7.25), packed with tasty vegetables and creamy goat's cheese, while evening offerings include generous plates of *petatou* (a Provençal potato and cheesecake, £13.50) and boeuf bourguignon (£14.50). A wine bar under the same management operates further along the street, and B&B rooms are also available. Mon–Sat 9am–11pm, Sun 9am–4pm; kitchen daily 9am–11am, noon–2pm & 6–9.30pm (Sun till 2.30pm).

Garden Café 16 Stony St ☎01373 454178, ⓦgardencafe frome.co.uk. In this relaxed haven from Frome's bustling centre, you can sip coffee or sample the tasty organic, ethical and locally sourced vegetarian dishes – for example cashew nut and bean patties (£10), flans (£10.50), Thai burgers (£11) or tapas (£4 each or £24 for a platter to share). There

are books to borrow, a paved garden with a children's play area, and a good selection of soft drinks. Mon 8.30am–6pm, Tues–Sat 8.30am–9pm, Sun 10.30am–5pm.

★ **Griffin Inn** 25 Milk St ☎01373 301251, ⓦgriffin frome.com. At the top of a steep hill, this affable neighbourhood pub brews its own beer and provides a pool table, a garden, huge burgers and a lively atmosphere. It's also one of Frome's best live music venues for local musicians, while other regular events include barbecue lunches on Sunday, Celtic music night on the last Tuesday of the month, and World Food Night every Wednesday, when you can dine royally for a fiver. Mon–Thurs 4–11pm, Fri & Sat noon–11pm, Sun noon–9pm.

★ **High Pavement Evening Café** 8 Palmer St ☎07967 222682, ⓦfacebook.com/thehighpavement. You won't find much choice on the menu of this slightly eccentric place on Catherine Hill, whose rugs, pictures and purple walls lend a theatrical ambience, but you won't be disappointed by the fare. The dishes are predominantly Spanish or Middle Eastern in style – tapas for starters, maybe slow-roast pork belly or roast aubergine with za'atar for a main course – and usually delicious, and there are some very zingy desserts too. The staff are marvellous, and there's a courtyard garden. Given its very limited opening hours, you should book well ahead. Starters are £3–6, mains around £14.50. No credit cards. Fri & Sat from 6.30pm; closed summer school hols.

AROUND FROME

Bath Arms Horningsham, near Longleat Ⓣ01985 844308, Ⓦbatharms.co.uk. Conveniently located outside the exit from Longleat, this upmarket Georgian inn shares some of the same jaunty spirit. The food in the bar or restaurant is traditional, local and usually good; you can have sandwiches (from £6.25) or choose from a wide range of dishes such as chicken, seabass, burgers and steaks (around £15). There's outdoor seating, and clean and comfortable accommodation upstairs (from £115). Mon–Sat 10am–11pm, Sun 10am–10.30pm; kitchen 7.30–10am, noon–2.45pm & 6–9pm (Fri & Sat till 9.30pm).

The George Inn Church St, Nunney Ⓣ01373 836458, Ⓦthegeorgeinnnunney.com. A stylish blend of antique and contemporary elements, this seventeenth-century coaching inn has bags of character as well as a top-class menu and a great selection of beers. Order sandwiches or panini (£7–8) from the bar, or go for a pan-fried salmon (£13), butternut squash risotto (£13.50) or lamb shank with couscous (£15), perhaps accompanied by a Wadworth's beer or chilled wine. There's a walled garden, and ten rooms upstairs provide B&B (from £120). Mon–Sat 10am–11pm, Sun noon–11pm; kitchen Mon–Fri noon–2.30pm & 5.30–9pm, Sat noon–9pm, Sun noon–7.45pm.

Spread Eagle Inn Stourton Ⓣ01747 840587, Ⓦspreadeagleinn.com. Part of the Stourhead estate, this slate-floored pub and restaurant is pricey but atmospheric, and the food is of a high standard. You can order ciabattas (about £8) or a full meal of such old favourites as duck breast, fish and chips and vegetable curry (around £12 at lunchtime, £13–18 in the evening), washed down with West Country beers. Coffees and cream teas are also served, and five rooms with period furnishings provide accommodation (£125). Mon–Sat 10am–11pm, Sun noon–10.30pm; kitchen noon–3pm (Sun till 4pm) & 7–9pm.

Salisbury and Stonehenge

SALISBURY CATHEDRAL

Salisbury and Stonehenge

The distant past is perhaps more tangible in neighbouring Wiltshire than in any other part of England. The chalky uplands of Salisbury Plain are littered with Bronze Age burial mounds and the remnants of ancient ceremonial structures, telltale signs of five millennia of pagan worship that reach their enigmatic zenith at Stonehenge, Europe's greatest Neolithic monument and a legendary site in every sense of the word.

At a sprightly eight hundred years of age, the great cathedral city of **Salisbury** is youthful in comparison but has more than its fair share of old-world atmosphere. The medieval Close and ensemble of half-timbered houses provide an aesthetic backdrop to the towering **cathedral**, while its compact core still bears the hallmarks of a deep-rooted mercantile tradition. Beyond the attractive old city, grassy water meadows grazed by sheep spread towards Harnham from the cathedral's southern edge.

The city itself has a number of worthwhile museums as well as a varied calendar of cultural events, but many visitors also find time to make the short walk or bus ride to **Old Sarum**, Salisbury's precursor. Its unusual double-ditch appearance – something akin to a grassy wedding cake – is just as much an attraction as the remains of the Norman castle that crowns it. In the other direction, and a model of accomplishment in comparison, lies sixteenth-century **Wilton House**, a real crowd-puller and one of Wiltshire's finest stately homes.

Just north of Salisbury begins the sea of swaying wheatfields and wildflower meadows that constitute **Salisbury Plain**. Much of it falls under the jurisdiction of the Ministry of Defence: signs warn motorists of tank crossings ahead, while flags deter casual trespassers from MOD firing ranges. Though now largely deserted except by forces families living in ugly barracks quarters, the Plain once positively throbbed with communities who lived, built, worshipped and died at Durrington Walls, Normanton Down and the other henges and barrows now conserved as the **Stonehenge World Heritage Site**. At the centre of this rich tapestry of ritualistic landmarks stands the famous circle of **Stonehenge** itself, an unmissable, frustrating, secretive and genuinely awe-inspiring monument that – some 3500 years after it was abandoned – still has the finest minds in archeological science scratching their heads and wondering what on earth it was really used for.

Salisbury and around

Huddled below Wiltshire's chalky plain in the converging valleys of the Avon and Nadder, **SALISBURY** looks from a distance very much as it did when Constable painted his celebrated view of it from across the water meadows, its tranquil **Close** fringed with fine Georgian houses and stately homes and focused around the city's magnificent **cathedral**. Stern-looking medieval gates (which are still locked every night) shelter the Close from the rest of the city; **North Gate** opens onto the centre's older streets, where narrow pedestrianized alleyways bear names like Fish Row and Salt Lane, indicative of their trading origins.

Many half-timbered houses and inns survive all over the centre, and the last of four market crosses, **Poultry Cross**, stands on stilts in Silver Street. Nearby **Market Square** still performs its historical role, its twice-weekly **market** (Tues 9am–3.30pm, Sat 9am–4pm) serving a large agricultural area, just as it did in earlier times when the city grew wealthy on wool. The Artisan Market adds home-made foods and handmade arts and crafts to the mix on the first Sunday of the month (March–Oct 10am–4pm).

STONEHENGE

Highlights

❶ Salisbury Cathedral The city's sensational cathedral is one of the finest buildings in England. See page 296

❷ Old Sarum The ruined remains of Salisbury's forerunner enjoy a dramatic setting on a hill just north of the city. See page 300

❸ Wilton House The pure panache of Inigo Jones's lavish state rooms almost steals the show from the superb art within. See page 300

❹ Haunch of Venison Lovely wood-panelled pub, small but perfectly formed, and with a large dose of quirkiness. See page 302

❺ Stone Circle Access Watching the sun rise from inside the sarsens, with only birdsong for company, is the only way to do Stonehenge justice. See page 304

❻ Walking the World Heritage Site There's more to Stonehenge than the stone circle – get out among the surrounding barrows, henges and processional pathways for an altogether different experience. See page 307

HIGHLIGHTS ARE MARKED ON THE MAP ON PAGE 296

Salisbury sprang into existence in the early thirteenth century, when the bishopric was moved from **Old Sarum**, an Iron Age hillfort settled by the Romans and their successors; the deserted remnants of Salisbury's precursor now stand on the northern fringes of the city and are – along with **Wilton House**, to the west – well worth working into your itinerary.

Salisbury Cathedral

The Close • Daily Mon–Sat 9am–5pm, Sun noon–4pm • Suggested donation £7.50 • Regular free tours (45min) • Tower tours (1hr 45min) £13.50; check website for times; advance booking recommended • ☎ 01722 555120, ⓦ salisburycathedral.org.uk

Begun in 1220, **Salisbury Cathedral** was mostly completed within forty years and is thus unusually consistent in its style, with one extremely prominent exception – the

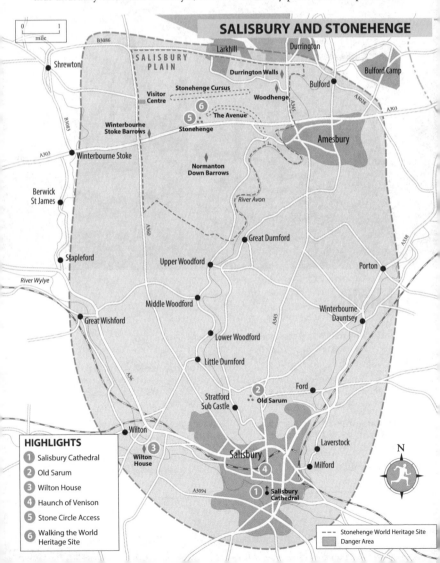

SALISBURY AND STONEHENGE

HIGHLIGHTS

1. Salisbury Cathedral
2. Old Sarum
3. Wilton House
4. Haunch of Venison
5. Stone Circle Access
6. Walking the World Heritage Site

- - - Stonehenge World Heritage Site

Danger Area

CONSTABLE IN SALISBURY

Though inextricably linked with the landscapes of Suffolk, **John Constable** (1776–1837) was greatly inspired by Salisbury and produced some of his finest work on the back of various visits to the city in the early half of the nineteenth century. A pencil drawing of *St Ann Gate* from his first trip here in 1811 – when he stayed with the Bishop of Salisbury – hangs in the Salisbury Museum (see page 299), but it's his later paintings that are more compelling. After honeymooning in the city in 1816, Constable returned to paint *Salisbury Cathedral and Leadenhall from the River Avon* (1820) and *Salisbury Cathedral from the Bishop's Grounds* (1823), which show the daring use of colour that made *The Hay Wain* such a revelation at the Paris Salon in 1824 – though the bishop famously made him redo the clouds for his third version of the "Bishop's Grounds". The contrast between these and Constable's later works, produced after the death of his wife Maria, is stark: his second *Salisbury Cathedral from the Meadows* (1831), painted a year after the first, is a raw, pain-filled picture, one whose sentiment, as he wrote in a letter to his friend David Lucas, "is that of solemnity".

10

spire, which was added a century later and at 404ft is the highest in England. Its survival is something of a miracle, for the foundations penetrate only about 6ft into marshy ground, and when Christopher Wren surveyed it he found the spire to be leaning almost 2.5ft out of true; he added further tie rods, which finally arrested the movement. You can get a better idea of how it all remains in place on one of the recommended tours of the **tower**, which take visitors up the 332 steps to the spire's base, offering sublime views of the city along the way.

The interior

The cathedral's **interior** might seem over-austere after James Wyatt's brisk eighteenth-century tidying, but there's an amazing sense of space and light in its high nave, despite the sombre pillars of grey Purbeck marble, which are visibly bowing beneath the weight they bear. Monuments and carved tombs line the walls, most notably the large marble memorial to Edward Seymour and Lady Catherine Grey (Lady Jane's sister) next to the **Trinity Chapel**, and the colourful tomb of Richard Mompesson and his wife, facing the "wrong way" on the south side of the huge **quire**. A striking modern addition to the nave is water sculptor William Pye's cruciform **font**, added in 2008; cast in bronze and clad in Purbeck stone, it mesmerizingly reflects the vaulting in its overflowing infinity pool-style surface.

The chapter house

Mon–Sat 9.30am–5pm (Nov–March 10am–4.30pm), Sun 11am–4pm • Free • No photography allowed

The largest cathedral cloisters in the country lead to the octagonal **chapter house**, with a beautiful vaulted ceiling fanning out above walls that are decorated with a medieval frieze of scenes from the Old Testament. The room displays a rare copy of the original **Magna Carta**, the best-preserved of only four surviving from 1215. The "great charter" established a national scheme for weights and measures, trial by jury and other civil liberties, though the 1215 version, sealed by King John, only lasted three months thanks to a controversial section (dubbed Clause 61) that gave great power to the barons over their king.

The Close

Surrounding Salisbury Cathedral, **the Close** is a peaceful precinct of lawns and mellow old buildings, their pathways lined with lavender. A slow circuit enables you to appreciate the cathedral from a variety of aspects – much like Constable did in the early 1800s (see box) – and to take in many of the city's finest houses along the way. Most of them have seemly Georgian facades, though some, like the **Bishop's Palace**, the

Old Deanery and **the Wardrobe** (once used as the bishops' clothes store and now home to the Rifles Museum), date from the thirteenth century.

Mompesson House

The Close • Mid-March to Oct daily 11am–5pm • £7.50; garden only £1.50 • NT • ☎ 01722 335659, ⓦ nationaltrust.org.uk

On the northern side of the Close, facing Salisbury Cathedral in the distance, **Mompesson House** was built by a wealthy merchant in 1701 and contains some beautifully furnished eighteenth-century rooms and decorative ceilings throughout;

10

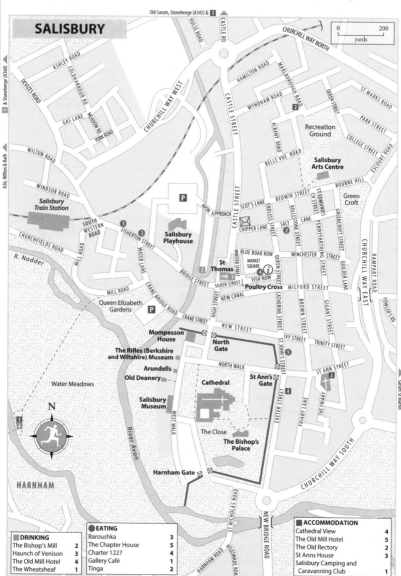

SALISBURY

even the underside of the oak staircase in the main entrance hall, which leads out onto a charming walled garden, is elegantly carved. The Queen Anne house still looks very much like it did in the 1700s, a fact not lost on the location team of Ang Lee's 1995 *Sense and Sensibility*, who used it for Mrs Jennings' London home.

The Rifles (Berkshire and Wiltshire) Museum

The Wardrobe, 58 The Close • Mon–Sat 10am–5pm; closed Jan & Dec • £5; garden only £2 • ☎ 01722 419419, ⓦ thewardrobe.org.uk

Backing onto a pretty, memorial-filled garden, the four rooms of **The Rifles Museum** house the collections of Berkshire and Wiltshire's infantry units; the Gloucester regiments, also part of the Rifles, are kept elsewhere. Its huge archive – the two thousand or so pieces on display at any one time constitute just over five percent of the total collection – spans the regiments' long history, with uniforms, medals, weapons and other military regalia adding colour to campaigns like the American War of Independence (from which they kept a cannon ball), the little-known nineteenth-century battles of Ferozeshah (India) and Tofrek (Sudan), and more recently the conflicts in Northern Ireland and Afghanistan.

Arundells

The Close • Mid-March to early Nov Sat–Tues 11am–5pm, Wed by hourly guided tour only (11am–3pm) • £7.50, garden and exhibition room only £3.50, guided tour £12 • ☎ 01722 326546, ⓦ arundells.org

The stately home partly shielded by gates on the western side of the Close is **Arundells**, a medieval canonry that was the residence of former prime minister Sir Edward Heath for twenty years until his death in 2005. Heath decreed that his foundation open the house to the public so that everyone could "share the beauty of Arundells" – try to visit on one of the Wednesday **guided tours**, which give visitors an insight into both Heath's charming home and the interesting life of the man himself.

Salisbury Museum

The King's House, 65 The Close • Mon–Sat 10am–5pm, mid-May to Sept also Sun noon–5pm • £8 • ☎ 01722 332151, ⓦ salisburymuseum.org.uk

At the southwestern corner of the Close, **The King's House** – so named because James I stayed here in the early seventeenth century – is home to the **Salisbury Museum**, an absorbing account of local history. Its enlightening section on Stonehenge includes five-thousand-year-old carved chalk plaques and the remains of the **Amesbury Archer**, whose 4300-year-old grave is the richest "Beaker" burial site ever found in Britain and contained the country's first objects made of gold.

The museum also focuses on the life and times of Lieutenant-General Augustus **Pitt-Rivers**, the father of modern archeology, who excavated many of Wiltshire's prehistoric sites. The collection of paintings and prints is extensive, though only one, a pencil drawing of St Ann Gate, is by **John Constable**, despite his affiliation with the city (see page 297).

St Thomas

St Thomas's Square • Mon–Fri 9am–5pm, Sun noon–5pm • Free • ⓦ stthomassalisbury.co.uk

Tucked behind Bridge Street, the dark, peaceful **church of St Thomas** – named after Thomas à Becket – is worth a look inside for its carved timber ceiling, decorated with Somerset angels (there are nearly 250 dotted around the church), and its "Doom Painting" over the chancel arch; dating from 1475, it depicts Christ presiding over the Last Judgement and is one of the largest of its kind in England.

The water meadows

ⓦ salisburywatermeadows.org.uk

Enclosed by the Nadder and Avon, on an island to the west of the cathedral, the **water meadows** reward walkers with the defining image of Salisbury: the cathedral's inspiring silhouette and the view made famous by Constable. It takes about twenty minutes to cross Town Path, the pathway that bisects them, and reach **Harnham**, where the riverside *Old Mill Hotel* (see page 301) serves refreshments to set you up for the return journey.

Old Sarum

Castle Rd, off the A345 • Daily 10am–6pm, Oct till 5pm, Nov to late March till 4pm • £5.40 • EH • ☎ 01722 335398, ⓦ english-heritage. org.uk; Old Sarum is served by Park & Ride #11 (every 15min; 10–15min; from the Beehive; see page 301) and Salisbury Reds (ⓦ salisburyreds.co.uk) bus #X5 (every 30min; 10min), while the hop-on-hop-off Stonehenge Tour bus (£16; ⓦ thestonehengetour.info) passes the ruins on its way back from the stones

The ruins of **Old Sarum** cap a bleak hilltop two miles north of Salisbury city centre. Possibly occupied up to five thousand years ago, then developed as an Iron Age fort (whose double protective ditches remain), it was settled by Romans and Saxons before the Norman bishopric of Sherborne was moved here in the 1070s. Within a few decades, a new **cathedral** had been consecrated at Old Sarum, and a large religious community was living alongside the soldiers in the central **castle** founded by William the Conqueror fifty years before.

Old Sarum was an uncomfortable place, parched and windswept, and in 1220 the dissatisfied clergy – additionally at loggerheads with the castle's occupants – appealed to the pope for permission to decamp to Salisbury (which is still known officially as New Sarum). When permission was granted, the stone from the cathedral was commandeered for Salisbury's gateways; once the church had gone, the population waned, and by the sixteenth century Old Sarum was deserted. Today, the dominant features of the site are its ditches, banks and huge, two-tiered earthworks, with a broad trench encircling the rudimentary remains of the Norman palace, castle and cathedral.

Wilton House

Wilton • **House** Mid-April to early Sept Sun–Thurs & bank hol Sat 11.30am–5pm • **Grounds** April to early Sept Sun–Thurs & bank hol Sat 11am–5.30pm • £15.50; grounds £6.50 • ☎ 01722 746700, ⓦ wiltonhouse.com; Park & Ride #3 (Mon–Sat) and Salisbury Reds (ⓦ salisburyreds.co.uk) buses #3 (Sun) and #8 (Mon–Sat) run from the city centre to Wilton House (every 15min; 20min)

Dominating its eponymous village five miles west of Salisbury, splendid **Wilton House** is home to the eighteenth Earl of Pembroke, whose family has occupied its stately rooms since the mid-sixteenth century. The original Tudor house, built on the site of a dissolved Benedictine abbey, was damaged by fire in 1647. It was rebuilt by Inigo Jones, whose hallmark Palladian style can be seen in the sumptuous Single Cube and Double Cube rooms, so called because of their precise dimensions. The **Double Cube Room**, in particular, is breathtakingly grand; one of the finest surviving staterooms in England, it was designed specifically with the fourth Earl of Pembroke's Van Dyck paintings in mind, and portraits such as *The Three Elder Children of Charles I* fit seamlessly onto its walls.

It's these easel **paintings** that make Wilton really special – in addition to Van Dyck, the collection includes works by Rembrandt, Poussin and Tintoretto, spread across only slightly less extravagant rooms throughout the first floor. In the grounds, which incorporate delightful little Japanese and rose gardens, Jones' famous **Palladian Bridge** has been joined by various ancillary attractions including an excellent **adventure playground** and, in the **Old Riding School**, a film on the colourful earls of Pembroke.

ARRIVAL AND DEPARTURE	SALISBURY AND AROUND

By train First Great Western and South Western Railway serve Salisbury train station, half a mile west of the city centre, on South Western Rd.

Destinations Basingstoke (every 30min; 40min); Bath Spa (hourly; 55min–1hr 5min); Bristol Temple Meads (hourly; 1hr 10–1hr 25min); Cardiff (hourly; 2hr); Crewkerne (hourly; 1hr); Exeter St David's (hourly; 1hr 50min); London Waterloo (every 30min; 1hr 25min); Portsmouth (every

SALISBURY INTERNATIONAL ARTS FESTIVAL

Arty Salisbury gets even artier every summer when it hosts the themed **Salisbury International Arts Festival** (May & June; ⓦ wiltshirecreative.co.uk), a fortnight of events – many of them interactive – that celebrate theatre, dance, comedy, film and spoken word performances from a dozen or so different countries each year.

30min; 1hr 15–1hr 25min); Southampton (every 30min; 30–45min); Woking (every 30min; 55min); Yeovil Junction (hourly; 50min).

By bus Buses stop at various sights around the city centre. Destinations Bournemouth (every 30min; 1hr 25min); Bath (daily; 2hr 50min); London (3 daily; 3hr 5min–3hr 20min); Southampton (hourly; 1hr 15min).

By car The main roads into Salisbury can get clogged with traffic, making the five Park & Rides (ⓦ salisburyreds.co.uk/parkride) that ring the city a sensible option. They're at the Beehive (north of Salisbury, on the A345); London Rd (northeast, on the A30); Petersfinger (southeast, on the A36); Britford (south, on the A338) and Wilton (west, on the A36). If you do drive into the centre, you'll find convenient car parks at Old George Mall and on Crane Bridge Rd.

10

INFORMATION AND TOURS

TOURIST INFORMATION

Tourist office Fish Row, just off Market Square (Mon–Fri 9am–5pm, Sat 10am–4pm, Sun 10am–2pm; ☎01722 342860, ⓦ visitwiltshire.co.uk).

WALKS AND TOURS

Salisbury City Guides Informative city walks (11am: April–Oct daily, Nov–March Sat & Sun; £6) and ghost walks (May–Sept Fri 8pm; same price), departing from the tourist office (☎07873 212941, ⓦ salisburycityguides.co.uk), plus tours of Old Sarum, Wilton and Stonehenge.

Salisbury and Stonehenge Guided Tours Recommended city walks and food tours, as well as tours of Stonehenge and Old Sarum (☎07775 674816, ⓦ salisburyguidedtours.com).

ACCOMMODATION
MAP PAGE 298

★**Cathedral View** 83 Exeter St ☎01722 502254, ⓦ cathedral-viewbandb.co.uk. Welcoming B&B in a Georgian townhouse just a few minutes' walk from the Close – which perhaps explains why the thoughtful hosts have such a good knowledge of what to do in town. Comfortable en suites (one with a bath) have excellent beds; as the name suggests, a couple of the street-facing rooms have views of the cathedral spire. Great choice at breakfast. No children under 10. **£100**

The Old Mill Hotel Town Path, West Harnham, half a mile southwest of Salisbury ☎01722 327517, ⓦ oldmill hotelsalisbury.co.uk. Wood-beamed riverside inn dating to the fifteenth century but with modern, fully equipped rooms, some boasting great views to the cathedral. It's a lovely 10min walk through tranquil water meadows from the city centre. **£117**

The Old Rectory 75 Belle Vue Rd ☎01722 415379, ⓦ theoldrectorybedandbreakfast-salisbury.co.uk. Once home to the rector of nearby St Edmund's Church (now Salisbury Arts Centre), this pleasant B&B, a short walk north of the centre, has three light, airy rooms, with one that can be made up as a twin and one a single (from £69). Breakfast is served in the conservatory overlooking the spacious back garden. **£95**

St Anns House 32–34 St Ann St ☎01722 335657, ⓦ stannshouse.co.uk. Stylishly furnished Georgian B&B with friendly family owners and a difficult-to-beat location on a quiet street just a few minutes' walk from the cathedral. Great breakfast spread, including a full English from local farm produce. There's also a homely one-bedroom apartment (sleeping four) just next door. Double **£70**, apartment **£95**

Salisbury Camping and Caravanning Club Hudson's Field, Castle Rd, 1.5 miles north of Salisbury ☎01722 320713, ⓦ campingandcaravanningclub.co.uk. Full-scale but friendly campsite close to Old Sarum (and Old Sarum Airfield), with plenty of room for kids to run around in the field next door (Hudson's Field itself). It's a good setup, though many of the pitches are on sloping ground. Two-night minimum stay. **£23.70**

EATING AND DRINKING
MAP PAGE 298

Baroushka 90 Fisherton St ☎01722 327628, ⓦ baroushka.com. Sophisticated Middle Eastern restaurant, mostly looking to the cuisines of Lebanon, Morocco and Turkey for its menu of cold and hot mezze, succulent grilled meats, tagines and salads; the *shish taouk* (chicken) skewers (£16.40) and rosemary and pistachio seasoned lamb cutlets (£19.40) are highly recommended mains. Daily noon–2pm & 5.30–10pm.

10

The Bishop's Mill 7 The Maltings ☎01722 412127. Enjoying a superb central riverside spot, *The Bishop's Mill* has a bare-brick-brasserie interior, and outdoor seating above the rushing weir. Pub grub is pretty standard (scampi and chips, sausage and mash; mains from £6.99), though a decent range of burgers (from £7.99) includes the Chicken Trio (buttermilk, piri-piri and Louisiana chicken) and a chickpea, red pepper and hoisin number. Daily 11am–11pm, Fri & Sat till midnight; food served daily noon–9pm.

The Chapter House 9–13 St John's St ☎01722 341277, ⓦthechapterhouseuk.com. Timber-framed grillhouse just outside St Ann's gate, with a South African, meat-focused menu that includes boerewors, bobotie and a range of burgers, ribs and steaks – choose the size and cut of your steak (from £18.50) and dress it in one of half a dozen sauces. Mon–Fri noon–2.30pm & 6–9.30pm, Sat noon–9.30pm, Sun noon–7.30pm.

Charter 1227 6–7 Ox Row, Market Square ☎01722 333118, ⓦcharter1227.co.uk. Housed above a *Costa Coffee* on Market Square, this informal but fine-dining restaurant serves beautifully presented Modern British and Mediterranean dishes such as glazed crab ravioli and roast lamb with piperade (mains from £15). Tues–Sat noon–2.30pm & 6–9.30pm.

★ **Gallery Café** Fisherton Mill, 108 Fisherton St ☎01722 500200, ⓦfishertonmill.co.uk. Set in a rustic old grain mill that's now home to a very browsable art gallery, this is a top spot for a light but tasty lunch – spinach, mushroom and garlic tart (£11.50), grilled lemon sole with chermoula (£16) or cheaper sandwiches – or a cuppa and a home-made cake. You can watch the artists at work – making jewellery, flower arranging – in their first-floor studios. Mon–Fri 10am–5pm (lunch noon–2.30pm), Sat 9.30am–5.30pm.

★ **Haunch of Venison** 1 Minster St ☎01722 411313. Tiny, richly atmospheric boozer, where you could easily lose an hour or two cradling a pint of Hopback's GFB or Summer Lightning. Creaky wooden stairs lead to a sloping-floored restaurant serving a menu that's dominated, as the name, suggests by one particular meat – choose from venison sausages, venison burger and venison steak, plus the signature pulled haunch of venison amongst other dishes (mains from £12.95). The pub's famous mummified hand of a nineteenth-century card player (still clutching his cards) lies locked behind an iron grill after it was repeatedly stolen. Daily 11am–11pm.

The Old Mill Hotel Town Path, West Harnham, half a mile southwest of Salisbury ☎01722 327517, ⓦoldmillhotelsalisbury.co.uk. Harnham's fifteenth-century paper mill enjoys a wonderful location on the Avon, and the hotel bar makes a good halfway stop for a pint of Abbot on a round trip across the water meadows. Daily 11am–11pm.

Tinga 2–4 Salt Lane ☎01722 504416, ⓦtingasalisbury.com. Fun Mexican restaurant and bar, where virtually every conceivable space is adorned with murals or draped in foliage. The menu of pretty authentic tacos, quesadillas, burritos and enchiladas (mains from £7.95) is accompanied by an ever-growing list of tequilas and mezcals. Mon–Thurs 5–9pm, Fri & Sat noon–9pm, Sun noon–7pm.

The Wheatsheaf Lower Woodford, 2 miles from the A360 ☎01722 782203, ⓦwheatsheaflowerwoodford.co.uk. There's a warm feeling to this Hall & Woodhouse pub, tucked away at the bottom of the lovely Woodford Valley on the back road to Old Sarum. The food – mostly pub classics like fish and chips, plus a decent range of vegetarian and vegan dishes (mains from £8.50) – is simple but satisfying, the interior varied (open in parts, cosier in others) and the service friendly. Mon–Sat 11am–11pm, Sun noon–10.30pm; food served daily noon–9pm, Sun till 8pm.

ENTERTAINMENT

As well as the events staged at the two venues below, there's a busy calendar of musical performances throughout the city – at the cathedral, Sarum St Martin (ⓦsarumstmartin.org.uk) and St Thomas, among others. For a diary of live music performances, from rock and ska to classical concerts, see ⓦsalisburygigguide.co.uk.

Salisbury Arts Centre Bedwin St ☎01722 320333, ⓦwiltshirecreative.co.uk. The old church of St Edmund's makes a great venue for an eclectic programme of music, theatre, film and dance, plus regular themed talks, contemporary art exhibitions and a variety of workshops.

Salisbury Playhouse Malthouse Lane ☎01722 320333, ⓦwiltshirecreative.co.uk. Respected regional theatre with two stages – the Main House and the more intimate Salberg – that produces a wide range of contemporary plays, costume dramas, pantomimes and comedies. Venue for the annual Theatre Fest West showcase for local theatre producers.

Salisbury Racecourse Netherhampton, 4 miles west of the city ☎01722 326461, ⓦsalisburyracecourse.co.uk. One of the oldest racecourses in the country, hosting sixteen flat races a season (May to early Oct), which normally attract a quality field. Tickets cost £15 for the Grandstand, £23 for the Bilbury Enclosure.

Stonehenge

No ancient structure in England arouses more controversy than **Stonehenge**, a mysterious ring of monoliths ten miles north of Salisbury. While archeologists argue over whether it was a place of ritual sacrifice or sun worship, an astronomical calculator or a royal palace, the guardians of the site struggle to accommodate its year-round crowds. Thanks to much-needed recent improvements, including the building of a new visitor centre and the closure of the intrusive A344, visiting Stonehenge is more rewarding than ever, though conservation remains an urgent priority, and unless you arrange for special access (see page 304), you must be content with walking around rather than among the stones.

10

INFORMATION

Opening hours Daily: April, May & Sept to mid-Oct 9.30am–7pm; June–Aug 9am–8pm; mid-Oct to March 9.30am–5pm; last admission 2hr before closing.

Entry fee £19; NT & EH; entrance by timed ticket, advance booking required; audioguides £3 extra or free if downloaded from the App Store or Google Play.

Access Shuttle buses run regularly from the visitor centre to the stones (10min), dropping off at the Fargo Plantation so you can walk the last stretch. Better still, you can follow a waymarked route across fields from the visitor centre (30min).

Tours Numerous companies run tours to Stonehenge, including The Stonehenge Tour Company (📞0203 506 1698, 🌐stonehengetours.com), Salisbury and Stonehenge Guided Tours (📞07775 674816, 🌐salisburyguidedtours.

com) and HisTOURies (📞01225 290858, 🌐histouries. co.uk), with departures from Salisbury, Bath and London. Several also incorporate the highly recommended Stone Circle Access in their itineraries (see page 304), though it's easy enough to book this direct with English Heritage.

Contacts English Heritage (EH) 📞0370 333 1181, 🌐english-heritage.org.uk; National Trust (NT) 📞01672 539920, 🌐nationaltrust.org.uk.

Getting there You can reach Stonehenge from Salisbury on either the A345 (via Amesbury) or the A360. The hop-on-hop-off Stonehenge Tour bus (£16 return; 🌐thestonehengetour.info) picks up from Salisbury train station and New Canal, taking just over half an hour to get to the visitor centre; it returns via Old Sarum (see page 300).

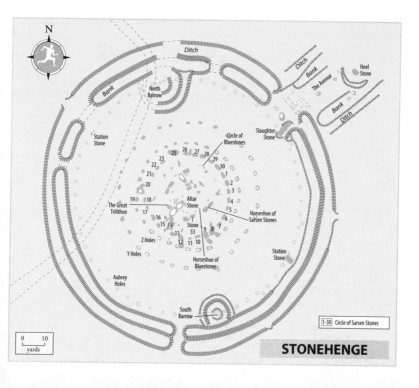

STONEHENGE

WHAT IS A HENGE?

A **henge** consists of a circular ditch enclosed by a bank, a feature best seen at Woodhenge (see page 309) and Durrington Walls (see page 310) – but not, ironically, at Stonehenge, which despite giving rise to the name in the first place is not actually a henge at all.

The visitor centre

A long time in the making (see page 305), the Stonehenge **visitor centre** lies around a mile and a half west of the stones and includes a shop, café and exhibition space. Among the varied treasures here are five-thousand-year-old antler picks retrieved from the base of the ditch around Stonehenge and ceramic cups found in burial mounds at Normanton Downs, although the most striking display is the skeleton (complete with eerily realistic re-created face) that was excavated from the long barrow at Winterbourne Stoke.

You can stand inside a 360-degree projection of the stones as it runs through the seasons, taking in the summer and winter solstices en route, and, outside, find out what life was like inside a Neolithic house or have a go at trying to shift a life-size Preseli bluestone.

The site

What exists at Stonehenge today is only a part of the original prehistoric complex, as many of the outlying stones were plundered for building materials, while posts have rotted away and ditches filled in over time. The site's **construction** is thought to have taken place in phases, starting with the surrounding earthworks and ending – nearly 1500 years later and with a few lengthy periods of inactivity in between – with the final adjustments to the great stone circle.

Specific dates within that timescale are open to debate, and archeologists still struggle to agree on the timings of some pretty significant events, including at what stage the first bluestones arrived from Wales and when the sarsen circle was actually erected. Thanks to advances in geophysical technology, our knowledge of Stonehenge is constantly evolving. In the mid-1990s, new discoveries aged the whole structure a thousand years overnight, while excavations of the Aubrey Holes in 2008 showed that the bluestones may have been here by 3000 BC, some five hundred years earlier than was originally thought. Incredibly, as the site enters its fifth millennium, the story continues…

INSIDE THE CIRCLE

Since 1978, a low, looping rope has encircled Stonehenge, keeping visitors at bay and, to a certain extent, adding to its general sense of mystery. While the path that runs around the perimeter is perfect for taking in the scale of its construction, you can only appreciate the primordial power of Stonehenge from within. Venturing inside the sarsens, wandering among the bluestones and getting close enough to make out the etchings of ancient graffiti is an experience to turn even the sternest of sceptics.

English Heritage's one-hour **Stone Circle Access** (book well in advance via the form on the English Heritage website, where you can also find out the latest availability; £45) allows you to do exactly that. As the name implies, it's not a guided tour, just a chance to visit outside of hours (the earliest "access" is at 5am in summer, the latest 8.45pm), when the site is quiet, the crowds have all gone home or are yet to arrive, and the A303 is merely an occasional hum in the background.

STONEHENGE TODAY

The **man-made landscape** at Stonehenge has changed greatly over the last few years. In 2011, after nearly 25 years of failed proposals and abandoned plans – an embarrassing state of affairs that once led a parliamentary committee to condemn it as "a national disgrace" – the authorities eventually reached a solution that would allow the site to finally fulfil its potential.

The high chain-link fence that shielded the stones was pulled down. The A344, which ploughed right through the Avenue, virtually clipping the Heel Stone en route, was grassed over, making the approach to the stones much more inspiring. And with the opening of the visitor centre in 2013, the site at last had the interpretative focus it had so sorely lacked. In March 2020, the government announced that money would be allocated to pay for the long-debated Stonehenge improvement scheme, specifically a tunnel to run the A303 under Salisbury Plain, thus returning the landscape to something that even Neolithic man might recognize.

10

The first Stonehenge (c.3000 BC)

The creation of Stonehenge began over 5000 years ago with the bank and outer ditch that still surround the stones today. There were at least two entrances into the circle: one aligned with the midsummer sunrise, to the northeast (which became the **main entrance**), and the other to the south, by the South Barrow. Just inside the banks is a ring of 56 pits (a sacred number), now marked by little concrete plaques; known as **Aubrey Holes** after the antiquarian John Aubrey, who discovered them in the seventeenth century, these are now thought to have contained **bluestones** from the Welsh mountains, which were later moved inside the sarsen circle.

The timber phase and the bluestones (c.2900–2500 BC)

Post holes show that not long after the banks were dug **wooden posts** were irregularly erected around the two entrances and in a zig-zagging passageway that ran from the southern entrance into the centre. Despite numerous excavations, nothing has been found in these – the wooden posts themselves disintegrated hundreds of years ago – though it was during this same period that the Aubrey Holes were filled with a mixture of earth and human ash, proving that one of Stonehenge's first uses was as a ceremonial monument and cemetery.

According to the most recent excavations, it was during the latter part of this phase that a double arc of approximately eighty great blocks of **bluestone** (a collective name for the various "foreign" stones at Stonehenge) was raised within the enclosure itself. Some experts have suggested that these monoliths were found lying on Salisbury Plain, having been borne down from the Preseli Hills in Wales by a glacier in the last Ice Age, but the lack of any other glacial debris on the plain would seem to disprove this theory – and in 2019, archeologists discovered Neolithic tools linked to Stonehenge in two Welsh quarries, 180 miles away, proving that the stones really were cut and then dragged here overland.

The sarsens (c.2500 BC)

The crucial phase in the creation of the site came during the next hundred years, when the bluestones were replaced with colossal **sarsens**, the "precious unhewn stones of Eden" according to William Blake's *Jerusalem*. Shaped from sandstone (from the Marlborough Downs, about twenty miles north), they were erected in a circle of thirty stones (seventeen of which remain), topped by lintels, and carefully dressed and worked – for example, to compensate for perspectival distortion, the uprights have a slight swelling in the middle, the same trick the builders of the Parthenon were to employ hundreds of years later.

Four **Station Stones**, only two of which survive, were also raised at this time (the positions of the other two are marked by the North and South Barrows), as were the

THE SUMMER SOLSTICE

Heralding sunrise on the longest day of the year, the **summer solstice** (Wenglish-heritage. org.uk) was once a guaranteed flashpoint between New Age travellers and the police. But since 2000 – fifteen years after open access was withdrawn following the notorious Battle of the Beanfield – it has been a relaxed and trouble-free event, despite drawing a mixed crowd of 25,000 or so druids, hippies, travellers and interested observers.

The site opens at 7pm the evening before the summer solstice (June 21) and closes at 8am the following morning, with the sun creeping up over the stones at around 5am. Buses ferry people from Salisbury train station and New Canal to the Visitor Centre (departing every 10min between 6.30pm and 1.15am, returning less frequently between 4am and 9.45am). You can park at the site, about half a mile from the stones themselves.

three sarsens that marked the main entrance to the circle. These all stood upright, meaning the one remaining stone, now known as the **Slaughter Stone**, could never have fulfilled the role of sacrificial altar that the Victorians so theatrically bequeathed it. The **Heel Stone**, or "Friar's Heel", standing in the middle of the Avenue (see page 309), was originally one of a pair, the gap between them aligning precisely with the rising sun on midsummer's morning.

The trilithons

Within the sarsen circle itself, a matching perimeter of bluestones was constructed around a horseshoe of five massive **trilithons** (two uprights crossed by a lintel), one – known as **stone 53** – carved with images of Bronze Age axeheads and a dagger resembling those from ancient Mycenae in Greece. The lintels in both the main circle and the sarsen horseshoe were held in place by mortise and tenon joints; the bobble topping the surviving upright of the **Great Trilithon** (45 tons of stone on its own) is a very visible example of the woodworking techniques that still keep some of the circle together.

Realigning the stones (c.2200 BC)

The final phase of building at Stonehenge saw the bluestones rearranged a number of times, finishing with a horseshoe setting that reflected the surrounding horseshoe sarsens. At their enclosed end – and partly hidden under the fallen upright and lintel of the Great Trilithon – lies the **Altar Stone**, a huge block of sandstone discovered by Inigo Jones during the first study of Stonehenge in 1620. Jones was markedly more adept at architecture than archeology, and named the stone to fit in with his theory that the site was once a Roman temple, rather than after any concrete archeological evidence.

The Z & Y Holes (c.1600 BC)

The last work carried out at Stonehenge was the creation of two concentric rings outside the circle, known as the **Z Holes** and **Y Holes**. The holes were never filled, so whether this phase – coming at a very late stage in Stonehenge's ceremonial life – was left unfinished, or whether the pits were used for something entirely different, remains unknown.

Their purpose – and indeed, the purpose of all the work at Stonehenge – remains baffling. The symmetry and location of the site (a slight rise in a flat valley with even views of the horizon in all directions), as well as its alignment towards the points of sunrise and sunset on the summer and winter solstices, tend to support the supposition that it was some sort of temple to the sun or a time-measuring device – though it has come to mean much to druidic orders, their association with the circle was a mid-eighteenth-century invention. Whatever it was, Stonehenge ceased to be used at around 1600 BC, and by the Middle Ages it had become a "landmark".

Stonehenge World Heritage Site

Only a fraction of the visitors who pull into the Visitor Centre car park at Stonehenge explore beyond the famous circle, and while the burial mounds and earthworks that make up the rest of the **Stonehenge World Heritage Site** can't match its visual drama, they hold just as much interest as the stones – with many, including **the Cursus**, predating them by over a thousand years. This is one of the richest ceremonial landscapes in Europe, yet despite the finds at **Durrington Walls** and **Woodhenge** and the obvious presence of dozens of **round barrows** dotted among the wildflower meadows, archeologists have still only scratched the surface.

10

INFORMATION

It's easy enough to visit the main attractions around Stonehenge on your own, but a guided tour will give you a much deeper insight into the history of this ancient landscape. The Stonehenge Cursus, the Cursus Barrows, the Avenue and King Barrows Ridge are accessed from the Visitor Centre off the A360; Durrington Walls and Woodhenge are on the A345; and the Winterbourne Stoke Barrows and Normanton Down Barrows are reached via footpaths leading off the A303. There are car parks at Stonehenge and Woodhenge.

Access The Stonehenge World Heritage Site is owned by a hotchpotch of organizations and individuals, including English Heritage and the National Trust, the Ministry of Defence, local farmers and private landowners. The Stonehenge Cursus, the Cursus Barrows, the Avenue, King Barrows Ridge and the Winterbourne Stoke Barrows are on National Trust open-access land, while the other sites covered below can be reached by public footpath.

Tours Some of the best tours are with Salisbury and Stonehenge Guided Tours (☎07775 674816, ⓦ salisbury guidedtours.com), whose tailor-made trips around Durrington Walls, the Stonehenge Cursus, Woodhenge and other sites are led by an informative guide with experience of working on excavations in the area. The National Trust runs an extensive programme of popular walks, including a highly recommended quarterly guided trip with an expert NT archeologist (£18; 3hr); for details, call ☎01672 539928 or see ⓦ nationaltrust.org.uk.

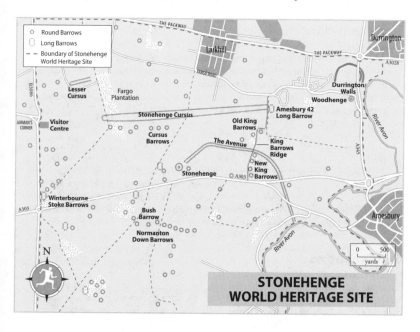

STONEHENGE
WORLD HERITAGE SITE

10

BARROWS: THE LONG AND THE ROUND OF IT

A defining feature of the landscape around Stonehenge, the conical humps that surge through the fields alongside the A303 are **round barrows**, Bronze Age burial mounds that appeared after the circle itself was built. Although often found alone, many round barrows were constructed in groups, with up to half a dozen individuals (usually family members) interred in satellite graves around a central primary mound, the whole acting as a kind of vertical cemetery. The vast majority were excavated during the eighteenth and nineteenth centuries by William Stukeley, William Cunnington and Sir Richard Colt Hoare, the owner of Stourhead. Their discoveries of grave goods – pottery, arrowheads, and jewellery made of gold and jet – have shaped much of our understanding of Beaker culture, but their rudimentary methods and incomplete digs (lacking the technology to analyse human remains, they simply reburied them) effectively ruined the sites for later archeologists.

On closer inspection, it is fairly easy to distinguish between the different varieties of round barrow. The most common, the **bowl barrow**, resembles an upturned pudding bowl and is usually surrounded by a ditch. The similar-looking **bell barrow** (generally used for male burials) is separated from its ditch by a gently sloping shelf (known as a berm), and hence has a very vague bell-like shape to it, while the **disc barrow** (generally used for female burials) is defined by a much smaller mound and therefore a much wider shelf, and with an external bank enclosing its ditch. The mounds on **saucer barrows** are much less distinct, while rarer **pond barrows** have no mound at all, with a hollow (rather than a ditch) enclosed by a lower bank than you'd find on a saucer barrow. Pond barrows were often used for "sky burials", wooden platforms supported by stilts and piled with bodies, which were exposed to the elements until only the bones remained.

The area contains far fewer examples of Neolithic **long barrows**, oblong-shaped burial mounds that often widen and rise at one end and were – unlike the later round barrows – used as communal burial chambers; there are notable examples at the western end of the Winterbourne Stoke group and behind King Barrows Ridge.

Stonehenge Cursus

Daily dawn–dusk • Free

The huge, drawn-out ellipse of the **Stonehenge Cursus**, or Greater Cursus (there's a Lesser Cursus nearby), stretches for nearly two miles across the fields north of the stone circle. Framed by two parallel sets of banks and ditches and varying between 350 and 500ft in width, it starts just beyond the trees of the Fargo Plantation (the gap between the copses is the Cursus) and finishes at a long barrow on King Barrows Ridge, a fact not properly established until 2008, when the Stonehenge Riverside Project (see page 310) discovered an enclosing ditch at its eastern end.

The Cursus was kept clean, but the few finds that have been made date it to around 3400 BC, nearly four hundred years before early Neolithic man had even started thinking about constructing the first phase of Stonehenge. William Stukeley, the antiquarian who discovered it in 1723, believed it had been used for chariot racing – *cursus* is Latin for racetrack. Modern-day archeologists aren't much closer to the truth, but the fact that it was too long and too low to be used as a defensive structure makes it likely to have been a ceremonial monument.

Cursus Barrows

Daily dawn–dusk • Free

Running partway along the southern side of the Stonehenge Cursus – and a useful landmark for finding it in the first place – the **Cursus Barrows** are the closest group to Stonehenge and one of the few features in the wider landscape to receive significant numbers of visitors. Like many of the barrows around Stonehenge (see box), they are Bronze Age Beaker burial mounds, a mixture of bowl and bell barrows that revealed human bones, fragments of pottery and amber beads when they were excavated by William Stukeley in 1723 and William Cunnington eighty years later.

King Barrows Ridge

Daily dawn–dusk • Free

The various burial mounds on **King Barrows Ridge** are some of the largest in the area. Normally an indication of age (these date from around 2300 BC, so are among the oldest of the area's barrows), here they are also likely a symbol of their occupants' importance, particularly as they run right across the route of the ceremonially significant Avenue. On the winter solstice, the area's inhabitants would have crossed the ridge after celebrating the sunset at Stonehenge on their way to watching the midwinter sunrise at Durrington Walls. The beech trees that surround the **New King Barrows**, the group that lies to the south of the line of the Avenue, inadvertently saved these from inquisitive Victorian archeologists, meaning that they may still hold valuable clues to unlocking some of Stonehenge's secrets.

The track running behind the ridge (and leading down to Woodhenge) traces the top of **Amesbury 42 Long Barrow**, which dates to the same time as the Stonehenge Cursus but has been added to over time; ironically, the track protected the barrow from the ravages of ploughing and continues to keep the roots of trees at bay.

The Avenue

Daily dawn–dusk • Free

Despite its measured appearance, **the Avenue** is largely a natural feature, its almost imperceptible gully (marked by two parallel ditches) the result of detritus being dragged across the landscape during the last Ice Age. By remarkable coincidence, it was carved in a position that aligned exactly with both the midsummer sunrise and midwinter sunset – it is because of the Avenue, therefore, that Stonehenge was built here at all. Used as a ceremonial pathway, it was lengthened in the later Bronze Age (around 2300 BC) and now doglegs over King Barrows Ridge and down to the River Avon; in 2009, the Stonehenge Riverside Project (see page 310) discovered a series of post holes by the river, a ring (dubbed "**Bluestonehenge**") that once held several of the Preseli stones that now stand inside the main circle itself.

Walking the original section back from King Barrows Ridge is by far the **best approach to Stonehenge**; the stones intermittently pop in and out of view until you crest the hill and see them looming directly ahead, the Avenue running past the Heel Stone and on into the circle.

Woodhenge

Daily dawn–dusk • Free

Compared to the mighty sarsens of Stonehenge, there's a lot less charisma about the reputedly significant Bronze Age site of **Woodhenge**, two miles to the northeast. The site, dating to around 2500 BC, consists of a circular bank about 160ft in diameter enclosing a ditch and six concentric rings of post holes, which would originally have held timber uprights, possibly supporting a roofed building of some kind; in 2006, it was discovered that standing stones were later erected on the same site. The holes are now marked more durably (if less romantically) by coloured concrete pillars – those with black tops signify where a hole was found that did not fit into the regular pattern. A child's grave was discovered at the centre of the rings, suggesting that it may have been a place of ritual sacrifice.

10

ALL IN THE NAME OF RESEARCH

With only a fraction of the World Heritage Site excavated so far, the one thing we know about Stonehenge that everyone can agree on is that we don't really know that much. A catalogue of key discoveries made by the **Stonehenge Riverside Project** over the last few years has gone a long way to increasing our knowledge but has also meant rewriting several parts of the story. The SRP, a supergroup of British archeologists led by Professor Mike Parker Pearson from Sheffield University, found that the Avenue was actually a periglacial feature (created by the action of glacial meltwater) that was extended rather than constructed completely, while their work around Durrington Walls proved that this was a year-round town and not simply a place for seasonal feasts. Their excavations of the Aubrey Holes around Stonehenge (see page 305), meanwhile, turned conventional thinking on its head, pointing to the fact that Stonehenge has been a stone monument for a lot longer than we originally thought.

Durrington Walls

Daily dawn–dusk • Free

In a landscape of burial mounds and ritual sites to the dead, **Durrington Walls**, the largest complete henge in Britain, is unique. Various finds of grooved-ware pottery and half-eaten animal bones (known as "feasting assemblages") had already established this as a place where people *lived* when, in 2005, archeologists working on the Stonehenge Riverside Project (see box) discovered the chalk floors of **houses** near the River Avon. They were so well preserved that even the hearthside indents remained where the occupants had kneeled down to rake out the ashes.

The houses were part of a vast village, the largest late Neolithic settlement in northern Europe, dispelling the notion that Durrington Walls was a temporary gathering place for ceremonial feasts. Given that they dated to the exact time the sarsens were going up at the great circle a couple of miles to the southwest, it is now thought that Durrington was in fact home to the builders of Stonehenge. The theory is lent more credence by the discovery that the earthworks were built after the houses, almost as if its creators wanted to seal it off as a kind of memorial.

The houses were covered up after the dig, and today Durrington Walls is again little more than the remains of a ditch and bank, albeit an enormous one, spreading for 500yds in a sweeping arc that is now partly cut through by the A345. You can't really get an idea of its size until you're standing inside it, in the area that was originally used for rituals and that once contained a number of timber circles, now mostly buried under the tarmac. The entrance to one of these, the **Southern Circle**, is aligned with the midwinter sunrise, the mirror image of Stonehenge. Like Stonehenge, Durrington Walls was connected to the River Avon by an "avenue", the river therefore effectively linking the land of the living with the resting place for the dead.

In 2015, a major discovery was made through ground-penetrating radar, which revealed that beneath the henge was a group of ninety standing stones, sixty of which are still extant. All had been deliberately pushed over in Neolithic times before the henge was built. The 4500-year-old monument is in a C-shaped formation and was thought to have been used as a ritual arena of some kind.

Normanton Down Barrows

Daily dawn–dusk • Free

Just west of Stonehenge, a turning off the A303 leads half a mile south down a bumpy, progressively rutted byway to **Normanton Down Barrows**, a fifty-strong round-barrow cemetery that contained the richest haul of Bronze Age grave goods found on Salisbury Plain. In 1808, while excavating a huge burial mound known as **Bush Barrow**, William Cunnington discovered the skeleton of an adult male, dating to around 1800 BC, who was surrounded by a treasure-trove of weapons and ornamentation: a bronze axe; bronze and copper daggers (traced back to Brittany); a fossil mace head (similar to those found at burial sites in Greece and Spain); and, most lavish of all, two diamond-shaped gold "lozenges" and a unique gold belt-hook. All the gold objects were very delicately worked, with the same parallel patterns of engraved lines on each; they're now on display at the Wiltshire Museum in Devizes.

Most of the barrows are on private land, but a few (including Bush Barrow) can be accessed on public footpaths.

10

Winterbourne Stoke Barrows

Daily dawn–dusk • Free

West of Stonehenge, a path from the A303 leads briefly through woodland to **Winterbourne Stoke Barrows**, over twenty barrows that encompass some two thousand years of ritual burial practices. The round barrows – bowl, bell, disc and the much rarer pond barrow – run in a line northeast from a well-preserved long barrow, recently dated to 3500 BC from human remains originally discovered in its northern end in the 1860s. You can climb the round barrow closest to the road for far-reaching views of Salisbury Plain and the grey dots of Stonehenge in the distance, though the noise from the adjoining roads detracts from the ambience somewhat.

RED DEER, EXMOOR

Contexts

History

For much of the last 500,000 years Somerset was covered by ice and snow, though this period was interspersed with warmer phases. The oldest evidence of human life in the region – and probably in the whole of Britain – is worked flints found in Westbury-sub-Mendip, from around 480,000 years ago, while Taunton's Museum of Somerset has examples of hand-axes from up to 400,000 years ago. Remains from about 12,000 BC have been found in the Cheddar Gorge, and a skeleton known as Cheddar Man has been dated to around 7000 BC – making this Britain's oldest complete skeleton.

Farming began about 6000 years ago, allowing people to settle year-round in permanent dwellings rather than being on the move in pursuit of prey and with the changing of the seasons. Funerary and religious shrines acquired special significance during this era, marked by numerous barrows (burial mounds) – such as that at **Stony Littleton** – and stone cairns, many found on the Mendip and Quantock hills and on Exmoor. Stone circles such as those at **Stanton Drew** and **Stonehenge** appeared in the late Neolithic and early Bronze Age (around 3500–2000 BC), though our knowledge about the purpose and function of these sites remains frustratingly slender. Pottery developed, important for the storage of food, metalworking began around 2500 BC, and the Bronze Age (roughly 3200–600 BC) saw the development of trade that extended beyond the British Isles.

During the late Bronze and early Iron Age (which began in the region around 650 BC), tribal territories became more defined and hillforts proliferated – important centres of crafts, trade and industry as well as power bases. The most significant ones were at **Ham Hill** – one of the biggest in Europe – and **Cadbury Castle**, though this site had been occupied for centuries beforehand. Smaller hillforts have been excavated at **Dolebury Warren**, in the Mendips; **Worlebury Hill**, outside Weston-super-Mare; **Solsbury Hill**, outside Bath; and **Brent Knoll**, near Burnham-on-Sea. Later on, lowland settlements became more established, for example the **Glastonbury Lake Villages** – settlements built on man-made islands in the Somerset Levels and specializing in jewellery and crafted artefacts.

In the course of the **Iron Age**, the territory was dominated by Celtic tribal groupings: the **Dobunni**, occupying the area now approximately covered by Gloucestershire and North Somerset, with their capital at present-day Cirencester; the **Belgae** and **Durotriges** to the south; and the **Dumnonii** in what is now West Somerset and Devon. These peoples were primarily farmers, shepherds and craftsmen, not warlike, and for the most part they quickly submitted to Roman rule, blending easily into the new Romano-British culture.

Romans, Saxons and Danes

The peaceful integration of present-day Somerset into the Roman Empire was effected soon after the **Roman invasion** in 43 AD. The new regime undertook some major

7000 BC	4000 BC	47 AD	410
Cheddar Man (now preserved as Britain's oldest complete skeleton) dies.	Farming develops in Somerset. Permanent settlements are established, replacing nomadic communities.	The Romans reach Somerset; Bath is developed as a Roman spa town soon after.	The Romans leave Britain, but Romano-British culture survives.

changes, including the deforestation of large areas and the building of such roads as the **Fosse Way**, which bisected Somerset on its route between Lincoln and Exeter. Roman Somerset was governed from **Ilchester**, a town on the Fosse Way, and Romano-British villas and bath complexes were scattered from **Pitney** to **Bruton**, though none so elaborate as the one at **Bath** itself, the only hot springs in Britain. The Romans also greatly expanded the mining activity that was already under way in parts of the region, particularly lead mining in the **Mendip Hills**.

Little is known about the region in the period following the Roman departure from Britain in around 410, but it is likely that the Romano-British culture endured for some decades afterwards. Eventually, though, Angles, Saxons and other Germanic peoples rushed in to fill the void during the sixth and seventh centuries. The shadowy figure of **King Arthur** – connected at least in myth with Glastonbury (see page 161) and Cadbury Castle (see page 187) – may have lived during this time, leading the Celtic Britons in their resistance to the newcomers. What is more certain is that the Britons suffered a major defeat at **Dyrham**, north of Bath, in 577, and the Saxons reached the River Parrett by around 660. By 845, Somerset formed part of the West Saxon kingdom of **Wessex**, whose capital was Winchester.

By this time, however, the **Danes** were already making incursions into the area, causing the Wessex king, **Alfred the Great**, to withdraw to **Athelney**, protected by the marshes of the **Somerset Levels**. In 878, Alfred rallied his forces to win a historic victory at Edington, near Westbury in eastern Wiltshire, blocking the Danish advance. The same year, a treaty dividing up southern England between Alfred and Guthrum, the Danish leader, was agreed at **Wedmore**, on the northern fringes of the Levels.

Wessex was the major bulwark against the Danes during the tenth century, but despite constant harassment Somerset itself was relatively unscathed. Edgar was crowned king of England in Bath Abbey in 973, and Christian foundations flourished, most notably **Glastonbury Abbey**, whose abbot Dunstan (909–88) was responsible for reforming the English monastic system and became Archbishop of Canterbury. The now-Christianized Danes tightened their grip on Wessex, culminating in the coronation of Cnut (or Canute) as king of England in 1016.

The Middle Ages

Having conquered England in 1066, the **Normans** maintained control by means of a chain of motte-and-bailey fortifications – essentially a mound surmounted by a keep and surrounded by a wall – throughout their new realm, including at **Dunster** and **Montacute**. Somerset, once at the heart of national life, found itself marginalized as William I established his capital in London rather than Winchester. As well as centralizing the government, the Normans consolidated trade and opened up European markets. Much of Somerset's growing wealth in the Middle Ages derived from the flourishing **wool and cloth industry**, centred in such towns as **Bradford-on-Avon**, **Frome**, **Yeovil** and **Taunton**. Landowners, merchants and other beneficiaries flaunted their prosperity by building and enriching churches, especially in the late medieval period – most of Somerset's exquisitely carved church towers, for example, date from 1450 to 1540. As well as parish churches, great cathedrals and abbeys were erected or rebuilt in

577	878	1066
The Britons suffer an overwhelming defeat by the Saxons at Dyrham, allowing the Saxons to occupy the Somerset region, which eventually becomes part of Wessex.	Alfred rallies his forces to win a decisive victory over the Danes at Edington. The Danish threat to Wessex is temporarily averted.	William, Duke of Normandy, conquers England and moves the capital from Winchester to London. Somerset loses its central role.

Bristol, Bath, Wells, Glastonbury and Salisbury, their magnificence often funded with money accrued from the huge landholdings they possessed – Glastonbury Abbey, for example, became one of the richest monastic houses in the country.

Many of the great treasures acquired by these institutions were destroyed during the **Dissolution of the Monasteries** – Henry VIII's radical appropriation of church property in the 1530s – while some houses were completely demolished. Parish churches, too, were vandalized in the puritanical zeal of the **Reformation**, losing much of their stained glass and statuary – though some items survived, such as the marvellous oak bench-ends still to be seen in the churches of the **Quantock Hills**. The landed gentry benefited from the decline of ecclesiastical power, with many former church estates converted into grand houses such as that at **Lacock Abbey**, taken over by Sir William Sharington in 1540.

Somehow, through all of these tumultuous events, trade continued to prosper. Warfare and commerce together engendered a strong seafaring tradition, and **Bristol** was fast becoming one of England's foremost ports. It was from here in 1497 that **John Cabot** sailed on the *Matthew* to what is now thought to have been Newfoundland – the first European to have set foot in North America since the Norsemen (see page 99). Claiming the land on behalf of the Crown, the Anglo-Italian sailor set in motion a long relationship between Bristol and the New World, for which the Bristol Channel became a major trading thoroughfare.

The English Civil War and the Monmouth Rebellion

In the Elizabethan and Jacobean periods, the wealthy directed their resources away from churches and castles and to their own abodes, and some of the region's greatest palaces, such as **Longleat**, date from this period. In the 1640s, Somerset was embroiled in the **Civil War**; most of the region's towns supported the Parliamentary cause, but many local families were divided in their loyalties. Large centres such as Bristol, Taunton and Bridgwater changed hands several times, and there were major engagements at **Langport**, in the Somerset Levels, **Dunster Castle** and **Lansdown**, outside Bath. Fortunes oscillated, but by 1645 almost the whole county was held by Parliament.

The reconciliation brought about by the **Restoration** of Charles II in 1660 proved all too brief. Like all of the king's other progeny, Charles's favourite son, James, Duke of Monmouth, was illegitimate and so could not inherit the throne, but this did not prevent him from becoming the focus of Protestant opposition to the new king, the Catholic James II. Returning from exile in Holland in 1685, Monmouth landed unopposed in Lyme Regis to launch the **Monmouth Rebellion** (see page 209). Assured of support in Somerset, he gathered forces en route and was proclaimed king in Taunton. However, the venture ended soon after with the duke's catastrophic defeat at **Sedgemoor** (or more accurately Westonzoyland), near Bridgwater, the last pitched battle on English soil, when more than three hundred rebels died and a further thousand were slaughtered as they fled (see page 174). A wave of oppression against the rebels was unleashed under Judge Jeffreys, who held two of his so-called **Bloody Assizes** in Wells and Taunton. Altogether, more than 1400 were tried, at least 300 were sentenced to be hanged and nearly 750 were transported to the West Indies.

1536–39	1642–49	1685
Henry VIII orders the Dissolution of the Monasteries, one of the defining events of the Reformation in England.	The Civil War breaks out between the Royalists, led by Charles I, and Parliament, ending with the execution of the king.	The Monmouth Rebellion led by the Protestant Duke of Monmouth against his Catholic uncle, James II, is crushed, and Bloody Assizes are set up across the county.

Three years later, James II was faced with another insurrection and was forced to flee the country when William of Orange landed in Torbay in the near-bloodless **Glorious Revolution** of 1688.

Bristol, meanwhile, was continuing to thrive as one of the country's great maritime cities. As well as its important trading role, it contributed to the settlement and colonization of the New World. Admiral William Penn, for example, took possession of Jamaica for the Lord Protector, Oliver Cromwell, in 1655, and his son, also called William Penn, established the Quaker colony of Pennsylvania in 1681, to which he (unwillingly) gave his name. Increasingly, however, Bristol's relations with the New World hinged on the **slave trade** – specifically the "triangular trade", whereby manufactured goods were exported to West Africa, the ships then transporting slaves to the West Indies from where they would bring sugar, tobacco and rum back to Bristol (see page 107).

The Georgian era

In contrast to the strife of the previous hundred years, the eighteenth century saw an extended period of peace – at least at home – and the growth of polite society. Bristol's burgeoning New World markets and the profits of the slave trade helped to finance grand mansions throughout the city, not least in its **Clifton** suburb. An even more dramatic transformation took place in Bath at about the same time, as the alleged health benefits of its spa waters made it an essential stop for England's fashionable elite. Its new status was reflected in a complete renovation of the city, filling it with architecture that revived classical Greek and Roman designs as filtered through the Italian Renaissance (courtesy of the sixteenth-century architect Andrea Palladio). During **Bath's Golden Age** (see page 54), the city became a centre for the arts – drawing writers such as **Jane Austen** and portrait painters such as **Thomas Gainsborough** – as well as the sciences, at least in the person of **Sir William Herschel**, who discovered (along with his sister Caroline Herschel) the planet Uranus in 1781.

It wasn't just the cities that witnessed significant changes during the eighteenth century: Somerset's grandees enhanced their rural seats with the help of some of the finest architects of the era, as at **Stourhead**, while designers such as **Capability Brown** were called in to apply the latest landscaping techniques to the parks of the great houses, as at **Longleat**. Elsewhere in the county, coalfields were opened up around **Radstock** in the 1760s, and a brick- and tile-manufacturing industry was established in **Bridgwater**. In the latter part of the century, large tracts of central Somerset were reclaimed from the marshes, increasing the productivity of the land, while agricultural reforms also helped to revive rural areas.

The Victorian age

Bath lost much of its kudos during the **nineteenth century**, but Bristol forged ahead. While the abolition in 1807 of the slave trade that had underpinned much of the city's prosperity seriously dented its commercial strength, the city was reinvigorated by **Isambard Kingdom Brunel**'s construction of the broad-gauge Great Western Railway

1700–50	1720–60	1763
Bath experiences a "Golden Age", becoming a hub of high society, and is rebuilt along Palladian lines.	Bristol's slave trade reaches its peak, with Bristol vessels carrying one third of Britain's total slave shipments in 1756.	Collieries start operating around Radstock, part of the great expansion of the Somerset coalfield.

between London and Bristol in 1841 (it was extended to Bridgwater and Taunton in the same year). Improved communications also came about through canal- and road-building, ending the isolation of much of the county. Somerset was soon crisscrossed by a dense network of railway lines owned by different companies (though these were cut to the bone in the 1960s). This greater ease of travel facilitated the growth of mass tourism in the later nineteenth century, leading to the development of Somerset's major seaside resorts, **Weston-super-Mare**, **Clevedon** and **Minehead**. Brunel also applied his genius to other engineering feats in Bristol, such as the first iron-clad ocean-going ship, the **SS Great Britain**, built in Bristol in 1843, and the city's **Clifton Suspension Bridge**, inaugurated after his death in 1864.

The expansion of the railways boosted the local economy in other ways, for example by encouraging businesses to invest in provincial centres. The town of **Shepton Mallet** became known for cider production in the 1860s, while iron ore was mined in West Somerset's **Brendon Hills** towards the end of the century, reviving the fortunes of West Somerset's only port of any size, **Watchet**, from where the ore was shipped out.

Modern times

World War I affected Somerset much as it did the rest of Britain, bequeathing a trail of bleak war memorials in towns and villages throughout the county. Many local industries closed down during the first half of the century, such as the Brendon Hills mines, and while production peaked in Somerset's coalfields in the 1920s, coalmining in the region disappeared completely over the next fifty years, priced out by the global market.

During **World War II**, Bristol became one of Britain's most bombed cities, losing much of its historic core (see page 96), and Bath too did not escape bombardment. The postwar rebuilding of Bristol added some architectural horrors to the city's skyline, including the bland **Broadmead** shopping precinct and a clutch of tasteless office blocks that catered to Bristol's burgeoning new role as a centre for business, finance and technology. The city's manufacturing base was sustained by the engineering works at Filton, including the Rolls-Royce factory that provided engines for the supersonic aircraft Concorde in the 1960s and 1970s. **Yeovil**, in South Somerset, similarly established itself with its Westland aircraft plant, which specialized in helicopter manufacture after World War II.

The construction of the **M5** motorway through Somerset in the 1970s and the expansion of **Bristol airport** in the 1990s further improved the region's infrastructure. However, an ill-advised reorganization of local government in 1974, whereby parts of Somerset were amalgamated with Bristol and parts of Gloucestershire to form the county of Avon, was faced with almost universal opposition, and the experiment was ended in 1996 with the creation of the unitary authorities of Bristol, North Somerset, Bath and Northeast Somerset (BANES or B&NES), and South Gloucestershire.

The trip-hop "Bristol sound" of the 1990s and the city's street art from the 1980s onwards have helped to raise Bristol's profile, while impressive new museums focusing on the local area were opened in Bristol and Taunton in 2011. But the creation and consumption of culture has taken second place to shopping in recent years; the

1807	1841	1941
Abolition of the slave trade, leading to the collapse of Bristol's trade with the West Indies.	The Great Western Railway reaches Bristol, Bridgwater and Taunton, largely financed by Bristol merchants.	Severe bombing of Bristol in World War II; the medieval quarter is gutted.

318 | CONTEXTS HISTORY

construction of the **Cribbs Causeway** retail complex outside Bristol in 1998 symbolized a shift of emphasis away from manufacturing to service and retail industries. Both Bristol and Bath celebrated the twenty-first century with the building of bold new inner-city shopping centres, respectively at **Cabot Circus** (2008) and **SouthGate** (2010). But the region as a whole – with the rest of Britain – suffered the dire effects of the **financial crash** of 2008, which among other consequences led to the radical slashing of Somerset's arts budget. Government cuts were also blamed for the failure to dredge rivers – one of the alleged causes of the catastrophic flooding that affected the **Somerset Levels** in 2014.

Two years later, the construction of two new nuclear reactors at **Hinkley Point**, on the Somerset coast, was given the official go-ahead, arousing sharp anxieties about the enormous cost and viability of nuclear power generation tempered by optimism for the local economy. In the **European referendum** of 2016, clear majorities in both Bristol and Bath and Northeast Somerset voted to remain in the EU, though most of Somerset's other parliamentary constituencies voted by slim margins to leave. Two of the UK's leading Brexiters, Jacob Rees-Mogg and Liam Fox, represent the Northeast Somerset and North Somerset constituencies respectively; the MP for Bath is Liberal Democrat Wera Hobhouse.

2013	2015	2017	2020
Somerset adopts a county flag: a red dragon against a yellow background.	Bristol is the UK's first European Green Capital.	Aerospace Bristol museum opens in Filton.	The UK leaves the EU.

Wildlife

Watching wildlife in Somerset is rewarding throughout the year, with spring offering the chance to catch mating displays and summer the time to spot seasonal visitors such as nightjar and hobby; while many mammals and reptiles hibernate in winter, it can be particularly good for bird-watching, when resident populations are boosted by arrivals from the Continent. The following field guide should help you identify some of the more common animals that you might see across the county; notes give clear pointers about the kinds of habitat favoured by each species, their appearance and behaviour and tips on spotting them.

MAMMALS

RED DEER
Cervus elaphus
Habitat Dense woodland and forest, and moorland, particularly Exmoor and the Quantock Hills.
Appearance and behaviour Magnificent beast, weighing over 440lb, with shaggy reddish-brown coat (grey-brown in winter); male has impressive highly branched antlers – the more branches, the older the deer; eats shoots, berries and leaves; volatile during rutting, when you should steer clear of males.
Sighting tips Most impressive during the October "rut", a breeding season characterized by warning bellows and occasional clashing of antlers.

BADGER
Meles meles
Habitat Undisturbed woodland.
Appearance and behaviour Stocky creature – the heaviest British carnivore – with two black stripes running from nose to back of neck and powerful front paws (name derives from *becheur*, French for "digger"); social, with large family groups living together in number of setts; varied diet, from bluebells to mice.
Sighting tips Mostly nocturnal; shy, though fierce if cornered, hence local saying "as mad as a badger"; keep downwind – keen sense of smell is around eight hundred times better than man's.

STOAT
Mustela erminea
Habitat Woodland and farmland, particularly the Mendips.
Appearance and behaviour Reddish-brown fur, with cream belly and black-tipped tail; shorter and stouter than weasel; eats mostly rabbits and game birds, which it kills with bite to back of neck.
Sighting tips Most easily seen on its morning hunt, particularly on open land that's attractive to rabbits.

OTTER
Lutra lutra
Habitat Rivers, lakes, marshland and coastal regions.
Appearance and behaviour Long brown furry body, with powerful tail and webbed feet; males slightly larger than females but both usually over 3ft long; can stay under water for three minutes; eats fish and crabs.
Sighting tips Usually swimming, with only head on view, though sometimes seen playing on the riverbank; tracks are fairly small, with only four of the five toes leaving an imprint.

WATER VOLE
Arvicola amphibus
Habitat Wetlands and fields around ponds, lakes and slow-flowing rivers and streams, particularly in the Somerset Levels.
Appearance and behaviour Largest vole in Britain, growing to 1ft in length; name stems from Norwegian for "field" (*voll*), their preferred habitat; also known as water rat; eats aquatic plants.
Sighting tips Nervy animals, so sightings are brief; look around riverbanks (where they live in burrows) and pathways between water.

LESSER HORSESHOE BAT
Rhinolophus hipposideros
Habitat Caves and buildings, particularly on the Mendips.
Appearance and behaviour At ten inches, wingspan is around six times length of body; name comes from horseshoe-shaped nose tip; finds food (moths and beetles) by echolocation.
Sighting tips Fairly rare, but between April and October can be seen inside caves or emerging from roosts half an hour or so after sunset.

BIRDS

GREY HERON
Ardea cinerea

Habitat Estuaries, rivers, ponds and wetlands, particularly Swell Wood, adjoining West Sedgemoor Nature Reserve.

Appearance and behaviour Largest European heron, measuring around 3ft tall, with uniform grey back and white breast, sinuous neck and black crests above eyes; long legs end in long toes, which help disperse weight across floating vegetation; usually solitary, though gathers to nest in single tree or group of trees (known as a "heronry").

Sighting tips Common; most often seen motionless on riverbank or in shallow water, stalking prey (mainly fish but also frogs and eels); flies with bent neck and bowed wings.

BITTERN
Botaurus stellaris

Habitat Dense reedbeds, particularly Ham Wall Nature Reserve in the Somerset Levels.

Appearance and behaviour Squat, chunky member of the heron family, its sandy brown plumage mottled with dark streaks; eats fish, amphibians and insects; growing in numbers since critical point in mid-1990s (when fewer than a dozen males in entire country) but still one of the most threatened species of bird in the UK.

Sighting tips Elusive and shy, and difficult to spot due to camouflaged plumage; call, a far-reaching "boom", can be heard in spring, though birds themselves are more visible during winter.

LAPWING
Vanellus vanellus

Habitat Wet meadows, worked farmland and marshes, particularly nature reserves in the Avalon Marshes.

Appearance and behaviour Iridescent purple and green back and wings, with red legs, white breast, black band around neck and distinctive crest; dithering flight, hence name; eats worms and insects; declining in recent years, and now on IUCN Red List.

Sighting tips Numbers swollen by autumn arrivals from northern Europe, with one of the largest groups of lapwing in the country wintering on the Somerset Levels; listen for high-pitched "pee-wit" call.

KINGFISHER
Alcedo atthis

Habitat Ponds, lakes, canals, slow-flowing rivers and streams, and (in winter) estuaries along the coast.

Appearance and behaviour Unmistakable sapphire blue and orange bird; dagger-like beak around a third the length of body – male's is all black, females have a reddish-orange lower beak; nests in riverside banks; eats mostly fish.

Sighting tips Usually darting above water surface, though sometimes spotted hunting fish from riverside branches; in summer, parents can be seen bringing fish (up to 100 a day) back to their burrows.

GREAT CRESTED GREBE
Podiceps cristatus

Habitat Lakes, reservoirs, gravel pits and slow-moving rivers, particularly Chew Valley Lake.

Appearance and behaviour Graceful-looking bird with black body and long white neck, easily recognized in early spring when it grows distinctive orange-and-black ruff and elaborate crest for breeding season; builds floating nests, carrying chicks on back for first few weeks.

Sighting tips Clumsy on land due to legs set far back on body, so rarely seen out of water – even prefers to dive to escape trouble, rather than fly; head-shaking courtship displays performed in February, when mating pairs hold themselves out of water by rapidly paddling.

WATER RAIL
Rallus aquaticus

Habitat Reedbeds, marshes, ditches and wetlands.

Appearance and behaviour Small, rounded body, with black-and-white striped flanks separating mottled brown back and grey underparts and face; long, slightly curving red beak; eats mainly small fish, snails and insects.

Sighting tips Fairly common but very secretive, though easier to see in winter, when more numerous and forced to break cover in search of food; more often heard than seen – odd-sounding call akin to squealing piglet.

SNIPE
Gallinago gallinago

Habitat Moors and wetlands.

Appearance and behaviour Squat, with striped brown back, dark streaks on chest and cream underparts; head has "humbug" streaking and long, arrow-straight bill; eats small invertebrates, including worms and insect larvae.

Sighting tips Most often seen on moorland during spring and summer, and round wetland pools in winter; performs acrobatic aerial displays during breeding season – thin whistling noise that accompanies these (known as "drumming") produced by male's tail feathers.

NIGHTJAR
Caprimulgus europaeus

Habitat Heathland, moors and woodland clearings, particularly Quantock Hills.

Appearance and behaviour Similar in shape to cuckoo, with grey-brown, mottled and streaked bodies, tapered wings and long tail; nocturnal; Latin name translates as "European Goatsucker", from belief it stole milk from goats during night; notes that make up male's strange song – rising and falling "jar" or "churr", which gives bird its English name – emitted up to forty times a second.

Sighting tips Summer migrant, in Somerset late April or mid-May to September; difficult to spot due to camouflaged plumage, but most likely seen on warm, still evenings, hunting moths on the wing.

BUZZARD
Buteo buteo
Habitat Farmland, moors, woodland, scrub and hills, particularly Mendips and Quantocks.
Appearance and behaviour Large raptor with short neck and tail, which it regularly fans out when soaring; variable brown plumage, with yellow legs and talons; eats birds, small rodents and rabbits, but will resort to earthworms and insects if necessary.
Sighting tips Commonest bird of prey in Somerset, most often seen soaring, though will also perch on fence posts and pylons; distinctive "pee-o" call can sound like a cat.

PEREGRINE FALCON
Falco peregrinus
Habitat Cliffs, quarries and rocky areas, particularly Cheddar Gorge.
Appearance and behaviour Medium-sized falcon with blue-grey back (dark brown in young) and head, spotted white chest and barred underparts, with distinctive black "moustache" across white face; eats small birds.

REPTILES AND AMPHIBIANS

GRASS SNAKE
Natrix natrix
Habitat Ponds, ditches and wetlands.
Appearance and behaviour Largest UK snake, males measuring around 3ft, females another nine inches or so; olive or dark green with yellow collar and black bars along flanks; strong swimmer, feeding on fish, frogs and newts.
Sighting tips Usually seen in or around water; hibernates under logs November to March.

ADDER
Vipera berus
Habitat Heathland and dunes.
Appearance and behaviour UK's only venomous snake, also called "viper"; dark zigzag pattern running down back, males are silvery-grey, females browner; eats small rodents and lizards.
Sighting tips Usually seen basking on exposed areas such as paths; hibernates underground November to February.

COMMON LIZARD
Lacerta vivipara

Sighting tips Most likely seen when at nest, in upper cliff ledges; incredibly agile flier, reaching speeds of up to 180mph.

MARSH HARRIER
Circus aeruginosus
Habitat Wetlands, marshes, reedbeds and surrounding farmland, particularly Catcott Lows and Shapwick Heath nature reserves in the Somerset Levels.
Appearance and behaviour Slightly bigger than buzzard, with streaked head and long grey tail (females larger than males and much darker brown, with cream-coloured heads); nests on ground among reedbeds; has recovered from near extinction but still on IUCN Amber List.
Sighting tips Easily identified in flight due to black wing tips; noticeable aerial displays during spring, when male inverts in mid-air to pass food to female.

SPARROWHAWK
Accipiter nisus
Habitat Woodland and open countryside.
Appearance and behaviour Small raptor, with blue-grey back and wings (less mottled than peregrine) and orange streaks on chest – females have browner back and wings, and brown barred underparts, both have long white "eyebrows"; eats small birds, mice and sometimes bats.
Sighting tips Common but secretive; flies close to ground, with several wing beats followed by a glide; males perform "rollercoaster" aerial displays in early spring.

Habitat Grassland, heathland and dunes.
Appearance and behaviour Up to six inches long; olive-green, speckled with black, brown and yellow markings; also known as viviparous lizard, as female hatches eggs moments before young are born.
Sighting tips Often seen basking on flat stones or logs, sometimes around water (they're good swimmers); hibernates between November and February.

GREAT CRESTED NEWT
Triturus cristatus
Habitat Ponds, pools and streams.
Appearance and behaviour Up to 6.5 inches long; has bright orange belly and bumpy skin (also known as warty newt); eats insects, worms and slugs; protected species, so is illegal to catch or handle one.
Sighting tips Name comes from large crest male grows along back during spring, which tells it apart from smooth and palmate newts, UK's other, similar-looking species (smooths have spotted throat, palmates webbed back feet); fairly easy to see (solitary) eggs laid on underside of aquatic plants; hibernates on land between November and February.

Books

FICTION

Jane Austen *Northanger Abbey* This tale follows 17-year-old Catherine Morland as she negotiates the sophisticated, vain and sometimes dishonest society of Bath, populated by characters you love and others you love to hate. Both a coming-of-age story and a satirical poke at the then-current vogue for Gothic literature.

Jane Austen *Persuasion* This is the more worldly-wise of Austen's two novels set (partly) in Bath, though the themes and narrative arcs are familiar – a young single woman in a world full of snobbery, social climbing and frustrated romance – and it's drenched with the usual Austen wit.

★ **R.D. Blackmore** *Lorna Doone* Swashbuckling Exmoor yarn of romance and inter-clan warfare during the time of the seventeenth-century Monmouth Rebellion. Don't let the archaic language and antiquated style put you off this page-turner.

Moyra Caldecott *The Waters of Sul* Immerse yourself in the shenanigans of Roman Bath in this historical novel by a Bath resident, in which competing cultures and cults vie for supremacy in the year 72 AD. Undemanding but well researched and entertaining, this is a perfect holiday read.

Helen Dunmore *Birdcage Walk* Set around Clifton Downs at the time of the French Revolution, Dunmore's last novel centres on the tense relationship between Lizzie, the daughter of a radical writer, and her property developer husband, reaching its denouement in the Avon Gorge.

Jennie Finch *Death of the Elver Man* Confident crime-thriller debut that beautifully evokes the haunting scenery and deep-rooted traditions of the Somerset Levels, as an outsider attempts to track down a killer amid the unusual setting of the eel-poaching underworld.

HISTORY AND ARCHITECTURE

H.G. Brown and P.J. Harris *Bristol England* If you're looking for a straight-up, no-nonsense history of the city, look no further. It's pretty ancient (taking us up to 1967) and long out of print, but you'll find it in libraries and online, and it provides the full lowdown on Bristol, its people and its buildings.

Bryan Little *Bath Portrait* It's getting on a bit (first published fifty years ago, updated in 1980), but this remains a first-class history of the city and the colourful characters who created it. Written in an easy, unpompous style, it's an entertaining and informative read, guaranteed to enrich anyone's visit to the spa town.

Timothy Mowl and Marion Mako *Historic Gardens of Somerset* This well-illustrated study of the county's gardens follows a thematic arrangement that imaginatively links gardens that share ideas, associations and physical features. Some of the places covered are well known, such as Prior

Park, Montacute House, Hestercombe and Tyntesfield, others less so, including Marston Bigot, Crowcombe Court, Poundisford Park and Camerton Court, but all are treated equally according to their significance. The appendices provide a helpful map, and a gazetteer gives visiting details and websites.

★ **Nikolaus Pevsner, et al** *The Buildings of England* Indispensable for anyone seriously interested in architecture and historic buildings in general, but a dry academic read for anyone else. The Pevsner guides were first written in the postwar years but updated and expanded by modern experts with greater resources. The editions on Bath; Bristol; Somerset: North and Bristol; and Somerset: South and West are authoritative and tell you everything you want to know about every building of note in the county – and plenty that you probably don't – but they're expensive.

GUIDES

WALKING

AA *50 Walks in Somerset* Handy little book describing walks of three to ten miles, with all the practical details you need and clear, large-scale maps. The walks are annotated with descriptions of local points of interest to visit along the way, plus tearooms and pubs, and there are suggestions for background reading on Somerset's history and wildlife.

Sue Gearing *Walking on the Mendip Hills* Subtitled "Twelve Circular Walks of Discovery", this is an excellent handbook for Mendip walkers, with most walks around five miles, though options are given for extending or shortening the walk. There's plenty of background information on history, topography, flora and fauna of the landscape.

John Gilman *Exmoor Rangers' Favourite Walks* Thirty circular walks to get the most out of Exmoor, originally written by a former head ranger and subsequently updated by National Park staff and volunteers. The routes vary from two to eight miles.

Derek Moyes *The West Mendip Way* Readable account of the thirty-mile walking route from Uphill, near Weston-super-Mare, to Wells. It's a bit old-fashioned in style, and the maps are appalling, but there are interesting asides on the countryside.

James Roberts *Walking in Somerset* This Cicerone guide has dozens of circular walks of three to twelve miles, of varying levels of difficulty, plus a chapter on the county's long-distance trails. There's plenty of information on places en route, with accommodation suggestions for every walk and at least one pub listed in most accounts. The directions are admirably detailed, though the maps are a bit sketchy.

★ *South West Coast Path* The official National Trail Guide to the coast path in four pocket-friendly volumes, with excellent 1:25,000 Ordnance Survey maps, copious information on background and things to see, and details of circular walks en route.

Woodland Trust *Exploring Woodland: The South West of England* One of a series of illustrated guides with maps and lots of descriptions of what there is to see, historical background and wildlife.

CYCLING

Nick Cotton and John Grimshaw *The Official Guide to the National Cycle Network* Covers all the routes of the National Cycle Network opened in the UK so far. Well presented with good maps and pictures, the guide also provides info on surfaces, traffic hazards and refreshment stops, and has useful advice for families.

Max Darkins *Mountain Bike Rides in & around Exmoor & Dartmoor* Beautifully produced guide to off-road biking in the region – not just the two moors but as far afield as Saunton and Truro – in a ring binder that can accommodate "expansion packs" (available from ⚉ roughrideguide.co.uk). There's also a collection of rides in Wiltshire and Dorset, with the same high-quality OS maps and directions.

Nigel Vile *On Your Bike Around Bristol and Bath* and *On Your Bike in Somerset* These spiral-bound cycling guides are clearly designed, well illustrated and beautifully produced on glossy paper, though you'll need a back-up map for some of the trickier routes. Each of the rides – most around twenty miles – has sections about some of the features en route.

GENERAL

Banksy *Wall and Piece* Published in 2005 but still the definitive introduction to Britain's most notorious street artist. The text – at turns humorous and unflinching – nicely complements the stinging satire of his work.

★ **Felix Braun** *Children of the Can: 25 Years of Bristol Graffiti* Lavishly illustrated journey through Bristol's street-art scene, penned by a graffer, and full of no-holds-barred insights from all the major players.

Paul Cresswell *Bath in Quotes* An enjoyable romp through the literary impressions of various visitors to Bath from Anglo-Saxon times onwards. The prose and verse extracts are arranged chronologically and include pieces from Pepys, Defoe, Thackeray and Dickens, with more recent contributions by Jan Morris and U.A. Fanthorpe.

Margery Fish *We Made a Garden* Charmingly detailed autobiographical account of East Lambrook Manor Gardens, and how a resolute Fleet Street secretary created the concept of cottage gardening.

★ **Rosemary Hill** *Stonehenge* Perhaps the most accessible account of Stonehenge, clearly presenting the myriad theories that have grown up around the great stone circle – it includes ideas by everyone from antiquarians to astrologists – and its wider portrayal in (and influence on) art and architecture.

Richard Jones *Bristol Music: Seven Decades of Sound* The musicians, DJs and producers that have emerged in the Bristol music scene since the 1950s are chronicled in this affectionate and knowledgeable volume, which includes images from the eponymous 2018 exhibition at Bristol's M Shed museum.

Maggie Lane *A Charming Place* Here's one for Jane-ites, a portrait of Bath seen through Jane Austen's life, books and letters. Sections include "Taking the Waters", "Public Entertainments" and "Shopping". Comes with a pull-out map of Bath in Jane's time.

James Russell *The Naked Guide to Cider* Knowledgeable and passionate introduction to the history of cider and the intriguing culture that surrounds this West Country staple – though Somerset is just one of several cider-producing regions covered. Plenty of mouthwatering photos, plus a cider-making guide for those who really get bitten by the bug.

Robin and Romey Williams *The Somerset Levels* Excellent volume that tells you everything you might want to know about this fascinating landscape. The story of human interaction with the wetlands is set against descriptions of the fauna and flora, and there are brief accounts of towns in the area – Wells, Glastonbury and Bridgwater, among others – and historical or semi-historical characters (including King Arthur and Alfred the Great), plus plenty of photos and illustrations.

David Worthy *The Old Quantocks: People and Places* Wonderful compendium of stories, photographs and paintings of the Quantock Hills by a local author. There are features on Nether Stowey, Kilve Priory and Fyne Court, among many others, all in full colour. If you haven't been there already, this will make you want to go.

Small print and index

Rough Guide credits

Managing editor: Rachel Lawrence
Cartography: Katie Bennett
Picture editor: Aude Vauconsant
Cover photo research: Aude Vauconsant

Senior DTP coordinator: Dan May
Head of DTP and Pre-Press: Rebeka Davies
Layout: Ruth Bradley

Publishing information

Third edition 2020

Distribution

UK, Ireland and Europe
Apa Publications (UK) Ltd; sales@roughguides.com
United States and Canada
Ingram Publisher Services; ips@ingramcontent.com
Australia and New Zealand
Woodslane; info@woodslane.com.au
Southeast Asia
Apa Publications (SN) Pte; sales@roughguides.com
Worldwide
Apa Publications (UK) Ltd; sales@roughguides.com
Special Sales, Content Licensing and CoPublishing
Rough Guides can be purchased in bulk quantities
at discounted prices. We can create special editions,
personalised jackets and corporate imprints tailored to
your needs. sales@roughguides.com.
roughguides.com

Help us update

We've gone to a lot of effort to ensure that this edition
of **The Rough Guide to Bath, Bristol and Somerset** is
accurate and up-to-date. However, things change – places
get "discovered", opening hours are notoriously fickle,
restaurants and rooms raise prices or lower standards. If
you feel we've got it wrong or left something out, we'd like
to know, and if you can remember the address, the price,
the hours, the phone number, so much the better.

Please send your comments with the subject line
"**Rough Guide Bath, Bristol and Somerset Update**" to
mail@uk.roughguides.com. We'll credit all contributions
and send a copy of the next edition (or any other Rough
Guide if you prefer) for the very best emails.

Reader's update

Thanks to all the readers who have taken the time to write in with comments and suggestions (and apologies if we've
inadvertently omitted or misspelt anyone's name):

Katie Bennett, Jennifer Gates, Anders Hanson, David Leffman, Trevor Surgenor and Charlie Wilde.

Acknowledgements

Rob Andrews would like to thank Rachel Yuan at Bath's Museum of East Asian Art, Emma Frayling at Visit Bath, and all the
various staff still working in the region's declining number of tourist offices, as well as Rachel Lawrence at Rough Guides
for her expert eye.

Rob Andrews is the author of the *Rough Guide to Devon & Cornwall*, among other titles.
Based for 30 years in Bristol, he is a connoisseur of rural walks, seaside piers and craft beers. His
tramps and rides around the byways of Somerset are usually interspersed by visits or revisits to
the region's brilliant collection of barrows, churches, castles and public houses.
Keith Drew grew up on the edge of the Mendips and can still often be found walking in the
Somerset Levels or cider-tasting his way round South Somerset. A former Managing Editor
at Rough Guides, he now runs the family-travel website ⓦ lijoma.com, creating inspirational
itineraries and providing expert advice on the practicalities of travelling with children.

Photo credits
(Key: T-top; C-centre; B-bottom; L-left; R-right)

Index

Map symbols

The symbols below are used on maps throughout the book

International boundary	Hospital	Wetland centre	Hills
State/Province boundary	Toilets	Museum	Peak
Chapter division boundary	Parking	Monument	Bus stop
Motorway	Place of interest	Castle	Airport
Pedestrianized road	Gardens/fountain	Observatory	Boat
Road	Statue	Campsite	Ferry/boat stop
Steps	Bridge	Cave	Church
Path	Gate	Windmill	Building
Railway	Tower	Radio mast	Stadium
Ferry route	Abbey	Spring	Park
Wall	Hide	Battle site	Beach
Post office	Cider farm	Ruin	Cemetery
Tourist information			

Listings key

Accommodation	
Eating	
Drinking	
Shopping	

YOUR TAILOR-MADE TRIP
STARTS HERE

Tailor-made trips and unique adventures crafted by local experts

Rough Guides has been inspiring travellers with lively and thought-provoking guidebooks for more than 35 years. Now we're linking you up with selected local experts to craft your dream trip. They will put together your perfect itinerary and book it at local rates.

Don't follow the crowd – find your own path.

HOW ROUGHGUIDES.COM/TRIPS WORKS

STEP 1

Pick your dream destination, tell us what you want and submit an enquiry.

STEP 2

Fill in a short form to tell your local expert about your dream trip and preferences.

STEP 3

Our local expert will craft your tailor-made itinerary. You'll be able to tweak and refine it until you're completely satisfied.

STEP 4

Book online with ease, pack your bags and enjoy the trip! Our local expert will be on hand 24/7 while you're on the road.

BENEFITS OF PLANNING AND BOOKING AT
ROUGHGUIDES.COM/TRIPS

PLAN YOUR ADVENTURE WITH LOCAL EXPERTS

Rough Guides' English-speaking local experts are hand-picked, based on their experience in the travel industry and their impeccable standards of customer service.

SAVE TIME AND GET ACCESS TO LOCAL KNOWLEDGE

When a local expert plans your trip, you save time and money when you book, even during high season. You won't be charged for using a credit card either.

MAKE TRAVEL A BREEZE: BOOK WITH PIECE OF MIND

Enjoy stress-free travel when you use Rough Guides' secure online booking platform. All bookings come witha money-back guarantee.

WHAT DO OTHER TRAVELLERS THINK ABOUT ROUGH GUIDES TRIPS?

Trip to Spain

This Spain tour company did a fantastic job to make our dream trip perfect. We gave them our travel budget, told them where we would like to go, and they did all of the planning. Our drivers and tour guides were always on time and very knowledgable. The hotel accommodations were better than we would have found on our own. Only one time did we end up in a location that we had not intended to be in. We called the 24 hour phone number, and they immediately fixed the situation.

Don A, USA ★★★★★

Trip to Morocco

Our trip was fantastic! Transportation, accommodations, guides – all were well chosen! The hotels were well situated, well appointed and had helpful, friendly staff. All of the guides we had were very knowledgeable, patient, and flexible with our varied interests in the different sites. We particularly enjoyed the side trip to Tangier! Well done! The itinerary you arranged for us allowed maximum coverage of the country with time in each city for seeing the important places.

Sharon, USA ★★★★★

PLAN AND BOOK YOUR TRIP AT
ROUGHGUIDES.COM/TRIPS